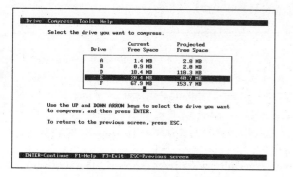

Doubling Your Disk Space

DoubleSpace makes it a snap to virtually double the space available on hard disks, floppy disks, and removable cartridge disks. DOS includes a full-screen management program (DBLSPACE.EXE) that makes it easy to manage and optimize the compressed disk volumes. A new /C switch on the DIR command provides information about the extent of newly available disk space on compressed drives. See Chapter 9 for a complete discussion of DoubleSpace.

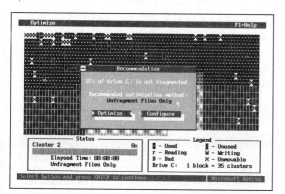

Disk Optimization and Defragmentation

The DEFRAG utility reduces defragmentation on your disk, thereby optimizing the arrangement of your file data. As explained in Chapter 18, both file and directory information can be optimized, making your system more efficient and improving the overall performance and throughput of all applications that attempt to access the disk. The program analyzes the degree of disk fragmentation and then makes recommendations about the best optimization approach to take.

Multiple Boot Configuration

DOS 6 offers the new ability to create multiple, independent configuration *blocks* within your single CONFIG.SYS file. Each "menuitem" seen here defines a unique Configuration Block within the CONFIG.SYS file, as explained in Chapter 9. Each separate configuration block defines a unique group of commands that will be executed if the user selects the associated menuitem choice during power-up.

For every kind of computer user, there is a SYBEX book.

All computer users learn in their own way. Some need straightforward and methodical explanations. Others are just too busy for this approach. But no matter what camp you fall into, SYBEX has a book that can help you get the most out of your computer and computer software while learning at your own pace.

Beginners generally want to start at the beginning. The **ABC's** series, with its step-by-step lessons in plain language, helps you build basic skills quickly. Or you might try our **Quick & Easy** series, the friendly, full-color guide.

The **Mastering** and **Understanding** series will tell you everything you need to know about a subject. They're perfect for intermediate and advanced computer users, yet they don't make the mistake of leaving beginners behind.

If you're a busy person and are already comfortable with computers, you can choose from two SYBEX series—**Up & Running** and **Running Start**. The **Up & Running** series gets you started in just 20 lessons. Or you can get two books in one, a step-by-step tutorial and an alphabetical reference, with our **Running Start** series.

Everyone who uses computer software can also use a computer software reference. SYBEX offers the gamut—from portable **Instant References** to comprehensive **Encyclopedias, Desktop References,** and **Bibles**.

SYBEX even offers special titles on subjects that don't neatly fit a category—like **Tips & Tricks,** the **Shareware Treasure Chests,** and a wide range of books for Macintosh computers and software.

SYBEX books are written by authors who are expert in their subjects. In fact, many make their living as professionals, consultants or teachers in the field of computer software. And their manuscripts are thoroughly reviewed by our technical and editorial staff for accuracy and ease-of-use.

So when you want answers about computers or any popular software package, just help yourself to SYBEX.

For a complete catalog of our publications, please write:

SYBEX Inc.
2021 Challenger Drive
Alameda, CA 94501
Tel: (510) 523-8233/(800) 227-2346 Telex: 336311
Fax: (510) 523-2373

SYBEX is committed to using natural resources wisely to preserve and improve our environment. As a leader in the computer book publishing industry, we are aware that over 40% of America's solid waste is paper. This is why we have been printing the text of books like this one on recycled paper since 1982.

This year our use of recycled paper will result in the saving of more than 15,300 trees. We will lower air pollution effluents by 54,000 pounds, save 6,300,000 gallons of water, and reduce landfill by 2,700 cubic yards.

In choosing a SYBEX book you are not only making a choice for the best in skills and information, you are also choosing to enhance the quality of life for all of us.

Mastering
DOS 6
Special Edition

Mastering
DOS® 6

Special Edition

JUDD ROBBINS

San Francisco • Paris • Düsseldorf • Soest

SYBEX®

ACQUISITIONS EDITOR: Dianne King
DEVELOPMENTAL EDITOR: Gary Masters
EDITORS: Doug Robert, Guy Hart-Davis
TECHNICAL EDITOR: John Maurer
BOOK DESIGNER/PRODUCTION ARTIST: Suzanne Albertson
CHAPTER ART: Rick van Genderen
TECHNICAL ART: Rick van Genderen
SCREEN GRAPHICS: Cuong Le
TYPESETTER: Deborah Maizels
PROOFREADER: Elisabeth Dahl
INDEXER: Matthew Spence
COVER DESIGNER: Archer Design
COVER PHOTOGRAPHER: Michael Lamotte
PHOTO ART DIRECTION: Ingalls + Associates

To Davey Sensei,
who first opened my mind to the Way of the Universe

ACKNOWLEDGMENTS

MANY people have contributed to the production of this book. Naturally, most of these people work for SYBEX. I thank all of you for your efforts before and during the analysis, design, editing, and production of this work of ours: Gary Masters, for his initial insights into content; Doug Robert, for his editorial insights and sense of organization, and for his careful shepherding of the project through two editions; Guy Hart-Davis, for helping Doug; John Maurer, for checking the technical accuracy of what I wrote against the new version of the program; and to all the people behind the scenes, to whom I never really get a chance to show my appreciation—the typesetters, production coordinators, proofreaders, and screen graphics personnel who moved the book quickly and efficiently from manuscript to finished pages. So thank you Deborah Maizels, Suzanne Albertson, Elisabeth Dahl, Janet MacEachern, Cuong Le, and anyone I've missed. Thanks also to Rick van Genderen, who provided the drawings for this and for the previous edition.

But not everyone works for SYBEX. Just as life is in many ways like a run-on sentence, the contributions of certain people go on and on: My wife Lin Van Heuit-Robbins contributes to every book I write, in terms of the time she spends talking with me about how it's going, the time she spends helping me to decide on some art image possibilities, the time she spends looking at some of the computer effects I've created for the chapters, the time she spends discussing my upcoming books and other technical efforts and plans, the time she spends commiserating with me on the vagaries of Beta cycles for, and the unpredictability of, unreleased software, the time she spends cooking, cleaning, shopping, and working part-time herself, so I am able to concentrate more fully and successfully on my current book, the time we both spend struggling to be good, loving, and effective parents, and the time she spends loving me and all of our children so I can continue to enjoy my life with her and with my entire family throughout the sometimes tiring process of writing thousand-page books.

Contents
AT A GLANCE

CONTENTS

PART FIVE OPTIMIZING YOUR DOS OR WINDOWS SYSTEM

APPENDICES

INTRODUCTION

IF YOU have an IBM or compatible computer, DOS is usually a required part of your computer system. Owing to its nature as an operating system, any improvements to DOS are available to all the application software packages that you run. In fact, many of DOS 6's improvements, such as doubling the space available on your hard disk, or making more memory available to each application, will dramatically improve the efficiency and functionality of your overall system.

This being the case, DOS 6 is well worth acquiring, whether as an upgrade of an earlier version or as the version of choice for your new computer. Of course, this doesn't address the question of why you should buy this book.

Admittedly, you don't need to know very much about DOS in order to run your favorite word processor, or database manager, or spreadsheet. But the fact is, there is so much to DOS 6 it would be a pity not to take advantage of it *all*. And to do that, you need a book—a thick book, because there is so much to DOS 6—written from the perspective of real users who want to get the most from their systems and applications with the least additional money.

This book can *save* you money, by showing you how to implement a variety of utility capabilities with DOS commands alone. A well-written DOS macro or batch file can often take the place of a costly piece of additional software. You'll learn how to use DOS to set up your own menu system, diskette-cataloging mechanism, backup procedure, text-searching facility, and much much more.

In fact, there are more than 100 batch files and DOSKEY macros scattered throughout the pages of this book. Some are discussed in the special pages labeled *EXTRA!*, while others are presented and listed in *Note* or *Tip* boxes, or in standard chapter text. All of them are available on a single high-density disk that you can order from the author—see the Order Form at the end of this book.

What Is New with DOS 6?

DOS 6 incorporates a variety of new and powerful features that make it exceptionally attractive to users of all earlier DOS versions. If you've never upgraded since you bought your computer, now is the time. The price is right even if you get this version only for the ability to double your hard disk space without having to spend the much greater amount of money to buy an additional hard disk. **The new DoubleSpace facility** that provides this capability for disk compression is now built into the operating system.

DoubleSpace makes it a snap to as much as double the space available on hard disks, floppy disks, and removable cartridge disks. DOS includes a full-screen management program that makes it easy to manage and optimize these compressed disk volumes. **A new /C switch on the DIR command** provides information about the extent of newly available disk space on compressed volumes.

You'll learn how to personalize your DOS system in many ways, one of which is to set up customized menus for your individual programs. This menuing facility alone formerly required you to purchase a third-party menu program. Now, in conjunction with the batch file facility, **a new CHOICE command** permits user input selection and data input, which represents a valuable new built-in feature of DOS itself.

DOS 6 also includes an ability to **specify multiple configuration menus within your single CONFIG.SYS file**. This multi-boot capability is an easy and inexpensive mechanism within DOS itself that makes it easy for several people to share a single computer, or for one person to use a single computer in several different ways.

DOS 6 includes **a memory-optimization program called Mem-Maker** that makes it easy to automate the process of moving device drivers (in CONFIG.SYS) and memory-resident TSR programs (in AUTO-EXEC.BAT) from conventional memory to upper memory blocks. **The MEM command has been enhanced** to display additional information about memory availability and program use of your system's memory. **The LoadHigh and DeviceHigh commands have also been improved** to provide the ability to specify one of several possible memory regions to use when loading programs or device drivers.

Under DOS 6, most application programs can actually run faster, and seem to exceed their former limits. As you will discover, your application programs will seemingly be able to manage larger databases, spreadsheets, or text files than before. Part of this is due to MemMaker's more efficient use of upper memory. However, part of this improvement is also due to the **enhancements to the EMM386.EXE device driver** that offer more upper-memory-block access and permit applications to access extended memory or simulate expanded memory when necessary.

The Undelete utility has been dramatically enhanced in DOS 6 to provide what is called **Sentry protection**. This enables you to recover any accidentally deleted files with almost 100-percent certainty, using hidden directories to store copies of deleted files for a specified number of days after deletion. **DOS and Windows versions of Undelete are included** as part of DOS 6.

The Backup command has been completely replaced with a powerful state-of-the-art backup program. **The new MSBACKUP command** uses fast DMA (Direct Memory Access) techniques to rapidly back up files from one or more disk drives onto either floppies or onto other hard disks. DOS 6 also provides a Windows version, called MWBACKUP, of the same backup facility.

The Microsoft Anti-Virus program is a third example of an important utility that is included in DOS 6 in both MS-DOS and MS-Windows versions. This program can detect and remove hundreds of known viruses from your system, and can also alert you to the possibility of other virus intrusions that may not yet even have an identifiable name.

During setup of DOS 6, you can decide whether to install the DOS or Windows sets of files (or both) for Undelete, Anti-Virus, and Backup. If you request installation of the Windows versions, Setup **creates a Microsoft Tools Program Manager group in Windows,** with icons for each program. In addition, Setup adds icons to the File Manager menu bar for easy startup of these programs.

DOS 6 enhances performance in a number of additional ways. **The SMARTDRV disk caching utility now includes delayed writeback,** which holds data to be written in a cache until system resource demand is lighter; when written this way, the timing is such that application throughput is enhanced. DOS 6 also **includes the SMARTMON program, a special Microsoft Windows monitor for disk caching activities.**

Connectivity has taken a dramatic leap forward in DOS 6. Included with this latest version of DOS is **a pair of programs, INTERLNK and INTERSVR, that enable you to transfer files between two computers,** using either parallel or serial ports and cables.

Finally, DOS 6 offers **a host of new and enhanced features for obtaining online help and diagnostic problem solving.** The enhanced HELP command now provides a complete full-screen reference for all DOS commands. The **Microsoft Diagnostics program (MSD)** obtains and displays information about system internals for your hardware and software DOS system. And during system booting, you can press one of two function keys (F5 for a **Clean Boot** or F8 for an **Interactive Boot**) to control which device drivers are loaded, which CONFIG.SYS commands are executed, and whether or not the AUTOEXEC.BAT file is processed at all.

Part
ONE

Getting Started

CHAPTERS

CHAPTER

1

The Fundamentals of
DOS

EVERY computer that uses disks (hard or floppy) must have a master program that coordinates the flow of information from computer to disk and from disk to computer. This is called the *disk operating system*, or *DOS*. In this book, you'll learn about the operating system used on the IBM PC and compatible microcomputers.

This chapter will teach you how DOS is used and what useful functions it can perform. You'll see what disks and diskettes are and how DOS provides you with commands to manage them. You'll learn how data is organized on disk, so you can make informed decisions about which disks are appropriate for your use.

In this chapter, you will concentrate on taking the first few critical steps toward becoming a proficient user of this powerful operating system. You'll learn the aspects of the DOS graphic shell interface, which presents you with the means to visualize and perform complicated operations without having to concern yourself with remembering every single step the system must take to accomplish its tasks. As you study and play around with each part of the shell's visual screens, you'll also discover the most effective ways to use your keyboard and mouse to select files and enter commands. And since certain commands cannot be initiated through the graphic shell, you'll learn how to issue commands from the command prompt.

► EXTRA!

Worried about Phosphor Burn-in
on Old Monitors?

Note: These "EXTRA!" sections offer specialized information in the form of additional details about a topic, insider tips, or files you can use for specific purposes. They are not necessarily related to the main text; you can peruse them at random or skip them as you please.

Do you wonder if one of your old monitors is a victim of monitor burn-in? Or are you interested in buying an old monitor and would like to somehow know if it has been victimized by a checkered past? Use the BURNIN.BAT batch file to test any monitor for character burn-in. Run the batch file, which reverses the screen video mode, then look around the screen for faint images of characters that have been burned into the phosphor. (First, though, be sure to load ANSI.SYS in your CONFIG.SYS file, to be sure that the special Esc code sequences used here are interpreted correctly. See Chapter 9 for further details about the ANSI.SYS driver.)

```
@ECHO OFF
Rem BURNIN.BAT helps you check old monitors for phosphor
Rem characters that have been burned in.
@ECHO ON
CLS
PROMPT $e[7m
CLS
@ECHO Take a good look around the screen now.
@PAUSE
PROMPT $e[0m$p$g
CLS
```

DOS and Disks

The disk operating system is assigned the responsibility of integrating the various devices that make up a computer system. This responsibility is broken into three major tasks:

- coordinating the input and output devices, such as monitors, printers, disk drives, and modems

- enabling the user to load and execute programs

- maintaining an orderly system of files on disk

The first of these tasks is almost entirely a behind-the-scenes type of operation; as long as your devices are designed to be compatible with each other and are connected properly, DOS takes care of their interactions with only a minimum of involvement from the user. The second and third tasks are intrinsically linked to the size and complexity of both your computer system and your programs. The relative speed and ease with which you will be able to deal with programs and files is itself a result of how well you interact with DOS as it deals with your computer's memory.

Computer memory has one basic drawback. The area of memory in which your programs and data are stored, called *random-access memory* (*RAM*), cannot store information after the electricity has been turned off, even for a fraction of a second. To store information in the computer, you must have some means of recording it. The most common devices for this task are *disk drives*, which are devices that can read or write to magnetic disks.

The typical computer system contains at least one hard drive and one floppy. Some manufacturers offer a powerful cross between hard and floppy disks: *Removable cartridges*, such as the ones offered by the Bernoulli Corporation, offer the speed and voluminous storage advantages (90 million and 150 million characters) of hard disks, while offering the flexibility, convenience, and removability of replaceable floppy diskettes. I use Bernoulli cartridges as additional hard drives on my system. I also store rapid backup copies of my work on them.

Although my system also includes a 250Mb backup *tape drive*, I'm increasingly interested in the latest "floptical" technology: *optical disks* that

➤ **EXTRA!**

Disk Drives Come in Two Flavors

Magnetic disks are generally divided into two categories: *hard disks* and *floppy disks*. Floppy disks are often referred to as floppies or simply as diskettes. On a hard disk the magnetic storage medium is rigid, or hard. Hard disks are called fixed or nonremovable disks if they are built into the drive itself; they are called removable cartridges if they can be inserted into and removed from the disk drive.

Information is stored magnetically on a disk as a collection of *characters* (to be explained momentarily). Hard disks usually hold at least 20 million characters, and larger models that hold more than 200 million characters are now available from a variety of manufacturers. (To give you an idea of just how many characters this is, consider that 1 million characters is roughly equivalent to 600 pages of double-spaced text.)

Floppy diskettes store less information. The most flexible and common type of floppy, the 5¼" diskette, can store several hundred thousand characters of information, depending on the density of the magnetic material on the disk's surface. A high-capacity 5¼" diskette can actually store 1.2 million characters. An increasingly popular type is the 3½" diskette, often called a *microfloppy* diskette. It owes its growing popularity to higher storage densities, holding as many as 2.88 million characters, although the typical microfloppy holds 1.44 megabytes. In addition, the microfloppy's small size makes it easier to store and transport, contributing to its growing popularity.

can store tremendous amounts of data. Commonly available now are 3½" disks that store 21Mb of information.

By now you understand that different types of disks store different amounts of information. However, all disks share information in the same way—as a collection of *characters*. Any keyboard character can be stored and represented by DOS as a series of eight *bits* (of binary 0's and 1's). In computer language, a series of eight bits is known as a *byte*. Because eight bits can be arranged in 256 different ways, a byte can represent any of 256 different characters. Some of these characters are the ones you can type in (A–Z, 0–9, and so on); others are simply interpreted by DOS as *control* characters. This classification includes all special character codes that control special operations, like sounding a beep or performing a carriage return on a printer. (See Appendix C for more information on character sets and numbering methods.)

NOTE   Approximately one thousand (actually 1,024) bytes are together called a *kilobyte*, which is abbreviated as *K*. Approximately one million (actually 1,048,576) bytes are together called a *megabyte*, which is abbreviated as *Mb*.

When you wish to store important personal or business data on a computer system, you do so by creating a computer *file*. This is simply a named and reserved area of a disk, within which you'll store your data. From the computer system's perspective, each file is a complete collection of related characters. A single disk can contain both *program files* (instructions for the computer) and *data files* (data stored by the user). On any one disk, each file must be given a unique name, by which the computer refers to the file in order to load it from the disk into the computer's memory.

As you will learn, DOS contains a host of commands and programs to enable it to store information on any disks connected to your computer. It also has full responsibility for arranging your files on these disks in ways that will contribute to easy and efficient retrieval when you need them.

Disk Organization

Generally, when you buy a box of diskettes, the diskettes in that box are *not* ready to be used with your computer. Unless the box displays a banner

➤ EXTRA!

Get System Information on Demand!

Use the SYSINFO.BAT batch program, with a parameter value of 1 to 9, to obtain up to nine separate pieces of information (e.g., memory, disk usage, system efficiency) about your system configuration:

```
@ECHO OFF
Rem SYSINFO.BAT displays information about system aspects
Rem Set %1 equal to a single digit to indicate your request:
Rem See the ECHO statements below for Request Codes.
Rem Syntax:     SYSINFO RequestCode
Rem
IF '%1'=='' Goto Help
IF '%1'=='/?' Goto Help
ECHO Just a moment please...
Goto %1
:Help
CLS
ECHO You must specify a first parameter value to request:
ECHO.
ECHO 1  Available conventional program memory.
ECHO 2  Contiguity information, if any fragmentation exists.
ECHO 3  Default drive's cluster (allocation unit) size.
ECHO 4  Free space on default drive.
ECHO 5  Size of current directory.
ECHO 6  Size of default drive.
ECHO 7  Space consumed by data files on default drive.
ECHO 8  Space consumed by directories on default drive.
ECHO 9  Space/Name info about hidden files on default drive.
Goto End
:1
MEM | FIND "executable"
Goto End
:2
CHKDSK *.* | FIND "non-"
Goto End
:3
CHKDSK | FIND "each"
Goto End
:4
DIR | FIND "bytes free"
Goto End
:5
```

```
DIR | FIND "(s)"
Goto End
:6
CHKDSK | FIND "total disk space"
Goto End
:7
CHKDSK | FIND "user"
Goto End
:8
CHKDSK | FIND "dir"
Goto End
:9
CHKDSK | FIND "hidden"
ECHO Now finding details about each one of these...
DIR \*.* /S /AH /OGN /P
Goto End
:End
```

announcing that the diskettes have already been *formatted*, you must prepare the diskettes with some of the special programs provided with your disk operating system. In fact, even hard disks must be prepared in this way, although your computer dealer usually does this prior to delivering your computer.

When a floppy diskette is taken out of the box, it is totally blank. So, too, is a hard disk. A primary difference between diskettes and hard disks lies in the arrangement of the magnetic material. This material can be arranged on one or both sides of a diskette; accordingly, the diskette is described as *single-sided* or *double-sided*. Nearly all diskettes today are double-sided.

Diskettes can also have different densities. The more densely the magnetic material is written onto a diskette, the more information it can hold. Hard-disk drives are designed to work with several *layers* of magnetic material, which means they can store even more information.

In order for the computer system to use any disk as a medium for storing information, the entire disk must be divided into sections organized so that every physical location on the disk has a unique *address*. This is the same concept as assigning zip-code numbers to various towns and cities. When DOS assigns addresses, it then has an orderly way in which to store and then find various pieces of information. You needn't be concerned about this addressing mechanism, since it is really only for DOS's benefit. You only have to know the names of your files and the storage capacity of your disks.

The system of magnetic storage used by DOS is one of concentric rings (see Figure 1.1). Each ring is called a *track*. There are 80 tracks (numbered 0 to 79) on each side of a high-density 5¼" diskette. Each track is

FIGURE 1.1

There are 80 tracks on a high-density 5¼" diskette, numbered 0 through 79.

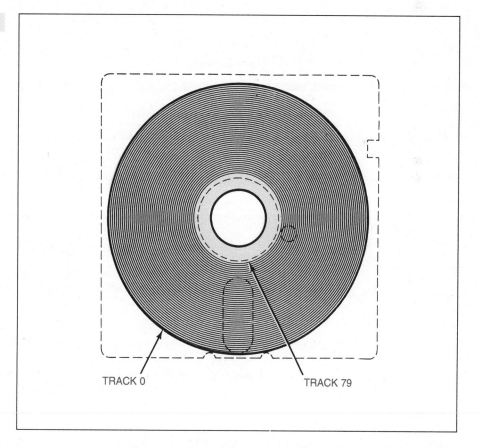

TRACK 0   TRACK 79

divided into smaller parts called *sectors*. Tracks and sectors are created when a disk is formatted. It is DOS's job to assign the necessary addresses for each track and sector.

The exact number of sectors per track depends on what type of diskette is being formatted (see Table 1.1). Standard double-sided double-density diskettes have 9 sectors per track, while the high-capacity diskettes available for the IBM PC-AT and compatibles have 15 sectors per track. Each sector can hold 512 bytes. The most common $3^{1}/_{2}$" diskettes, containing 1.44Mb, have 80 tracks per side, each track holding 18 standard 512-byte sectors. The newest $3^{1}/_{2}$" diskettes can store as much as 2.88Mb.

TABLE 1.1: Diskette organization

	$5^{1}/_{4}$" DISKS		$3^{1}/_{2}$" DISKS		
TRACKS	40	80	80	80	80
SECTORS PER TRACK	9	15	9	18	36
CHARACTERS PER SECTOR	512	512	512	512	512
TOTAL SECTORS	720	2400	1440	2880	5760
TOTAL CHARACTERS	360K	1.2Mb	720K	1.44Mb	2.88Mb

Some of the formatted disk space is not available to you for storing data— about 6K on a $5^{1}/_{4}$" diskette, and up to about 18K on a $3^{1}/_{2}$" diskette. When a disk is formatted, some of the sectors are set aside for keeping track of the information stored on that disk. Every formatted disk has these areas. Together, they serve as a catalog of the contents of that disk. These areas are called the *file allocation table (FAT)*, the *boot record*, and the *directory table*. The details of their use are beyond the scope of this book, but at least you are now aware of their impact on disk-space usage.

➤ EXTRA!

Password-Protect Your System When You Walk Away!

Use PASSWORD.BAT to blank your screen until you are ready to un-blank it. See the **DEBUG** section of Chapter 16 for explanation of how to create the CODESCAN.COM file, or use the Order Form at the end of this book to send for the Companion Disk which includes all programs and batch files from this book.

```
@ECHO OFF
Rem PASSWORD.BAT blanks screen until Ctrl+F10 is pressed.
IF EXIST CODESCAN.COM Goto OK
ECHO The CODESCAN.COM file must be available to PASSWORD.BAT
Goto End
:OK
ECHO Press any key to blank the screen.
ECHO Or press Ctrl+C if you don't know the password.
PAUSE > NUL
CLS
:Nope
CODESCAN
IF ERRORLEVEL 103 IF NOT ERRORLEVEL 104 Goto Yep
Goto Nope
:Yep
ECHO Welcome Back
:End
```

Understanding the DOS Shell Screen

To let you know that DOS is active, the computer displays its readiness in different ways, according to your system configuration. You can set up

DOS so that you see the screen entitled *DOS Shell*, which is the main control screen for all actions with DOS. If you do not see this screen, you can usually type **DOSSHELL** to bring up the shell, an example of which can be seen in Figure 1.2.

The different visible portions of the DOS shell enable you to keep track of and to exert control over different aspects of DOS. Figure 1.2 shows how the shell displays and provides access to directories (names of file groupings), individual files, and programs, both active (running) and inactive (ready to run). The next several chapters of this book will explain all of the various areas of the DOS shell in depth. You will learn what can be done with DOS, what will appear on the DOS shell screen, and how to request and initiate any of the available operations.

In this section, you should concentrate on understanding the various portions of the DOS shell screen, because you will probably be working with it every time you use your computer.

The top line is called the *title bar*; it contains a centered title for the screen contents. At times, other programs and utilities will appear to run on this graphic screen, displaying smaller rectangular windows of information. When these windows appear, they are always displayed with their own unique title bar that contains an identifying label for the window.

FIGURE 1.2

An example DOS shell screen, displaying some of the different areas available to aid you in your file-management and program-management tasks. (This is an example. Your screen will not initially look like this.)

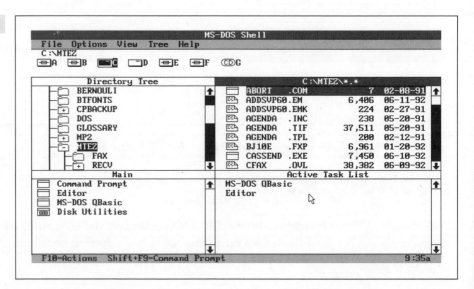

The line below the title bar contains what is known as the *menu bar*, which lists the names of the *menus* available while this screen is displayed. The menus themselves are boxed lists of commands and operations. When you select a menu name, by means of your keyboard or a mouse, the corresponding menu is displayed directly below the menu bar, as you can see in Figure 1.3. This type of menu is often called a pull-down menu.

FIGURE 1.3

The DOS shell's File menu displays commands and operations related to working with files.

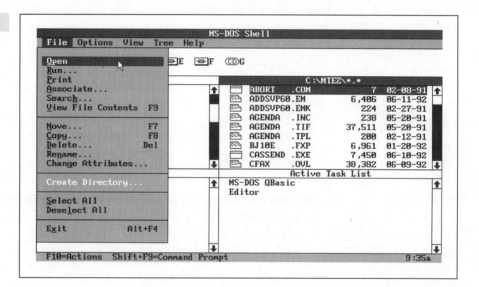

Just as the appearance of the shell can change, according to your personal configuration selections, so can the list of options on each pull-down menu change. I'll point out relevant distinctions at appropriate points during the discussions and examples in the next several chapters.

T I P

Also visible on the shell's menu bar is the Help choice. You'll discover later in this chapter how this choice can display one or more windows containing information explaining the shell's features and procedures.

> ➤ **EXTRA!**

The Guts of Your Screen Is the Selection Area

The largest area on the shell screen, the space between the top three screen lines and the bottom one, is called the *selection area,* because it is where you will make any necessary selections from the choices shown. All the important information about your system is accessible to you through this portion of the screen.

The selection area can contain several components, as you saw in Figure 1.2:

- **drives area** Displays the disk drives available on your system

- **Directory Tree** Lists the names of your disk's file groupings in a "tree" arrangement

- **files area** Lists and describes the files in the group selected in the Directory Tree area—in this case, it lists the *C:\MTEZ* directory

- **programs area** Lists available programs, or subgroups of programs

- **Active Task List** Lists currently running programs

Directly below the menu bar is the name of the *currently selected drive and directory*. In Figure 1.2 the current directory is C:\MTEZ.

The three areas discussed so far take up only the top three lines of the shell screen. The bulk of the rest of the screen—between the top lines and the very bottom line—is called the *main area* or *selection area*. This will show different contents depending on what you intend to do in the shell. The shell displayed in Figure 1.2 showed the main area split into five portions: the drives area, a directory tree, a files list, a program group, and an active task list. This arrangement will change according to the view you have selected. The titles of these different portions may also change. When a directory tree or active task list appears on your screen, it is always titled as such. The titles of the other portions, if they are titled at all, will reflect your system configuration and your earlier menu choices. For example, the group title *Main* (in the lower left area of Figure 1.2) is simply the heading for one of the groups of program choices available from the DOS shell.

Figure 1.4 shows an arrangement where the selection area displays only a program group window. I will show you later how to arrange your own shell in the same way; for now I just want to illustrate the different possibilities available.

Each choice in a program group either begins a program immediately or displays another group. If the choice displays another group, that choice becomes the new group title, replacing the previous one.

As you can see in Figure 1.4, the graphic symbol to the left of each of these choices can differ. (If your own screen is in "text mode" rather than "graphic mode," you will not see any of these symbols on your screen—you'll see only a small arrow to the left of the choice that has been highlighted.

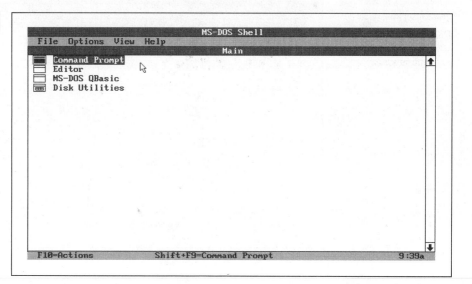

FIGURE 1.4

One view of the DOS shell shows only the program group window, occupying the whole selection area.

You'll learn shortly how to control this and other aspects of your screen display by means of a variety of choices from the Options menu.) The symbol beside the first three choices indicates that a specific program will be run if you select one of them. This symbol, or *icon*, is supposed to be a miniature screen window representing the executing program. The fourth choice (*Disk Utilities*) has an icon that is similar but which appears to contain something. This icon is intended to suggest that Disk Utilities represents not a program, but another group of choices, actually a separate group of programs. As Figure 1.5 shows, the Disk Utilities screen simply lists for selection a special group of DOS *utilities*, programs that are used for routine tasks. You'll learn below about copying and formatting disks (using the *Disk Copy*, *Quick Format*, and *Format* utilities), and you'll learn in Chapter 11 about backing up and restoring your hard disk (using the *Backup Fixed Disk* and *Restore Fixed Disk* utilities). Finally, in Chapter 19 you'll learn about recovering erased files (using *Undelete*).

You've now seen two views of the DOS Shell screen, one showing five possible areas and the other showing just one area. Since both screens are handled by the shell, the first two lines (title bar and menu bar) remain

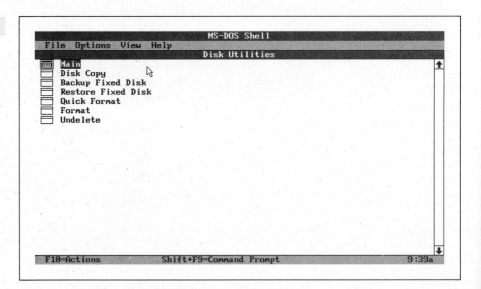

➤ EXTRA!

Extend DIR and CHKDSK Capability with DOS Macros

The DOSKEY utility (see Chapter 15) enables you to write and incorporate your own customized new commands into DOS. Here are three simple ones to demonstrate how easy it can be. To create any of these macros, you must have first loaded the DOSKEY utility.

CHKDSK2 automatically runs the **CHKDSK** command on two drives (C and D); modify it if your system has more than two hard drives. *DIRN* displays the current directory sorted by name. *DIRE* displays the current directory sorted by name within extension.

All three new commands can be created by typing these three lines at a command prompt:

```
DOSKEY CHKDSK2=FOR %i IN (C: D:) DO CHKDSK %i
DOSKEY DIRN=DIR /ON /P
DOSKEY DIRE=DIR /OEN /P
```

the same. The bottom line on all screens shown by the shell also remains the same. It is called the *key definition line* or *status bar*. It lists the most important function keys that are currently active. (It also displays the system time.)

In Figure 1.5, the key definition line reminds you that F10 (one of the numbered F keys—*function keys*—on your keyboard) moves the selection cursor to the menu bar for actions that can be taken, and it reminds you that pressing Shift+F9 leads to the *command prompt* (the topic of an upcoming section). Throughout this book, you will learn about a variety of special-purpose keystrokes. Shift+F9 is called a *combination keystroke*, which means that you must keep one key pressed down (in this case the Shift key) while pressing the other key (in this case function key F9).

In the following sections, you will learn how to select and activate one of the programs from the Main group of available programs. Then you'll learn how to work with a group of programs, such as the group seen in the Disk Utilities screen you saw in Figure 1.5.

Using Your Mouse or Keyboard in the Shell

If you have not yet managed to get DOS working on your computer, you should either refer to Appendix A for instructions on installing DOS on your hard disk or refer to Chapter 2 for instructions on getting DOS up and running. If you have done what you need to start your computer and load DOS, this is a good time to learn the various selection techniques. Moving the cursor, highlighting choices, and actually making selections are all simple chores; in fact, reading about them will take more time than just doing them. Using your keyboard or mouse when you read something here will ensure that you immediately understand what is explained.

Although the keyboard is essential to normal DOS operations, and the mouse is optional, most shell operations prove to be simpler when performed with a mouse. However, since you might not have a mouse on your system, this section will explain how to control shell functionality with either device.

In order to initiate a program or a DOS operation, or *select* a screen item for a subsequent action, you must first learn how to *highlight* a screen item. Remember that your shell screen may look slightly different from the one in this book, depending on how your system is configured. That will not detract from your ability to try the mouse and keyboard instructions offered in this section. Before learning more about highlighting and selecting items, let's take a closer look at the different portions of your DOS shell.

Beyond offering you an interface for selecting commands from menus, the shell is responsible for managing your application programs and files. As you probably suspect, the shell uses different areas of the screen for program management and file management. Program management may include displaying menus from which you can select commands to initiate programs, or display submenus of additional choices. It may also include a list of actively running programs, or *tasks*.

The file management aspect of the shell may use up to three portions of the screen to display information about your file system:

- the drives on your system (A, B, C, and so on)
- the directories (the names of the file groupings) created on those drives
- the names of the individual files in a particular directory

You will learn later how to determine for yourself which of these screen areas appears at any given moment in the shell. Regardless of which areas appear, however, you must follow the same general procedure to make anything happen from the shell:

1. You must first highlight a desired screen item.

2. You must then initiate a command or operation to carry out on that item.

TIP

Don't worry if you notice some apparent inconsistency in DOS's responses to single clicks and double clicks. In general, a single click highlights a choice and a double click actually activates a choice. However, since this is not always true—for example, with menu choices in a menu or with buttons in a dialog box—you can at times become frustrated. If a single click unintentionally runs a program, it's not a big deal. You can just return to the shell by selecting the appropriate *Exit* or *Quit* choice from that program's pull-down menu.

Table 1.2 indicates that each of these two steps can be accomplished with a mouse by moving the mouse pointer to a screen item and clicking Button 1 (usually the left button) on the mouse. Sometimes both steps can be accomplished at once by double-clicking on the item or by "dragging" the item with the mouse. I'll explain those operations in a moment. Keyboard users can achieve the same results by using the arrow keys to move the screen highlight to the desired item and then pressing the Enter key (or sometimes the spacebar).

TABLE 1.2: General mouse and keyboard techniques for the DOS shell

	HIGHLIGHTING	SELECTING
MOUSE	Click on item	Double-click on item
KEYBOARD	Use the arrow keys	Press the Enter key or the spacebar

Using the Mouse

If you have a mouse on your system, a mouse pointer is displayed somewhere on screen. Moving the mouse itself causes the mouse pointer to move correspondingly. If you want to highlight something on the screen using your mouse rather than your keyboard, you first move the mouse pointer to the desired item, then quickly press and release Button 1. This is called *clicking*. For example, move the mouse pointer to any file name and click on it; the file name line becomes highlighted. Try moving the mouse pointer to any directory name in the tree area; the directory name is highlighted, and the file area changes to display the file names found in that directory area.

N O T E

The mouse pointer appears as an outline of an arrowhead if your screen is in graphics mode, and as a solid rectangle if your screen is in text mode.

Notice how the item on which you click the mouse pointer is redisplayed immediately in reverse video. This extended reverse-video highlight on a screen item is called the *selection cursor*. Once an item is highlighted in this way, you can be confident of what item has been chosen for a subsequent operation.

Using the Keyboard

The procedure for highlighting items is more cumbersome for keyboard users. Whereas you can move the mouse pointer anywhere on the screen, the keyboard's arrow keys are more constrained. If you do not use a mouse for choosing items, you may use the four arrow keys to move the selection cursor, but only within one portion of the screen. Since there are a number of logically distinct areas of the DOS shell, keyboard users must first tell DOS which area they wish to be in. Once you've moved this *control focus* to a particular portion of the screen, the arrow keys can highlight one of the displayed items within that portion, and the Enter key can then initiate or activate the operation.

As Figure 1.6 indicates, you can press the Alt or F10 key at any time to switch the control focus between the menu bar and one of the shell areas. No matter what areas currently appear on your DOS shell screen, pressing F10 or the Alt key will switch from that area to the menu bar. Pressing F10 (or the Alt key) once more will switch back from the menu bar to the shell area that formerly contained the selection cursor.

When you first press F10, the word *File* will become highlighted on the menu bar, and the first letters of each of the other menu names on the menu bar will become underlined. You can then press the right and left arrow keys to change from any menu to its neighbor.

When a menu name is highlighted, pressing the Enter key will pull down the associated menu. You can then use the down and up arrow keys to highlight an item on the pull-down menu. Pressing Enter will then select, or activate, that particular choice.

THE FUNDAMENTALS OF DOS

FIGURE 1.6

Switching the control
focus using the
keyboard

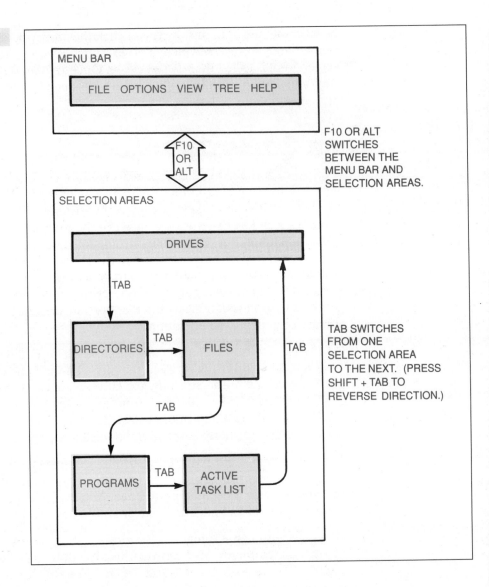

F10 OR ALT
SWITCHES
BETWEEN THE
MENU BAR AND
SELECTION AREAS.

TAB SWITCHES
FROM ONE
SELECTION AREA
TO THE NEXT. (PRESS
SHIFT + TAB TO
REVERSE DIRECTION.)

N O T E   If you press the left or right arrow key when a menu is pulled down, you will pull down the neighboring menu without having to take the intermediate step of first choosing the *name* of that menu.

Whenever a letter is underlined on a menu choice, you can type that letter on your keyboard and the choice will be activated immediately. Note that typing an underlined letter is faster than using the combination sequence of arrow keys to highlight plus Enter key to select.

When your DOS shell displays multiple information areas, you can successively move the control focus from area to area by pressing the Tab key, as suggested in Figure 1.6. When you press Tab, the next screen area becomes the focus of your next keyboard action. The area title (such as *Directory Tree*) is highlighted, and one entry in the area is also highlighted. If you have not previously moved the control focus to that area, the first item in the list is highlighted; otherwise, DOS keeps track of the last item highlighted in each area and highlights that item again. You can then use the up and down arrow keys to choose a different item.

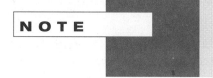
N O T E   The *Active Task List* is treated somewhat differently than the other areas. This subject will be covered in Chapter 5.

Using the Command Prompt

There are a great many commands possible in DOS. You can activate only some of them through the graphic screens of the DOS shell. In order to run the other commands, you must activate a command prompt, which enables you to *type* your instructions to DOS.

Initiating the DOS Command Prompt

When the *Command Prompt* choice is highlighted, as it is when the shell first displays the Main program group, you need only press Enter to initiate it. If your shell does not currently display the Main program group, you can initiate the command prompt by simply pressing the Shift+F9 key combination, as noted on the screen's key definition line. If the Main group *is* currently displayed, it might be faster to use the mouse and double-click on the Command Prompt program listed there.

If you have a mouse, try the double-clicking method now to activate the Main group choice called Command Prompt. Remember that to do this you move the mouse pointer onto the words *Command Prompt* and quickly press Button 1 (the primary mouse button) two times in a row. If this produces only the highlighting and nothing else happens, try pressing the button twice again but more quickly. Double-clicking is time-dependent; you must click twice in a very short time interval for it to be recognized as a double-click. Otherwise, it may be misinterpreted as Button 1 pressed two separate times.

(If you just have a keyboard and simply wish to explore the alternate method of selecting items, use the down or up arrow key to highlight *Command Prompt*. Remember that you will first need to press F10 to return the selection cursor back to the Main group choices if one of the items on your menu bar is currently highlighted. Again, once *Command Prompt* is highlighted, you only need to press the Enter key to activate it.)

When the command prompt is activated by any of these methods, you receive a more-or-less blank screen showing a "prompt"—usually the name of the current drive and directory. For example, you may see simply

```
C:\games>
```

Your prompt may be somewhat different; we'll discuss how you can modify it to your liking in Chapter 9. When the command prompt first appears, DOS usually also displays a couple of preliminary lines that include manufacturer, version, and copyright information.

When you see the prompt, you can issue any of the commands I present in this book. DOS 3.*X* (and earlier) users received this type of command prompt automatically when DOS was booted up. In these earlier versions, the *only* way to give instructions to DOS was from a prompt. In DOS versions 4 and higher, however, you can switch back to the graphic shell interface by entering the **EXIT** command (typing **EXIT** then pressing Enter) at the command prompt.

NOTE

As you may have noticed, I'll be using boldface to identify commands and words or characters you would be expected to type. I'll show longer command strings and phrases, however, in a different font, on separate lines.

The presence of the DOS command prompt is a simple indication that DOS is ready for your instructions. The prompt indicates the directory that is currently active; unless otherwise specified, all commands will affect data in that directory only. The presence of the prompt also tells you that you are not actively working in an application program.

In DOS 6, as you have seen, you have a choice between the graphic shell interface and the command-prompt interface. If you are an experienced user of an earlier version of DOS, you may want to switch to the command-prompt interface to initiate familiar commands. DOS 6 includes many new commands, but accepts nearly all earlier commands. DOS includes an on-line reference to the syntax and functionality of all its commands. (I'll present this reference in Chapter 2.)

Whenever a DOS feature is available through the graphic interface, this book will primarily explain how to activate the feature from the shell. Of course, you can also use the command prompt whenever you like, even if the feature has an easier, shell activation procedure.

► EXTRA!

Interpreting the Results of Using CHKDSK

Error messages about lost clusters are usually not serious. They occur when a program allocates space on the disk but never correctly completes the proper steps. This can occur when the program crashes, for instance, or when it runs into an error (such as insufficient disk space) that it doesn't properly handle.

Run the **CHKDSK/F** command to direct DOS to gather all of the lost (i.e., incompletely assigned) allocation units into files. If CHKDSK discovers lost allocation units, it will display a message similar to:

```
23 lost allocation units found in 5 chains.
Convert lost chains to files?
```

If you respond with Yes, the disk space in question, and the data within it, will be stored in files for you to later peruse or use.

You can then look at the data—CHKDSK stores it in files having .CHK extensions in the root directory. However, you can't do much with this information unless it is strictly ASCII text that can be easily handled by your word processor.

If the message you receive from the CHKDSK program does not identify lost allocation units, it may instead identify one or more files that have become "entangled" with each other. File entanglement means that more than one file has been assigned the same disk allocation units for storage of data. This is called *cross-linking*, and it is quite serious, usually resulting in the loss of some or all of the file data. The problem occasionally occurs after power problems or program crashes. When you run CHKDSK /F after this type of situation, you may receive a message like:

```
<Filename> is cross linked on allocation unit <UnitNumber>
```

Your best bet now to recover some or all of the cross-linked file is to use the **COPY** command to copy the cross-linked file to another disk location, then delete the original filename. You can then run the newly copied program, or use the data in the file, to determine if this recovery technique was successful.

Giving Commands to DOS

Since some commands *must* be entered from the command prompt, you need to fully understand how to enter and edit commands directly while you are not in the graphic shell.

When the blinking cursor is positioned at the DOS prompt, all you need to do is type in a valid DOS command and press the Enter key. The cursor moves as you type so that it always indicates the position of the next character to be typed. DOS does not process your request until it determines that you have actually pressed Enter. I will not specify that you press Enter after each command; instead, you should learn to use the key as an automatic end to each of your direct commands.

N O T E

Some DOS computers label the Enter key *Return;* others label it *Enter;* still others label it with only a ⏎ symbol. All are equivalent. In this book I will use *Enter* when I need to identify the key by name.

Additional qualifications for command requests include *parameters* and *switches*. Parameters identify the objects you want the command to act upon. When presenting parameters, I will use italics to characterize the information you need to type in (or enter by other means) when you give a DOS command. For example, to use the command **RENAME *OldFile NewFile*,** you would replace the descriptive terms for the *OldFile* and *NewFile* parameters with the actual old and new names of the file you want to rename. You might note that I used no space between the words in each parameter. I did this on purpose to indicate that spaces are not allowed within file names.

A switch slightly changes how a command executes. *What* the command does remains the same; only *how* the command executes its task changes because of the added switch. Modifying a DOS command with a switch is therefore analogous to modifying a verb with an adverb. For example, the command:

    CHKDSK

will analyze the files and organization of a disk drive (i.e., CHecK a DiSK). If the analysis discovers some disk problem, you will be alerted to it but DOS will do nothing about it. Adding the switch /F to the request, however—

    CHKDSK /F

—produces the same analytical report, but in addition instructs DOS to fix the problem.

As you learn new commands in this book, you'll also learn the most important and useful parameters and switches available with each command. In some cases, more switches exist, but their purpose is either obscure or not frequently needed.

Summary

This chapter introduced you to DOS—what it is, what it does, and how it is used. This chapter also contains specific information to guide your first steps with your new operating system. You discovered many important facts about DOS.

- You learned that information is stored on a disk in circular patterns called tracks, which are broken up into easily addressable, 512-byte portions called sectors.

- You learned that DOS arranges and maintains the physical and logical arrangement of information stored on the disks. Your programs and data are stored on the disk in collections of bytes called files.

➤ EXTRA!

How the Simple DIR Command Has Grown Up

You use the **DIR** command to ask DOS to display a listing of what files exist on a disk, or in some portion of the disk. Without this command, it would be extremely difficult, if not impossible, to operate a computer system of any size. The detailed format is shown here, since certain switches are well worth pointing out here:

```
DIR [FileSpec][/A:attributes][/B][/C][/L]O:order][/P][/S][/W]
```

Note that all parameters represented by FileSpec here are completely independent of one another. They can be used in any combination, either alone or together, to limit the directory listing.

FileSpec is an optional drive and path, including the file name and extension, of the file that is the object of the command.

/A limits the display to only those files whose attributes match the ones you specify. You can enter any sequence of the following attributes after the colon; spaces are not necessary between entries:

h | -h	Hidden (or not hidden) files
s | -s	System (or nonsystem) files
d | -d	Directory (or nondirectory) names
r | -r	Read-only (or read-write) files
a | -a	Archivable (or already archived) files

/B displays filenames only ("bare" format).

/C displays compression ratio of Dblspace volume files.

/L displays information in lowercase.

/O arranges the displayed entries in one of the following specified orders:

e | -e	By extension, alphabetical or reverse alphabetical
c | -c	By compression ratio, lowest (or highest) first
d | -d	By date and time, chronologically or reverse chronologically
g | -g	Group directories before, or after, other files
n | -n	By name, alphabetical or reverse alphabetical
s | -s	By size, increasing or decreasing

/P causes the computer to pause the directory listing and prompt you to continue listing the files if the listing is longer than one screen.

/S lists file entries in the specified directory and all subdirectories located below it hierarchically.

/W causes the directory listing to be displayed in a wide format (without listing the file size and date and time of creation or modification), with entries listed in a columnar arrangement.

You can preset the values of any of these switches in an environmental variable named DIRCMD. To later override a value that has been preset with the DIRCMD environmental variable, run DIR and prefix that switch with a hyphen (e.g., */-S*). For example, you could add the following line to your AUTOEXEC.BAT file:

```
SET DIRCMD = /OE /P
```

This would ensure that DOS would list all files in order of extension, and would pause after each screenful, whenever you simply typed **DIR** at any command prompt.

- Pressing the Shift+F9 key combination from the DOS shell displays the command prompt, which is needed only for those less frequently used commands not initially included in the DOS shell.

- Almost all of DOS's features and functions are available through the new graphic windowing interface (the shell), either by keyboard controls or with an installed mouse.

- Switches modify the operation of a DOS command, giving you the same sophisticated control over DOS commands that adverbs give you over verbs when you construct a sentence.

Now that you've learned the fundamentals of DOS, turn to Chapter 2 to get your DOS system up and running right now.

CHAPTER
2

Up and Running

YOU'VE learned what operating systems are. DOS is installed on your computer system, and you have taken your first few simple steps with it. Now that you can use your keyboard and mouse to control your DOS system, it's time to take a few larger steps. You should learn how to perform some essential system operations, such as copying your original DOS diskettes to protect them. In the process, you'll explore the major possibilities open to you when you first get your system up and running each day.

In addition, you'll learn to prepare disks for storing your valuable data and file information, as well as for booting up your system. Backing up your original system disks and exploring the status of a disk are necessary skills you'll also acquire here. In short, this chapter starts to teach you the ropes of DOS.

Before anything else, you'll learn how to get help whenever you need it using the online help system. Then, you'll set up your computer system so that all the rest of your work with DOS is visually pleasing. The DOS shell offers a variety of options that affect the appearance of the shell screen itself. In this chapter, you'll experiment with the options that control the screen colors and resolution. You'll learn how to control the remaining options in subsequent chapters.

Next, you'll actually run the important *Disk Copy* and *Format* utility programs included in the shell's Disk Utilities group. These utilities are necessary for safeguarding your original investment in DOS, and are equally important for proper preparation of the disks you'll be using for your applications.

Obtaining On-Screen Help

Getting Help in the Shell

Whenever DOS is displaying any of its graphic screens—that is, whenever you are using the shell—you can always press F1 to display a help window containing context-sensitive information. Context-sensitive means the help text is relevant to the current screen being displayed. If you have activated a program or process that displays a subordinate window, such as was done earlier with the *Disk Copy* choice, F1 displays text pertaining to that subordinate process. Figure 2.1 shows the help window you will see if you press F1 when the Disk Copy window is displayed.

Clicking on the *Index* button at the bottom of each help window provides you with direct access to *all* DOS help topics. (You can, alternatively, select the *Index* option from the shell's Help menu.) The help index presents a list of the shell's functions and features organized by category.

FIGURE 2.1

The help window displayed if you press F1 when the *Disk Copy* facility is active in the shell. This is an example of *context-sensitive help.*

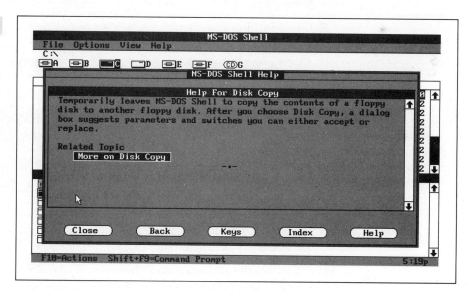

By choosing any of these topics with your keyboard or mouse, you can move through the help text system. Each successive selection displays a help text window that replaces the preceding one. Figure 2.2 shows the Help Index window that has replaced the Disk Copy help window.

The screen in Figure 2.2 has more text to display than can fit in the window being shown. This is why a *scroll bar* appears on the right side of such a help window. Mouse users can click on the down arrow symbol at the bottom of the scroll bar to scroll more text into the window in order to view the additional information. Keyboard users can simply press the keyboard's down arrow key to accomplish the same task. Naturally, you can scroll upward by pressing the up arrow key.

Getting Help at a Command Prompt

While you are entering commands at a DOS command prompt, you may need some immediate help in formulating an individual command. Help is also available to you here. It is not extensive, being limited to a brief description of the command's use and the formal syntax required when using that command. To obtain command-screen help, you merely type the command's name and add */?* before pressing the Enter key. You can

FIGURE 2.2

The Help Index window, which directs you to help on any topic, is obtained by selecting the *Index* button at the bottom of another help window or by selecting *Index* from the Help menu.

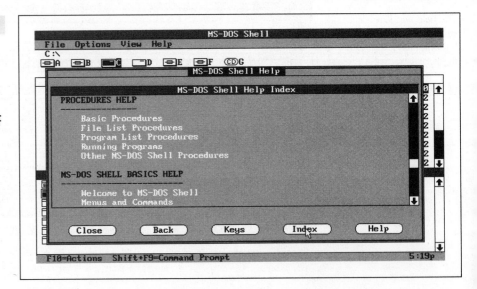

➤ EXTRA!

Use a Slider Box to Zip through Data!

Mouse users have more powerful control than keyboard users do over the display of information. Mouse users are able to drag the scroll bar's *slider box*, which appears as a vertical rectangle inside the scroll bar, between the up and down arrow symbols. The bottom screen in Figure 2.2 shows a help window after the text has been scrolled downward several lines—notice the position of the slider box.

The slider box moves inside the scroll bar relative to the length of the window's entire text, showing you how far along in the contents you've progressed. The size of the slider box changes from one help topic to another to give you an idea of how much information there is to scroll through. Think of the box as representing the current window and the rest of the scroll bar as representing the total amount of information to scroll through. Therefore, if the slider box fills half the scroll bar, the current window contains roughly half of the information to scroll through.

To use this slider box, position the mouse pointer over it, press Button 1, and then move the mouse without releasing the button. (This is called *dragging*.) When you finally release Button 1, the window is redisplayed at the new position in the text.

All of the shell's help screens operate this way, offering you a consistent interface to be used with either the keyboard or the mouse. In fact, you use a similar scroll bar in many other DOS operations that involve the display of more information than can be fit into one graphic window.

obtain the same result by typing **HELP** and the command for which you want information. Figure 2.3 shows the result when requesting help about the **FORMAT** command by typing:

```
FORMAT /?
```

Notice how brief the help is here. The shell's help system offers much more detail, usually including examples, notes, and complete syntax.

The result of using the /? switch after a command entered at a command prompt. This type of help is usually limited to explanations of the command's parameters.

```
C:\>FORMAT /?
Formats a disk for use with MS-DOS.

FORMAT drive: [/V[:label]] [/Q] [/U] [/F:size] [/B ¦ /S]
FORMAT drive: [/V[:label]] [/Q] [/U] [/T:tracks /N:sectors] [/B ¦ /S]
FORMAT drive: [/V[:label]] [/Q] [/U] [/1] [/4] [/B ¦ /S]
FORMAT drive: [/Q] [/U] [/1] [/4] [/8] [/B ¦ /S]

    /V[:label]   Specifies the volume label.
    /Q           Performs a quick format.
    /U           Performs an unconditional format.
    /F:size      Specifies the size of the floppy disk to format (such
                 as 160, 180, 320, 360, 720, 1.2, 1.44, 2.88).
    /B           Allocates space on the formatted disk for system files.
    /S           Copies system files to the formatted disk.
    /T:tracks    Specifies the number of tracks per disk side.
    /N:sectors   Specifies the number of sectors per track.
    /1           Formats a single side of a floppy disk.
    /4           Formats a 5.25-inch 360K floppy disk in a high-density drive.
    /8           Formats eight sectors per track.

C:\>
```

➤ EXTRA!

Use DOS Macros for Information and Deletion Control

The DOSKEY utility (see Chapter 15) enables you to write and incorporate your own customized new commands into DOS. Here are three simple ones to demonstrate how easy it can be. (To create any of these macros, you must have first loaded the DOSKEY utility.)

CLUSTER displays the cluster (i.e., allocation unit) size. *DEL* ensures that an attempted deletion is always confirmed. *DIRSIZES* prints the number of bytes consumed by each directory on the current drive. It ignores any slack space at the end of the file's last cluster.

All three new commands can be created by typing these three lines at a command prompt:

```
DOSKEY CLUSTER=CHKDSK $b FIND "each"
DOSKEY DEL=DEL $1 /P
DOSKEY DIRSIZES=DIR \ /S $b FIND "i" $g PRN $t ECHO ^L$g PRN
```

Although the shell's help offers more information, the value of the /? switch is that you can use it directly from the command prompt to obtain immediate assistance.

Controlling Your Screen Appearance

To this point, you've learned how to make screen choices and select items from any place on the screen. Let's use those skills now with your mouse or keyboard to set up your screen for the most pleasing color combinations, and the most useful screen resolution. To access either set of choices, you must move to the menu bar and pull down the Options menu (see Figure 2.4).

FIGURE 2.4

The Options menu offers expanded control over certain file operations and permits you to change your screen appearance.

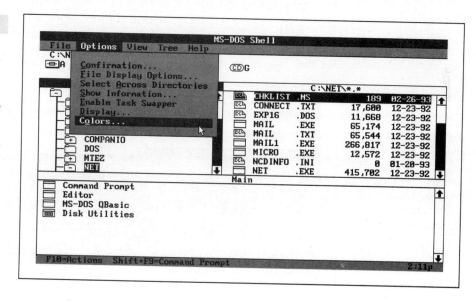

TIP Remember that if your screen is still at a command prompt that you reached from the shell, you can return to the main DOS Shell screen by typing the command EXIT and pressing Enter. If you've left the shell completely, you can initiate it again by typing DOSSHELL and pressing Enter.

Note that Figure 2.4 and the remaining figures show file information in the top half of the shell and program group lists in the bottom half. This is the default display of the DOS shell, though you are free to select a different screen arrangement from the View pull-down menu. You will learn below the meaning of all display choices on this menu. For now, let's concentrate on the Options menu.

Exploring Dialog Boxes

Selecting *Colors* on the Options pull-down menu brings up the screen shown in Figure 2.5. The window that appears in the center of your screen is a typical *dialog box*, which temporarily overlies whatever currently

FIGURE 2.5

A Color Scheme dialog box for changing the screen color combinations appears on screen after you choose *Colors* from the Options menu.

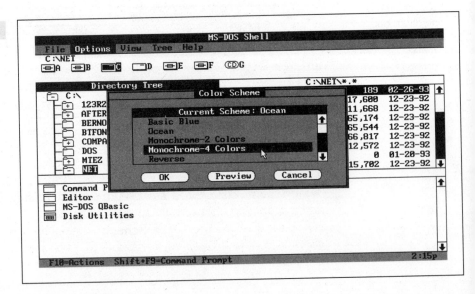

appears on your screen. These boxes, common in many application programs, offer a simple means of specifying additional requirements for selected actions.

A dialog box often has its own title, as you saw earlier in the help-window dialog boxes when you learned about on-screen help. In this example, the dialog box is titled *Color Scheme*. Within the dialog box, information is laid out for you in different ways, depending on the task being accomplished by each dialog box. Scroll bars appear in many dialog boxes, and a slider box within the scroll bar appears when more information is to be displayed than can fit within one window. The Color Scheme dialog box offers this type of scroll bar to allow you to see the additional choices.

When a dialog box first appears, the screen cursor is positioned in the center area above the on-screen pushbuttons. This indicates the location of the dialog box's control focus. Pressing Enter at that moment would tell DOS that the currently selected choice (e.g., *Monochrome-4 Colors* in Figure 2.5) is acceptable. If you wish to change the screen's color scheme to one of the available alternatives, you must first highlight the appropriate choice, then press Enter or select the OK pushbutton.

Keyboard users can press the Tab key to move the selection cursor from the center area to the pushbuttons. When you first press Tab, DOS moves the cursor to the *OK* pushbutton, then successively to *Preview* and *Cancel*, and lastly back to the central area of the window that contains the list of color schemes.

Once you've highlighted one of the color schemes, choosing the OK pushbutton instructs DOS to adopt that color combination for all subsequent shell displays. DOS will even remember your selected color scheme the next time you power up your computer and activate the shell.

If you wish to temporarily see how the shell would appear in a particular color combination before you decide whether you want to accept it, just select *Preview* after highlighting a color scheme. DOS will immediately redisplay your entire screen using the new color combination. Since the Color Scheme dialog box itself reappears in the new colors as well, you have a chance to choose *Preview* repeatedly for different color schemes. If you select *Cancel*, the Color Scheme dialog box disappears, and your screen is restored to the color scheme that was in effect before you chose *Colors* from the Options pull-down menu.

> ➤ EXTRA!

Use the Keyboard to Control Everything!

Keyboard users can press the Tab key to successively rotate the control focus within a dialog box. As you press the Tab key, the focus switches through each pushbutton and each selection area found in the dialog box. Many dialog boxes contain more pushbuttons than just the OK and Cancel seen so far.

Once a choice has been made, pressing Enter will complete the selection. If you want to practice, try one of these methods now with the Color Scheme dialog box to change your screen's colors.

Changing the Screen Color Combinations

Figure 2.6 depicts the result after previewing *Reverse* from the list of choices in the Color Scheme dialog box. Depending on the type of monitor you are using, the appearance of your screen will differ from mine in color, resolution, and emphasis. Therefore, this figure merely represents, in black and white, the general appearance your DOS screens will take on if you select a different color combination.

The name of the current color scheme is indicated just above the list of possibilities. If you like the color, just press the Enter key; the dialog box will disappear and DOS will adopt that scheme for all subsequent screen displays. DOS will also recall this color scheme the next time you power up your machine. Take a moment now to try each of the possibilities and decide on the best color combinations for the rest of your work with DOS.

FIGURE 2.6

The appearance of a reverse-color screen depends on the monitor you are using.

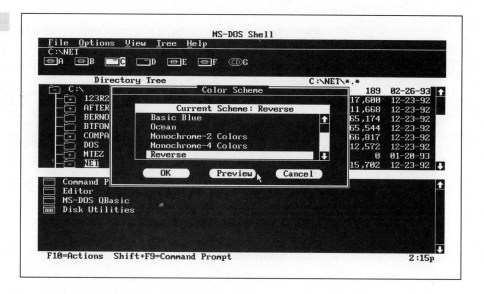

Selecting the Best Screen Mode

In addition to changing colors, the shell offers a limited ability to control screen *modes*. Return to the Options pull-down menu (see Figure 2.4) and select the *Display* choice. This brings up the Screen Mode dialog box shown in Figure 2.7. Your screen may be slightly different, depending on the particular video board that you have installed.

By selecting one of the modes shown, you can control whether DOS uses high or low screen resolution, and whether the shell appears in text or graphics mode. There are valid reasons for choosing each of these possibilities. For example, my monitor has the option of displaying in either graphics or text mode, with low or high resolution, so I could choose any of the listed options. I find graphics mode more eye-appealing and I find low resolution easier on my eyes for the amount of time I spend looking at the monitor; therefore, I normally use the low resolution capability (25 lines are displayed) in graphics mode, as seen in Figure 2.7.

The *Display* choice on the Options menu brings up a dialog box for controlling the screen *mode*—that is, the size and style of the characters and symbols.

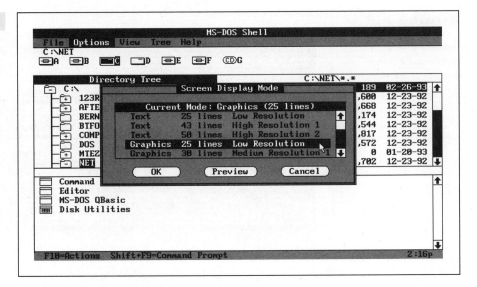

If your monitor is capable of displaying in different modes, you can switch screen modes to suit your needs. For example, Figure 2.8 depicts the shell when previewing low-resolution *text* mode.

You'll notice several visible changes in text mode. The mouse pointer now appears as a reverse-video solid rectangle, and the icons that were beside most of the items have been removed. Only a small arrow remains to indicate the currently chosen screen item; in this sample screen, the selection cursor is located at the low resolution text choice in the Screen Mode dialog box. The arrow just to the left of this entry will automatically move to another portion of the screen when you exit from this dialog box and move the control focus to one of the other screen areas.

TIP Use text mode to obtain faster response from DOS.

Notice how the icons that were formerly visible beside the directory names in the directory tree area have changed from symbolic file folders to textual brackets. When DOS displays its screens in text mode, no

FIGURE 2.8

Viewing the shell in
text mode

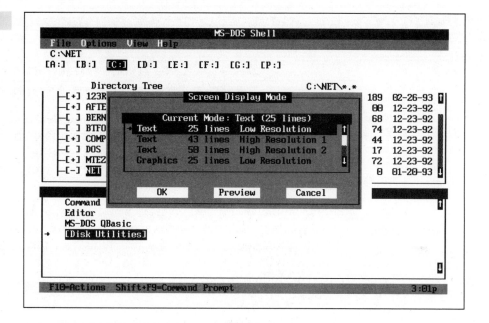

graphic characters are used. If you and your applications do not require
the graphic icon displays, you can obtain faster response from DOS by
using the text mode.

Exploring the Primary DOS Utilities

DOS incorporates several key operations in the Disk Utilities group of
programs. Each of these utilities has a direct DOS command equivalent,
which will be presented in the corresponding section below. You needn't
execute these commands directly, since they can easily be executed from
the Disk Utilities group in the shell. However, it's useful to begin to understand how the shell's choices actually are just a simpler way of executing DOS commands. In the following sections you will be given the
opportunity to use some of these commands just to see the difference.

> ► **EXTRA!**

See More Information with High-Resolution Modes

If you have a high-resolution monitor, you can take advantage of the higher screen resolutions—in either text or graphics mode. Higher resolution allows the same information to be shown in a smaller area of the screen. This means that you can potentially see more total information at the same time.

For example, on my system DOS will show up to 50 lines of information in the higher resolution mode versus the more conventional 25 lines in the lower resolution mode. Some programs can take advantage of these modes to display more information. Depending on your equipment, the Screen Mode box may offer even more choices in regard to the number of lines.

In order for a program to take advantage of the shell's display mode and resolution, you must switch the mode appropriately before running such programs. Further, such programs must be run *from the shell,* not from the command prompt. Many programs that use their own display mode will be unaffected by changes you make to the DOS shell.

Preparing Your Disks for Use

As you learned in Chapter 1, all disks must be prepared correctly before you can use them. This goes for hard disks as well as all 5¼" and 3½" diskettes. All disks, once formatted, can store any information you like, including programs. Such disks are called *data disks*, or, when they contain only programs, *program disks*.

If you also want a diskette to be able to start your system (in other words, to *boot* it), then you must include special DOS files on that disk, and you must prepare it in a special way. Once you've followed these steps, the disk is called a *system disk*. Note that, as a consequence of adding these special DOS files to the disk, there will be less room remaining to store data and programs.

NOTE

Hard disk users will not normally need to take additional steps to make their hard disk a system disk, since their hard-disk drive is prepared during the installation process to boot DOS.

The next sections will teach you how to format data disks and how to create system disks. The Format utility (or **FORMAT** command) is the primary tool for doing both operations. As you'll see, you simply add a special switch to create a system diskette. A number of other switches allow you to specify different diskette densities and layouts. You can always use the on-screen help system to explore these other possibilities.

Formatting a Data Diskette

Use a *scratch diskette* to try the following preparation commands. A scratch diskette is one that is fresh out of the box from your local computer store or is any old diskette that contains information you don't care about. If you do not have one, you should get one before you continue reading.

In order to prepare any diskette for use, you must select *Format* from the Disk Utilities group. However, it is possible that the Disk Utilities program group is not yet visible on your DOS Shell screen. In order to bring up this menu and begin the formatting process, you should move to the menu bar, pull down the View menu, and select *Program List*. (You'll explore the choices on this pull-down menu further in Part Two of this book.)

Making this choice will display either the Main program list or, if you've already been using the program-management feature of the shell, the most recently used program list. If the Main group appears, first make the appropriate choice to display the Disk Utilities group.

What's So Unique about a System Disk?

A system disk is any disk that contains the files necessary to boot a DOS system. There are two ways of looking at the special files included on system diskettes:

- hidden vs. visible
- internal vs. external

You should understand both to fully understand when to create and use system diskettes.

A large part of DOS is invisible to the user, but still requires space on a system diskette. DOS has two parts, one of which, the *hidden files* part, is stored on the disk but does not appear on the disk directory. The other part is a file called COMMAND.COM, which is visible on every diskette used to start up or boot the system. In DOS 6, COMMAND.COM occupies approximately 52K, while the two hidden system files together occupy almost 80K. All together these files constitute over 130K; you will pay this price in disk space on every system (boot) disk you create.

The many other actions performed by DOS are divided into two types. *Memory-resident*, or *internal*, commands are essential or frequently used actions. These commands are automatically loaded into the computer's memory during the booting process. They are actually included in the COMMAND.COM file, so they will be able to execute immediately when you want.

Disk-resident, or *external*, commands are really for special purposes. These are found in separate files on your hard disk so that they do not typically consume valuable memory space. They are loaded into memory only as called for (for example, on entering the specific command name).

You can find lists of DOS's internal and external commands under the *Internal commands* and *External commands* entries in the Glossary.

On this Utilities menu you can see two choices that have to do with formatting disks. The most inclusive choice is *Format*; it brings up the dialog box seen in Figure 2.9, which permits all the capabilities of the **FORMAT** command. Naturally, the time it takes to complete a disk format depends on the speed of your hardware and the size of the disk being formatted.

TIP

If the first thing you do with the cursor in an entry field is to type a letter, DOS deletes the contents of the entry field and simply shows the letters you type. To simply *add* characters to an existing entry, first position the cursor somewhere *within* the field and then move it to where you want to start typing.

In this example, the *a:* parameter is automatically inserted into the dialog box's entry field. If you have two floppy drives, you might intend to format diskettes in your B drive. If this is the case, you must ensure that the parameter entered in the dialog box is *b:*. Do this by simply typing **b:** when the dialog box appears. If the first thing you do with the cursor in an entry

FIGURE 2.9

The Format utility's dialog box shows a *Parameters* entry field for you to identify which drive you want to use. For this example, *make sure you enter only the letter identifying one of your floppy-disk drives!* (usually A: or B:)

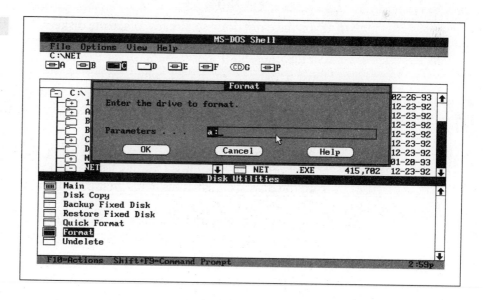

field is to type a letter, DOS deletes the contents of the entry field and simply shows the letters you type. Pressing Enter will then invoke the **FORMAT** command with one parameter, that being the drive containing the diskette to be formatted.

TIP

You can use the UNFORMAT command (see Chapter 19) to retrieve much of the data from an accidentally formatted disk. If for security reasons you want to ensure that a format operation totally eradicates any previously existing information on a disk, enter the /U switch after the drive parameter for the FORMAT command.

Once this command begins, the Format utility program will ask you to place a diskette in the drive you've specified. For example, in the case where you are using a hard disk to format a disk in drive A, you will see the following prompt:

```
Insert new diskette for drive A:
and press ENTER when ready...
```

If you have not done so already, place the diskette in the drive at this point. When you are ready to begin the formatting process, press Enter. DOS will take over and erase any data on your diskette. It electronically lays down a pattern of marks, which make up the tracks and sectors you learned about in Chapter 1. The number of seconds it takes to format the diskette varies, depending on the size of the diskette (double-density, high-capacity, etc.).

To prevent unauthorized users from formatting disks, you can rename the *Format* entry on the Disk Utilities list, or you can remove it completely from the displayed list. This helps guarantee that disks with valid data will not be formatted and have their data destroyed. You can go even further by password-protecting the *Format* choice on the Disk Utilities screen. Chapter 5 explains how to control all of these possibilities.

➤ **EXTRA!**

Don't Cut Corners When You Format Your Disks!

You can speed up a format in some instances by selecting *Quick Format* from the Utilities menu, but I recommend against using this brief timesaver. Let me explain why.

A Quick Format can only be accomplished on a disk that has been formatted previously. Because much of the track and sector work would already have been done during the previous formatting process, a Quick Format can complete in a relatively short amount of time. It does this merely by erasing the disk's root directory and file allocation table. Although this is a faster process, it reminds me of the saying "penny wise and pound foolish."

Since such a Quick Format does not check the entire disk for areas that have failed, as a complete format does, you may later lose data that could otherwise have been stored and retrieved successfully. Data can indeed be written to sectors that have gone bad since the last complete format—which is to say, data can be stored in places you'll never be able to retrieve it from. During a complete format, any areas that are noted to be bad are forever restricted from use. Hence no data will ever be written to such areas, so you are far less likely of losing important data.

Diskettes can be formatted as many times as you like. You can even format some diskettes that were used previously by another computer. Of course, any information stored by the other computer on that diskette will be wiped out.

Although the default size for formatting is established by the disk drive used, diskettes are rated according to certain production characteristics. Therefore your data will be safest if you buy and format diskettes with the same rating as the drive on your system. For example, if your system has a 1.2Mb 5¼" floppy-disk drive, do not attempt to squeeze 1.2Mb out of a double-sided, double-density diskette whose manufacturer's rating is 360K. The reverse warning is also true, but for a different reason. Because of hardware incompatibilities, it is unsafe for your data if you attempt to format a 360K diskette in a 1.2Mb drive, then later use that diskette in a different 360K drive.

When the formatting is complete, you are automatically prompted to enter a textual label for this newly formatted diskette:

```
Volume label (11 characters, ENTER for none)?
```

When the overall process is done, DOS shows you how much space was found on the disk, and how much space remains available for your files. For example, the total bytes formatted is 362,496 bytes on a double-sided, double-density diskette or 1,213,952 bytes on a high-capacity diskette. In addition, DOS also creates and writes a hidden file (named UNFORMAT.DAT) which can be used by the **UNFORMAT** command to recover a disk that has been accidentally or erroneously formatted. This explains the 14,848-byte entry seen in the following example.

You are also told how many bytes exist in each physical block on the disk (often called a *cluster*; formally called an *allocation unit*), and how many of these blocks are available. DOS also assigns a unique serial number to each formatted diskette and writes that number on the first (reserved) sector of the diskette. For example,

```
1213952 bytes total disk space
  14848 bytes used by system
1199104 bytes available on disk
    512 bytes in each allocation unit
   2771 allocation units available on disk

Volume Serial Number is 1550-0BFF
```

DOS will then ask you if you want to format another diskette. If you type **Y** for Yes and press Enter, the process will begin again, and you will be prompted to insert another diskette in your selected drive. If you are done, you enter **N** for No. The format operation will end, returning you to DOS. DOS is now ready for your next command, and your formatted diskettes are ready to accept information.

➤ EXTRA!

Adjust the Date/Time Stamp on Any File

Use the DATETIME.BAT batch file to adjust the date and time stamp of any file. Run this batch program by specifying the name of the target file, or files using a wildcard specification, as the first parameter. After running the batch program, the target file(s) will then reflect the current system date and time:

```
@ECHO OFF
Rem DATETIME.BAT adjusts a file's date/time stamp from
Rem its existing values to the current date/time.
Rem Allows a wildcard spec to update multiple files at once.
Rem Syntax: DATETIME FileSpec
:ANOTHER
IF %1Z==Z GOTO END
FOR %%X IN (%1) DO COPY %%X /B + > NUL
SHIFT
GOTO ANOTHER
:END
```

Making a System Diskette

There are various circumstances that require system diskettes:

- If you ever need to run DOS on an old system that does not have a hard disk, you will need to boot the system from a floppy.

- If many users share a single computer and they are not all comfortable with the same version of DOS, different versions of DOS can be placed on different system diskettes. Each user can place the desired boot disk in the A drive before powering up the system. The most popular version can be installed on the hard disk so that in most cases the system can be powered up without a disk in the A drive.

- In order to meet the special requirements of some older application programs, you can always boot an earlier DOS version from a floppy system diskette that has been specially configured to run your applications. After this application has run, you can reboot your system to once again run your newest applications under DOS 6.

- You may find situations where you want to run the same version of DOS but with different configurations. For example, you might need to prepare a system diskette with the same version of the DOS system files that exist on your hard disk, but with different CONFIG.SYS and AUTOEXEC.BAT files to control both startup and configuration setup. (These files will be discussed in Chapters 9 and 14, respectively.)

- Whenever you will be making configuration changes to your system, you should *first* make a system disk with copies of your current CONFIG.SYS and AUTOEXEC.BAT files, in case those important files change irretrievably. This will enable you to reboot your system from this system disk, if your hard disk refuses to boot because of your configuration modifications.

Making a system diskette requires you to understand the difference between a system disk and a non-system disk. An MS-DOS system disk is one that contains three special files: IO.SYS, MSDOS.SYS, and COMMAND.COM. If you want to boot up DOS with a disk, that disk must contain these system files. Only if this is true can the DOS boot-up program find them, load them, and bring up DOS properly.

If you look at a directory listing of a system disk, you will generally see only COMMAND.COM listed. The other two files are purposely hidden from view to avoid any accidental erasure or modification of them. There is an easy way to list the hidden files as well, but for now just accept that these files are contained on any system diskette you create using the procedure to be presented in this section. The three DOS files account for all necessary tasks for managing your hardware and running your applications. COMMAND.COM is the primary file and handles the interpretation of each of your command requests, whether submitted at a command prompt or from the shell. The IO.SYS file contains the software programs for sending data to and receiving data from peripheral devices like printers and disks. The MSDOS.SYS file contains the logic and routines for managing the data organization itself. In essence, the more nitty-gritty signal and data communications are handled by routines in IO.SYS, and the file and program-management aspects of DOS are controlled by logic in MSDOS.SYS.

These files contain most of the information that you have been calling DOS. When you turn on the computer, one of the first things it does is seek the information in these files and read it into memory. The appearance of the DOS shell or the availability of the command prompt indicates that these files have been read and stored in the computer's internal memory.

What would happen if you turned on the computer and the boot drive did not contain these system files? The computer would not load DOS and would therefore not be capable of using the disk drives. You would then receive a message requesting that a DOS system diskette be placed in the boot drive:

```
Non-System disk or disk error
Replace and strike any key when ready
```

To correct the situation, you would insert a diskette that has the DOS files and reboot the system. At this point, simply pressing Enter (or any other key) is sufficient for rebooting.

Occasionally, you will see this same message even though you have a properly prepared hard disk that contains all the necessary DOS files. This occurs when a nonbootable data diskette has been left in the A drive from the last work that someone did with this computer. The solution is simply to remove the data disk and press Enter for DOS to continue the booting process with the files from your hard disk.

You can see that having DOS on a disk is important. When you used the **FORMAT** command previously, you created a nearly blank diskette. This was not a system diskette, because it did not have the three crucial DOS files on it. Now you will learn how to format a diskette and copy the system's files to it at the same time.

To format a system diskette in the A drive, you choose *Format* from the Disk Utilities group as you did in the last section. When the Format dialog box appears, you should first press the right arrow key to move the cursor beyond the *a:*. Then, you can type **/S** and press Enter. The */S* (the System switch) tells the computer to add the DOS system files to the diskette in drive A when completing the formatting process. Pressing Enter once again invokes the **FORMAT** command with *a:* as the drive identifier and */S* as the switch requesting that a system disk be prepared. When the process is done, DOS tells you how much space on this disk was consumed and how much remains available for your use. In this example, the diskette in drive A will now be a system disk. You can use it to get the computer started.

➤ EXTRA!

Organize Your Floppies with Printable Labels!

Use the FLOPPY.BAT batch file below to produce an editable file (DIRLIST.TXT) that contains a printable list of file names found on each floppy diskette. Use your word processor to arrange the information as you like, then print out a label for each floppy diskette.

```
@ECHO OFF
Rem FLOPPY.BAT produces an editable disk directory file.
IF EXIST DIRLIST.TXT ERASE DIRLIST.TXT
:NewFloppy
CLS
ECHO Place a floppy disk in drive A:
PAUSE
LABEL A:
DIR A: /W /ON >> DIRLIST.TXT
CHOICE "Disk Logged. Do you have another to log"
IF ERRORLEVEL 1 IF NOT ERRORLEVEL 2 Goto :NewFloppy
Rem Users of earlier DOS versions should remove the preceding
Rem two command lines and use the next four lines instead.
REM ECHO Disk Logged. Press Enter if you have another to log.
REM ECHO Press Ctrl+C if you have no other floppies to catalog.
REM PAUSE >> NUL
REM Goto :NewFloppy
:End
```

Backing Up a Floppy

In this section you'll see how to make backup (duplicate) copies of diskettes to reduce the risk from losing or damaging them. Once you've made copies of your original diskettes, you can then employ the backup diskettes while carefully storing and protecting the originals.

The *Disk Copy* choice from the Disk Utilities group will make an exact copy of another diskette. (It cannot be used to copy a hard disk.) When you make copies of any diskettes, be sure to use diskettes that are the same size and density (e.g., $3\frac{1}{2}$" low or $3\frac{1}{2}$" high density, or $5\frac{1}{4}$" double or $5\frac{1}{4}$" high density) as the originals.

The shell's Disk Copy utility uses the **DISKCOPY** command behind the scenes. It is the fastest way for DOS to copy an entire diskette. This disk-copying procedure is valid for making copies of any diskettes, whether they are financial data diskettes or third-party application programs. However, the procedure differs depending on how many floppy-disk drives you have.

N O T E

DOS prompts you several times during the disk-copying operation, referring to your original diskette (which you are copying) as the *source* diskette, and referring to the blank or scratch diskette (to which you are making your copies) as the *target,* or *destination,* diskette.

Copying with Only One Floppy-Disk Drive

The following exercise will use the Disk Copy utility and a single floppy drive to create an exact copy of each of your DOS 6 diskettes. You will need as many scratch diskettes for this purpose as your version of DOS ($3\frac{1}{2}$" or $5\frac{1}{4}$") comes with.

➤ **EXTRA!**

Write-Protection Differs on 5¼" and 3½" Disks

Each box of new 5¼" diskettes includes a sheet of small adhesive tabs called *write-protect tabs*. On the side of each of the diskettes is a square notch called a *write-protect notch*. If you place one of the tabs over a diskette's notch, it becomes impossible to write information onto that disk.

Before copying any of your original diskettes, it is wise to place write-protect tabs over the original diskette's notch. That way, if you make a mistake in handling the diskettes during the copy procedures, DOS will not erroneously overwrite your original data.

3½" diskettes have a different write-protection mechanism. It is built into the diskette housing itself. In the upper right corner of the diskette (upper right when you're holding it with the metal faceplate down) is a small rectangular window. Normally, you cannot see through this window because a slide switch (located on the back of the diskette) covers the opening. If you wish to write-protect this diskette, you must slide the switch so that the opening is revealed.

Conceptually, these techniques are very different. On the larger diskette the notch must be covered, and on the smaller diskette the hole must be uncovered, in order to inhibit the drive from writing any data onto the disk.

First select *Disk Copy* from the Disk Utilities group. You will see the Disk Copy dialog box shown in Figure 2.10.

The default parameters are *a:* and *b:*. Backspace over the *b:* since you are making a copy using only one drive (the A drive), and change the parameters so that the second entry is replaced by *a:*. DOS will then use drive A to read a source diskette and then use drive A again to write the

FIGURE 2.10

To copy an entire diskette, choose the *Disk Copy* utility from the Disk Utilities program group, and enter the source and destination (original and copy) drive(s) in the Parameters field.

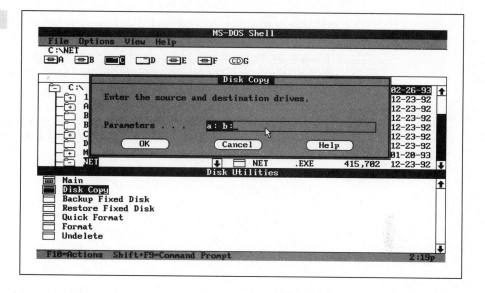

target diskette. When the disk copy command executes, DOS will first prompt you like this:

```
Insert SOURCE diskette in drive A:
Press any key to continue...
```

In this single-diskette environment, DOS will first ask you to place the source diskette in drive A and then later ask you to place the target diskette into the same drive.

Once you have inserted the diskette and pressed the Enter key, DOS will give you an informative message as it copies your diskette. This message will vary according to the diskette's storage density and its number of sides. For example,

```
Copying 80 tracks
15 Sectors/Track,2 Side(s)
```

When DOS has read as much as it can from the diskette, it will prompt you to

```
Insert TARGET diskette in drive A:
Press any key to continue...
```

At this point, take a label and write the name of the original disk you are copying, and place the label on one of your scratch diskettes. Remove the source diskette, place the newly labeled diskette in drive A, and press Enter. DOS will then copy to the scratch diskette whatever part of the source diskette it was able to read in its first pass. The amount will depend on the total size (in bytes) of your source diskette and the amount of memory your computer has available for this kind of task. If the diskette's contents cannot be read completely into memory and/or copied in only one pass, DOS will again prompt you to insert the source diskette and to press any key to continue. If you receive this message, you should remove your target diskette and put the original source diskette in, so that DOS can continue reading information from it. DOS will then prompt you to insert the target diskette again in order to copy more information in a second pass. Depending on the amount of memory you have on your computer, this juggling of diskettes will continue until all of the information from the original diskette is read, and all of it can be written to the destination diskette. The process is summarized in Figure 2.11.

At the end of this cycle, DOS asks if you would like to

```
Copy another diskette (Y/N)?
```

Type **Y** (for Yes) or **N** (for No) and hit Enter.

Copying with Two Floppy-Disk Drives

If your system has two compatible diskette drives, that is, the same drive type and same diskette type, copying the diskettes can go much faster because no juggling is required. You place a source diskette in drive A, and place a labeled scratch target diskette in drive B. With two diskette drives, the original dialog box seen in Figure 2.10 requires no changes. You just press Enter at that point, since the default is for a source diskette in drive A and a target diskette in drive B. DOS will not automatically know if you have inserted the disks already, so it will prompt you as follows:

```
Insert SOURCE diskette in drive A:
Insert TARGET diskette in drive B:
Press any key to continue...
```

DOS will prompt you as before, except that each diskette will be copied in its entirety before DOS asks if you want to copy another diskette.

The steps for using *Disk Copy* with a single diskette drive.

1. SELECT DISK COPY FROM THE DISK UTILITIES PROGRAM GROUP.

2. DOS PROMPTS YOU TO INSERT THE SOURCE (ORIGINAL) DISKETTE.

3. DOS READS AS MUCH AS IT CAN FROM THE SOURCE DISKETTE, THEN PROMPTS YOU TO REMOVE THE SOURCE DISKETTE AND TO INSERT THE TARGET DISKETTE.

4. AFTER COPYING THE SOURCE DISKETTE'S FILES FROM MEMORY TO THE TARGET DISKETTE, DOS PROMPTS YOU TO REMOVE THE TARGET DISKETTE.

5. IF THE ENTIRE CONTENTS OF THE SOURCE DISKETTE DID NOT FIT INTO THE COMPUTER'S MEMORY ON THE FIRST PASS, DOS WILL PROMPT YOU TO REPEAT THE PROCEDURE, STARTING AGAIN FROM STEP 2.

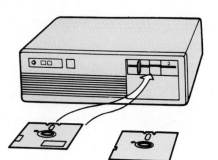
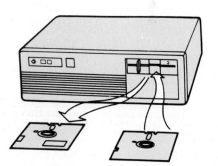

Summary

The DOS shell screen represents a new graphic interface to most of DOS's commands and utilities. You learned in this chapter how to access important features of DOS from the initial DOS shell screen.

- When in the shell, you can always press F1 to get on-screen help, which is information that is relevant to the currently selected screen item. You can also select the Help pull-down menu from the menu bar.

- When in the shell, you can always press F1 to get on-screen help, which is information that is relevant to the currently selected screen item. You can also select the Help pull-down menu from the menu bar.

- When at the command prompt, you can obtain help about any command by adding the /? switch. DOS will display syntax and usage information.

- You can change the shell's color combinations and screen mode easily and quickly.

- The primary DOS utility operations of Disk Copy and Format are available from the Disk Utilities subgroup in the Main program group. You will learn in Chapter 5 how to add other DOS utility programs to this default list.

- All disks, hard or floppy, must be formatted before you use them. You've seen how to use the Format utility to prepare a scratch or blank diskette for storing files. This diskette can also be used to boot the system if you add the /S switch to the parameters field in the Format dialog box. However, the /S switch does cost you storage space on the diskette; less space is then available for your files.

- You use the Disk Copy utility, which automatically formats your target disks as needed, to make exact copies of diskettes.

Part

TWO

Understanding the DOS Shell

CHAPTERS

CHAPTER

3

Introducing the File System

BY NOW, you've learned the fundamentals of DOS, and you've seen what it can do. You've entered simple commands and prepared your disks. In this chapter, you will learn about directories and how to access your files.

When you work with DOS, you will always deal with files of one sort or another. Program files you purchase must be stored in some portion of your disk; data files you create must be stored in another portion. The more practiced you become at defining and accessing these disk portions, or directories, the more success you will have with DOS.

The DOS shell incorporates a file-management facility which is your primary connection to DOS directories, DOS files, and application programs. This chapter introduces you to the DOS file system, showing you how to access your computer's various drives, directories, and files.

Moving Around in the File System

As you learned in Chapter 2, the DOS shell screen can take on a variety of appearances. It is up to you to choose the particular view of DOS you prefer or require. To do so, you can move to the menu bar and pull down the View menu. In Figure 3.1, you can see the View menu as well as the result of selecting the first choice, *Single File List*.

Naturally, your system will have different directories and file names. This screen is very clearly organized. Using the Single File List view means that the entire screen is primarily devoted to displaying the files in a single directory. Some of the screens you saw in the preceding chapter contained

FIGURE 3.1

The View pull-down menu and a single list of files

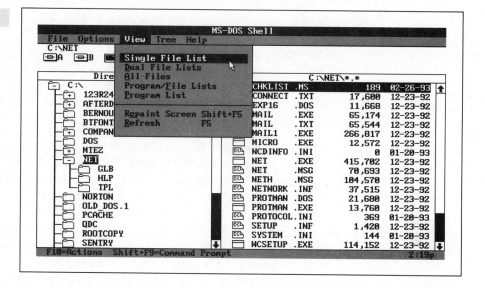

file-management elements as well as program-management portions. These are just different views. We'll explore these and other possible shell views in the next two chapters. In this chapter we will concentrate on the Single File List view.

In Figure 3.1, you see the default full-screen shell, containing a title bar on the top line and showing the currently available principal keystrokes on the bottom line. Just below the title bar is the menu bar, containing five primary menu names: File, Options, View, Tree, and Help. Four of these choices are always available from a shell screen; the Tree menu appears only when you are working in one of the file-management areas of the shell, as in Figure 3.1. When you select one of these menu names, you can perform many operations by choosing commands from the pull-down menu that appears. Chapter 4 focuses on the range of file and directory manipulations that are accessible from these menu choices.

Below the menu bar are three other primary portions of the file-management screen. In these three areas you specify the disk drive you want to work on, the group of files (the directory) you want to work with, and the individual file names you want to access. Although you were briefly introduced to these areas in Chapter 2, you will now take a much closer look at them.

Switching Your Control Focus

The *control focus* is just a fancy term for the area of the screen that has DOS's attention. Formally, it is the area that will be affected by your immediate keystrokes. (If you're not using a mouse, remember that you can switch from each of these areas to the next by pressing the Tab key on your keyboard.)

When a shell screen that includes file-management information first appears, as in Figure 3.1, the current drive (normally the boot drive) is automatically selected, and the symbol or *icon* that represents the boot drive is initially highlighted. You can switch your attention to the data on another drive by simply clicking on one of the other displayed drive icons. To use the keyboard to switch drives, you press the left or right arrow key until the desired drive letter is highlighted, and then press Enter. Alternatively, you can simply press Ctrl+X, where X is the drive letter, to quickly change drives. For example, pressing Ctrl+D on my system would cause DOS to display the directory and file entries on drive D. Try each of these methods now on your system to change the file-management displays from one drive to another. (The number and letters of the drive icons will vary according to the hardware you've installed on your system.)

➤ EXTRA!

Use DOSKEY to Locate File Names Quickly!

Use **DOSKEY** (see Chapter 15) to create a *LOCATE* macro that will enable you to display all file names that match a file specification (parameter one) on a specified drive (parameter two). If a second parameter is not specified, this macro uses the current drive:

```
DOSKEY LOCATE=DIR $2\$1 /B /S /P
```

For example, you could then quickly locate all batch files anywhere on the current drive by typing:

```
LOCATE *.BAT
```

You might notice a slight delay the very first time you ask DOS to switch to a new drive. During this delay, a small screen window will open that tells you that DOS is reading the directory and file information from the disk in that drive:

```
Reading Disk Information...
```

From that point forward, as you work with the information on that drive, there will be instantaneous response because DOS will have stored all the information in memory. However, this efficiency technique does have one downside. If you press Shift+F9 to exit from the shell to a command prompt and make some directory or file changes, those changes will not affect the in-memory directory/file table that the shell set up when you first selected that drive. When you return to the shell by typing the **EXIT** command, some of the displayed file-management information may therefore be incorrect.

To ensure that the shell displays are made current, you will have to reselect any drive affected by changes. Do so by double-clicking on the drive letter, by highlighting the letter in the drive area and pressing Enter, or by pressing F5 while in the directory tree or files area. DOS will reread the file and directory information from that drive and then update its internal table.

Using Files in Different Directories

Once you've selected the correct drive, you will want to find the file grouping, or *directory,* containing the files you're interested in. Switch to the directory tree area of the screen and highlight the directory you want, using the keyboard or mouse techniques presented in the previous section.

As you can see in Figure 3.2, or on your own system if you are trying these techniques while you read, the file names displayed on the right side of the screen are those contained in the directory you've highlighted on the left side of the screen.

The complete name of the current directory (my C:\BERNOULI directory in Figure 3.2—note that I had to change the spelling of Bernoulli to

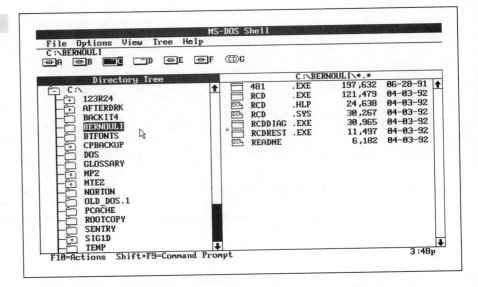

fit it into DOS's eight-letter filename limit) is displayed on the line just above the drives area (between the drives areas and the menu bar) regardless of the location of the control focus. This line changes whenever you highlight a different directory. As you highlight different directories, DOS also redisplays the file names contained within that directory. These new file names appear within the files area on the right side of your screen.

Before you can copy, delete, or perform any action on your files, you must highlight the directory that contains the desired files. In order to then perform specific operations on your files, you must select the individual file(s) to work with. As you'll soon see, there are various ways to select various combinations of files. You can then pull down one of the menus to display a variety of actions that can be performed on the selected file(s).

Selecting Files

The various options that are available from the shell's menus can apply to one file or to many files at once. When you study them in the next chapter, you'll learn which of these commands apply to single files and which can apply to multiple files. For now, you'll learn how to prepare DOS for one of these actions by first selecting the file(s) with which to work.

WARNING   If you inadvertently press Enter when selecting a file, DOS will attempt to open or start it.

Do not press the Enter key during any of these highlighting steps. Doing so will inadvertently request DOS to open, start, or run the selected file. Depending on the type of file, many different actions can occur automatically at this point. In all likelihood, none of them is what you want. Usually all you can do at that point is press the Esc key to attempt to cancel the mistaken request.

Selecting Single Files

It's easy to select a single file for any subsequent action. You merely switch the control focus to the files area and highlight the file name. To do this with the keyboard, you first press the Tab key until the focus moves to the files area. Then you press the down arrow or up arrow keys until the desired file name is highlighted by the selection cursor. In graphics mode, the adjacent icon is highlighted at the same time. In text mode, as shown in Figure 3.3, a small triangle appears next to a selected file.

Notice also how, in text mode, a horizontal arrow appears to the left of the entry being highlighted. If the control focus were to move back to the directory tree area, the arrow would move to the left of the current directory. Even though the highlighted file and associated triangle remain visible on the right, the arrow would indicate that the control focus has moved back to the directory tree area. Pressing the down or up arrow key changes selections only in the area that contains the control-focus arrow.

If you change your mind about the file you've highlighted, just move the selection cursor to another file name. This will simultaneously highlight the new name and remove the highlight from the previously highlighted

FIGURE 3.3

A file highlighted in text mode shows a small triangle next to the file name.

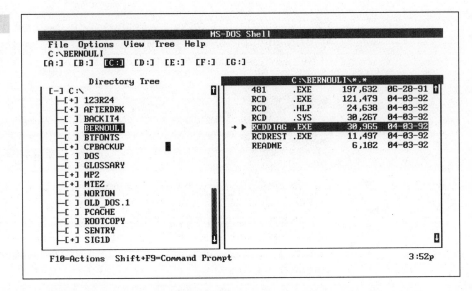

name. To deselect a file without choosing another file, press the Ctrl+spacebar key combination.

Try this now. Move to the files area and highlight any file shown. Now move the control focus back to the directory tree area. Notice how the file highlight is retained. A number of menu choices (e.g., *Copy* and *Move* on the File menu) will be available to you because of your file selection. After returning the focus to the files area, press Ctrl+spacebar; the file or icon highlight disappears. Certain pull-down menu options (e.g., *Print* and *Delete* on the File menu) will no longer be available or meaningful now that there is no highlighted file to work on. You'll explore this issue of option availability in more depth in the next chapter.

Selecting Multiple Files

You can select either consecutive or nonconsecutive files from the listing you see in the files area. These two different operations require slightly different techniques. In each of these two cases, I'll first explain how to use your mouse to select more than one file, then I'll explain how to use the keyboard to perform the same chore.

Selecting a Consecutive Group of Files

Selecting multiple files requires that you use the Shift key. To select multiple adjacent files with a mouse, start by clicking on the first file name you want to select. (As with a single file selection, you can change your mind about this first file by simply pointing to a different file name and pressing Button 1 again. This will deselect the former file and select the new one.) After selecting the first file, press and hold down the Shift key. Then click on the last file of the desired group. This selects and highlights all files from the first one you selected to the last one.

Figure 3.4 depicts the result after I selected RCD.EXE and then held down the Shift key and clicked the mouse on RCD.SYS.

Regardless of whether you select one file or fifty-one files, the next operation you ask DOS to execute will be performed for each selected file. You might select a group of files with the intention of then pulling down the File menu from the menu bar and asking DOS to delete them all. You'll learn exactly what is involved in asking DOS to do this in the next chapter.

Notice that two different types of file icons are used in the files area. A rectangle with one corner turned over, symbolizing a piece of paper, represents a data file. You can see this icon beside some of the files in Figure 3.4. A

FIGURE 3.4

Select multiple adjacent files by selecting the first file then holding down the Shift key while you select the last file.

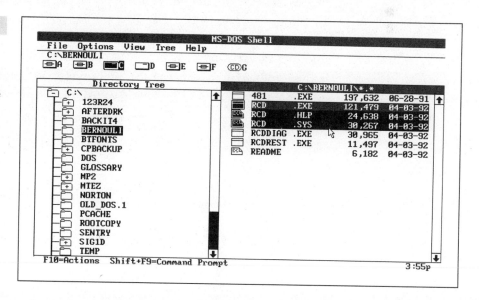

rectangular icon, symbolizing a signpost, marks a program or file that can be executed. You can see this beside the .EXE file entries in Figure 3.4.

An executable program or command always has an extension of .BAT, .COM, or .EXE. Only files with one of these three extensions are symbolized by the rectangular icon. All other files are represented by the paper icon.

Suppose that you wanted to select this same group of files with your keyboard alone. In this case, you simply move the selection cursor to the first file you want to select, press and hold the Shift key, then use the down arrow key to move the selection cursor down to the last file you want to select. Because the Shift key is held down, each intervening file is highlighted as you move the cursor to it.

➤ EXTRA!

Lay a Trail of Bread Crumbs to Find Your Way Home!

Batch files sometimes run programs that change the current directory. After the program runs, your batch file may lose its bearings. But by adding several lines to any batch file that runs other .EXE files, you can ensure that the batch file will always find its way back to where it started.

Your first step is to create a small text file (let's call it WHEREAMI) that contains three characters: the letters C, D, and a space character. Next, add the following two lines at the beginning of any batch file that will run an executable program that changes the current directory:

```
COPY \UTILITY\WHEREAMI \UTILITY\WHEREAMI.BAT
CD >> \UTILITY\WHEREAMI.BAT
```

The first line here creates (or recreates) an executable WHEREAMI.BAT file that contains a **CD** (Change Directory) command. The second line augments the CD command with the current directory, prior to any possible changes to it from within your batch file.

At the end of your batch file, you only need to add the following line:

```
CALL \UTILITY\WHEREAMI.BAT
```

which runs the created WHEREAMI.BAT file, whose only chore is to Change Directory back to the directory that was current when your batch file began. You can replace my \UTILITY directory in these three commands with your own subdirectory in which you keep such utility programs or batch files.

If you really want to get fancy, and make your batch file run faster, you can use a **TEMP** environmental variable. For efficiency purposes (see Chapter 18), TEMP is usually set to the name of a directory on a RAM disk. Assuming that your system has already set TEMP, you can replace the above commands with the following variations.

At the beginning of your batch file, place:

```
COPY \UTILITY\WHEREAMI %TEMP%\WHEREAMI.BAT
CD >> %TEMP%\WHEREAMI.BAT
```

At the end of your batch file, place:

```
CALL %TEMP%\WHEREAMI.BAT
```

This use of the TEMP variable does assume that you've set TEMP to some directory other than a root directory of a drive. Because of the limit on the number of file entries that a root directory can accommodate, you should not set TEMP to a root. If you choose to do so anyway, you would have to modify this sample batch code slightly.

Selecting a Nonconsecutive Group of Files

You use the Ctrl key to select multiple files that are not adjacent. If you use a mouse, simply press and hold down the Ctrl key while you click on each file name. When you click Button 1 the file is selected. Because you continue to hold down the Ctrl key, subsequent clicks will select new file names without deselecting any of the former files. Figure 3.5 depicts this situation after I selected a variety of miscellaneous file names in my BER-NOULI directory.

If you wish to deselect any single file, continue to keep the Ctrl key depressed and click the mouse on the individual file you wish to deselect. As long as you keep the Ctrl key pressed down, you remain in multiple selection (and deselection) mode. If you change your mind about the entire group selection, just release the Ctrl key and click the mouse on any file. All other file names will be deselected. Remember that pressing Ctrl+spacebar will deselect even this last file. The absence of a highlighted icon is your confirmation that a file has been deselected.

FIGURE 3.5

Select multiple nonadjacent files by holding down the Ctrl key while you highlight each file separately.

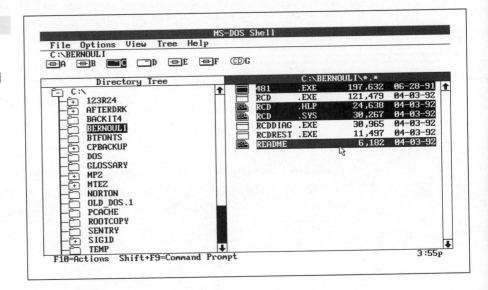

Using the keyboard for nonadjacent multiple file selection is a bit cumbersome. To switch DOS into this nonadjacent selection mode, you press Shift+F8 once. The word *ADD* appears on the right side of the bottom screen line. Use the down or up arrow keys to move the selection cursor to each file name you wish to select, and press Ctrl+spacebar to select it. As long as you remain in multiple selection mode, you can also move the selection cursor to any selected file and press Ctrl+spacebar to deselect it.

Table 3.1 summarizes the different possible sequences for selecting adjacent or nonadjacent files using either the mouse or keyboard.

TABLE 3.1: Selecting multiple files

	ADJACENT FILES	NON-ADJACENT FILES
MOUSE		
	1. Click first file.	1. Press and hold down Ctrl key.
	2. Press and hold down Shift key.	2. Click on each desired file.
	3. Click last file.	
KEYBOARD		
	1. Move selection cursor to first file.	1. Move selection cursor to first file.
	2. Press and hold down Shift key.	2. Press Shift+F8.
	3. Move selection cursor to last file.	3. Move selection cursor to next file to be selected; press Ctrl+spacebar to select it.
		4. Repeat Step 3 for each file you want to select.

Selecting More Files Than You Can See

As you select multiple files, you are not limited to selecting files whose names fit in the small directory tree area on your screen. If you wish to select multiple files whose names do not appear on the same screen, simply keep the appropriate key (Shift or Ctrl, or both) depressed while scrolling to another portion of the file list (using the arrow keys, or, with a mouse, the vertical scroll bar on the right side of the files area). Completing the selection process will then include files that may not be visible at the same time. DOS keeps track of any or all files you've selected, no matter where they are located in your file list. As you will learn in Chapter 4, you can also select files from more than one directory at a time.

➤ EXTRA!

View Long Text Files One Screen at a Time!

Use the SHOWBATS.BAT batch file to display one or more text files, specified as parameters. Wildcards are supported. A temporary text file gathers the output, then pipes it through the **MORE** command in order to display text one screen at a time.

```
@ECHO OFF
Rem SHOWBATS.BAT
Rem Syntax: SHOWBATS Filenames...
:Again
IF '%1'=='' Goto End
Rem Use FOR to handle wildcards
FOR %%F IN (%1) DO TYPE %%F >> TEMP.TXT
SHIFT
Goto Again
:End
TYPE TEMP.TXT | MORE
ERASE TEMP.TXT
```

Exploring the Disk Directory Structure

As you know, a hard disk will store many times the amount of data or number of files that can be stored on a floppy diskette. For example, if the average size of your files is 20,000 bytes, then a 120-megabyte hard disk would hold approximately 6,000 uniquely named files. If the average file is smaller (say, 10,000 bytes), then you could have 12,000 different files on the disk. The sheer number of potential files raises the problem of keeping order among them all. To deal with this problem, DOS allows you to create *directories* and *subdirectories*—units of organization that divide a disk into sections.

This ability to create directories and subdirectories—in other words, to create and maintain groupings of files—is DOS's most powerful organizational facility.

Distinguishing between Directories and Subdirectories

Directories are like separate drawers in a filing cabinet. Subdirectories are like the file folders within each drawer. Files are stored in subdirectories and are isolated from other files. Figure 3.6 depicts this organizational concept.

Just as a well-organized filing cabinet promotes efficiency in the office, a well-organized set of DOS directories and subdirectories enables you to quickly and easily store and retrieve your program and data files.

The key to understanding DOS's directory and subdirectory structure is understanding that it is *hierarchical*, which means in effect that every item can contain other items. Consider the typical office filing cabinet. Each

FIGURE 3.6

One way of picturing how files can be organized in directories

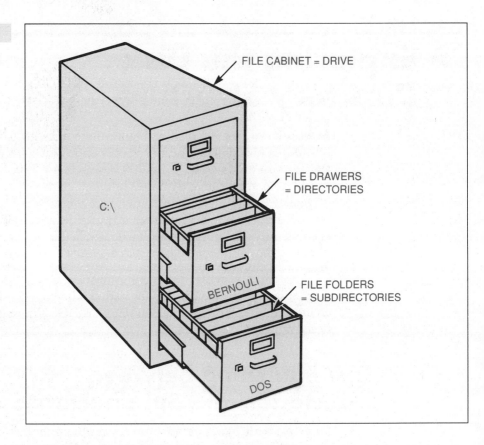

FILE CABINET = DRIVE

FILE DRAWERS = DIRECTORIES

FILE FOLDERS = SUBDIRECTORIES

C:\

BERNOULI

DOS

filing cabinet contains file drawers, each file drawer contains file folders, and each file folder itself can contain more file folders.

In logical terms, every item contained by another item in a hierarchy is considered below that item. Thus we speak of *sub*directories that belong to directories, and *sub*-subdirectories that belong to subdirectories, and so on.

Note that any subdirectory is still considered a directory. The use of the prefix *sub* merely indicates the relationship of one directory to another. In writing about DOS, I will use the *sub* prefix only when I need to indicate the status of one directory in relation to another.

The item at the top of the hierarchy is ultimately the equivalent of the filing cabinet itself—the thing that contains all the file drawers and file folders. In a DOS directory structure, this is somewhat confusingly called the *root directory*, the primary object from which the entire hierarchy grows. The reason this may be confusing is that it is conventional to describe the branching structure of a directory system as a tree, and most people visualize a tree root as being at the bottom of the structure. In fact, the important point to remember about the root directory is that there is only one per drive; consider it the *main* directory for the drive.

Changing the Default Directory

Just as DOS allows you to select a default drive, it also allows you to select a default directory for a disk. When you first access a disk, the root directory of that disk is the assumed default directory. The root directory is represented by a backslash after the drive specification. That is why C:\ is the directory whose file contents were displayed in Figure 3.1 when you first activated the shell from the hard disk. (You will see the backslash symbol often in DOS because it is used to represent the break between one level on the hierarchy and the next level. Thus you will see it to the left of each directory and subdirectory name when DOS identifies the full directory path to a file.)

NOTE   The backslash symbol can be used by itself (without the drive specification) to represent the root directory of the default drive.

Summary

To use your computer effectively, you need to understand how data, programs, and information of any sort are stored in files and how to properly manage these files. In this chapter, you learned the following:

- The *Single File List* choice on the View pull-down menu provides you with complete graphic access to files, directories, and drives.

- You can easily switch the command focus between drives, directories, and individual files with either special keystrokes or the mouse.

- You can easily select individual or multiple file entries with either your mouse or with special keystrokes. All pull-down menu choices for file operations will then apply to the selected file(s).

In the next chapter, you'll take a closer look at DOS's hierarchical directory structure and at the pull-down menus. You'll also learn about the various actions you can initiate in DOS while you explore the range of commands for managing files.

➤ EXTRA!

Rid Your Disk of Leftover Zero-Length Files!

Some programs don't clean up after themselves. They may leave files on your disk that contain no information yet clutter your directories. Other programs may crash after opening up files, never having the opportunity to erase their temporary data sites. In any case, the ZEROSIZE.BAT file below can discover the existence of such files. You can then use standard deletion techniques for erasing the files.

Note that the file names are stored in a text file named ZEROSIZE.TXT. The last line of the batch file is currently a **Rem** command, which causes the batch file to refrain from deleting the ZEROSIZE.TXT file after creating it. You can then use the file at your convenience later to delete the discovered zero-length files.

Note that this batch file itself creates some zero-length files with its redirection and filtering techniques. These files have completely weird names, consisting of nonsensical character sequences, and can be ignored since they'll be deleted automatically.

```
@ECHO OFF
Rem ZEROSIZE.BAT discovers and displays names of all files
Rem which have zero length.
DIR \*.* /S | FIND " 0 " > ZEROSIZE.TXT
CLS
ECHO These files have zero size (if any).
TYPE ZEROSIZE.TXT
Rem ERASE ZEROSIZE.TXT
```

Changing your default directory can save you time by allowing you to work with only the files contained within a certain directory without having to specify the directory's location every time you want to deal with one of those files. In the following example, I'll continue to use the simple **DIR** command. However, as you move through this book and learn other commands, the same file-referencing techniques will apply.

Suppose that you are in the root directory and want to see a listing of the files in a subdirectory. Naturally, if you are simply manipulating files from the shell, you can change directories by simply selecting a different directory from the directory tree. When at the command prompt, you must enter **DIR** followed by—for each directory above your directory—a back-slash and the name of the directory. Once you make the subdirectory (rather than the root) the default directory, simply entering **DIR** at the command prompt will give you your directory's listing.

The command used to change directories when at the command prompt is the **CHDIR** or **CD** command. For example, entering

```
CD \UTIL
```

makes the UTIL subdirectory the current DOS default whenever you make references to files on the current disk drive.

CHAPTER

4

Manipulating Files and Directories

LEARNING more about files and directories will give you more confidence and control over your system. In this chapter you will learn how to display the contents of text files, how to erase old files that you no longer need or that are occupying too much space, and how to make copies of any files onto 5¼" or 3½" diskettes so you can free disk space for new work.

As an aid in keeping your work organized, you will see how to easily rename files. If simple renaming isn't enough, you will learn to rapidly move and regroup files between disk drives and between directories.

You will also discover the myriad of possibilities for graphic display of your disk's files. Lastly, you will learn about some special options for file selection and presentation.

Managing Your Screen Display

For convenience, and for minimum distraction, start by pulling down the View menu and selecting *Single File List*, as you did in the preceding chapter. Remember, you can move the mouse pointer to the menu bar and click on the menu name and then click on the *Single File List* choice, or you can press Alt-V on the keyboard and then press *S*.

In this section, you'll learn more about managing your display screen more effectively. To that end, you should pull down the Options menu. In Chapter 2, you learned about the last two choices on this menu (shown in Figure 4.1). *Display* controls whether your screen appears in high or low resolution, as well as whether DOS uses text mode or the slower, more detailed graphic mode. *Colors* offers a selectable color scheme, depending on your monitor's capability for color display. The third choice from the bottom, *Enable Task Swapper*, is a special program-management feature that will be explained in depth in Chapter 5. It provides the ability to initiate many programs at the same time, allowing you to pause one program and switch to another quickly and easily.

You'll concentrate in the remainder of this chapter on the first four choices. They offer a variety of file-management controls. By appropriately using the options available through these choices, you'll make much more efficient use of your DOS system. In particular, you will find it much easier to manage files and control the actions you can take with them.

FIGURE 4.1

The Options menu provides a miscellany of controls for the DOS shell. You can control which types of files are displayed, and in what order, limit or open up the selection process, select the colors and detail of the display itself, and display file and program status.

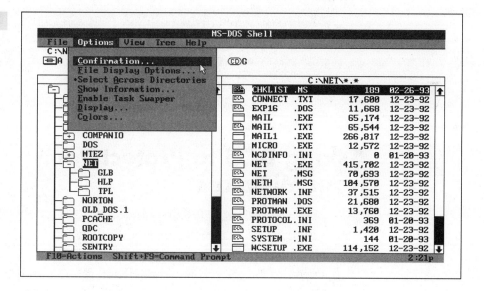

➤ EXTRA!

Use Macros to Move around the Directory Tree!

The DOSKEY utility (see Chapter 15) enables you to write and incorporate your own customized new commands into DOS. Here are three simple ones to demonstrate how easy it can be. (To create any of these macros, you must have first loaded the DOSKEY utility.)

DOS6 demonstrates how to set up a typographical shortcut to my DOS6 directory, located deep within my system's directory tree. You can change the name, and the specific directory changed to, to gain the same rapid changing facility on your system.

MCD first makes, then changes to, a new directory. You name the desired directory in the first parameter (*$1*). *SUBDIR* lists all subdirectories found within any directory (specified as the first parameter, or *$1*).

All three new commands can be created by typing these three lines at a command prompt:

```
DOSKEY DOS6=CD \SIG1D\DOCS\DOS6
DOSKEY MCD=MD $1 $t CD $1
DOSKEY SUBDIR=DIR $1 /AD /ON
```

Asking DOS to Protect You from Mistakes

Let's take a look at the first choice on the Options menu: *Confirmation*. This displays the dialog box seen in Figure 4.2.

As you'll see later in this chapter, DOS displays a *confirmation box* on the screen whenever you issue a deletion request and the *Confirm on Delete* toggle is set (displays an X). This confirmation box warns you that the file will be deleted and prompts you to confirm your request (select OK) or withdraw it (select Cancel). Since deleting a file with confirmation will not be a single-step operation, it requires a few extra seconds to execute.

FIGURE 4.2

Three file-confirmation options are available. You can ask the system to alert you or not whenever a file deletion or replacement is about to take place, as a result of a menu command or as the result of dragging files with the mouse.

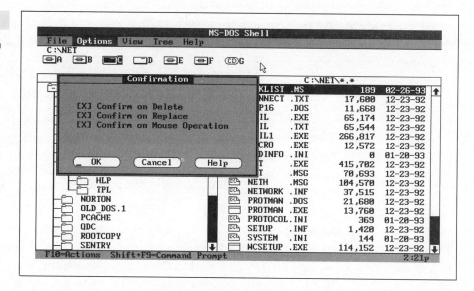

However, these few extra seconds may be all you'll need to realize that you made a mistake. Withdrawing the request at the point of confirmation is simple, requiring no time-consuming recovery operations. Without confirmation, you must do a bit of work to recover from a mistake. You'll see examples of confirmation boxes later in this chapter.

The *Confirm on Replace* choice is necessary for moving or copying files, two operations that can also involve the deletion of files. As you'll see later in this chapter, you can ask that an existing file be *copied* from one place to another on your disk, so that you have the original file in one place and a copy of it in another. You can also *move* a file from one place to another, so that you have only the original file, in a new location. In each operation, the new site for the file may already have a file with the same name. This existing file will be overwritten (obliterated, in effect) by any file of the same name you've explicitly asked DOS to place there. The *Confirm on Replace* setting protects you by displaying a confirmation box on your screen and prompting you to confirm whether or not to actually complete the requested operation.

➤ EXTRA!

Use DOS Toggle Switches to Protect Yourself

All three choices on the Options menu are called *toggles*; that is, they are either on (active) or off (inactive). You select or deselect these options by clicking on each choice with mouse button 1 or by moving the cursor with your keyboard's arrow keys to the desired choice and then pressing the spacebar. Each click, or keypress, switches or toggles the setting from on to off, or off to on. An x indicates that the setting is on.

Each of these options can help to protect you from inadvertent erasure of one or more files. In Figure 4.2 all three options have been turned on. When you work with files, the actions of deleting and replacing (both discussed later in this chapter) can be potentially dangerous activities. You can lose quite a bit of work by accidentally erasing a file from the disk or overwriting it with data from another file.

After you turn on the first two options in this dialog box, DOS will automatically prompt you later to confirm selected file deletions or replacements before completing them. The third option, when toggled on, asks DOS to display a prompting box whenever you initiate a mouse operation involving a file move or copy.

Since these are so valuable as protective mechanisms, all of these toggles are set to On by default. You would have to consciously turn them off to lose the protection. Theoretically, some of you may wish to turn these toggles off because it may save some time when later deleting or replacing files. Don't do it. The little bit of time you save can be more than made up by the time it takes to reenter lost data. It only takes one disastrous loss of an important file that was inadvertently included in a deletion operation to see the value of these settings.

The final choice in the Confirmation dialog box, *Confirm on Mouse Operation*, offers the same sort of protection as the second choice. The difference is in the method you choose to actually cause a file replacement to occur. With the second choice, as you will see later in this chapter, you will only receive the confirmation box if you have used the menus to initiate a move or copy operation. However, as you'll also see, you can actually move or copy files without selecting a move or copy command, by selecting them in one directory with a mouse and *dragging* them into another directory. When using the mouse like this, you needn't spend the time to pull down the File menu and type the destination for the selected files. If the *Confirm on Mouse Operation* toggle option is set, DOS will display a dialog box requesting confirmation whenever an existing file is threatened with erasure because of a mouse-initiated move or copy operation.

Controlling the File Names That Appear

The second choice on the Options menu, *File Display Options*, enables you to specify which subset of files are to be displayed from each directory you select, and what order they are to be displayed in. You can ask DOS to display files according to any of the following:

- their base name
- their file extension
- their date of creation or last modification
- their size in bytes
- the order they are actually stored on your disk

You can also specify whether to display hidden and system files.

Figure 4.3 shows the dialog box that appears after you select *File Display Options* from the Options menu. There are two primary portions to this dialog box. By default, your cursor is at the Name area in the upper left portion of the window when the window first appears. The *.* in the Name entry field represents DOS's method of identifying all files in the directory. You can change this *.* indicator to another expression if you want to restrict which file names are displayed.

FIGURE 4.3

The File Display Options dialog box enables you to specify whether or not hidden and system files are to appear in the file lists. You can also define here the order in which the file names will appear, and by what criteria they are to be sorted.

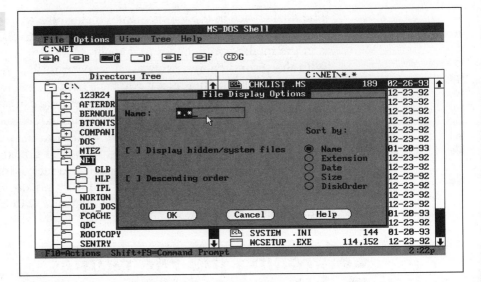

Using Wild Cards to Limit the File Display

Although the DOS files area is initially set up to display file names in alphabetical order, some practical problems require other arrangements. Although a directory may contain hundreds of files, there may be only a handful that fit your needs at the moment. For example, you might want to view the names of all initialization files in your WINDOWS directory—those with the filename extension .INI. If you simply scan the entire default list of file names, you might be hard pressed to pick out just the .INI files. It might be better to narrow the display to just the files that have the .INI extension. This will make it much easier to find the name of a particular file among the existing names.

DOS allows you a certain degree of ambiguity in asking for files. This means that you can ask for different groupings of files from the directory. The asterisk is used as a *wild-card* symbol to indicate your criteria. For example, if you want to list all files ending with the extension .INI, you enter ★.INI in the Display Options entry field, as shown in Figure 4.4.

FIGURE 4.4

You can restrict the display of file names to those that meet your specification. To do so, just type a wild-card specification into the Name: field. In this example, only files that end in .INI will now appear in the files area.

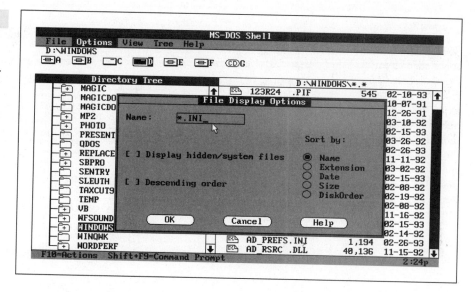

After selecting the OK pushbutton, DOS redisplays just the file names that meet this specification. Figure 4.5 shows the resulting, more limited display.

You can now easily see all the file names that fall into this more specialized sublist. DOS has displayed a smaller number of files—only those that end in .INI.

You can use wild cards to select listings of files by their base names as well as by their extensions. Suppose you want to display all the initialization file names in your WINDOWS\SYSTEM subdirectory that had anything to do with the *Arial* TrueType font.

As Figure 4.5 indicates, the SYSTEM subdirectory within \WINDOWS is not even visible at this moment, so first you must expand the directory tree in order to access the files in that subdirectory. Mouse users can just click on the **+** icon to the left of *WINDOWS* in the directory tree area. Keyboard users can move the control focus to the directory tree area, highlight *WINDOWS*, then press the shortcut Plus (**+**) key.

At that point, DOS will display any subdirectories within WINDOWS. You can move the highlight down to the *SYSTEM* directory and use the Display Options dialog box to look at specific files within that directory.

FIGURE 4.5

Setting the wild-card specification from Figure 4.4 results in a list that is restricted to just the *.INI file names for the current directory. Notice that the restricted specification appears in the bar at the top of the files area of the screen.

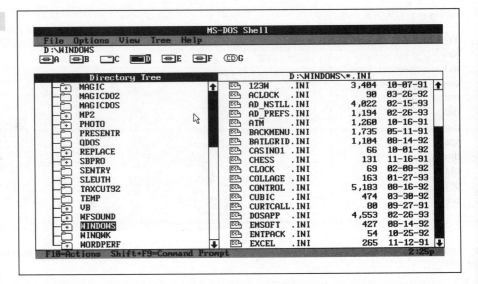

If the files were originally given names that began with the letters A, R, I, A, and L, you could use a wild card to ask DOS to display just these names. Since you do not care what letters come after *ARIAL*, you use an asterisk for the rest of the base name and another for the extension. Thus, by returning to the Options menu, selecting *File Display Options*, and entering **ARIAL*.*** in the Name field, you can produce a new display, such as the one seen in Figure 4.6.

In the selected directory (D:\WINDOWS\SYSTEM), DOS lists all the files that begin with the letters *ARIAL*, continue with any other letters at all (the first *), and have any extension at all (the * after the period).

Another way to search for names is to use the **?** symbol. The question mark is a wild-card symbol for a single character, as opposed to the asterisk symbol, which stands for any number of characters (up to the eight-character maximum for base names, and up to the three-character maximum for file extensions). For example, entering **ARIAL?.TTF** in the Display Options dialog box would result in a display containing ARIAL.TTF and ARIALI.TTF. In other words, the two file names with bases that are up to six characters long and that begin with the characters *ARIAL* (and that have a .TTF extension) are displayed.

FIGURE 4.6

Whenever you're looking at a file list in the shell, you can discover whether or not the list is showing all the file names in a directory, or just a specified group in that directory, by looking at the file specification at the top of the files area.

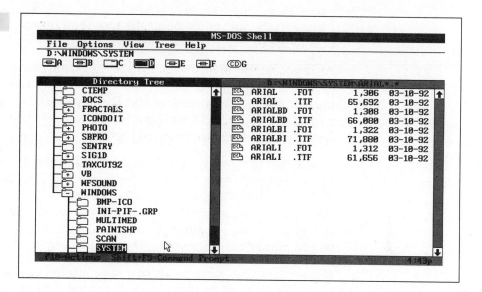

In the Display Options dialog box, there is one more toggle switch that affects which file names appear in the file area. On the left side of the box is a toggle called *Display hidden/system files*. Whenever you see the square brackets to the left of a choice, as you do here, you can be confident that you are looking at a toggle switch of some sort. By selecting this choice, you can request DOS to include or exclude in the file area all files that have the hidden or system file attributes. Other than COMMAND.COM, all the other DOS system file names are hidden from display. If you wish to explore or affect them for some reason, DOS provides this switch for your convenience. (However, unless you are already an advanced user, it is wisest and safest to leave this toggle set to *off*.)

Chapter 19 explains hidden files in more depth when it presents the **ATTRIB** command.

Specifying the Sorting Order for Files

After limiting which file names are to be displayed, you can switch to the *Sort by* area in the Display Options dialog box. Keyboard users must remember to press the Tab key to switch over to this area of the dialog box and to use the arrow keys to change the different display arrangements.

Mouse users can simply point the mouse to one of the selection circles next to the ordering choices and press button 1.

After you've specified any changes to the Name field and indicated which sorting order to follow, simply press Enter, or click your mouse on the OK pushbutton at the bottom of the Display Options dialog box. For example, if you specified a sorting order based on size for the *.INI files, you would receive the screen seen in Figure 4.7.

Notice that the sizes are shown in descending order. This is controlled by the *Descending Order* toggle at the bottom left of the Display Options dialog box. If this toggle is not set on, as it was when I created Figure 4.7, then the default order will be ascending. Ascending name and extension orders will be alphabetical (from A to Z), while ascending size ordering will be numerically increasing. Date orders will be chronological.

If more files that meet the display specification exist than can be shown in the files area of the screen, the scroll bar becomes active and a slider box appears for mouse users. Also notice that the active file specification is displayed just above the files area. Up to now, this had been *.*, but in Figure 4.7 the current and more restrictive *.INI specification is shown.

FIGURE 4.7

To quickly identify which files are the largest in your directories, first sort your files by their Size in the File Display Options dialog box. Then, make sure that you've checked the Descending Order box in that same dialog box.

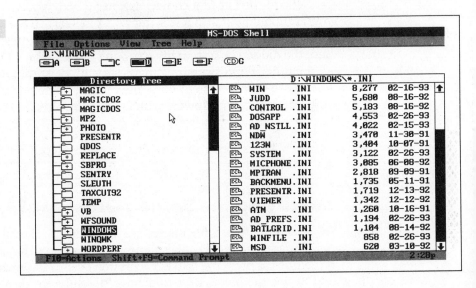

In a similar manner, you can select *Date* as the sorting order to request that DOS display the selected files in chronological order. An ascending sort based on Date displays the oldest files first, while a descending sort based on Date shows the newest files first. *Extension* sorts the files alphabetically by their extensions.

If you select *DiskOrder*, the files are listed in the default order that DOS actually stores them in its directory tables on the disk. Sorting by *Name* alphabetizes the file names using both base names and extensions.

➤ EXTRA!

Discover Duplicate File Names in Two Directories!

Use the DOUBLES.BAT file to list any file names that appear in two separate directories.

```
@ECHO OFF
Rem DOUBLES.BAT discovers duplicate filenames.
Rem Syntax:    DOUBLES FirstDir SecondDir
Rem DOUBLES leaves you in the first dir when it ends.
IF '%1'=='' Goto Omission
IF '%2'=='' Goto Omission
ECHO Please wait ... Checking filenames now.
CD %1
FOR %%j IN (*.*) DO IF EXIST %2\%%j ECHO %%j appears twice.
Goto End
:Omission
ECHO You must specify two directory names as parameters.
ECHO Syntax is:    DOUBLES FirstDir SecondDir
ECHO For example,
ECHO              DOUBLES C:\DOS C:\OLDDOS
:End
```

Operating on Files Located in Different Directories

The third choice on the Options menu, *Select Across Directories*, is very powerful. Like the earlier Confirmation choices, this choice is merely a toggle. When you select it from the Options menu, a diamond-shaped symbol appears to the left of the choice in the menu itself. This indicates that the toggle has been selected, and is on. If you subsequently wish to deselect it, by clicking on the choice once again, the diamond symbol will disappear. The ability to select files from more than one directory means that you can choose files to copy, erase, move, etc., from anywhere on your disks.

Most file selections occur within the confines of a single directory. If *Select Across Directories* is off, you can select files within a single directory only, and if you switch the directory tree to a different directory, any former

➤ EXTRA!

Change to Any File's Directory Instantly!

Write a DOSKEY macro to make directory changes a snap. In particular, the following macro will enable you to rapidly make any one of perhaps many parallel-level directories (*$1*) current:

```
DOSKEY CHANGE=CD ..\$1
```

For example, suppose that you bought my *DOS Magic Tricks* book (SYBEX 1992). The installation disk sets up more than eighty separate directories under a MAGICDOS directory. To try out any one of the programs, you must switch among the subdirectories before running each program. With this macro in place, you only need type **CHANGE TEAMTRIS** to be ready to play a version of the popular game Tetris, either with or against a friend. You can then type **CHANGE BUGFRY** to prepare to enjoy an animated and sound-enhanced version of a backyard-porch bug zapper.

selections are automatically deselected. No accumulation of selected files can occur unless you turn on this toggle switch. When *Select Across Directories* is turned on, however, you can direct DOS to apply specified actions to files that are located in many different directories. DOS keeps track of all selected files in all directories.

Select Across Directories is an extraordinarily useful feature. With it, you can easily issue single commands which can act on files located in multiple places. For example, you can regroup miscellaneous files scattered among your disks into one directory. Merely turn on this selection switch, then move to the various directories to mark all desired files. Then with one single Move command you can reassemble all the files into one directory.

Displaying Detailed Drive, Directory, and File Information

The fourth choice on the Options menu is called *Show Information*. This pop-up window, shown in Figure 4.8, displays four categories:

- **File**   Name and attributes of the currently highlighted file
- **Selected**   Number of files selected—and on which drives—with total number of bytes occupied by all selected files
- **Directory**   Number and total size (in bytes) of files in the current directory
- **Disk**   The organization of the current drive, including total used and available space, and number of files and directories

When you select the *Show Information* choice, your entire current system status is displayed. For example, although the files area in Figure 4.8 shows only four selected files (the icons for the four highlighted files are in reverse video), the Show Information box also indicates that nine files in total have been selected here and elsewhere on drive C. The box also shows that three files have been selected on drive D, which means that the *Select Across Directories* toggle was turned on before making those various selections.

TIP

Use the *Show Information* choice when selecting files for transfer to a diskette to ensure that the total number of bytes to be transferred does not exceed the available space on the diskette.

As you can see in Figure 4.8, the total size of the 9 selected files is 1,540,479 bytes. The current directory is AFTERDRK, which contains 4,633,093 bytes spread among 76 files. The current drive is C, as indicated at the top of the files area. You can see in the Show Information box that it does not have a volume label (i.e., name). Approximately 20 megabytes of the drive's total space is unused and currently available; the remaining space is consumed by 2,417 files spread across 58 directories.

Selecting the *Show Information* option is valuable whenever you want to learn more about how a particular disk is being used. It is particularly important when you need to quickly get a sense of the available space on a drive, and it is invaluable when you've made multiple file selections and need some visible feedback about how far along in your selection process you've gone.

FIGURE 4.8

Use the Show Information window to display overall status information. You can see at a glance the attributes of a single file, the number and size of all selected files, and the size of the current directory. You can also make a quick analysis of the space available on your current disk.

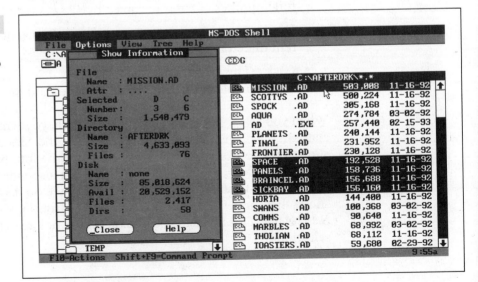

Note that the nine files selected in this example are clearly located across two separate disk drives. Three files on drive D and six files on drive C have been selected. When you turn on the *Select Across Directories* toggle (in the Options menu), the selected files can be in any directories and on any drives on your system.

➤ EXTRA!

Avoid Copying New Files over Existing Files!

Have you ever copied one file to another disk location, discovering too late that a preexisting file of the same name has been irrevocably overwritten? Use the NEWCOPY.BAT batch file instead of DOS's **COPY** command and you'll never worry about this problem again:

```
@ECHO OFF
Rem NEWCOPY.BAT protects against accidental erasure when
Rem COPYing one file to another location.
Rem Uses the CHOICE command to request user decision making.
Rem Syntax NEWCOPY Sourcefile DestinationFile
IF NOT '%2'=='' Goto Test2
IF NOT '%1'=='' Goto Test2
ECHO Please specify Source and Destination Filenames.
Goto End
:Test2
IF EXIST %1 Goto Test3
ECHO Cannot find the filename you specified as the Source.
Goto End
:Test3
IF EXIST %2 GOTO :Problem
COPY %1 %2
GOTO :End
:Problem
CHOICE "The file %2 already exists. Overwrite?"
IF ERRORLEVEL 1 IF NOT ERRORLEVEL 2 COPY %1 %2
:End
```

Taking Advantage of File-Display Arrangements

The View menu can be seen in Figure 4.9. You use this menu to configure your DOS Shell screen in one of several fashions.

The *Single File List* display is the one you've seen thus far in this chapter. Only one directory is highlighted in the directory tree area, and the files contained in that directory are shown on the right side of the screen. The second choice, *Dual File List*, splits the screen in two, giving you the ability to simultaneously view and select files in two directories at once. You'll learn how to do this in just a moment.

When the *Dual File List* option is active, as in Figure 4.9, you can switch back to *Single File List*, switch to an *All Files List* (which is discussed below), or bring up the two alternative program-management displays. As long as the display is set to *Dual File List*, the Dual File List option is not

FIGURE 4.9

Although you can display file information using a *Single File List*, the *Dual File Lists* option on the View menu is helpful for displaying both source and destination directories. Use program-oriented views if you are running utilities or applications, and especially if you will be switching among programs.

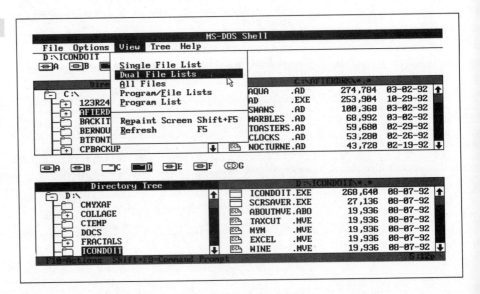

currently available as an alternative choice. You can highlight it just to read it, but otherwise it will appear either grayed or in a lighter color on your screen. This technique is what DOS uses whenever a pull-down menu choice is unavailable for any reason.

The AFTERDRK directory from drive C has been chosen in the top directory tree section, and the files in that directory are shown on the right. Both the directory tree and the files area have active scroll bars, since the file-management display is now less than half of its former size and cannot fit all possible entries. As usual, pressing the Tab key will shift the control focus successively among all the screen sections. In Figure 4.9, the focus will move from the top drives area to the top directory tree to the top files area. Then it will move to each of the equivalent areas in the bottom portion of your screen before returning to the top drives area again.

In the bottom directory tree section, the ICONDOIT directory on drive D has been selected. Notice that just above the bottom directory tree is the familiar line of disk drive icons, which means that you can clearly select a different drive for this second directory tree. In each half of the screen, you can first select one of the drive icons, then move into the directory tree area to highlight the desired directory. Then, of course, you can move into each files area to select one or more files for a particular DOS operation, such as moving or copying the files between disk locations.

The third choice on the View menu is an *All Files* list. The effect of this unique DOS feature can be seen in Figure 4.10.

In this special view of your files, you can scroll continuously through *all* the files on your selected disk drive. Since all files from the selected drive appear on this list, you have no need for the directory tree portion of the display. Consequently, it is replaced by the Show Information display that you saw earlier. As you highlight and/or select different files, the information displayed on the left changes accordingly.

The files are displayed according to the sorting order that is currently selected from the *File Display Options* choice on the Options menu. You can see in Figure 4.10 that the files are now sorted by name, in ascending alphabetical order. As each file is highlighted on the right, its actual

FIGURE 4.10

The *All Files* choice on the View menu allows you to view all the files on a selected drive regardless of directory groupings. This makes it easy to identify if there are multiple files of the same name located in different directories. This can be very helpful when you wish to eliminate extra copies of the same file.

```
                              MS-DOS Shell
 File  Options  View  Tree  Help
 C:\
 [=]A   [=]B   [=]C   [=]D   [=]E   [=]F   (CD)G
                                         *.*
                                CODESCAN.TXT      762    01-01-93   3:33a
 File                           COLLEGE .FMT      294    09-28-92   3:34p
   Name  : COMMAND.COM          COLLEGE .WK1    5,976    09-28-92   3:34p
   Attr  : r...                 COLOR   .BAT       68    06-15-87  12:13p
 Selected      D       C        COLOR   .BAT       68    06-15-87  12:13p
   Number:      0       1        COLOR   .BAT       68    01-01-93   3:33a
   Size  :     52,925           COLOR   .BAT       68    01-01-93   3:33a
 Directory                      COLOR   .DSP    5,382    07-22-91   5:27p
   Name  : \                    COLORAD2.GSD   19,237    11-13-92   1:00p
   Size  :    553,875           COLORADO.GSD   19,183    11-13-92   1:00p
   Files :         24           COMMAND .BAT      527    02-23-93   9:58a
 Disk                           COMMAND .COM   52,925    02-12-93   6:00a
   Name  : none                 COMMAND .COM   52,925    02-12-93   6:00a
   Size  : 85,018,624           COMMAND .COM   53,460    12-23-92   6:00a
   Avail : 18,610,176           COMMAND .COM   52,841    01-28-93   6:00a
   Files :      2,491           COMMLOAD.COM   14,592    01-01-80  12:15a
   Dirs  :         61           COMMS   .AD    90,640    11-16-92  12:00a
                                COMPA123.V22    4,158    04-30-91  11:33a
 F10=Actions   Shift+F9=Command Prompt                            2:30p
```

directory location appears on the left of the screen. This particular arrangement is helpful for identifying files that may have the same name though they are located in different directories on the disk.

COMMAND.COM, for instance, appears several times in the file area on the right. This is because over time I have installed various DOS versions when installing separate application programs. Some application programs made copies of COMMAND.COM, the main DOS command file that was active at the time, placing those copies in specific subdirectories. This type of display can help me to update those separate directories, or, better yet, to update the configuration of those individual applications so that they use the newest version of the DOS command file.

Sometimes, this duplication is purposeful. For example, I use a different dBASE IV memory-setup file for both my financial applications (located in an ADMIN directory) and my mailing list application (located in a MAIL-LIST directory). Each of those directories contains its own uniquely configured ADMIN.MEM file. Often, however, you will discover an outdated version of a file, or an unnecessary second copy of a file, in different directories. You can therefore use the All Files List choice to help you eliminate wasted disk space by deleting the unneeded files.

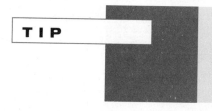

TIP

If you already know the name of a file that you suspect can be found in different directories, use the *Search* option on the File menu to display the full path names for that file name.

The next major choice on the View menu—*Program/File Lists*—comes in handy when you want to continue working with the file-management aspect of the shell, but also wish to run a particular program. In the next chapter you'll see how to use this option to manage a directory and file list in the top half of your screen and actually display and run the program-management facility of the shell in the bottom half. The final choice—*Program List*—displays only the program-management portion of the shell. In the next chapter, you'll learn about the power for program management behind both of these two selections.

➤ EXTRA!

The Shell Screen Is Not Always Correct!

An important choice on the View menu is *Refresh*. Refreshing the screen is necessary when your file structure has somehow changed but is not reflected in the shell's displays. This can easily occur when you bring up a command prompt by pressing Shift+F9 and make some file adjustments on your own, or with a DOS application program. When you return to the shell's file-management display, it can easily have become out-of-date.

This seeming flaw occurs because although the DOS shell reads the current directory structure automatically, it does so initially and only for shell operations. When it first brings up the shell, the entire disk status is stored in memory. If you make changes from the shell, as you will below by moving or deleting files, they will be instantly reflected in the displays.

But if your changes are done at a command prompt, you'll have to refresh the shell display to show the changes. Note that pressing F5 anytime you are in a file-management area of the shell will have the same effect as selecting *Refresh* from the View menu.

Performing the Major File Operations

Figure 4.11 shows the primary menu that appears when you select File from the menu bar. Depending on which files are selected when you pull down this menu, some of the file-operation choices may be grayed, indicating that they are currently unavailable. In this particular display, for example, no file has previously been selected in the files area on the right of the screen. Consequently, many file operations are grayed and therefore unavailable. It makes sense: if you've selected no file, there is no file to print, or move, or copy, and so on. You'll explore the most important of the File menu operations in this section. But in each case, you must usually first select one or more files to be acted on by the menu operation.

FIGURE 4.11

You must select files in the files area before you can perform actions that apply to file names. For example, because no files are selected in this figure, all the file-oriented choices on the File menu are grayed and therefore unavailable for choice.

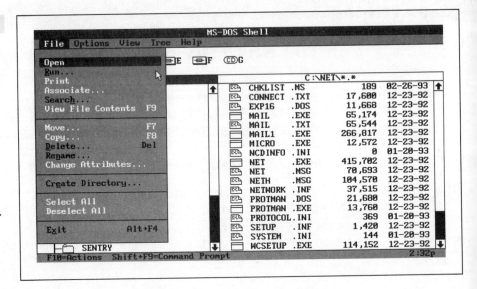

Viewing the Contents of a File

One of the most common tasks you'll perform with DOS is freeing up space on your disk. Files seem to proliferate, and occasionally it becomes necessary to delete some files that are no longer needed. In the case of readable text files, as contrasted with unreadable executable files, you can use the *View File Contents* command (shortcut key: F9) to quickly see the contents of these text files. This can help you to make a decision about whether to retain or delete them. When you are finished viewing the file, press Esc to return to the shell.

Some applications create files that are textual, yet may contain special codes. These are still readable with the *View File Contents* command, although you will have to know what those special codes mean when seen in the View screen. This is more useful for programmers. In fact, the F9 keypress (during viewing operations) is purposefully provided to enable programmers to look at certain files in an obscure (but meaningful to them) form called *hexadecimal*.

NOTE   You can view only one file at a time.

After first selecting a file (from the right side of the screen) to examine, selecting the *View File Contents* choice on the File menu results in the screen shown in Figure 4.12. If you had selected more than one file and then pulled down the File menu, the View choice would have been unavailable: DOS would not allow you to make this selection, because only one file may be selected for viewing.

Notice the PgUp and PgDn icons near the top of this View screen. They indicate that you can move through large files by successively pressing the PgUp or PgDn key, or by clicking the mouse on these icons. Try viewing

FIGURE 4.12

Viewing a text file is easy with the shell. Just select a single file name in the files area and press F9 (the shortcut key for *View File Contents* on the File menu).

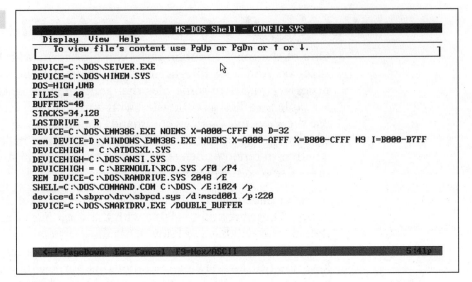

```
                        MS-DOS Shell - CONFIG.SYS
   Display  View  Help
  [      To view file's content use PgUp or PgDn or ↑ or ↓.                  ]
  DEVICE=C:\DOS\SETUER.EXE
  DEVICE=C:\DOS\HIMEM.SYS                    ⌖
  DOS=HIGH,UMB
  FILES = 40
  BUFFERS=40
  STACKS=34,128
  LASTDRIVE = R
  DEVICE=C:\DOS\EMM386.EXE NOEMS X=A000-CFFF M9 D=32
  rem DEVICE=D:\WINDOWS\EMM386.EXE NOEMS X=A000-AFFF X=B800-CFFF M9 I=B000-B7FF
  DEVICEHIGH = C:\ATDOSXL.SYS
  DEVICEHIGH=C:\DOS\ANSI.SYS
  DEVICEHIGH = C:\BERNOULI\RCD.SYS /F0 /P4
  REM DEVICE=C:\DOS\RAMDRIVE.SYS 2048 /E
  SHELL=C:\DOS\COMMAND.COM C:\DOS\ /E:1024 /p
  device=d:\sbpro\drv\sbpcd.sys /d:mscd001 /p:220
  DEVICE=C:\DOS\SMARTDRV.EXE /DOUBLE_BUFFER



  Ctrl=PageDown  Esc=Cancel  F9=Hex/ASCII                              5:41p
```

any text file on your system now with this File menu option. (You'll have to wait until Chapter 6 though to learn how to edit, or change, this file.)

Moving Files between Drives and Directories

DOS lets you move files between locations in a single operation. Coupled with DOS's ability to select one or more files from different directories, you now have a powerful and simple way to reorganize your disk. Building on what you've learned so far, take a look at Figure 4.13.

In this figure, you're using the split screen to verify the status of the disk before and after the move operation. Two files (APPA and APPB) are selected from the DOS6 directory in the top half of the screen. The destination directory (BOOKS) is highlighted in the bottom half—you can tell this from the bottom file area's title bar. (Remember that mouse users must press and hold the Shift key to select adjacent files, and press and hold the Ctrl key to select nonadjacent files.) Once you have selected the file(s) you want to move, you can then initiate the move through the File menu by using the Move command or directly by using the mouse.

FIGURE 4.13

Multiple files can be selected for most file operations. Even files in different directories can be selected for common operations. If including files from different drives, remember to check the *Select Across Directories* toggle option on the Options menu.

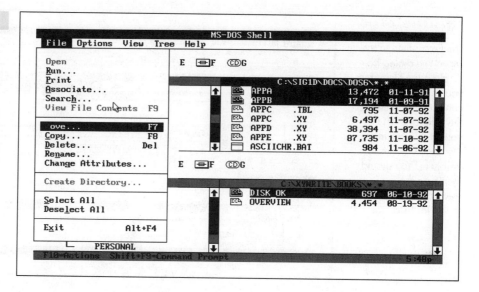

Moving Files Using the Move Command

Selecting the *Move* choice from the File menu brings up the dialog box shown in Figure 4.14. This dialog box is representative of what you'll see during many similar file operations. The currently selected file names are displayed for you in the From: entry field. You cannot type in this field— you must select all desired files before invoking a particular file operation. If the selected file names do not completely fit into the From: field, there's no problem; DOS keeps track of all selected names. To see the rest of the file names in the From: field, you would simply move your cursor or mouse pointer to it and use the right arrow to scroll right.

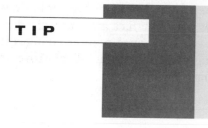

T I P

You can move files across drives by specifying the destination drive in front of the directory designation, or, if you are moving files by dragging them with your mouse, by pressing Alt while dragging the files.

FIGURE 4.14

The From: field in the Move File dialog box displays the file names you've selected. You can scroll this field to the right and left if you've selected more file names than can visibly fit. You should then type the destination directory in the To: field.

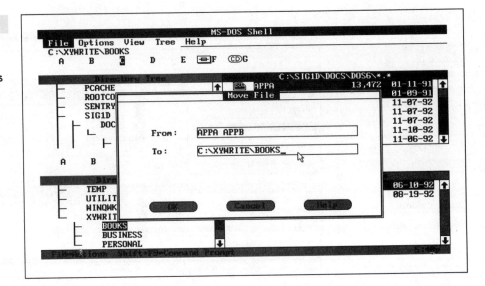

You are permitted to change the destination drive and directory in the To: field of the dialog box. (As usual, keyboard users can press the Tab key to switch among all active fields and pushbuttons in the dialog box.) Pressing Enter or clicking the mouse on OK in the dialog box initiates the Move operation. The results can be seen in Figure 4.15. As you can see, the listing of the DOS6 directory at the top no longer contains the two selected files, and the BOOKS directory at the bottom of the screen does.

Moving Files Using the Mouse

If you are using a mouse, you can perform the Move operation even more quickly. First make sure the destination directory is visible in the directory tree area. (If you're moving from one drive to another, you will have to display Dual Files Lists from the View menu.) Once you have selected the files you want to move, simply keep button 1 depressed, hold down the Alt key, and drag the selected files from the files area into the directory you want. As shown in Figure 4.16, the mouse pointer changes its appearance when you're performing this operation. This Move mouse pointer looks like several overlapping pages.

FIGURE 4.15

Use the Dual Files List view to verify the results of file operations. In this example, you can see that your APPA and APPB files now appear in their new BOOKS directory location and have disappeared from their former DOS6 directory location.

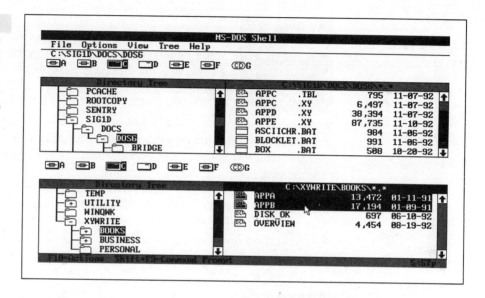

FIGURE 4.16

The mouse pointer turns into a special Move mouse pointer of overlapping pages when you drag the selected files into the directory tree or the drives area. Check the status bar at the bottom of the screen to see a description of the mouse operation you are performing.

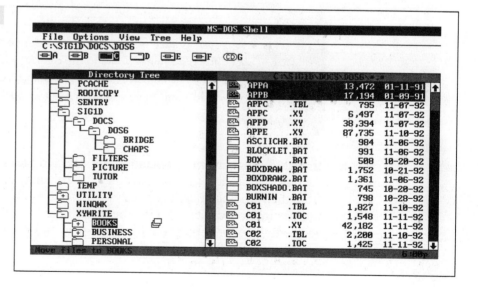

NOTE   You can cancel a mouse move or copy operation
instantly by releasing the mouse button when the
pointer is in the files area instead of in a directory
tree area.

As you move the mouse pointer in the directory tree area, a message appears on the status bar at the very bottom of the screen. This message will inform you of which mouse operation you are in the midst of performing and which destination directory has been chosen, based on the current location of the mouse pointer. When you have reached the correct destination directory, you can release button 1 on the mouse. If you had set your Confirmation options earlier so that the *Confirm on Mouse Operation* toggle was on, you would receive a box asking you to verify the move.

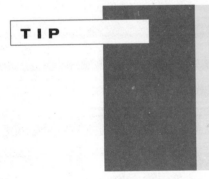

TIP   DOS also includes an explicit MOVE command that
you can invoke from the command prompt. You can
move one or more files to a different directory by
typing each file name (separated by a space) and
the path name of the target directory all on the
same command line. To save typing, you can use
wild cards to specify the names of the files you
want to move.

In fact, during any move operation, the selected files are first copied to the destination location (the *To:* directory); after being copied, they are deleted from their original location (the *From:* directory). If a file already exists in the destination directory with the same name, DOS protects you from accidentally overwriting that file by displaying yet another type of confirmation box. As shown in Figure 4.17, you are told both the byte size and the file dates of the two files.

DOS can warn you about possible file replacement (which effectively involves a file deletion). To help you to determine if you should continue with the replacement, the confirmation box displays the existing file's size and date as well as the size and date of the file that would replace it.

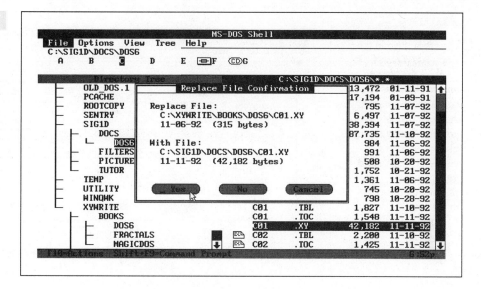

Prior to making a final approval of the move operation, which will obviously result in the overwriting of the earlier file data, you can determine whether you really meant to perform this replacement. If you are not sure of the contents of the preexisting file, it would be wise to cancel the Move operation and press F9 (*View File Contents*) to look more closely at the contents of the files in question.

Copying Files

Making copies of files is a very common and important operation. In this section I'll show you how to copy files for a variety of purposes.

Copying Files across Directories

The *Copy* command works in a way similar to the Move command. You can choose the *Copy* command in the File menu or drag selected files with your mouse (no need to use the Alt key in this case).

In Figure 4.18 three files have been selected from the DOS6 directory and *Copy* has been chosen as the desired operation.

FIGURE 4.18

The From: field in the Copy File dialog box displays the file names you've selected. You can scroll this field to the right and left if you've selected more file names than can visibly fit. You should then type the destination directory in the To: field.

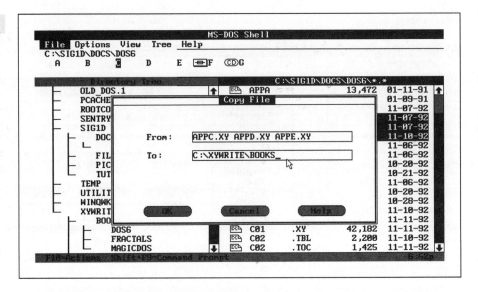

As you just saw with the shell's Move operation, the source (From:) files are simply the ones you select before choosing *Move*. If you had previously activated *Select Across Directories* from the Options menu, your source files could have come from other directories in addition to the current one.

As in the Move File dialog box, if the selected file names do not completely fit into the From: field, there's no problem; DOS keeps track of all selected names. To see the rest of the file names in the From: field, you would simply move your cursor or mouse pointer to it and use the right arrow to scroll right.

Once again, you can type the name of your desired destination directory if the default one shown is not the one you want. In this case, I've typed **C:\XYWRITE\BOOKS** into the To: field to indicate where these selected files are to be copied. Since this is a Copy operation, the three source files will still exist in the From: directory after new copies of them have been added to the C:\XYWRITE\BOOKS directory.

TIP

Remember, you can also copy files by simply dragging them with your mouse from the files area to the directory you want.

You will find many uses for the *Copy* command. You might want to make a secondary copy of a file you are working on, or you might want to make a backup copy of a file on another disk for precautionary reasons. You might want to make a replica of several files at the same time, perhaps from someone else's disk to yours. The following sections explore these and other uses of the *Copy* command.

➤ EXTRA!

Protect Yourself with Secondary and Backup Copies

A second working copy of a file can be made easily with the *Copy* command. You can retain the original while working on and modifying the copy. To create the secondary copy, you would select the first file name (say BUDGET.BAT) before choosing the *Copy* command. The original file name will appear in the From: field; you can then type the same base name with a .BAK extension in the To: field (**BUDGET.BAK**).

After the copying operation is completed, a listing of your current directory would show two files where there had previously been only one, since the new copy (BUDGET.BAK) would be created in the same directory as the source file (BUDGET.TXT). The *Copy* command uses the directory containing the selected file as the default destination for the file copy.

With *Copy*, you can also make a safe backup copy on a completely different disk. Suppose that you want to copy your PHONES.DAT file to the diskette in drive B. You could do this by selecting PHONES.DAT, invoking the *Copy* command from the File menu, and then entering **B:** in the To: field. This sequence creates a copy of PHONES.DAT on the diskette in drive B, using the same name. Put this backup diskette away to protect yourself against inadvertently losing your original file or disk.

Making Multiple Copies

Multiple files can be copied simultaneously by using any of the file selection techniques you learned in this and the preceding chapter. Just use the mouse or keyboard methods to select multiple adjacent or nonadjacent file names, then run the *Copy* command. If the multiple file names you wish to copy have similarly constructed names, you could perhaps select them more quickly by using the *File Display Options* choice from the Options menu to select all files with similar file names.

For example, Figure 4.19 shows a Copy dialog box after setting *File Display Options* to display only *.TIF files. In addition, I chose *Select All* on the File menu to then quickly select the entire set of file names. These include more .TIF files than appear in the screen window; you can tell that is the case because the slider box on the right of the file area does not occupy the entire scroll bar. Consequently, you can assume that there are other entries that would be seen after scrolling.

In the dialog box itself, all the .TIF files are displayed in the From: field. (You can scroll this field to the right to view all the actual names.) Naturally, you can type in the destination for these file copies. I've typed the name of my D:\COLLAGE directory, but I could have just as easily typed A: to send copies out to a diskette in the A drive.

FIGURE 4.19

You can copy any group of files, regardless of whether they are in the same directory or even on the same drive. Just make sure you've toggled *Select Across Directories* on, then select the source files, and finally select File ➤ Copy or drag the last selected files with your mouse. All the files you have selected will be copied.

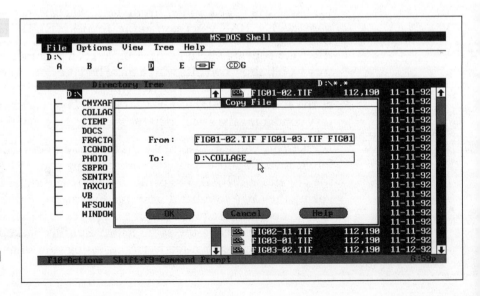

New users frequently ask if two copies of a file can be created on a disk by copying it twice to the same disk. The answer is, Not unless you're copying it to different directories. DOS will not allow two files to have exactly the same name in the same directory. Unfortunately, if a file is copied to a directory that already has a file with that name, DOS erases the old file and then copies the new file to that file name. If this happens, the old file is *overwritten* by the new file, and you are *in big trouble!*

The DOS shell can prompt you to confirm that you want this overwriting to occur. Remember that this is controlled by the *Confirm on Replace* toggle (one of the choices reached through the *Confirmation* choice on the Options menu). This minimizes the risk of copying a different file of the same name to that disk and accidentally erasing all the information contained in the original file.

TIP

You should always have the *Confirm on Replace* option set on to protect against accidentally overwriting files.

If you absolutely refuse to spend the time on confirmation of such operations, at least take a moment to look at the destination directory before completing the operation. Check the contents of this directory to ensure that no unexpected duplicate file names will be accidentally overwritten. If you discover a file with the same name, figure out whether you should rename it (an operation covered later in this chapter) prior to the Copy operation, or whether it is okay to copy over it.

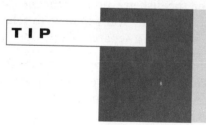

TIP

Use the FC (*File Compare*) command to compare two ASCII files against each other. The differences, line by line, will appear on your screen. Specify each of the two files to be compared as the first and second parameter after the command name.

Take a moment to practice with the *Copy* command. If a colleague or friend has some spreadsheet or database files or even games that you've been wanting to take a look at, now's the time. Of course, you should only make copies if there will be no copyright violation involved.

Making Complete Disk Copies

One of the most common uses of the *Copy* command is to copy all the files from one diskette to another. This is necessary because diskettes can become worn out from use over a long period of time. Copying the files to a new diskette will solve this problem. Also, keeping multiple copies of important files protects you against computer problems, human errors, or accidents such as fires.

You've already been introduced to the *Disk Copy* command in the Utilities program group for making a complete copy of one disk to another disk. Why should you consider using *Copy* instead of *Disk Copy*? The difference is subtle. Disk Copy makes an exact replica of the original disk, *retaining all noncontiguity*. The Copy command will usually rewrite files to contiguous tracks and sectors on the new disk, and thereby improve future disk-access speed. The net result is that the performance or responsiveness of all your programs may improve.

As an example, suppose you have two diskette drives on your system. To copy all the files from the diskette in drive A to that in drive B, you should first select drive A from the drives area of the DOS Shell screen. Next, you can select all files listed in the files area. Lastly, you can pull down the File menu and choose *Copy*, specifying **B:** in the destination field. There is one somewhat dangerous aspect to this copying procedure. The *Copy* command copies only the actual files contained in a particular directory. If you have created a directory structure on the diskette, none of the files located in subdirectories are included in the copying. You will have to select and copy those possibly additional file names in a separate Copy operation.

If you change your mind before completing a Copy operation, the File menu also provides a means to *deselect* all files as well. This is important if you do not actually run an operation after selecting files.

WARNING

If the destination diskette already contains some files, it may not have enough space for all additional files from your Copy request. If this occurs, DOS will display the message "Insufficient Space." The best solution is to use a freshly formatted diskette or to erase files on the destination diskette before issuing the Copy command. This ensures that there is enough space for the source diskette's files.

Removing and Renaming Files

There are just a few more file operations you should know about to aid you in your activities at this point. Of course, many other commands exist, but you'll need them only in more advanced situations, which are covered later in this book. You should now become comfortable with deleting and renaming files.

Deleting Files and Directories

Many computer users accumulate a variety of utility programs over the years, and only rarely take the time to clean up their disk and actually erase certain files that are no longer needed or useful.

Suppose you select three files from the C:\UTILITY directory, then issue the *Delete* command from the File menu, or simply press the Del key. This brings up the dialog box seen in Figure 4.20. You must now explicitly press Enter or click on OK with the mouse to ask DOS to complete the deletion request.

If the *Confirm on Delete* toggle option from the Options menu is on, you will then receive a follow-up Delete File Confirmation box, which successively displays the name of each file to be deleted and asks you to confirm the deletion of each file individually. With this feature, you could conceivably select all the files in a directory and then confirm the deletion of just the particular files (three in this example) that you no longer need.

FIGURE 4.20

The Delete File dialog box contains a single field that identifies all the file names selected for erasure. Remember that if you do not scroll the contents of this field you might not see all the names listed for deletion.

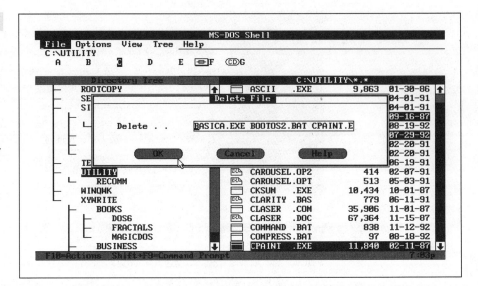

You would want to use this technique whenever you intend to eliminate most of the files within a directory. It gives you a chance to think about each file name (during the confirmation pause) and to make individual deletion decisions on the spot. Figure 4.21 shows an example of this Delete File Confirmation box.

As you can see in Figure 4.21, you must confirm the deletion of each file. In this opening box, the first of three files (BASICA.EXE) is shown. You can avoid deleting this one by selecting the No pushbutton in the dialog box. To actually delete the file, you select Yes. After either response, the confirmation box automatically displays the next file name to be considered for deletion. You can always terminate the entire deletion sequence by choosing the Cancel pushbutton.

Changing the Name of a File

There may be times when you want to change some file names so that you can use the **?** or ***** wild card to manage blocks of files. At other times, you may simply wish to give a file a more understandable name. You can change the name of a file without affecting its contents.

FIGURE 4.21

The Delete File
Confirmation box
appears only if you
had previously
checked *Confirm on
Delete* in the Options
menu's Confirmation
dialog box. This
dialog will then
appear for each file
selected for deletion.
Specifying this
confirmation is well
worth the extra couple
of seconds required.

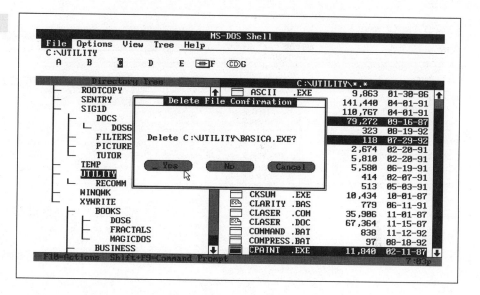

As the *1 of 1* in the dialog box in Figure 4.22 suggests, whenever a series
of files has been selected, the Rename File dialog box will display each one
in turn, showing its place in the series and the total number of files
selected. In this dialog box, you could enter a new file name for each of
the selected files. DOS automatically submits a **RENAME** command behind the scenes when you enter each new file name.

NOTE

You cannot use RENAME to specify a new directory
or subdirectory for a file. You also cannot specify a
drive for the new file name. In other words, a
renamed file does not move; it stays in its same
location.

You can use the Rename command only for renaming files on a single disk
drive. You *cannot* use the Rename command to simultaneously copy a file

FIGURE 4.22

The Rename File dialog box displays the old file name and accepts a single typed replacement name. The dialog box repeats for each file that had been selected prior to choosing the Rename operation.

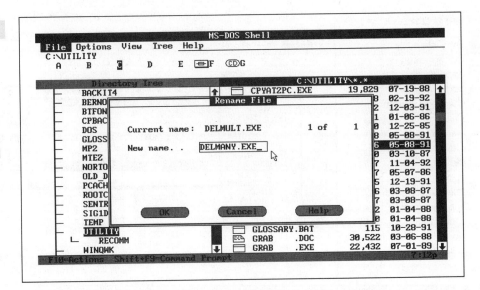

from one disk to another while renaming it—use the Copy command to do that particular chore. Rename only changes the name of the file, whereas Copy creates an entirely new file. With Copy, you begin with one file and end up with two; with Rename, you begin with one file and end up with the same file.

You can use the Rename command to gain a limited degree of protection. You may not be the only person with access to your computer and disks. In that case, you may want to safeguard some of your data files. You can rename an obvious file like BUDGET.WK1 to TEMP.NDX, a clearly misleading name. Prying eyes are not as likely to notice the renamed file.

Take a moment now to try this renaming technique on any files for which you'd like to restrict access. But be careful: first, don't select a dispensable name (like TEMP.NDX) if anyone else using your disk is at all likely to delete files; second, don't forget the new file name you choose.

➤ **EXTRA!**

Remove Unneeded Clutter from Your Hard Disks!

The most common use for the *Delete* command choice is to clean up disks that have been in use for a while. Old versions of data files often proliferate; early copies of memos and other word-processed documents always seem to expand to fill any available space on your disk. If you have a disk that fits this description, now is a good time to use one of DOS's deletion facilities to clean it up.

As you know, you can use the shell's *Delete* choice to delete a previously selected file or group of files. You can also use it to delete a directory. However, deleting a directory from the shell requires that you first erase all files and possible subdirectories within that directory. If the directory you are deleting has any hidden files, which would prevent you from being able to delete it, you will be informed of their existence when you try to delete it.

If you wish to save considerable time, and are willing to be extremely cautious, you can delete an entire subtree with a single command. The **DELTREE** command (not a shell menu option—you have to type it on a command line) will erase a directory, along with all contained subdirectories and files, in a single step. In its basic format the command requires confirmation, which can be very useful in preventing you from making a mistake in haste. You can force DOS to skip the confirmation step by using the **/Y** switch. Remember, though, that in either case this command will erase files you might not be aware of—i.e., hidden files—without any signal that it is doing so. It's very convenient when you know what you're doing, but you can mess things up in a hurry if you are careless.

Shutting Down the DOS Shell

You will typically select the *Exit* choice on the File menu when you have finished manipulating all your files and directories. At that point, the shell screen will disappear and the original DOS command prompt will appear. You could also exit from the shell by simply pressing F3, or by pressing Alt+F4. Remember that once you've returned to the DOS command prompt, you can always reactivate the shell by typing **DOSSHELL**.

Summary

In this chapter, you have examined the pull-down menus of the DOS shell. You learned the following things:

- The *File Display Options* choice from the Options menu enables you to specify which files will be displayed for each directory. It also allows you to specify a sorting order for the file entries.

- The *Confirmation* choice enables you to have a confirmation box displayed before you delete or replace files.

- Selecting across directories is a powerful feature in DOS. You can select any number of files from any number of directories if the *Select Across Directories* toggle choice is set on. Then you can choose any of the file operations to act on those files.

- DOS's *Show Information* option displays system-wide summary data, including byte totals for the drive, directory, and selected files.

- You can request the shell to display file names in several screen arrangements, including a single-directory display, a split-screen display of two directories, and a system-wide display that lists all file names on a drive, cutting across directory distinctions.

- You can also ask the shell to display groups of executable program names. You can combine program and file information by displaying file information in one half of the screen and program-group selections in the other half.

- Files can be easily viewed on your console with DOS's *View File Contents* option on the File menu.

- DOS offers a combined Copy and Delete command called *Move* on the File menu.

- Files can be easily copied into and among various disk directories with the *Copy* command. The Copy capability in DOS is one of its most powerful features, spanning many standard application needs.

- You can use the *Delete* choice on the File menu to delete either files or directories from your disk hierarchy. However, DOS will only delete a directory if it contains no other directories or files.

- Any file or directory can be quickly renamed (on the same drive) by using the *Rename* option on the File menu.

In the next chapter, you will continue your study of the DOS shell by exploring the program-management facility. You will learn about selecting, grouping, and running DOS commands and application programs on your hard disk.

CHAPTER

5

Running Application
Programs

RUNNING programs on a hard disk is much more convenient than using diskettes, but to take full advantage of a hard disk you must learn how to organize it. This chapter will show you how to arrange and manage your disk so that you can simplify your work and get the most out of your programs.

Running programs is the major subject of this chapter. You'll use appropriate directory commands to set up your hard disk for three common and very popular types of programs: a word processor, a spreadsheet, and a database-management system. You'll also discover how to add selected DOS commands as well as your own utility and application programs to the DOS program groups. Finally, you'll learn how to activate multiple programs and quickly switch among them without having to wait until any one of them completes. With the techniques you learn here, you will be able to efficiently set up your hard disk for any collection of applications.

The Basics of the Directory Structure

This chapter will give you the complete understanding of the disk and directory structure that you need to run your application programs and utilities. Since many application programs need to navigate the directory structure in order to access relevant files, I'll show you how to set up DOS so that this requirement is easily met.

Creating and Deleting Directories

It is always a good idea to create a separate directory for files that are related to one another. Having similar and related files together makes it easier and faster to use them.

Selecting the *Create Directory* choice on the File menu of the shell tells DOS to make a new directory within the current directory. Figure 5.1 shows the dialog box that appears when you choose the *Create Directory* option. In this example, I've highlighted the DOCS directory under the SIG1D directory in the directory tree area. As you can see at the top of the screen, drive C is the current drive.

All you are required to do at this point is to type in a new name for the directory that you have asked DOS to create. In this example, I typed in **WIND-NT** and pressed Enter. The immediate result is seen in Figure 5.2. The WIND-NT directory is displayed along with any existing subdirectories, in alphabetical order.

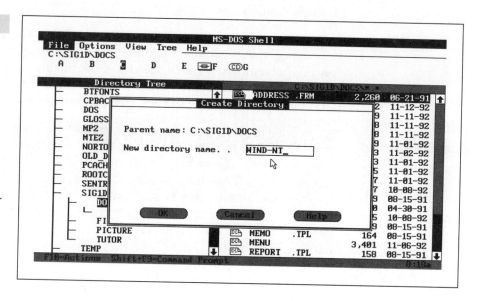

FIGURE 5.2

The directory tree is updated immediately whenever directory-oriented operations complete in the shell. (Similarly, file-oriented operations are reflected immediately in the shell display if the operations were initiated from the shell.)

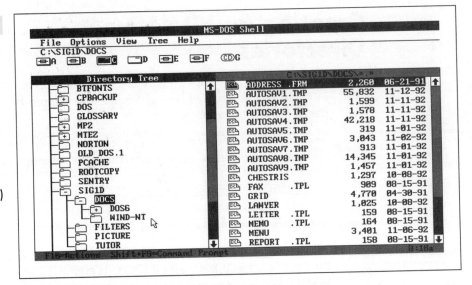

The graphic directory tree is instantly updated to show drive C's added directory. You can now do what you like with the new directory, treating it like any other one on your disk.

Since you can always see the current directory and drive in the shell, managing your directories is quite easy. Each new directory is created on the current drive and under the current directory. And in graphics mode, the visual feedback of location is augmented by the new file folder icon that appears beside the new directory name in the directory tree.

As you saw in Chapter 5, if you want to delete a directory from a disk, you must first remove all its files. Only after you empty a directory of all its contents (both files and other subdirectories) can you delete it from the directory tree. When the directory is empty, you can select it in the directory tree, and then select *Delete* from the File menu. If *Confirm on Delete* from the Options menu was turned on, a confirmation box would now appear and wait for your choice. Answer Yes to delete the directory whose name appears in the Delete Directory Confirmation box.

Understanding Paths

The combination of a drive prefix, a destination directory, and any sub-directory (or subdirectories), as in

```
C:\SIG1D\DOCS\WIND-NT
```

is called a *full path name*. DOS attaches path names to subdirectories and files so that it can keep track of them. A *path* is a linked series of directories that leads to a subdirectory or file. For example, in order to get to the WIND-NT directory, you must first pass through the DOCS and the SIG1D

➤ EXTRA!

Changing Directories Is a Snap with DOS Macros!

The DOSKEY utility (see Chapter 15) enables you to write and incorporate your own customized new commands into DOS. Here are two simple ones to demonstrate how easy it can be. To create any of these macros, you must have first loaded the DOSKEY utility.

CD... is somewhat like the **CD** command that specifies a single parameter (..) that moves up to a parent directory. This macro name, however, is five characters long, including the letters CD and three periods. When you type it, the macro changes directory to the parent's parent (i.e., two directories up).

The *CDD* macro enables you to change both drive and directory without having to enter multiple commands, and without having to type a single backslash. *CDD* first changes to drive $1 (the first parameter), then to dir $2 (the second parameter) within the root, then to $3 in $2, $4 in $3, and $5 in $4. And it does it all in one step!

Both new commands can be created by typing these two lines at a command prompt:

```
DOSKEY CD...=CD.. $t CD..
DOSKEY CDD=$1: $t CD \$2 $t CD $3 $t CD $4 $t CD $5
```

directories. This requirement to follow a path to any particular directory can be compared to climbing a tree. To get to any particular branch you have to first climb past the larger branches leading to it. Any branch on the tree is analogous to a DOS directory or subdirectory.

Each branch of a tree can have new branches, or subdirectories, growing from it. Just as each branch may also have fruit or leaves on it, each subdirectory may have program or data files stored in it.

In the shell, the full path name to the files in the current directory is displayed just above the drives area of the screen. Thus, in Figure 5.2 every file in the DOCS directory has a path-name prefix of C:\SIG1D\. Similarly, each file placed in the new WIND-NT directory would have a prefix of C:\SIG1D\DOCS\.

The path system in DOS subdirectories allows you to create increasingly complex but organized groupings. By taking advantage of this system, you can easily manage several levels of subdirectories.

Viewing and Printing the Structure

The directory tree display in the shell provides you with a clear visual representation of a disk's directory structure. If you are at the command prompt, you can see a similar representation by using the **TREE** command to obtain a printed summary of the directories and subdirectories on a disk.

TREE is an *external*, or disk-resident, utility command. This means that it will not work in every circumstance. **TREE** is really a program file provided with DOS. If the file, TREE.COM, is not present on one of the disks in your system, you cannot execute the TREE command. If your system is installed on a hard disk, then TREE.COM must be in an accessible directory. The usual place for this and other DOS utilities is the DOS directory, located in the root of the boot drive. Entering

TREE ¦ More

will list the volume label and serial number of the disk in the current default drive, and will list all directories and any subdirectories. (The extra broken vertical bar, and the word MORE, help to show you the directory tree one screenful at a time.) By adding a couple of different special symbols to this command, you can send a copy of the entire tree to your system printer:

```
TREE >PRN
```

This command uses a special feature called *redirection* (discussed in Chapter 10). You can also specify a drive parameter if you want to print the tree structure of another drive without changing the current default drive. For example, entering

```
TREE B: >PRN
```

will print information about all the directories on the diskette in drive B. You can get a more detailed tree display that prints the file names in each subdirectory by entering the **TREE** command's **/F** switch:

```
TREE/F >PRN
```

N O T E

The TREE command uses the same graphic characters for lines connecting the directory names that you see in the directory tree area of your DOS Shell screen. Depending on your printer, however, you may or may not receive these line-drawing graphic characters. If your printer does not support these graphic screen characters, use the following variation on the command: TREE /A > PRN to have DOS will print the directory tree using plus signs, minus signs, and slashes to simulate the graphic tree characters.

Navigating the Directory Structure

While subdirectories are essential for good organization, they can nonetheless be confusing at times. DOS provides the **PATH** and **APPEND** commands to help you maneuver through the complex tangle of directories. In order to help the DOS shell perform its operations successfully, you should set the **PATH** command before initiating the DOSSHELL program. This is typically done as part of the AUTOEXEC.BAT file. Chapter 14 explains how to set up an AUTOEXEC.BAT file. In this section, you'll learn how to properly prepare the **PATH** and/or **APPEND** commands for inclusion in the system startup (AUTOEXEC.BAT) file.

Running Programs from Your Default Directory

Now that you understand how the DOS directory structure organizes your files, you should learn how application programs use that structure when they actually run. As you'll see later in this chapter, you can set up your shell to display menus that include your desired application and utility programs.

Most of your work occurs when you are running application programs. Usually you set the working directory to the one that contains your application program. Related files are then read from and written into that directory. Sometimes, you will want to run a utility program that is in a different directory from the one you are working in. For instance, you may want to run the **CHKDSK** program while you are working in the DOS directory.

You may wonder why this is important at all. Surely you should be able to select a directory from the directory tree area, then point to and choose an application program from the file area to run. Isn't that what the DOS shell is supposed to do for you? Well, yes... most of the time. And you'll learn later in this chapter just how to perform that very sequence. But as you become more familiar with DOS, you'll discover how to perform more sophisticated combinations of requests. You'll see how application programs must sometimes be guided through the hierarchy of the directory structure in order to store and retrieve information files.

In this main section, you'll learn what goes on behind the scenes in DOS. Whether you activate a program from the shell or from a command prompt, the program must be able to access the DOS directory structure. Since *you* often decide which files are stored in which directories, DOS

➤ EXTRA!

Easily Add or Remove a Directory on the Current Path

Use the following batch file to add a directory to the current path, or to remove a previously added directory. (Note that your DOS environment must contain enough free space for this technique to work. If it does not work, you may need to expand the amount of available environment space in your CONFIG.SYS's **SHELL** command.)

```
@ECHO OFF
Rem PATHMOD.BAT
Rem Syntax:  PATHMOD [A or R] DirName
Rem          where A means to Add the DirName to the PATH
Rem          and   R means to Restore the previous PATH.
Rem Only one directory at a time can be added/restored.
IF '%1'=='' Goto OMISSION
FOR %%j IN (A a) DO IF %1==%%j Goto ADD
FOR %%j IN (R r) DO IF %1==%%j Goto RESTORE
:Omission
CLS
ECHO First parameter must either be A (Add) or R (Restore)
ECHO If A, the second parameter should be a valid directory name.
Goto End
:ADD
SET SAVEPATH=%PATH%
PATH=%PATH%;%2
Goto End
:RESTORE
PATH=%SAVEPATH%
SET SAVEPATH=
:END
```

provides the **PATH** and **APPEND** commands (available only from the command prompt, unless you add them to a program group in the shell) in order for you to inform application programs of your organizational decisions. Even when you don't make the explicit decisions, as for instance when an application program itself sets directories for default purposes, you will often have to know which directories were used.

Suppose, for example, that after installing all the necessary files for a new database management program (in a DBMS directory), you now want to see how much space is left on your hard disk. If you switch to a command prompt, you can enter **CHKDSK** to analyze the disk. However, if you have not prepared your system completely, you may just receive the message

```
Bad command or file name
```

because DOS will not know where (that is, in which directory) to find the CHKDSK.EXE program in order to run it.

The CHKDSK program is stored in the DOS subdirectory. How can you tell DOS to check the DOS subdirectory if it hasn't found CHKDSK in the current directory? You can certainly type the complete path name of the CHKDSK.EXE program whenever you want to run it:

```
C:\DOS\CHKDSK
```

However, instead of specifying the path name every time you want to run a program, you can set up the PATH *command*. It tells DOS which subdirectories, in addition to the current one, it should check from that point on whenever you submit the name of a program to run.

To open a path to the DOS subdirectory, for example, you would enter the following command at a command prompt:

```
PATH \DOS
```

(Be sure to prefix this with the drive specification for the DOS subdirectory if it is on a different drive than your command prompt is currently using.)

The CHKDSK command would now execute properly from any command prompt, because the path to the subdirectory that contains the command is now open. In fact, all of DOS's utility programs are now accessible to you no matter what your current working directory happens to be.

➤ EXTRA!

Put Yourself in Charge of Your Path!

You can open a complex path by separating a list of directory names with semicolons. As an example, when I first started working on this book, I had an earlier release of Xywrite on my D: drive. As a DOS path, I could enter

```
PATH \DOS;\WP;\LOTUS;\DBMS;D:\XYWRITE
```

(Remember not to leave any spaces between the entries on the path list. DOS stops reading the line when it comes across the first space on the list.)

If a program I try to run can't be found in the current default directory, DOS will first look for it in the DOS subdirectory. If it isn't there, DOS will then successively look in the WP, LOTUS, and DBMS subdirectories on the boot drive, and then the XYWRITE subdirectory on the D drive. DOS will only return the "Bad command or file name" message to you if it doesn't find the specified program in any of these directories. Note that the **PATH** command does not change the active directory. It simply tells DOS to search other directories if the program requested is not in the current directory.

You can set the default directory before you start up a main application program. Whenever your program reads or writes files, it will use the default directory. For example, to do database work with a set of accounting files while at a command prompt, you could set the DOS default directory to the DBMS\ACCOUNTS directory. If you then set the path to \DBMS, you can invoke commands from your database-management program. For example, in the following,

```
CD \DBMS\ACCOUNTS
PATH \DBMS
DBASE
```

the first **CD** (short for CHDIR, or change directory) command sets the default directory. After this particular sequence, the default directory will be ACCOUNTS, so the program you're working with will expect to find all data files in that directory. It will hunt for its own management programs along the directories specified on the path, finding them in \DBMS.

It is necessary to execute the **PATH** and **APPEND** commands from a command prompt *before* activating the shell if you wish the PATH or AP-PEND specifications to affect shell operations. If you run these commands from a Shift+F9 (shell) command prompt, the specifications will affect activity only during that command-prompt session. When you exit from this command prompt (using **EXIT**) back to the shell, your latest PATH and APPEND specifications are given up in favor of the original ones that were active when you first activated the shell with the **DOS-SHELL** command.

Searching Paths

There will be instances when you will need to reach a file in a directory other than the one you're working in (that is, other than the default directory). For example, while using drive D and my new Signature word processor to write these chapters, I switched among the following three items:

1. SIG.BAT, the batch file that runs my main word-processing program, and which is located in my C:\UTILITY directory

2. The DOS utilities, which are located in the C:\DOS directory

3. The individual data file in the C:\SIG1D\DOCS\DOS6 directory that contains the chapter you are now reading.

You can open a path to several directories at once by entering a series of path names separated by semicolons (and no spaces). By specifying the following PATH command in my AUTOEXEC.BAT file, I was able to quickly access all executable files in any of the three directories:

```
PATH C:\SIG1D\DOCS\DOS6;C:\DOS;C:\UTILITY
```

Use the SUBST command (see Chapter 19) to reduce the number of characters required to type a PATH statement. For example, if you substitute K: for the much longer path to the DOS6 directory—for example, SUBST K: C:\SIG\DOCS\DOS6—you will have fewer typing errors later. Also, you will avoid confronting the 127-character limitation imposed by DOS on the length of complex command lines.

If you find that DOS generally takes a while to locate your programs, you may want to redefine your **PATH** command for those files. Since DOS searches the path in the order in which you list directory names, you should list the directories in the order most likely to succeed.

For now, you should plan to use a single **PATH** command that enables DOS to hunt for and find all of your main programs, for example:

```
PATH \DOS;\UTIL;\LOTUS;\WP;\DBMS
```

In this way, you will be able to set up one **PATH** command in your system's AUTOEXEC.BAT file. Since the DOS shell is initiated from this system startup file, you will have no trouble running any programs from the shell once this **PATH** command is set up properly. Later, you can experiment with changing the **PATH** commands during the execution of various batch files.

You can only use the **PATH** command to search for files with the extensions .COM, .EXE, and .BAT. The first two types are executable programs, and the last is a DOS batch file. (See Chapters 12 through 14 for more on batch files.) As DOS will not search the path directories for files with other extensions, you cannot use it to access *data* files not found in the current directory.

Some programs require special *overlay* files that are usually not loaded into memory until they are needed. The *PATH* command itself will not enable DOS to locate and load these files. Some of the newest programs requiring overlays are able to run because they are smart enough to use DOS's path information themselves to locate their overlay files. Some older programs, however, may require that you run the application program from within the directory that contains both the main and overlay files.

➤ EXTRA!

Take the PATH of Least Resistance!

Include a **PATH** command line in your AUTOEXEC.BAT file. This ensures that DOS will later know where to look for your executable files. However, do not include too many subdirectories in your path. Since DOS will potentially search every directory on the path, system performance may suffer when too many directories are searched.

If you run some application programs infrequently, you can avoid placing their home directories on the path at all. This can often avoid the overhead of DOS having to search through extra directories. To do this, you can write a batch file that first changes to the correct directory, then executes the program name.

For example, I keep the latest version of Lotus 1-2-3 in the C:\123 directory. However, I don't use 1-2-3 very often, so I wrote a simple batch file:

```
c:
cd \123
123
```

This runs the actual 123.EXE program after first ensuring that the current drive and directory are correct. Since this batch file is itself located in a directory (C:\UTILITY) on my path, along with a number of other such useful batch files, I can have a minimum of directories on my system's path.

You can also improve system efficiency by carefully ordering the names of the the directories on your path. Place first the directory name that contains the most frequently referenced executable file names. Place second the directory name that is next most frequently referenced, and so on.

You might also note that this simple 123.BAT batch file would leave you in the \123 directory after running the 123.EXE program, even though it saved you the trouble of having C:\123 on your path all the time. There is another, more sophisticated alternative. Your 123.BAT file, or a comparable batch program for your favorite application, can temporarily *augment* the path with the desired directory. With this technique, the batch file can run the desired program and when it is finished can restore the path that existed prior to running the application.

For example, to run the NORTON.EXE program, you should usually have the C:\NORTON directory on the path. My NORTON.BAT file:

```
@ECHO OFF
Rem NORTON.BAT
SET SAVEPATH=%PATH%
PATH=C:\NORTON;%PATH%
NORTON.EXE
PATH=%SAVEPATH%
SET SAVEPATH=
```

uses the sophisticated technique of *environmental variables* (See Chapter 19) to first save the existing path, temporarily add C:\NORTON to the system path, run the NORTON.EXE program, then restore the original path (which was saved in a special variable named SAVEPATH).

The **APPEND** command enables you to set up a searching path to overlay files and data files, effectively removing DOS's former inability to locate these files. To create an **APPEND** command, you list the directory names containing the files you want DOS to find after the command name itself. For instance,

```
APPEND \WP;\DBMS\PROGRAMS
```

establishes a searching path that DOS will use to locate overlay files for a word processor, and database files for your database-management system.

➤ EXTRA!

Check the Path If You're Having Problems

After working in several different directories, you may not be sure which path DOS will take to search for files not found in the current directory. If this is the case, you can see what the current path is by entering **PATH** at the command prompt. DOS then lists the current path.

You can redefine the path by simply reentering a complete path statement with a new sequence of directory names. Entering a path statement is known as *opening*, or defining, the path.

To *close* the path, enter the **PATH** command with a lone semicolon (;) as follows:

```
PATH ;
```

After you've entered this command, asking DOS for the current path will produce the message:

```
No Path
```

You should consider running the **PATH** command with no parameters whenever an application program seems to be having trouble running. Just asking DOS to display the current path list in this way may be all it takes to suggest the solution to the problem. You may find that you did not include the required directory names in your **PATH** command.

Creating Multiple Subdirectories for Your Program's Files

Many programs allow you to change the subdirectory used to store program data. In fact, if you work in an office where more than one person uses the computer, each person's work can be stored in a different subdirectory.

➤ **EXTRA!**

Installing Is Different from Configuring!

When you copy a program to a hard disk from a floppy diskette, you have only *installed* the program; it is not necessarily *configured*. Configuration is the setup process that gives the program all of the information unique to your system, such as what type of screen display and printer are being used. In addition, some programs require you to specify the default data drive and directory. Lotus 1-2-3 is one of those programs.

Just because the program (let's say Lotus 1-2-3) was installed on your hard disk, it does not follow that 1-2-3 knows what drive you want to use for data. When 1-2-3 is installed on a hard-disk drive, it makes default assumptions about which drive and directory to use for worksheet creation. To change the default disk and directory for any program like this, there is usually a command in the software itself that can be invoked. Refer to your software's user's guide to discover it. In 1-2-3, it is the /WGDD command.

You can also store work for different projects in separate subdirectories if that suits your office better.

To see how this works, you must return to DOS. Since subdirectories are organized in a hierarchical order, LOTUS, which is a subdirectory of the root in Figure 5.3, can also have subdirectories of its own.

Suppose that in your office, three people—Sue, Harry, and Alice—will be working with Lotus 1-2-3. To keep their work from getting confused, it might be useful to separate and store their files into unique subdirectories. All you need do to manage this is to select LOTUS from the directory tree area, then choose the *Create Directory* command three times, specifying the name for the subdirectory each time. Assuming that you had earlier created a WP directory for word processing in the root (\), and that your DOS files themselves are stored in a \DOS directory, your hard disk will now be structured as shown in Figure 5.3. Figure 5.4 shows another way to visualize the directory structure.

FIGURE 5.3

The DOS directory structure is analogous to a growing tree. Everything stems from a root, and each successive branch (i.e., directory) can parent or give rise to another branch (i.e., subdirectory).

Running Programs in Subdirectories

At this point you have set up a directory that contains the main program files and subdirectories for its data files. (You could use this setup for your word processor as well.) To run the program, you would change the current directory to LOTUS, run the program, and then tell the program which subdirectory you wish it to work in. This type of request from within a program varies with each program, but the concept remains the same.

FIGURE 5.4

The DOS directory structure can also be visualized much like an organizational chart. Here, the lines represent hierarchical relationships, and the circles represent individual directories.

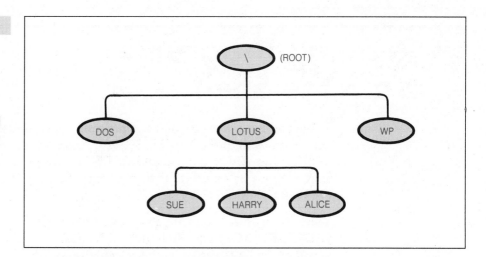

T I P

Because every program has different assumptions about default directories, you may at times try to retrieve a file and not find it. Check the program's default directory. The solution is often as easy as resetting it to the directory that you regularly use for file work.

In 1-2-3, the command to change default subdirectories is the File Directory command (/FD). The program will first display the current directory setting. Because you started 1-2-3 when you were in the main LOTUS directory, 1-2-3 automatically sets the default to C:\LOTUS. To change directories, you would enter the full path name of the subdirectory that you want to use. If you were Alice, for instance, you would specify to 1-2-3 that it should use your directory. Including the drive as well, you would submit the following at 1-2-3's command-entry line:

```
C:\LOTUS\ALICE
```

All files would then be saved in or retrieved from the subdirectory LOTUS\ALICE. In this way, Alice can have her work separated from Harry's and Sue's. If Harry or Sue later logged on, they could go through a similar sequence to ensure that they had access to the files in their respective subdirectories.

Running Programs from the Shell

There are many ways to initiate a program under DOS. In this chapter, I demonstrate all of the possibilities; you can select the ones that will work best for you. I will initiate DOS's **CHKDSK** program in my first examples, since it is a utility that will come in handy when you set up and work with your directory structure.

The shell provides you with a variety of ways to initiate any program (like CHKDSK.EXE). The first three methods require that the program's location, the DOS directory, be selected in the directory tree.

- You can highlight CHKDSK.EXE in the files area with your keyboard using the Tab and arrow keys. You could then press Enter to initiate the program.

- You can use your mouse to run CHKDSK by simply double-clicking on the line containing the name CHKDSK.EXE.

- You can select CHKDSK.EXE with either the mouse (single click) or the keyboard (Tab and spacebar). Then you could select File from the menu bar. Since the CHKDSK.EXE program is already selected, it will be run if you simply choose *Open* from the File menu.

When you run a program using any of these methods, it executes immediately. If there is any screen output, it temporarily takes the place of the shell screen, and you are not returned to the shell until you respond to the prompt

```
Press any key to return to MS-DOS Shell
```

This gives you time to read the output at your leisure.

A fourth method of running programs, the *Run* choice on the File menu, enables you to execute any program on any disk at any time. It also pauses the video screen when the program completes its execution. In Figure 5.5, while the current directory is clearly \SIG1D\DOCS, I've selected the

FIGURE 5.5

The Run dialog box offers an easy way to execute any application from within the shell. You can type any single command or command filename into the Run dialog box. (The field will scroll if your command line exceeds the visible width.) Press OK when you've typed the complete command line.

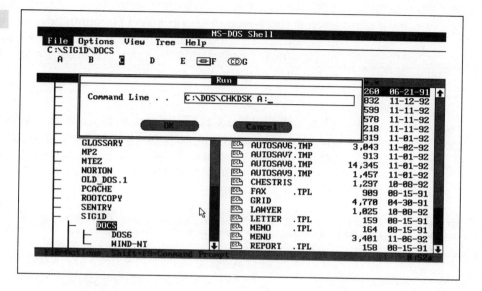

Run choice on the File menu. This displays a dialog box into which I've typed the complete path name of the program I wish DOS to run, followed by a parameter indicating the drive name to check:

```
C:\DOS\CHKDSK A:
```

You will use this Run dialog box throughout the remainder of the book to execute simple application programs and DOS utilities. Although you will shortly learn how to implement your own menu applications, listing for simple selection any applications you will frequently run, this Run dialog box is most convenient for running programs that are only occasionally required.

Running Commands and Utilities Directly

You can run any program by simply typing its name at a command prompt. For example, entering **CHKDSK** will initiate DOS's CHKDSK program if it is in the current directory, or if you had previously used the **PATH** command (discussed earlier in this chapter) to specify its location.

Even if you have not set up a **PATH** command, you can still run a program located in another directory or on another disk by prefixing the file name with the command's complete path name and drive identifier. For example, if you enter

```
C:\DOS\CHKDSK A:
```

DOS will find the CHKDSK program in drive C's DOS directory, then run it for the diskette in drive A. The normal output of CHKDSK is a full-screen display, as seen in Figure 5.6. When you use the full path name for a program, it doesn't matter what directory you are in.

➤ EXTRA!

Instantly View a File in the Program That Created It!

You can *associate* a program with one or more file extensions, such as .TXT, .XY, .DOC, or .WP. In this way, whenever you double-click or press Enter on a data file that has one of these extensions, DOS will automatically run the associated program file. It will also automatically load the selected data file.

As you'll learn elsewhere in this chapter, when you associate programs with file extensions, you can instruct DOS to either run the program immediately with the selected data file or first display a dialog box that will prompt for other information (i.e., switches or parameters) required by the program.

Note: Every DOS program and command has its own unique set of possible parameters and switches. Use the help screens to learn all of a command's parameters and switches.

FIGURE 5.6

The CHKDSK command displays information about total and free disk space, the space consumed by the files in the current directory, and information about memory usage.

```
C:\>CHKDSK A:

   1457664 bytes total disk space
   1200128 bytes in 25 user files
    257536 bytes available on disk

       512 bytes in each allocation unit
      2847 total allocation units on disk
       503 available allocation units on disk

    651264 total bytes memory
    419216 bytes free

C:\>
```

Managing Application Programs from the Shell

Individual program names like CHKDSK can be placed in the shell's program areas and run quickly by simply selecting them. You'll learn later in this chapter how to add any programs you wish to existing program groups, and you'll learn how to construct your own separately selectable lists of programs and make them available from the shell.

When you incorporate your own application programs into the shell, you'll learn how to control whether DOS pauses the screen after the program runs. As well, you'll learn how to display your own dialog box with which to request further user input. You can then use this dialog box to include any desired parameters, such as a specified disk drive for the **CHKDSK** command.

For example, in Figure 5.7, I've run the Format utility. A dialog box appears, to request any desired parameter or switch entries for this behind-the-scenes command.

As you can also see on this screen, the program-management aspect of the shell appears to be running and displaying the Disk Utilities group in the bottom half of the screen. The purpose of the *Program/File Lists* choice on the View menu is to enable you to easily access and run programs while also managing your file system. This view uses the lower half of the shell screen as a mini window within which to display the DOS-shell hierarchy of program names. You can then select the Disk Utilities group, followed by the *Format* choice in that group.

The *Format* command in the shell's Disk Utilities group displays a dialog box with the most common parameter (the A: drive) already visible. To format a disk in another drive, or to add other switch settings or parameters, modify the Parameters field before selecting OK.

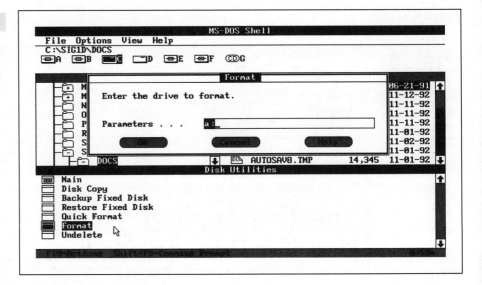

Running Programs Automatically

Remember that you can run any program at a command prompt by simply typing its name and pressing Enter. You do not need to enter an extension, although operations may be slightly faster when you do. Whenever you enter an extensionless word at the beginning of any command line, DOS assumes that you are either specifying an internal command to run or an external program name. If the name you enter is not found in the built-in table of internal commands (stored in the COMMAND.COM file itself), DOS looks for a file name with a .COM extension (first), or an .EXE extension (second), or a .BAT extension (third). This will typically cover all external commands, utility programs, and your application programs.

One of the most common parameters entered after the program name is the name of a data file to be used by the program you are running. For example, if I include a data file as an optional parameter for my word-processing program (SIG.EXE), then that file is automatically loaded into memory, ready to be used in the word processor. In other words, entering

SIG 1099.FRM

at the command prompt will start up my word processor and also load the 1099.FRM text file. Remember that this file-name reference will only work when both program and data files are in the current directory, or when you have properly set the path list.

Associating Application Programs with Data Files

Establishing an association between an executable program and your data files' extensions is straightforward. You can do this in two ways. First, you can select a file with one of the desired extensions (like .XY), then associate that extension with a specified executable program. Whenever you

➤ EXTRA!

Avoid Bringing Up a Second Copy of the DOS Shell!

You might find that you occasionally initiate the DOS shell by accident when you already have it running. This can happen sometimes after you bring a command prompt from within the DOS shell, then forget that the shell is already active. It is easy to forgetfully type **DOSSHELL** from within this embedded command prompt.

This can be a problem because it consumes memory resources. To avoid this mistake, you can modify the *Command Prompt* program item in the shell's Main program group. Choose the File ➤ Properties option for this item and modify the *Commands* field. Initially, this field simply contains **COMMAND** which means that the COMMAND.COM file will run when you click on this item. You should replace this entry with:

```
Set PROMPT=(SHELL)%PROMPT% ; COMMAND
```

Now when you are working at a command prompt you reached from the shell, your command prompt will include the phrase **(SHELL)** to remind you that the shell is still running. Be sure to leave a blank space on either side of the semicolon in this multiple-command entry.

later select a file with that extension, the associated program will automatically execute. In order to establish this association, you first select a data file name from the files area, then pull down the File menu and choose *Associate*. The dialog box that appears allows you to enter the name of the program you want to associate with that extension. You must enter the full path name of the executable file, as shown in Figure 5.8.

Alternatively, you can first select the executable program you'll want to run and then pull down the File menu and select *Associate*. Lastly, you can enter into the resulting dialog box the extensions that you want the shell to associate with that executable program. Use this approach when you know that you want one program to handle a variety of file extensions.

For example, I wanted DOS to automatically run my word-processing program whenever I selected any text file, whether its extension is .XY (my own specifier), .TXT or .DOC (common standard extensions), or .WP (used by other text processors on my system).

First I selected the SIG1D directory from the directory tree. Next I chose the SIG.EXE program from the files area. Finally, I pulled down the File menu and selected *Associate*. DOS then displayed the Associate File dialog box seen in Figure 5.9. The entry window in this dialog box is initially blank—you must enter the extensions that you wish to associate

FIGURE 5.8

After associating files of a particular extension with one executable program, opening such a file will automatically run the associated program. To associate extensions, first select any file having the desired extension, choose File▶Associate and fill in the name of the executable file.

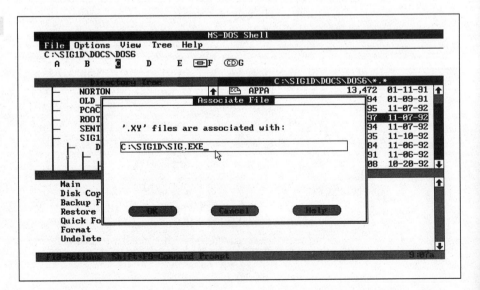

with a program, as I did here. Separate each extension with a space, then press Enter when you've typed in all the possible extensions.

From this point on, all you need do to run the SIG.EXE program is to double-click on a text file that has one of the now-associated extensions or, using the keyboard, press Enter to run the selected file.

FIGURE 5.9

If you first select an executable file name, like SIG.EXE, and then choose File➤Assoc-iate, you can easily associate one execu-table program with many extensions. In this example, SIG.EXE will run whenever you later open any file with a .XY, .DOC, .TXT, or .WP extension.

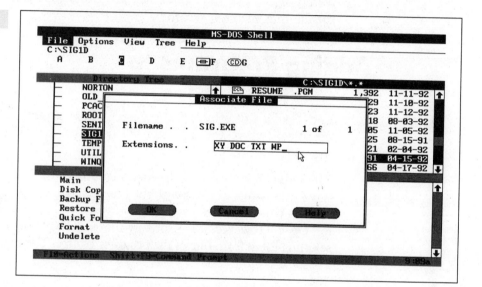

Setting Up Program Lists

You've learned how to run programs from both the shell and from the command prompt. As you have now seen several times, the View menu contains two choices that enable you to initiate application programs. If you are quite comfortable with managing both files and programs from the shell screens, you can display and access both of these features of the shell by selecting *Program/File Lists*. If you have no need for manipulating files and simply wish to initiate specific applications, you can display the simpler screen obtained by selecting *Program List*.

Since you are now familiar with these screens, I will show you how the Main and Disk Utilities program groups can be modified to extend DOS's program-management capability. You will learn how to add your own program names or other DOS utilities to these group listings. You will even discover how to define your own completely new program group, listing your favorite and most commonly run programs. By creating your own program list, you can initiate programs more quickly than if you use the file-management screens.

Adding Programs to a Group Listing

Let's take a closer look at the Disk Utilities group. From this portion of the screen, when you can select File from the menu bar, you see the menu shown in Figure 5.10.

The *Open* choice on the File menu is similar to the *Open* choice that you saw earlier when dealing with the file-management portion of the shell. It enables you to initiate whichever program you had selected before choosing *Open*. However, it is probably more comfortable to run programs by selecting them from one of the program groups. The program and program

FIGURE 5.10

The File menu changes according to the shell's context. If you highlight one of the choices in a program group, such as *Disk Copy*, the File menu displays options that apply to programs. In this example, none of the file-oriented choices (like *Move* or *Copy*) appear.

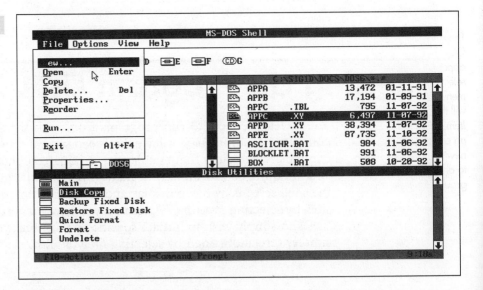

group names within these lists can be renamed so that they are easier to understand than the .EXE or .COM file names in the files area of the shell.

You can add other utilities to this list quite easily. To do so, you first select *New* from the File menu, in order to bring up the New Program Object dialog box seen in Figure 5.11.

This dialog box offers two choices. A new entry can be either an executable program (*Program Item*) or a group of choices (*Program Group*). Let's first select *Program Item*, in order to add a new utility program to the existing Disk Utilities group.

After selecting *Program Item*, the Add Program dialog box appears. You can now give DOS the name of any utility program to run, and also rename it with a more understandable title or expression to display for users. For instance, suppose you want to run the **CHKDSK** program but want it to be listed in the menu as *Check Disk*. You would fill in the first two fields as shown in Figure 5.12 and then press Enter, or click on OK. We will return later to augment this entry by selecting *Properties* on the File menu.

The title, which will be displayed in the Disk Utilities list (see Figure 5.13), will be *Check Disk*, and the underlying program that will

FIGURE 5.11

The New Program Object dialog box appears whenever you select New from the File menu. Generally, you will then select *Program Item* if you are adding an entry (such as a new program choice) to one of the existing groups.

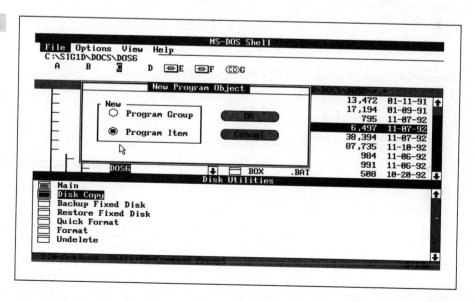

FIGURE 5.12

The Add Program dialog box permits you to define a good deal about what happens behind the scenes when you add a new program-group item. The user sees only what you type in the *Program Title* field. The *Commands* field specifies what actually runs when the user chooses the menu item.

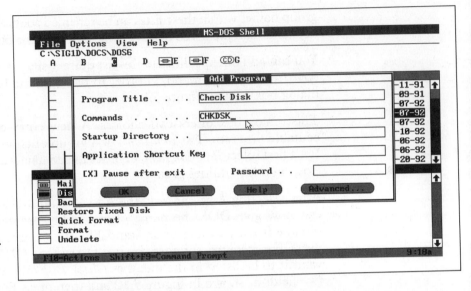

FIGURE 5.13

Each new program item that you add to any menu immediately appears on the shell's menu list.

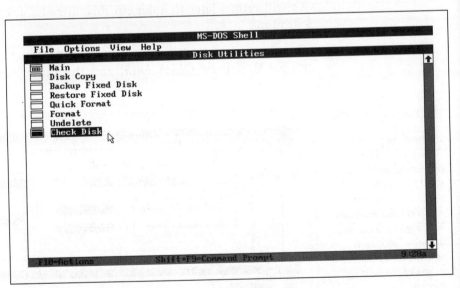

automatically be run will be CHKDSK.EXE. (For this and subsequent figures, I've used the View menu to switch to a program-list-only display. This way, each figure will allow you to concentrate more fully on the effects of your actions on the program list entries.)

As it stands now, the CHKDSK program will run with no additional parameters; therefore, only the boot drive will be checked. In addition, since the *Pause after exit* toggle was initially set on by default (see Figure 5.12), DOS will pause after the CHKDSK.EXE program completes. As noted earlier in this chapter, this means you can take your time reading the output display, then press any key to tell DOS to redisplay the shell screen.

Customizing Program Startup

Other setup options appear in the Add Program dialog box. All of the options in this dialog box are known as *properties*. Once you've added a program entry to a program group list, you can later change any of the initial properties. To do this, you merely select *Properties* from the File menu after you've highlighted the program entry whose characteristics you wish to modify.

Other than the *Program Title* and *Commands* entry, the remaining properties are optional. They afford you more control over the access to and execution of your programs:

- **Startup Directory** defines the directory that will be current when your program runs.

- **Application Shortcut Key** offers a quick, single-keystroke method of selecting and executing a program. This enables you to use what is known as a *hot key* to switch to individual executing tasks.

- **Pause after exit** defines whether or not DOS pauses the screen display after the program has completed, and before the shell screen redisplays.

- **Password** will enforce some restriction on who can actually run the program. Only someone who knows the password and can enter it when prompted by DOS can actually cause the program to begin executing.

TIP

You can switch instantaneously to any executing program by assigning a *shortcut key* to that executable program name. To assign such a shortcut key, highlight the program name on the Active Task List or on the Main program group and pull down the File menu. Select the *Properties* choice and move to the *Application Shortcut Key* field. Press any desired shortcut key (you can use any combination of Alt, Ctrl, and Shift keys plus another character), then select OK.

Suppose that you typically work on the D drive, although your boot disk is the C drive. As you've currently defined this new program item, only the boot drive is checked by the CHKDSK program. You could modify this behind-the-scenes work with another choice on the File menu. First, highlight *Check Disk* on the Disk Utilities list. Then pull down the File menu, and select the *Properties* choice to bring up the Program Item Properties dialog box seen in Figure 5.14. Through this dialog box, you can make adjustments to the same underlying characteristics you saw in

FIGURE 5.14

The Program Item Properties dialog box enables you to adjust any or all of the behind-the-scenes information for a menu item. Just highlight the relevant program item before selecting *Properties* from the File menu.

the Add Program dialog box. For example, you can specify or change the title that appears on the group itself. You can specify how many (and if any) parameters are to be expected and solicited from a user who makes this choice. The other entry fields, toggle options, and pushbutton choices represent more detailed aspects that underlie each simple group choice.

In this simple example, I've only made the simple change of adding **%1** to the *Commands* field in the dialog box. When you later select *Check Disk* from the group menu, this %1 entry will force DOS to prompt for a single additional parameter: the drive identifier of the disk a user wants to check. After selecting *OK*, this new property will be stored, and DOS will request additional information for the %1 property, as shown in Figure 5.15.

I've already filled in the four fields required. They are blank the first time you specify a percent entry with a program name. (If you later *change* properties, these fields would display your earlier entries so that you could modify them.) Later, when you select *Check Disk* in the Disk Utilities group, DOS will display a special prompting box that forces you (or any user) to provide the additional information you specified in the Program Item Properties dialog box. In this simple example, a user who selects *Check Disk* from the Disk Utilities group will be prompted for the desired disk drive identifier, as shown in Figure 5.16.

FIGURE 5.15

Use the percent-sign+numeral technique in the *Commands* field to ask DOS to display a special input dialog box (to define what the *%n* parameter is to actually be) whenever the user selects this program item. Additional information will also be requested for later prompts to the user.

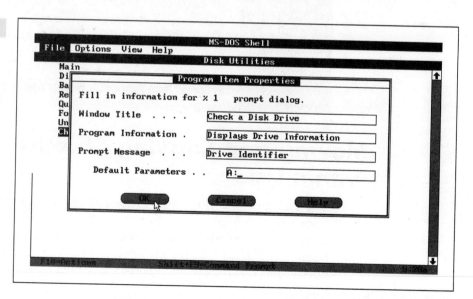

FIGURE 5.16

An example of a user-specified prompting box when running applications. This is the result of specifying in Figure 5.14 a *Commands* property that referenced *%1* for the *Check Disk* program choice, which brought up the variable-parameter definitions box I further filled out in Figure 5.15.

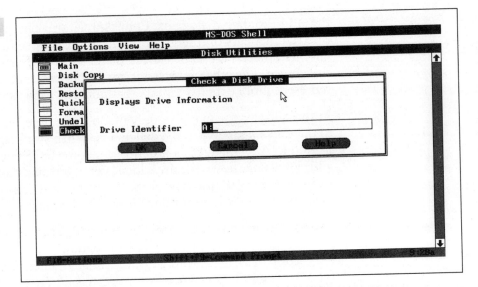

N O T E

When you run programs that allow optional parameter entry, as does the CHKDSK command for specifying a drive identifier, it is up to you to know the allowable parameters and their individual purpose(s). If the program you are entering into a program group requires or allows more than one optional parameter, you can simply add %2, %3, and so on to the Commands list shown in the Program Item Properties dialog box of Figure 5.14.

Moving and Copying Choices within Lists

The *Delete* choice in the File menu enables you to remove any program from a program group list. For example, you may decide to remove one of the initially standard entries, such as the *Backup* or *Restore* option. (You might want to do this, for instance, if your system uses a special backup device that includes its own software for backing up and restoring your files.)

You will not need the File menu's *Copy* choice very often, so I won't discuss it in detail here. You only use it after you've set up several group listings and want to quickly copy a complete entry from one group to another without having to reenter all the properties of that program item. Use this technique when adding new entries to program groups that are the same or almost the same as an existing entry in another group.

In addition to copying and deleting program names from a program group listing, you can also reorder them. To rearrange the order in which the choices are displayed, you use the *Reorder* option. As an example, suppose you want to make your new entry, *Check Disk*, the first entry on the list. You need to first highlight *Check Disk*, then pull down the File menu, and select *Reorder*. You'll be prompted to

```
Select location to move to, then press Enter. Press ESC to cancel
```

Next, move the highlight to the desired new location (let's say the top of the list) and press Enter. The selected entry (*Check Disk*) is then placed in this new entry location, and it will be redisplayed there every time you select the Utilities group. Behind the scenes, the program-management aspect has kept track of all existing properties of the program item known to you as Check Disk.

Defining Your Own Program Groups

Suppose that you wish to do more than just add an individual choice to the Disk Utilities group. You may have an entire set of application programs that you use frequently, and a completely separate menu group for those programs may be in order. As you may have noticed in Figure 5.12, you can add a new program group to any existing shell group. The new group object will have a file-folder icon beside it, and you can insert this new group choice into the Main program group or any subgroup you like. (When you first install DOS, the only subgroup in the shell is the Disk Utilities.)

As an example, let's return to the Main program group and add a new group called *Applications*. After choosing *New* from the File menu, and

Program Group from the New Program Object dialog box, the Add Group dialog box appears. Use this to enter the Applications group title, as I have done in Figure 5.17. Note that you can use lowercase and uppercase letters in your *Title* field.

Entering **Applications** in the *Title* field directs DOS to add that new group name to the Main program list. Entering a password during this Add Group procedure ensures that only authorized users can gain access to the program items (which you will be including shortly in the group list itself).

You can also enter textual help information into the *Help Text* field. Users will be able to read this text whenever they select your Applications group from the Main screen and press F1 for help. You can enter up to 255 characters of help text. To do this for a program group, select *File Properties* and type your text into the *Help Text* field. When you add a new program *item*, you must choose the *Advanced* pushbutton of the Add Program Item dialog box to make the *Help Text* field accessible.

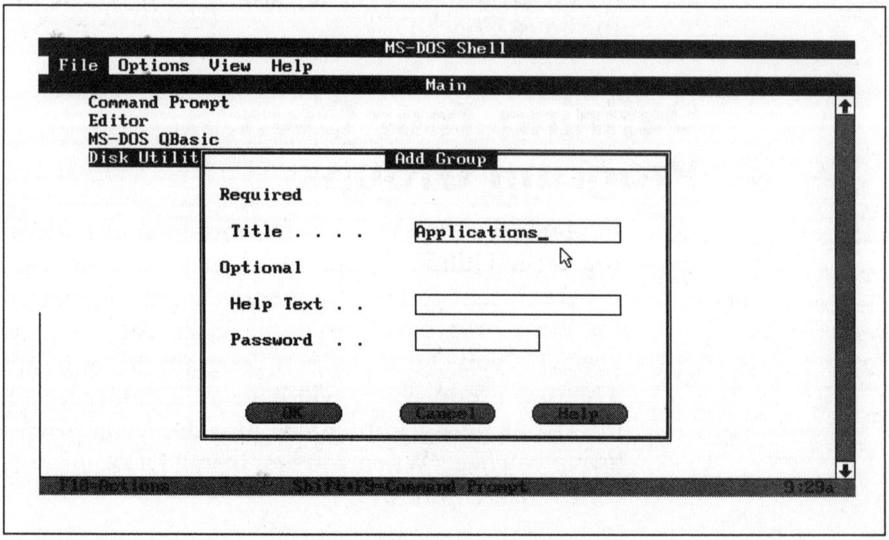

FIGURE 5.17

You can customize the DOS shell by creating your own group of program choices. The Add Group dialog box enables you to create and name a new program list (which will initially contain no program choices).

TIP

If you are entering multiple phrases of help text for a program group or program item, type ^M at the end of each phrase. DOS will then insert a carriage return there when it displays the text in the help window. (Note that ^M is a two-character sequence, consisting of the caret symbol followed the letter M. It is not a Ctrl+M single-character control code, which is sometimes represented in books as ^M.)

After completing all desired entries on the Add Group screen of Figure 5.17, you select *OK* to store the information. DOS immediately updates the Main group screen to reflect this new group item. Figure 5.18 shows the Main group with its added Applications group.

When you first select a newly defined group item, like Applications, only one entry appears on the group list. That entry is the choice that will restore the preceding menu to your screen. In this case, the new Applications screen would list Main as the only selectable choice.

FIGURE 5.18

It's easy to add your own group. The Applications group name now appears in the Main group. When selected, it will display a separately defined group of program items.

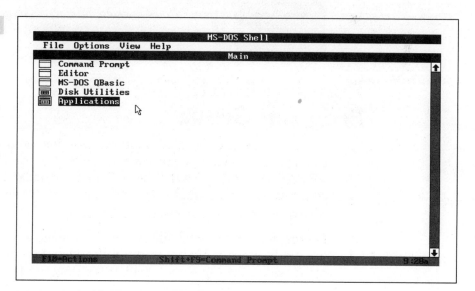

In order to define application-program entries for this new Applications group, you must pull down the File menu and select *New* to add your first program to this group. This initiates the same procedure you followed earlier to add an entry to the Disk Utilities group. I followed this procedure several times to add other customized applications to my Applications group. You can see my completed Applications list in Figure 5.19.

TIP

Since most of us frequently edit the AUTOEXEC.BAT and CONFIG.SYS files, why not just create two special program items—*Edit Autoexec.bat* and *Edit Config.sys*—in a program group? This would save time and reduce typographical errors when you need to update one of these important controlling files. Each item can have a Commands field that runs the *EDIT* program and brings up the particular file that is frequently updated. For example, you could have Update Autoexec.bat appear in the group (i.e., as the Program Title). Clicking on this choice would execute the contents of the Commands field (e.g., EDIT C:\AUTOEXEC.BAT).

Running Batch Files from a Program Group

When I originally installed Ventura Publisher on a hard disk, it went through an installation process that created a special batch file called VP.BAT. (See Chapters 12 through 14 for detailed presentation of the concepts and techniques of batch files.) I must execute this batch file whenever I want to run Ventura.

In order to have the batch file executed automatically when I select it from my Applications program group in the shell, I specify the **CALL** command within the *Commands* field of the Program Item Properties dialog

FIGURE 5.19

To create a customized new program group, such as the one in this figure, you must first *Add a Program Group* entry, then select that group, and finally select *Add Program Item* for each program to add to the group.

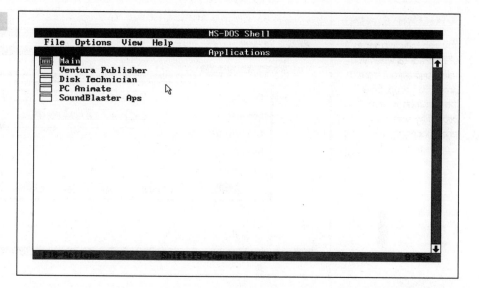

box. This ensures that once I exit the called program, it returns control to the program that called the batch file. In other words, when I am finished with Ventura, I am returned to the shell instead of to the DOS command prompt.

Since I keep my Ventura program files on a different drive, I also want to change to that drive whenever I want to run the program. Figure 5.20 shows how I filled out the Program Item Properties dialog box to accomplish both of these taskswhen I choose Ventura Publisher from my Applications group.

(Remember, to reach this dialog box, you would first highlight Ventura Publisher in the program group, then select *Properties* from the File menu, and finally enter the required commands in the *Commands* field.)

When specifying multiple commands in a Program Item Properties dialog box, you must put them in sequence and you must separate each command from adjacent ones by a space and a semicolon. When listed on separate lines, the commands you see in Figure 5.20 would appear as:

```
E:
CD \
CALL VP.BAT
```

FIGURE 5.20

FIGURE 5.20

You can initiate a series of commands when you select a program from a program group. Enter the commands, separated by semicolons and spaces, in the *Commands* field.

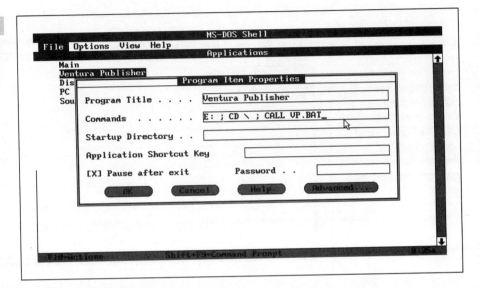

These commands make E the current drive, change the current directory to the root of the drive, and call up the VP.BAT batch file (which initiates the Ventura program).

Running Multiple Programs—The Task Swapper

Up to now, you've learned a variety of ways in which to initiate utility or application programs. In each case, you had to wait until one program was completed before you could begin a new program. In fact, the DOS shell includes a special feature that enables you to initiate multiple different programs, and quickly switch from one to another without having to wait for one to finish in order to begin another program. In order to activate this feature, you must pull down the Options menu and select the toggle choice *Enable Task Swapper*. When you do this, the right portion of the program-management aspect of the screen is then used to display a list of program names you have initiated.

Figure 5.21 displays this *Active Task List* window just after enabling the Task Swapper.

No programs are active the first time you activate this Active Task List window. However, the current program group is still visible, and available, on the left side of the screen. You can use standard selection techniques to choose any program to run from that area of the screen, and the program will begin to execute as expected. However, rather than having to wait until it finishes, you can press the Ctrl+Esc key combination to interrupt it and switch to another task. When you press Ctrl+Esc, the shell screen reappears with the interrupted program's name on the Active Task List. You can now perform any other shell operation you like, including the initiation of another program.

It doesn't matter how you activate a program. You've learned several ways now. For example, in Figure 5.22 I've activated six programs. The ASQ.EXE program was initiated directly from the files area in the upper portion of the screen—I switched to directory UTILITY, and opened the ASQ.EXE program. The Ventura Publisher and Disk Technician tasks

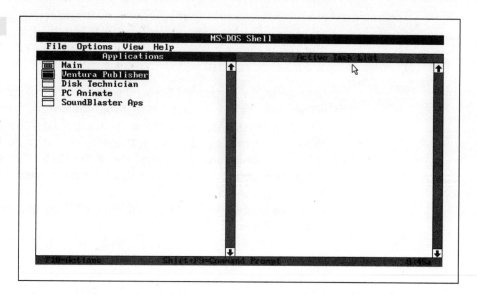

were initiated from my personal Applications program group (now seen, after several deletions and a reordering, in the lower left portion of the screen). The Disk Copy utility was activated from the Disk Utilities group. The Editor and the QBasic programs were initiated from the Main program group.

➤ **EXTRA!**

Task Swapping in DOS Is Different from Multitasking in Windows!

DOS manages the available memory in your system to switch between each application you initiate. It does not run these applications and utilities simultaneously. This facility of DOS is called *task swapping* or *context switching*. This enables you to switch from one executing program (or context) to another.

This facility is not as powerful as the multitasking available under Microsoft Windows, which manages time and control to permit multiple programs to continue executing commands and operations in the background. By comparison, under the control of the DOS shell, only the program (or "context") that is active on your screen is actually running. Any other active tasks are computationally frozen until you once again activate them. They are simply interrupted in the middle of what they are doing, and suspended until you switch back to them.

If you refer to Figure 5.22, you'll see that I first successively initiated six active tasks. That is, after each program began, I pressed Ctrl+Esc to return to this primary shell screen. (I also pulled down the View menu and selected *Program/File Lists* to give myself access to both file-management and program-management aspects of the shell.) In fact, while this shell screen is showing, none of the so-called active tasks is executing at all. I must select the one that I wish to truly become active; that is, the one that I want to actually gain control of the CPU and the screen to continue its own execution.

FIGURE 5.22

You can activate programs in different ways. Selecting an executable program from the files area or from a program group will initiate the program. Selecting an executable program name from the Active Task List will transfer control of the CPU back to a program that had been previously initiated.

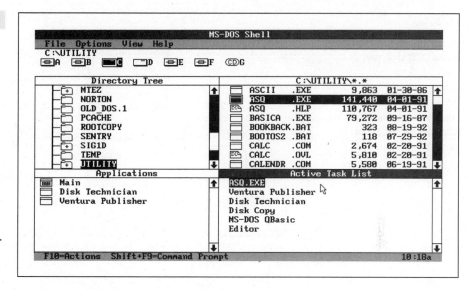

After activating a program, the Ctrl+Esc key combination restores the most recent shell screen. You can then use keyboard (i.e., the Tab and Enter keys) or mouse techniques to do whatever you want from the shell, including switching to another program on the Active Task List. Alternatively, you can press Alt+Esc to move from one active task to the next without returning to the shell screen between each selection. This technique returns you to the shell screen only after you switch from the last program in the Active Task List. Use this alternative keystroke to quickly explore the existing status of the active tasks. Figure 5.23 depicts how the Ctrl+Esc and Alt+Esc combinations control the two possible switching sequences.

One more special key combination exists to make your management of multiple tasks easier. If you press and hold down the Alt+Tab key combination, your screen will clear and the name of the next active task will appear in a single line at the top of your screen. You can quickly display the names of each active task by keeping the Alt key depressed, while successively releasing and then pressing the Tab key. Each time you press the Tab key while keeping Alt pressed down, another active task name will very quickly appear on the top line of your screen. When the task name appears that you would like to directly swap into active status, simply release the Alt key. DOS will immediately switch to that task. This is

FIGURE 5.23

Press Ctrl+Esc to return to the DOS shell, and its Active Task List, from within any active program. Press Alt+Esc to rapidly switch execution control from one active program to the next.

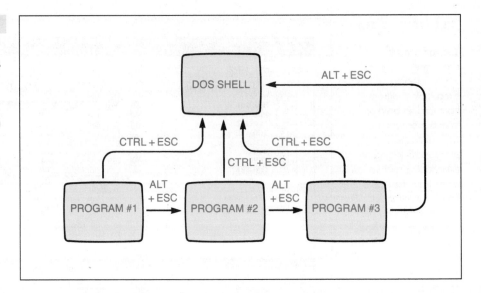

equivalent to, yet faster than, pressing Ctrl+Esc, then selecting the desired task from the main shell screen.

These key combinations for switching from task to task or task to shell can be summarized thus:

Alt+Esc	Switches from current program in Active Task List to next program in list.
Alt+Tab	Switches from current program to blank screen identifying next program in list. Pressing Tab repeatedly while holding down Alt lets you cycle through the list to quickly reach the program you want. Release Alt to drop directly into that program.
Ctrl+Esc	Switches from current program to the shell.

Remember that an active task is only active in the sense that DOS has *initiated* it. The underlying program receives the attention of your computer (CPU) only when you have switched to it. When you switch to a task, the executing program takes over the video monitor, just as you would expect.

There is one last important fact to realize. Once you've activated the swapper, you will not be allowed to exit from the shell until all you have exited all the active tasks. If you pull down the File menu, the *Exit* choice will be grayed to signify that it is unavailable. If you try to get around it by using the Exit shortcut (Alt+F4), DOS will merely beep at you and ignore the request.

Summary

In this chapter, you have explored the many ways you can run programs in DOS. All versions of DOS share certain common techniques for setting up hard-disk structures and initiating programs. DOS offers additional ways to run programs from its graphic display screens.

You have learned the following methods of working with directory structures and running programs:

- You learned how to create new directories in any existing directory.

- You can use the **PATH** command to direct DOS to search through a specified series of directories for .EXE, .COM, and .BAT files that are not located in the current working directory.

- You learned how to set up your hard disk for a word processor, a spreadsheet, and a database-management system. Using these examples, you should be able to set up an efficient directory structure for all your application software systems.

- You can run programs by selecting them directly from one of the shell program groups.

- You learned how to associate data and text files with program files, such as word processors and database managers, so that you can automatically run the program by simply selecting a file whose extension is associated with the executable file.

- You can set up your own customized groups of program files to be initiated from a shell screen. You can then run a single program or a sequence of commands automatically by selecting it from the group.

- When you set up your program-group choice, you can create a related help window for it. You can also password-protect each group or group item individually.

- DOS can initiate multiple programs and switch between them. You enable the Task Swapper from the Options menu, and use the Alt+Esc, Ctrl+Esc, or Alt+Tab keystroke combinations to switch among all active tasks.

In Part Three of this book, I will teach you how to control the flow of information to the screen, to the printer, and even to other devices through the DOS communications ports.

Part

THREE

Managing Your PC

CHAPTER

6

Using the Full-Screen Editor

BESIDES being able to process numbers and large amounts of data, computers are exceptionally good at manipulating text. There are many different word-processing programs available for doing this. All of these programs include the standard features for creating and editing files. As text editors have become more sophisticated, they offer more advanced features that facilitate copying, moving, and searching through existing text. Many of these programs include margin and tab controls, header and footer capabilities, and facilities for working with multiple columns.

DOS includes a full-screen, menu-based text editor called EDIT (I'll also refer to it as "the Editor"). It does not offer pagination and page-layout controls (e.g., for margins, headers, or columns), so it is most appropriate for tasks that do not require these facilities. You can use EDIT to create any text-based file, including files of information to be used by your other application programs. You can also use it to write programs. In DOS, there are two primary program applications for EDIT. First, you will need it to prepare the customized application programs that you may write using the QBasic program language (see Chapter 16). Second, you will use it to write batch files (see Chapters 12 through 14) that can help you to customize your DOS system.

This chapter explains how to get started with the EDIT program. You will learn how to create new text files and enter text into them. Then you will learn the most important techniques needed to work with the text. These will include the most common facilities for inserting new text, changing existing text, and deleting text that is no longer needed. Additionally, you'll learn some of the more sophisticated features such as moving, copying, searching, and replacing text.

> **EXTRA!**

Manage and Display Text with DOS Macros

The DOSKEY utility (see Chapter 15) enables you to write and incorporate your own customized new commands into DOS. Here are three simple ones to demonstrate how easy it can be. To create any of these macros, you must have first loaded the DOSKEY utility.

LINECNT counts the number of lines in a text file, specified by parameter one (*$1*). *SHOWTEXT* is a fancy replacement for the TYPE command, allowing wild cards and multiple parameters specifying filenames. *VGA* resets the number of lines shown on your display adapter to the number specified by parameter one (must be *25*, *43*, or *50*, depending on your adapter's capability).

All three new commands can be created by typing these three lines at a command prompt:

```
DOSKEY LINECNT=FIND "^&@*" $1 /V /C
DOSKEY SHOWTEXT=FOR %%j IN ($*) DO TYPE %%j
DOSKEY VGA=MODE CON: LINES=$1
```

Getting Started with Edit

In Chapter 5, you learned how to start programs in several ways. Any of those methods can initiate the EDIT text-processing program. The easiest and fastest way is simply to select *Editor* from the Main program group. As part of DOS's initial configuration, a dialog box (see Figure 6.1) appears, to request the name of the text file you wish to modify. Initially, the *File to edit?* field is empty. I've typed in an example entry in Figure 6.1.

FIGURE 6.1

FIGURE 6.1

You can run the DOS Editor (EDIT.EXE) by selecting *Editor* on the Main program group. You are given the opportunity to specify a file name to use when the Editor begins.

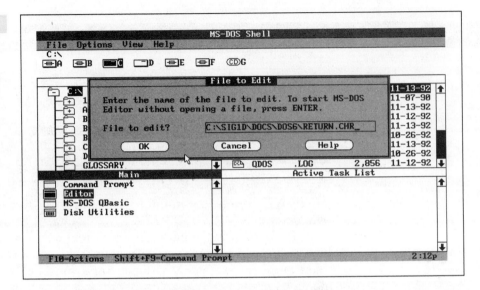

(You can leave this field empty if you simply want to create a new file; you'll be given the opportunity to specify a file name from within the Editor when you are ready to save the file.)

Remember that this dialog box represents one aspect of the program-group nature of the shell. As you learned in Chapter 5, you can configure the shell to have a dialog box appear in order to prompt for additional parameters whenever you select one of the executable names listed in a program group. If you run the EDIT program from a command prompt, you will not be prompted for a file name, but you can direct the Editor to display a specified file immediately on opening by typing the file name as part of the **EDIT** command.

NOTE

If you cannot get the Editor to run, you need to make sure that the QBASIC.EXE file is in the same directory with EDIT.COM, or that it can be found in the current directory or on the search path. QBASIC.EXE is required for the DOS full-screen editor to be able to run.

Creating a New File

If you wish to create a completely new file, you can assign it a name in the opening File To Edit dialog box. Just type its name and press Enter. If you wish the Editor to create this new file in a directory other than the current one, include a full path name as I've done in Figure 6.1. In either case, the Editor will display its opening screen. If you're not sure what name to assign to the file you are about to create, you can just press Enter

► EXTRA!

Display All Extended ASCII Codes Whenever You Like!

There are often times when you need to use and incorporate one of the extended ASCII codes (128–255) into a text file. Other sidebars in this chapter demonstrate a number of useful examples of this technique, from creating large block letters on the screen to dressing up your output with various types of boxes and drop shadows.

Just type ASCIICHR after creating the ASCIICHR.BAT file, and your screen will display both the ASCII code and its corresponding character:

```
@ECHO OFF
Rem ASCIICHR.BAT displays all extended ASCII characters.
Rem These correspond to ASCII 128 through 255.
CLS
ECHO 128 Ç 129 ü 130 é 131 â 132 ä 133 à 134 å 135 ç 136 ê 137 ë
ECHO 138 è 139 ï 140 î 141 ì 142 Ä 143 Å 144 É 145 æ 146 Æ 147 ô
ECHO 148 ö 149 ò 150 û 151 ù 152 ÿ 153 Ö 154 Ü 155 ¢ 156 £ 157 ¥
ECHO 158 ₧ 159 ƒ 160 á 161 í 162 ó 163 ú 164 ñ 165 Ñ 166 ª 167 º
ECHO 168 ¿ 169 ⌐ 170 ¬ 171 ½ 172 ¼ 173 ¡ 174 « 175 » 176 ░ 177 ▒
ECHO 178 ▓ 179 │ 180 ┤ 181 ╡ 182 ╢ 183 ╖ 184 ╕ 185 ╣ 186 ║ 187 ╗
ECHO 188 ╝ 189 ╜ 190 ╛ 191 ┐ 192 └ 193 ┴ 194 ┬ 195 ├ 196 ─ 197 ┼
ECHO 198 ╞ 199 ╟ 200 ╚ 201 ╔ 202 ╩ 203 ╦ 204 ╠ 205 ═ 206 ╬ 207 ╧
ECHO 208 ╨ 209 ╤ 210 ╥ 211 ╙ 212 ╘ 213 ╒ 214 ╓ 215 ╫ 216 ╪ 217 ┘
ECHO 218 ┌ 219 █ 220 ▄ 221 ▌ 222 ▐ 223 ▀ 224 α 225 β 226 Γ 227 π
ECHO 228 Σ 229 σ 230 µ 231 τ 232 Φ 233 Θ 234 Ω 235 δ 236 ∞ 237 φ
ECHO 238 ε 239 ∩ 240 ≡ 241 ± 242 ≥ 243 ≤ 244 ⌠ 245 ⌡ 246 ÷ 247 ≈
ECHO 248 ° 249 · 250 · 251 √ 252 η 253 ² 254 ■ 255
```

at the opening File To Edit dialog box, and you'll be taken to a slightly different opening screen, which we'll discuss when we come to Figure 6.3. As seen in Figure 6.2, the entire center of this screen is almost blank, allowing you ample space in which to type your text. The menu bar at the top displays a new set of menu names for your work in the Editor. The name of the file, as you entered it into the dialog box, appears on the title line below the menu bar.

FIGURE 6.2

The Editor's opening screen displays the file name being edited at the top of the screen. If you have specified an existing file, its contents will be visible in the center of the screen. Otherwise, the screen center will be blank, awaiting your initial text.

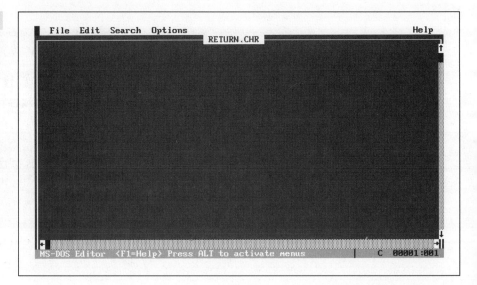

At this point, you can type whatever text you like into the central editing portion of the screen. The cursor initially appears here and the standard typographical keystrokes all apply. You'll practice and learn the standard typing techniques for inserting and modifying text in the next major section of this chapter, "Editing Your Text Files."

If you were not sure what name to assign in the initial File To Edit dialog box and you simply pressed Enter, no name is assigned, and the opening screen appears as in Figure 6.3.

The title line, which includes the name of the file being worked on, is now displayed as *Untitled*. No name has been assigned yet; you must later

If you do not specify a file name when you first start the Editor, the opening screen looks like this. Press Esc to go immediately into editing mode and start writing your file, or press Enter to display help.

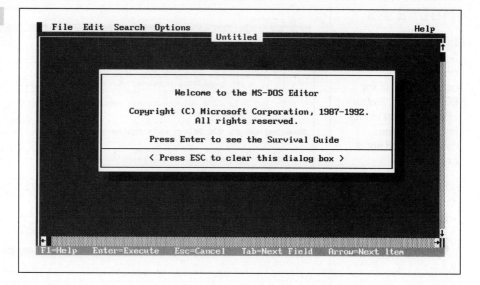

```
 File  Edit  Search  Options                              Help
┌──────────────────────── Untitled ────────────────────────┐
│                                                            ↑
│                                                            │
│          ┌──────────────────────────────────────┐        │
│          │   Welcome to the MS-DOS Editor         │        │
│          │                                        │        │
│          │ Copyright (C) Microsoft Corporation, 1987-1992. │
│          │        All rights reserved.            │        │
│          │                                        │        │
│          │ Press Enter to see the Survival Guide  │        │
│          │                                        │        │
│          │ < Press ESC to clear this dialog box > │        │
│          └──────────────────────────────────────┘        │
│                                                            │
│                                                            ↓
└────────────────────────────────────────────────────────────┘
  F1=Help   Enter=Execute   Esc=Cancel   Tab=Next Field   Arrow=Next Item
```

assign a disk file name when you save whatever text you type. You will shortly learn how to do this by selecting one of the options on the Editor's File menu. If you need some initial help to use the Editor, you can initiate the Editor's "Survival Guide" by pressing Enter at this opening screen.

Using the "Survival Guide" Help System

If you assigned a file name at the opening dialog box, you can access the beginner's help screen—the Survival Guide—by pressing F1 at the opening blank screen. This is the same help screen that appears if you press Enter from an "Untitled" opening screen. It is shown in Figure 6.4.

If you don't have your DOS documentation, this help system is actually sufficient to get going with the Editor. Notice that Untitled, the text-editing portion of the screen, has not been completely replaced by the help portion. The screen has actually split into two different-size windows. The top portion contains the help text; the bottom portion contains the smaller, yet still accessible, text-entry and editing area.

FIGURE 6.4

The help system's Survival Guide explains how to activate and use the EDIT program. It also offers hypertext entries into other screens containing additional help text.

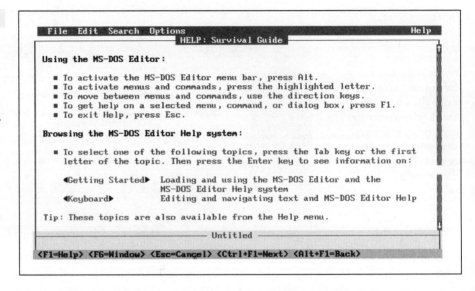

```
  File  Edit  Search  Options                                    Help
                        HELP: Survival Guide
 Using the MS-DOS Editor:

   ■ To activate the MS-DOS Editor menu bar, press Alt.
   ■ To activate menus and commands, press the highlighted letter.
   ■ To move between menus and commands, use the direction keys.
   ■ To get help on a selected menu, command, or dialog box, press F1.
   ■ To exit Help, press Esc.

 Browsing the MS-DOS Editor Help system:

   ■ To select one of the following topics, press the Tab key or the first
     letter of the topic. Then press the Enter key to see information on:

     ◄Getting Started►   Loading and using the MS-DOS Editor and the
                         MS-DOS Editor Help system
     ◄Keyboard►          Editing and navigating text and MS-DOS Editor Help

 Tip: These topics are also available from the Help menu.
                              Untitled
 <F1=Help> <F6=Window> <Esc=Cancel> <Ctrl+F1=Next> <Alt+F1=Back>
```

As the bottom line of the screen suggests, you can press F6 to switch your cursor between these two windows. In this way, you can carry out all necessary text entry and modifications, using relevant help screens whenever necessary. You can, for example,

1. Type in the lower window,

2. Press F6 to obtain help in the upper window about any Editor topic, and

3. Press F6 once again to return the cursor to the editing window at the bottom of the screen.

If you actually use both windows very often, you may want to adjust their relative sizes. Pressing Alt+plus (Alt and the plus key together) increases the current window (the one containing the screen cursor) by one line each time you press the key combination. Pressing Alt+minus decreases the current window by one line each time you press this key combination.

➤ EXTRA!

Put Messages on Your Screen in Large Block Letters!

The extended ASCII characters include a number of line-drawing characters. Some of these are lines that can be connected to create rudimentary line drawings. Others are solid or semi-solid rectangles (see the next sidebar in this chapter) that can be used to create boxes and drop shadows.

You can use these different rectangle shapes to create your own customized large block letters. Just combine enough of them to create larger symbols or characters, as in the BLOCKLET.BAT batch file seen below:

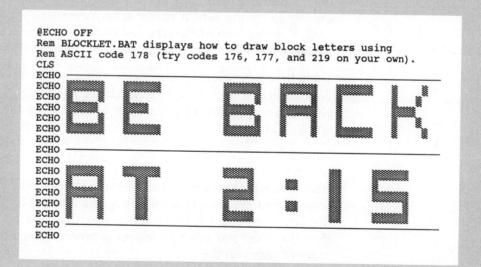

To ensure that you can get going quickly, the Survival Guide lists the essential startup techniques. As in the DOS Shell, pressing the Alt key moves the selection cursor to and from the menu bar. Pressing arrow keys moves the highlight from one menu choice to the next. You can always get into the help system by pressing the F1 key, and out of the help system by pressing Esc.

Just as with the DOS shell's help system, the Editor's help system is a series of linked text screens. This type of help is sometimes called a *hypertext system*. In addition to displaying information on the topic selected, each screen contains the name of one or more related topics, indicated by colored or reverse-video triangles. In Figure 6.4, there are two such topics: Getting Started and Keyboard. These items can be used to display other text screens from the hypertext system.

To move among the different topics of a hypertext system, you must select one of the displayed choices. Keyboard users can press the Tab key to quickly move the screen cursor from one triangle-flanked topic to the next. Pressing Enter when the cursor appears between the bookend-like triangles will select that topic.

If you have a mouse, the mouse pointer appears as a reverse-video rectangle; double-click to select a topic. (On Microsoft-compatible mouses, you can also single-click Button 2 to instantly call up the highlighted hypertext screen.) The selected help text screen appears, as in Figure 6.5.

Once you've ventured into the set of hypertext screens, you can select new screen topics, as you see here. You are also offered a means—Alt+F1, or Back—to return to any preceding screen. Notice that the size of the two screen windows adjusts according to the amount of help text there is to display. If less space is necessary in a particular screen, as in Figure 6.5, then the lower text-editing window is expanded automatically to display more of your text file.

If you wish to leave the help system completely, just press the Esc key. The entire screen is once again devoted to your text editing work. While later working with any of the Editor features, you can return to the hypertext help system in one of two ways. You can pull down the Help menu, seen at the far right on the menu bar, and make a selection, or you can simply press the F1 key.

FIGURE 6.5

The help system is a hierarchical set of linked screens. Known as hypertext, each screen is reachable from other screens by clicking on a high-lighted word or phrase.

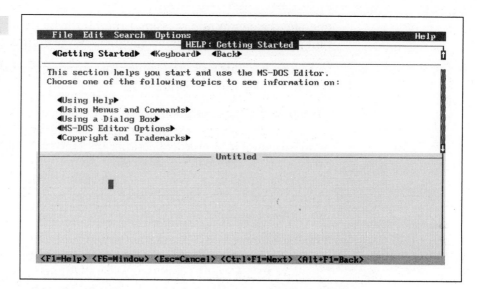

```
 File  Edit  Search  Options                                    Help
                          ┌─ HELP: Getting Started ──┐
   ◄Getting Started►  ◄Keyboard►  ◄Back►                              ↕
   This section helps you start and use the MS-DOS Editor.
   Choose one of the following topics to see information on:

      ◄Using Help►
      ◄Using Menus and Commands►
      ◄Using a Dialog Box►
      ◄MS-DOS Editor Options►
      ◄Copyright and Trademarks►
   ─────────────────────────── Untitled ───────────────────────────

               ▌


   <F1=Help> <F6=Window> <Esc=Cancel> <Ctrl+F1=Next> <Alt+F1=Back>
```

T I P

If you become confused at any time while working with the Editor, simply press F1. The Editor itself will come to your rescue with an appropriate help screen.

Pressing F1 has a special benefit. If you have selected a particular menu item or command, or have activated a dialog box or Editor operation, F1 causes the Editor to display help text relevant to the current item or screen. This is known as *context-sensitive help*, since the specific help screen that appears depends on the screen context (i.e., what you were doing) when you pressed F1.

Changing an Existing File

Assuming that you run the Editor by selecting its name from the Main program group, you can use the opening dialog box to easily access and modify any existing file. Doing this is as easy as typing its name into the opening dialog box and pressing Enter. If the file is not located in the current directory, you must naturally include the complete path prefix.

In Figure 6.6, I've run the Editor after entering BUSINESS.TXT in the opening dialog box of Figure 6.1.

This example file is as good as any to demonstrate the Editor's features. It is a simple series of text lines, organized into apparent columns. Many people maintain simple collections of data such as this in their word processing or text editing programs. Although many other people use database management systems—sophisticated application programs that maintain such tables of data—you can certainly use the DOS Editor for the simplest of these types of information tables.

You'll see examples in Chapter 16 of how the Editor is used to write QBasic application programs (with .BAS file extensions) under DOS. Further, in Chapters 12 through 14 you'll see how the Editor is also used to write batch files (with .BAT file extensions). In this chapter, you'll explore how to manipulate text of any kind with the Editor. The examples here will use the text you see in the BUSINESS.TXT file.

FIGURE 6.6

The BUSINESS.TXT file contains text aligned in columns. This file will be used in this chapter's subsequent examples, which show techniques for manipulating the text of any file with the Editor.

```
 File  Edit  Search  Options                                        Help
                          BUSINESS.TXT
Cantonese Imports    134  Roberts   Joseph 212/656-2156
Brandenberg Gates    754  Bennett   Mary   415/612-5656
Sole Survivor,Inc.   237  Evans     Gail   415/222-3514
Presley Plastics     198  Presley   Robert 716/245-6119
Plymouth Granite Co  345  Williams  Peter  617/531-6145
Bucket Dance Wear    276  Lewis     Ann    415/635-2530
Intelli-Strategies   743  Griffiths Robert 415/362-9537
Benicia Balloons     983  Franklin  Marie  212/524-4157
Standard Shelters    690  Rucker    Sally  415/532-1107
Panama Rain Corp.    576  Cook      Freda  408/534-9739




 MS-DOS Editor  <F1=Help> Press ALT to activate menus        C  00001:001
```

Use Boxes and Drop Shadows to Dress Up Your Screen!

A variety of line-drawing codes exist in the extended ASCII character set (codes 128-255). Remembering them can be difficult while you're in the middle of an editing session. After creating the BOXDRAW.BAT file below, you only need to type **BOXDRAW** to quickly display these sample boxes, along with the codes necessary to create them.

In the lower portion of the file, you can see the different effects obtainable by using ASCII codes 176, 177, and 178 for 25%, 50%, and 75% gray scale. You can use ASCII code 219 for a solid drop-shadow effect.

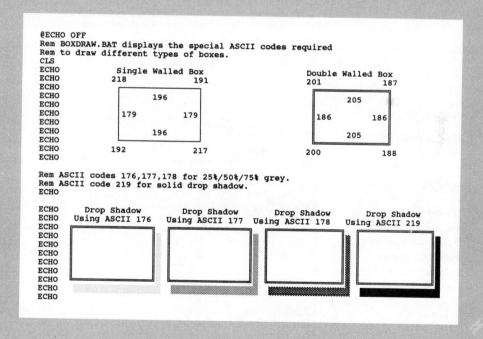

Using the Editor's Menu Bar

The Editor's menu bar contains five pull-down menu choices: File, Edit, Search, and Options, as shown in Figure 6.7. You will discover as you gain experience with the Editor that the first menu item (File) is the most important and the most frequently used. This is because it contains the options to:

- create new text (*New*),
- edit existing files (*Open*),
- store your editing work in the file from which it was retrieved (*Save*) or in a newly named file (*Save As*),
- print your work (*Print*), and
- return to the operating system (*Exit*).

FIGURE 6.7

The File menu offers standard options for creating new text files, opening existing files for editing, saving the current file, saving the current file under a new name, printing the current file, or returning to the DOS prompt.

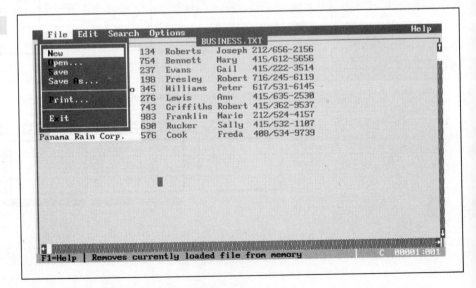

I'll discuss the other menu options where appropriate in the remainder of this chapter. For the moment, they are briefly summarized in Table 6.1.

You've learned how to obtain help while you are working with the Editor. Since it is entirely possible that you will be experimenting on your own before you finish reading this chapter, it is important to explain at this point how to end your editing session, so that you can save your work successfully.

TABLE 6.1: The Editor's pull-down menu choices

MENU	COMMAND	DESCRIPTION
File	New	Begins a new text-editing session
	Open	Reads an existing file into memory
	Save	Backs up current text-editing work
	Save As	Copies current text-editing work to a specified disk file
	Print	Sends current text-editing work to the printer
	Exit	Returns to the operating system prompt, or the shell
Edit	Cut	Removes currently selected text from the current file and places it in memory (on "the Clipboard") in order to copy it in another location using *Paste*
	Copy	Copies (does not remove) currently selected text from the current file and places it in memory (on "the Clipboard") in order to copy it in another location using *Paste*
	Paste	Copies a Cut or Copied portion of text from the Clipboard to the current position of the screen cursor
	Clear	Deletes currently selected text; does not move or copy it to the Clipboard

TABLE 6.1: The Editor's pull-down menu choices (continued)

MENU	COMMAND	DESCRIPTION
Search	Find	Locates a specified string of textual characters
	Repeat Last Find	Searches for another instance of the previously specified string of characters
	Change	Replaces one string of characters with another
Options	Display	Controls screen colors and special video display options
	Help Path	Specifies the directory containing the EDIT.HLP hypertext file
Help	Getting Started	Displays the primary entry screen to the hypertext set of initial Editor control screens
	Keyboard	Displays the primary entry screen to a series of help screens that describe the use of the keyboard
	About	Displays version information about your copy of the Editor program

In Case You've Jumped Ahead: How to End Your Editing Session

When you have completed all your editing work, you should select the *Exit* choice on the File menu. If you have previously saved your work and have made no new changes to the file since that last save, the Editor immediately returns you to the operating system. In order to protect you from inadvertently losing your work, however, the Editor will warn you if you have forgotten to save the current file. A small dialog box will appear in the center of the screen, with the confirmation request:

```
Loaded file is not saved. Save it now?
<Yes> <No> <Cancel> <Help>
```

Pressing Enter asks the Editor to save a disk copy of your file at this time. This is equivalent to selecting the Yes choice. If you were working on a specific file (for example, the BUSINESS.TXT file in Figure 6.7), the Editor replaces the former disk copy with your current in-memory work. If you had not yet assigned a file name to completely new editing work, the Editor asks you for a name at this time. After the save operation is completed, the Editor returns control to the operating system.

As Figure 6.8 suggests, you can do several things with your file editing work. Once you have brought up the Editor, you may choose to make modifications to one file, print it, save it, and then return to the operating system for

FIGURE 6.8

The relationship between the various commands on the File menu and the copy of your editing work that exists in memory or on disk.

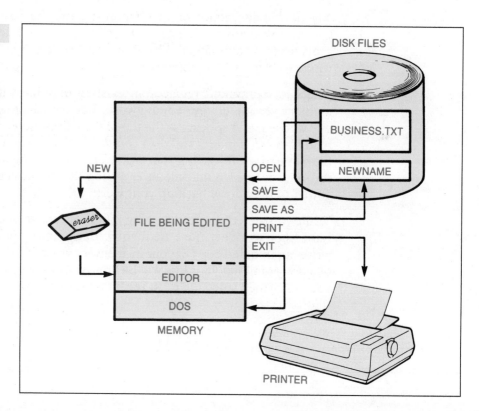

additional application work. On the other hand, you may just as readily choose to stay within the Editor and make adjustments to some other disk files. You needn't go back to the operating system in between your work on individual files. Similarly, you needn't return to the operating system after performing an intermediate save of your work. You can continue editing, secure with having backed up a copy of your work to that point.

Saving Your Editing Work during a Single Session

You can use the straightforward commands on the File menu to work on one file, save your work, and then begin work on another file. The DOS Editor does not allow you to work on more than one text file at a time. (However, there are some tricks that you can use to involve multiple files. I'll present them later in this chapter.)

The next major section of this chapter explains the various editing actions you can take with the Editor. Of the choices on the File menu, the Editor provides two commands to back up your work and two commands with which to begin new editing work.

The *Save* command replaces an existing disk file with the current in-memory version of your editing work. The disk file that is replaced is the one whose name appears at the top of the editing screen, if it does not still read *Untitled*. If it does still read *Untitled*, you are prompted to enter a disk file name to use for saving your work. This prompting procedure is exactly the same as you would encounter during the *Exit* selection if you had forgotten to previously back up your work.

While you are editing and making modifications to your text, you should remember to select *Save* frequently. Each time you do so, the Editor writes an updated copy of your in-memory work to a disk file. In the event of a power failure, your loss will be limited to whatever amount of editing you performed since the most recent Save operation.

➤ EXTRA!

Create Your Own Online
Note-Taking System!

Use the NOTES.BAT batch file below to type quick notes to yourself while on line. Type **NOTES** to enter a new note, or **NOTES D** to display all stored notes, or **NOTES C** to clear the notes file of all saved notes.

Each note that is entered is automatically date-and-time stamped. But this feature requires the existence of a RETURN.CHR text file that contains the Carriage-Return and Line-Feed pair of characters. To create this file at a command prompt, type:

```
COPY CON RETURN.CHR
```

Then, press the Enter key, the Ctrl+Z key combination, and then the Enter key once more. Here is the batch file:

```
@ECHO OFF
Rem NOTES.BAT allows for quick notes to oneself.
Rem Syntax      NOTES [D or C]
Rem
IF '%1'=='' Goto :Startup
If %1%==D Goto Display
If %1%==d Goto Display
If %1%==C Goto Clear
If %1%==c Goto Clear
:Startup
IF EXIST NOTES.TXT Goto :AddNote
Rem This is the online Quick Notes file > NOTES.TXT
:AddNote
ECHO Type your notes now, pressing Enter after each line.
ECHO When done, press Ctrl+Z, then Enter once more.
ECHO . >> NOTES.TXT
IF NOT EXIST return.chr Goto Missing
DATE < RETURN.CHR | FIND "Current" >> NOTES.TXT
TIME < RETURN.CHR | FIND "Current" >> NOTES.TXT
```

```
Goto Continue
:Missing
ECHO Cannot find the required RETURN.CHR file.
ECHO Will be unable to date/time stamp your notes.
:Continue
COPY CON TEMP.TXT > NUL
COPY NOTES.TXT+TEMP.TXT > NUL
rem COPY NOTES.TXT+TEMP.TXT /B
Goto End
:Display
CLS
TYPE NOTES.TXT | MORE
Goto End
:Clear
ECHO This is the online Quick Notes file > NOTES.TXT
:End
```

Sometimes, you may wish to retain different versions of your text file. Corporate users often send similar reports to different personnel, including extra information for certain groups of employees. Programmers often need to write two programs that perform similarly in most circumstances, yet act differently under special conditions. In such cases, the *Save As* choice on the File menu should be used.

When you select *Save As*, the Editor prompts you to enter a file name. Make sure it is different from the one your file already possesses. As long as the name is different, the *Save As* choice will ensure that the changes you have made to the file are written out to a different disk file. In this way, the file to be modified—or even a file you have already modified—can be stored under the new name, and the original file will remain, unchanged, with the name it was last saved under.

Whenever you use *Save As* to create a new file from an old one, the Editor uses the new file name for continued in-memory work. This protects your old file from accidentally being overwritten by new text editing. For example, on my own computer, I chose *Save As* and typed **BUSINESS.DTA** as a different name under which to store the BUSINESS.TXT information. The Editor stored the information in a new file called BUSINESS.DTA, immediately updating the title line of the screen to reflect that all sub-sequent file edits would apply to the new BUSINESS.DTA file, and not to the old BUSINESS.TXT file. BUSINESS.TXT remained unchanged, because from that point on I was working with the BUSINESS.DTA file.

Beginning New Text-Editing Work

The *New* command completely erases all in-memory text-editing work, returning the file name line at the top of the screen to *Untitled*. Use this command when you have completed your work on a current file and wish to begin typing completely new text. The *Open* command is provided when you have completed your work on a current file and wish to begin working on a different, yet existing, disk file.

Both commands have the same built-in protection that the *Exit* command offers. If you haven't saved your work, the Editor asks if you want to save it before carrying out your latest request. A *New* request, after dealing with the question about saving any existing work, simply clears the screen. You can then begin typing in new text. An *Open* request, on the other hand, displays the dialog box shown in Figure 6.9.

FIGURE 6.9

When you attempt to Open an existing text file for editing, the Open dialog box permits you to select a file from the Files list seen here. To display file names that meet your own specification criteria, just fill in the File Name field before selecting OK.

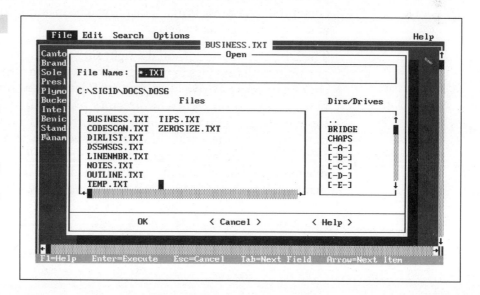

The cursor initially appears in the File Name: portion of the dialog box. If the file you want is listed in the Files area of the box, simply highlight it and select it. If it isn't listed, type in the name and press Enter. The dialog box will disappear, the file name will appear in the title line of the screen, and the text from that file will appear in the center portion of the editing screen.

NOTE   The default file name list contains only the file names that have a .TXT extension. In order to see *all* the files in a directory, you must enter the full *.* wild-card file specification.

If you do not know the name or location of the desired file, you can ask the Editor to help you. In the File Name: area, you can either specify the actual file name you wish to open, or you can enter a more general file specification that includes the * or ? wildcards.

For example, if you know you want to work with a batch file but you can't remember exactly how you spelled its name, you could enter *.**BAT** to display all the .BAT files in the current directory. (The current directory is identified between the File Name: field and the Files window.) Once you see the file you want, you can double-click on it or move the selection cursor to it and press Enter. The file will be instantly loaded into memory and displayed on the screen.

The Dirs/Drives window on the right side of the screen offers you the opportunity to access files in other directories and on other drives. When you click on or select a drive identifier, the Files window displays the specified files—if any—on the current directory on that drive, and any subdirectories that exist in that current directory are listed in the Dirs/Drives window, replacing the earlier listing of directories and drives. From this Dirs/Drives window, you can also click on or select any directory name that appears. This causes the Editor to display all the files in *that* directory that match the specification you've entered in the File Name field.

Once you've opened an existing file (using *Open*) or erased the current file from memory (using *New*), you can begin to use the various editing techniques necessary for text insertion, modification, and removal.

Editing Your Text Files

There are three primary editing tasks that you must learn in order to work with text. Although there are more sophisticated techniques available (you will learn about them later in this chapter), you can successfully edit text files with the three methods presented in this section.

First, you must understand how to type new text into your file. This new text may be added to the end of text that you've already typed, or it may be inserted into the middle of the existing text. Second, you need to learn how to correct and change information that you've already typed. Lastly, you should learn how to remove text.

Inserting New Text

To incorporate new text to the end of your file, you only need to position the cursor and begin typing. If you'd like to add new text to the end of existing text, just move the cursor below your last line of text and begin typing the new information. Mouse users can simply click at the position in the text where they want to begin typing. Table 6.2 summarizes for keyboard users the principal keystrokes responsible for cursor movement.

TABLE 6.2: Keystrokes to control cursor motion

PRESS ...	TO MOVE CURSOR ...
Left arrow	One character to the left
Right arrow	One character to the right
Ctrl+left arrow	One word to the left
Ctrl+right arrow	One word to the right

TABLE 6.2: Keystrokes to control cursor motion (continued)

PRESS ...	TO MOVE CURSOR ...
Up arrow	One line up
Down arrow	One line down
Home	To beginning of line
End	To end of line
Ctrl+Home	To first line of text
Ctrl+End	To last line of text

N O T E

Even though this is a full-screen editor, it is still line-oriented. Each line can contain at most 255 characters. If you attempt to type more than this, or to insert additional characters that increase the total on a line to more than 255, the Editor will beep and refuse to accept the new keystrokes. At that time, you will have to move to a new line before typing any additional characters.

Suppose I wanted to add a new business contact to the group of ten shown earlier in this chapter. I simply move the cursor to the first character position in line 11, just beneath the entry for Panama Rain Corp, and begin typing in the new text.

Suppose I decide to separate the eleven contact businesses in my current BUSINESS.DTA file into two groups: Active and Inactive accounts. You can insert new text to identify which is which by simply moving the cursor to the desired point in the file and beginning to type your new information. For example, Figure 6.10 shows the BUSINESS.DTA file after adding some blank and dashed lines, and inserting two group name lines.

N O T E

Notice in Figure 6.10 that the cursor is currently at the far right side of the last line inserted. The Editor always keeps track of cursor location for you. On the bottom line of the screen, you can see the indicator 00016:055. This indicates the location of the cursor, in *line:column* format. In Figure 6.10 the cursor appears at line 16 and in column 55. This cursor-location feature becomes useful when you are trying to line up text that appears on different lines of your file. Sometimes those lines do not fit on one screen, so it is helpful to know the columnar orientations. (The bottom line of the screen also indicates whether you have the CapsLock or NumLock key active by displaying *C* or *N.*)

FIGURE 6.10

Inserting new text is simple. Just move the cursor to the point where you want the new text to begin, and start typing.

```
 File  Edit  Search  Options                                  Help
┌───────────────────────── BUSINESS.DTA ──────────────────────────┐
│ACTIVE ACCOUNTS                                                   │
│===============                                                   │
│Cantonese Imports    134   Roberts   Joseph 212/656-2156          │
│Brandenberg Gates    754   Bennett   Mary   415/612-5656          │
│Sole Survivor,Inc.   237   Evans     Gail   415/222-3514          │
│Presley Plastics     198   Presley   Robert 716/245-6119          │
│                                                                  │
│INACTIVE ACCOUNTS                                                 │
│=================                                                 │
│Plymouth Granite Co 345   Williams  Peter  617/531-6145           │
│Bucket Dance Wear    276   Lewis     Ann    415/635-2530          │
│Intelli-Strategies   743   Griffiths Robert 415/362-9537          │
│Benicia Balloons     983   Franklin  Marie  212/524-4157          │
│Standard Shelters    690   Rucker    Sally  415/532-1107          │
│Panama Rain Corp.    576   Cook      Freda  408/534-9739           │
│Garden Park Events   139   Cetaskey  Jean   617/222-1029          │
│                                                                  │
│                                               ■                  │
└──────────────────────────────────────────────────────────────── ┘
MS-DOS Editor  <F1=Help> Press ALT to activate menus        00016:055
```

This is a good point to take a break from reading this chapter and try the Editor itself. Run it from the Main program group on your DOS Shell screen. Begin typing some text. Then insert some new text in the middle of what you've typed. Add some text at the end of the existing text. Use both your keyboard and your mouse if you have one to control the cursor location. Try out the *Save* option to create a disk-file version of your editing work, or to back up your work under the name you may have typed into the opening dialog box. Then continue in the next section to learn how to make changes to your text.

➤ EXTRA!

Let Your Personal Style Guide Your Mode Selection

There are two different keyboard insertion modes; they are known as *Insert* and *Overtype*. Your keyboard is always in one or the other; the Ins key toggles between the two. You can recognize which is the active mode by the appearance of the cursor. When in Insert mode, the cursor appears as a flat blinking underscore symbol. When in Overtype mode, the cursor expands to a large, solid blinking rectangle. Overtype mode will be discussed in the next section, in connection with deleting text.

When your keyboard is in Insert mode, all text that you type is squeezed into the file at the point of the cursor. Any text that currently exists on the line is pushed off to the right, thereby making space for the new text that you are typing. Text that is pushed off to the right in this manner will not wrap around to the next line, as in some more sophisticated word processors. Instead, once the line reaches its maximum (which is 255 characters), it will simply balk at any more characters you try to insert and your computer will beep at you. You have to break the lines yourself, by pressing Enter at the point you want the line to break.

You must also use the Enter key to insert any completely blank lines in your text. Just move the cursor to the first character position in a line and press the Enter key.

Changing Existing Text

There are two common methods for changing existing text. First, you can replace old text with new text. The new text can be shorter or longer than the original text. Second, you can simply delete or remove text from your existing file.

If you are a first-time user of an editing program, it is easiest to follow simple steps. To replace old text with something new, first check to see if your keyboard is in Insert mode (the cursor appears as a flat underscore symbol). If it isn't, press the Ins key on your keyboard to switch to Insert mode. Then move the cursor to the point where you'd like your new text to appear, and type the new text.

When you've finished typing the new text, and are satisfied that you no longer need the old text, you can simply press the Del key repeatedly to erase the older text, one character at a time. (If you press and *hold* the Del key, the text is erased more quickly.) Once you become comfortable with these simplest replacement and deletion procedures, you'll want to learn some faster, more efficient techniques. Table 6.3 summarizes the special keystrokes related to text deletion.

As you can see, some of the keystrokes mentioned in Table 6.3 refer to "selected" text. In the next section, you'll learn the techniques for selecting text and how to perform a number of advanced operations.

TABLE 6.3: Keystrokes to delete text

PRESS...	TO DELETE...
Del	Character at the cursor, or all selected text
Backspace	Character to the left of the cursor
Ctrl+T	Remainder of word in which the cursor is located
Shift+Tab	Leading spaces on the current line
Ctrl+Y	The entire line containing the cursor
Ctrl+Q+Y	All characters from current cursor location to the end of the line
Shift+Del	Selected text (but a copy is placed on the Clipboard)

Advanced Editing Techniques

The concept of selecting a block of text is important to many of the advanced operations available to you with the DOS Editor. Rather than affecting only one character at a time, you can define a larger group of characters at once. The entire group (it could be a word, a paragraph, a series of complete screens, or any contiguous block of characters) is then acted on at one time by your subsequently specified operation. This is similar to the method of marking a group of files in the DOS Shell and then acting on the entire group by selecting an action from one of the pulldown menus.

Within the DOS Editor, you can delete single characters or entire blocks of specified or selected text. This is called *clearing*. You can also make complete replicas of portions of your text without having to retype anything. This is called *copying*. Similar to copying is *cutting and pasting*, which enables you to reinsert an entire block of deleted text into a different location in your text file. In this section, you'll explore all of these powerful operations. Additionally, you'll learn about the Editor's capability for searching through your text to find specified character sequences.

➤ EXTRA!

Use ANSI Escape Characters in Your Editor Files!

In order to insert the Escape character (ASCII 027) into a text file with the DOS EDIT program, you must first press Ctrl+P, then press the Esc key. To generate this character with many other word processors, you must press Alt+027 (or Ctrl+Alt+027 for some) on the numeric keypad. Earlier DOS users of the EDLIN program may remember that generating the Esc character required the obscure sequence of Ctrl+V followed by the left bracket symbol ([).

Selecting Text for Subsequent Operations

Regardless of whether you intend to delete, move, or simply copy a block of text, you must first mark the text in some fashion. Marking a block of text is called *selecting*, which can be performed by either keyboard or mouse actions. Table 6.4 summarizes the keystrokes that control text selection. Mouse users can manage similar selections by moving the mouse pointer while pressing Button 1.

In every case, regardless of how you select text, the Editor highlights the selected text in reverse video (or in a different color) to identify it. Only when you are sure that the desired block of text has been completely and correctly highlighted are you ready to continue. You can then move on to one of the following sections which explain how to move, copy, or delete selected text.

TABLE 6.4: Keystrokes to select text

PRESS...	TO SELECT...
Shift+left arrow	Character to the left of the cursor
Shift+right arrow	Character to the right of the cursor
Shift+Ctrl+left arrow	Word to the left of the cursor
Shift+Ctrl+right arrow	Word to the right of the cursor
Shift+down arrow	Current line
Shift+up arrow	Line above the current line
Shift+PgDn	A full window's worth of lines in the down direction
Shift+PgUp	A full window's worth of lines in the up direction
Shift+Ctrl+Home	All lines in the file above the current line
Shift+Ctrl+End	Current line through the end of the file

NOTE

Be aware that once you've selected text, you must do something with that text as your very next step. As you'll now learn, you can erase it permanently (i.e., *clear*) or temporarily (i.e., *cut*), or make a copy of it elsewhere in this or any other file. But if you do not use the text before doing anything else, and instead perform some scrolling or other cursor movement, the selected text is deselected. If this happens, you'll have to select the text again before you can then use it in one of the upcoming operations.

As Table 6.4 suggests, you can begin the marking of selected text at any place in the file. If you use any of the keystrokes in this table, the highlighting begins at the location of the cursor and continues until you stop pressing any of these selection keystrokes. You should take a few moments now to practice on your computer. Select some portions of text by using these keystrokes.

Mouse users have a simpler procedure to follow, although the sensitivity of your mouse may affect how easy it is to highlight text areas with it. To select text with a mouse, first move the mouse pointer to the first character or line you wish to select. Then, press Button 1 and keep it pressed. Without releasing Button 1, move the mouse pointer to the last character or line you wish to select. Only then should you release Button 1.

The highlighting expands as you move the mouse pointer, and stays visible even after you release Button 1 to conclude the highlighting. If you've made an error, perhaps by not selecting the exact block of characters you wanted, you can repeat the mouse sequence again. Or, you can fine-tune the selection by using any of the selection keystrokes shown in Table 6.4. Try some text selection now with your mouse, and then with both your mouse and keyboard.

Cutting and Pasting Selected Text

You may wish to remove text from one portion of your file and move it to some other portion, or even to another file. The Editor uses a reserved portion of memory called *the Clipboard* to do this. The Clipboard temporarily stores text that has been cut or copied from your file, holding it there until you replace it with other text. Editing operations that use the Clipboard are shown in Figure 6.11.

Cutting removes a single block of selected text and places it in the Clipboard. The reverse operation, called *pasting*, places a copy of that text wherever you specify with your cursor.

Once you've highlighted the text you wish to move, you can cut it from the file in one of two ways. You can pull down the Edit menu and select *Cut*, or you can use the shortcut keystroke Shift+Del.

As an example, suppose you were working with my BUSINESS.DTA file and you wanted to move two business clients from inactive to active status. You would first highlight the two accounts. Then you could pull down the Edit menu and select *Cut*, as shown in Figure 6.12. Both highlighted lines are instantly removed from the screen. However, since you selected Cut, the text involved is actually written to the special area of memory called the Clipboard, as was depicted in Figure 6.11.

You have now removed two lines of information from the inactive accounts portion of the BUSINESS.DTA file. To now insert it, or *paste* it, into the active accounts portion, you must first move the screen cursor to the point you wish to insert it. In this case, to position the text at the end of the Active Accounts group, you would position the cursor in the first column on the line below the last account in the group.

Once you've positioned the cursor where you'd like the cut text to be pasted, you can either pull down the Edit menu and select *Paste* or you can use the Shift+Ins shortcut key (to save the time of pulling down the Edit menu). In

FIGURE 6.11

Cutting and Copying both place a copy on the Clipboard; the difference is that Cutting removes the text from your original file, while Copying leaves the original untouched. Use Clear (or just press Del) to simply remove text without copying it to the Clipboard.

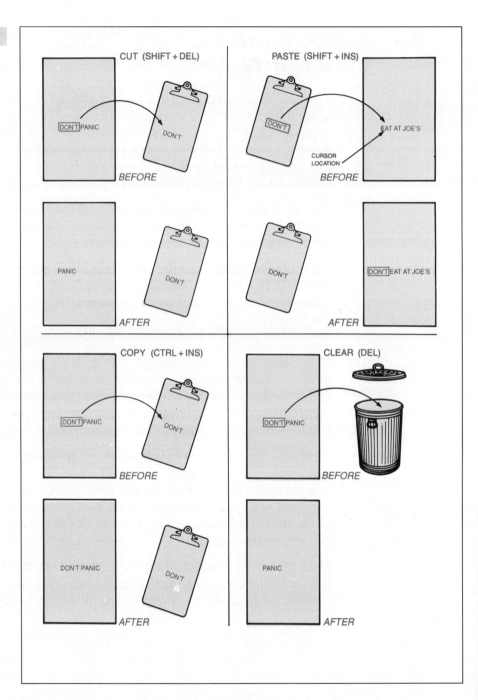

Cut text with the Edit
menu if you don't
remember the shortcut
keystroke.

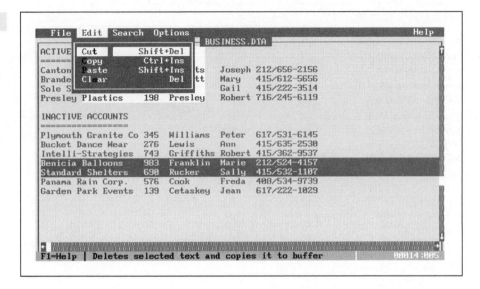

either case, the entire text that was cut and placed into the Clipboard is
now rewritten into your file. Figure 6.13 represents the final result of the
Paste procedure when used with our BUSINESS.DTA example.

One extremely powerful benefit of cut-and-paste lies in moving text from
one file to another. You can cut a block of text from one file, then open
another file, and paste the cut block into this second file. You have effectively transferred text from one file to another without retyping.

TIP

You can cut and paste a tremendous amount of
text at any one time. However, the capacity of the
Clipboard *is* limited by the amount of memory
available on your system.

FIGURE 6.13

You should never have to retype something that already exists somewhere in your file. Here is the final result of cutting and pasting from INACTIVE ACCOUNTS to ACTIVE ACCOUNTS.

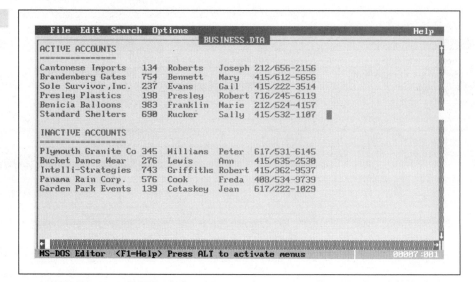

Clearing (Deleting) Selected Text

The *Clear* choice on the Edit menu simply erases the selected text. As you might intuitively expect, you can also just press the Del key to remove any highlighted, selected text. Unlike the Shift+Del or *Cut* option, clearing text from a file just throws it away completely.

If you change your mind about a block of text that you've cleared, or deleted, you have no choice but to retype it. If you're not completely sure about whether you want to completely erase a large block of text, you should therefore consider cutting it rather than clearing it. In both cases, the selected text is removed from your file, but you can always retrieve text that has been cut, at least up until the next time you use the Clipboard to store newly cut or copied text.

➤ EXTRA!

Making Additional Text Copies within a Document

Typically, you will use *Cut* and *Paste* to excise text from one portion of a file and place it in another. However, you may at times wish to leave the original text intact, and simply place a *copy* of it in another portion of your file.

Using the *Copy* choice on the Edit menu, or pressing the Ctrl+Ins shortcut key, enables the Editor to write a copy of the selected text into the Clipboard, leaving the original text unchanged. You can then use the Paste operation to write the copy into another portion of your file. In fact, you can use the *Paste* option repeatedly to paste the same text from the Clipboard as many times as you want, into as many files as you want. This is because *Paste* does not empty the Clipboard—it only pastes a copy of whatever you cut or copied to the Clipboard. The contents of the Clipboard remain unaffected by *Paste*. Once you have caused text to be written into the Clipboard, it remains in that special memory area until another block of text is written into it. It doesn't matter what you do in the meantime. For example, you can paste the text anywhere, within any Editor files, as many times as you want, until you turn off your machine. You could even return to the DOS Shell screen and do some file-management operations and then come back and be able to paste the same piece of text you left in the Clipboard. It's not likely you would have a reason to do this using the sample accounts file in this chapter; however, there are many situations in which you can save considerable time by doing so—for example, when creating a group of similar QBasic subprograms (see Chapter 16) or similar batch files (see Chapter 14).

Searching and Scrolling through Your Text

The last major feature of the Editor is concerned with moving through your text. At times, all you want to do is simply scan your text to look at it. Without any more specific a goal than this, the scrolling instructions in Table 6.5 and the following section may be all you need. Of course there will be times when you need to do more than just scan your work.

You may wish to find specific strings of characters in a long file. In programming, as you'll see in the next chapter, you may wish to discover where certain commands or program references occur. In text data files, such as BUSINESS.DTA, you may wish to find all references to a specific person's name, or company name, or zip code. In the sections following the scrolling instructions, you will learn both how to search for such text strings and how to automatically replace strings with other strings. Finally, you will learn how to mark a file in as many as four locations to enable you to move directly to frequently accessed data.

➤ EXTRA!

Scrolling May Be All You Need!

Mouse users can easily scroll through large amounts of text. Just press Button 1 and move the mouse pointer to the edge of the screen. This procedure highlights the text and, if there is more text beyond that edge, scrolls more text onto the screen.

The Editor scrolls the unseen text into view from beyond whichever of the four sides you touch with the mouse pointer. Remember to keep Button 1 depressed as you perform this step. Release Button 1 when you wish to stop the scrolling. Then click the mouse once to remove the highlight.

Actually, you may find that using the keystrokes indicated in Table 6.5 is easier than using a mouse. The keystrokes allow more precision in the exact number of lines and columns that are scrolled onto or off the screen.

TABLE 6.5: Keystrokes to scroll the text screen

PRESS...	TO MOVE SCREEN...
Ctrl+up arrow	One line up
Ctrl+down arrow	One line down
PgUp	One page up
PgDn	One page down
Ctrl+PgUp	One window to the left
Ctrl+PgDn	One window to the right

Searching for Specific Character Sequences

The Editor offers various means for searching, replacing, and marking text and positions in the file:

- To search for a specified string of characters, select *Find* from the Search menu, or press Ctrl+Q+F.

- To repeat your last text search, select *Repeat Last Find* from the Search menu, or press F3.

- To replace some or all occurrences of a specified string of characters, select *Change* from the Search menu, or press Ctrl+Q+A.

- To mark the current cursor location for quick return later, press Ctrl+K plus 0, 1, 2, or 3. (You can have four separate marked positions—"bookmarks"—in a file.)

- To return to a marked file position, press Ctrl+Q plus the number of the marked position (0, 1, 2, or 3).

Suppose you answer the phone and the caller simply says "Hi. This is Freda Cook. It's been a while since we last spoke." Perhaps you have no trouble remembering who she is. On the other hand, your account list may be several hundred names long by now and it may be three years since you last spoke. If your account file happens to be on the screen in front of you (as it might if you were in fact doing some telephone work with your accounts), you can let the Editor help you to remember by finding whatever information you have on file for Freda Cook.

To ask the Editor to find a specified string of characters, such as the name of your caller, pull down the Search menu and select the *Find* option. Or, simply press the Ctrl+Q+F key combination. When the Find dialog box appears, type in the desired character string. In this case, you might type in *Freda*, as shown in Figure 6.14, and press Enter.

Note that two toggle options appear in the center of this dialog box. By default, the search mechanism will find the sequence of letters that you type regardless of whether they appear in your file in upper or lower case, or even "proper case" (first letter capitalized). Since you may not know how some other data-entry person actually typed earlier entries, it's usually best to leave this toggle off. If you choose to set it on, only strings of characters in your text that precisely match the Find What: field entry (both characters and capitalization) will be displayed for you. The Whole Word toggle restricts the search to complete words, rather than discovering occurrences of the string that may exist within other longer words. This is also best left off unless you are sure that you want to impose the restriction.

FIGURE 6.14

Use the Search menu to find occurrences of a specified character string. Use the check boxes seen here to direct the Editor to find only exact matches for case and/or to find whole words only (not strings that might exist within longer words).

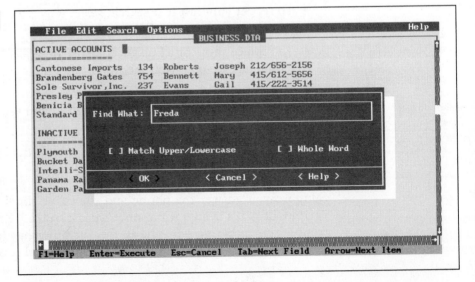

The result of the Find request for *Freda* appears in Figure 6.15. The Editor instantly finds the first occurrence of the specified string in your text, highlights it, and moves the cursor to the first character in that string.

Sometimes, you will search for a different purpose. For example, suppose you just received a notice from the telephone company about a change in area code from 617 to 508. You may simply wish to find out which of your clients may be affected. As a shrewd marketer, this may be one of those perfect excuses for a quick contact call. So you follow the same procedure, using the *Find* option on the Search menu. After the first 617 area code entry is highlighted, you can quickly highlight the next entry by pressing F3. This performs the same task as selecting *Repeat Last Find* on the Search menu.

As you successively press F3, the Editor successively continues searching for the specified text string (previously entered in the Find What: field). When the Editor reaches the bottom of the file, it will continue its search from the top of the text file. This is called *wrapping around*. No matter where in a file your cursor happens to be when you initiate a search, this wrap-around technique assures that your entire file will be searched. In this way, the Editor is sure to find all occurrences of the desired search string.

FIGURE 6.15

A successful search moves the cursor and highlights the found string. Press F3 to search quickly for the next occurrence of the same string in your file.

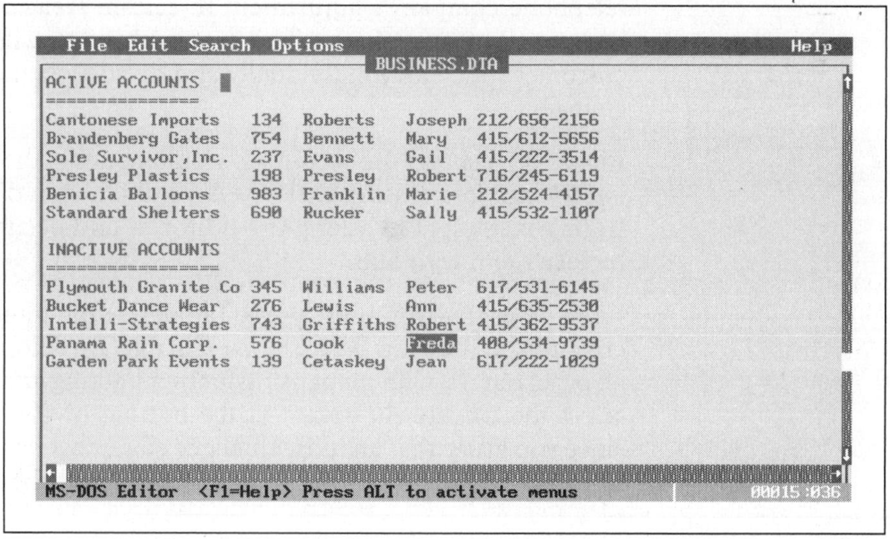

```
  File   Edit   Search   Options                              Help
                              BUSINESS.DTA
ACTIVE ACCOUNTS
================
Cantonese Imports    134   Roberts   Joseph 212/656-2156
Brandenberg Gates    754   Bennett   Mary   415/612-5656
Sole Survivor,Inc.   237   Evans     Gail   415/222-3514
Presley Plastics     198   Presley   Robert 716/245-6119
Benicia Balloons     983   Franklin  Marie  212/524-4157
Standard Shelters    690   Rucker    Sally  415/532-1107

INACTIVE ACCOUNTS
=================
Plymouth Granite Co 345   Williams  Peter  617/531-6145
Bucket Dance Wear   276   Lewis     Ann    415/635-2530
Intelli-Strategies  743   Griffiths Robert 415/362-9537
Panama Rain Corp.   576   Cook      Freda  408/534-9739
Garden Park Events  139   Cetaskey  Jean   617/222-1029




MS-DOS Editor  <F1=Help>  Press ALT to activate menus          00015:036
```

You must remember to specify all search strings sufficiently. For instance, typing 415 is insufficient if you wish to identify only customers in the BUSINESS.DTA file with 415 area codes. Successive F3 keypresses will eventually highlight the 415 that occurs in the middle of the phone number for the Benicia Balloons company. To avoid this problem, the proper search string should be 415/, the extra slash character ensuring that only phone numbers that begin with 415 and a slash will be discovered and displayed during the search procedure.

Replacing Old Text with New Text

The time always comes when your data must be updated. To continue with our BUSINESS.DTA file example, the day eventually arrives when you must switch area codes. To do this, the Editor includes a *Change* option on the Search menu. This option is essentially a combination of the *Find* option with a replacement feature.

Some changes apply to all occurrences within a text file. For example, your text file may include several references to a name (e.g., company name, person's name, file name). For one reason or another, that name may have to be changed throughout your text. Other changes, such as the telephone company's adjustment to certain area codes, may affect some but not all of your clients. This means that you will have to look at each customer's file entry individually and decide whether or not to make the change.

Figure 6.16 shows the screen after pulling down the Search menu, selecting *Change* (or pressing Ctrl+Q+A), and filling in the two required fields. In this example, I'm asking the Editor to find occurrences of 617 and to replace them with 508.

Remember that you must press Tab or use the mouse to move the entry cursor from the Find What: to the Change To: field. If you want to change all occurrences, with no pausing for highlighting and display, you can then select the *Change All* option at the bottom of the dialog box. However, since you know that an individual decision must be made about each possible 617 occurrence, you should instead select the *Find and Verify* choice

The Change dialog box offers what some people refer to as a Search-and-Replace facility. You can type the desired search string in the Find What: field, and the replacement text in the Change To: field.

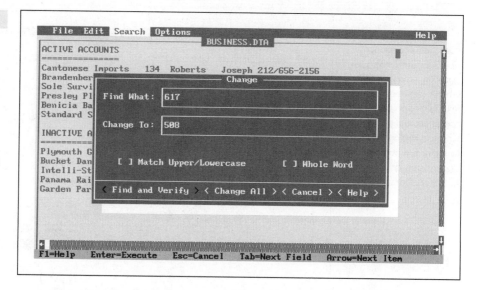

at the bottom of the dialog box. The result is a new verification dialog box, which appears in Figure 6.17.

As the Editor finds occurrences of your specified text, it highlights them and displays a secondary dialog box. You must tell the Editor now whether this highlighted occurrence of 617 (in the Plymouth Granite line) should be changed or not. If you choose *Change*, it will be instantly replaced with 508, and the next occurrence of 617 will be found and highlighted. The Change dialog box will redisplay, prompting you for a decision about what to do with that next occurrence.

If you decide that you do not wish to change this occurrence of the Find What: string (i.e., 617), but you do wish the automatic searching to proceed, you should select the *Skip* choice. The displayed occurrence of 617 is left intact, and the next occurrence is found and displayed. This procedure of finding each 617 occurrence in your file will continue automatically, one occurrence at a time. It stops only when all occurrences have been found and processed, or when you select *Cancel* from the Change dialog box.

When the Change procedure is complete, a final dialog box appears announcing this fact. The cursor is restored to the point in your file where it was before you began the search-and-replace sequence.

For each occurrence of a specified string, you can easily decide whether to change the text as previously specified in the Change dialog box or to leave the text unchanged and skip to the next occurrence.

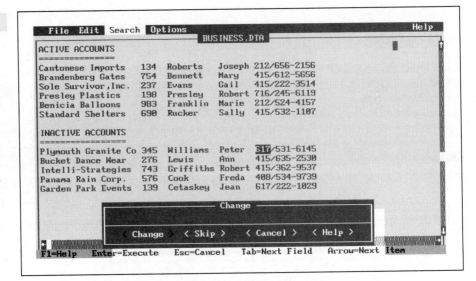

Using "Bookmarks" to Position the Cursor

In the course of creating large amounts of text, there will often be times when you wish to mark one or more places that you wish to come back to quickly. Rather than use the generic scrolling keys to find these places, you can mark them precisely just as you might place a bookmark on a page of a book. These bookmarks are helpful and time-saving when you know precisely where in a file you wish to move the cursor. The Editor permits four such places in your text to be marked for quick and easy returns.

For example, in my BUSINESS.DTA file, I may be adding all my account information into either the Active Accounts portion or the Inactive Accounts portion. Assume for this example that the newest accounts are being added by your clerical assistants. They will add new entries for active accounts to the *top* of the Active list, and new entries that are currently inactive to the *bottom* of the Inactive list. This is simply to provide an easier context (i.e., either at the start or at the end of the file) for entering all entries. Your data-entry people needn't concern themselves any further with the arrangement of the entries. All the names in each list can always be sorted at any later time by name, account code, company, or phone number during separate utility operations.

The person doing the data entry with the Editor will have to switch back and forth between the Active list of names and the Inactive list of names. Since the Ctrl+End key combination always takes you to the bottom of your text, you can have them press that key combination to enter inactive account information. But new active accounts must be inserted below the Active Accounts line and below the line of dashes.

Rather than having your assistant use the cursor-movement keys, you can set a bookmark. Move the cursor to the first character of the first line. Press Ctrl+K. The characters *^K* appear on the right side of the bottom line of your screen. Now press the digit 1. You've now defined that character position in your file with the number 1 bookmark. You can define up to four bookmarks, by using the digit 0, 1, 2, or 3 during your ^K definition.

After defining a specific bookmark location, you can return to perform any text entry or manipulation you like. For instance, you can type in a new active account, press Ctrl+End to move to the bottom of your file and enter three new inactive accounts, then make corrections to some other lines in your file. No matter where your cursor is located, you can request that the Editor instantly reset the cursor location to the first entry line in the Active Accounts section simply by pressing Ctrl+Q. A *^Q* symbol appears on the right side of the bottom screen line. Now press the bookmark number (0, 1, 2, or 3), and the Editor quickly moves the cursor to that bookmark location.

If you attempt a ^Q bookmark movement without having first defined the bookmark location with a ^K sequence, the Editor simply beeps and does nothing.

Printing Your Text

As you learned at the beginning of this chapter, you should be backing up your work as you go along. Normally, just before leaving the Editor, you will make a final backup copy of your work. If you forget to do so, but attempt to end your editing session by using the File▶Exit command, the Editor will remind you to save your work.

After you save your file to disk, and before exiting from the Editor, you will usually want to print out a copy of your work. In fact, you may wish to print out intermediate copies of your work during your editing session.

WARNING

Since printer connections are often the cause of computer output problems, remember to save your work *before* attempting to print your text.

You can print all or only a part of your text file, sometimes called a *document*. To do so, you only need to select *Print* from the File menu. As you can see in Figure 6.18, a dialog box appears to offer the choice of printing selected text or the entire text file.

If you had just highlighted a portion of your text, then the Editor assumes that you wish to print only that portion. The diamond symbol to the left of the *Selected Text Only* choice indicates this. If you have not selected any text prior to choosing the Print request, the diamond indicator appears beside the *Complete Document* choice. Even if you have selected some text, you can override the selection and print the entire document by moving the diamond symbol down to the *Complete Document* choice.

When you press Enter or select OK, you ask the Editor to send your text choice directly out the printer port for immediate printing.

FIGURE 6.18

If you've selected any text in your file, the *Selected Text Only* option appears highlighted when you initiate the *Print* option from the File menu. Simply choose *Complete Document* if you would rather print the entire file.

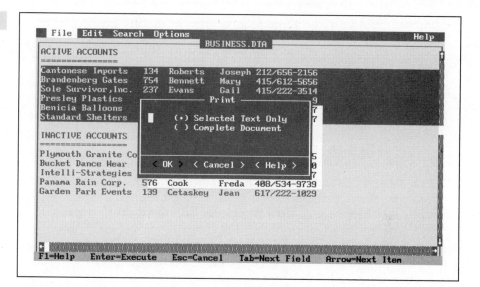

NOTE

You will have to eject the last printed page yourself. The Editor does not transmit a form-feed character to the printer when it has completed sending your requested text.

Summary

This chapter has explained how to use the DOS Editor. You have learned the following information:

* How to create a new text file, or make changes to an existing file, with the Editor.

* How to obtain on-line, context-sensitive help, and how to use the hypertext system of linked help screens.

- How to insert text or modify existing text.
- How to select text for subsequent block operations.
- How to use the File menu to:
  - begin new text files
  - read old files into memory
  - save your editing work
  - print part or all of your text file
  - exit from the Editor back to the operating system
- How to use the Edit menu to:
  - cut and paste selected text
  - copy and delete selected text
- How to use the Search menu to:
  - search and scroll through your text, using up to four special-purpose "bookmarks" to identify specific locations for rapid cursor positioning
  - search for specific text strings, and optionally replace them with new strings of characters

Over the course of this book, you'll use this editor extensively as you write batch files or explore the QBasic programming environment.

CHAPTER

7

Printing

COMPUTERS can do many marvelous things, and do them all at lightning speeds. However, the magic of the computer would be all for naught if there were no way to see the results. In this chapter, you'll learn a wide range of output capabilities in DOS. You'll discover some easy methods, some "quick-and-dirty" techniques, and some sophisticated commands for controlling when output will occur, where it will go, and what it will look like. You'll also learn why these alternatives work as they do.

Printing simple screen images of both text and graphics screens is the easiest kind of output to master quickly, so you'll learn that right away. Since printing onto paper is unquestionably the standard method for obtaining hard-copy results from programs, the principal focus of this chapter will be on producing paper output.

Indirect printing plays a very important role in more and more systems. The last section in this chapter will take an in-depth look at this feature. With indirect printing, you can continue to work on your computer while it sends output to a printer. This is DOS's first step into the world of multitasking and multiprocessing, where more than one program can execute at one time and more than one user can share the system's capabilities.

Printing Screen Images

It's often easier to generate results on the video screen than on any other output device. However, as you'll learn in this chapter, anything that can be displayed on your video screen can also be transferred to your printer.

Although many users never need DOS commands for printing (their application programs have built-in commands for managing output printing), you can easily obtain hard copies of any important textual data that is being displayed on your monitor simply by using DOS commands. In this case, your printed output may not appear pretty or nicely formatted. Nevertheless, you will be able to obtain the key data itself, usually the important results of some application program's processing. This may be all you ever need to be satisfied with the printed output from your computer system. To accurately replicate a screen image that was created in graphics mode instead of text mode, however, you must have a printer capable of creating graphics.

If you are using older equipment or programs, you might have a Color Graphics Adapter (CGA) monitor, which can generate graphics images using an array of pixels (dots) that is 640 pixels wide by 200 high. This density—128,000 pixels—is acceptable for many text applications, although most programs produce more pleasing and detailed results using denser output screens. An Enhanced Graphics Adapter (EGA) monitor has a density that is nearly twice that of the CGA. Its graphics mode produces an array of 640x350 pixels, while its principal successor, the Video Graphics Array (VGA), produces 640x480.

The VGA has several additional display modes, a popular one being the 720x400 resolution for increasing the number of text lines displayed. The most popular current extension of VGA screens is an 800x600 (or Super VGA) mode.

If neither you nor your dealer has yet connected your printer, you should do so now. If you need to do more than simply connect your printer and cable to the appropriate ports, consult Chapter 8, which covers communications in detail.

DOS requires you to press the PrtSc or Print Screen key to print a copy of whatever is on the screen. This should work on any video monitor if the information being displayed is in standard text characters. To see how it works, turn on your computer and bring up any program at all, or just use a simple directory listing. Turn on your printer and press PrtSc. It's as simple as that to obtain hard copy.

NOTE Some of the older keyboards require that you press the Shift key in combination with the PrtSc or Print Screen key.

Assuming you have a printer capable of generating graphics images, you can also create printed images of graphics by following a simple preparatory procedure. The **GRAPHICS** command in DOS is a disk-resident program that enables the same PrtSc key to capture a graphics screen image for printing. You must invoke this command *before* attempting to print a graphics screen.

The simplest form of the command is invoked by typing **GRAPHICS** at the command prompt. (Just as with the **PRINT** command, you should run the **GRAPHICS** command *before* you start up the DOS shell.) Invoking **GRAPHICS** causes future presses of the PrtSc key to reproduce on your printer all screen images, including graphics images. Graphics images cannot be printed without taking this crucial step.

➤ EXTRA!

Output a Fixed Number of Blank Lines!

You can generate a controlled number of blank lines of output from any batch file, with only a single instruction line, by using the **FOR** command (see Chapter 13):

```
FOR %%I IN (1 2 3 4 5 6 7) DO ECHO.
```

In this example command, I've placed the numbers 1 to 7 in the parentheses. This specifies that the **ECHO.** command, which by itself produces a blank line of output, will repeat seven times. To control how many blank lines are output, just place that many single digits or characters in the parentheses.

If you have a graphics program or an integrated package that includes graphics, try running that program now. Press PrtSc to attempt to print one of the graphics images. First try it without executing **GRAPHICS**, then go back to DOS and run the **GRAPHICS** command. Return to your program, and try PrtSc with the same graphics image.

The **GRAPHICS** command has some flexibility when it comes to output appearance. Its general and simplest form is

```
GRAPHICS PrinterType /B /R
```

where *PrinterType* is one of the possible parameter values defining printer type, as shown in Table 7.1. The **/B** and **/R** switches are used for background color and reverse video, as you will see shortly. As always, if the GRAPHICS.COM file is not in the current directory or in your path statement, you should precede the **GRAPHICS** command with the drive and directory where it can be found. When you run the **GRAPHICS** command from your DOS directory in the shell, you can also enter the optional **/R** and **/B** switches.

TABLE 7.1: *PrinterType* parameters for the **GRAPHICS** command

PARAMETER	PRINTER TYPE
COLOR1	IBM Personal Computer color printer with a black ribbon
COLOR4	Color printer with a red/green/blue and black ribbon
COLOR8	Color printer with a cyan/magenta/yellow and black ribbon
DESKJET	Hewlett-Packard DeskJet printer
GRAPHICS	IBM Graphics printer, IBM Proprinter, and the IBM Quietwriter printers
GRAPHICSWIDE	IBM Graphics printers with wide carriages
HPDEFAULT	Hewlett-Packard PCL printer

TABLE 7.1: *PrinterType* parameters for the **GRAPHICS** command (continued)

PARAMETER	PRINTER TYPE
LASERJET	Hewlett-Packard Laserjet printer
LASERJETII	Hewlett-Packard Laserjet II printer
PAINTJET	Hewlett-Packard PaintJet printer
QUIETJET	Hewlett-Packard Quietjet printer
QUIETJET PLUS	Hewlett-Packard Quietjet Plus printer
RUGGED WRITER	Hewlett-Packard Rugged Writer printer
RUGGED WRITERWIDE	Hewlett-Packard Rugged Writerwide printer
THERMAL	IBM PC Convertible thermal printer
THINKJET	Hewlett-Packard Thinkjet printer

The **GRAPHICS** command has a variety of advanced capabilities. See the help system for a listing of all the available switches and options.

Figure 7.1 shows a sample graphics screen from a spreadsheet program. This figure is the output of a special "screen-capture" program, so it is an almost exact representation of what appears on my video screen. If you try to print this screen with the PrtSc key without first running the **GRAPHICS** command, the result will be unsatisfactory, as you see at the top of Figure 7.2. However, if you use the **GRAPHICS** command with the appropriate parameter for your printer, and *then* use PrtSc, the printed result, as shown at the bottom of Figure 7.2, will be what you want to see.

If you specify *PrinterType* as **COLOR4** or **COLOR8**, you have the option of printing the background screen color by using the **/B** switch when you invoke the command—for example,

```
GRAPHICS COLOR4 /B
```

FIGURE 7.1

A typical graphics screen on a video display. (The detail depends on the screen's resolution.)

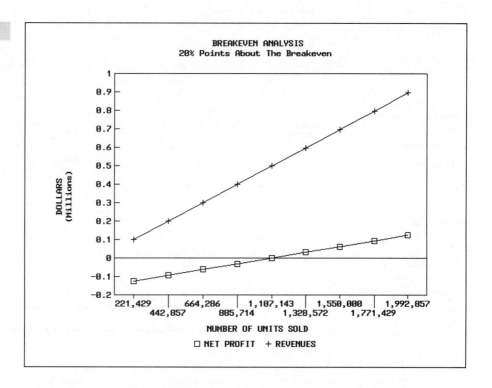

As an alternative, the **/R** switch with this command produces a striking *reverse-video* image (white letters on a black background). For example, typing

```
GRAPHICS COLOR4 /R
```

would produce the reverse-video printing shown in Figure 7.3.

Finally, note that printing a screen that contains only text is reasonably quick with PrtSc (well under a minute for most printers). Printing a screen containing graphics can take several minutes, depending on the graphics resolution and screen contents, as well as the speed of your printer. Printing a reverse-video image will naturally require more time than printing a normal black-on-white image.

FIGURE 7.2

By default, most printers expect text and are not prepared to properly deal with graphics characters. The top image shows the first attempt at using the PrtSc key to print out the screen seen in Figure 7.1. The bottom image shows the results of using the same key after first issuing the **GRAPHICS** command from a command line. Your printer will then be able to print images that include extended ASCII graphics characters.

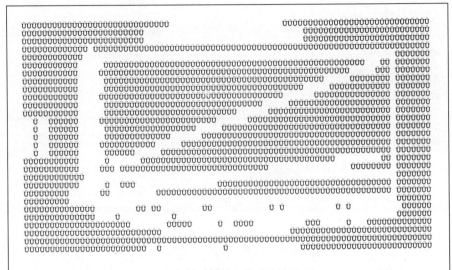

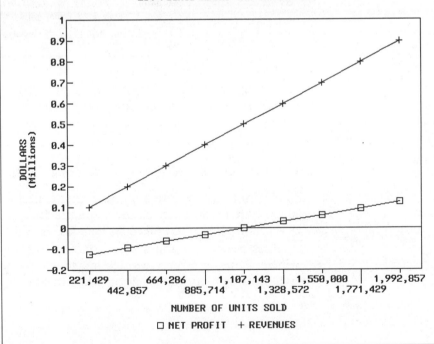

FIGURE 7.3

Reverse-video print-out of the screen from Figure 7.1. The **/R** switch on the **GRAPHICS** command reverses black for white and white for black when printing.

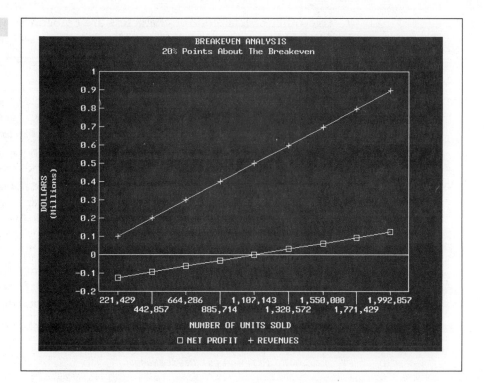

Printing Files

Creating printouts of displayed data with the PrtSc command and the **GRAPHICS** command is easy, but it is limited to one screenful of information at a time. There will be many times when you need a printed copy of an entire data file.

Printing Standard ASCII Files

Many data files are created as standard ASCII files, which usually contain only standard letters, numbers, and punctuation. In addition, each line of an ASCII file has a carriage return and line feed (CR/LF) at the end of it.

(No other special control characters are embedded within the file.) An ASCII file can be printed in several ways, as you will see in the following sections.

NOTE If a file is stored in a special format (as it is for spreadsheet programs, database programs, and many word-processing programs), you will need to print it from within the program that created it (or translate it to a format that can be handled by one of your application programs) in order to obtain an acceptable hard copy.

At the command prompt, the simplest way to print one or more data files is to use the **COPY** command. Remember that if you are only running one command while you are in the shell, you can pull down the File menu, select *Run*, and then type the desired command. The general form of the **COPY** command is

```
COPY FileName(s) DeviceName:
```

where the destination parameter, *DeviceName*, is the printer's *reserved device name*. DOS reserves several special names like LPT1 or COM1 for the hardware ports to which printers are connected. (You will learn about these names in Chapter 8.)

TIP Get in the habit of following reserved device names (e.g., LPT1, LPT2, COM1, COM2) as well as drive names (A, B, C, and so on) with a colon in your commands. This lets DOS know where the device or drive name ends and the sequence of parameter values begins.

➤ EXTRA!

Control Your Printer Better with These DOS Macros

The DOSKEY utility (see Chapter 15) enables you to write and incorporate your own customized new commands into DOS. Here are three nifty ones to demonstrate how easy it can be. (Remember, to create any of these macros, you must have first loaded the DOSKEY utility.)

FF sends a Form-Feed character to your printer. This can be particularly helpful if your printer does not automatically eject the last page of a printed document. What a pain in the neck to have to go over to the printer, turn it offline, press the Form-Feed button, then turn it back online again. But no more; just type **FF** at the command prompt and the task is done!

PRINTDIR prints an alphabetized listing of directory $1. *PRINTIT* prints a specified text file ($1), then ejects the page of paper in your printer.

Create these new commands by typing the following lines at a command prompt. (Note that the "female symbol" control character is created using the ASCII code 012).

```
DOSKEY FF=ECHO ♀ $g PRN

DOSKEY PRINTDIR=DIR $1 /ON $g PRN $t ECHO ♀ $g PRN

DOSKEY PRINTIT=TYPE $1 $g PRN $t ECHO ♀ $g PRN
```

If the file you want to print is called KEYS.DTA, then it can typically be printed by specifying the following command:

```
COPY KEYS.DTA LPT1:
```

In this command, LPT1 is a name for the first parallel printer port. (See Chapter 8 for additional information about using multiple printers and using serial ports for printing.) The printer will be engaged immediately, and the entire file will be printed, even if it takes multiple pages. You will now have to wait until the printout is completed before the DOS prompt will return. Nothing else can be done by your DOS system or by you until the printing terminates.

Printing Multiple Files

You know that you can copy multiple files with one command by using a wild-card specification. In this situation, you can also initiate the *printing* of multiple text files with a wild card. For instance, as shown in Figure 7.4, you could initiate the printing of all the .TXT files in the C:\DOS directory by running this command:

```
COPY C:\DOS\*.TXT LPT1:
```

FIGURE 7.4

You can print one or more text files from the shell by copying them to the port connected to your printer. Select the *Run* option from the File menu and enter the **COPY** command, specifying your printer port after the file(s) to copy.

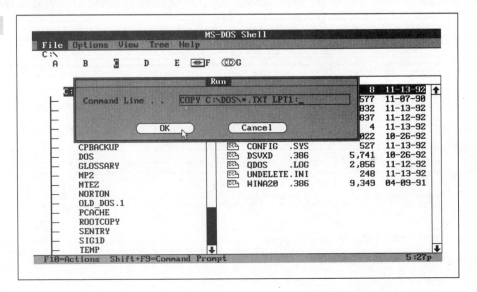

DOS will respond to this request by successively displaying on the screen the name of each .TXT file. After displaying each name, it will transmit all the contents of that file to the printer. Only then will it move on to the next file that meets the .TXT file specification in the specified directory. Once again, you will not regain control until all of the specified files have been printed.

Indirect Printing and Spooling

In the previous section, the **COPY** command allowed you to transfer files to a printer. However, **COPY** will not relinquish control of the system

➤ EXTRA!

Use ECHO to Type Single Lines Directly to Your Printer

You can use **ECHO** to send a single line of text to the printer. For example, typing:

```
ECHO Hello > LPT1:
```

will cause **Hello** to be printed. You can also use **ECHO** to print lines directly to a file: just replace the device name in the example above with a file name.

Note that if you wish to print a character that has a special meaning for DOS, you must enclose it in double quotation marks. For example, you would have to type

```
ECHO The ">" symbol is used for redirection
```

to properly print the > character as part of the sentence; otherwise DOS would treat the > sign as a redirection operator, as it did in the first sentence above.

until the print transfer is complete. Consequently, you are unable to enter any other DOS command or do anything else while the printing proceeds. The **PRINT** command is DOS's solution to the problem of idling its users.

Printing Files with the PRINT Command

The **PRINT** command is functionally similar to **COPY**. You could enter either of the following to print files on a standard system printer:

```
COPY FileName(s) PRN:
```

or

```
PRINT FileName(s)
```

You could also use the equivalent *Copy* or *Print* options from the shell's File pull-down menu. However, in order to use the *Print* option on the File menu, you must first execute the **PRINT** command once from the command prompt to set up the *spool queue*. To do this, you should first exit from the shell entirely by pressing Alt+F4, and enter the **PRINT** command without any parameters. Then restart the shell by typing **DOSSHELL**.

> **WARNING**
>
> Before you run any memory-resident or TSR program or command from the shell, you should first exit the shell entirely (don't simply "shell out" by pressing Shift+F9) and run the program first from the initial command prompt.

After running **PRINT** once, you have prepared DOS properly to manage the simultaneous printing of selected text files. Unlike the **COPY** command, which requires an output destination such as LPT1, **PRINT** *knows* that its job is to send the specified file names to a printer. Although you can use one of the special switches, discussed later in this section, to indicate which printing device the files are to be printed on, it's not really necessary. If you haven't specified the switch, DOS will prompt you for a destination the very first time you invoke the **PRINT** command:

```
Name of list device[PRN]:
```

At this point, you could just press Enter to accept the default device name, or you could enter a specific reserved device name (like COM2) for your system.

T I P

As mentioned previously, the *Print* option on the File menu is available only after the print spool has been initially set up by entering PRINT at a command prompt. Because it is easiest to do this *before* bringing up the DOS shell, you may want to set it up from your AUTOEXEC.BAT file, which is discussed in Chapter 14.

For the rest of your computing session, you can send files to your printer and then immediately continue working in DOS while the printing proceeds. In Figure 7.5 I have used the shell to do this by selecting the

FIGURE 7.5

In order to use the print spool from within the DOS shell, you should first have entered the **PRINT** command from a command prompt before invoking the DOS shell. Once in the shell, simply select the files you want printed, then select the *Print* option from the File menu.

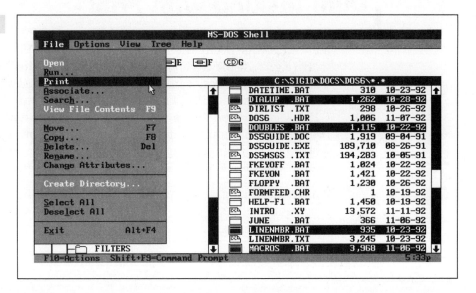

Print command on the File pull-down menu. In this example, I selected four .BAT files before initiating the command.

Stop now briefly and try the *Print* option to print any text files (.TXT, .BAT, .DTA, and so on) you have on your system. Just enter the **PRINT** command at the regular DOS prompt (not with the *Run* option from the File menu). When DOS asks you for the name of the list device (the destination), just press Enter. Then, start the shell and select a series of file names from the files area. Finally, pull down the File menu and select *Print*. (Note that DOS limits you to a maximum of ten files in the print queue at once, unless you increase the maximum value when you first initiate spooling. You will learn shortly how to do this.)

WARNING

When using the PRINT command, only the file *name* is queued, not the file *data*. Remember this if you are changing a file's contents and saving it after you queue it for printing; DOS will print the changed file, not the version existing when the printing request was made.

Dual Tasking with Print

The major difference between **PRINT** and **COPY** is apparent immediately after you specify the file names to print. DOS continues with other work (e.g., redisplays a command prompt or the shell) right after **PRINT** begins its work. You can invoke other programs or commands while **PRINT** prints your files. The effect is apparently simultaneous action: the CPU seems to be managing the printing job at the same time it is responding to your new requests at the DOS prompt for nonprinting work. The indirect printing, or spooling, is called a *background task*, while your principal new work (if any) is called the *foreground task*.

This dual-tasking technique is actually electronic chicanery—a silicon sleight-of-hand. A DOS computer has only one central processing chip

(CPU), and it can really only do one thing at a time. However, it *can* do things very quickly. In any given period of time, a CPU can rapidly shift its processing attention repeatedly from a slow printer to a slow typist to a not-really-so-fast disk drive before the typist even notices that the CPU has performed the other work.

In Figure 7.6 I have issued the **PRINT** command for the first time since DOS was brought up. This example shows my request for the printing of a single text file, PHONES.BAT, as a background task, and, on the following line, DOS's prompt for the name of the desired printer (referred to by the formal specification "list device"), at which point I simply pressed Enter to accept my single parallel printer as the default print device.

FIGURE 7.6

During the very first use of **PRINT** for background printing, you are asked to name the port connected to your system's printer. This sequence installs the memory-resident portion of PRINT.EXE, which will handle print spooling now as well as during later print requests.

```
C:\>PRINT C:\SIG1D\DOCS\DOS6\PHONES.BAT
Name of list device [PRN]:
Resident part of PRINT installed

  C:\SIG1D\DOCS\DOS6\PHONES.BAT is currently being printed

C:\>
```

When you enter the **PRINT** command from a command prompt, DOS displays the name of the first file it is about to print from its queue. Succeeding file names from the queue will print unattended, and unannounced. You can always find out the current status of the queue by typing **PRINT** with no parameters. As shown in Figure 7.7, **PRINT** will respond by listing the name of the file currently being printed, as well as the names of the remaining files in the queue. After this status message is displayed,

FIGURE 7.7

You can always inquire about the current status of the print queue by simply typing PRINT at any command prompt. All file names that reside in the queue will be identified, as well as whether or not one of them is presently printing.

```
C:\>PRINT

  C:\SIG1D\DOCS\DOS6\HELP-F1.BAT is currently being printed
  C:\SIG1D\DOCS\DOS6\VIDEO.BAT is in queue
  C:\SIG1D\DOCS\DOS6\SHORTCUT.BAT is in queue
  C:\SIG1D\DOCS\DOS6\JUNE.BAT is in queue
  C:\SIG1D\DOCS\DOS6\PHONES.BAT is in queue
  C:\SIG1D\DOCS\DOS6\WAIT.BAT is in queue

C:\>
```

the standard DOS prompt reappears. If you now initiate any other command or program, DOS will simply shift its processing power back and forth between the new job and the currently running print job.

Depending on how much slack time exists in your new program (for example, keyboard or disk waiting), the new program may not get held up to any noticeable extent. Usually, however, the print job can never run as fast as it could if it were not contending with a foreground task for the processor's attention. DOS will do its best to efficiently juggle the time-sharing between tasks.

Using Switches with Print

DOS provides you with certain switches that give you performance controls for indirect printing. Detailed analysis of these switches is beyond the scope of this book. In fact, using these switches at all may be unnecessary for most users. If future versions of DOS permit multitasking, these parameters will be more useful for fine-tuning your individual DOS.

In the example that was shown in Figure 7.6, I did not specify any switches. DOS set its own intelligent initial values for the performance parameters. However, you can specify other values for these parameters. The memory-resident setup will follow defaults unless you specify other values by switches. Note that some of these switches can only be used the first time **PRINT** is invoked. If you wish to change the values set by these switches, you will have to reboot and issue a new **PRINT** command using the changed values.

➤ EXTRA!

Get More for Your Money with Print Spooling!

Unlike the **COPY** command, which prints directly to your printer, the **PRINT** command causes printing to occur indirectly. **PRINT** sends information out to a disk file to indicate which data files are to be printed. Then, later, while you are doing other work, DOS will independently read this disk file to discover which data files should be printed. The printing will occur simultaneously with other work you may then be doing with DOS and your computer system.

Indirect printing is often called *spooling*, an acronym for "simultaneous peripheral operations on-line." Spooling is the only form of limited multitasking available in the current version of DOS. As discussed earlier, multitasking is the apparent simultaneous operation of different programs or computer tasks.

The biggest complaint about the system performance associated with spooling traditionally centers on the long waiting time for slow peripheral devices like printers and plotters. The **PRINT** command, when used intelligently with switches and wild cards, can help to address that complaint.

Print Switches Available Initially Only

Of the six switches available to you only the first time you invoke **Print** (see Table 7.2), the only one that you might want to consider setting is **/Q**, the Queue switch, which indicates how many separately named files can be managed by the **PRINT** command. A *queue* is just a waiting line, like a line of people waiting for a bus or bank service. In this context, a queue is a list of files to be printed. There must be at least 4 files in a queue. DOS allows 10 as a default maximum, but you can enter a different value after the **/Q** switch.

TABLE 7.2: Switches and parameters for the first **PRINT** command

SWITCH AND PARAMETER	EFFECT
/D:*Device*	Specifies the device to which print output is to be sent (COM1, LPT2, and so on).
/Q:*QueueSize*	Specifies how many files can be accepted by the **PRINT** command at one time for background printing. Maximum number is 32, minimum number is 4, and the default value is 10.
/M:*MaxTicks*	Specifies the maximum number of CPU clock ticks to be used by the **PRINT** command each time it is given control by the CPU. Range of allowable values is 1 to 255, with a default value of 2.
/B:*BufferSize*	Specifies the number of bytes in memory to be used for data to be printed. 512 bytes is both the standard and a minimum value, but it can be increased in 512-byte increments up to a maximum of 16,384.
/U:*BusyTicks*	Specifies how many clock ticks to wait for a printer that is still busy with earlier printing. Allowable range is 1 to 255, with a default value of 1.
/S:*TimeSlice*	Specifies how many clock ticks to allocate to this **PRINT** command. Range is 1 to 255, with a default value of 8.

Figure 7.8 shows what happens if you try to print more files than there are queue entries. As you can see, I tried to queue up all 39 .BAT files for printing. Even though there are 39 files that match the wild-card specification (*.BAT), only the first 10 were accepted for printing into the queue. (Since the **/Q** switch has not been used, the default queue size is 10 slots.)

In this situation, the DOS shell displays a dialog box with important information and options. It first indicates that while attempting to place the 11th specified file into the print queue, it determined that the print queue

FIGURE 7.8

The number of files printed is limited by queue size. The default number of entries is 10, but you can save memory by setting it as low as 4. Increase the print spool entries to a maximum of 32 if you expect to print large numbers of files in that session.

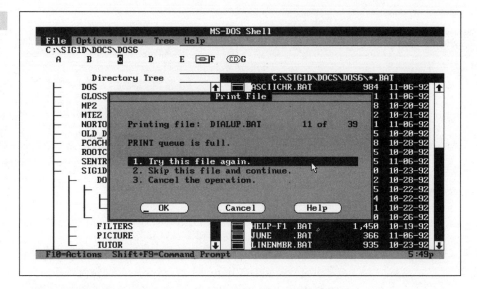

was full. It then offers three options. You can take Choice 1, which resubmits the file name to the print queue. Assuming that at least one of the ten queue entries has completed printing by the time you select Choice 1 here, this file name will be added to the queue for printing. It will be printed after the remaining queue entries have been printed.

You can select Choice 2 to skip this specific file name, and go on to the next possible file for which printing was requested. That would redisplay the same dialog box but with the 12th file name from the group of 39 selected .BAT files.

The last choice, number 3 in Figure 7.8, would cancel the request. In this case, the first ten file names that did fit into the queue will continue to print in the background while you go on with any other work you like, but the remainder of the file names that did not fit into the queue would not print at all. The remaining .BAT files that were not initially accepted into the queue for printing will have to be queued up with other **PRINT** commands after these first ten finish printing. At best, other **PRINT** commands that are issued when some of the slots open up will fill the open slots. However, the total number of queued files can never exceed the maximum queue size. Trying to queue more than that produces another dialog box such as the one you saw in Figure 7.8.

> EXTRA!

TSRs Are Neither Black Nor White!

Notice in Figure 7.6 that a message appears informing you that the resident part of **PRINT** has been installed. **PRINT** is an example of a *terminate-and-stay-resident* program, or *TSR*. A TSR is neither a completely internal (memory-resident) nor a completely external (disk-resident) command. In fact, **PRINT** permanently expands the resident memory requirements of DOS when it runs.

Although the extra memory requirement reduces the memory remaining for your primary application program, this cost is a small price to pay for the ability to continue using your computer while printing proceeds. Until you actually need it, it looks like any other disk-resident command, residing on disk as an unobtrusive .COM or .EXE file. It takes up no room in memory until it is needed. When it is invoked for the first time, it installs itself into memory. When it has completed its task(s), however, it does not free the memory space it used. Instead, it continues to reside in memory to be rapidly used again when needed.

Print Switches Always Available

Three other switches are always available to you for management of the queue and its entries—they can be used each time you use the **PRINT** command. As you can see in Table 7.3, they are **/P** (Print), **/C** (Cancel printing), and **/T** (Terminate all spooling).

You'll probably use **/P** least often, since it is already the system default. You will only need to use it when you construct and directly submit to DOS more complicated print requests.

If you want to cancel the printing of one or more files already in the queue, you can do so at a command prompt (or with File➤Run within the shell)

TABLE 7.3: Switches and parameters for any **PRINT** command

SWITCH AND PARAMETER	EFFECT
FileName **/C** *AdditionalFileName(s)*	Removes the specified file name(s) from the queue.
FileName **/P** *AdditionalFileName(s)*	Adds the specified file name(s) to the queue; this is the default.
/T	Terminates the printing of all files in the print queue.

with the **/C** switch. For instance, to remove the BOX.BAT, BUR-NIN.BAT, and DIALUP.BAT entries from the queue, effectively canceling the former print request for those three files, enter

```
PRINT BOX.BAT /C BURNIN.BAT DIALUP.BAT
```

Notice that the **/C** applies both to the file name immediately preceding the switch in the command line and to files listed after it. This allows a complex but useful construction in which you can simultaneously add and remove queue entries by putting more than one switch in the command line. For example, in the next example, BOX.BAT, BURNIN.BAT, and DIALUP.BAT are removed from the queue with **/C**, while JUNE.BAT is added with **/P**:

```
PRINT BOX.BAT /C BURNIN.BAT DIALUP.BAT JUNE.BAT /P
```

NOTE

Like the /C switch, the /P switch applies to the file name immediately preceding it on the command line.

If the file you wish to cancel is currently printing, the printing will stop and you will receive a message to that effect. If the file you cancel is elsewhere in the queue, it will be removed, and the new status of the print queue will be displayed on your monitor.

Finally, the **/T** switch will cancel all file names in the queue. If you find that the paper has jammed, or an ink-jet cartridge has run dry while printing, you may like to cancel all outstanding print requests and then restart the output spool, naming specific files in your desired order. Simply enter the command

```
PRINT /T
```

➤ EXTRA!

Attention CAD Programmers and Graphics Designers!

If you use a plotter and your software allows offline plotting (that is, the software doesn't have to control the plotting process directly), you can use the **PRINT** command to queue several plots at once. Plotters are notoriously slow, and waiting for a detailed plot can contribute to hair loss at worst and graying hair at best.

Print spooling is often an easy way to regain control of your CPU quickly. In this way, your boss can happily see you working on your next design or drawing right away. Let the **PRINT** spooler worry about communicating with that slow plotter.

Refer to your plotting program's documentation for further details. It will usually include any explanations having to do with setup for automatically linking program output and plotter input.

➤ EXTRA!

Generate a Numbered Printout of Any Text File!

Use the LINENMBR.BAT batch file below to create a new file from any existing text file. The newly created file, LINENMBR.TXT, will contain all text lines from the specified file (parameter one), with each one numbered for easy identification or referencing:

```
@ECHO OFF
Rem LINENMBR.BAT
IF '%1'=='' Goto Missing
FIND /N /V "*&$#" %1 | FIND /V "---------- " > LINENMBR.TXT
Goto End
:Missing
ECHO You must specify a text file name as the first parameter.
:End
```

Summary

Printed output from your system is fundamental for nearly all software applications. This chapter has presented a variety of methods for obtaining printed output for both simple screen images and files:

- You can easily obtain hard-copy printouts of screen images consisting solely of text characters by using the PrtSc key combination.

- You can generate printed images of graphics screen images with the same PrtSc combination, provided that you first run the **GRAPHICS** command and include the appropriate printer type.

- You should type **GRAPHICS** at the regular command prompt before starting the shell (don't type it at the *Run* option from the shell's File menu). You can follow the command with useful switches for "special effects." The **/B** switch prints a separate background screen color if you are using multicolor printer ribbons. The **/R** switch produces the dramatic effect of white letters on a solid black background.

- You can use **COPY** to print text files that don't fit on one screen, by simply copying the files to a printer instead of to another file. However, you cannot use the *Copy* option on the File pull-down menu to print files.

- You can use **PRINT** to print files indirectly while you work at the same time with other DOS programs or commands. You must first invoke **PRINT** once from the command prompt before you can use the *Print* option from the shell's File pull-down menu.

- You can add more files to a print queue with the **/P** switch, remove files from the queue with the **/C** switch, and terminate all spooling operations by removing all files from the queue with the **/T** switch.

Now that you've learned several methods of printing with DOS, you can extend these techniques with the information in the next chapter. Printing is only one form of data communications. Chapter 8 will take you on an extended tour of other DOS communications capabilities which permit information to be transferred to many other output devices besides printers.

CHAPTER

8

Communicating with Other Devices

PRINTING is only one form of system communications; you learned about it first (in Chapter 7) because of its central role in any computer system. This chapter concentrates on the "speaking and listening" that goes on between computer devices. As you'll see, there are many other devices to understand besides printers in any complete computer system. Beyond simply connecting these devices, you will learn in this chapter how to get them started and how to transfer information to and from them. Learn this information well, and you will no longer be at anybody else's mercy when it comes to buying and hooking up new equipment.

This chapter will help you understand the differences between *parallel* and *serial* communications, so you can make intelligent decisions about which is right for you. You will also learn enough about the various aspects of these two kinds of communications to use the DOS communications setup commands properly.

One major DOS command in particular, the **MODE** command, is central to an understanding of data transfer to printers, serial ports, and the video display. You'll learn what it can do for you and when to use it. It will give you control over

- Your printer (for improving the appearance of your hard-copy output),

- Your video screen (for enhancing all displayed information),

- Your keyboard (for getting more out of each key than simply what is printed on the key), and

- Just about any additional device at all that connects to one of the communications ports (plugs) in the back of your computer. This includes devices such as plotters, modems, and digitizers.

➤ EXTRA!

Computers Speak Their Own Special Language!

A computer and all its connected devices (*peripheral* devices) can be thought of as a large collection of very tiny electronic parts. Each of those parts can receive—or *not* receive, according to the logic built into the computer—a small voltage. The voltages affect the bits of magnetic material that store data for you or store instructions for the computer itself.

If a bit is energized with a small voltage, it has a value of 1. If it receives no voltage, it has a value of 0. The word *binary* means two; as you see, a single bit has two possible values, 0 or 1.

You may not realize it, but in communicating with others, you usually perform a variety of tasks based on simple yes/no answers or simple directives. Everything can be broken down into smaller and smaller components, from hitting a baseball properly, to conducting an interview, to carrying out a superior's orders.

Similarly, in a computer system, everything can be broken down into component bits. Complex logic and decision-making are broken down into sequences of bits that either receive voltage or do not receive voltage—values of 1 or 0. Perhaps this is not as rich an alphabet as A through Z, but it serves the same purpose.

System Communications in General

To understand computer communications, you need to understand the concept of data structure and storage. When you enter keyboard characters into programs, either as data or instructions, you enter them as numbers, letters, or punctuation marks, as represented on the face of the key.

Each of your keystrokes is interpreted by the computer as a well-defined string of *binary digits*, the 0's and 1's you may already know about. Computers talk in a binary language rather than in English. When computers communicate with each other and with peripheral devices they speak in binary sequences of 0's and 1's, akin to our own native language which uses sequences of words.

Communication between people is a sequence of sentences, which consist of a sequence of words, which in turn consist of a sequence of letters. These sequences are broken up by verbal pauses or inflections, or by written punctuation marks, intended to help the listener or reader better understand. Pauses and punctuation, therefore, help to *synchronize* the communication of information. To synchronize computer communications, a sequence of 0's and 1's is grouped into seven or eight data bits, each group representing a character. Characters can be letters (A–Z), numbers (0–9), or special symbols or codes (* # % " : > ? and so on).

To understand why some communications use seven data bits while others use eight, let's briefly look at the binary number system. One bit can have the value 0 or 1. Therefore, two bits in a row have four possible combinations of values, since each bit has two possible values:

- 0 followed by 0, or 00
- 0 followed by 1, or 01
- 1 followed by 0, or 10
- 1 followed by 1, or 11

Taking this a step further, three bits in a row can have eight possibilities:

- 0 followed by 00, or 000
- 0 followed by 01, or 001
- 0 followed by 10, or 010
- 0 followed by 11, or 011
- 1 followed by 00, or 100

- 1 followed by 01, or 101
- 1 followed by 10, or 110
- 1 followed by 11, or 111

As you can see, the binary system is based on powers of the number 2. With one data bit, there are two possibilities (2^1); with two data bits, there are four possibilities (2^2); and with three data bits, there are eight possibilities (2^3). Continuing this progression will result in the following:

- Four data bits = 16 possibilities (2^4)
- Five data bits = 32 possibilities (2^5)
- Six data bits = 64 possibilities (2^6)
- Seven data bits = 128 possibilities (2^7)
- Eight data bits = 256 possibilities (2^8)

The standard keyboard and ASCII character set is more than covered by the 128 possibilities contained in seven data bits. However, there are additional characters (graphics characters, foreign-language characters, and so on) that constitute what is called the *extended ASCII set*. When these additional characters must be transmitted, the eight-bit form of data communications is used. Appendix C covers this issue more fully. You will usually see characters represented as eight bits, and communicated as such. This conventional eight-bit unit is a *byte*, the fundamental storage and data unit you deal with throughout DOS.

The groups of bits we have been examining represent either data or controlling information. In a conversation, you gain someone's attention by saying their name or saying something like "Hey, you!" Computer communications use special groups of bits to gain the attention of another device. Once the attention is obtained with this *control code*, or special sequence of bits, the actual data transmission can begin.

Computers also use additional bits to ensure synchronization. *Stop bits* follow each unique character code (string of bits) to set it off from other transmitted information. In order to minimize sending or receiving errors, a *parity bit* is also sent after the data bits. This bit is used by both the transmitting and receiving equipment. (How it is computed and used is beyond the scope of this book.)

➤ EXTRA!

Let Your Computer Do the Walking for You!

Modify the DIALUP.BAT batch file below to include your favorite or frequently dialed phone numbers. Assuming that your telephone line is connected to the same line as your computer's modem, this batch file will dial for you when you type your friend's name. For example, I can call Lin with this program by simply typing:

```
DIALUP Lin
```

at a command prompt. (Note that this works only for Hayes-compatible modems.) Here's the DIALUP.BAT file for you:

```
@ECHO OFF
Rem DIALUP.BAT is a batch file dialer for your telephone.
Rem Assumptions: 2400 baud line is connected to COM1.
Rem Syntax:   DIALUP Name  to actually dial the phone
Rem          or DIALUP /?    to display all possibilities.
MODE COM1:2400 > NUL
IF '%1'=='' Goto :Listing
IF %1==/? Goto :Listing
IF %1==Jackie ECHO ATDT1-516-922-2345; > COM1:
IF %1==Sandy  ECHO ATDT1-212-945-5496; > COM1:
IF %1==Lin    ECHO ATDT524-1841;        > COM1:
IF %1==Home   ECHO ATDT525-5033;        > COM1:
ECHO -------------------------------------------
ECHO When computer dialing is complete, you may
ECHO pick up your handset and press any key on
ECHO the keyboard to disconnect the modem.
ECHO -------------------------------------------
PAUSE
ECHO ATH > COM1:
Goto End
:Listing
CLS
ECHO To use the DIALUP program, you should type:
ECHO.
ECHO DIALUP Name
```

```
ECHO.
ECHO where Name is one of the entries seen below.
ECHO Be sure to use the same upper/lower case as
ECHO was entered into the batch file itself.
ECHO For example, you might call Sandy by typing:
ECHO DIALUP Sandy
ECHO.
FIND "ATDT" DIALUP.BAT | SORT /+8
:End
```

Parallel versus Serial Communications

When you type a capital **J** from the keyboard, a code is sent to the computer's input routines, which translate it into the binary digits 01001010. The letter itself is echoed back to the video screen to confirm what you typed (see Figure 8.1). Remember that the video screen is part of the system's console; the keyboard is the input part of the console and the video screen is the output part. The passing of information between these parts is called *data transmission*.

There are two methods of data transmission: *parallel* and *serial*. Nearly all DOS microcomputers are connected with peripheral devices using one of these two communication techniques. Although most printers use the parallel method of data transmission, some use the serial method. Other peripheral devices like plotters, digitizers, modems, and mice usually transmit data serially.

FIGURE 8.1

Keyboard echoing is a simple form of data transmission. The keyboard hardware identifies the character pressed, and the same ASCII code is sent (i.e., echoed) to the video monitor to be displayed.

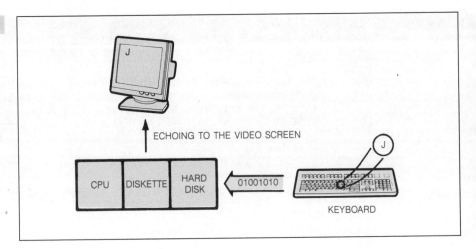

If a peripheral device is connected to a serial port and is designed for serial transmission, each bit will be sent to or received from the central processing unit one bit at a time, and only one transmission wire will be used. If the peripheral device is connected to a parallel port and is designed for parallel transmission, then eight separate bits will be transmitted simultaneously over eight separate wires. (In both cases, other wires are used for additional purposes, such as the synchronization of signals or grounding; however, it's sufficient in this context to understand the concept in terms of one wire versus eight.)

Let's return to the example of keyboard data transmission. Say you type in the word **JUDD** and you want the CPU to send it to a peripheral device. Your keystrokes will be translated into the following ASCII character codes:

J	01001010
U	01010101
D	01000100
D	01000100

➤ EXTRA!

Airlines Understand Parallel vs. Serial Concepts!

Consider the following simple analogy. In the figure below, an airport's baggage terminal has eight conveyor belts, and passengers' suitcases are being unloaded from eight flights simultaneously. This is like parallel communications. In the figure below that, however, the airport has only one conveyor belt, and the baggage from all eight flights is being unloaded onto it. This is like serial communications.

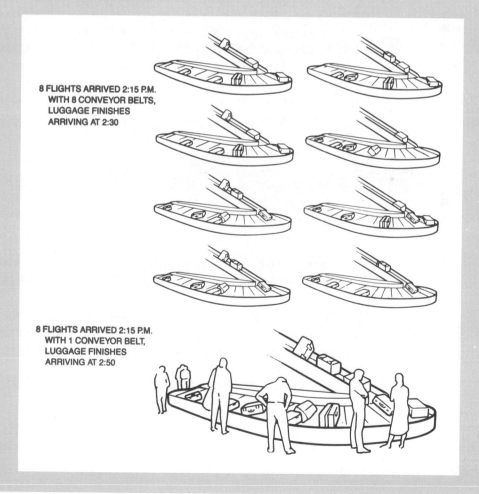

8 FLIGHTS ARRIVED 2:15 P.M.
WITH 8 CONVEYOR BELTS,
LUGGAGE FINISHES
ARRIVING AT 2:30

8 FLIGHTS ARRIVED 2:15 P.M.
WITH 1 CONVEYOR BELT,
LUGGAGE FINISHES
ARRIVING AT 2:50

The passengers in the serial situation might have to wait eight times as long as those in the first airport, and they probably won't be happy about it. Then again, the airline officials may not mind, since they spent one eighth the amount of money on the conveyor mechanism and the ongoing expenses for maintenance and terminal-space rental.

It's a trade-off of time versus money. In this analogy, you are the airline officials. You make the decision about what equipment you buy and use, deciding whether to spend more money on parallel connections or less money on serial connections, which require more waiting time for certain peripheral devices. In fact, most computers now come with both parallel and serial ports. Simply understand that devices that are connected to the parallel port have the opportunity to move data around faster.

NOTE

Serial communications are often referred to as *asynchronous communications*, because the sending and receiving devices do not send and receive simultaneously, or synchronously. Instead, each uses an agreed set of electrical signals to indicate when to stop and start actual data transmission (see the MODE command later in this chapter).

Figure 8.2 shows a parallel transmission of these characters. As you can see, eight wires are used. A serial transmission of the same characters would require only one wire, as you can see in Figure 8.3. However, the transmission of data would be much slower. This explains why virtually all printers that print faster than several hundred characters per second *must* use parallel transmission and be connected correctly for parallel transmission.

FIGURE 8.2

Parallel data transmission uses a group of wires to simultaneously send bit values for different characters. The **J** for instance is represented by the 01001010 bits sent at the same time on eight wires.

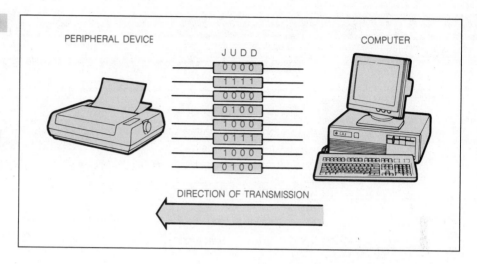

FIGURE 8.3

Serial data transmission uses a single wire to send the same ASCII codes. Each of the identifying bit values must be sent successively, rather than simultaneously. This is slower. Choose parallel over serial if you have a choice for a peripheral device.

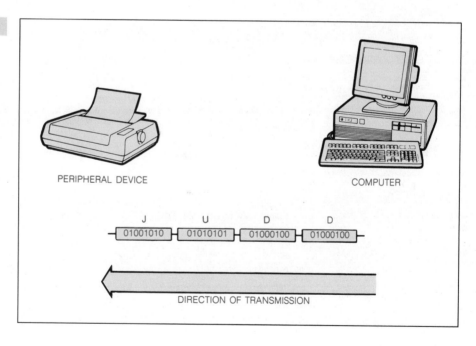

➤ EXTRA!

Maintain Your Own Online Directory Assistance!

Use the following PHONES.BAT batch file to provide yourself with an online directory-assistance facility. In the example PHONES.BAT, sample phone entries appear for letters A, B, and C. You can fill in the rest of the alphabet for your customized version of this batch file.

This batch file merely refreshes your memory with someone's phone number and address. If you want your computer to actually dial someone's number, use the DIALUP.BAT file shown in an earlier *EXTRA!* in this chapter.

```
@ECHO OFF
Rem PHONES.BAT looks up all entries in a phone directory
Rem and displays them on the screen.
Rem Syntax: PHONES FirstLetterLastName
CLS
Rem If the user does not specify a value for %1,
Rem display the required syntax.
IF '%1'=='' Goto NoParameter

Rem Allow uppercase or lowercase letters A-Z.
FOR %%i IN (A B C D E F G H I J K L M N O P Q R S T U V W X Y Z) DO IF '%%i'=='%
FOR %%i IN (a b c d e f g h i j k l m n o p q r s t u v w x y z) DO IF '%%i'=='%
Goto NotAlphabetic

:A
Rem All phone entries look like this
ECHO Arthur, Viola
ECHO 643 Bay Street
ECHO Wellesley, MA 02181
ECHO (617) 235-3749
ECHO.
ECHO Anderson, Lynn
ECHO 2 Berkeley Court, Apt 3D
ECHO Albany, CA 94706
ECHO (510) 444-3498
Goto End

:B
ECHO Bingham, Quisley
ECHO 17 Cheshire Court
ECHO Massapequa, NY 11729
ECHO (516) 923-0349
Goto End

:C
Goto NoEntriesYet

:D
Rem Customize this batch file by replacing each
Rem "Goto NoEntriesYet" line with a set of lines
Rem defining the person's name/address/phone #. Leave the
Rem NoEntriesYet line for letters having no phone information.
Rem And so forth up to the letter Z.
Goto NoEntriesYet
:Z
Goto NoEntriesYet

:NoEntriesYet
ECHO No names begin with %1
Goto End
```

```
:NotAlphabetic
:NoParameter
ECHO You should specify the first letter of the last name
ECHO For example, type:     PHONES R
ECHO to obtain all entries beginning with the letter R.
:End
ECHO.
```

DOS Devices versus Files

As you've seen many times already, you specify the source and destination of the data in your software commands. The consistency with which DOS lets you reference hardware devices (like the console) or software devices (like a disk file) makes it easy to learn both new commands and new concepts. Commands like **COPY** work in precisely the same way for a data transfer from a CPU to a disk file and for a data transfer from a CPU to a peripheral device (a printer).

DOS is designed to understand and permit the referencing of certain typical peripheral devices. The following is a not atypical system setup for many users:

DOS RESERVED NAME	DEFINITION	SAMPLE CONNECTION
LPT1	First parallel port	Fast draft printer
LPT2	Second parallel port	Color printer
LPT3	Third parallel port	Laser printer
COM1	First serial port	Mouse

DOS RESERVED NAME	DEFINITION	SAMPLE CONNECTION
COM2	Second serial port	Plotter
COM3	Third serial port	Modem
COM4	Fourth serial port	Digitizer

Unlike file names, which you can make up yourself (as long as you obey certain rules), device names are restricted to certain reserved names, shown in Figure 8.4. DOS allows only three specific parallel device names (LPT1, LPT2, and LPT3) and four serial device names (COM1, COM2, COM3, and COM4). It assigns these automatically according to the order in which the devices are connected and turned on.

The additional device names in Figure 8.4, AUX and PRN, are called standard device names. They are used to communicate with the first serial and parallel ports to be connected, respectively. When using commands that refer to port devices, you can use these nonspecific device names if

FIGURE 8.4

DOS reserves four device names for serial communications, and three device names for parallel communications. Your programs send data to a COM port (when connected to a serial device) or an LPT port (when connected to a parallel device).

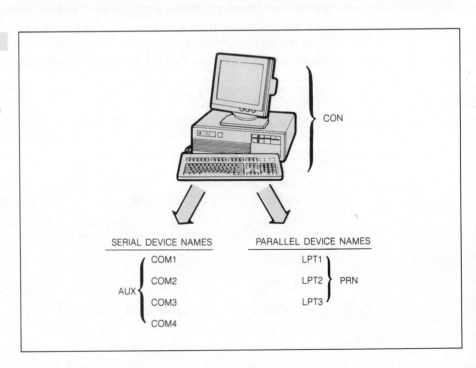

you don't want to be bothered with the details of which communications port is connected to your printer or device. Programs don't necessarily have to know which device is connected to which port. They can simply reference PRN, and the output will be routed to the first connected parallel port; or they can reference AUX, and the output will be routed to the first connected auxiliary communications (serial) port.

NOTE   Like the drive names in previous chapters (A, B, C, and so on), reserved device names should be followed by a colon in your commands. This lets DOS know when the device name ends and the sequence of parameter values begins.

Keep in mind that you must purchase the actual hardware to make the proper connections. In other words, DOS may understand what it means to send data to a serial port called COM1, but you must have a serial connector on your system, and it must be connected to a serial device, or the request is meaningless.

➤ EXTRA!

You Can Connect More Devices Than You Have Ports!

Even if you have purchased various pieces of peripheral equipment and sufficient add-in boards to connect them, DOS may not be able to address all of them. For instance, if your setup is like that described next to Figure 8.4, there are no more reserved names available if you decide to buy another serial device (perhaps an inexpensive networking alternative).

In this case, you would have to buy some form of switch. You would need to connect the switch to one port (say, COM1) and then connect two peripherals (the mouse and the modem, for example) to the switch.

Once all this hardware has been connected, you still must exercise great care to ensure that your software will work. The key to this is to make sure that two or more devices connected to the same switch do not try to transmit data at the same time. Your first reaction may be that this isn't a complication you expect to run into very often. On the other hand, you may have a computer with only one serial port (COM1), and you might want to use a graphics package that requires a mouse for input and a plotter for output.

Short of buying another serial-port connector, you can run your software by using a switch for the two devices. You might not think that there will be any problem because you plan not to allow both devices to use the same serial line simultaneously. However, what actually happens is that you'll probably become impatient with the slowness of the plotter, and long to regain control of the computer while the plot progresses independently (perhaps using the concept of print spooling that was explained in the preceding chapter).

If you choose to save money with this technique, or if your hardware simply cannot sustain any more separate interrupts for devices, you must be careful. When you are using the same serial line for two purposes, one operation must wait for the other to finish. If you are plotting, you cannot throw the switch to activate the mouse until all the plotting data has been transmitted to the plotter. And when you are using the mouse to control cursor movement and menu selections, you cannot switch over to the plotter for output until all mouse movements have been completed.

Initializing Devices and Ports

Different peripheral devices require special setup sequences when connected to the computer. The **MODE** command permits you to initialize aspects of your printers and your serial-port devices, as well as to redirect output from parallel to serial ports, and even to control some features of your video display. Other capabilities of **MODE** for the support of foreign-language characters will be discussed in Appendix D.

WARNING   Installing memory-resident programs while in the shell can misuse your system's memory. Since some forms of the MODE command consume memory, it is safest to run MODE from a command prompt only *before* invoking the DOS shell.

Figure 8.5 depicts the principal capabilities of the **MODE** command that you'll explore in this section.

FIGURE 8.5

The MODE command has extensive capabilities for controlling and configuring different devices. Refer to DOS's online help for extensive syntax and examples.

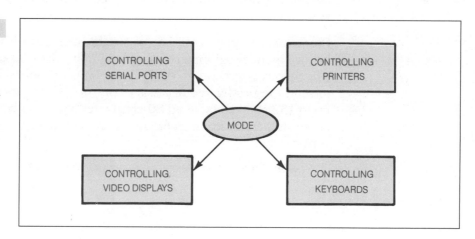

In all four situations depicted in Figure 8.5, the **MODE** command can be invoked like any other disk-resident DOS command. You'll see below that certain features of the **MODE** command are memory-resident and require that you run **MODE** from a command prompt to be safe. Assuming **MODE** is either in the current drive and directory or on the path you have specified, you would enter

    MODE *Parameters*

at a command prompt. For example, the following command for a parallel printer connected to the LPT1 port would set the columns per inch to 132 and the lines per inch to 8:

    MODE LPT1: COLS=132 LINES=8

Depending on what parameters you specify, one of the four versions of this command will be activated. The four major versions of this command almost act as four separate commands.

Controlling the Printer

An operation that is often desired by users is to turn on *compressed print*. Wide spreadsheets and database records are often hard to read when the number of characters per line exceeds the standard 80 characters. Most printers assume a normal default of 80 characters, because most programs generate data using an 80-column video screen. Printers also assume a default value of 6 lines per vertical inch, but you can control that as well.

Programs that can scroll left and right, like spreadsheets and database management programs, can generate more than 80 columns on a line. The following version of **MODE** gives you a simple way to instruct DOS to send the printer the necessary control codes requesting it to squeeze up to 132 characters on an 80-chartacter line, or to squeeze up to 8 lines of output per vertical inch on the paper. The general form of this **MODE** command is

    MODE *PrinterPort CharactersPerLine LinesPerInch*

Filling in the parameters with values, you could issue the following command to initialize the printer port to **LPT1**, the characters per line to **132**, and the lines per inch to **8**:

```
MODE LPT1: COLS=132 LINES=8
```

WARNING

This version of the MODE command assumes you are using the most common kind of printer: an EPSON MX series, an IBM graphics printer, or a compatible. Any other printer (including the popular HP Laserjet II) may require different control codes, making this DOS command useless to you.

Figure 8.6 shows different outputs from the same printer after different **MODE** commands are executed.

With the **MODE** commands for compressed print, DOS will respond to your command entry by displaying information about the new settings for columns and lines per inch. You will then be prompted to

```
Press any key to continue ...
```

Dot-matrix and laser printers make the horizontal compression occur by printing the dots closer together.

TIP

The MODE command has limited capability for sending control codes to printers. Some applications like Lotus 1-2-3 and dBASE IV let you send control codes directly to a printer. In fact, you can use the DOS Editor (EDIT.COM) or your own word processor to include a sequence of control codes in a file (say, CTRLCODE.TXT) and then send the file directly to a printer with the *Print* choice on the File menu, or the simple command-prompt instruction COPY CTRLCODE.TXT PRN.

FIGURE 8.6

Output of different mode commands, showing different combinations of CPI (columns per inch) and LPI (lines per inch). Use CPI=80 and LPI=6 for the most easily readable output. Use CPI=132 and LPI=8 for the most detailed output, such as is needed by wide and long spreadsheets.

```
--------------------------------------------------------------------------------
This short file was printed after entering MODE LPT1: COLS=80 LINES=8
        These four lines take up 1/2 inch vertically
        because, at LINES=8,
        four lines take 4/8 inches
        (which of course is the same as 1/2 inch)
.........10........20........30........40........50........60........70........80
The numbers above cover the full width of the paper
because COLS=80 (that is, 80 columns, or characters, per line).

Notice how any information that takes up more columns than the mode specifies "w
raps around" from one line to the next.

--------------------------------------------------------------------------------


--------------------------------------------------------------------------------
This short file was printed after entering MODE LPT1: COLS=80 LINES=6
This is the default printer setting for DOS.

        These four lines take up 2/3 inches vertically
        because, at LINES=6,
        four lines take 4/6 inches
        (which of course is the same as 2/3 inches).

.........10........20........30........40........50........60........70........80


--------------------------------------------------------------------------------


----------------------------------------------------------------------------------
This short file was printed after entering MODE LPT1: COLS=132 LINES=8
    These four lines again take up 1/2 inch vertically
    because LINES=8.
    The width of the characters has changed, however,
    because now COLS=132:
.......10.......20.......30.......40.......50.......60.......70.......80.......90.......100......110......120........132
Wide spreadsheet rows or database records typically require this 132-column mode.

----------------------------------------------------------------------------------


----------------------------------------------------------------------------------
This short file was printed after entering MODE LPT1: COLS=132 LINES=6

    As noted previously, when LINES=6,
    these four lines take up 2/3 inches vertically.
    We still have 132 columns or characters per line
    as you can see below:

.......10.......20.......30.......40.......50.......60.......70.......80.......90.......100......110......120........132


----------------------------------------------------------------------------------
```

➤ EXTRA!

Connecting Serial Printers to COM Ports

Printed output usually goes to a PRN device (usually a parallel port like LPT1). In the specific case where the serial device you have connected to a COM port is a printer, an additional version of the **MODE** command is required. You must redirect output to a COM port with the command

```
MODE LPTx:=COMy
```

The single digit represented by the x and the y should hold the specific numbers of your chosen ports.

Assuming that you have first initialized the communications parameters for the port so that the device and the CPU are synchronized, as in the last section, you can redirect the LPT1 port to the COM2 port with

```
MODE LPT1:=COM2
```

DOS will confirm the redirection for all succeeding print output requests with the following:

```
LPT1: rerouted to COM2:
```

Most application programs assume that output will go to the LPT1 port, unless otherwise directed. This explains why DOS provides this redirection option for sending print output to one of the available serial ports. However, the reverse is not possible. You cannot redirect to a parallel port any output that is specifically being sent to a serial port.

Initializing Serial Communications Ports

Synchronization is a difficult problem when serial devices are connected to computers. For example, if a computer sends data out to the serial port at a rate of 1200 bits per second, any printer connected to that port must be set (by means of hardware switches or software initialization) to receive this information at the same rate.

A second version of the **MODE** command allows you to correctly set a number of parameters for this and other aspects of serial communications. The general form of this **MODE** command is

```
MODE SerialPort BaudRate, Parity, DataBits, StopBits, Retry
```

The parameters have the following meanings:

- *SerialPort* indicates which one of the four possible peripheral connectors is being used by DOS for a particular device.

- *BaudRate* sets the speed at which data bits will be transmitted through the serial port. You only need to use the first two digits of the possible values (shown in Table 8.1).

- *Parity* represents the number of binary 1's, if any, that are used in a data transmission; this is used for error detection.

- *DataBits* specifies the number of bits used to represent actual transmitted data.

- *StopBits* represents the one or two bits used at the end of the data bits to indicate that end.

- *Retry* indicates how **MODE** is to respond to another system request for the serial port.

Table 8.1 contains the allowable values for these parameters.

TABLE 8.1: Possible parameter values when configuring serial ports

PARAMETER	POSSIBLE VALUES
SerialPort	**COM1, COM2, COM3,** or **COM4**
BaudRate	**11** (110), **15** (150), **30** (300), **60** (600), **12** (1200), **24** (2400), **48** (4800), **96** (9600), or **19** (19,200). (Use first two digits only.)
Parity	**n** (none), **o** (odd), **e** (even), **m** (mark), **s** (space)
DataBits	**5, 6, 7,** or **8**
StopBits	**1, 1.5,** or **2**
Retry	**E** returns an error to a busy port's status check. **B** returns a busy signal to a busy port's status check. **R** returns a ready signal to a busy port's status check. **N** (the default value) specifies that no retry action will be taken. **P** returns a message telling the other requester to persist in its request until the port is free.

TIP

Don't bother initially with this serial communications version of the MODE command; follow the initialization instructions in your software program's manual or in your serial device's instruction book. Usually this is all you need for success—only if this fails will you need to understand these MODE parameters more fully.

As an example, the following command issued at the command prompt would set the second serial port to transmit at 9600 baud, with no parity, using eight data bits with one stop bit:

```
MODE COM2: 96,n,8,1,r
```

The last parameter value, **r,** requests that DOS automatically try again to send data to a communications port when the first request is met by a control signal indicating that the device is still busy processing the last transmission. This setting is particularly useful with printers, which process data significantly slower than the computer's central processing unit.

This version of the **MODE** command is disk-resident, but it does require that a permanent part of physical memory be reserved for its processing and buffering chores. This means that when you run the command for the first time, it will take up a small additional amount of memory, extending the memory requirements of your DOS's memory-resident portion.

Programs that act in this manner are called terminate-and-stay-resident, or TSR, programs. Whenever you want to run such a program, you should first exit completely from the shell by pressing Alt+F4, then run the program or command from the command prompt.

After the initial **MODE** command runs, DOS issues a message to confirm the port settings:

```
Resident portion of MODE loaded
COM2: 9600,n,8,1,r
```

The requested task is complete and the **MODE** command terminates for the moment. At this point you can restart the shell by typing the command **DOSSHELL**. Because certain instructions remain resident in memory to handle the communications through the port, there is now slightly less memory available for your application programs.

Normally, serial devices are accompanied by instruction manuals that describe the required settings. The best advice is to follow scrupulously the suggested settings for connection. Switches often have to be set on or in the printer, as well as on the board that is controlling your serial port itself. In addition, the software product you are using might need to be initialized as well, since it may send its data directly to the port.

All of these locations and parameters are opportunities for error or frustration in connecting serial devices to computers. Unfortunately, there is no consistent standard for serial communications as there is for parallel communications. You must determine the characteristics of your serial device and issue the proper **MODE** command *before* using the port in any way. Good luck!

➤ **EXTRA!**

Reconfiguring Your Hardware
Connections with CTTY

If you have a special system configuration or another workstation connected through one of the auxiliary serial ports (AUX, COM1, COM2, COM3, or COM4), the **CTTY** command can change the current input and output device (which is usually the keyboard and screen) to something else. The proper format to use the command is:

```
CTTY Device
```

where *Device* is any valid device name.

Note that the keyboard and monitor will be reset as the main console when you use programs that do not use DOS-function calls. Also, be careful—since specifying a noninput device such as LPT1 in a **CTTY** command will hang the system. The computer will try to input data from this port, which cannot be done.

Those of you who write batch files may occasionally use output redirection to discard unwanted and distracting messages. For example, you may have a series of command lines such as:

```
COPY %1 %2 > NUL
XCOPY C:\*.* /S E: > NUL
```

Rather than type **> NUL** at the end of each of perhaps many individual commands, you can nest the entire sequence of commands in two **CTTY** commands:

```
CTTY NUL
Command Line 1
Command Line 2
Etc.
CTTY CON
```

This will have the same effect as each of the individual NUL redirections, yet be easier to type. However, be aware that if your batch file crashes before the **CTTY CON** command executes, you will not be able to regain control of your system at your keyboard without rebooting your machine. So don't even think about using this technique unless you've completely debugged the batch file, and are very confident that it will not crash. Even then, think twice before giving up control of your keyboard to this advanced technique.

Controlling the Mode of the Video Display

Certain video characteristics can be controlled with the following version of the **MODE** command. This version is used most often when you purchase nonstandard equipment, when you connect multiple monitors to your computer, or when you are using older equipment such as CGA or EGA monitors. The command is used to tell DOS which monitor is receiving the video-display request; it also allows you to adjust the video image in several ways. It does not work for all types of monitors.

To control both the number of lines and columns shown on your video monitor, you can use this version of the **MODE** command:

```
MODE CON: LINES=xx COLS=yy
```

All monitors can accept a value of 40 or 80 for *xx*, which determines whether 40 double-size characters or 80 standard-size characters appear on each line.

To use the **LINES** switch, you must have previously installed the ANSI.SYS device driver (see Chapter 9) in your CONFIG.SYS file. The **LINES** parameter can take values of *25* (the standard on all monitors),

43 (an EGA option), or *50* (only available on VGA or higher resolution monitors).

If your monitor accepts one of the two higher numbers, then you can squeeze more lines of information onto a single screen. This has an obvious advantage of providing more output data at a single go, but has the distinct disadvantage of being harder to read for most viewers.

The **COLS=80** mode is the standard for business applications, although some games reset the mode to 40 columns. Naturally, the **COLS=40** mode produces larger, more legible characters on the video monitor. This can be handy for users with vision problems.

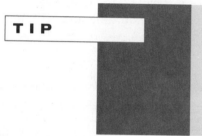

TIP

If you use 40-column mode with your word processor in order to have larger, more legible text on your monitor, remember to reset your margins as necessary to standard width before printing your documents. (Note that not all application software will adhere to the 40-column video setting.)

Changing the LINES or COLS values for your video console will not affect the current status of the monitor's color. You can explicitly enable or disable color by preceding the column number by **CO** (to enable color) or **BW** (to disable color, leaving a black-and-white image). If you have an IBM monochrome display, the proper parameter value is **MONO**. In fact, if your system has both a monochrome *and* a color monitor, you can switch output between them by simply entering

```
MODE MONO
```

to switch output to the monochrome monitor, and

```
MODE CO80
```

to switch output to the color monitor, using 80 columns with color enabled.

Setting Your Keyboard's "Typematic" Rate

The "typematic" keyboard repetition feature of the **MODE** command enables you to set the rate at which a keystroke is repeated as you hold a key down. It also enables you to specify the delay time that DOS will wait before the repetitions begin.

You can submit the **MODE** command using the special **RATE** and **DELAY** optional parameters:

```
MODE CON SetRate SetDelay
```

As a simple example, the following entry will set the typematic rate to two repetitions per second and the delay time for automatic repetitions to one second:

```
MODE CON RATE=1 DELAY=4
```

The *SetRate* parameter actually ranges from a value of 1, standing for 2 repetitions per second, to a value of 32, standing for 30 repetitions per second. (You can consult your DOS user's manual for a detailed listing of all possible settings for these parameters.) The range of values for the *SetDelay* parameter varies from 1 to 4, standing for delay times of $1/4$, $1/2$, $3/4$, and 1 second.

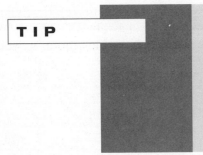

TIP

Create a DOSKEY macro to easily and quickly speed up your keyboard to its maximum settings: DOSKEY KEYFAST=MODE CON RATE=32 DELAY=1. That way you won't have to remember the particular parameters for the MODE command. You'll be able to just type KEYFAST to speed up your keyboard to its maximum values.

➤ EXTRA!

BBS Users—Save Time and Effort after Downloading!

After downloading several zipped files from a Bulletin Board System, you usually cannot unzip (decompress) the files in the same directory, because some file names are repeated (e.g., README). The OPENZIP.BAT batch file lets you specify a zipped file name as parameter 1. It then creates a directory of the same name, changes to that directory, and unzips the ZIP file within that subdirectory.

This program assumes that PKUNZIP.EXE is on your DOS path, and that you specify just the base name as the first parameter. For example, if you've downloaded a zipped file called TETWIN.ZIP, you would type:

```
OPENZIP TETWIN
```

Here's the OPENZIP.BAT batch file:

```
@ECHO OFF
Rem OPENZIP.BAT PKunzips programs into their own directories.
Rem Requires PKUNZIP.EXE to be on your PATH.
Rem Syntax: OPENZIP filename.zip
MD %1
CD %1
PKUNZIP ..\%1
CD ..
```

Summary

This chapter covered important communications aspects of DOS. Output from your system is fundamental to effectiveness, and in this chapter you learned quite a bit about data transfer and system output in general. Here is a brief review:

- Files and hardware devices share certain similarities, which permits you to use them interchangeably in a number of commands.

- Devices communicate with the central processing unit of your computer in one of two ways: by parallel or serial data transmission. Parallel communications send data bits out to a device on separate wires simultaneously. Serial communications send the same data bits out to a device on a single wire successively, using additional control characters and bits to help distinguish when and where the transmission and characters begin and end.

- Each bit of magnetic memory—that is, each data bit—can be either energized with a voltage or not energized, with a value of 1 or 0, respectively. Eight bits make up the proverbial byte, and each byte can represent up to 256 different codes. These codes can represent either standard letters, numbers, and punctuation, or special control codes, foreign-language characters, and graphics characters.

- DOS can send and receive bytes of information to and from three parallel devices connected to hardware ports. These devices and their parts are addressed by programs as LPT1, LPT2, and LPT3.

- DOS can send data to and accept data from as many as four separate devices connected to four serial communications ports. These serial ports are addressed by the names COM1, COM2, COM3, and COM4.

- The **MODE** command is the principal DOS command for controlling serial communications. It handles both the setup and status of certain serial and parallel output devices. It is also necessary in order to properly initialize the communications between a computer and a printer or plotter. Several parameters defining the command must be carefully set in order to synchronize the CPU and the device, or the data transfer may not work at all. The parameters include the baud rate, the parity of the transmission, the number of data bits and stop bits, and the transmission instructions for handling busy ports.

- Another version of the **MODE** command allows you to control multiple display monitors, which can be either color or black-and-white and can display either 40 or 80 columns across.

- The **MODE** command also lets you set the keyboard repetition (typematic) rate and the delay time before repetitions begin.

By now you've certainly learned many new things about DOS and have no doubt begun to use your disk and hardware capabilities more efficiently. In the next chapter, you'll take a look at some possibilities for customizing and optimizing the DOS system that you have created so far.

Customizing:
Optimizing DOS for
Your System

SO FAR, everything you've seen about DOS has been clearly defined. Every feature has had a concrete definition and strict limits on how it could be used and what results you could expect. Behind the scenes, however, there are several additional aspects to DOS itself that have considerable flexibility, and that you can control.

DOS is like your home: you can walk in and accept everything as it is, or you can adjust the environment to your liking. In your home, you can open some windows and close others, you can turn the lights on or off, you can set the thermostat to a different temperature; you can even rearrange the furniture. DOS also has a certain way in which it appears when you walk in, or start it up. This internal configuration, and how you can adjust it, is the subject of this chapter.

In DOS, you can customize your system in many ways. In this chapter you'll focus on customizing some of the inner workings of DOS itself. In later chapters (12, 13, and 14) you will concentrate on the batch-file mechanism for complete online adjustments.

Even if your system has already been customized by someone else, you can use the information presented in this chapter to revise the customizing settings. If you're concerned about losing the former customizing settings, make a copy of the CONFIG.SYS and AUTOEXEC.BAT files before making any changes to them. If you name the copies **CONFIG.BAK** and **AUTOEXEC.BAK**, you can always restore the previous configuration. To do that, you only need to rename (or delete) your changed CONFIG.SYS and AUTOEXEC.BAT, then restore your backed-up versions, using the following four commands in sequence:

```
RENAME CONFIG.SYS CONFIG.NEW
RENAME AUTOEXEC.BAT AUTOEXEC.NEW
RENAME CONFIG.BAK CONFIG.SYS
RENAME AUTOEXEC.BAK AUTOEXEC.BAT
```

Using the CONFIG.SYS file, you can optimize memory usage (see Chapter 17) and you can enhance performance (see Chapter 18). In this chapter, you'll look at other mechanisms to improve overall system efficiency. You'll learn how to protect your system from viruses, fully control system bootup alternatives, and double the available space on your hard (and floppy!) disks.

You'll also use CONFIG.SYS to load additional drivers such as ANSI.SYS, which enables you to redefine keys and control the display.

You can create RAM disks, emulate expanded memory, and move much of DOS's own work into available extra memory, freeing up conventional memory for your important application programs. In this chapter, you'll learn all these customization methods.

➤ EXTRA!

Save Copies of Your Most Important System Files Automatically!

Whenever you or any application programs adjust the system's CONFIG.SYS file, there is the possibility of later difficulties. You can always try to remember to make a backup of CONFIG.SYS and AUTOEXEC.BAT, but you may not always remember. One technique that can help is to include the following line in your AUTOEXEC.BAT file:

```
COPY C:\*.* C:\ROOTCOPY
```

First, you should create a new directory named ROOTCOPY in the root of your boot drive. Each time you power up, the current versions of all your root directory files will be copied to the ROOTCOPY directory. If you discover a problem in any session, just change to the ROOTCOPY directory to obtain the former version of your affected file(s).

Using the CONFIG.SYS File

When a microcomputer is turned on, it runs through a well-defined sequence of steps. At the end of this procedure, you are ready to use your system and run your applications. Figure 9.1 depicts the entire startup procedure.

First, your hardware runs through a built-in "bootstrap" program. The time-consuming part of a typical bootstrap is a memory test. The more memory you have, the longer the test will take; if you ever expand the memory of your system, you will probably notice the difference.

Following the memory test, the bootstrap attempts to find the disk-resident portion of DOS (within the COMMAND.COM file and in the two hidden system files IO.SYS and MSDOS.SYS) on one of the drives in the system, usually beginning with drive A. That is why the light on drive A comes on before the hard drive is accessed, even if you have a hard disk. It is also why anyone can circumvent a menu system set up on your hard disk—one can always place a DOS system disk in drive A, boot the system from that disk, and then access any files on the hard disk.

When the system drive is found (the one that has a copy of the DOS files on it), the computer reads the information into its memory. The next thing DOS does is to scan the root directory of the drive from which it has read the DOS files for a special file called CONFIG.SYS. If this file is not present, DOS initializes your system according to built-in default values. If a file called AUTOEXEC.BAT exists (see Chapter 14 for a detailed explanation of this file), DOS then proceeds with the instructions in that file and displays the DOS prompt (usually A> or C>, depending on which drive contained the system files).

If a CONFIG.SYS file is present in the root directory DOS scans, it will contain a list of special statements that define a nonstandard system

Power-up procedures on a DOS system include system checking of memory chips (during a "cold boot"), loading of the resident portion of DOS, establishing the configuration of device drivers and internal DOS table sizes, and initial activation of some programs.

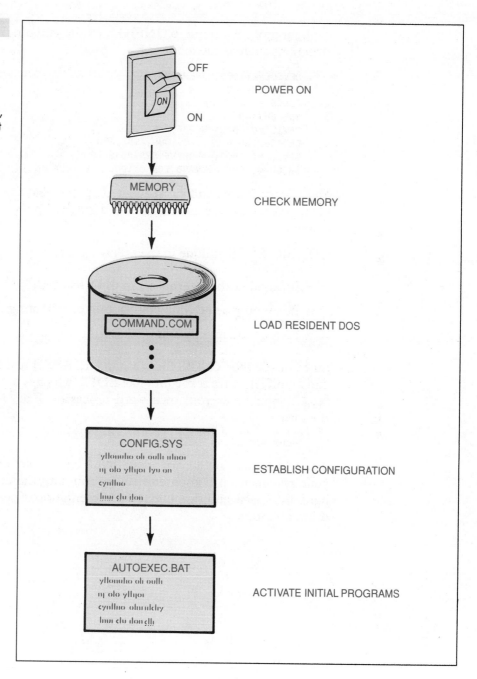

configuration. A sample CONFIG.SYS file contains a series of text instructions such as the following:

```
DEVICE=C:\DOS\HIMEM.SYS
DOS=HIGH,UMB
FILES = 40
BUFFERS=40
DEVICE=C:\DOS\EMM386.EXE NOEMS
DEVICEHIGH = /L:1 C:\DOS\ANSI.SYS
DEVICE=C:\DOS\RAMDRIVE.SYS 2048 /E
SHELL=C:\DOS\COMMAND.COM C:\DOS\ /E:1024 /p
```

You'll learn in this and subsequent chapters what the commands in this file represent, as well as a number of additional possibilities for your own system.

CONFIG.SYS is unique in the following ways:

- It can alter the internal setup of DOS itself.
- It can only be activated by booting or rebooting the computer.
- It can contain only a limited set of commands.

Since the CONFIG.SYS file is a standard ASCII text file, you can create and modify it with a text editor like **EDIT** (which is provided with DOS—see Chapter 6) or your own word processor. Each line in this file has the form

Command=Value

The commands you'll learn about in this chapter are critical to protecting your system from computer viruses, doubling the amount of available hard disk space, and simplifying the presentation of configuration choices during bootup.

➤ **EXTRA!**

The SHELL Command Has Unexpected Power!

The **SHELL** command is not always needed on a DOS system, but it does offer some useful capabilities. In fact, the key switches I'll talk about here have to do with the command processor that is specified in the **SHELL** command itself. The **SHELL** command specifies the location and name of the command processor to use, and the subsequent switches are readily recognized by the command processor that is specified.

Many of you already know about the **/E** switch, which enables you to specify an environment that is larger than the usual default. Applications that require you to set many environmental variables often need extra space. My system has a number of such programs, so my CONFIG.SYS's **SHELL** command uses a **/E:1024** switch setting to ensure that 1024 bytes are reserved for the environmental variable values.

Undocumented features are sometimes documented in later versions. Microsoft does not guarantee that it will support any undocumented feature, but here's an unusual one that is so helpful, I've installed it in my CONFIG.SYS file. The **/F** switch directs DOS to default to a choice of "Fail" whenever an error condition would otherwise display the "Abort, Retry, Fail" message.

Instead of waiting for you to choose one of these three options, DOS will default to Fail and merely return to a command prompt, displaying the message:

```
Current drive is no longer valid.
```

This is a power-user's convenience, enabling you to conveniently and quickly go on with your work without the minor annoyance of responding to this bothersome question. Of course, you can never know what underlies the appearance of an "Abort, Retry, Fail" message. If it is as simple as a disk drive not being ready, this technique can be a time-saving one. Realize, however, that this message might appear because of some grievous internal problem in one of your applications. In that case, proceeding through the automatic choosing of Fail could cause damage to the data that program is managing.

Protecting Your System from Computer Viruses

Computer viruses are like real viruses—they can wreak havoc or they can just be annoying. In many cases, they come and go quickly. In other cases, they linger indefinitely. Usually, their origin is unknown. Fortunately, there are preventive measures you can take before your system is infected. And there are curative measures you can take if a virus successfully invades your system.

In this section, you'll learn about the **VSAFE** program, which is a memory-resident program included with your DOS system. It can guard your system against the unwanted effects of virus intruders. You'll also learn about the **MSAV** program (**M**icro**S**oft **A**nti-**V**irus), which can detect existing system viruses and clear them out of your system after detection.

As you'll learn shortly, you should use the MSAV program to regularly detect the possible existence of viruses. If you are willing to give up the memory required for the VSAFE program, then you can have the protection enabled continuously.

Preventing Viruses in Advance

Viruses invade your system in different ways. If the virus is contained within a data file, it can be transmitted onto your system if you unwittingly open the file and attempt to use it in one of your applications. If the file is contained in the boot sector of a disk, it can easily spread to any diskette that is read from or written onto in that infected computer. Carrying the infected disk to another computer generally spreads the virus to that other computer system.

Once a virus has been introduced into your system, it can spread in a variety of ways. Understanding these ways is the key to preventing viruses from gaining a foothold on your system in the first place. Typically, the ways in which viruses subsequently spread is the same way in which your system is initially infected.

> **EXTRA!**

The Doctor Is Out When It Comes to Computer Viruses!

In real life, a virus is itself a microorganism. It gets into your body and tries to do its own thing. That may produce unwanted coughs, headaches, or unusual and uncomfortable symptoms. In a computer, a virus is not unlike a miniature organism. Your normal computer software represents the usual application functions. A virus is generally a small block of coded instructions that somehow obtain control of your computer's CPU and direct it to perform unusual and often uncomfortable actions.

Some viruses consist of coded commands that produce humorous or nasty messages. These are annoying but not destructive. Other viruses are more malicious, destroying your data files or your hard disks. The most common way in which viruses are classified is to place them in one of three categories, depending on how they seem to infect a computer system.

A *boot-sector virus* is a 512-byte block of code that has somehow replaced the boot sector of your computer. It performs the usual booting control operations, so it is difficult for you to recognize the infection. Unfortunately, such a virus can do just about anything it wants. Once your computer boots up, the virus is always resident in memory. Since it is in immediate control of your system at power-up time, it can infect every disk on your system, including each new diskette that is processed on any diskette drive.

A *file infector virus* is a block of infected code that is maliciously added to an executable program or driver file, such as those with .EXE, .COM, or .SYS extensions. This virus can only be activated when the infected program is actually run. However, depending on the nature of the virus, it once again can do whatever it likes once it's been activated and becomes memory-resident.

A *trojan horse virus* is a visible but disguised virus program. It may be given to you under certain pretenses, such as a program whose intention is to produce a particular result. However, when you actually run the program, it produces a far more debilitating and unexpected result such as erasing a file or a directory, or even formatting your entire hard disk!

There are many good suggestions for minimizing the likelihood of virus infection. But this advice can sometimes be constrictive, and other times be bothersome:

- Don't use programs that were obtained from a BBS, user group, or a friend. Naturally, this requires some temperance, since even commercial products sometimes arrive with a virus in place. Whenever you *do* use new programs, scan them first with **MSAV**.

- Write-protect your COMMAND.COM file. It is one of the most frequent targets of attack for viruses, since all systems must contain a COMMAND.COM file.

- Place write-protection (tabs for 5¼" diskettes, slide switches for 3½" diskettes) on all original program diskettes. Do not store data on these original diskettes.

- Inspect any new disks before using them. Use the **MSAV** program discussed below.

- Install a sentry-type program like **VSAFE**, especially if you frequently use programs, files, or disks from other systems on your computer.

TIP

Windows users of VSAFE should be sure to load the necessary TSR program by adding (or modifying) the appropriate WIN.INI line: LOAD=MWAVTSR.EXE. Including this line will facilitate the display of VSAFE messages to you while Windows is running.

DOS offers the VSAFE program for continuous monitoring of virus infection. This memory-resident program uses 22K of memory if you choose to install it on your system through your AUTOEXEC.BAT file. Using one or more special invocation options, you can ask VSAFE to display a warning when it finds evidence of possible virus infection. To install the program in memory, use this syntax:

```
VSAFE /[option[+ | -] ...] /NE /NX /Ax /Cx /N /D /U
```

where the *option* value controls how VSAFE monitors for viruses. Use a plus or minus sign (**+** or **-**) after the option value to turn that option on or off. There are eight possible options, and seven possible switches. All of them are briefly described in Table 9.1.

TABLE 9.1: Options for the VSAFE program

OPTION	EXPLANATION
/?	Displays help text
/1	Warns about hard-disk low-level format (Default=On)
/2	Warns of resident virus (Default=Off)
/3	Establishes general write protection (Default=Off)
/4	Checks infected files (Default=On)
/5	Warns of boot-sector infection (Default=On)
/6	Protects the hard-disk boot area (Default=On)
/7	Protects the floppy-disk boot area (Default=Off)
/8	Establishes write protection for executable files (Default=On)
/A*x*	Use Alt+*x* as the hotkey
/C*x*	Use Ctrl+*x* as the hotkey
/D	Disables creation of a checksum
/N	Network driver will be loaded after VSAFE
/NE	No expanded memory should be used
/NX	No extended memory should be used
/U	Unloads VSAFE from memory

As you can see, you needn't specify any of the first eight options at all, if the default settings are acceptable. As an example, you might incorporate the following line in your AUTOEXEC.BAT file to install VSAFE:

```
VSAFE /2+ /N /Av
```

This invocation (the **/2+** option setting will now be *on*) would ensure that VSAFE will warn you of any program's attempt to stay in memory. Use this if you are not expecting any memory-resident software to be installed after VSAFE is active.

The **/N** switch enables your subsequent network software to be installed without triggering a VSAFE alarm. Lastly, the **/Av** switch specifies that Alt+V is the hotkey that will later display the VSAFE status screen. The status screen displays the on/off status of the eight option settings. While that screen is visible, you can press Alt+U to "uninstall" VSAFE and remove it from memory.

Detecting Viruses on Your System

The best preventive plans can sometimes go awry. Viruses may sometimes make it onto your system. The best initial advice to deal with viruses is to:

- Run a detection program like MSAV frequently, especially if you are not running a sentry-type program all the time.

- Stay alert. If operations begin to slow down noticeably, or if occasional difficulties arise in booting or reading files, you may have a virus in its early stages. Run MSAV immediately to try to isolate and remove the virus.

The MSAV virus-detection utility can minimize the potential damage to your computer's memory or disks. It can do this by both detecting and removing viruses. To run the MSAV program, you can initiate it at any command prompt with the following command line:

```
MSAV [drive:lpath] [/Sl/C][/R][/A][/L][/N][/P][/F][/VIDEO]
```

Table 9.2 briefly explains all of the possible switch settings. You can limit the virus detection to a particular path or directory path by specifying the first parameter.

TABLE 9.2: Options for the MSAV program

OPTION	VALUE	EXPLANATION
/?		Shows help information
/A		Scans all drives other than A or B
/C		Scans disk and files for viruses; then removes any discovered viruses
/F		File names are suppressed. Use with **/N** or **/P**.
/IM		Disables mouse function
/L		Scans only local (non-network) drives other than A or B
/LE		Exchange left/right mouse-button functions
/N		No information display during scanning operations. Will display MSAV.RPT text report file, if it is created
/NGM		Use default mouse character rather than graphics symbol
/P		Uses command-line (instead of graphic) display mode
/PS2		Restores mouse cursor if it disappears
/R		Turns on the Report option, which creates MSAV.RPT to list files checked, and any viruses found and removed
/S		Scans disk and files, but does not remove any discovered viruses (without this switch, it would remove them by default)

TABLE 9.2: Options for the MSAV program (continued)

OPTION	VALUE	EXPLANATION
/video		Sets screen display mode, according to value of *video*:
	25	25 line mode (the default)
	28	28 line mode (VGA adapter only)
	43	43 line mode (EGA/VGA adapters only)
	50	50 line mode (VGA adapter only)
	60	60 line mode (Video 7 adapter only)
	IN	Use color scheme (regardless of adapter)
	BW	Use black and white scheme
	MONO	Use monochrome scheme
	LCD	Use LCD color scheme
	FF	Use fast screen updating
	BF	Display video from BIOS
	NF	Do not use alternate fonts
	BT	Allow graphic mouse in Windows

For example, to check memory (always checked by default) and all the files on drive D:, remove any viruses discovered, and create a complete summary report, enter the following line:

```
MSAV D:  /C  /R
```

If you just want to bring up the full-screen graphic interface seen in Figure 9.2, just type **MSAV** at any command prompt.

Generally, you would choose the *Select new drive* option, if the current default drive (C:, as you can see in the lower right corner) is not the one you'd like to scan. If you choose this, MSAV will display a line of drive identifiers near the top of your screen. Just highlight the one you'd like to scan, then press Enter.

FIGURE 9.2

The Microsoft Anti-Virus main screen. You can bring up MSAV any time you introduce new software into your system, or you can automate running MSAV via your AUTOEXEC.BAT file.

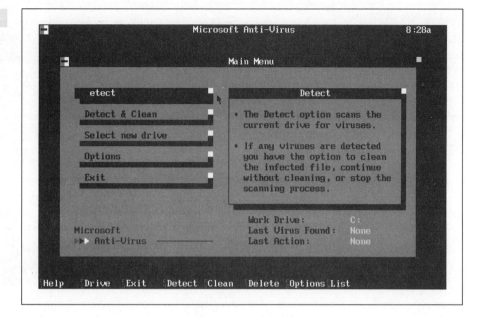

Next, you'd typically choose the *Options* choice to display the choices visible in Figure 9.3. As you can see, these options settings are equivalent to a group of switch settings from Table 9.2 that you might otherwise specify from a command line.

T I P

After running the MSAV.EXE program, you may discover the existence of a number of CHKLIST.MS files (one in each directory that is scanned). These files contain *checksums* for each executable file in the directory. Later executions of MSAV will compare checksums against the information stored in this file. If a program's checksum has changed, it is treated as a possible indication of a virus infection. This will generate a screen alert.

The first two choices speak for themselves. If you select *Detect and Clean*, the second choice, MSAV will first scan and then automatically remove

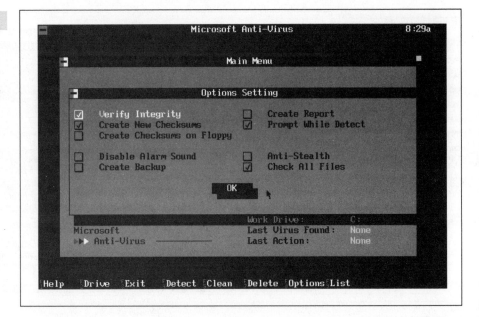

any viruses found. Selecting *Detect*, the first choice, identifies viruses found on your system. Progress windows will appear during the scanning operations to inform you of results. (Memory is scanned first; then directories and the files within them are scanned.) If any viruses are found or suspected, you'll be offered choices as to how you'd like to deal with them.

For example, Figure 9.4 depicts how MSAV noted a possible virus infection, based on the fact that my CONFIG.SYS file changed since the last run of MSAV. (CONFIG.SYS—and other executable files—are often the target of viruses.) This Verify Error window appears because I selected the *Verify Integrity* and *Prompt While Detect* options in the screen shown in Figure 9.3.

My decisions at this point are visible at the bottom of the Verify Error window.

Select *Update* if you know about the possible problem, and recognize that it is not a real virus. In my example, I chose *Update* because I knew that I

FIGURE 9.4

MSAV identifies possible virus infections with the Verify Error window. If the identified change is OK, press *Update*. If the change is undesired, press *Delete* to remove the new version of the identified file. Press *Continue* to bypass the check and explore the cause yourself.

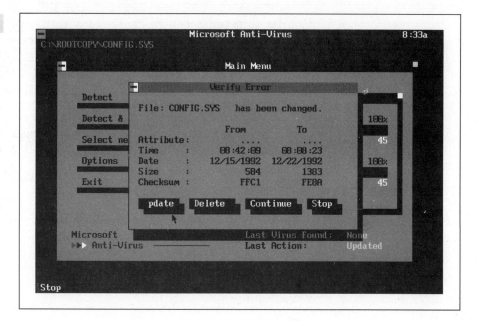

made the CONFIG.SYS changes myself. If I make no further changes to CONFIG.SYS in the future, subsequent runs of the MSAV will no longer alert me because the internal data stored by MSAV will have been updated.

Select *Delete* if you wish to delete the currently existing (and possibly infected) CONFIG.SYS file. MSAV will restore your previous version of CONFIG.SYS. If you want to conduct your own explorations, neither deleting nor confirming the validity of CONFIG.SYS, just choose *Continue*. The virus scanning will continue, but the internal MSAV data will not be updated. A future run of MSAV will similarly alert you to a changed CONFIG.SYS file.

If you receive a Verify Error window and cannot immediately determine what you should do, it may be safest to choose *Stop*. This stops scanning and allows you to immediately launch some form of investigation.

Unlike the sometimes benign causes of a Verify Error window, when a known virus is found MSAV displays a Virus Found window. The *Update* choice you saw in Figure 9.4 would be replaced with a *Clean* choice. Select *Clean* if you wish MSAV to remove the virus from the infected file and restore the program or disk data to its original condition.

If you specified the *Create Report* option in the screen in Figure 9.3 (or the **/R** switch on a command line), MSAV would finish its scanning operations by displaying a summary screen (see Figure 9.5).

When you have finished scanning one disk, the MSAV main screen (see Figure 9.2) reappears. You can select a new drive to scan, or new options to apply to any subsequent screen. When you finally select the *Exit* choice, the Close Microsoft Anti-Virus window will appear. It offers a checkbox which can save your most recent configuration of options settings. Typically, you would want to check this box to save yourself the trouble of respecifying a desired group of options settings the next time you use the MSAV program.

FIGURE 9.5

The summary report screen after scanning is done. This is most useful if you set MSAV on automatic, requesting during option setting that it proceed to detect and clean without informing you along the way.

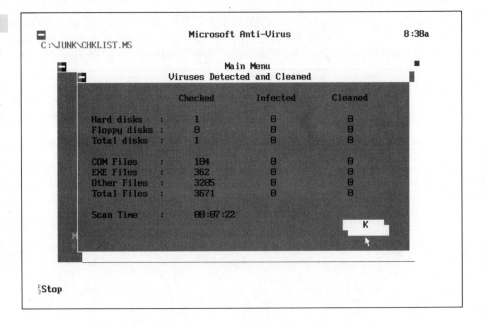

Controlling the System Startup

As you learned at the beginning of this chapter, your system's initial configuration depends on the contents of your CONFIG.SYS file. Furthermore, the contents of your AUTOEXEC.BAT file dictate which programs are first run, as well as which startup conditions (e.g., environmental variables) might be set.

T I P

When the message "Starting MS-DOS" appears, press F5 (or Shift) to completely skip all CONFIG.SYS and AUTOEXEC.BAT commands. This is called a *clean boot*. Alternatively, you can press F8 to request single command confirmation for each key line in CONFIG.SYS, with a single request to skip or run the AUTOEXEC.BAT file as well. This is called an *interactive boot*. You can disable all of these special keystroke controls by including the command SWITCHES /N in your CONFIG.SYS file. DOS will refuse to recognize the unique operations associated with pressing the F5, F8, or Shift keys during power-up processing.

In this section, you'll learn how to further control the actions of both your CONFIG.SYS and AUTOEXEC.BAT files. In particular, you'll learn how to bypass all or part of the actions of these files, and how to set up your system for multiple configurations.

Bypassing CONFIG.SYS and AUTOEXEC.BAT Commands

Unfortunately, there may be times when your system does not perform properly, or even does not perform at all. Usually, these times occur when you add new hardware or software into your computer. The documentation for these new entries into your system will sometimes suggest that you rename or remove your CONFIG.SYS and AUTOEXEC.BAT files temporarily in order to begin the process of isolating the problem.

In fact, some problems that involve CONFIG.SYS will disallow you from even starting up your computer. DOS offers an easy way to bypass *this* problem and allow you to begin the process of isolating your *computer's* problem.

To skip all commands in both CONFIG.SYS and AUTOEXEC.BAT, just press the F5 key (or the Shift key) when DOS displays the power-up message:

```
Starting MS-DOS...
```

Pressing the F5 key at this time will skip all startup commands in both of your system's critical opening control files. Naturally, DOS will start at this point but it will use certain minimum and default values. For example, since no environmental variables will be set (a chore normally performed during your AUTOEXEC.BAT processing), your system **PROMPT** will be the default boot-drive identifier (C> for example).

In addition, your search **PATH** will not be set. This means that to test out any programs, you will have to type the complete path name and file name for all executable files. At least, you will have to do this unless you manually set the path yourself at a command prompt.

The CONFIG.SYS file contains the **SHELL** command, which enables you to specify a location for COMMAND.COM if it is other than the root directory of the boot drive. Many people do this to avoid maintaining two copies of COMMAND.COM (i.e., one in the root directory, and one in the installation \DOS directory). If your CONFIG.SYS performs this chore, you'll receive a message during F5 booting that there is a:

```
Bad or missing command interpreter
```

This is easily circumvented. Just type the full path name to the command interpreter and press Enter:

```
C:\DOS\COMMAND.COM
```

The booting will continue, using this specified command interpreter for subsequent operations.

Bypassing all CONFIG.SYS and AUTOEXEC.BAT file operations also means that no installable drivers will load. That means no mouse driver, no expanded or extended memory drivers, and no removable cartridge disk systems, and so on, will load.

Hopefully, solving your system problem will not require that any of these drivers be loaded. However, if you must install drivers such as these, or programs that require these drivers to have first been loaded, you must move to the next section and bypass only some of the CONFIG.SYS and AUTOEXEC.BAT commands.

Confirming Individual Startup Commands

During the course of problem resolution, you will often wish to load some drivers and programs, while skipping others. DOS offers one more keystroke for an extra measure of control during the startup procedures.

Instead of pressing F5 to bypass all CONFIG.SYS and AUTO-EXEC.BAT commands while the "Starting MS-DOS" message appears at power-up time, you can press F8. This will offer individualized control. Each command in the CONFIG.SYS file will appear, followed by a [Y,N] request as to whether you wish DOS to process (Y) or skip (N) this command.

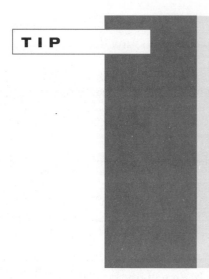

T I P

You needn't press F8 to require confirmation of individual CONFIG.SYS commands. You only need to place a question mark after a command name, and before the equals sign. Regardless of whether or not you press F8, DOS will prompt you about that particular command. For example, including DEVICE?=RCD.SYS in my CONFIG.SYS will ensure that DOS prompts me each time it boots as to whether or not to install my RCD.SYS Bernoulli cartridge disk driver. If a particular session will not be requiring it, you can just answer No. The device driver will not load and the memory otherwise used by the driver will remain available to other programs.

This mechanism is extremely helpful during tough debugging sequences. Rather than have to edit the CONFIG.SYS command file over and over again, making sure to disable (through a **REM** statement) various commands, you don't even have to make any actual changes. You just reboot, press F8, and tell DOS each time which CONFIG.SYS commands to process. This enables you to easily check any combination of commands as part of your debugging regimen.

Unfortunately, this same command-by-command decision-making is not available when the AUTOEXEC.BAT file is processed. Instead, the F8 individualized-control keystroke merely asks you (after processing your selected CONFIG.SYS commands) if you wish to:

```
Process AUTOEXEC.BAT [Y,N]?
```

If you answer Yes to this question, then DOS runs all the command lines from your AUTOEXEC.BAT file. If you answer No at this point, DOS will skip the entire set of AUTOEXEC.BAT instructions. There is no in-between.

Using a Startup Menu for Multiple Configurations

One of the most interesting and helpful facilities in DOS is the ability to create a specialized startup menu within the CONFIG.SYS file itself. This facility enables you to choose among several possible configurations when you power up your system.

In the past, if you wished to configure your system in different ways at different times, you had to create several different CONFIG.SYS files. You then had to be sure to name, rename, or relocate the preferred configuration file in the root directory of the boot drive just prior to powering up or rebooting your system.

What a pain in the neck this was. Those of you who wanted lots of memory for special DOS configurations, such as computer-aided design (CAD) projects, needed one set of CONFIG.SYS instructions. Those of you who needed a special set of drivers to support your network needed a different CONFIG.SYS. Those who wanted a unique configuration of memory-resident programs had their own CONFIG.SYS file. For Windows users, there is a wide range of optimization adjustments that are possible, making CONFIG.SYS a chameleon-like location for software tugs and tweaks.

Controlling Code Groups within CONFIG.SYS

DOS now offers a special set of configuration commands that manage the incorporation of many different system configurations within the definition of a single CONFIG.SYS file. As you'll learn below, this same multiple-configuration facility can extend to the processing of different groups of commands in your AUTOEXEC.BAT file as well. Table 9.3 summarizes the special commands themselves.

TABLE 9.3: Commands used in CONFIG.SYS startup menu blocks

COMMAND	EXPLANATION
include *BlockName*	Shorthand notation for all the commands in a different configuration block elsewhere in the CONFIG.SYS file
menucolor *Textcolor,ScreenBackground*	Sets foreground text and background screen color
menudefault *BlockName,[timeout]*	Specifies default block to execute, after either an Enter keypress, or a *timeout* (in seconds) occurs
menuitem *BlockName,[menutext]*	Specifies a configuration block name, and an optional text string to display on the startup menu
numlock *On ¦ Off*	Turns on or off the NumLock key status
submenu *BlockName,[menutext]*	Defines a second-level menu of configuration command options

Figure 9.6 shows a sample CONFIG.SYS file that has been modified to include a startup menu, some of the special commands shown in Table 9.3, and various configuration blocks. You can create your own customized CONFIG.SYS file, using this example to get you going.

The commands seen in Table 9.3 are uniquely meaningful, but only within the framework of a startup menu. As you can see in Figure 9.6, the main startup menu begins with a heading line that consists of the square bracketed expression *[Menu]*. Each line that follows the menu block header line must be one of the special commands from Table 9.3.

Although we won't discuss the possibility further, you may in fact complicate your CONFIG.SYS file to another entire level by developing submenus within existing configuration blocks. Personally, I don't recommend it, just because of the complications introduced and the much increased difficulty in later understanding the actual flow of execution through your CONFIG.SYS file.

FIGURE 9.6

A sample CONFIG.SYS with three configurations. Three menu items (*LotsOfFreeMem*, *Normal*, and *OptimumWindows*) appear at power-up. Choose one of them to force DOS to process the related (and identically named) block of commands. All configurations process *[Common]* commands.

```
[Menu]
menuitem=LotsOfFreeMem,Minimum Installation Only
menuitem=Normal,Normal DOS/Windows Installation     } STARTUP MENU
menuitem=OptimumWindows,Optimized for Windows
menudefault=Normal,20
menucolor=14,2
numlock=On

[LotsOfFreeMem]  ←──────BLOCK HEADER
DEVICE=C:\DOS\HIMEM.SYS                            }
DOS=HIGH,UMB                                        } CONFIGURATION BLOCK
FILES = 20
BUFFERS=20
DEVICE=C:\DOS\EMM386.EXE NOEMS

[Normal]
DEVICEHIGH=C:\DOS\SETVER.EXE
DEVICE=C:\DOS\HIMEM.SYS
DOS=HIGH,UMB
FILES = 40
BUFFERS=40
STACKS=34,128
LASTDRIVE = R
DEVICE=C:\DOS\EMM386.EXE NOEMS
DEVICEHIGH = /L:1 C:\DOS\ANSI.SYS
SHELL=C:\DOS\COMMAND.COM C:\DOS\ /E:1024 /p /f
devicehigh = /L:1 d:\sbpro\drv\sbpcd.sys /d:mscd001 /p:220

[OptimumWindows]
DEVICE=C:\DOS\HIMEM.SYS
DOS=HIGH,UMB
FILES = 40
BUFFERS=40
STACKS=34,128
LASTDRIVE = H
DEVICE=C:\DOS\EMM386.EXE NOEMS M9 I=B000-B7FF WIN=D700-DAFF
DEVICEHIGH = /L:2 C:\DOS\ANSI.SYS
SHELL=C:\DOS\COMMAND.COM C:\DOS\ /E:1024 /p /f
devicehigh = /L:2 d:\sbpro\drv\sbpcd.sys /d:mscd001 /p:220

[Common]
DEVICEHIGH = C:\DOS\DBLSPACE.SYS                    }
DEVICEHIGH = C:\BERNOULI\RCD.SYS /F0 /P4            } COMMON BLOCK
DEVICEHIGH = /L:1 C:\ATDOSXL.SYS
```

In essence, the lines below the [Menu] header define the nature of the menu that will appear on your screen when you boot up your computer. The *menuitem* command is the most common command line you'll use. Each menuitem defines a unique configuration block that exists elsewhere in the CONFIG.SYS file. Each separate configuration block defines a unique group of commands that will be executed if the associated menuitem choice is made by a user during power-on choices.

You define a separate menuitem command for each unique configuration you use. In the example of Figure 9.6, DOS would boot up this system and display the following menu:

```
MS-DOS 6 Startup Menu
=====================
1. Minimum Installation Only
2. Normal DOS/Windows Installation
3. Optimized for Windows
Enter a choice: 2
```

At the bottom of this same startup screen, DOS reminds you that you can further control startup processing by pressing one of the special keys just discussed in the preceding sections:

```
F5=Bypass startup files F8=Confirm each CONFIG.SYS line [No]
```

Look back at Figure 9.6 once again. You can see three menuitem command lines. Each one specifies the three text expressions that you see numbered here (as choices 1, 2, and 3). After the equals sign in the menuitem command, the first expression is treated as the name of a unique configuration block, seen only in the CONFIG.SYS file itself. There are three configuration blocks in the CONFIG.SYS of Figure 9.6, named *LotsOfFreeMem*, *Normal*, and *OptimumWindows*. Following the configuration block name with a comma enables you to then type the text that you wish to appear to the user at power-up time as a numbered choice. My three text expressions appear in the MS-DOS Startup Menu and are numbered for easy selection.

When you see the Startup Menu, one of the choices is assumed to be the default. This will always be number 1, unless you include the *menudefault* command as I have done in my Figure 9.6 example. Include the menu-default command if you wish a configuration block other than the first one to be assumed to be the default. In my example, choice 2 would be highlighted as the default, and the number 2 would appear in the "Enter a Choice" question. Pressing the Enter key would immediately begin the processing of all the commands in the configuration block named *Normal*, or whatever you've named the number 2 configuration block in your CONFIG.SYS file.

The menudefault command also allows a second parameter, which specifies how many seconds to wait for a response before defaulting to this particular choice (block 2 in this example). If you type any number when the menu appears, DOS stops its timer countdown and waits for you to press Enter to continue the CONFIG.SYS processing.

Note the use in Figure 9.6 of a *[Common]* configuration block at the end of this CONFIG.SYS file. I've placed three commands after the block header. These commands, and in fact any other commands that I later add, will always be executed regardless of which of the other three configuration blocks is selected during power-up choices. In essence, the commands found in a [Common] block are always *common* to all CONFIG.SYS command processing, just as if they had been repeated within each of the other configuration blocks.

In Figure 9.6, I've also used two other startup-menu configuration commands. The *menucolor* command specifies two colors for the foreground characters in the menu, and the background screen color. I've chosen *14,2*, which dictates yellow characters on a green screen. You can type:

```
Help menucolor
```

at any command prompt to display the series of screen colors that are alternatively allowable.

Lastly, this example CONFIG.SYS explicitly turns the NumLock key on by using the *numlock=On* menu command. Depending on whether or not you prefer to use the numeric keypad for responses, you can control whether those keystrokes will be interpreted at startup as cursor-control or numeric-entry keys.

You can also include multiple [Common] blocks if you wish, and if they make sense. DOS will execute all commands found in that block wherever you've placed it. Generally, it makes the most sense to include common commands at the beginning (i.e., FILES=, BUFFERS=, DOS=HIGH, and so on) or at the end (i.e., drivers that should always be installed in all your configurations) of a CONFIG.SYS file.

Those of you who are programmers can use a familiar command within your CONFIG.SYS file. An *Include* line can specify the name of a different configuration block. Rather than repeating the commands listed in

➤ EXTRA!

Beware of Inadequate Software Installation Programs!

Automatic installation programs that update CONFIG.SYS and AUTO-EXEC.BAT files do not always perform their updates correctly or completely. To minimize possible problems later, you should always have a *[Common]* block at the end of your CONFIG.SYS file, even if you do not have any commands that are truly common to all unique configurations.

It's okay to just have a *[Common]* line at the end of CONFIG.SYS, even if no commands follow it. This becomes very important if you later install software that updates your CONFIG.SYS file. Generally, such updates consist of added lines at the end of CONFIG.SYS. If you do not have a [Common] block awaiting the addition of such commands, they will only take effect if a user chooses the last physical configuration block in your CONFIG.SYS file. This is probably not what you actually want to happen.

In fact, some installation software may not be aware of your multiple-configuration CONFIG.SYS file at all. Since some software packages make changes to existing lines within your CONFIG.SYS file, you should check to ensure that automated installation routines have correctly modified all necessary lines, in possibly several configuration blocks. If this has not been done, you'll have to determine manually what changes are necessary and edit each of your separate configuration blocks.

that other configuration block, you can include those commands by referencing the block. For example, your CONFIG.SYS file may offer five configuration-block choices, each named by a menuitem command. If the block header names are *Windows*, *DOS*, *Network*, *WinNet*, and *DosNet*, you might save time and effort by placing the following command somewhere in the DosNet configuration block:

```
Include=DOS
Include=Network
```

This shorthand notation would ensure that, during the processing of the configuration block named DosNet, all the commands found within the DOS and the Network blocks would also be processed.

Controlling Code Groups within AUTOEXEC.BAT

Once you establish a startup menu in your CONFIG.SYS file, it then also becomes possible to control which portions of your AUTOEXEC.BAT file are executed. This ability relies on the fact that DOS manages multiple configurations by creating an environmental variable named *CONFIG*. Its value is equal to the block header of the choice you make from the startup menu that appears during bootup.

For example, suppose you select choice 2 from the startup menu created in Figure 9.6. DOS would create the CONFIG environmental variable and set it equal to *Normal*, since this is the block header name assigned to the second startup menu item. It's as if you had incorporated the following **SET** command in your CONFIG.SYS file:

```
SET CONFIG=Normal
```

What this now means is that you can use labels and conventional flow-of-control commands in your AUTOEXEC.BAT file to determine which groups of commands will be executed there. Figure 9.7 depicts my AUTOEXEC.BAT file, which relies on the known configuration group names seen earlier in the associated CONFIG.SYS file. (Note that the **PROMPT** line has been split only to fit it all into the figure width.)

This AUTOEXEC.BAT file always performs the instructions at the beginning of the file, which set **ECHO** off, make a backup copy of the files in the root directory, and load the UNDELETE utility in upper memory. At that point, the **GOTO** command transfers control to one of three labeled blocks of code.

FIGURE 9.7

Controlling configuration-group processing in AUTOEXEC.BAT. Use the **GOTO** command and the *CONFIG* environmental variable to direct the flow of control to an appropriate block of instructions. DOS sets CONFIG equal to the menuitem name that was selected by you during powerup.

```
@ECHO OFF
REM These commands always execute:
COPY C:\*.* C:\ROOTCOPY > NUL
LOADHIGH C:\DOS\UNDELETE /LOAD
PATH C:\DOS;D:\WINDOWS;C:\;C:\UTILITY

REM Choose the same section as CONFIG.SYS startup
GOTO %CONFIG%
:LotsOfFreeMem
rem Don't load any of the optional TSRs
Goto Common

:Normal
c:\dos\mscdex /v /d:mscd001 /m:15
loadhigh d:\windows\mouse
loadhigh C:\PCACHE\PCACHE
C:\DOS\smartdrv /L
PROMPT $p$g
LOADHIGH C:\DOS\DOSKEY /BUFSIZE=2048
CALL C:\SIG1D\DOCS\DOS6\MACROS.BAT
Goto Common

:OptimumWindows
d:\sbpro\drv\mscdex /v /d:mscd001 /m:15
loadhigh d:\windows\mouse
loadhigh C:\PCACHE\PCACHE
C:\DOS\smartdrv /L
PROMPT $e[s$e[H$e[1B$e[K$e[H$e[K$e[1;24H$e[1;37;41mCalc,Calendr
,Seekeasy,Ring,Dazzle$e[H$e[1;32;40m$t$e[1;67H$d$e[u$p$g$e[K

:Common
set comspec=c:\command.com
set dircmd=/on
set qdos=c:\utility
set qlog=c:\utility
set temp=c:\
set backit=c:\backit4
set bkout=c:\backit4
set nu=c:\norton
set sound=d:\sbpro
set blaster=a220 i2 d1 t2
:End
```

TIP

Some of your batch files (see Chapters 12, 13, and 14) can now incorporate sophisticated decision-making based on the configuration chosen at power-up time. Just make your IF tests based on the value of the *CONFIG* environmental variable.

The transfers of control depend on the text value contained in the CONFIG variable. If a user had selected choice 1 from Figure 9.6, the screen choice would have read:

```
1. Minimum Installation Only
```

and DOS would already have executed the instructions inside the configuration block headed by *[LotsOfFreeMem]* in CONFIG.SYS. Now that processing has flowed to this point in the AUTOEXEC.BAT file, the **GOTO** command transfers control to a label with the same name. As you can see in Figure 9.7, the labeled block *:LotsOfFreeMem* in AUTOEXEC.BAT does nothing. None of the optional memory-resident programs are loaded, leaving a good deal of available memory for application processing that doesn't require any of these TSRs that will not be loaded.

If the user had earlier selected choices 2 or 3 during CONFIG.SYS processing, the AUTOEXEC.BAT processing would either flow to the label marked *:Normal* or the one marked *:OptimumWindows*. As you can see, the :Normal processing here involves loading four memory-resident programs, setting the **PROMPT**, loading one more TSR, and finally executing the MACROS.BAT file.

The :OptimumWindows processing involves loading the same first four TSRs, setting a different **PROMPT**, not loading the final TSR, and not running the MACROS.BAT program. When running a Windows-based system, this configuration saves conventional memory by loading the DOSKEY utility and initializing the macros within a DOS session.

Notice that, after all the separate blocks of code in AUTOEXEC.BAT, there is an explicit instruction that directs control to flow to the *:Common* statement. Although the final block doesn't require such an instruction, this code mechanism ensures clean and easily readable code. All the final commands listed after :Common are executed at the end of AUTOEXEC.BAT, regardless of which configuration has been selected.

Using Device Drivers to Customize DOS

The CONFIG.SYS file is also used to load additional software *drivers* into DOS. Drivers are special-purpose programs which can control specific peripheral devices, or which can manage special functionality. DOS can't be responsible for knowing all the control codes for all possible external devices; operating systems in general leave the details of communicating with and controlling these devices to the special driver programs.

Drivers extend the command range of DOS. Naturally, they also take up more memory, which is one reason why they are optional. On my system, I include drivers for a plug-in 105Mb hard disk from Plus Development Corporation, a CD-ROM reader from Sony Corporation, and a cartridge-disk subsystem from Bernoulli Corporation.

Also on my system, I include drivers for two special features that are available to any DOS users. The first is the DBLSPACE.SYS driver, which is arguably the most attractive new feature of DOS 6. It enables you to nearly double the usable space on your hard, floppy, and removable cartridge disks. The second is a driver called ANSI.SYS, which extends the functions of DOS to include reprogramming or redefinition of keys and screen colors in DOS.

NOTE

Do not use the DEVICE command to load COUNTRY.SYS or KEYBOARD.SYS; these files are loaded automatically by DOS when it boots up.

DOS also has a driver that is used to create a *RAM disk* (sometimes called a *virtual disk*). The RAM disk is not really a disk—it is an area in memory that simulates the operations of an additional disk drive. Using this driver can dramatically improve the performance of your DOS system.

A critical aspect of this mechanism is that any files placed on the RAM disk are really memory-resident. They can therefore be retrieved at the speed of memory, which is usually microseconds or nanoseconds. Files on actual mechanical disk drives are slower, usually in the millisecond range. The difference in speed can be noticeable over the course of accessing the millions of bits of data that might be required in some operations. See Chapter 18 for an in-depth discussion of establishing and using RAM disks.

Doubling the Amount of Usable Disk Space

This is probably the best and most useful tool in DOS 6, at least for the great majority of DOS system users. The **DBLSPACE** command offers you an easy mechanism to nearly double the usable space on your hard disks, removable hard disk cartridges, and even on your floppy drives. If you don't have DOS 6 at this moment, go out and buy it immediately. The convenience and power of DBLSPACE will more than pay for itself immediately.

The very first time you type **DBLSPACE** from a command prompt, the DoubleSpace Setup program will execute. You'll receive a screen that offers two choices:

```
Express Setup (recommended)
Custom Setup
```

You should accept the *Express Setup* choice this first time, and Double-Space will compress your normal and current boot drive. Virtually every system has at least one hard disk, from which normal booting occurs. DoubleSpace can dramatically increase the available space for files on this disk.

As you can see in Figure 9.8, the DoubleSpace Setup program displays a confirmation screen after you select *Express Setup*. You must press *C* to compress the selected drive (by default, the boot drive C:), or you can press Esc to withdraw the request.

The more file space that is in use on a drive that you want to compress, the more time it will take DoubleSpace to compress it. In the case of

FIGURE 9.8

DoubleSpace estimates the time required to compress a drive. All existing files and directories will be compressed into a single hidden file, usually named DBLSPACE.000.

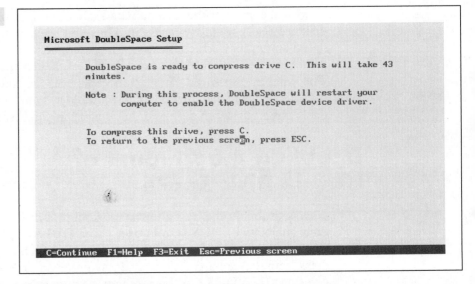

```
Microsoft DoubleSpace Setup

        DoubleSpace is ready to compress drive C.  This will take 43
        minutes.

        Note : During this process, DoubleSpace will restart your
               computer to enable the DoubleSpace device driver.


        To compress this drive, press C.
        To return to the previous screen, press ESC.




    C=Continue   F1=Help   F3=Exit   Esc=Previous screen
```

Figure 9.8, for my drive C:, DoubleSpace had to compress over 70Mb of disk space. It estimated about three quarters of an hour to compress, but the final result was over 140Mb of usable space on the same drive.

The DoubleSpace Setup program compresses your hard disk drive and loads the DBLSPACE.BIN program into memory. DBLSPACE.BIN is the actual portion of your DOS system that provides access to compressed drives.

After this initial setup sequence, you can always just type **DBLSPACE** at any command prompt to start the DoubleSpace program in full-screen interface mode. In this graphic mode, DoubleSpace can list all available drives and provide menu access to various compression facilities.

It is possible to activate all of DoubleSpace's tasks via the pull-down menus in the full-screen mode, or by specifying appropriate switches when entering **DBLSPACE** from a command prompt. Table 9.4 lists and explains all of the **DBLSPACE** command-prompt switch values. In the course of this section, you'll learn the pull-down menu choices for the most important of these options.

TABLE 9.4: DBLSPACE command-line switches

SWITCH	EXPLANATION
/CHKDSK	Checks validity of internal file structure
/COMPRESS	Compresses a hard disk or a mounted floppy disk
/CREATE	Creates new compressed drive in existing disk's free space
/DEFRAGMENT	Optimizes the organization of a compressed disk
/DELETE	Removes a compressed drive permanently
/FORMAT	Formats a compressed drive
/INFO	Displays miscellaneous status information
/LIST	Displays list of non-network drives on your system
/MOUNT	Makes compressed files available on a removable disk
/RATIO	Modifies a drive's estimated compression ratio
/SIZE	Modifies the megabyte size of a DoubleSpace drive
/UNMOUNT	Administrative support for physically removing a compressed volume

Understanding What DoubleSpace Really Does

Compression techniques have become increasingly common on PC computer system. Most of these methods enable you to squeeze out of a file the many blank-space and redundant characters that account for so much wasted disk space. Naturally, there are many additional aspects to compression beyond simply eliminating the redundancy involved with repeated characters.

Until now, most compression methods were used to save space in backup media, or to reduce the size of the data that is transmitted over phone lines. This reduced both the cost of the communications and the time spent waiting for a particular amount of data to be transmitted or received. Now, however, DOS offers a dramatic new way to effectively use compression techniques.

The DOS 6 DoubleSpace utility enables you to gain the benefits of compression technology with none of the usual burdens of having to actually compress your file data. In fact, once you establish or activate the Double-Space compression facility for a particular drive, you don't have to do anything different at all. Just reference your files and drives by their familiar

► EXTRA!

Behind the Scenes with DoubleSpace

DOS includes a number of memory-resident capabilities. The DBL-SPACE.BIN file, found in your DOS directory, constitutes the control portion of MS-DOS that gives you access to your compressed drives.

At power-up time, DOS loads the DBLSPACE.BIN file into memory. It does this before it executes any other commands from your CONFIG.SYS and AUTOEXEC.BAT files. Since it must load before anything else, it always occupies a small part of conventional memory: access to upper memory is not provided until the necessary device drivers themselves load up during CONFIG.SYS processing.

You can see, after installing DoubleSpace, that there will be a device driver command in your CONFIG.SYS file that loads up a DBLSPACE.SYS file. This driver does not itself provide access to your compressed drives and files. This .SYS file only does the job of defining where the actual control file (DBLSPACE.BIN) resides in your system's memory. If you use a standard **DEVICE** command to load DBLSPACE.SYS, then DBLSPACE.BIN will be moved to a location in the bottom of conventional memory. If you use a **DEVICEHIGH** command to load DBLSPACE.SYS, and if you have a sufficient number of free upper memory blocks, DBLSPACE.BIN will be moved into upper memory, and will execute its compressed-drive control functions from there.

names and identifiers, and you'll never have to know what, how, or when the data was ever compressed.

You'll just gain the benefit of having much more available disk space than you could have believed possible. That 80Mb hard disk that you thought was getting a bit tight may now have 70Mb of free space, as if you had bought a 160Mb hard disk in the first place. Figure 9.9 depicts how the DoubleSpace mechanism appears to you as a user.

Your disk is still the same physical size it always was. But **DBLSPACE** compresses the free space on the disk so that it can store about twice the former amount of information. Using what it calls its *estimated compression ratio*, it guesses that about twice as much file information will be able to be compressed and then stored on the drive. As you later create files and directories, the DBLSPACE.BIN portion of DOS compresses the data as it writes on the disk.

In fact, the actual compression varies slightly according to the disk you are using, and the nature of the data being compressed. You'll see shortly that

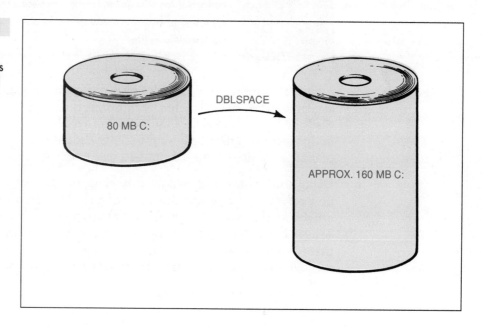

the compression ratio on my drive C: averages out to be approximately 1.7 to 1, while the estimated ratio for future files is still assumed by DOS to be 2 to 1. Actual compression calculation is based on the original size of the files before and the final size of the stored files after compression. On my disk below, I've gained seventy percent additional space with an actual compression of 1.7 to 1.

Estimated compression is a ratio, which you can increase or decrease, that is used to calculate how much additional, usable space remains on the compressed drive. Although we won't cover compression-ratio modification any further here, it is one of the many subtle controls you can exercise in how you use the DoubleSpace facility.

TIP

If you seem to run out of room on a compressed drive, even though a CHKDSK display suggests that you should have more room, then the estimated compression ratio is set too high. You'll need to reduce it (as discussed in the next section of this chapter) to bring it more into line with the actual compression ratio.

Figure 9.10 shows how DoubleSpace performs its magic. First, it finds an available drive identifier. In the figure, it is drive H:, but it could just as easily be drive L:, as is the case with another DoubleSpace drive seen later in this section. This newly acquired drive identifier is assigned to your actual physical drive, and maintained by DoubleSpace.

Using a mechanism known as *drive swapping*, DoubleSpace tells DOS to now refer to the physical drive as drive H. This permits booting and any other actual hardware-related activities to proceed successfully. However, so as to not adversely affect any of your application programs or batch files that rely on previously set path names, your files and directories are compressed and stored in a single large file on this physical H: drive.

The compressed DoubleSpace file that houses the entire formerly uncompressed contents of a disk drive is called a *compressed volume file* (or *CVF*). In Figure 9.10, you can see that this is named DBLSPACE.000,

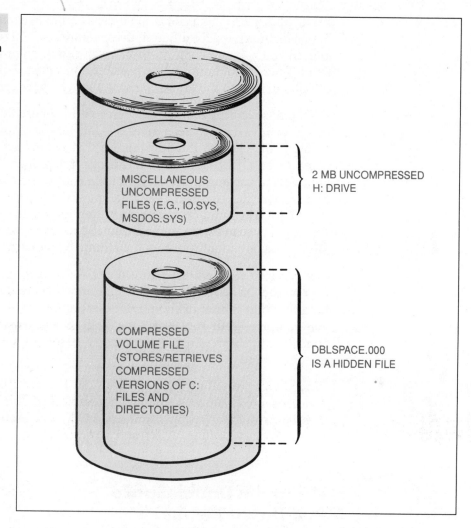

FIGURE 9.10

What really is going on during DoubleSpace operations. Your physical drive receives a new drive letter (H:), but the hidden DBL-SPACE file (a *CVF*, or *Compressed Volume File*) is treated on the fly as your new, seemingly much-larger C: drive.

MISCELLANEOUS UNCOMPRESSED FILES (E.G., IO.SYS, MSDOS.SYS)

2 MB UNCOMPRESSED H: DRIVE

COMPRESSED VOLUME FILE (STORES/RETRIEVES COMPRESSED VERSIONS OF C: FILES AND DIRECTORIES)

DBLSPACE.000 IS A HIDDEN FILE

the .000 extension representing the first of possibly several compressed volumes that can be created and stored on a single physical disk drive. I won't be discussing multiple compressed volume files any further, other than to note that you can create them out of available free space on any of your drives. Subsequent CVFs on the same physical drive would receive the name DBLSPACE.*xxx*, where *xxx* would be 001, 002, and so forth.

Using multiple CVFs is not going to be a common occurrence, unless you have a distinct need for different drive identifiers. There would not be any gain in space by creating multiple compressed volume files on a single drive. There would only be the possible convenience of having a measure of separateness to the file referencing that you later can use.

Let's talk specifically about the example of Figure 9.10 again. Double-Space ensures that any references to a former uncompressed C: directory or file is matched to the information that is now actually stored in the compressed DBLSPACE.000 file. Since it is a single file that contains a compressed version of possibly thousands of other files, it is maintained as a hidden file. You won't see it in any directory listing, unless you use the **ATTRIB** command to unhide it. Remember, to even get close to the file, you'd have to switch to the DoubleSpace swapped drive (D: in the example) that is actually housing the DoubleSpace compressed volume file.

You can also see from the figure that DoubleSpace reserves some space beyond the DBLSPACE.000 file. This uncompressed space is reserved to hold files that cannot or should not be compressed at all. For example, if you compress your root drive, the IO.SYS and MSDOS.SYS files that constitute the heart of the DOS memory-resident system itself will remain uncompressed.

When I compressed my former drive C, as Figure 9.10 suggests, Double-Space reserved 2Mb for such uncompressed files. This left 78Mb for compression, resulting in approximately 156Mb of usable disk space after DoubleSpace was done. This result assumed a 2-to-1 estimated compression ratio.

Using the DoubleSpace Pull-Down Menus

Simply typing **DBLSPACE** at a DOS command prompt will display the principal DoubleSpace control screen, seen in Figure 9.11. Just prior to displaying this screen, DoubleSpace spends a few moments searching

FIGURE 9.11

The primary Double-Space full-screen interface offers access to all of the facilities of the program. Currently available (i.e., *mounted*) compressed drives appear in the screen center. Menu options offer access to other DoubleSpace services.

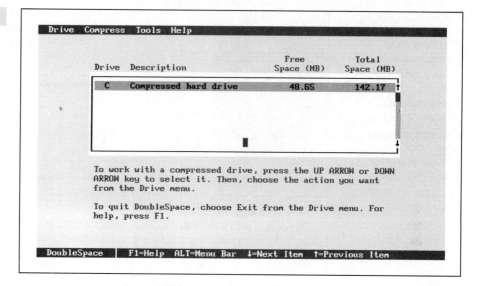

through all available drives on your system. The center portion of Figure 9.11 will always reflect details about any CVFs (Compressed Volume Files) that are found.

In the case of Figure 9.11, DoubleSpace only discovered that drive C:, the main hard drive on my computer, was already compressed. As you'll see below, it is possible that *any* of my system's removable media (diskette drives or Bernoulli removable cartridge drives) housed a CVF. If any of those drives contained a diskette or cartridge that had been previously compressed, then that drive would have been listed as an additional entry on this screen. You'll see such a case shortly.

As with most windowing programs, DoubleSpace offers up a menu bar with choices that can be activated with either a mouse or with keyboard selections. Selecting the *Drive* choice in Figure 9.11 will display the menu seen in Figure 9.12.

Each of the choices on the Drive menu refers to the compressed drive that you chose first by highlighting its line in Figure 9.11. In this case, there is

FIGURE 9.12

The Drive menu enables you to redefine existing drives, and to mount or dismount removable media DBLSPACE volumes. You must have previously compressed a diskette or cartridge in order to gain the compression benefits of DoubleSpace.

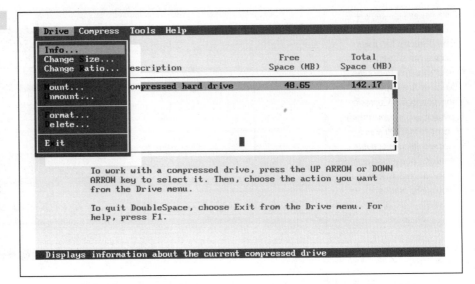

only one compressed drive, so the *Info* choice will offer up the information seen in Figure 9.13.

This screen provides a detailed view of the compressed drive selected from Figure 9.11. Note that you received information about both the actual physical disk drive (now disk-swapped and viewed by the system as drive H: on my system) and the new enlarged DoubleSpace drive that bears the same drive identifier as my original C: drive.

In Figure 9.13, you can see that the total physical space on my drive (the *Uncompressed Drive H* column) is 80Mb, but after compression, DoubleSpace makes 142Mb available as the apparent total space on *Compressed Drive C*. Of those totals, the actual drive has 79.31Mb consumed. This consists of a couple of uncompressed megabytes, and a large DBLSPACE.000 file that actually holds the compressed-drive file/directory data.

The *Space Used* entry for the compressed DoubleSpace drive C: is 93.51Mb. This number represents the actual storage that would have been used by files and directories on drive C, had they been stored on a larger physical drive in uncompressed fashion.

The compressed drive information screen. The physical drive (H:) displays known details, while the compressed volume (C:) uses mathematical projections to estimate free and total space.

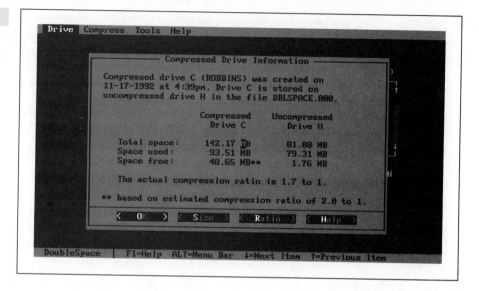

The *Space Free* for the uncompressed drive (1.76Mb) is an exact value; that free space is physically calculable. However, the Space Free for the DoubleSpace volume is an estimate. As the screen suggests, this free space is estimated using a compression ratio of two to one. This means that there are roughly 24Mb remaining in the DoubleSpace volume file, allowing a presumed 48Mb of file storage at the estimated compression ratio. It's not exact, but it's close enough to give you what you need to know—an idea of how much more data the disk will hold.

It is possible to use other menu choices to create DoubleSpace volumes out of free space on drives. Consequently, you may wind up at times wishing to use additional free space to enlarge an existing DoubleSpace drive, or to shrink an existing DoubleSpace volume in order to reclaim the remaining free space on the physical host drive. The *Change Size* choice on the Drive menu displays a dialog box that shows the largest and smallest values for the DoubleSpace volume on this drive. You can adjust the compressed volume size directly within those limits.

If you decide that the estimated ratio (2.0 to 1 in Figure 9.13) is not close enough for you, you can use the *Change Ratio* choice on the Drive menu to correct it. As you can see, the actual compression ratio on my drive C: (in Figure 9.13) is 1.7 to 1. This means that the particular mix of files on my drive can only be compressed by seventy percent. Since the 48Mb of free space on my compressed drive in Figure 9.13 was calculated by multiplying the ratio of 2:1 times the available space in the DoubleSpace volume, this must mean that roughly 24Mb of uncompressed space really was free when I snapped the picture for Figure 9.13.

If I were to continue adding files to my C: drive that actually compressed at the 1.7:1 ratio, then only 1.7*24Mb, or 40.8Mb, of new file data is all that could fit before the DoubleSpace drive would really fill up. The drive would have no more space free after only 40 more megabytes, rather than the 48 suggested in Figure 9.13. Leaving the compression ratio alone might mislead you as to how much you can really fit on drive C:. Consequently, you might want to adjust the compression ratio, so the information screen estimates (as well as output from other programs like CHKDSK) would more accurately reflect the probable space that will really be usable on a DoubleSpace drive.

➤ EXTRA!

When Should You Change a Drive's Compression Ratio?

Ideally, you want the estimated compression ratio for a DoubleSpace drive to be as close as possible to the actual compression ratio for the files stored on that drive. This means that all information displays concerning estimated free space will be as close as accurate to reality.

DoubleSpace's Drive menu offers up the Information screen (see Figure 9.13) that displays both the estimated compression ratio and the actual compression ratio. The actual ratio is based on the nature of the files on your disk and how easily they are compressed. You can always discover for yourself how compressible individual files are by using the */C* switch on the **DIR** command.

The figure below depicts the results of the following command, which looks at the nondirectory entries in my F drive's root directory:

```
DIR /A-D /C F:
```

```
Volume in drive F has no label
Volume Serial Number is 09D0-3758
Directory of F:\

BACKUPC       <DIR>       02-19-93   2:23a
BACKUPD       <DIR>       02-19-93   2:24a
EXP16    DOS      11668 12-23-92   6:00a   1.9 to 1.0
NETWORK  INF      37515 12-23-92   6:00a   2.4 to 1.0
PROTMAN  DOS      21680 12-23-92   6:00a   3.0 to 1.0
PROTOCOL INI        369 01-20-93   8:25a  16.0 to 1.0
SETUP    INF       1420 12-23-92   6:00a   8.0 to 1.0
SYSTEM   INI        144 01-20-93   8:28a
WORKGRP  SYS       7268 12-23-92   6:00a   1.3 to 1.0
                 2.5 to 1.0 average compression ratio
         9 file(s)     80064 bytes
                           0 bytes free
```

You can see that the very smallest files compress at a ratio of 16 to 1. In fact, most batch files and worksheet files compress consistently at ratios of 8 or 16 to 1. To see a file-by-file compression ratio display on a compressed drive, just change to the drive and type:

```
DIR \ /C /S
```

You will not only learn about individual files, but you will learn the average compression ratio achieved for your groups of files, by directory. You can then decide whether or not to change a drive's compression ratio. If you have a large number or highly compressible files on a drive, then increase the drive's compression ratio. If your drive contains many dense files, such as already compressed .ZIP files, then you will need to reduce the drive's compression ratio.

Ensuring that your drive's compression is accurate is more important than just guaranteeing more accurate information displays. DOS and some application programs use the estimate of file space available to make decisions when files are moved, copied, or created. If, for instance, your compression is too low, then some file operations may not be allowed because there appears to be insufficient space, when in fact there may be more than enough free space on the actual drive.

There is a certain artificiality to the *Format* and *Delete* commands on the Drive menu. To Format a compressed drive is really only to erase the entire contents of the representing compressed volume file, such as a DBLSPACE.000 file. Although DoubleSpace will not allow you to erroneously perform this Format on your C: drive, it will enable you to quickly erase all the files and directories of any other compressed drive with this choice. Use this only when you want a very fast way to erase everything on a DoubleSpace volume.

The *Delete* choice goes one step beyond *Format*. In addition to clearing out the contents of the DoubleSpace CVF, the Delete option will actually delete the DBLSPACE.000 file itself. This eliminates any trace of the compressed volume. Use this option only when you want to once again use the drive in its former uncompressed manner. *Format* recaptures all compressed space on a drive for subsequent use; *Delete* removes all possibility of using the compressed drive at all.

The *Mount* and *Unmount* choices on the Drive menu are so important and useful that they deserve their own presentation. I'll discuss them in the context of the next section.

Compressing Diskettes and Removable Cartridges

The second menu is the *Compress* menu, which displays only two choices:

```
Existing drive
Create new drive
```

Compressing an *Existing drive* (the first choice) enables you to select any drive on your system and compress all files and directories that currently reside there. Creating a *New* (compressed) *drive* enables you to carve out a new drive identifier that represents a block of compressed space that is carved out of space available on an existing drive. This creation choice does not strike me as such a big deal. I envision most users compressing an entire existing drive, not bothering to retain uncompressed space at all, if possible.

The first option, to compress an existing drive, is much more powerful, especially if the drive is used for removable media. Naturally, all diskette drives enable you to use removable diskettes. If you use this *Existing drive* choice to compress a diskette, you are creating the DBLSPACE.000 hidden file (and swapped drive identifier) on the specific diskette that resides in the drive when you make this choice.

The same applies to removable cartridges. When I selected *Existing drive*, I had an empty 20Mb cartridge in the E: drive of my system. At the completion of the compression step, the original drive identifier contained compressed information, additional free space, and was able to be treated as a DBLSPACE.000 drive. This means, as you learned above, that DoubleSpace renamed the original E: drive to some new and available drive identifier. Also, DoubleSpace retained as accessible on this uncompressed volume any files that cannot or should not be compressed. In this case, since there is nothing critical to the system on my removable Bernoulli drive, the free space is virtually completely doubled.

Selecting *Existing drive* from the Compress menu can display a screen such as the one in Figure 9.14. The central window on this screen provides information about:

1. All configured hard drives on your system that are not already compressed (that is only drive D: in this example).

2. Any floppy diskette drive that has an uncompressed diskette loaded into it, and which has sufficient free space remaining to warrant bothering with the overhead of doubling that space.

3. Any removable cartridge drives that have uncompressed cartridges in them when you make this menu choice (drives E: and F: in this example).

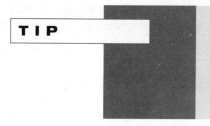

T I P

Double the storage capacity of your 1.44Mb or 1.2Mb floppies by using the *Existing drive* choice on the Compress menu. You'll have to later select *Mount* from the Drive menu to actually gain access to the compressed file space.

FIGURE 9.14

You can select a removable drive to compress if the drive has a diskette or cartridge in it, and if there is a sufficient amount of free uncompressed space on it. This amount varies according to the drive.

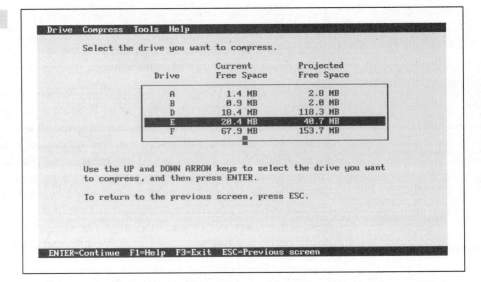

```
 Drive  Compress  Tools  Help

    Select the drive you want to compress.

                        Current         Projected
            Drive      Free Space      Free Space

             A          1.4 MB          2.8 MB
             B          0.9 MB          2.0 MB
             D         18.4 MB        118.3 MB
             E         20.4 MB         40.7 MB
             F         67.9 MB        153.7 MB

    Use the UP and DOWN ARROW keys to select the drive you want
    to compress, and then press ENTER.

    To return to the previous screen, press ESC.



 ENTER=Continue  F1=Help  F3=Exit  ESC=Previous screen
```

If you press Enter when Figure 9.14 appears, a new screen appears that provides information about the results of going ahead with the Double-Space operation. For example, the screen would indicate the new drive identifier that will be assigned to the uncompressed DoubleSpace swapped drive, as well as the amount of free space that will be retained in uncompressed fashion. Besides the DOS system files on drive C:, there are a number of examples of files that must remain uncompressed or their related programs will not work properly. The Windows permanent swap file is such a file, as is the hidden print-cache file used by the third-party PCACHE print spooling program.

One final screen appears in this process. This screen estimates the time necessary to compress the indicated removable cartridge or diskette. If you decide to go ahead with the compression, just press *C* at this point. Otherwise, cancel the request by pressing the Esc key.

WARNING   Compression is a one-way street. Once you have compressed a drive, it cannot be uncompressed.

Since a compressed drive can store more file information than the same drive when uncompressed, there may not be enough room on the uncompressed drive to store all the file information that has been placed there. If you want to reverse the process, you'll have to copy all the directories and files from a DoubleSpace drive to a different, uncompressed drive.

While DoubleSpace is compressing your removable cartridge or diskette, it will display a time-keeping screen. You'll be able to see when compression began, and when DoubleSpace estimates the process will complete. After compression completes, DoubleSpace automatically initiates the *defragmentation* program in order to optimize the file space on the new compressed drive.

In Chapter 18, I discuss the powerful **DEFRAG** program included with DOS. It enables you to easily optimize the arrangement of files on a drive in your system. The Tools menu offers a *Defragment* choice that can perform this optimization on the file structure stored within a DoubleSpace volume. You should use this choice from time to time to ensure that you receive optimum response from DOS's file access to compressed files.

When all aspects of the compression process are completed, you'll receive a completion screen like the one seen in Figure 9.15.

If the drive that was just compressed has any impact on your Windows system, then the DoubleSpace program updates your Windows SYSTEM.INI file. Similarly, if the compression affects your DOS system, it may also update your CONFIG.SYS and AUTOEXEC.BAT files.

After rebooting, you can gain access to a compressed DoubleSpace volume that resides on removable media. To do so, enter the **DBLSPACE** command, pull down the Drive menu, and select *Mount*. DoubleSpace will display a brief message on the screen:

```
DoubleSpace is scanning your computer for unmounted compressed
drives.
```

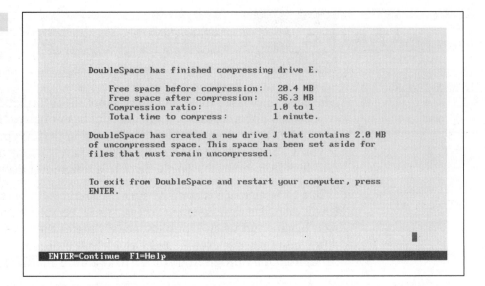

```
        DoubleSpace has finished compressing drive E.

            Free space before compression:    20.4 MB
            Free space after compression:     36.3 MB
            Compression ratio:                1.0 to 1
            Total time to compress:           1 minute.

        DoubleSpace has created a new drive J that contains 2.0 MB
        of uncompressed space. This space has been set aside for
        files that must remain uncompressed.


        To exit from DoubleSpace and restart your computer, press
        ENTER.




 ENTER=Continue   F1=Help
```

Assuming that the diskette or cartridge that you've previously compressed is in its drive, it will appear as a choice in the window that appears (see Figure 9.16).

Note that Figure 9.16 indicates that currently only one removable compressed drive (stored on the physical drive as DBLSPACE.000) exists. Remember that this was a 20Mb drive, with 2Mb reserved for uncompressed space. There are 18Mb remaining for the compressed volume file. Selecting OK on the screen shown in Figure 9.16 will ask DoubleSpace to mount the cartridge, making all of the compressed file space available to your system.

The result can be seen in Figure 9.17. The main DoubleSpace information window now displays the E: drive, in addition to the C: drive, as a compressed DoubleSpace drive. Note also how the total space available is 36Mb, just as you'd expect from a formerly empty 18Mb of drive space.

FIGURE 9.16

Mounting a compressed drive. **DBLSPACE** displays here all removable media that were previously compressed and are currently accessible in a system drive. Select one and choose OK to make the Compressed Volume File available for use.

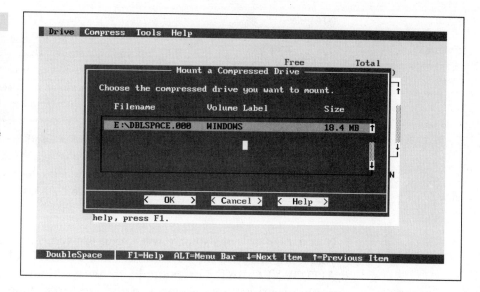

FIGURE 9.17

After mounting a removable cartridge drive, the compressed volume file can be treated with other **DBLSPACE** commands. First, highlight the desired DBLSPACE.000 volume. Then, pull down the appropriate menu that contains the action you wish to apply to that volume.

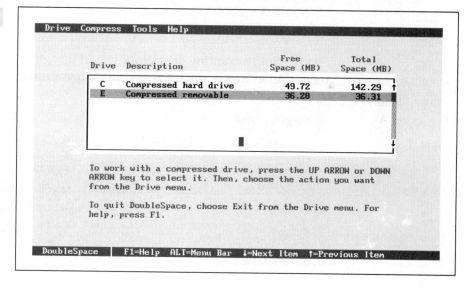

WARNING

You must enter DBLSPACE only from a true DOS prompt; you cannot run it from a DOS session within Windows. In fact, do not try to access a compressed DoubleSpace volume on a removable cartridge unless you have first *Mounted* it. If you forget to run DBLSPACE and mount all the required DoubleSpace CVFs prior to starting Windows, you'll have to leave Windows and mount those volumes. Only then will you have access to the compressed files within the DoubleSpace volumes.

If you plan to consistently use a compressed, removable cartridge on your computer, you should consider adding a **MOUNT** command to your AUTOEXEC.BAT. For example, to always mount the removable Bernoulli cartridge just seen, I could add the following line to my AUTOEXEC.BAT file:

```
DBLSPACE /MOUNT E:
```

The required mounting operations would be carried out without bothering to display any of the normal DoubleSpace information screens.

TIP

DOS automatically unmounts a DoubleSpace diskette or removable cartridge when you physically remove it from the drive. CVFs are also unmounted when you reboot your computer. You must perform a new mount before being able to access the compressed files on any other DoubleSpace volume that you then place into the drive.

Adding Power with the ANSI System Driver

The ANSI (American National Standards Institute) system allows you to modify the default setup of your screen and keyboard. For example, you can change the characteristics of the screen, including both the cursor position and, with a color monitor, the screen colors. You can also redefine the expected value of keys on your keyboard, so you can customize the use of your function keys, as well as how the Ctrl, Shift, or Alt key affects them.

In order to obtain any of these customizing capabilities, you must have the ANSI.SYS driver installed in your system. The **DEVICE** or **DEVICEHIGH** line of CONFIG.SYS that loads ANSI.SYS does just that:

```
DEVICE=C:\DOS\ANSI.SYS
```

Some special-purpose application programs like SuperKey, a keyboard redefinition program, also require that you include this type of command in your CONFIG.SYS specification. If so, it is best that you specify the full path name to the ANSI.SYS file; as you can see in this example, ANSI.SYS is located in the DOS directory on drive C:.

Using the **DEVICEHIGH** command here instead of simply using **DEVICE** takes further advantage of DOS's memory-management capabilities. Specifically, this command requests that DOS load the ANSI.SYS device driver into available memory in the system reserved area between 640K and 1Mb. In order to use **DEVICEHIGH**, DOS must first have established appropriate addressing connections to these memory addresses. The **DOS=** command in the example CONFIG.SYS above (see Figure 9.6) did this by specifying a UMB parameter:

```
DOS=HIGH,UMB
```

The HIGH parameter instructed DOS to allocate a portion of high memory for DOS's own memory requirements. The UMB parameter further established linkage with upper memory block addresses in the system reserved area. These approaches enable you to retain extra conventional memory for your applications in two significant yet easy ways. First, as the bottom of Figure 9.6 demonstrates, you can load device drivers into upper memory blocks with the **DEVICEHIGH** command. Chapter 17 discusses this facility in more depth. You will also learn in Chapter 17 how you can load memory-resident application programs into these upper memory blocks by using the **LOADHIGH** command.

Even if you are not yet using application software that requires the ANSI.SYS driver, the possibilities in the next section will probably inspire you to include this line in your CONFIG.SYS specification all the time.

> **EXTRA!**

Set Up Hotkeys for Your Favorite Applications!

You can develop your own Windows-like hotkey combinations for your favorite programs when running under DOS. The SHORTCUT.BAT batch file is a simple example of how few lines are necessary to gain this time-saving benefit on your system. See the chapter text for more details.

```
@ECHO OFF
Rem SHORTCUT.BAT defines the following three hot keys
Rem using ANSI.SYS codes: Alt+C, Alt+D, and Alt+U
ECHO [0;46;"CHKDSK"p
ECHO [0;32;"DOSKEY"p
ECHO [0;22;"UNDELETE"p
```

ANSI.SYS and the Prompt Command

The **PROMPT** command, as you might guess, lets you determine the appearance of the DOS command prompt itself. The **PROMPT** command can also be used to access the ANSI.SYS driver in order to control the screen's appearance when at the DOS prompt. (Remember you can also change your graphic screen from the Options menu in the shell.)

The form of the **PROMPT** command used to change the color of the screen is

```
PROMPT $e[Attribute(s);Colors;m
```

The *$e* combination instructs DOS to invoke the ANSI driver. The possible screen attributes and colors that you enter after the opening bracket are listed in Tables 9.5 and 9.6. You can enter as many of these parameters

TABLE 9.5: Values for video-screen attribute parameters

ATTRIBUTE	PARAMETER VALUE
All attributes off	0
Bold	1
Low intensity	2
Italic	3
Underline (monochrome monitors only)	4
Blinking	5
Rapid blinking	6
Reverse video	7
Hidden	8

TABLE 9.6: Values for video-screen color parameters

COLOR	FOREGROUND VALUE	BACKGROUND VALUE
Black	30	40
Red	31	41
Green	32	42
Yellow	33	43
Blue	34	44
Magenta	35	45
Cyan	36	46
White	37	47

as you need between the opening bracket and the lowercase letter *m*; however, be sure to separate them with semicolons if you use more than one color or attribute. Be aware that some of these video attributes may not be available on your particular monitor.

NOTE

The letter *m* in the PROMPT escape sequence signifies the end of your sequence of attribute settings. It must be lowercase.

Controlling the Screen Display

It's up to you to decide if you like the standard white letters on a black background (which you usually get even if you've bought a color monitor), or if you prefer something flashier. Using the **PROMPT** command with the attribute and color codes shown in Tables 9.5 and 9.6, you can customize things as you like.

For example, To switch the display to dark letters on a light background (see Figure 9.18), you would use an attribute value of 7, for reverse video:

```
PROMPT $e[7m
```

All future output on your screen will now appear as reverse video—black on white. Note that in Figure 9.18, the only prompt that appears after the **PROMPT** command has been executed is the underline cursor—the C:\> prompt at the top of the screen has been stripped of its information. This is because the **PROMPT** command in this instance was used to set screen attributes only. You will learn in the next section how to specify the appearance of the command prompt.

To return to normal video (see Figure 9.19), you would use an attribute value of **0**, which turns off all special attributes:

```
PROMPT $e[0m
```

FIGURE 9.18

Setting reverse video requires the *$e[7m* ANSI escape sequence. All such sequences can be applied with the **PROMPT** command, assuming that you've loaded the ANSI.SYS driver in your CONFIG.SYS file.

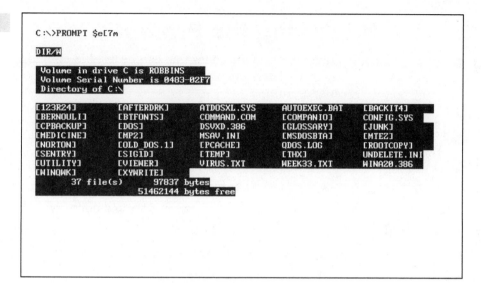

FIGURE 9.19

After any video attribute modifications, you can always reset your monitor to normal settings. To do so, use the **PROMPT** command and the *$e[0m* ANSI escape sequence.

```
[UTILITY]        [VIEWER]        VIRUS.TXT       WEEK33.TXT      WINA20.386
[WINQWK]         [XYWRITE]
         37 file(s)        97837 bytes
                      51462144 bytes free

PROMPT $e[0m

DIR/W

 Volume in drive C is ROBBINS
 Volume Serial Number is 0483-02F7
 Directory of C:\

[123R24]         [AFTERDRK]      ATDOSXL.SYS     AUTOEXEC.BAT    [BACKIT4]
[BERNOULI]       [BTFONTS]       COMMAND.COM     [COMPANIO]      CONFIG.SYS
[CPBACKUP]       [DOS]           DSVXD.386       [GLOSSARY]      [JUNK]
[MEDICINE]       [MP2]           MSAV.INI        [MSDOSBTA]      [MTEZ]
[NORTON]         [OLD_DOS.1]     [PCACHE]        QDOS.LOG        [ROOTCOPY]
[SENTRY]         [SIGID]         [TEMP]          [THX]           UNDELETE.INI
[UTILITY]        [VIEWER]        VIRUS.TXT       WEEK33.TXT      WINA20.386
[WINQWK]         [XYWRITE]
         37 file(s)        97837 bytes
                      51462144 bytes free
```

Modifying the Prompt

Table 9.7 lists the codes that can be used in conjunction with the **$** character to determine the appearance or informational content of the command prompt.

TABLE 9.7: $ codes for command prompts

SYMBOL	MEANING
e	The Esc key
p	Name of current drive and directory
g	The > character
n	Current drive identifier
d	System date
t	System time
v	DOS version number
l	The < character
b	The ¦ character
q	The = character
h	A backspace (deletes character to left of cursor)
_	(underscore, not hyphen) The carriage-return/line-feed sequence
$	The dollar sign

For instance, to display the name of the current directory, you would enter

        PROMPT $p

To display the name of the current directory and the > symbol, you would enter

        PROMPT pg

Combining Multiple Attributes

All of the preceding possibilities can be combined to create more complex prompt effects. The simplest combinations only involve two attributes at once. For example, to create a reverse-video display that blinks, you can combine the codes for blinking (5) and reverse video (7):

    PROMPT $e[5;7m

Future output will be seen as black characters that blink on a light background. To set things back to normal again, you would enter

    PROMPT $e[0m

To display the current directory and the > symbol, *and* to set to boldface all future video output, you would enter

    PROMPT pg$e[1m

The results of this command are shown in Figure 9.20.

You can enter text into your prompt by simply typing it with no special codes; text can also be embedded between any special-purpose screen

FIGURE 9.20

You can readily combine any sequence of characters and escape sequences in the **PROMPT** command. *$p* displays the current directory. *$g* shows the > symbol. And *$e[1m* turns boldface on for subsequent video display. See the chapter tables for other possibilities.

```
[UTILITY]       [VIEWER]        VIRUS.TXT       WEEK33.TXT      WINA20.386
[WINQWK]        [XYWRITE]
        37 file(s)       97837 bytes
                      51462144 bytes free

PROMPT $p$g$e[1m

C:\>DIR/W

  Volume in drive C is ROBBINS
  Volume Serial Number is 0483-02F7
  Directory of C:\

[123R24]        [AFTERDRK]      ATDOSXL.SYS     AUTOEXEC.BAT    [BACKIT4]
[BERNOULI]      [BTFONTS]       COMMAND.COM     [COMPANIO]      CONFIG.SYS
[CPBACKUP]      [DOS]           DSVXD.386       [GLOSSARY]      [JUNK]
[MEDICINE]      [MP2]           MSAV.INI        [MSDOSBTA]      [MTEZ]
[NORTON]        [OLD_DOS.1]     [PCACHE]        QDOS.LOG        [ROOTCOPY]
[SENTRY]        [SIGID]         [TEMP]          [THX]           UNDELETE.INI
[UTILITY]       [VIEWER]        VIRUS.TXT       WEEK33.TXT      WINA20.386
[WINQWK]        [XYWRITE]
        37 file(s)       97837 bytes
                      51462144 bytes free

C:\>
```

codes. For example, you can change the prompting message to *Your Command?* and display it in high intensity with the following:

```
PROMPT $e[1mYour Command?$e[0m
```

The beginning *$e[1m* turns high intensity on for the phrase *Your Command?* and the ending *$e[0m* turns it off.

NOTE

Complicated or long screen prompts can wrap around to a second screen line as you type them in, but you should not press the Enter key to get to the second line—the Enter key terminates your prompt-string input. DOS will wrap a multiple-line command request on its own.

Color monitors present other interesting alternatives. Using the color codes of Table 9.6 and the prompt codes of Table 9.7, it's easy to set any desired combination for foreground and background colors. For example, the following command will set a three-line prompt that changes the screen color.

```
PROMPT $p$_$d$_$t$g$e[34;43m
```

The first line will contain the current directory (code **p**). The carriage-return/line-feed sequence (code **_**) ensures that the system date (code **d**) appears on the next line. The time (code **t**) and the > character (code **g**) will be on the third line, and all succeeding text (including the future prompting strings) will be displayed as blue characters on a yellow background.

A slight change to this command could provide the same information content while using reverse video to highlight particular portions. In this way, the same **PROMPT** command could be used for both color and monochrome monitors. Notice in Figure 9.21 that the display of commands and output is in normal video, since the reverse-video code is reset immediately after the > symbol is output:

```
PROMPT $e[7m$p$_$d$_$t$g$e[0m
```

FIGURE 9.21

A three-line, reverse-video prompt. Note that each line's output is separated from the others because of the $_ included in the **PROMPT** sequence.

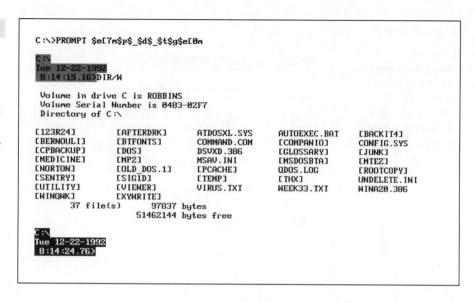

```
C:\>PROMPT $e[7m$p$_$d$_$t$g$e[0m

C:\
Tue 12-22-1992
8:14:19.16>DIR/W

 Volume in drive C is ROBBINS
 Volume Serial Number is 0483-02F7
 Directory of C:\

[123R24]      [AFTERDRK]     ATDOSXL.SYS    AUTOEXEC.BAT    [BACKIT4]
[BERNOULI]    [BTFONTS]      COMMAND.COM    [COMPANIO]      CONFIG.SYS
[CPBACKUP]    [DOS]          DSVXD.386      [GLOSSARY]      [JUNK]
[MEDICINE]    [MP2]          MSAV.INI       [MSDOSBTA]      [MTEZ]
[NORTON]      [OLD_DOS.1]    [PCACHE]       QDOS.LOG        [ROOTCOPY]
[SENTRY]      [SIGID]        [TEMP]         [THX]           UNDELETE.INI
[UTILITY]     [VIEWER]       VIRUS.TXT      WEEK33.TXT      WINA20.386
[WINQWK]      [XYWRITE]
       37 file(s)         97837 bytes
                       51462144 bytes free

C:\
Tue 12-22-1992
8:14:24.76>
```

You might not like the multiline appearance of this information. You could just as easily put the same information on one line with the following variation:

```
PROMPT $e[7m$p    $d     $t$g$e[0m
```

The spaces in this command are critical to the separation of the directory name, date, and time. The results are shown in Figure 9.22.

There are many more fanciful things you can do with the **PROMPT** command to control the video display. The codes required would go well beyond the scope of this book, but you can manipulate the cursor and its location in a variety of ways.

Use the **PROMPT** command now to redefine your own DOS prompt to provide more information. Issue the proper command to display the DOS version number on one line, the system date on the next line, and the current directory on the third line of this multiline prompt. On a fourth line, generate the text string

```
Enter next command, please :
```

If you have a monochrome monitor, have this message appear in reverse video. Remember to reset the video attribute so that the rest of the video

FIGURE 9.22

A one-line,
reverse-video prompt.
Note that spacing in
the eventual DOS
command prompt is
controlled by the num-
ber of spaces inserted
at appropriate points in
the **PROMPT** line itself.

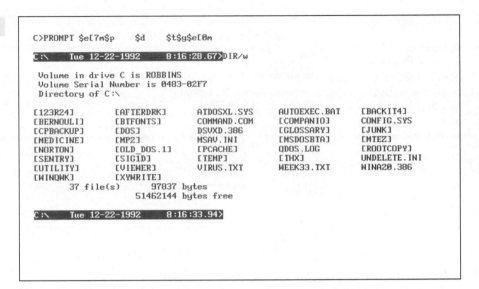

```
C>PROMPT $e[7m$p     $d     $t$g$e[0m

C:\     Tue 12-22-1992      8:16:28.67>DIR/w

Volume in drive C is ROBBINS
Volume Serial Number is 0483-02F7
Directory of C:\

[123R24]        [AFTERDRK]      AIDOSXL.SYS     AUTOEXEC.BAT    [BACKIT4]
[BERNOULI]      [BTFONTS]       COMMAND.COM     [COMPANIO]      CONFIG.SYS
[CPBACKUP]      [DOS]           DSVXD.386       [GLOSSARY]      [JUNK]
[MEDICINE]      [MP2]           MSAV.INI        [MSDOSBTA]      [MTEZ]
[NORTON]        [OLD_DOS.1]     [PCACHE]        QDOS.LOG        [ROOTCOPY]
[SENTRY]        [SIGID]         [TEMP]          [THX]           UNDELETE.INI
[UTILITY]       [VIEWER]        VIRUS.TXT       WEEK33.TXT      WINA20.386
[WINQWK]        [XYWRITE]
        37 file(s)      97837 bytes
                     51462144 bytes free

C:\     Tue 12-22-1992      8:16:33.94>
```

display appears in normal video. If you have a color monitor, have this
message appear as white letters on a red background. Also, remember that
your new fancy prompt will only remain until you shut your system down.
If you wish to make a new prompt more permanent, you'll have to include
that **PROMPT** command in the AUTOEXEC.BAT batch file, as explained in Chapter 14.

Redefining Keys

In addition to changing screen colors, you can use the ANSI system to
reprogram some of your keys to type out commands or phrases. You can
define any of the ASCII keys or the extended-keyboard keys (F1–F12,
Home, End, and so on). Some people have even used this technique to
redefine individual keys to represent other individual keys, so that the keyboard assumes a different layout.

Like screen attributes, key reassignment begins with the special symbol
for the Esc key (**$e**) and continues with the opening bracket ([). If you
want to assign new values to a normal key, like the A key or the = key, you

enter the ASCII value of the key, like 96 for the letter A or 61 for =. (The ASCII values of all the characters are given in Appendix C.) However, if you want to reassign values to the special keys on your keyboard (which is a more common goal), you must begin the key assignment with a zero and then follow it with the special code given the key by DOS (see Table 9.8).

TABLE 9.8: Function-key redefinition codes

FUNCTION KEY AND CODE	WITH SHIFT	WITH CTRL	WITH ALT
F1: 59	Shift+F1: 84	Ctrl+F1: 94	Alt+F1: 104
F2: 60	Shift+F2: 85	Ctrl+F2: 95	Alt+F2: 105
F3: 61	Shift+F3: 86	Ctrl+F3: 96	Alt+F3: 106
F4: 62	Shift+F4: 87	Ctrl+F4: 97	Alt+F4: 107
F5: 63	Shift+F5: 88	Ctrl+F5: 98	Alt+F5: 108
F6: 64	Shift+F6: 89	Ctrl+F6: 99	Alt+F6: 109
F7: 65	Shift+F7: 90	Ctrl+F7: 100	Alt+F7: 110
F8: 66	Shift+F8: 91	Ctrl+F8: 101	Alt+F8: 111
F9: 67	Shift+F9: 92	Ctrl+F9: 102	Alt+F9: 112
F10: 68	Shift+F10: 93	Ctrl+F10: 103	Alt+F10: 113
F11: 133	Shift+F11: 135	Ctrl+F11: 137	Alt+F11: 139
F12: 134	Shift+F12: 136	Ctrl+F12: 138	Alt+F12: 140

For example, F11 has the reassignment code 133. Suppose you wanted to have the F11 key automatically type the command **DOSSHELL**. You would enter

```
PROMPT $e[0;133;"DOSSHELL";13p
```

> **EXTRA!**

Customize Your Function Keys As You Like!

You can use the techniques discussed in this chapter to customize the interpretation of any keys on your keyboard. In particular, the FKEYON.BAT file seen below demonstrates how to set up F1 to F10 to easily run some of the useful DOSKEY macros and batch files presented elsewhere throughout this book.

Naturally, you can modify the appropriate lines as you see fit to make this batch file work for you. If you run *FKEYON* to set up the function keys, you can run the additional FKEYOFF.BAT file also seen below to restore the function keys to their original settings.

```
@ECHO OFF
Rem FKEYON.BAT defines your ten function keys F1 - F10.
Rem Change the contents in quote to customize this program.
Rem Use FKEYOFF.BAT to reset original function key definitions.

SET CURRENTPROMPT=%PROMPT%
ECHO ON

Rem Define F1 to F7 as macros from this book.
PROMPT $e[0;59;"CHKDSK2";13p
PROMPT $e[0;60;"FF";13p
PROMPT $e[0;61;"KEYFAST";13p
PROMPT $e[0;62;"LISTMACS";13p
PROMPT $e[0;63;"SAVEMACS";13p
PROMPT $e[0;64;"DIRN";13p
PROMPT $e[0;65;"DIRE";13p

Rem Define F8 and F9 as simple batch files from this book.
PROMPT $e[0;66;"ASCIICHR";13p
PROMPT $e[0;67;"BOXDRAW";13p

Rem Define F10 as a HELP key for the defined function keys.
PROMPT $e[0;68;"REM F1=FF F2=SAVEMACS F3=LISTMACS F4=KEYFAST
F5=CHKDSK2";13;"REM F6=DIRN F7=DIRE F8=ASCIICHR F9=BOXDRAW";13p

ECHO OFF
SET PROMPT=%CURRENTPROMPT%
SET CURRENTPROMPT=
------------------------------------------------------------------
@ECHO OFF
Rem FKEYOFF.BAT to reset your ten function keys F1 - F10.
Rem Use FKEYON.BAT to customize the ten function key definitions.
```

```
SET CURRENTPROMPT=%PROMPT%
ECHO ON

PROMPT $e[0;59;0;59p
PROMPT $e[0;60;0;60p
PROMPT $e[0;61;0;61p
PROMPT $e[0;62;0;62p
PROMPT $e[0;63;0;63p
PROMPT $e[0;64;0;64p
PROMPT $e[0;65;0;65p
PROMPT $e[0;66;0;66p
PROMPT $e[0;67;0;67p
PROMPT $e[0;68;0;68p

ECHO OFF
SET PROMPT=%CURRENTPROMPT%
SET CURRENTPROMPT=
```

First, *$e[* tells DOS that an ANSI command is being entered. Next, *0* tells DOS that the key to be redefined is part of the extended keyboard. The *133* selects F11 as the key to be redefined. *DOSSHELL* is the text of the command. (Note that these text characters are enclosed in quotation marks to indicate that they are not codes for ANSI.SYS to interpret.) The number *13* is the code for the Enter key, which is required after the **DOS-SHELL** command, just as it would be if you typed in **DOSSHELL** (or any other command) at the keyboard yourself. The last character in a key redefinition is always *p*, just as the last character in the video redefinition was an *m*.

Finally, some very fancy custom menu systems can be set up simply with the **PROMPT** command and a well-thought-out group of function-key assignments. There are potentially 12 function keys (F1–F12), 12 Shift+function-key combinations, 12 Ctrl+function-key combinations, and 12 Alt+function-key combinations. These provide 48 assignment possibilities. The extended code numbers for redefining these keys are also shown in Table 9.8.

The following **PROMPT** commands redefine several keys. The first will cause the shifted F4 key to type **FORMAT A:**. The second will cause the

Ctrl-F6 combination to type **CHKDSK,** and the third will cause the Alt-F8 combination to type **CD \:**

```
PROMPT $e[0;87;"FORMAT A:";13p
PROMPT $e[0;99;"CHKDSK";13p
PROMPT $e[0;111;"CD \";13p
```

NOTE Some programs reset the function-key definitions when they begin, and you will not be able to use the PROMPT command for key redefinition. When you encounter such a situation, the best solution is to purchase and use a keyboard redefinition program (from a third-party utility vendor) which will allow you to redefine any key while another program is operating.

You must assign a key its original code value in order to reset it. The following will reset all three of the example function-key sequences:

```
PROMPT $e[0;87;0;87p$e[0;99;0;99p$e[0;111;0;111p
```

The nicest thing about all these possibilities is that they are cumulative—that is, you can issue any number of key-redefinition requests and they will accumulate. Until you reset each one or end your session at the command screen, they will retain their new definitions while you are at the DOS prompt level.

One final note about these key redefinitions is in order here. After any of these escape (*$e*) sequences, the visible prompt will disappear on the screen unless you also issue a **PROMPT** command using the **$** codes from Table 9.7. Typically, you may redefine screen attributes or keyboard definitions with a sequence of *$e* codes; then, to display the current drive and directory, follow these with a single **PROMPT** command using a **$** code sequence, such as

```
PROMPT $p$g
```

Try out these techniques now. Use the information in Table 9.8 and ANSI.SYS to program your F7 function key to perform a **CHKDSK** command. Don't forget to make sure you have a CONFIG.SYS file in your root directory, and be sure it contains a **DEVICE** specification that loads the ANSI.SYS driver. If your keyboard contains an F12 key, determine and test out the **PROMPT** command necessary to switch back to the shell after switching to a command prompt (that is, using Shift+F9, not Alt+F4). You'll need to assign **EXIT** with a carriage return to the key. Use Table 9.8 to determine the key code associated with the F12 key.

Summary

In this chapter, you've learned some very powerful methods in DOS to customize your system for both power and convenience:

- The CONFIG.SYS file permits you to offer custom bootup menus during initialization, specifying completely different configurations according to user choice at power-up time. The same choice can be extended to control different startup groups in your AUTOEXEC.BAT file as well.

- Your entire system can be protected from computer viruses by installing the **VSAFE** program to warn of virus incursions, and by running the **MSAV** (**MicroS**oft **A**nti-**V**irus) program to detect and remove viruses that have already invaded your system.

- The **DEVICE** command allows you to incorporate any number of specialized peripheral device drivers into your DOS configuration. The **DEVICEHIGH** command loads the same device driver file into upper memory blocks (640K–1Mb), assuming that your CONFIG.SYS file contained an earlier **DOS=** command that specified the UMB parameter. (Chapter 17 will present more extensive details and examples.)

- The **DBLSPACE** program enables you to double the free space available on hard drives, as well as on removable diskette or cartridge hard disks.

- The ANSI.SYS device driver provides extraordinary controls over both the video monitor and the keyboard. It provides a number of special codes, which give you the ability to redefine any keys and to control the video output. Using these codes with the **PROMPT** command allows you to make your system more intelligent, useful, and fun to operate.

In the next chapter, you'll learn about another fundamental aspect of controlling your DOS system. Chapter 10 will focus on DOS's ability to redirect and filter all input and output information.

CHAPTER
10

Redirecting and
Rearranging Your
Information

IN THIS chapter, you'll concentrate on three related features: redirection, filters, and pipes. These features offer you additional ways to control input and output in your system, as well as new ways to process your information. They are of great interest to programmers designing automated applications for DOS systems; they are also of practical value for anyone using DOS.

Controlling the Flow of Information by Redirection

Redirection refers to the ability of a program or a DOS command to choose an alternative device or file for input or output. As you know, most programs and commands have a default device. For example, when you enter the **DIR** command, the computer assumes that you want a directory to be displayed on the screen. This is because the default for **DIR** is the console (CON), which comprises the screen as the output device and the keyboard as the input device. You can assign a different device or even a file to be the command's output destination by preceding the device or file name with the > symbol. Similarly, you can assign a device or file to be a command's input by preceding the device or file name with the < symbol.

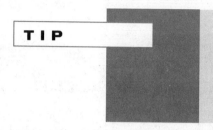

TIP

Use the DOSKEY utility (see Chapter 15) to create an *ARRANGE* macro to sort the contents of one file (parameter one) line by line and write the sorted text into another file (parameter two): DOSKEY ARRANGE=SORT $L $1 $G $2.

Storing Screen Output in a Disk File

As you know, DOS doesn't have to direct its output only to the screen. It can also direct the output to a text file. This means that the information displayed on the screen can be sent to a file on disk.

This redirection technique has many practical uses. If you're in a hurry and don't want to wait for printed output, you can quickly send the information to a disk file and then peruse it at your leisure. You can read it into your word-processing program and make modifications to it, or include it in reports. You can read it with a database-management program and perform file-management functions based on the information sent by DOS into the disk file.

An excellent use of redirection is to create a file that is a catalog of the contents of several diskettes. If you were working with a word processor or a database program, you could then get a master listing of all the files you have stored on all your working diskettes. If you were working with a hard disk, you could make a catalog of your backup disks.

The first step in creating your own diskette catalog is to decide where the master list will be placed. Let's assume you want to place the data in a file called CATALOG. The first cataloged directory will be that of the diskette in drive A:. Entering

```
DIR A: > CATALOG
```

at the DOS command prompt produces no visible result on the screen. That's because you just told DOS to store the information in a file called

➤ **EXTRA!**

Sending Screen Output to the Printer

You often need a hard-copy printout of the information that appears on your computer screen. As you learned in Chapter 7, the PrtSc key (or Shift+PrtSc on some keyboards) is limited to only one screenful of information at a time. However, it is usually more useful to send a command's complete output to the printer. DOS has a simple way of redirecting the complete output, no matter how many screenfuls of data are involved.

Including **>PRN** in a command line tells DOS to redirect that command's output to the printer. For example, the following command will redirect the standard DOS directory listing to the printer instead of to the video screen:

```
DIR >PRN
```

As with all the example commands in this chapter, you can try this at a command prompt, or with the *Run* choice on the shell's File menu. When the shell is running, you can always see the files contained in the currently selected directory. Although using the PrtSc key can print the screen image (after using the **GRAPHICS** command), it won't print all the file names if they don't fit within the files area of your screen. Using the above **DIR** command at the command prompt will print the entire listing regardless of how many files are in the directory.

The same principle of redirection applies to any DOS command that sends data to the screen. For example, entering

```
CHKDSK >PRN
```

will generate a status check of disk and memory and send it to the printer rather than to the video screen.

CATALOG rather than to display the directory on the screen. If you were watching, you would have seen the A: drive light come on as the CATALOG file was being written.

TIP

Use the NUL device to discard undesired and frequently annoying DOS messages. Just redirect a command's output to NUL and those distracting messages will disappear. For example, the XCOPY command normally displays several expected messages, such as "Reading source file(s)...", as well as the actual names of the files being copied. The command XCOPY *.COM \COMFILES > NUL will copy all the .COM files to the specified COMFILES directory, but will discard all the annoying messages. The DOS prompt will just return and the chore will have been done.

To check the results of this command, you can view the contents of the CATALOG file from the shell. The resulting display will contain the directory contents just as if you had typed in the **DIR** command. Of course, this display only represents what the directory looked like at the time the original CATALOG file was created by DOS. It is like a snapshot of the original directory; if you add or delete files on the A: drive the directory listing you see in the CATALOG file will not reflect any of the changes.

Try the following sequence now to reinforce your understanding of redirection. Redirect the output from the **DIR** and **CHKDSK** commands at the DOS prompt to a disk file. You can call this file CATALOG, or you can give it a name of your own. Then use File▸View in the shell to verify that the output was generated properly. Later on, you can see that the contents of this file are unchanging. After doing some other work with the system, issue a **DIR** or **CHKDSK** command at the DOS prompt again. Then compare the results to the snapshot contained in your CATALOG file.

Adding Output to an Existing File

Redirection also allows you to add the directory display of another drive to the CATALOG file. This requires a slightly different command. Look at the following two commands:

```
DIR A: > CATALOG
DIR A: >> CATALOG
```

What is the difference?

The first command simply replaces the old CATALOG file with a new one. The second command, on the other hand, causes the output from the **DIR** command to be *appended* to (added to the end of) the existing CATALOG file. The directory listing of the new diskette placed in drive A: will be appended to the directory listing of the diskette previously placed in drive A:.

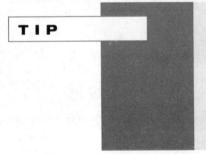

TIP

Use the redirection operator (>) to direct a program's output to a file or to a device. In the case of a file, this new output will completely replace any existing data in the file. Use the append operator (>>) to redirect new data to an existing file. This new data is appended to, or added to the end of, the current contents of the file.

You can continue this process by placing other diskettes in drive A: and repeating the >> command. CATALOG will grow as you store your diskette directories in it. If you are a hard-disk user, you can place your diskettes in drive A: and update your CATALOG file on drive C:. When you then view your CATALOG file the result will be a consolidated directory that spans the contents of a number of diskettes.

If you need a hard copy of the directories, you can use the *Print* choice from the File menu. Naturally, this assumes that you've already activated the printer's spooling queue, as explained in Chapter 7. Alternatively, you can redirect the data to your printer by using the **TYPE** command:

```
TYPE CATALOG > PRN
```

You can edit this command's output with your word processor, print the results on gummed labels, and attach them to your original diskettes. Some companies sell programs for fifty dollars just to do this simple task.

WARNING   Using TYPE on a non-ASCII file could display meaningless symbols on your screen. It could also lock up your system entirely. If this happens, you'll need to reboot.

Try the redirection feature yourself right now. Create your own CATALOG file, listing all the file names on several diskettes. If you're interested only in the names themselves and not in the size or date and time information, use a **DIR/W** command to direct the output to your CATALOG file. Remember to use a single **>** sign to create a new file and a pair of them (**>>**) to append directory output to an existing file. Dual-diskette users should place the diskettes to be cataloged into drive B:, creating the CATALOG file on drive A:. Hard-disk users should place their diskettes into drive A:, creating the CATALOG file on drive C:.

Receiving Input from Text Files

DOS can receive input from a text file. This means that instead of waiting at the console to enter data, make responses, or otherwise generate input for a DOS command or a program, you can type your responses in advance. DOS will then take each response from the input file as it is needed. Let's look at a simple example.

You may have noticed that some DOS commands require the user to enter additional keystrokes after the program has begun. For example, the **FORMAT** command will always pause after you press Enter and ask you to press any key before actual formatting takes place. This safety precaution protects you from errors, giving you a moment to take a deep breath (and to check the disk in the drive) before actually committing yourself to the formatting process.

You could avoid that extra keystroke by creating an input file to be used with the **FORMAT** command. The input file would contain any keystrokes that you wanted typed in while the program was running. In this case, a simple press of the Enter key will do. To create a file containing the Enter character, you could use the DOS Editor (see Chapter 6), or your own word processor.

You can even create an input file from the DOS prompt by using the **COPY** command you learned earlier. Let's call the file *KEYS*. Enter

```
COPY CON: KEYS
```

at the command prompt, or from the File➤Run option in the shell, and press Enter. Press Enter twice more to store the actual code for the Enter key two times in the newly created file: once to tell DOS you have put the diskette into the drive and once to tell DOS you don't want to create a volume label. While you're at it, type the letter **N** and press Enter. This is for the No response to the **FORMAT** command's final request "Do you want to format an additional diskette?" Then press Ctrl+Z to insert the end-of-file code, which is displayed on screen as

```
^Z
```

and press Enter. The KEYS file now contains the responses needed for the **FORMAT** command.

To indicate that these responses are coming from a file and not from you at the keyboard, the < symbol is used. When you select the *Format* choice from the Disk Utilities program group, you can enter the following as the parameters in the dialog box that appears:

```
B:/S < KEYS
```

When you submit this completed command, the formatting does not pause—the Enter keypress has been input from the KEYS file. When the single disk is completely formatted, the N tells FORMAT you're done, and the DOS prompt reappears. As you can see, this kind of feature can save you time and effort, and can be useful in many situations.

Processing Your File Information with Filters

Another powerful feature of DOS is its use of *filters* to process data directly. Just as a camera filter changes what you see through the lens, a DOS filter can process in unique ways any data that passes through it and can change what you see on the screen. There are three filters included in DOS: **SORT**, **FIND**, and **MORE**. They are stored on disk as the SORT.EXE, FIND.EXE, and MORE.COM files.

Arranging Your Data with the Sort Filter

Let's look first at one of the most useful filters, the **SORT** filter. **SORT** rearranges lines of data. Take a look at the sample data files in Figures 10.1 and 10.2. The information is arranged into neat columns. These lists could have been prepared with a word processor, a database manager, a spreadsheet, or even with DOS itself. In general, you can align information by using tabs or a sufficient number of space characters. Since each program's tab settings can be different, the techniques in this chapter assume that you've separated your columnar data with a proper number of *space* characters, not tabs. If in fact you've created your own files by using tabs, you should first convert the files to a space-only (non-tab) format. Most word processors include a special output mode wherein each tab

FIGURE 10.1

An example of a typical business contact list. It's straight text, so it could just as easily have been created in a database program, a word processor, or a spreadsheet.

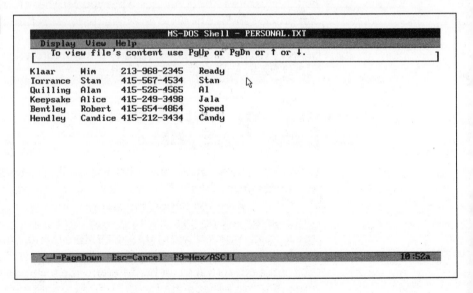

```
                              MS-DOS Shell - BUSINESS.TXT
   Display  View  Help
 [    To view file's content use PgUp or PgDn or ↑ or ↓.                        ]

 Cantonese Imports    134  Roberts   Joseph 212/656-2156
 Brandenberg Gates    754  Bennett   Mary   415/612-5656
 Sole Survivor,Inc.   237  Evans     Gail   415/222-3514
 Presley Plastics     198  Presley   Robert 716/245-6119
 Plymouth Granite Co  345  Williams  Peter  617/531-6145
 Bucket Dance Wear    276  Lewis     Ann    415/635-2530
 Intelli-Strategies   743  Griffiths Robert 415/362-9537
 Benicia Balloons     983  Franklin  Marie  212/524-4157
 Standard Shelters    690  Rucker    Sally  415/532-1107
 Panama Rain Corp.    576  Cook      Freda  408/534-9739




 <─┘=PageDown  Esc=Cancel  F9=Hex/ASCII                              10:51a
```

FIGURE 10.2

A personal phone list is another example of a typical text file that many people maintain on their computers. There are no fixed guidelines on the number of data columns, their width, or their contents.

```
                              MS-DOS Shell - PERSONAL.TXT
   Display  View  Help
 [    To view file's content use PgUp or PgDn or ↑ or ↓.                        ]

 Klaar     Wim     213-968-2345  Ready
 Torrance  Stan    415-567-4534  Stan
 Quilling  Alan    415-526-4565  Al
 Keepsake  Alice   415-249-3498  Jala
 Bentley   Robert  415-654-4864  Speed
 Hendley   Candice 415-212-3434  Candy










 <─┘=PageDown  Esc=Cancel  F9=Hex/ASCII                              10:52a
```

character is replaced by a proper number of space characters to ensure continued visual alignment.

Lists like these usually grow in size, with the new entries added chronologically as your business acquires new clients or as you make new friends and acquaintances. Every once in a while, you probably rewrite your own personal phone list. You usually want the list in last-name order, but you might want a special printout in nickname or first-name order. Even more often, businesses need to reprint their client list in some other usable order. Perhaps the telephone receptionist needs an updated list in company-name order. The marketing department may need the same list printed in telephone-number order. Then again, the accounts payable department may want the list in customer-ID order. All of these are very easy to obtain with the **SORT** filter.

Using the redirection concept presented in the previous section, you can take each of the representative lists above and rearrange the data to suit your needs. One form of filtering is to enter the following command at the DOS prompt:

```
SORT < BUSINESS.TXT
```

Remember that you have the choice of using the command prompt or using the Run dialog box. I present the main parameter options for the commands in this chapter. You can then choose how to enter them. The sample screens all represent DOS shell outputs, using the File➤Run choice, since I find it to be faster for single commands than waiting for the command prompt to appear after pressing Shift+F9.

In Figure 10.3 I've only specified the file name BUSINESS.TXT, since the current directory is the one that contains this file. You can see the current directory (C:\SIG1D\DOCS\DOS6) in the drives area of the screen, just below the menu bar. If you use a file that is located in a different drive and directory, you'll naturally have to prefix the file name with this specifying information.

Sorting the BUSINESS.TXT file results in the list ordered alphabetically by company name, as shown in Figure 10.4.

FIGURE 10.3

You can run the **SORT** command from the DOS shell to arrange the data in any text file. The < redirection operator is used here to guide the data from the BUSINESS.TXT file into the SORT command. Output will go by default to the video screen.

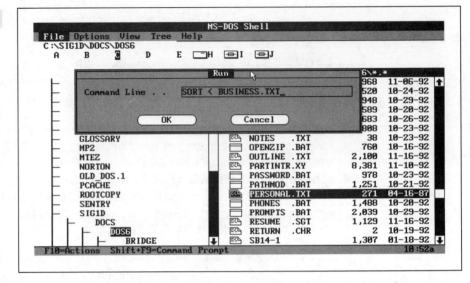

FIGURE 10.4

The BUSINESS.TXT file is sorted by company name, but only because the company's name appears in the first columns of the text file. The **SORT** command by default arranges data by column, from left to right.

```
Benicia Balloons      983  Franklin  Marie   212/524-4157
Brandenberg Gates     754  Bennett   Mary    415/612-5656
Bucket Dance Wear     276  Lewis     Ann     415/635-2530
Cantonese Imports     134  Roberts   Joseph  212/656-2156
Intelli-Strategies    743  Griffiths Robert  415/362-9537
Panama Rain Corp.     576  Cook      Freda   408/534-9739
Plymouth Granite Co   345  Williams  Peter   617/531-6145
Presley Plastics      198  Presley   Robert  716/245-6119
Sole Survivor,Inc.    237  Evans     Gail    415/222-3514
Standard Shelters     690  Rucker    Sally   415/532-1107
```

Press any key to return to MS-DOS Shell

A similar arrangement of your personal phone list can be obtained by entering

```
SORT < PERSONAL.TXT
```

In this case, the arrangement is by last name. That is because these lists are sorted by whatever data comes first on the line.

Improve Efficiency by Combining Input and Output Redirection

In the examples you've just read about, the .TXT files were directed to be *input* to the **SORT** command. Since there was no redirection specified for output, the sorted results appeared on the video screen by default. Each of these commands could also specify an output redirection that would place the sorted results in a disk file. You could then work with the sorted file as you like, perhaps delaying the printing until a convenient time. For example, the two sorted lists could be saved in the files CLIENTS.TXT and PHONES.TXT with the following commands:

```
SORT < BUSINESS.TXT > CLIENTS.TXT
SORT < PERSONAL.TXT > PHONES.TXT
```

In longer command lines like these you must remember that the > and < symbols relate the words that follow them only to the *command* preceding them on that line. Although at first glance it might appear that the middle item in each of the lines above is being directed to the SORT command on the one hand and to the CLIENTS.TXT or PHONES.TXT file on the other hand, in fact you should read the line in terms of the command only: "The command **SORT** is being directed to take its input from the < file and to send its output to the > file."

Figure 10.5 shows how you can use the **TYPE** command to verify your results. Figure 10.6 depicts how the **SORT** filter works to create the PHONES file from the PERSONAL file.

FIGURE 10.5

Use output redirection to sort data (e.g., from the PERSONAL.TXT file) and send the sorted results into a newly created file (e.g., the PHONES.TXT file). The **SORT** command arranges all the lines in order, treating each line as a single collection of characters.

```
C>TYPE PERSONAL.TXT
Klaar      Wim      213-968-2345    Ready
Torrance   Stan     415-567-4534    Stan
Quilling   Alan     415-526-4565    Al
Keepsake   Alice    415-249-3498    Jala
Bentley    Robert   415-654-4864    Speed
Hendley    Candice  415-212-3434    Candy

C>SORT < PERSONAL.TXT > PHONES.TXT

C>TYPE PHONES.TXT
Bentley    Robert   415-654-4864    Speed
Hendley    Candice  415-212-3434    Candy
Keepsake   Alice    415-249-3498    Jala
Klaar      Wim      213-968-2345    Ready
Quilling   Alan     415-526-4565    Al
Torrance   Stan     415-567-4534    Stan

C>
```

FIGURE 10.6

The **SORT** filter can work in conjunction with the redirection operators to take input from one file and send output to another file.

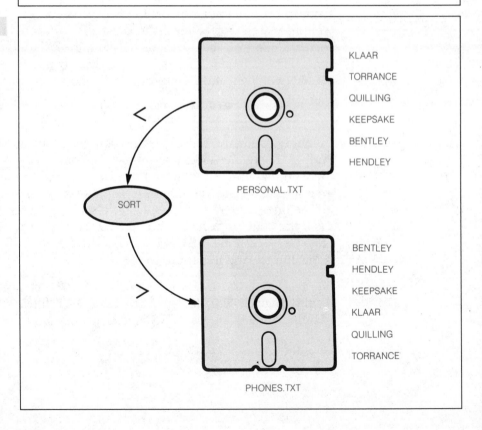

The **SORT** filter also enables you to sort data in several different ways. For example, the **/R** switch tells the program to sort in reverse order. **SORT** also allows you to specify the column on which you want the sorting to take place.

Normally, **SORT** begins with the first character in the line. However, using the **/+n** switch, you can tell **SORT** to sort from the *n*th column in the data line, which allows you to sort the data from a file in a variety of ways. Of course, you can use the **SORT** filter for data that you create at the console or obtain from a file.

For example, by choosing the forty-third column in the BUSINESS.TXT file, you could just as easily sort the entries by phone number (see Figure 10.7). Character column 43 gets you past the columns containing names and ID numbers.

```
SORT  < BUSINESS.TXT /+43
```

You can use the **/+n** switch to sort rows of information according to a portion of the data. Sorting by phone number, for example, requires that you correctly identify that the phone number begins in column 43 of this file's data.

```
C>SORT < BUSINESS.TXT /+43
Benicia Balloons     983  Franklin  Marie  212/524-4157
Cantonese Imports    134  Roberts   Joseph 212/656-2156
Panama Rain Corp.    576  Cook      Freda  408/534-9739
Sole Survivor,Inc.   237  Evans     Gail   415/222-3514
Intelli-Strategies   743  Griffiths Robert 415/362-9537
Standard Shelters    690  Rucker    Sally  415/532-1107
Brandenberg Gates    754  Bennett   Mary   415/612-5656
Bucket Dance Wear    276  Lewis     Ann    415/635-2530
Plymouth Granite Co  345  Williams  Peter  617/531-6145
Presley Plastics     198  Presley   Robert 716/245-6119

C>
```

Performing Text Searches with the Find Filter

Let's look at another DOS filter, the **FIND** command. It permits you to scan any text file for a series of text characters and to locate any lines in the file that contain the specified characters. For instance, let's take the business contact list from Figure 10.1 and try to find all clients located in the area code 415:

```
FIND "415" BUSINESS.TXT
```

This command will locate all lines that contain the specified *character string* (the first parameter) in the specified text file (the second parameter). The quotation marks around your character strings are delimiters. You must use them. They assist DOS in distinguishing a character string from the command line's other characters, which represent commands, file names, or parameters.

N O T E

When you are doing character searches in DOS or any other processing language, the case (upper or lower) of alphabetic characters is critical. Unless you incorporate the /I switch to ignore case, you must always specify the characters in the string *exactly* as you expect to find them in the file.

Figure 10.8 shows the command request, while Figure 10.9 demonstrates the results.

Note that the first line of the output identifies the input text file.

This is a typical database extraction request that has been handled by DOS *almost* satisfactorily. Notice that the Benicia Balloons company has been included in the results, even though its area code is not 415. You asked DOS to find every line in the file that included 415 anywhere in the line, and 415 is in the last four digits of that company's telephone number (524-4157). Therefore, the line was filtered into the resulting selection.

FIGURE 10.8

Use the **FIND** filter to extract data from a text file of row-oriented information. FIND will display all lines of data that contain the specified search string (415 in this example).

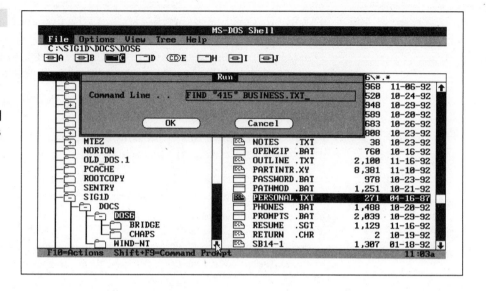

FIGURE 10.9

Results of the search for 415. Each line that contains the three-character string 415 is identified. Note that 415 is correctly identified in all lines, even though you may be surprised to discover that the string exists in more than just the obvious place.

```
---------- BUSINESS.TXT
Brandenberg Gates     754   Bennett    Mary    415/612-5656
Sole Survivor,Inc.    237   Evans      Gail    415/222-3514
Bucket Dance Wear     276   Lewis      Ann     415/635-2530
Intelli-Strategies    743   Griffiths  Robert  415/362-9537
Benicia Balloons      983   Franklin   Marie   212/524-4157
Standard Shelters     690   Rucker     Sally   415/532-1107
```

Press any key to return to MS-DOS Shell

To solve this problem, specify a space as the first character in the character string. By including the extra space before the digits 415, you will be sure to extract only the telephone numbers that *begin* with the desired digits, i.e., those following a space. (Remember, the examples in this chapter are set up with spaces, not tabs.) Enter

```
FIND " 415" BUSINESS.TXT
```

Figure 10.10 shows this command entered at the command prompt and its results. Your command has selected the correct lines from the file.

FIGURE 10.10

You must make sure that your character string is sufficiently defined to identify only the text lines you want. Since the phone number is always preceded by a space, you can include the extra space in the search string to limit the results to the desired phone numbers.

```
C>FIND " 415" BUSINESS.TXT

---------- BUSINESS.TXT
Brandenberg Gates   754   Bennett    Mary    415/612-5656
Sole Survivor,Inc.  237   Evans      Gail    415/222-3514
Bucket Dance Wear   276   Lewis      Ann     415/635-2530
Intelli-Strategies  743   Griffiths  Robert  415/362-9537
Standard Shelters   690   Rucker     Sally   415/532-1107

C>
```

You can also name more than one file as input to the **FIND** filter. With the command shown in Figure 10.11, you could quickly see if any of your business clients from area code 617 appeared on your prospects list as well. This is an example of how DOS can help you find duplicate or redundant entries.

FIGURE 10.11

You can use FIND to discover duplicate entries in multiple lists. Simply type the search string as the first parameter, followed by one or more file names in which to search for the existence of the string.

```
C>FIND " 617" BUSINESS.TXT PROSPECT.TXT

---------- BUSINESS.TXT
Plymouth Granite Co 345  Williams  Peter  617/531-6145

---------- PROSPECT.TXT
Williams  Peter   Plymouth Granite Co 617/531-6145
Kingland  Benson  Ranger Treadmills   617/222-4543
Brandeis  Judd    Scholar Support,Inc 617/298-4455

C>
```

Other tools that you've already learned to use can check for duplicates throughout all the area codes at one time. First use the **COPY** command to join the two business files into one temporary file, which you can delete later; then use **SORT** to filter the resultant file. Duplicates would appear one right after the other in the output listing. Using either File▶View or **FIND**, you could proceed to find any subset of records of interest (for example, the 617 calling area). In each case, you would not have to look back and forth between two lists.

WARNING

When you are joining two files to create a third, or when you are creating any temporary file, make sure your disk has enough space on it for the operation.

Pausing Screen Output with the More Filter

The last filter available in DOS is named **MORE**. It causes the screen display to pause, just as the **/P** switch does with the **DIR** command. Since some DOS commands accept the **/P** switch to process data one screenful at a time, you only need the **MORE** filter for commands that do not allow screenful processing. For example, the **TYPE** command displays an entire text file at once. In order to pause the output each time the screen fills up, you need to use the **MORE** filter.

➤ EXTRA!

Which File Contains a Particular Text String?

Use the SEARCH.BAT batch file to look into all files in a particular directory for a specific sequence of characters:

```
@ECHO OFF
Rem SEARCH.BAT finds all occurrences of a specified text
Rem string, within a specified directory,
Rem and within a specified wildcard set of filenames.
Rem Syntax:   SEARCH "string" Filespec DirName

Rem Example:  SEARCH "Robbins" *.TXT C:\DOSBOOK
Rem           will find all occurrences of 'Robbins' in the
Rem           TXT files in the DOSBOOK directory.
Rem Note: Embedded blanks are not allowed in the text string.
Rem If %3 (DirName) is missing, use current directory.
Rem If %2 (Filespec) is missing, use *.* for Filespec.
Rem If you specify a DirName, you must specify a Filespec
IF NOT '%2'=='' SET Fspec=%2
IF '%2'=='' SET Fspec=*.*
IF '%3'=='' FOR %%j IN (%Fspec%) DO FIND /N /I %1 %%j
IF NOT '%3'=='' FOR %%j IN (%3\%Fspec%) DO FIND /N /I %1 %%j
SET Fspec=
```

To display any text file that exceeds the size of a single screenful, use input redirection and the MORE filter to display one screenful of text at a time. For example, to display a long text file named REPORT.TXT, screenful by screenful, type:

```
MORE < REPORT.TXT
```

Connecting DOS Operations with Pipes

You've seen how the **SORT** and **FIND** filters can work with data files as input. Now you'll explore how filters can work in connection with other programs or DOS commands. When these connections are made, the filters are called *pipes*. Earlier in this chapter, you saw how you could change DOS's default input and output devices using redirection. Pipes allow you to combine the power of redirection with that of filters. You can simultaneously change (filter) your data while it is being moved (redirected) from one location to another.

Even with the redirection techniques you have learned so far in this chapter, if you want to do several things in a row, you might still have quite a bit of work to do. You might need to run one program, send its results to a disk file, and then run another program to process the resulting data. Then you might have to take the next program's input from that disk file to continue the processing chain, perhaps creating several intermediate files before getting the final result.

Piping allows you to take the output of one command or program and make it the input of another command or program. You can do this several times in a row. An entire series of programs that generate intermediate output for one another can be automated by using the sophisticated combination of filters and pipes.

Many of the batch files scattered throughout this book as examples (especially in the *EXTRA!* sidebars) demonstrate how to successfully combine DOS commands and operations with pipes. You can do many interesting, novel, and valuable new operations by intelligently combining the techniques of this chapter with other facilities of DOS.

For example, the *EXTRA!* in this section shows how to construct a batch file that can display (or easily print) the system date or time. You can **CALL** either of these batch files to date or time-stamp whatever else you may be doing on your system. The fundamental technique that makes these batch files work is redirection and piping:

```
DATE < RETURN.CHR | FIND "Current"
```

➤ EXTRA!

Want to Output the Current System Date or Time?

The system commands **DATE** and **TIME** normally display the date or time, then pause until a user accepts them or corrects them. If you just want to display the current values, without experiencing any pause for input, you can use one of the two batch files below. If you want to include this date or time information as a stamping mechanism within other text files, you can use the **>>** redirectional operator to append the results to an existing text file. This is an exercise best left to you, but I'll get you started by telling you that you only need to add **>>** and a file name to the **DATE** or **TIME** lines in the batch files below.

Both batch files require the existence of the RETURN.CHR file. This simple file contains a two-character sequence, consisting of a carriage-return and line-feed. You can create this file by typing:

```
COPY CON RETURN.CHR
```

at any command prompt. Then press the Enter key, then the Ctrl+Z key combination, and finally the Enter key once more.

Here's the first file:

```
@ECHO OFF
Rem CURRDATE.BAT outputs system date.
IF NOT EXIST return.chr Goto Missing
DATE < RETURN.CHR | FIND "Current"
Goto End
:Missing
ECHO Cannot find the RETURN.CHR file which must contain the
ECHO CR/LF (Carriage Return + Line Feed) ASCII characters.
:End
```

Here is the second file:

```
@ECHO OFF
Rem CURRTIME.BAT displays system.
IF NOT EXIST return.chr Goto Missing
TIME < RETURN.CHR | FIND "Current"
Goto End
:Missing
ECHO Cannot find the RETURN.CHR file which must contain the
ECHO CR/LF (Carriage Return + Line Feed) ASCII characters.
:End
```

The contents of the RETURN.CHR file are first redirected into the **DATE** command. The output of the **DATE** command is then piped into the **FIND** filter which looks for the line containing the word "Current." This line alone is then output to the screen. Naturally, you could append an output redirection to send this **DATE** stamp to the printer or to a file.

Many other examples can easily be constructed. For example, suppose that you wanted to obtain some system information. Piping could readily use DOS commands to first obtain normal output, then extract only the specific data that you want. Table 10.1 contains a group of such piping examples.

TABLE 10.1: Piping Examples

TO FIND THIS OUT...	...USE THIS PIPING COMMAND
Available conventional program memory	MEM ¦ FIND "executable"
Contiguity information about current drive	CHKDSK *.* ¦ FIND "non-"
Default drive's cluster (allocation unit) size	CHKDSK ¦ FIND "each"
Free space on default drive	DIR ¦ FIND "bytes free"
Size of current directory	DIR ¦ FIND "(s)"
Size of default drive	CHKDSK ¦ FIND "total disk space"
Space consumed by data files on default drive	CHKDSK ¦ FIND "user"
Space consumed by directories on default drive	CHKDSK ¦ FIND "dir"

Summary

In this chapter, you've learned about powerful DOS features for specialized utility operations. You've seen that redirection allows you to specify alternative input and output devices for DOS commands. Pipes enable you to direct the flow of information with precision from one command to another. Filters permit you to process the data as it flows through your central processing unit under your direction. The chapter presented the following important points:

- Special symbols are used by DOS during redirection operations. The > sign indicates a new output device, and < indicates a new input source. If you use the >> sign, the output is appended to the specified file.

- Certain DOS commands can filter data. This data can be input at the keyboard, from an existing file, or even from another program or command.

- The **SORT** filter can easily arrange the lines of output from any command or data file. Optional switches add significant power to this command: **/R** produces a reverse-order listing, while **/+n** sorts the file by the *n*th character space instead of the first. This allows you to sort your data in meaningful orders.

- The **FIND** filter displays lines that contain the specified characters.

- The **MORE** filter performs the simple task of making the display pause when output fills the screen. This gives you the opportunity to read the complete display before continuing the processing.

- Pipes are preceded by the ¦ symbol. They transmit the output from one command to another, in effect making one command's output the next command's input.

- Pipes can be combined with both filters and redirection in sophisticated ways to produce powerful results.

The examples in this chapter should serve to spark your imagination—you can now create your own useful utility extensions. With the tools from this chapter, you can now develop your own programs for file sorting, text searching, and diskette cataloging. Now that you've rounded out your knowledge of DOS fundamentals, you can turn to Part Four to begin refining your understanding of the possibilities with DOS.

Making Backups and
Restoring Files

ONE OF THE disadvantages of hard disks is that if they fail, or "crash," all the information stored on them can be lost. Much more is at stake than just one floppy diskette's worth of contents. Back up your hard disk regularly or run the constant risk of losing your data!

Of course, the reason for backing up your files onto floppies or onto another hard disk is so you can rewrite the files back onto your hard disk in the unfortunate event that the hard-disk version has been deleted, destroyed, or corrupted. You may never need to restore a file, but your backup files will provide you with some inexpensive protection against hardware or software failure.

This chapter describes in depth how to protect your programs—and more importantly, your data—from loss due to operator error or hardware failure. However, you must remember to back up your files on a regular basis to keep the backup floppy diskettes up to date with the changes you've made on your hard disk. Depending on how frequently you generate new data files or update old ones, you may want to back up your disk every week or every month (or more or less frequently). Experience seems to be the best teacher in all things, and most people who back up files regularly do so because they have experienced an uncomfortable loss of data at some point. The more data they lost, the more frequently they now back up.

Types of Backups

To be truly useful, you must back up your computer work at regular intervals. Anyone who works with changing files daily should perform some form of backup at the end of each day. If your files do not change much from week to week, you could possibly plan on weekly backups. DOS offers backup programs that can back up all of your files, or only those that have changed since a preceding backup. A *backup cycle* is the entire span of time that begins with a complete (i.e., Full) backup of an entire set of files, and includes all subsequent changes to those files (i.e., Incremental and Differential backups). These three backup options—Full, Incremental, and Differential—offer their own advantages and disadvantages.

A *full backup* copies all the files you indicate, regardless of whether some or most of them have remained unchanged since your last backup. You can

➤ EXTRA!

At What Special Times Should You Back Up Your Files?

In addition to the backups you should make regularly, there are three special situations that necessitate backing up your hard disk:

1. Your computer is going to be moved. Especially if your computer will be traveling in airplane cargo holds or in shipper's trucks, you should back up your data before the trip. Your hard disk may not survive the physical handling (or occasional abuse).

2. You are running out of space on your hard disk, and you decide to take an hour or two to delete some files, consolidate some directories, and create new branches in your directory tree. With such a massive project, you should protect yourself against your own enthusiasm and fatigue by doing a backup.

3. You are going to defragment your disk with **DEFRAG** (see Chapter 18), or compress your disk's files with **DBLSPACE** (see Chapter 9). Programs like these can improve system performance as well as make more efficient use of hard disk space. During the optimization or compression process, however, your entire hard-disk contents are liable to loss in the event of a power failure. Do a complete disk backup just prior to running such a program.

opt for an *incremental backup* to copy only files that have been changed since a time you specify. Files that are unchanged will not be written to the backup media, making for a faster and smaller backup. *Differential backups* make copies of all files changed since the last full backup. This may include some files that may have been written on the last incremental backup. Trade-offs among the three types of backups are analyzed in an *EXTRA!* later in this chapter.

N O T E   MSBACKUP does have an internal limit of 2046 subdirectories per drive. If the drive you are backing up contains more subdirectories than this, you will have to back up partial directories. Alternatively, you should probably reassess your directory organization—it may help if you can eliminate or combine some of your directories.

Activating the Microsoft Backup Facility

If you're using a dual-diskette system, you can easily use **DISKCOPY**, **COPY**, or even **XCOPY** (see Chapter 19) to back up diskette files onto another diskette. Protecting yourself from the major trauma of losing an entire hard disk, however, requires more effort than that. **DISKCOPY** is designed for floppy diskette copies only, and the **COPY** and **XCOPY** commands have a fundamental weakness: the destination for your copied files is limited to what can be stored on that one diskette. If the current directory contains more files than can fit on one destination diskette, or even if it contains one extremely large file that exceeds the capacity of the backup floppy, the **COPY** and **XCOPY** commands simply can't handle the job.

In order to allow you to back up files onto a series of floppy diskettes or another fixed (hard) disk, DOS provides a command called **MSBACKUP**. You can activate this command from the DOS shell by choosing *Backup Fixed Disk* in the Disk Utilities program group. This command is usually used to back up the files from a hard disk and distribute them as necessary over a series of floppy diskettes.

As with all the shell programs, you can activate MSBACKUP from a command prompt as well. To do so, you would use this syntax:

```
MSBACKUP SetupFile [/BW | /LCD | /MDA]
```

The *SetupFile* is the name of a file that contains the specifications of the backup to be performed. It includes the directories and file names to back up, as well as which type of backup to perform (Full, Differential, or Incremental). If you neglect to define a setup file at all, then MSBACKUP will use a standard group of assumed settings stored in a DEFAULT.SET file.

The three switches that can optionally be used when running **MSBACKUP** from a command prompt each force the program to use a different screen mode. Depending on your system, you might not need any of these at all. **/BW** is for black-and-white output. **/LCD** is for laptop-compatible video-mode output. **/MDA** is for output to a monochrome display adapter.

When **MSBACKUP** runs, it presents the main graphic screen seen in Figure 11.1. If this is the first time that you've run the MSBACKUP program, however, you'll first receive the following Alert message:

```
The disk compatibility test has not been performed on this
system. Reliable disk backups cannot be guaranteed until the
compatibility test has been completed successfully.
```

If you get this message, choose OK to display the screen in Figure 11.1, and choose the *Configure* choice, in order to run the compatibility test.

In the center of the screen, this interface offers four primary actions—*Backup, Restore, Compare,* and *Configure*. We'll take a look at each of these primary options in a slightly different sequence in the rest of this chapter.

FIGURE 11.1

The primary MSBACKUP interface screen. From here, you can initiate an extensive backup or restore. You can also ensure restorability by comparing your backup data with the original files. Finally, you can configure your backup system, which is usually done only once.

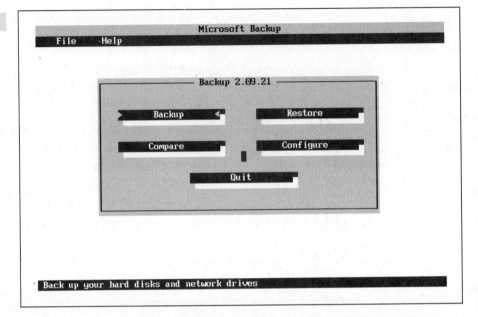

- *Configure* enables you to set up the entire MSBACKUP program to perform efficiently within your environment. In actual fact, you'll probably select *Configure* before any other choice, but you'll do this only once. This choice enables you to make some important first-time compatibility tests between MSBACKUP and your hardware. (It also enables you to later install new devices, or make changes in mouse and screen settings. However, you will not typically use *Configure* in the course of usual backup processing.)

- Choose *Backup* to make copies of specified files on any kind of backup medium. The medium is usually floppy disks, but can just as easily be something faster and larger, such as tape drives or removable cartridge disks. In fact, you can use any device that can be specified to DOS with a drive identifier, such as another fixed disk on your system.

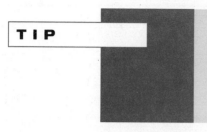

TIP

Use the *Backup* and *Restore* options of MSBACKUP to easily *copy* a large number of files from one system to another. Just back up on the first system, then restore from your backup medium to the second system.

- Use *Compare* to ensure that the backup was successful, and that the data stored on the backup medium is indeed an accurate replica of the specified original files. Essentially, you are simply asking MSBACKUP to do a file-by-file comparison of the backed-up files to the original ones remaining on your hard disk.

- *Restore* offers you the opportunity to copy backed-up files back onto a hard disk. Typically, this enables you to restore normal use after a hard disk has failed and you've replaced it. However, this same restoration procedure can be just as effective in reestablishing a backup copy of single files that have become corrupted or irretrievable for some other reason.

Configuring MSBACKUP to Your System

You should select the *Configure* choice from the initial backup screen (Figure 11.1) the very first time you use MSBACKUP. Doing so will bring up the dialog box seen in Figure 11.2, which will enable you to specify the type of mouse and video monitor you'll be using.

To ensure both efficient and successful backups, MSBACKUP must correctly identify your video and mouse hardware. Accordingly, if you select the *Video and Mouse:* field at the top left of this dialog box, the Screen and Mouse Options screen (Figure 11.3) appears.

FIGURE 11.2

The Configure dialog box provides options for specifying your video monitor type, your mouse characteristics, and the possible backup devices that you may use. You can also run a compatibility test to assure that your equipment will accurately back up your data.

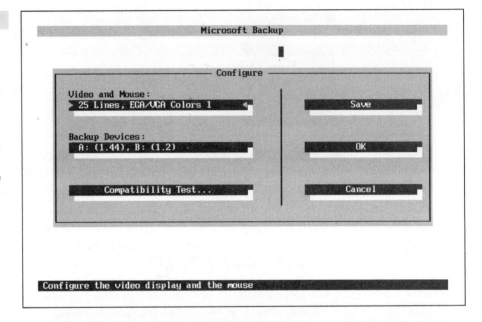

FIGURE 11.3

The Screen and Mouse Options window from the Configure dialog box. Configuring the screen and mouse options involves a range of possible settings. All of these have standard default values, but can be customized to you and your hardware.

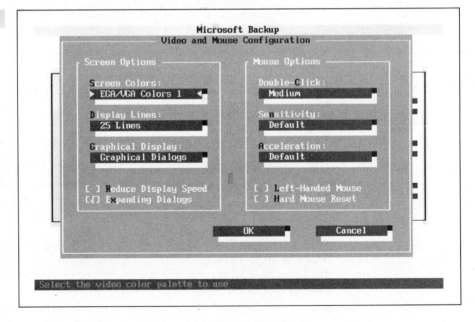

The default values determined on my system were just fine, and I left them exactly as you see them and clicked on the button. You will probably want to do the same.

If you feel like experimenting with the various Configure options or just viewing the various alternatives in the Configure dialog box, move the cursor highlight to each field in turn and select it. To do this, you can either press Enter after the cursor has moved to the field (by pressing the Tab key), or you can double-click on the desired field with your mouse.

For example, if you select the *Backup Devices:* field, you'll receive the window shown in Figure 11.4, which enables you to specify precisely the floppy drives you will be using. Generally, you won't even have to bother with this choice. If you change floppy hardware or add a floppy to your system, however, you will have to choose it and then click on the *Auto Config* button in this screen. MSBACKUP will then automatically test your hardware for you. Usually, this is sufficient to identify most floppy-drive types.

FIGURE 11.4

The Backup Devices window from the Configure dialog box. You can use this screen to specify the types of backup diskettes you plan to use in your drives. Usually, you can just click on *Auto Config* to allow MSBACKUP to automatically identify the hardware and use the conventional size and type diskettes for that equipment.

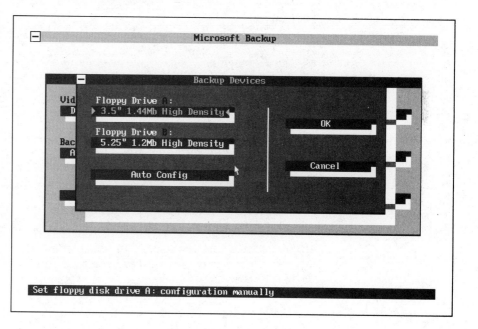

When you click on the *Auto Config* button, MSBACKUP performs a *Floppy Drive Change Line Test*. This special test requires that you remove any diskettes in the drives. MSBACKUP checks the hardware to verify that disk changes can later be readily and speedily ascertained. This will enable backups to be performed most efficiently on those floppy drives. Once this verification is complete, the Backup Devices window of Figure 11.4 reappears; you receive no special notice that the test was successful.

Running the Compatibility Test

You must click on the *Compatibility Test* button in the Configure dialog box before you can back up at all the first time. This instructs MSBACK-UP to verify that your system is prepared to back up files successfully. This test automatically performs its own small file backup, followed by a file compare. Other than specifying the drive to send your backup files to, the rest of the test is completely automated.

WARNING

If you run Windows on your system, do not run this compatibility test from within a DOS session under Windows. Run it directly from a DOS command prompt after fully exiting Windows.

MSBACKUP uses Direct Memory Access (DMA) buffers for speedier backup. If your system does not allot these DMA buffers, or allots an insufficient number of them, the compatibility test will abort with a message similar to this:

```
EMM386 DMA buffer is too small.
Add D=64 parameter and reboot.
```

If you receive this message, you will probably have to edit your CONFIG.SYS file by adding the **D=** switch, as in this example:

```
DEVICE=C:\DOS\EMM386.EXE NOEMS D=64
```

After rebooting, return to the compatibility test and rerun it. You will see an entire sequence of file selection, file backup, and file compare screens appear. If the entire process proceeds with no hitches, a final message will appear that tells you that the test was successful, and MSBACKUP is now prepared to back up files for you whenever you choose.

When you've run through and specified all possible configuration options and buttons and have completed the tests, you can save all your specifications in a single configuration file. Just click on the *Save* button and MSBACKUP will save your configuration to your hard disk. These various changes will affect your immediate backup session, and will remain in effect when you next start up the Backup program.

Selecting and Backing Up Your Files

When you are ready to actually back up some or all files from a hard disk, select *Backup* from the main MSBACKUP screen (Figure 11.1). This will bring up a screen similar to that shown in Figure 11.5.

FIGURE 11.5

The primary Backup initiation screen. From here, you can specify the files to back up, where to write the files, and the type of backup (Full, Incremental, or Differential). Or, you can choose a *setup file* that already contains all your backup specifications.

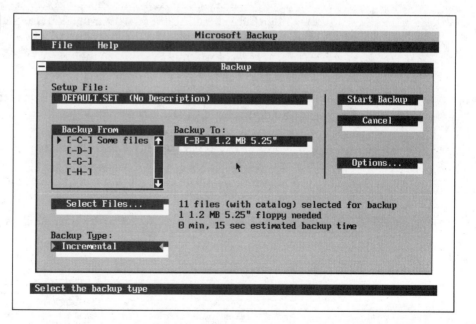

Most of Figure 11.5 should be fairly obvious. At the top of the screen, the *Setup File:* field indicates the current backup-specification file. As you can see, DEFAULT.SET is indicated the first time you display this screen. Initially, this specifies a complete backup of drive C: to floppies in your A: drive. (I've already customized this screen by selecting just a few files from drive C: for backup.) If you want to change your backup specification, you will do so by working with the other choices available on this screen. You can then pull down the File menu to reveal choices for saving your specifications in your own setup file.

➤ EXTRA!

Trade-Offs in Selecting a Backup Type

The Backup Type: field in Figure 11.5 offers three choices: *Full, Incremental,* or *Differential* backups. In each choice, MSBACKUP decides whether or not to copy each of your selected file choices. You must specify how it determines this before starting a backup.

In a *Full* backup, all your selections are copied to the backup media. Naturally, your selections may be just an eclectic group of chosen files, but they might also be all the files with a particular extension, or all the files on a drive. This can take the most amount of time, because so many files can be written in a single backup session. However, this type of backup is the easiest for restoring any one or more of the backed up copies later.

In an *incremental* backup, the intent is to only write copies of files that have *changed* since the last full or incremental backup. This allows you to maintain emergency backup copies of file versions as they change. You should use an incremental backup if you work with many different files. Each new incremental backup set will capture the latest version of all changed files. This is the method of choice if you need to maintain and have access to intermediate versions of your files.

Because fewer files are written during such a backup (unchanging files are not written), incremental backups are much faster than full backups and require less space (or fewer diskettes). However, since each incremental backup builds on the preceding full and incremental backup sets, you must retain the various sets. Later restorations will require the preceding full backup and each subsequent incremental backup set.

A *differential* backup will copy to your backup media just the last version of a file. In this instance, MSBACKUP writes the latest versions of files that have changed since the last *full* backup. This is sort of a cross between a full and an incremental backup. You should use this method if you work with virtually the same set of files daily.

Differential backups are not as large as full backups, since only files that have changed since the last full backup are written. However, they are larger than incremental backups, since files that have changed since the last incremental backup are also written. So this method is slower than an incremental backup, and requires more space or backup diskettes. Nevertheless, restoration will be faster because you will not have to use as many backup sets to reconstruct the latest version of your files.

Basically, if you can afford the space and time, use a full backup every time, and simply maintain separate sets of backup diskettes. If you don't mind the administrative overhead of maintaining multiple sets of incremental backups, save time by performing incremental backups. If you work with a limited number of different files daily, use the differential backup method as a balanced approach to time and effort, both for initial backup and subsequent possible restoration.

TIP

For instant backup of your entire hard disk onto diskettes in the A: drive, just start MSBACKUP, press B (for *Backup*), and S (for *Start Backup*). The defaults in the DEFAULT.SET setup file will be used. If you wish to quickly back up a different hard disk, or send the copies to a different drive, or change any other settings, such as verification or compression, you can save your settings to your own uniquely named .SET file.

In general, a setup file consists of information that specifies several key characteristics of the backup process. These settings can all be set or modified via the fields in the primary backup initiation screen shown in Figure 11.5. They include:

- The source of the files to copy (*Backup From:*)
- The destination medium to which the copies will be written (*Backup To:*)
- The specific group of files to be copied (*Select Files...*)
- The type of backup to create (*Backup Type:*)

The *Backup From:* choice is pretty straightforward. Click on it to display a list of system drives from which to choose.

The *Backup To:* choice is similar. Here, you are also given the choice "MS DOS Drive and Path," which opens a field for you to type the path name of a specific directory on your backup medium, which could include a removable cartridge drive or a network drive. If you specify the backup destination to be a shared network directory, be sure to use the correct nomenclature. For example, remember that you will often refer to a shared directory on a network computer (for example, \\SERVER\BACK-UPS) as if it were a root directory on a unique disk drive (for example, K:). Also, be sure that you actually have the authority to write into (as opposed to merely being able to read) that shared network directory.

The *Select Files...* button brings up a window that lets you specify precisely which files and/or file types to back up. You will need to use this choice every time you want to include or exclude files from the current setup-file specification.

The first two buttons on the right of the screen are for simply starting or canceling the backup as specified. The third button, *Options...*, provides a variety of choices concerning backup verification and password protection.

Of the screens available from the main backup initiation screen, only two really require more discussion: the Select Backup Files screen and the Disk Backup Options screen. These are the topics of the next sections.

Selecting the Files You Want Backed Up

Before you can back up anything less than a complete hard drive, you must first instruct MSBACKUP which files you want to back up. To do this, you must choose the *Select Files* button from the backup initiation screen in Figure 11.5. This displays the selection screen depicted in Figure 11.6. This screen offers a number of controls for determining precisely

FIGURE 11.6

The Select Backup Files screen from the primary backup initiation screen. You can quickly identify the files to back up from this screen. Press the spacebar when highlighting a directory name to quickly toggle an entire directory.

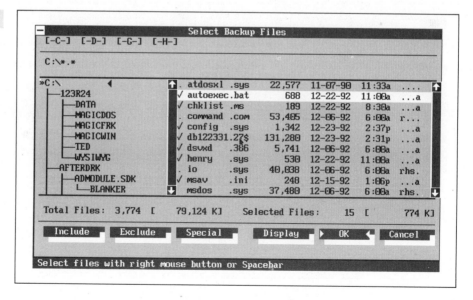

what files are to be backed up when you finally ask MSBACKUP to start the backup.

To select individual files, you should first move the cursor highlight to the desired directory in the graphic tree area on the left of the screen. As you highlight a directory name, the files contained within the directory appear in the files area to the right of the screen. To select all the files in a directory, move the highlight into the files area and just press the spacebar when the directory name is highlighted. To select (or deselect) an individual file name, press the spacebar when the file name itself is highlighted.

TIP

Mouse users can select all the files in a particular directory by clicking the right mouse button on the directory name. To select (or deselect) all the files in multiple directories, click and hold the right mouse button on the first directory name, then drag the mouse to the last directory name and release the right mouse button.

As you select files in the screen shown in Figure 11.6, MSBACKUP instantly updates the selection line below the directory and files areas. In Figure 11.6, this line indicates that 15 files (774K) have currently been selected out of a total of 3,774 files (79,124K).

Besides the *OK* and *Cancel* buttons at the bottom of the screen, there are four other buttons you can use to further specify the set of files to back up. The *Include* choice enables you to use wild cards to ensure that particular groups of file names are always included in the file-name list. The *Exclude* choice enables you to always skip certain file names, guaranteeing that they will never take up space unnecessarily on your backup disks. The *Special* and the *Display* buttons display their own screens with additional choices for working with certain types of files and for rearranging the file names in the files area.

TIP

Use the *Exclude* choice to save time and space each time you back up. Exclude such commonly unneeded files as .BAKs and .TMPs. Also exclude caching or swapping files, if they are large and visible on your system. Some third-party applications use these type of files to speed up your system, but backup copies of them won't do you any good. They are only support tools while the caching or multitasking program is executing. Use the *Special* button to quickly exclude all files that fall into one of the following categories: hidden, system, read-only, or copy-protected.

Special: The Special Selections Screen

Choosing the *Special* button in Figure 11.6 will display the Special Selections screen seen in Figure 11.7.

FIGURE 11.7

Use the *Special* pushbutton at the bottom of the Select Backup Files screen to display this screen, which enables you to include or filter out specific groups of files, such as hidden or system files, or files within a particular date range.

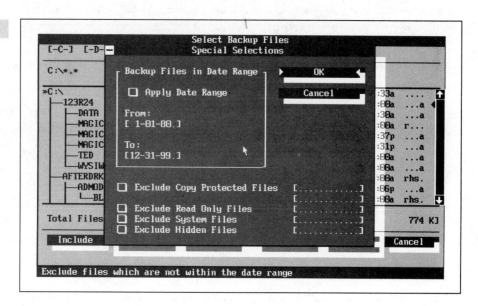

This screen contains five checkboxes that enable you to include or exclude unique groups of files. Checking the first checkbox (*Apply Date Range*) will instruct your backup set to back up only those files whose file dates are within the From–To range that you specify. Checking one or more from the bottom group of checkboxes is an easy way to exclude from backup any files that fall into the categories listed: *Copy-Protected*, *Read-Only*, *System*, and *Hidden*.

The normal default is to include these types of files in your backup. But many hidden files in particular are very large, and backup copies of them are usually very useless. For example, the swap file on my Windows system is larger than eight megabytes. Backing it up does no good because its contents are meaningless beyond representing the current state of my Windows multitasking environment when it is actually running. It wastes time and backup space to back up such a file.

The five small text boxes at the bottom right of the screen are meant for you to use if you check the *Exclude Copy-Protected Files* box. In that case, you can move the pointer to each of the five text boxes and explicitly type in the name of up to five copy-protected files that you wish to exclude from the backup. (Even if it is possible to copy such files, you might want to exclude them from your backup because copies of copy-protected files are often useless, due to the copy protection mechanism itself.)

Display: The Display Options Screen

Selecting the *Display* button from the bottom of the Select Backup Files screen shown in Figure 11.6 brings up the Display Options screen shown in Figure 11.8. This figure enables you to specify various orders for the file names that are included in your selection display.

This Display Options screen is useful for sorting the file names by one of several properties: *name*, *extension*, *size*, *date*, or *attribute*. The first four are common and self-explanatory. The fifth sorting option, *attribute*, can be especially useful. If you select this one, file names that have the archive attribute set (and consequently need most to be backed up) will appear at

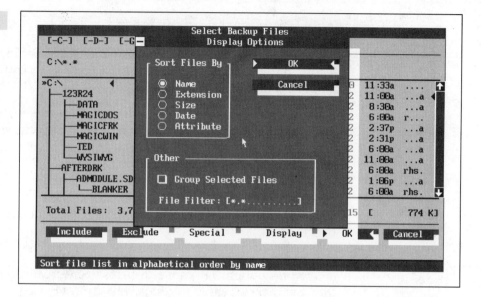

FIGURE 11.8

Use the *Display* pushbutton at the bottom of the Select Backup Files screen to display this screen, which enables you to specify how your backup files should be ordered and grouped. *Sorting* controls the individual file-name order within broader arrangements controlled by the *Group* facility.

the beginning of the list. This can be particularly helpful if you are running a partial (i.e., an incremental or differential) backup. Chapter 19 explains in depth the different attributes that a DOS file can have, as well as the **ATTRIB** command for setting or resetting those attributes.

Check the box named *Group Selected Files* if you intend to back up only a few files from one or more large directories. Checking this box ensures that the file names you've selected will appear at the top of the file lists when you display the contents of each directory in the Select Backup Files window.

Finally, use the *File Filter:* field if you plan to back up only a certain type of file. Only files that match the wild-card specification will appear in the file lists. For example, if you create a backup set to back up your Lotus 1-2-3 worksheet files, you can set the filter equal to *.WK1. This field value is temporary and is always reset to *.* whenever you return to the *Select Files...* choice on the main Backup screen.

Miscellaneous Backup Options

Returning to the primary backup initiation screen of Figure 11.5, the *Options...* button on the right side of the screen displays the Disk Backup Options screen seen in Figure 11.9.

Most of these options speak for themselves. For example, you would opt for a *Password* if the data you're saving should be secured from easy view—for example, when you're working with financial or other secret information. You might opt for *Prompt Before Overwriting Used Diskettes* if you have so many diskettes lying around that you're worried you might accidentally use an important one during a backup. I always enable this option because it offers a final view of the contents of an old disk before I overwrite it with backup data.

Personally, I would especially recommend using the *Use Error Correction on Diskettes* option. This not only helps to ensure the integrity of the saved files, but makes it easier to restore files from a backup set which may have experienced partial destruction of the backup disks themselves.

FIGURE 11.9

Clicking on the *Options...* button from the primary backup initiation screen brings up this screen showing miscellaneous options that apply to the entire backup process. Turn on or off an individual option setting by pressing the spacebar after highlighting the option line.

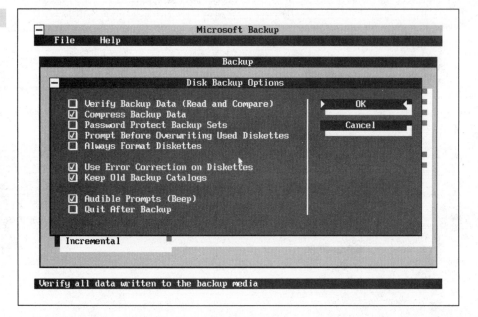

Saving Your Backup Specifications in a Setup File

You can pull down the File menu on the main Backup screen (Figure 11.5) at any time to reveal four choices for managing setup files:

- *Open Setup*
- *Save Setup*
- *Save Setup As*
- *Delete Setup*

Select the first choice (*Open Setup*) to switch this session's specification to the settings in a differently named setup file. Select the *Save Setup* choice to update the file currently being used. (That would be DEFAULT.SET in Figure 11.5.)

If you make changes but do not want to modify the currently selected setup file, you can create a new one by choosing the third option (*Save Setup As*). You'll have to type in the name you wish to use; MSBACKUP will create a new setup file with that name and the currently modified group of program settings. Finally, you can delete one or more setup files by choosing the *Delete Setup* choice and specifying the setup file(s) to erase.

Backup Complete: The Summary Screen

After making a number of modifications to my backup settings, my final test backup included only 11 critical files. During the actual backup, MSBACKUP displays timing, progress, and compression statistics. At the end of the process a Backup Complete box appears in middle of this display, as you can see in Figure 11.10.

The Backup Complete box merely summarizes the overall procedure. You probably already know some of the information, since file counts and times were displayed as the backup progressed. Once it is over, however, this box gives you a sense of the overall performance of MSBACKUP. In fact, if you look closely, it gives a bit of a view of your performance as well. Notice that MSBACKUP spent a total of 30 seconds backing up my 11 selected files. It appears that I wasted 22 of these seconds putting the backup disk into the drive after MSBACKUP prompted me for it. Obviously, I had better improve my technique if I expect to back up a full hard disk onto twenty or more diskettes.

FIGURE 11.10

A backup summary appears at the end of the backup process. This offers a satisfying, though somewhat unnecessary, sense of accomplishment.

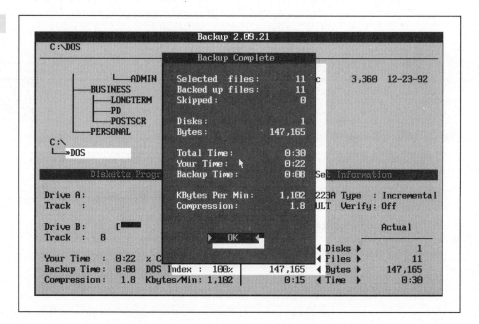

➤ EXTRA!

Network Users Can Maintain Personal Configurations!

Suppose you use MSBACKUP from a network drive that only allows read-and-execute access to the files on it. Under normal conditions, MSBACKUP will use the configuration data, as well as the backup sets and catalogs, that it finds on that network drive.

But you can divert MSBACKUP's attention to your local drive for this same information by specifying the **MSDOSDATA** environmental variable. By setting this variable equal to a directory on your local drive, MSBACKUP will then create, update, and access all configuration information, backup sets, and backup catalogs on your local drive.

For example, suppose that the network drive containing MSBACKUP is drive G:. If you want to maintain your personal backup configuration in the \DOS directory of your C: drive, you can simply add this line to your local computer's AUTOEXEC.BAT file:

```
SET MSDOSDATA=C:\DOS
```

As you'd expect, you can start the backup program on the network drive by typing **G:\MSBACKUP** at any command prompt. All subsequent catalog and configuration writes will take place in the DOS directory of your C: drive.

Comparing Original Files with the Backed-Up Versions

Once you've completed a backup, you can use the *Compare* choice in the original Backup screen (Figure 11.1) to make doubly sure that your backed-up files can be restored onto your hard disk. If this choice were only to give you a second method of file verification (beyond the *Verify* option that can be set during backup), this main MSBACKUP option would seem to be unnecessary. Of course, it can provide more than just that.

> **TIP**
>
> Be sure to turn on the *Verify Backup Data* option seen in Figure 11.9. This option alerts you to bad sectors on your backup diskettes so that you can immediately discard such a diskette and replace it with another.

You can use the *Compare* choice to easily determine which files from the backup set have changed on the hard disk since the backup set was written. In doing this, you can ask MSBACKUP to compare either all the files on the backup set, or simply one or more of the files. In fact, as you'll soon see, you can even compare files from a single backup set to files on a different computer, or in a different drive and directory from the original versions of the files.

According to Microsoft, there is an additional reason to use the *Compare* option. This option is able to detect individual variations in the mechanics of individual disk drives, which can vary slightly. If a Compare sequence verifies that the backed-up files are precise copies of your originals, then you can be more completely certain that the files can readily be restored when and if you need to do so.

Figure 11.11 shows the screen that initially appears when you select *Compare* from Figure 11.1.

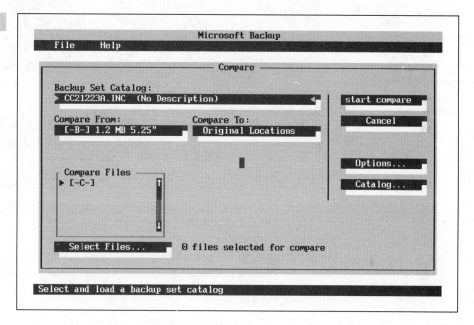

The primary control in this screen is the *Backup Set Catalog* field. The catalog contains the file names and directory locations of the files written to your backup medium during a particular backup. To choose a particular (perhaps different) backup catalog, such as the CC21223A.INC that appears in Figure 11.12, you can select the *Catalog...* button on the right side of the screen.

The *Catalog...* button displays a list box that contains all catalog file names available in the MSBACKUP directory. Just select the one that you want to use. If you're not completely sure that a catalog name is the one you want, you can then choose *Select Files...* at the bottom of the screen. This displays the Select Compare Files screen seen in Figure 11.12.

FIGURE 11.12

Clicking on the *Select Files...* button in the Compare screen brings up this screen for selecting the file names to compare. As with Backup, press the spacebar to toggle on or off a highlighted file name, or a highlighted directory to select an entire directory of file names.

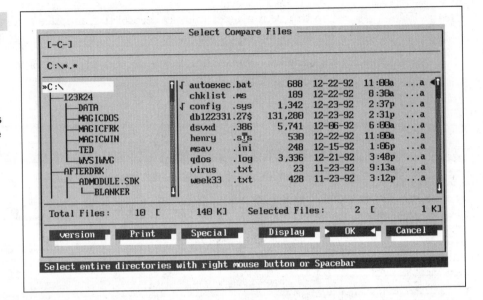

From this screen, you can then select the *Print* button (at the bottom of the screen) to produce a descriptive listing of the contents of the currently selected backup set catalog. For instance, performing the Print sequence from the point illustrated in Figure 11.12 would result in the catalog listing seen in Figure 11.13. The .INC extension on the catalog file name means that this was an incremental backup.

The mechanics of running a Compare are very similar to performing the original Backup. As you can see in Figure 11.12, there is a directory area and a files area. You use the same techniques you used for selecting files to back up when you select files to compare. You can also use the *Special* and *Display* buttons at the bottom of the screen to impose a number of file restrictions and filters to aid you in identifying the file names to compare.

As with the original backup procedure, MSBACKUP displays the running times for both you and the program during the actual compare process. At the end of the procedure, a summary window appears that includes information about files, times, disks, bytes, and comparison errors.

FIGURE 11.13

Each backup generates a catalog file. The catalog contains a text listing of all the files backed up. The extension of the catalog file name defines the type of backup (e.g., .INC for Incremental).

```
Backup    Catalog Listing                    12-24-92  8:28a

          Catalog File:       CC21223A.INC
          Backup Date:        12-23-92
          Setup File:         DEFAULT.SET
          Backup of Drives: C


          --------------   ----------   --------   ------   ------   --------
C:\
          autoexec.bat            688   12-22-92   11:00a   .a..        1
          chklist .ms             189   12-22-92    8:30a   .a..        1
          config  .sys          1,342   12-23-92    2:37p   .a..        1
          db122331.27$        131,280   12-23-92    2:31p   .a..        1
          dsvxd   .386          5,741   12-06-92    6:00a   .a..        1
          henry   .sys            530   12-22-92   11:00a   .a..        1
          msav    .ini            248   12-15-92    1:06p   .a..        1
          qdos    .log          3,336   12-21-92    3:48p   .a..        1
          virus   .txt             23   11-23-92    9:13a   .a..        1
          week33  .txt            428   11-23-92    3:12p   .a..        1
```

Restoring Files from a Backup Set

Restoring files is very similar to comparing files. Most of you will do restoration and comparison very infrequently. In ten years of backing up files several times a week, I've only had to restore backed-up versions a few times. However, those few times were more than traumatic enough to justify having spent the original time backing up files.

When you first select *Restore* (from the main Backup screen, shown in Figure 11.1), you'll receive a screen that looks almost identical to the Compare screen of Figure 11.11. This Restore screen, shown in Figure 11.14, lets you specify exacly which files to restore and to which hard disk.

FIGURE 11.14

Restoring files from a backup set is of course the reverse of a backup. You can restore backed-up files to the same or a different disk. You can also choose the *Select Files...* button to specify whether to restore all or only some of the files that were backed up.

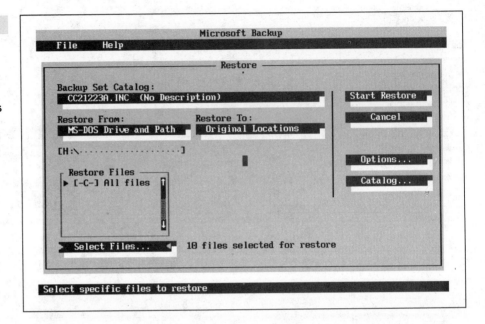

First, you should be sure to select the *Backup Set Catalog* that contains the files you wish to restore. Double-clicking on this field will display a list box containing the names of all available backup set catalogs. Next, make sure to select and fill in the correct choices for the *Restore From:* and *Restore To:* fields. Normally, you will be restoring from the diskette drive that contains the backup files. However, in Figure 11.14, you can see that I selected *MS-DOS Drive and Path* from the choices available in the *Restore From:* field in order to enter the drive letter for my removable disk cartridge.

You must always choose the *Select Files* button at the bottom of the screen before you can start the restore itself. In fact, the *Start Restore* button will not even become available until you have selected some files for restoration. In Figure 11.14, I had already displayed the Select Files screen and selected all the backed-up files for restoration. To select all the files, I simply pressed the spacebar when the cursor highlight was over the C:\ directory name, since all the backed-up files came from this root directory.

Restoring files is pretty straightforward. Once you select the *Start Restore* button, the process proceeds unimpeded. At the end of the restore, a summary screen once again appears. By now, the entire sequence should be easy.

The hardest part of using MSBACKUP is in getting comfortable with the various selection and settings screens in the first place. In the next section, you'll take a look at some of the sophisticated considerations that you can make while you are using MSBACKUP.

Ensuring That Your Backups Are Performed Optimally

To this point, I've spoken about the mechanics of backing up, comparing, and restoring files from your hard disk. Many of the mechanical settings have distinct performance consequences. In this section, you'll learn some of the costs and trade-offs of these various settings.

As a first example, suppose that your system contains more than one hard drive. You can save a good deal of time by using MSBACKUP's ability to back up files from multiple hard drives in a single backup session. Figure 11.15 depicts this capability.

To specify files to back up that reside on multiple hard drives, you should successively move the cursor highlight in the *Backup From:* area to each drive that contains files you wish to back up. While the drive in question is highlighted, tab over to (or click on) the *Select Files...* button. Then just select the files on that drive you wish to back up. Press OK to return to the Backup screen of Figure 11.15.

MSBACKUP keeps track of the total number of files and the total bytes of storage space required on your backup medium. In Figure 11.15, the

FIGURE 11.15

You can back up files
from multiple drives in
a single backup
session. To do so, first
highlight the desired
source drive in the
Backup From: list box.
Then choose *Select
Files...* and specify
which files are to be
included.

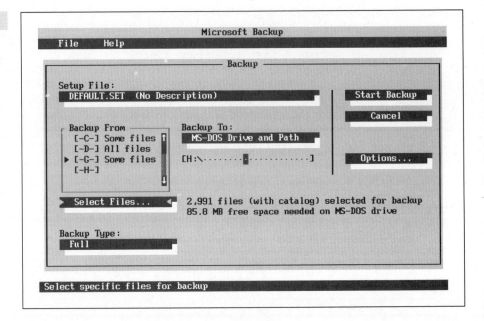

backup set will contain some files from drives C: and G:, and all the files
from drive D:. This amounts to 2,991 files and requires 85.8Mb of backup space.

One of the options seen in Figure 11.9 is for compressing backup data.
You can speed up your backup by checking this option. If you have turned
on compression, then MSBACKUP will compress data that is read from
your hard disk(s). Even though compression requires additional CPU
time, MSBACKUP tries to use free waiting time that already exists between hard-disk reads and floppy-diskette writes. In addition, compression means that the data being written to the backup medium requires less
space than in its original form. Consequently, the backup data involves
less time to write the compressed information. A compressed backup is
therefore faster.

TIP

Do not turn the verification option off in an attempt to speed up your backups. Also, do not turn off the error correction option. Both options will speed up your backups, but they will also reduce the likelihood that your backup sets contain valid data. In particular, the verification option will alert you to the existence of bad sectors in your backup medium. Further, the error correction option can make it easier to later restore data from diskettes that have themselves gone bad to some degree.

MSBACKUP can write backup data to a variety of media, including both low- and high-density diskettes. Use high-density diskettes for optimum speed, preferring the slightly larger 3½" high-density diskettes if you have the choice. Because a 1.44Mb 3½" disk holds slightly more data than a 1.2Mb 5¼" disk, overall backup speed will be slightly higher, if only because you may have to change diskettes less often. Further, the hard casing on a 3½" diskette makes it a safer medium for storing your backup data than the flexible 5¼" diskettes, which are more prone to damage.

Summary

This chapter has taught you how to back up your disks. Power failures do occur in businesses, brownouts occur even more frequently, and a multitude of other incidents can cause the intermittent loss or corruption of important files. Therefore, making backups is critical for avoiding disaster. This chapter has presented the following backup information:

- You should back up your files before moving your computer, when you are close to filling up your hard disk, and just before running a disk-optimization or fragmentation-reduction program.

- The **MSBACKUP** command can make three types of backups of your files: *Full*, which includes all files specified; *Incremental*, which includes all files that have recently changed; and *Differential*, which includes all files that have changed since the last Full backup.

- The full-screen interface to the **MSBACKUP** command facilitates easy configuration (or reconfiguration) of your system. A special compatibility test for your equipment can be performed the first time you run the backup program.

- MSBACKUP provides a button for comparing backup versions of files with their original disk versions. It also provides a *Restore* button for copying back to your hard disk all or some of the backed-up versions.

- MSBACKUP offers the facility of storing *setup files* for backing up different sets of files, backup types, and destination drives. Save time by creating different setup files for different purposes.

In the next part of this book, you'll learn techniques for totally customizing your DOS system. Specifically, you'll discover how to write your own programs, add commands to DOS, and create your own shortcut keystrokes.

Part
FOUR

Designing Power
Shortcuts

CHAPTERS

CHAPTER

12

The Power of DOS Batch Files

IN THIS chapter, you will begin to learn about batch files. You've already learned several DOS features that give you added power. Batch files can *multiply* the power of DOS, not just add to it. This chapter will show you what batch files are, and how they can be created and used. You will learn why they are so important to you and to your effectiveness as a DOS user.

Up to this point, you've learned quite a bit about individual DOS commands. You know that when you want to execute a DOS command, you type in the command at the prompt or invoke it in the shell. When the command is complete, DOS displays the prompt or shell again; then you can enter another command. You've seen that when you work with DOS, you must enter these commands one at a time.

Batch files allow you to enter a *group* of DOS commands automatically. A batch file is a series of ordinary DOS commands that the computer can execute automatically as a group (a *batch*) instead of one at a time.

You create batch files to automate DOS activities that require more than one DOS command. Sometimes you may even create a batch file to automate only one command that happens to be long or complex. As you will see, the simple idea of a batch file has some unexpected benefits. DOS's ability to understand simple batch files allows you to create sophisticated DOS programs. Just as QuickBASIC programs can contain commands, variables, subprograms, and conditional statements, so can a DOS batch file contain such elements. However, whereas a QBASIC program is used to control customized processing of data, a batch file is used to control customized execution of applications.

Building a Batch File

Batch files can be as simple or as complex as you want them to be. In Chapter 9, you learned how to use the PROMPT command to customize your DOS system's command prompt. You learned that you can issue a series of such PROMPT commands to specify the color, position, and contents of your DOS command prompt. Suppose that you find yourself frequently switching from the shell to a command prompt and back again. If you exit completely from the shell (by pressing Alt+F4) to access the original command prompt, you must type DOSSHELL and press Enter to start up the shell again when you need it. If you bring up a secondary command prompt from within the shell (by pressing Shift+F9), you must type EXIT and press Enter to return to the shell. Figure 12.1 summarizes these cases.

FIGURE 12.1

Type DOSSHELL to run the DOS shell. Once there, press Shift+F9 to run a secondary command processor. Type EXIT from it to return to the shell. To return to the original DOS command prompt from the shell, you can press Alt+F4 at any time.

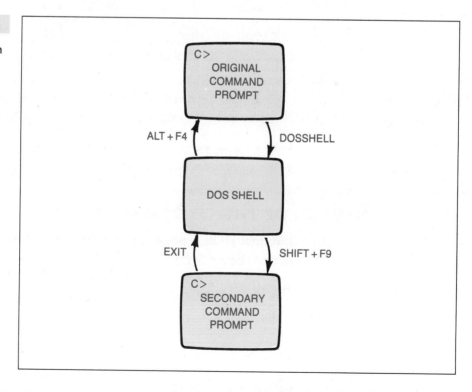

Wouldn't it be nice to press a single key to return to the shell, just as you press a single key combination to leave the shell in each of these two situations? Using the PROMPT command and ANSI.SYS techniques discussed in Chapter 9, you could successively enter each of the following DOS commands at a command prompt to obtain the desired result:

```
PROMPT $e[0;133;"DOSSHELL";13p
PROMPT $e[0;134;"EXIT";13p
PROMPT $p$g
```

The first command redefines the F11 key to enter the DOSSHELL command. The second command line redefines the F12 key to enter the EXIT command, and the last PROMPT command ensures that the command prompt displays the current directory followed by a > symbol. Press Alt+F4 now to exit from the shell back to the original command prompt. Type the three commands above, and then test them by using all four methods for switching to the shell: the two shown in Figure 12.1, and F11 and F12. If your keyboard does not have an F11 or F12 key, use a different key code (see Chapter 9) to replace the 133 and 134 in the command lines above. Remember that if you perform these commands from the original command prompt, the key redefinitions will remain in effect at all subsequent command prompts, original or secondary, until you reboot.

To complete this keyboard redefinition task, you had to type three separate commands. If switching to a command prompt is a task that you perform often, and it probably is, you could automate the task with a batch file that contains these commands. To do so, however, you first need to know the rules for building batch files.

Rules for Batch Files

To ensure that DOS properly recognizes and processes a file as a batch file, you must follow several rules. These rules apply to

- file type
- file name

Batch Files Must Be ASCII Text Files

Standard text files contain normal ASCII characters, and each line ends with a carriage return (CR) and a line feed (LF). This definition may not mean much to novice computer users; it is more important to know how to produce such files.

You can create a batch file using the EDIT program or any word-processing program that can create an ASCII standard file or convert its files to ASCII standard. For example, some of the more common word-processing programs produce ASCII files directly, including

- WordPerfect, using TEXT IN/OUT
- WordStar in nondocument mode or with the UNFORM format
- Microsoft Word, saving the file as UNFORMATTED
- DisplayWrite, using ASCII COPY TO FILE
- Framework IV, using DISK EXPORT ASCII

➤ EXTRA!

How to Make Batch Files Work for You

Make batch files work for you by following these guidelines:

1. Each batch file should be a completely ASCII file with a .BAT filename extension.

2. Each command line should end with a carriage return and line feed pair of characters.

3. Choose a base name of up to eight characters, but be careful not to use a name already used by one of DOS's standard command names.

4. Finally, choose a name that is meaningful to you or the batch file's expected users.

- Microsoft Word for Windows, using FILE, SAVE AS, SAVE FILE AS TYPE, TEXT ONLY
- Write for Windows, using SAVE AS, TEXT ONLY

You can use programs such as the following to convert files to DOS standard text files after they have been saved as word-processing files:

- Software Bridge, using format selection menus
- RDocX, using format selection menus
- Symphony, using the PRINT FILE command

The best way to create and manipulate your batch files is to use DOS's EDIT program, or your own favorite word processor. Your word-processing program probably offers a wider range of commands for manipulating text. However, EDIT does have the advantage of being available with DOS.

WARNING

When you create your batch files, be sure to use a completely ASCII or nondocument mode in your word processor. This special mode will ensure that no hidden formatting codes are inserted into your newly created files. Some editing programs insert these hidden codes to control the overall appearance of the word-processed text. However, appearance is not of critical importance to DOS batch files. If such codes make their way into your batch programs, they will definitely cause your batch file to work unreliably.

Because you may not have a word processor, I will assume that you are using EDIT to create and manipulate your batch files. If you need to refresh your memory on EDIT, refer to Chapter 6.

Adhering to Batch-File-Naming Conventions

You've learned by now that there are certain classes of files on your system: .COM and .EXE program files, .BAS BASIC language files, .WK1 spreadsheet files, .DBF database files, and many others. DOS must be able to distinguish a batch file from these other types of files on your system.

You can give a batch file almost any name you like, as long as you use the .BAT extension. Of course, the name must adhere to standard DOS file-naming rules, with no more than eight letters or numbers in the base name. SIMPLE.BAT and SETUP.BAT are examples of acceptable batch-file names.

► EXTRA!

Don't Confuse Matters with Poor Batch File Names

You should never create a batch file that has the same name as a DOS command (for example, DIR.BAT or FORMAT.BAT). If you do, DOS will not know whether you want to execute the command with that name or the batch file with that name. DOS always assumes you want to execute a DOS command first. The only exception to this would be if you clicked on the batch-file name (e.g., DIR.BAT) in the files area of the DOS shell.

Only if DOS can't find a DOS command (or any .EXE or .COM files) with that name will it look to see if there is a batch file with the name that you typed in. DOS expects you to enter the command or batch-file name without typing the extension. Thus, although you could create a file named DIR.BAT, you could never use it from a command prompt or from a batch file—DOS would always assume when you entered DIR that you wanted the Directory command, not the DIR.BAT file.

Batch Files Have Certain Limitations

Only commands that work at the DOS prompt can be included in a batch file. You'll soon see that there are some additional controlling commands (called subcommands) that can be used in a batch file. You can also use variable input parameters, which will be covered in detail later in this chapter. However, the main commands that do something for you are always going to look just as they would if they were typed at the DOS prompt.

Running and Stopping Batch Files

Executing all the instructions within a batch file is as simple as typing the name of the .BAT file containing those instructions. As with commands and programs, however, if you don't precede the batch-file name with a drive identifier and a directory name, the assumption will be that the batch file exists in the current drive and current directory.

Normally, you can run any batch program from the shell by simply selecting it from the files area. If you or other users will use the batch programs repeatedly, you may want to install them in one of the program groups. However, if the chores performed by the batch file have special system implications, as do the PROMPT commands demonstrated earlier in this chapter, you will want to run them directly from the original command prompt.

You can stop batch-file execution at any time by pressing the Break key (Ctrl+Break) combination on your keyboard. DOS will display ^C on the screen and then ask you if you want to terminate the batch job. Usually, you answer Y for Yes, since that's why you pressed the Break combination in the first place. However, if you have a change of heart and answer N, the current step in the batch file will be ignored and the rest of the commands will be executed.

WARNING

Users of diskette systems should be aware that exchanging a diskette containing an executing batch file for another diskette will force DOS to stop after it completes the current instruction and prompt you to reinsert the original diskette. Only then can the next instruction in the batch file be executed properly. You may already have experienced this situation without realizing it. Many application programs are installed by running a SETUP.BAT or INSTALL.BAT program from the first of several installation diskettes. In this case, you are usually asked to reinsert the very first diskette just prior to completing the entire installation.

Creating Your First Batch File

Take a moment now to create your first batch file. Create your own version of SETUP.BAT, including all the statements seen in Figure 12.2. Use the EDIT program unless you are familiar with an available word processor and plan to use it for all your batch-file work.

The first two PROMPT commands in Figure 12.2 represent escape sequences that define what will happen when the F11 or F12 keys are pressed on your keyboard. You will learn shortly how to define (or redefine, if they are presently defined differently) any two keys on your keyboard. You could also define any series of keys with a series of escape-sequence PROMPT commands. Unless you redefine the same key every time, each command will augment previous definitions, creating an increasingly customized environment for your DOS operations.

FIGURE 12.2

The SETUP.BAT file demonstrates how to set up your system's F11 and F12 keys. You can customize your SETUP.BAT file by replacing my example DOSSHELL and EXIT commands with your own desired command or program names. SETUP always initializes F11 and F12 in the same way.

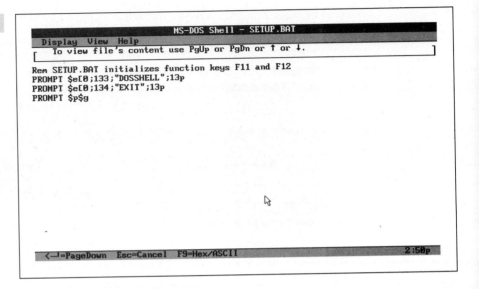

```
                     MS-DOS Shell - SETUP.BAT
  Display  View  Help
[     To view file's content use PgUp or PgDn or ↑ or ↓.              ]

Rem SETUP.BAT initializes function keys F11 and F12
PROMPT $e[0;133;"DOSSHELL";13p
PROMPT $e[0;134;"EXIT";13p
PROMPT $p$g




                                                      ⌐


  ◄─┘=PageDown  Esc=Cancel  F9=Hex/ASCII                        2:50p
```

The third PROMPT command:

    PROMPT pg

specifies the contents of the command prompt itself. It replaces any earlier definition of the prompt line. In this case, the prompt becomes the current drive/directory followed by a greater-than (>) symbol.

Remember that when you use EDIT, you are entering text into a file. This means that nothing appears to happen when you type in a command. Only after the SETUP.BAT file has been saved will you tell DOS to read, process, and execute the instructions contained in it.

Write the file now using EDIT. When you exit the Editor and return to DOS, press Alt+F4 to leave the shell and return to the original prompt. You are now ready to execute this particular batch file. You should do this by typing in its name *without* the .BAT extension:

    SETUP

The results of typing in this one-word command are the same as those produced when all three PROMPT commands are typed in separately at consecutive command prompts. DOS executes each of the commands automatically, one after the other, without further assistance from you. Notice how DOS displays each batch-file instruction as it executes it.

Like programs or disk-resident DOS commands, batch files can be located on any disk and in any directory, and they can be referenced by simply specifying the full path name to them. For example, if SETUP is located in a directory called UTILITY\MISC on drive C, you could execute it by entering

```
C:\UTILITY\MISC\SETUP
```

You'll learn in the next chapter about a number of special commands to use primarily within batch files. For instance, the Rem command at the top of the SETUP.BAT file is known as a Remark command. It provides the same ability to document your instructions that the apostrophe affords in QBasic programs (see Chapter 16).

Variables in Batch Files

What you've seen so far is a batch file that has been designed for a specific use. In particular, SETUP.BAT redefines two specific keys (F11 and F12, represented by key codes 133 and 134) to perform two specific chores (automatically typing DOSSHELL or EXIT for you). In such cases, the batch file works with unchanging values (133, 134, DOSSHELL, EXIT).

If batch files could accept variables, as more sophisticated programming languages do, they could be much more flexible. You could then use the same batch file, for instance, to redefine certain keys within a range of keys whenever you liked. If you write such a batch file correctly, you can run it anytime, even redefining the same keys to perform different chores at different times.

You can write DOS batch files that will permit such flexibility. Variables in any language allow you to construct programs that differ in a well-defined way each time the program is run. In other words, the program stays the same, but the values used by the program to complete its tasks vary. You can consider the DOS batch-file feature to be a simple programming language.

Recognize Function Keypresses in Your Batch Files!

Ever want to set up a menu of choices, allowing a user to press one of several specified function keys? The TESTSCAN.BAT batch file below demonstrates how to do this, using a special CODESCAN.COM program that you can create on your own. See the DEBUG section of Chapter 16 for an explanation of how to create the necessary CODE-SCAN.COM program; CODESCAN will recognize the scan code transmitted by hardware after you press any function key.

The CODESCAN program transmits an ERRORLEVEL value equal to the scan code received. You can build your own batch files using similar IF tests to control execution of your own logic.

```
@ECHO OFF
Rem TESTSCAN.BAT batch file code segment shows how to test
Rem a user's keypress of any one of the first ten
Rem function keys F1 through F10.
Rem It uses the CODESCAN.COM program that can be created
Rem with the DOS DEBUG program and an assembler script file.
ECHO Press any function key from F1 to F10.
CODESCAN
IF ERRORLEVEL 59 IF NOT ERRORLEVEL 60 ECHO Scan code 59 (F1)
IF ERRORLEVEL 60 IF NOT ERRORLEVEL 61 ECHO Scan code 60 (F2)
IF ERRORLEVEL 61 IF NOT ERRORLEVEL 62 ECHO Scan code 61 (F3)
IF ERRORLEVEL 62 IF NOT ERRORLEVEL 63 ECHO Scan code 62 (F4)
IF ERRORLEVEL 63 IF NOT ERRORLEVEL 64 ECHO Scan code 63 (F5)
IF ERRORLEVEL 64 IF NOT ERRORLEVEL 65 ECHO Scan code 64 (F6)
IF ERRORLEVEL 65 IF NOT ERRORLEVEL 66 ECHO Scan code 65 (F7)
IF ERRORLEVEL 66 IF NOT ERRORLEVEL 67 ECHO Scan code 66 (F8)
IF ERRORLEVEL 67 IF NOT ERRORLEVEL 68 ECHO Scan code 67 (F9)
IF ERRORLEVEL 68 IF NOT ERRORLEVEL 69 ECHO Scan code 68(F10)
```

Let's take a moment to look at the terminology involved. As you have seen throughout this book, many DOS commands accept a variety of parameters. These parameters are just additional pieces of information needed by DOS to clarify the task specified in the command. For example, the command:

```
COPY REPORT.DOC FEBRUARY.DOC
```

contains the COPY command, and the REPORT and FEBRUARY documents are its respective source and destination parameters. Next month, however, you might want to run the COPY command again, with the REPORT.DOC file as the source once again but with the MARCH.DOC file as the destination:

```
COPY REPORT.DOC MARCH.DOC
```

The second parameter can be considered a variable parameter, since it needs to be changed each month.

Batch files can accept variables as easily as they can accept DOS commands. Variables always begin with a percentage sign (%) and are followed by a number from 0 to 9. DOS allows variables named %0, %1, %2, and so on.

To see how this system works, create a variation of the first batch file now. Call this new file START.BAT and type in the commands seen in Figure 12.3.

In START, I've changed the documentation lines at the beginning of the file. This version of the batch file can initialize *any* two function-key combinations whenever you run it. The first three lines in the batch file are now remarks for the reader's benefit only. They briefly describe what the file does and how to run it.

In the remaining four lines, the only difference between SETUP.BAT and START.BAT is the replacement of the unchanging keycodes 133 and 134 with the variable parameters %1 and %2. This means that %1 can stand for any keycode you want to press to make DOS type DOSSHELL for you. Similarly, the variable %2 is used to stand for the second key whose purpose is to type EXIT. Each time you run this batch file, you specify which keycode %1 stands for DOSSHELL and which keycode %2 represents EXIT.

FIGURE 12.3

You can use variable parameters in the START batch file to define any two function keys. The key codes you enter as parameters to the START program will vary the identity of the keys chosen by the ANSI escape sequences (for example, the $e[0;%1 and $e[0;%2 sequences).

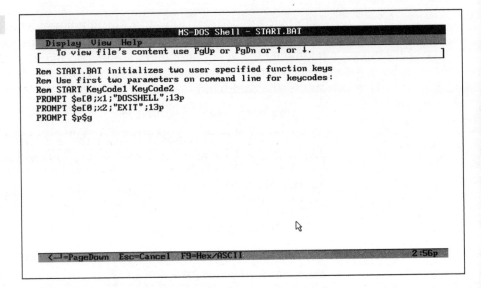

```
                    MS-DOS Shell - START.BAT
 Display  View  Help
     To view file's content use PgUp or PgDn or ↑ or ↓.
[                                                                    ]
Rem START.BAT initializes two user specified function keys
Rem Use first two parameters on command line for keycodes:
Rem START KeyCode1 KeyCode2
PROMPT $e[0;%1;"DOSSHELL";13p
PROMPT $e[0;%2;"EXIT";13p
PROMPT $p$g




                                         ⍨


 ←─┘=PageDown  Esc=Cancel  F9=Hex/ASCII                        2:56p
```

Here's how the % symbol works. When you type in any DOS command, DOS automatically assigns variable names to each section of that command. DOS internally assigns %0 to the first phrase, %1 to the second phrase, %2 to the third phrase, and, if there are other parameter entries on the line, % values up to %9. Our batch file incorporates the variable names %1 and %2; therefore, it will use the two phrases you enter after the first, or variable %0, phrase (START) on the command line. For example, if you execute START.BAT with the command START 67 68, then the first PROMPT line in the batch file

```
PROMPT $e[0;%1;"DOSSHELL";13p
```

will execute as if you had actually typed

```
PROMPT $e[0;67;"DOSSHELL";13p
```

The next line in the batch file,

```
PROMPT $e[0;%2;"EXIT";13p
```

will execute as if you had actually typed

```
PROMPT $e[0;68;"EXIT";13p
```

When the batch program runs, it will redefine F9 (which has keycode 67) to type DOSSHELL and F10 (which has keycode 68) to type EXIT.

Running the batch file again with different values for the two variable parameters will generate different results. For instance, entering

```
START 102 103
```

would redefine Ctrl+F9 and Ctrl+F10 to type DOSSHELL and EXIT for you.

The technique that uses variable parameters is called *deferred execution,* since the decision as to what value will be used is deferred until the time of batch-file execution. In this example, the same two PROMPT commands as before will be executed. However, the decision as to which specific keys are redefined is deferred until the batch file has actually been called and the %1 and %2 parameters have been specified after the batch-file name.

Using variable parameters has enormous possible benefits. In START, you improved the batch file's flexibility by enabling the user to specify which keys would be used to quickly type DOSSHELL or EXIT. You could just as easily have used additional variable parameters to defer specifying the character strings to be automatically typed.

Suppose you wanted to have the ability to redefine any one function key combination so that it represented any user-specified string of characters. Your batch file would only need this one command:

```
PROMPT $e[0;%1;"%2";13p
```

Assuming that you also wanted to retain the directory prompt, you could write the simple batch file (KEYDEFS.BAT) seen in Figure 12.4. You can then run KEYDEFS each time you wish to redefine any function-key combination. The %1 parameter controls which key is redefined, and should be one of the redefinition codes presented in Chapter 9. The %2 parameter should be the character string you would like to be automatically typed for you when you press the specified key.

For example, to define function key F11 as DOSSHELL, you would submit this line at the command prompt:

```
KEYDEFS 133 DOSSHELL
```

FIGURE 12.4

You can use variable
parameters to further
extend the flexibility of
the PROMPT command.
KEYDEFS uses the first
parameter (%1) to
specify the function
key to use, and the
second (%2) to specify
the character string
definition.

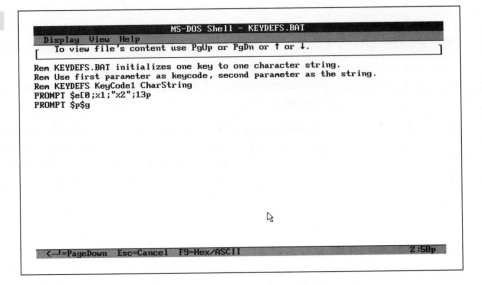

Later, if you also wish to define function key F7 to type the name of a
commonly used application program, say dBASE, you enter this line at
the command prompt:

```
KEYDEFS 65 DBASE
```

Typing this last example line produces the sample output seen in Figure 12.5.

As you can see in Figure 12.5, the %1 and %2 variable parameters have
been respectively replaced with 67 and DBASE prior to the actual command line being submitted from the batch file to DOS. The batch-file
mechanism takes care of inserting 67 between the semicolons where the
%1 *place holder* was located. The character string DBASE is also inserted
between the quotation marks in place of the %2 variable parameter seen
in the actual batch-file code.

Since you may well wish to use one or more of these example batch files
immediately, it would be good to know how to reset a key that has been
changed. According to the instructions in Chapter 9, you must transmit
an escape sequence that contains the key code twice. For example, to reset
F11 to its original status, you would issue:

```
PROMPT $e[0;133;0;133p
```

FIGURE 12.5

Escape sequences can produce cumulative effects. The KEYDEFS batch file seen here uses PROMPT once to assign the character string "DBASE" to the key represented by keycode 67. The next PROMPT command then augments this effect by adding current directory and >.

```
C>KEYDEFS 67 DBASE

C>Rem KEYDEFS.BAT initializes one key to one character string.

C>Rem Use first parameter as keycode, second parameter as the string.

C>Rem KEYDEFS KeyCode1 CharString

C>PROMPT $e[0;67;"DBASE";13p

PROMPT $p$g

C:\SIG1D\DOCS\DOS6>
C:\SIG1D\DOCS\DOS6>
```

But why type this entire line every time you wish to reset a redefined key? You could more easily use a batch file, such as KEYREDEF.BAT, seen in Figure 12.6.

Once you've added this batch file to your system, you only need to type KEYREDEF and the key code for the key you want to reset in order to produce the necessary PROMPT command.

As you can begin to sense, running a batch file can usually save considerable time in typing, retyping, or correcting errors. In the next two chapters, you'll begin to see even more reasons for studying this facility closely. You will explore even further how variable parameters can serve you well in managing your DOS system.

You should already be starting to think of the tasks that you perform frequently on your system. Any repetitive chores are prime candidates for batch files. Keep those tasks in mind as you continue to study the facilities available within the batch-file feature of DOS.

FIGURE 12.6

Once you've adjusted the definition of a function key combination, you can restore its original functionality with the KEYREDEF batch file. This batch program only requires as a single parameter the keycode for the key you're resetting.

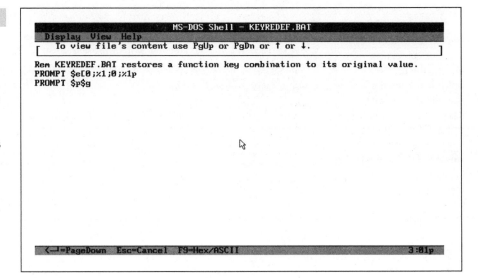

```
                            MS-DOS Shell - KEYREDEF.BAT
  Display  View  Help
 [     To view file's content use PgUp or PgDn or ↑ or ↓.                    ]

Rem KEYREDEF.BAT restores a function key combination to its original value.
PROMPT $e[0;%1;0;%1p
PROMPT $p$g




                                         ⌐

 <─┘=PageDown  Esc=Cancel  F9=Hex/ASCII                              3:01p
```

Summary

In this chapter, you took your first look at the DOS batch-file mechanism. It extends the power of your operating system by allowing you to build your own new set of commands. The new set of commands can be used just like any existing DOS command, except that it is your customized batch file that executes when requested, and not a prewritten command provided by DOS.

You learned the following key points about batch files:

- Batch files execute commands exactly as if they were entered at successive command prompts.

- DOS displays each batch-file command as it executes the command.

- Batch files can be invoked as easily as any DOS command—by simply typing the base name of the batch file at the command prompt or selecting it from the Files area of a shell screen. This allows you to create your own set of specialized add-on DOS commands.

- You can terminate the execution of your batch program by pressing Ctrl+Break.

- Variable parameters make your batch files very flexible. These variables are referred to as %0, %1, %2, %3, and so on through %9.

The next chapter will take your batch-file construction skills one giant step further. You'll learn about the set of specialized subcommands designed to work only within the batch-programming mechanism. These unique commands can be incorporated into any batch file, making DOS comparable to a high-level computer language.

CHAPTER

13

Using Subcommands
in Batch Files

BATCH files have their own set of specialized support commands, known as *subcommands.* You don't need them to create simple batch files, but you greatly expand your possibilities when you learn them. You'll learn about all of these extra built-in tools in this chapter. Depending on what type of batch program you write, you may need to use one or several subcommands.

Some subcommands will be commonplace in your batch files; for example, you will frequently use ECHO or REM to insert messages and documentation both into the batch file itself and onto the video screen. You'll use others only occasionally; for example, you'll use PAUSE only for batch files that must allow users sufficient time to read information on the screen. Still others will be used in specific situations only. In this category, you'll see the FOR subcommand, which allows the repetition of operations, the IF subcommand, which provides decision making, and the GOTO subcommand, which manages the flow of control.

There is another subcommand, SHIFT, that provides the esoteric capability of running a batch file that can process more than the maximum number of variable parameters (%0 to %9). The SHIFT command takes no parameters. Each time you include a SHIFT line in a batch file, DOS shifts the remaining variable parameters to the left by one position. Many DOS books make you struggle through the concept of shifting parameters, using trumped-up examples. Although no realistic batch file needs more than a few input parameters, you can use SHIFT to create some sophisticated trick situations. You'll see a few examples of this subcommand in various EXTRA! sidebars throughout this book.

In the preceding chapter, you looked at some simple examples of batch files, in which each command was executed in the order you created it. DOS also allows you to execute these commands nonsequentially, according to your own specified order. Changing the order of command execution is known as modifying the flow of control, or simply *branching*.

This chapter deals with elements that make the DOS batch-file feature into a simple but practical high-level programming language. A final section in the chapter discusses the distinction between creating a standard batch-file *chain* (which allows you to transfer control of execution from one file to another) and emulating true programming *subroutines*.

Incorporating Messages into Batch Files

In the preceding chapter's batch files, each command was displayed on your video monitor as it executed. The ECHO subcommand controls the display of the commands themselves while a batch file is processing. You can turn off command display (known as *echoing*) with an ECHO OFF instruction in your batch file; conversely, you can turn it back on again with an ECHO ON instruction.

TIP

To keep screen clutter at a minimum when batch files execute, use @ECHO OFF as the very first command line in your batch file. The ECHO OFF suppresses the echoed display of all subsequent batch-file commands, and the @ prefix suppresses the display of the ECHO OFF command itself.

As you saw in the last chapter, you don't need to include ECHO ON at the beginning of your batch file in order to have the commands display while the batch file is being processed. The effect itself is ON by default until you explicitly enter ECHO OFF to suppress the command display.

In most of the batch files seen in this chapter and in Chapter 14, the first instruction in the file turns echoing off. This simply reduces unnecessary clutter on your screen. However, displaying instructions as they execute can be quite useful when you are debugging a new batch file.

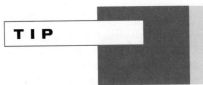

T I P

Use ECHO ON for debugging batch files, in the same way as you use the TRACE ON facility when debugging a QBasic program (see Chapter 16).

As you will see in this section, ECHO has some other uses as well. For example, if ECHO is followed by text instead of by ON or OFF, it will display that text on your screen. Thus, ECHO can also be used to display information on your video monitor during the execution of a batch file.

To see how this type of ECHO command works, create the following batch file called HELPTXT1.BAT. It should contain several ECHO subcommands, each of which contains helpful information for a user, as seen in Figure 13.1.

FIGURE 13.1

The HELPTXT1.BAT file uses the ECHO command to display informational text to a user. Since ECHO OFF opens the batch file, the user only sees the text and not the ECHO command words themselves. Note that ECHO followed immediately by a period generates a blank output line.

```
REM HELPTXT1.BAT
ECHO OFF
CLS
ECHO The batch file KEYDEFS.BAT requires two input parameters
ECHO to initialize any function key combination. Parameter 1
ECHO is the extended key code from the table below. Parameter
ECHO 2 is any string of characters to be automatically typed
ECHO when you later press the selected key combination.
ECHO.
ECHO FUNCTION KEY   Unshifted   Shift+   Ctrl+   Alt+
ECHO -------------------------------------------------
ECHO     F1            59          84      94      104
ECHO     F2            60          85      95      105
ECHO     F3            61          86      96      106
ECHO     F4            62          87      97      107
ECHO     F5            63          88      98      108
ECHO     F6            64          89      99      109
ECHO     F7            65          90     100      110
ECHO     F8            66          91     101      111
ECHO     F9            67          92     102      112
ECHO     F10           68          93     103      113
ECHO     F11          133         135     137      139
ECHO     F12          134         136     138      140
ECHO.
ECHO Example: KEYDEFS 133 DOSSHELL
ECHO initializes F11 to the string "DOSSHELL" + the Enter key
ECHO.
```

This batch file will offer explanation on demand to explain how the previously created KEYDEFS.BAT file can be used. When you run this batch file by typing in

HELPTXT1

at the DOS prompt, or by selecting HELPTXT1 from a Files list in the shell, the result is the screen shown in Figure 13.2.

Notice that the second line of the HELPTXT1 file in Figure 13.1 sets ECHO to OFF, and the third line clears the screen. As a result, the remaining "echoed" messages appear without your seeing the actual word ECHO at the beginning of each line. Regardless of whether ECHO is on or off, the textual information on an ECHO line is always displayed. ECHO OFF only suppresses the display of succeeding DOS commands in the batch file.

FIGURE 13.2

Results of executing the HELPTXT1.BAT batch file. Notice the blank lines used for separation are the results of the ECHO command followed immediately by a period.

```
The batch file KEYDEFS.BAT requires two input parameters
to initialize any function key combination. Parameter 1
is the extended key code from the table below. Parameter
2 is any string of characters to be automatically typed
when you later press the selected key combination.

FUNCTION KEY    Unshifted   Shift+   Ctrl+   Alt+
-------------------------------------------------------
    F1             59         84       94     104
    F2             60         85       95     105
    F3             61         86       96     106
    F4             62         87       97     107
    F5             63         88       98     108
    F6             64         89       99     109
    F7             65         90      100     110
    F8             66         91      101     111
    F9             67         92      102     112
    F10            68         93      103     113
    F11           133        135      137     139
    F12           134        136      138     140

Example: KEYDEFS 133 DOSSHELL
initializes F11 to the string "DOSSHELL" + the Enter key

C:\SIG1D\DOCS\DOS6>
```

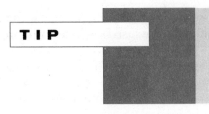

TIP Use the TYPE command to display a large body of predefined text (stored in a text file) to a user. This is much faster than including a series of ECHO statements in your batch file.

Interrupting Batch Files during Execution

There are two kinds of interruptions in life: temporary and permanent. DOS provides batch-file equivalents to these types of interruptions with the PAUSE subcommand and the Break-key combination (Ctrl+Break), respectively.

➤ EXTRA!

Rewrite REM Statements Including Redirection Symbols

REM statements are usually treated as strictly textual comments. However, if your REM statement includes any of the three special redirection symbols (<, >, or |), DOS will try to perform the seemingly requested redirection operation. If you truly mean to incorporate a redirection symbol as text only, you should enclose the symbol in standard double quotation marks (e.g. "|"). Here is an example:

```
Rem NOTES.BAT uses this syntax: NOTES [C | D]
```

Unless you rewrite this REM line, the vertical bar will be misinterpreted by DOS. The batch file will produce an unusual error message even though the remainder of the batch file's logic may work just fine.

When a PAUSE subcommand is used in a batch file, the execution of the commands in the file stops temporarily, and DOS displays the message "Press any key to continue ...". When you press the Enter key, the spacebar, or any alphabetic key, the next command in the batch file will execute.

➤ EXTRA!

Be Sure to Suppress REM Statements!

In batch files, you should usually suppress the display of all REM (remark) statement lines. You will see many REM statements in batch-file listings. Here is an example:

```
REM This is a simple internal commenting line.
REM So is this ... for the TYPICAL.BAT file
```

A REM statement is used for internal documentation in a batch file, and is used in the same way as an apostrophe line in a QBasic program. Lines that begin in this way usually contain notes to the programmer or to the future user of the batch program. Displaying them during the execution of a batch file serves no useful purpose.

As far as documentation goes, anything from the name of the file to information about algorithms and techniques will be welcomed by someone trying to understand the inner workings of a batch program. The word REM itself can be in lowercase or uppercase, or a combination of cases, according to your personal taste. Nearly all of the remaining batch files in this book will have at least the REM statement that contains the name of the batch file itself.

If ECHO is set to OFF, then the REM statements will not be shown on the video screen during program execution. The more complex or obscure your batch-file logic, the more you need to have several REM lines built into it.

The PAUSE subcommand is not necessary to the functioning of the program, but it has a practical function. Filling the screen with a lot of instructions is a sure way to lose a user's attention. Instead, you can display a little information, pause the display, clear the screen, and display a little more information. This will keep the user alert.

TIP

In batch files that display text, it's often a good idea to include PAUSE as a final command so that the screen information can be read. Information that is displayed to a user is usually only one part of a more complex batch file; pausing the execution allows the user to read the messages before continuing the program.

HELPTXT2.BAT (see Figure 13.3), an expanded version of the batch file that you saw in the last section, represents a two-screen help system. This is implemented by inserting the two commands PAUSE and CLS into the middle of the batch file. PAUSE temporarily interrupts the execution of the batch file, prompting you to press any key when you are ready to go on. CLS simply erases the messages you've already read, so that you can concentrate on the new messages displayed. When you run the HELPTXT2.BAT program, the results are as shown in Figure 13.4.

When a PAUSE subcommand is issued, almost any key will cause the batch-file processing to resume. One exception to this is the Ctrl+Break key combination. When you press Ctrl+Break, DOS first displays a ^C on the screen and then asks if you wish to terminate the batch job. In fact, you can press Ctrl+Break at any time during the execution of a batch file. Figures 13.5 and 13.6 demonstrate what your screen might look like if you pressed Ctrl+Break while the first help screen was being written.

FIGURE 13.3

The HELPTXT2.BAT file demonstrates how a PAUSE command followed by a CLS enables you to manage multiple screen text displays. The CHOICE command could also be used to manage a more sophisticated selection of multiple possible screen displays.

```
REM HELPTXT2.BAT
ECHO OFF
CLS
ECHO The batch file KEYDEFS.BAT requires two input
parameters
ECHO to initialize any function key combination. Parameter 1
ECHO is the extended key code from the table below.
Parameter
ECHO 2 is any string of characters to be automatically typed
ECHO when you later press the selected key combination.
ECHO.
ECHO    FUNCTION KEY   Unshifted   Shift+   Ctrl+   Alt+
ECHO    -------------------------------------------------
ECHO       F1            59          84       94      104
ECHO       F2            60          85       95      105
ECHO       F3            61          86       96      106
ECHO       F4            62          87       97      107
ECHO       F5            63          88       98      108
ECHO       F6            64          89       99      109
ECHO       F7            65          90      100      110
ECHO       F8            66          91      101      111
ECHO       F9            67          92      102      112
ECHO      F10            68          93      103      113
ECHO      F11           133         135      137      139
ECHO      F12           134         136      138      140
ECHO.
ECHO Press Ctrl-BREAK key to restore the command prompt,
ECHO Or, to display another screen with KEYDEFS examples,
PAUSE
CLS
ECHO Examples:
ECHO.
ECHO KEYDEFS 133 DOSSHELL
ECHO initializes F11 to the string "DOSSHELL" + the Enter
key
ECHO.
ECHO KEYDEFS 90 EXIT
ECHO initializes Shift+F7 to the string "EXIT" + Enter
ECHO.
ECHO KEYDEFS 105 WORDPERF
ECHO initializes Alt+F2 to the string "WORDPERF" + Enter
ECHO.
```

FIGURE 13.4

PAUSE displays
"Press any key to con-
tinue...". A user can
press Ctrl+Break to
exit the batch file, or
any normal key to see
the second text screen
in this two-screen help
system.

```
The batch file KEYDEFS.BAT requires two input parameters
to initialize any function key combination. Parameter 1
is the extended key code from the table below. Parameter
2 is any string of characters to be automatically typed
when you later press the selected key combination.

FUNCTION KEY   Unshifted   Shift+   Ctrl+   Alt+
------------------------------------------------------
    F1            59         84       94     104
    F2            60         85       95     105
    F3            61         86       96     106
    F4            62         87       97     107
    F5            63         88       98     108
    F6            64         89       99     109
    F7            65         90      100     110
    F8            66         91      101     111
    F9            67         92      102     112
    F10           68         93      103     113
    F11          133        135      137     139
    F12          134        136      138     140

Press Ctrl-BREAK key to restore the command prompt,
Or, to display another screen with KEYDEFS examples,
Press any key to continue . . .



Examples:

KEYDEFS 133 DOSSHELL
initializes F11 to the string "DOSSHELL" + the Enter key

KEYDEFS 90 EXIT
initializes Shift+F7 to the string "EXIT" + Enter

KEYDEFS 105 WORDPERF
initializes Alt+F2 to the string "WORDPERF" + Enter


C:\SIG1D\DOCS\DOS6>
```

In Figure 13.5, your Y answer causes the batch file to cease immediately
and return control to the DOS prompt. This is a permanent interruption.
Notice in Figure 13.6 that the ^C occurred in the middle of writing the
F9 keycode information line. Because you answered N, the currently executing statement (the F9 line in the batch file) does not complete, and
the batch file continues executing with the next line. In short, DOS's message gets in the way of normal batch-file output, which is one important
reason to avoid asking a batch file to continue after you interrupt it.

FIGURE 13.5

Pressing Ctrl+Break displays ^C on the screen and requests confirmation that you want to permanently stop the execution of the batch file.

```
The batch file KEYDEFS.BAT requires two input parameters
to initialize any function key combination. Parameter 1
is the extended key code from the table below. Parameter
2 is any string of characters to be automatically typed
when you later press the selected key combination.

FUNCTION KEY   Unshifted  Shift+  Ctrl+  Alt+
------------------------------------------------
   F1             59        84      94     104
   F2             60        85      95     105
   F3             61        86      96     106
   F4    ^C

Terminate batch job (Y/N)?Y

C:\SIG1D\DOCS\DOS6>
```

FIGURE 13.6

Continuing a batch file after interruption always misses the completion of the instruction that was executing when you interrupted the program. Note how the F9 line did not complete in this example.

```
is the extended key code from the table below. Parameter
2 is any string of characters to be automatically typed
when you later press the selected key combination.

FUNCTION KEY   Unshifted  Shift+  Ctrl+  Alt+
------------------------------------------------
   F1             59        84      94     104
   F2             60        85      95     105
   F3             61        86      96     106
   F4             62        87      97     107
   F5             63        88      98     108
   F6             64        89      99     109
   F7             65        90     100     110
   F8             66        91     101     111
   F9^C

Terminate batch job (Y/N)?N
  F10             68        93     103     113
  F11            133       135     137     139
  F12            134       136     138     140

Press Ctrl-BREAK key to restore the command prompt,
Or, to display another screen with KEYDEFS examples,
Press any key to continue . . .
```

➤ EXTRA!

Want to Display Blank Lines in Your Batch File Output?

It's easy to insert a blank line for readability into the sequence of command lines of an actual .BAT file. It's easy, but not as straightforward to incorporate blank lines into the output of a batch file. In the programs of this chapter, you will see that visual separation is achieved by including a special ECHO line:

```
ECHO.
```

Do not leave a space between the word ECHO and the period symbol. DOS will not display the period, but will instead just show a blank line. Alternatively, you can display a special ASCII character that is not visible, either on your screen or in the .BAT file's instruction list. This special technique also works in all earlier versions of DOS.

This special nondisplaying character is ASCII 255, which is obtainable in most word processors and editors by holding down the Alt key, pressing the digits 2, then 5, then 5, and finally pressing the Enter key. Some word processors, like Xywrite and Signature, require that you actually hold down both the Ctrl and Alt keys while then pressing the three-digit ASCII code.

To make use of this feature, you should type ECHO, then press the spacebar, and finally follow the method required to enter this single undisplayable ASCII character into your .BAT file. Your batch file command line may look like:

```
ECHO
```

when, in actual fact, the ASCII characters for a space and the invisible ASCII character 255 are also on the line. Some books show this as:

```
ECHO <Alt+255>
```

or possibly

```
ECHO <Ctrl+Alt+255>
```

The Break-key combination will also work with DOS commands that have built-in pauses, such as FORMAT and DISKCOPY. When these commands display such messages as "Press ENTER when ready," the Break combination will cancel the command. You may also want to use Break to stop the execution of a batch file that does not seem to be working correctly or that is stuck in an infinite loop.

Managing the Flow of Control

While executing batch files, you can guide the execution with IF and GOTO statements. In one case (IF), you can make decisions about whether or not to execute an instruction. In the other case (GOTO), you can explicitly force execution to continue in a separate section of the batch file.

Making Decisions in a Batch File

To get an idea of the usefulness of the IF and GOTO statements, let's enhance the KEYDEFS.BAT file from the preceding chapter. In that file, you had to know the key code that represented a function-key combination before you could successfully initialize the keystroke. In file KEYDEFS2.BAT (see Figure 13.7), you needn't know the codes at all. This batch file is written to allow a user to type an easily remembered mnemonic for the first parameter that represents the key being redefined. For example, to redefine the Alt+F11 key combination with this batch file, you can type

```
KEYDEFS2 AF11 DOSSHELL
```

➤ **EXTRA!**

Distinguish between Conditional and Unconditional Transfers!

DOS can test the value of certain variables and parameters during the execution of a batch file. Performing this test is known as *decision making*, or *logical testing*. A logical test can control *conditional branching* within a program, which means that different actions will be performed based on the results of the test.

In English, a conditional branching statement might look like this:

```
If something = something else, do this; otherwise do that
```

A more formal way of stating this is

```
If A = B then perform action C; otherwise perform action D
```

A=B is called a *logical expression*. As in any language, it can stand for such things as Wage=500 or Lastname=Robbins. If A=B is a true statement, then C will happen. On the other hand, if A=B is false, then action D will take place. This branching ability allows you to create batch files that evaluate circumstances and perform different actions according to the conditions found.

A second form of branching in DOS is the GOTO statement. You can direct the flow of control to move immediately from one statement to another statement located elsewhere in the program with such an instruction. The GOTO instruction is called an *unconditional* branching statement. You'll explore examples of IF and GOTO in the upcoming examples in this chapter.

FIGURE 13.7

The improved KEYDEFS2.BAT file does not require you to know anything about keycodes. The first parameter can be a recognizable acronym for the key combination. For example, F7 means the function key F7, while CF7 means Ctrl+F7. The batch file does the work of interpreting.

```
@ECHO OFF
Rem KEYDEFS2.BAT initializes one key to one character string.
Rem First parameter tells which key, using common identifiers:
Rem        F1..F12 for one of the twelve function keys.
Rem        SF1..SF12 for Shift + function key.
Rem        CF1..CF12 for a Ctrl+ function key.
Rem        AF1..AF12 for Alt + function key.
Rem Second parameter is the string you want DOS to type.
Rem Use this syntax: KEYDEFS2 Key CharString
SET KEY=0
IF %1 == F1 SET KEY=59
IF %1 == F2 SET KEY=60
IF %1 == F3 SET KEY=61
IF %1 == F4 SET KEY=62
IF %1 == F5 SET KEY=63
IF %1 == F6 SET KEY=64
IF %1 == F7 SET KEY=65
IF %1 == F8 SET KEY=66
IF %1 == F9 SET KEY=67
IF %1 == F10 SET KEY=68
IF %1 == F11 SET KEY=133
IF %1 == F12 SET KEY=134

IF %1 == SF1 SET KEY=84
IF %1 == SF2 SET KEY=85
IF %1 == SF3 SET KEY=86
IF %1 == SF4 SET KEY=87
IF %1 == SF5 SET KEY=88
IF %1 == SF6 SET KEY=89
IF %1 == SF7 SET KEY=90
IF %1 == SF8 SET KEY=91
IF %1 == SF9 SET KEY=92
IF %1 == SF10 SET KEY=93
IF %1 == SF11 SET KEY=135
IF %1 == SF12 SET KEY=136

IF %1 == CF1 SET KEY=94
IF %1 == CF2 SET KEY=95
IF %1 == CF3 SET KEY=96
IF %1 == CF4 SET KEY=97
IF %1 == CF5 SET KEY=98
IF %1 == CF6 SET KEY=99
IF %1 == CF7 SET KEY=100
IF %1 == CF8 SET KEY=101
IF %1 == CF9 SET KEY=102
IF %1 == CF10 SET KEY=103
IF %1 == CF11 SET KEY=137
IF %1 == CF12 SET KEY=138
```

FIGURE 13.7

(continued)

```
IF %1 == AF1 SET KEY=104
IF %1 == AF2 SET KEY=105
IF %1 == AF3 SET KEY=106
IF %1 == AF4 SET KEY=107
IF %1 == AF5 SET KEY=108
IF %1 == AF6 SET KEY=109
IF %1 == AF7 SET KEY=110
IF %1 == AF8 SET KEY=111
IF %1 == AF9 SET KEY=112
IF %1 == AF10 SET KEY=113
IF %1 == AF11 SET KEY=139
IF %1 == AF12 SET KEY=140
IF %KEY% == 0 GOTO :END
ECHO ON
PROMPT $e[0;%KEY%;"%2";13p
PROMPT $p$g
:END
@ECHO ON
```

Remember that the earlier KEYDEFS batch file forced you to know or learn the extended key code for the Alt+F11 key combination, thus

`KEYDEFS 139 DOSSHELL`

Figure 13.8 depicts the logical steps and flow of control performed by the instructions in KEYDEFS2.BAT. The first instructions, ECHO OFF and the REM commands, are familiar to you by now. The @ sign that precedes the ECHO OFF instruction is a special technique that suppresses the screen appearance of the *current* instruction. Remember that batch file instructions are not suppressed until *after* an ECHO OFF command executes. Without the @ symbol, the first ECHO OFF command itself would appear on the screen.

The next subcommand is new: the SET subcommand. It creates a variable and stores a specific value into it for later program purposes. Since the program no longer requires the user to know and enter a key code, this particular KEY variable will be used within the batch file to control what happens if the user types an incorrect mnemonic.

FIGURE 13.8

Flow of control in the KEYDEFS2.BAT file. Setting KEY to 0 at the beginning ensures that, after the subsequent IF tests, KEY will still equal zero unless a valid acronym was specified as the first parameter.

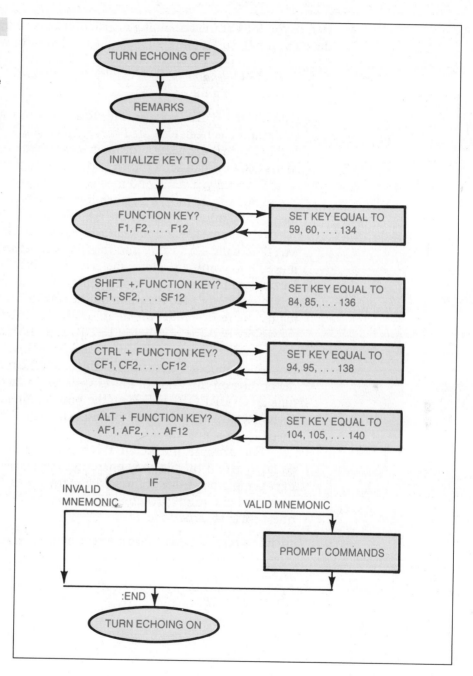

Before you look at the remaining instructions, take a moment to first understand the IF subcommand. It can be used in three ways in a batch file:

1. **IF EXIST** *filename* or **IF NOT EXIST** *filename*. This form of IF tests to see if a file exists.

2. **IF ERRORLEVEL** *number*. This form tests to see if the preceding command has been executed correctly. Certain DOS commands and individual application programs executed by means of COMMAND.COM can set a return code equal to a number from 0 to 255. Usually, a value of 0 means that the preceding command completed successfully; a number greater than 0 indicates a failure, the specific value indicating the specific reason for that failure.

   Only some DOS commands, such as XCOPY and FORMAT, actually set a value into this variable return code. If any of these DOS commands fails, the error level can be compared to a particular number found in the command's documentation, and action can be taken depending on the severity of the error. The higher the return code, the more severe the error.

   Note that the number in IF ERRORLEVEL *number* means a return code of that number *or greater*. The IF statement can control which succeeding section of the batch file receives control, depending on the value of this error level. In fact, you can combine an IF ERRORLEVEL on the same command line as another IF ERRORLEVEL to more precisely control the execution for a specific error level value.

   For example, the XCOPY command returns an error level equal to zero if the file copy operation was successful. The following example batch-file command congratulates the user in this particular situation (presumably after an XCOPY command request was just processed):

```
IF ERRORLEVEL 0 IF NOT ERRORLEVEL 1 ECHO Congratulations!
```

TIP

To test whether or not a user has specified a required parameter when running a batch file, you can use a special version of the IF subcommand. In the following example, you can test to see if parameter number one (%1) has been omitted by using IF '%1'=='' AnyDOSCommand. There is no space between the second pair of apostrophes. If parameter one was omitted, then %1 is treated as nonexistent (or NULL) and the expression on the left of the == marks also becomes equal to ''. In this case, the comparison becomes True, and the specified AnyDOSCommand is executed.

3. **IF A==B or IF NOT A==B.** This form tests the equality of A and B, where A and B represent character strings. Note that DOS uses the double equals symbol == to stand for equality (as opposed to the single equals for assignment—see Chapter 16). The character strings can be literals or variables. A *literal* (also known as a constant) is any unchanging character string, such as JUDD or CF3. A variable is one of the changing parameters %0 through %9, which you learned about in Chapter 12. For example, the command IF %1==CF3 tests to see if the first variable parameter in the batch-file command, %1 (a variable), is equal to the characters CF3 (a literal). This is the most common use of the IF subcommand; there are 48 examples of this type of command line in KEYDEFS2.BAT.

WARNING

When you are testing for the equality of groups of characters, as you do with the IF and the FIND subcommands, case matters. If you enter cf3 with lowercase letters as the first parameter when you run the batch file, DOS will evaluate the IF expression %1==CF3, with uppercase letters, as false. You must enter the uppercase letters *CF3* for the logical expression to be true.

This batch file uses the IF A==B version of the IF subcommand to make a series of tests. The main block of 48 IF statements tests the first parameter, %1, to determine what mnemonic code was entered. If any of these tests finds a TRUE equality (i.e., the characters entered equal F1 or F2 and so on or SF1 or SF2 and so on), then the KEY variable is reset from its initial value of zero to the appropriate key code seen in Figure 13.5.

Transferring Control Directly

The final IF statement is the crucial branching test to determine whether a user has entered any of the valid mnemonics. If one of the possible mnemonics has not been entered, then KEY will still equal its initial value of zero. In this case, the GOTO instruction sends the flow of control to the end of the program:

```
IF %KEY% == 0 GOTO :END
```

The GOTO subcommand tells DOS to continue executing the batch file at some other preferred location. END is a special placeholder, or *label*, that you enter into the batch file to indicate that desired location. In Figure 13.7, you can see *:END* on the next-to-the-last line. It is called a *non-executable instruction,* because it does not represent any steps that the processor takes. It is simply a label for that place in the program. It can be compared to the address on your house, which is just a label that helps friends and the postal service find their way to you.

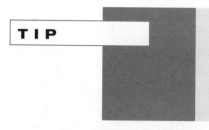

TIP

If you reference a nonexistent (or misspelled) label with a GOTO subcommand, the batch file will terminate immediately. You'll receive a "Label not found" error, and no further batch-file commands will execute.

If the value of KEY is still zero when the GOTO statement is reached, then batch-file processing jumps directly to the :END instruction. The label line does nothing except facilitate this jumping, so the actual instruction that is next executed is found on the line following the label (the @ECHO ON command). All branching techniques like these are referred to as the *flow of control*.

The GOTO statement itself can appear in stand-alone fashion on its own line, or, as you see here, it can be a part of an IF statement. Only if the A==B condition (IF %KEY%==0) proves to be TRUE does the GOTO statement even execute. If it does, it initiates an *unconditional transfer of control*. In the case of this batch file, you only want to execute the PROMPT commands if a user has correctly entered a valid mnemonic for the first parameter, %1.

TIP

Do not use long labels in your batch file. Only the first eight characters are used by DOS to transfer control. If more than one long label begins with the same eight characters, control is transferred only to the first such label. A seemingly unique, but long, label name is not truly unique from DOS's point of view.

There is always a different, and often better, way to program anything on a computer. You can usually improve the coding of any sequence of instructions. This batch file demonstrates how to handle an erroneous first parameter value. You initialize a variable to zero, then reset it to other values depending on the actual input for the first parameter. When the resetting is finally done, you can tell if there was an input error by whether the variable still equals zero. Currently, this batch file contains no error checking for the second parameter.

TIP

Use the GOTO %1 command to transfer control to a label that is exactly the same as the first parameter specified by a user. Use multiple labels (one after the other, and all of them just preceding a block of instructions) in your batch file when you're unsure of which of several, possibly similar, parameters a user may specify.

In the next chapter, you'll learn other methods for checking input, including what to do if the user forgets to enter a required parameter. With a little bit of thought, it's easy to see that this batch file can be written in countless other—perhaps simpler—ways. However, you've used an IF subcommand, a GOTO subcommand, the label mechanism, and variable parameters. Learning about those subcommands is the main point of this batch file, not the actual job being performed. You can now use these tools to write new batch files, which will do meaningful work for you on your own system.

➤ EXTRA!

Flash through Batch-File Text!

If you place a good deal of documentation in your batch files, you can make the batch file run faster with this technique. Just place this line:

```
GOTO AFTER
```

right before all your text lines, and place this line:

```
:AFTER
```

just after all your text. Virtually no processing time will be spent in reading and interpreting each of your text lines. If you use this technique, you don't even have to bother making your text into a series of REM lines.

Using Looping and Repetition in Batch Files

The FOR subcommand in DOS batch files offers you a facility that is similar to commands in other programming languages. In particular, this

> ➤ **EXTRA!**

Batch Files Offer Programming Language Features!

Often, one or more commands in a program need to be repeated, sometimes a fixed number of times and sometimes a variable number of times. In either situation, the FOR subcommand enables you to meet this need. The general form of the FOR subcommand is

```
FOR %%Letter IN (Possibilities) DO Command
```

Letter can be any single alphabetic letter. It is similar to the variable parameters you saw in Chapter 12 (%0, %1, %2, and so on). With the FOR command, however, double percent-sign variables are used (but only in batch files: from a command line, only a preceding percent sign is used). The %% tells DOS that you are referring to a batch-file variable in the looping FOR statement.

The *Command*, which will be executed repeatedly, can change slightly during each repetition. This works similarly to the variable parameter method, which required you to write the batch file originally using %1 or %2 to refer to possible first or second input parameters. As you learned in Chapter 12, the variable parameter technique defers execution so that when the batch file actually executes, it uses the actual values typed in after the batch-file name, instead of using the placeholder % expressions.

In a FOR subcommand, execution is similarly deferred until the command executes. At that time, the *Possibilities* are evaluated, and the *Command* is executed for each possibility. When written into a batch file, this command can represent a more concise form of coding.

command facilitates repetition, much like the DO command in QBasic that you'll learn about in Chapter 16.

Let's take a look at a typical example of the FOR command in action. Suppose you have a program called QRTLY.EXE that generates a quarterly business report. This program requires only that you specify the desired quarter for the current fiscal year. Entering the following at the DOS prompt would produce a report for quarter 3:

```
QRTLY 3
```

At the end of the fiscal year, you might want to generate current copies of the quarterly reports for each quarter. You would enter

```
QRTLY 1
QRTLY 2
QRTLY 3
QRTLY 4
```

and press Enter after each line. You will quickly discover that you must wait for each report to completely finish before you can type in the next QRTLY request. However, all four of these successive requests could be replaced in a batch file called REPORTS.BAT with one automatic FOR subcommand, as shown in Figure 13.9.

FIGURE 13.9

The REPORTS.BAT file uses the FOR command to replace four separate but similar runs of the QRTLY program. %%A is replaced four times, for each of the variable values 1, 2, 3 and 4, generating QRTRLY 1, QRTRLY 2, QRTRLY 3, and QRTRLY 4.

```
@ECHO OFF
REM The REPORTS.BAT File
REM Produce the Four Quarterly Reports
FOR %%A IN (1 2 3 4) DO QRTLY %%A
ECHO ON
```

Using this looping mechanism does not require you to wait for each quarterly report to finish before you request the next to begin:

```
FOR %%A IN (1 2 3 4) DO QRTLY %%A
```

Your first reaction might be that this is an awfully complicated-looking expression just to save typing in four simple QRTLY report requests. Again, it just demonstrates the technique. If you had a monthly report program called MONTHLY.EXE, you could just as easily request the printing of twelve monthly reports with:

```
FOR %%A IN (1 2 3 4 5 6 7 8 9 10 11 12) DO MONTHLY %%A
```

The modified REPORTS file would look like REPORTS2.BAT, shown in Figure 13.10.

FIGURE 13.10

The REPORTS2.BAT file is as simple to write as the REPORTS batch file. This time, however, the FOR line takes the place of twelve separate but similar runs of the MONTHLY report program.

```
@ECHO OFF
REM The REPORTS2.BAT File
REM Produce the Twelve Monthly Reports
FOR %%A IN (1 2 3 4 5 6 7 8 9 10 11 12) DO MONTHLY %%A
ECHO ON
```

As you've just seen in the general form of the FOR subcommand, there can be only one *Command* parameter executed after the DO portion of the command. It can be a program name (with its own parameters), as you've just seen demonstrated, or it can be another DOS command, like DIR or CHKDSK. The following FOR subcommand exemplifies this:

```
FOR %%A IN (%1 %2 %3 %4) DO DIR %%A
```

This command would perform a DIR command for each variable parameter (up to four different file names). If this FOR subcommand were in a batch file called HUNT.BAT, as shown in Figure 13.11, you might

FIGURE 13.11

The HUNT.BAT file demonstrates that variable parameters can be combined with the FOR command to form the first steps in a powerful search facility.

```
@ECHO OFF
REM The HUNT.BAT File
FOR %%A IN (%1 %2 %3 %4) DO DIR %%A
ECHO ON
```

invoke HUNT in the following manner to determine if any of the specified files were located in the current directory:

```
HUNT HEART.EXE LUNGS.EXE LIVER.COM
```

The result of executing this command might look something like Figure 13.12. The files HEART.EXE and LIVER.COM were found, but LUNGS.EXE was not.

Even though you've suppressed the display of the DOS commands themselves with ECHO OFF, the remaining output still appears cluttered. Using a batch subcommand as the object of DO (the last keyword in the FOR subcommand's required syntax) can produce a more concise and

FIGURE 13.12

Executing HUNT.BAT to repeat the DIR command. It's useful when information is found, but the display gets a bit crowded when other data is repeated.

```
C:\MEDICINE>HUNT HEART.EXE LUNGS.EXE LIVER.COM

 Volume in drive C is ROBBINS
 Directory of C:\MEDICINE

HEART    EXE    15796 10-26-92   6:00a
         1 file(s)        15796 bytes
                       76824576 bytes free

 Volume in drive C is ROBBINS
 Directory of C:\MEDICINE

File not found

 Volume in drive C is ROBBINS
 Directory of C:\MEDICINE

LIVER    COM     1754 04-13-93   6:00a
         1 file(s)         1754 bytes
                       76824576 bytes free

C:\MEDICINE>

C:\MEDICINE>
```

attractive result. An IF subcommand can even be used to replace the DIR command:

```
FOR %%A IN (%1 %2 %3 %4) DO IF EXIST %%A ECHO %%A FOUND
```

I replaced the FOR command in HUNT.BAT with this new FOR command, creating HUNT2.BAT in the process. Figure 13.13 first displays the four instructions that constitute the HUNT2.BAT file, then shows the results of running the file to hunt out the same three medical files, as in Figure 13.12. This time, the desired information about whether the files exist is not obscured by the full directory information. In this FOR subcommand, the actual command executed by DO is

```
IF EXIST %%A ECHO %%A FOUND
```

Try out all of the sample batch files in this section to affirm your understanding of the subcommands. In some cases, you will have to change the directory references to references that will work on your system. Also, remember that in all of these batch files the first ECHO OFF command is preceded by the @ prefix. ECHO OFF ensures that DOS turns the echoing feature off for all succeeding commands, and the @ symbol suppresses the display of the ECHO OFF command as well.

As an exercise, in addition to or in place of the examples in this section, create a new batch file—perhaps called GYRO.BAT—that will provide extra information to a user about your chosen topics. The batch file should be invoked as

```
GYRO HEART
```

```
C:\MEDICINE>TYPE HUNT2.BAT
@ECHO OFF
REM The HUNT2.BAT File
FOR %%A IN (%1 %2 %3 %4) DO IF EXIST %%A ECHO %%A FOUND
ECHO ON

C:\MEDICINE>HUNT2 HEART.EXE LUNGS.EXE LIVER.COM
HEART.EXE FOUND
LIVER.COM FOUND

C:\MEDICINE>

C:\MEDICINE>
```

to determine if a text file called HEART.HLP existed. If it did, the screen would clear and the contents of the HEART.HLP file would be displayed. If it did not, the message "No help is available on subject HEART" would be displayed. Create your own sample .HLP text files to test your batch file.

► EXTRA!

Batch Chaining Differs from Subroutine Calling!

Since a batch file can execute any command that otherwise could be entered directly at the DOS prompt, a batch file can invoke or run another batch file. By simply entering the name of the second batch file somewhere in the first one, you can pass control from the first to the second file. Execution continues with the instructions in the second batch file and does not return to the first batch file. This is known as *chaining*. It is different from the calling procedure familiar to programmers.

Chaining is also different from what occurs when you run a .COM or a .EXE program by typing its name. When such a program completes, execution continues from the point it was run (either the command prompt or its typed location within the batch file). When you simply type a batch file's name, control passes to it and does not automatically return.

In contrast to this, true subroutines provide you with the ability to write modular batch files that perform well-defined task sequences, and to leave one batch file *temporarily*—to execute a sequence without losing your place in the first batch file. If you need to run a batch file while in the middle of another batch file, you can use the CALL subcommand:

    CALL BatchFileName

When the batch file has executed all its commands, control will be returned to the very next line—the one *following* the CALL instruction— in the calling batch file, and execution will continue from there.

Using Batch Chains and Batch Subroutines

Batch files can run programs or other batch files. However, care must be taken to ensure that your intentions are performed by DOS properly. To do this, you must understand the difference between *chaining* execution from one batch file to another, and *calling* one batch file from another.

Look at the listings of the three batch files in Figures 13.14, 13.15, and 13.16. These three files together demonstrate both the capabilities and the limitations of chaining. Carefully read the steps of each of the three batch files, while looking at the output results in Figure 13.17.

The first batch file executes three "instructions" and then invokes the second batch file as its last instruction. The simulated instructions take the place of any other successive batch-file commands that you might write. You should focus on the chaining here, rather than on these example command lines; the simulated instructions are displayed merely to give you a representative context for the chaining technique.

FIGURE 13.14

FIRST.BAT demonstrates batch file chaining. Invoking SECOND as the last line here transfers control irrevocably to the SECOND.BAT batch file. Such a purposeful transfer should nearly always be in the last line of a batch program.

```
@ECHO OFF
REM The FIRST.BAT File
ECHO Simulated Instruction 1 in First.bat
ECHO Simulated Instruction 2 in First.bat
ECHO Simulated Instruction 3 in First.bat
SECOND
```

SECOND.BAT transfers control via chaining to the THIRD.BAT file. However, it does it before the actual last line is reached. This means that the last instruction line in this batch file is never executed at all.

```
@ECHO OFF
REM The SECOND.BAT File
ECHO Simulated Instruction 1 in Second.bat
ECHO Simulated Instruction 2 in Second.bat
ECHO Simulated Instruction 3 in Second.bat
THIRD
ECHO Last Instruction in Second.bat
```

The THIRD.BAT file doesn't do much except simulate running three separate instructions, which might be anything you like if you had written such a batch file. It ends the FIRST-SEC-OND-THIRD chaining sequence.

```
@ECHO OFF
REM The THIRD.BAT File
ECHO Simulated Instruction 1 in Third.bat
ECHO Simulated Instruction 2 in Third.bat
ECHO Simulated Instruction 3 in Third.bat
```

This is the visible output from batch-file chaining sequence managed by running FIRST, which chains to SECOND, which chains to THIRD. Notice how the final instruction in SECOND is clearly never reached or executed.

```
C>FIRST
Simulated Instruction 1 in First.bat
Simulated Instruction 2 in First.bat
Simulated Instruction 3 in First.bat
Simulated Instruction 1 in Second.bat
Simulated Instruction 2 in Second.bat
Simulated Instruction 3 in Second.bat
Simulated Instruction 1 in Third.bat
Simulated Instruction 2 in Third.bat
Simulated Instruction 3 in Third.bat
C>
```

After FIRST is done, it passes control to SECOND by invoking as its last instruction the name of the file (SECOND) to which control will be passed. Then batch file SECOND executes another three simulated instructions before passing control to batch file THIRD. THIRD executes its own three simulated instructions before the chain process is complete. The line "Last instruction in Second.bat" is never executed, because the third batch file was invoked *in the middle* of the second batch file!

T I P

Proper *chaining* of batch files requires the new batch-file name to be the last instruction of the preceding batch file in the chain. Proper *nesting* of batch files requires that you use the CALL subcommand. You can call one batch file from any position within any other batch file.

Look again at the THIRD.BAT file shown in Figure 13.16, and then look at FOURTH.BAT, shown in Figure 13.18. The results of running FOURTH.BAT, as shown in Figure 13.19, are different from the results of chaining.

FIGURE 13.18

The FOURTH.BAT file demonstrates a true calling sequence, based on a CALL subcommand. Because THIRD is executed with a CALL, control will return to the last instruction here after the instructions in THIRD.BAT have completed.

```
@ECHO OFF
REM The FOURTH.BAT File
ECHO Simulated Instruction 1 in Fourth.bat
ECHO Simulated Instruction 2 in Fourth.bat
ECHO Simulated Instruction 3 in Fourth.bat
CALL THIRD
ECHO Last Instruction in Fourth.bat
```

FIGURE 13.19

DOS supports true subroutines with the CALL subcommand. Clearly, control transfers through the FOURTH batch file, then through the THIRD batch file via a CALL command, and finally back to the FOURTH batch file to execute its last instruction.

```
C>FOURTH
Simulated Instruction 1 in Fourth.bat
Simulated Instruction 2 in Fourth.bat
Simulated Instruction 3 in Fourth.bat
Simulated Instruction 1 in Third.bat
Simulated Instruction 2 in Third.bat
Simulated Instruction 3 in Third.bat
Last Instruction in Fourth.bat
C>
```

Running FOURTH by this method results in the same first three simulated instructions as with chaining. When those three have executed, control is transferred to the THIRD batch file, at which point *its* three simulated instructions execute. However, unlike the previous chaining example, control then *returns* to FOURTH, which can execute its next instruction. If there were still other instructions following that, they would all execute consecutively in the normal way. As you can see, sophisticated, structured application environments and systems can be built up by using only DOS commands and the batch-file mechanism.

TIP

It is possible to program a recursive batch file; that is, a batch file can CALL itself. If you do this, however, be sure to include at least one command within the batch file that can exit from the batch file under one or more circumstances.

Summary

In this chapter, you extended your understanding of batch files. You learned about a variety of specialized commands that only work from within batch files. These subcommands provide DOS with the kind of features normally reserved for a high-level computer language:

- Messages can be included for internal documentation with the REM subcommand. You can also include messages to be displayed during the execution of the batch program with the ECHO subcommand.

- Normally all batch-file command lines are displayed on the console as they execute. You can suppress any particular one by preceding it with the @ character in column 1 of the command line, or you can suppress all succeeding command lines with the ECHO OFF command.

- Batch files can contain the standard logic seen in most programming languages. Branching is managed by the GOTO subcommand in conjunction with simple labels like :END.

- Decision making is provided with the IF subcommand. DOS allows decisions based on whether a file exists or not (EXIST) and on whether character strings equal each other or not (==). DOS also allows decisions based on the severity of command errors (ERRORLEVEL *number*).

- The FOR subcommand controls the sophisticated features of looping and command repetition.

- You can interrupt your own batch program temporarily with the PAUSE subcommand or permanently with the Break-key combination (Ctrl+Break).

- You can implement true programming subroutines by using the CALL subcommand.

Now that you possess these fundamental batch-file construction skills, the next chapter will make a more advanced user out of you. While demonstrating actual sophisticated batch files, you will learn many tricks and techniques that will lead you to develop fancy implementations and systems of your own.

CHAPTER

14

Sophisticated Batch-File Examples

YOU'VE learned that the primary role of batch files is to allow you to conveniently group together a collection of DOS commands, other programs, and other batch files. You've also seen how this entire collection of commands can be run by entering the batch-file name with any special parameters at the DOS prompt.

There are two situations in which you should write batch files:

- When you have a time-consuming sequence of unattended operations to be performed.

- When you need to run a complex sequence of commands frequently, and you would like to ensure that they are performed consistently.

In this chapter, you will see a wide range of batch files. These examples provide you with usable programs, from virus detection to password protection. You can type them in yourself, or you can send for a diskette with the files already on it (see the order form at the end of this book). These examples will also give you ideas for creating similar programs for your own computer system.

NOTE

As is often the case with examples designed to illustrate specific concepts, certain files presented in this chapter may not be the fastest, most efficient, or most elegant files, but they do illustrate the topic at hand. They will also do the job until you feel comfortable enough to refine them on your own.

Automating System Jobs with AUTOEXEC.BAT

When you turn on your computer, DOS looks for and reads the contents of any CONFIG.SYS file to configure your system. After this first internal configuration, DOS then scans the root directory of your system's boot disk for a batch file called AUTOEXEC.BAT. If it finds that file, it executes the commands within it automatically.

➤ EXTRA!

Don't Let a New Application Overwrite Your AUTOEXEC.BAT!

DOS does not supply a default AUTOEXEC.BAT file. However, many application programs do supply one on their system disks. When loading a new application program, be sure that the program's adjusted or new AUTOEXEC.BAT file does not overwrite an existing AUTOEXEC.BAT file that you previously created.

You can make it easier to monitor adjustments to your AUTO-EXEC.BAT file by making it into a two-line program:

```
@ECHO OFF
AUTOREAL.BAT
```

Then, place all of your AUTOEXEC.BAT command lines in the AUTOREAL.BAT batch file. If any installation program makes changes to your standard AUTOEXEC.BAT file, you can easily identify what they are later. Then, you can carefully correct or modify your AUTOREAL.BAT file, which really contains the startup instructions you desire.

AUTOEXEC.BAT is a valuable tool. In both diskette and hard-disk systems, it can be used to automatically execute any number of DOS commands or other programs. For example, you can configure your PROMPT and MODE commands for specific serial-port and video-screen requirements. There is no limit to the variations you can make in your AUTOEXEC.BAT file.

Let's take a look at some of these AUTOEXEC.BAT variations. You'll look first at how to load and run a specific program automatically when you power up your computer. Then you'll see how to use an existing batch file to customize your command prompt and the F11 and F12 keys. Finally, you'll explore some possibilities for more complex system setups.

Automating the System Startup

It's easy to add an automatic startup feature to your system disk. As soon as DOS is loaded, the computer will run a particular program. Typically, the default is to run the DOSSHELL program and display the initial DOS Shell screen. If you have a self-contained executable program, you can also run it automatically from this AUTOEXEC.BAT file by including its name on its own instruction line. An example AUTOEXEC.BAT file can be seen in Figure 14.1.

After a series of other command instructions, the last one executed in my AUTOEXEC.BAT file is the DOSSHELL.EXE program. This runs and brings up the DOS shell on your monitor. However, suppose that you don't want to use the shell at all. Suppose that you only want to use the QuickBASIC program and nothing else. On a hard-disk system, all you need to do is change your AUTOEXEC.BAT to make \DOS the current directory and run the QuickBASIC program. To do this, you would replace the DOSSHELL line with:

```
CD \DOS
QBASIC
```

On a floppy-disk system, you can prepare a system disk that contains the QBasic program and an AUTOEXEC.BAT file that will run QBasic when you power up. To do this, you should first use the COPY command to place copies of QBASIC.EXE and any necessary support programs (i.e., QBASIC.HLP and QBASIC.INI) on your new system disk.

FIGURE 14.1

An example
AUTOEXEC.BAT file. If
a batch file exists in
the root directory of
your boot drive, DOS
will automatically
execute the instruc-
tions found within it
at power-up time.

```
@ECHO OFF
LOADHIGH C:\PCACHE\PCACHE
LOADHIGH D:\WINDOWS\MOUSE
LOADHIGH C:\DOS\UNDELETE /LOAD
C:\DOS\SMARTDRV
D:\SBPRO\DRV\MSCDEX /V /D:MSCD001 /M:15
LOADHIGH C:\DOS\DOSKEY /BUFSIZE=2048
PATH C:\DOS;D:\WINDOWS;C:\;C:\UTILITY
PROMPT $p$g
SET COMSPEC=c:\command.com
SET DIRCMD=/ON
SET TEMP=C:\
SET SOUND=d:\sbpro
SET BLASTER=A220 I2 D1 T2
Call SETUP
DOSSHELL
```

N O T E

The AUTOEXEC.BAT file must be stored in the root
directory of the disk. It will be ignored if it is stored
in any other directory. If DOS cannot find your
AUTOEXEC.BAT file, either because you have
misplaced it or because you have not created one at
all, then the DATE and TIME commands are
automatically executed. You may adjust the system
date and time at this point, and the DOS system
prompt will then appear.

Assume that your intended system disk is temporarily in drive B (e.g., for the
copying operation) for a dual-diskette system. You would use the command

```
COPY QBASIC.* B:
```

If your dual-diskette system uses the smaller 360K floppies, you will have
to place the .HLP file on a different floppy because it is too large to fit on
the same floppy as the QBASIC.EXE file.

It is a simple task for your AUTOEXEC.BAT file to submit the name of
a particular application program you want to execute. The principle
shown here will apply to any program that you want to start up automatically when your system boots. For this example, you'd like to invoke

QBASIC.EXE automatically on startup. Use whatever text-editing method you like to create an AUTOEXEC.BAT file containing the one line that invokes the QBASIC program:

```
QBASIC
```

As you can see from the sample AUTOEXEC.BAT, there is no limit to how many individual programs you can run automatically in a AUTO-EXEC.BAT file. Besides setting the PATH, this AUTOEXEC.BAT file loads a variety of programs (PCACHE, MOUSE, UNDELETE, SMARTDRV, MSCDEX, DOSKEY, and DOSSHELL) and a batch file named SETUP. Your AUTOEXEC.BAT file can be as simple as one line or as complex as you like. If you'd like to automate running your word processor—say, WP.COM—make sure you copy WP.COM to the new system disk, or change directories to the one containing WP.COM. In this case, your AUTOEXEC.BAT file will contain the following line:

```
WP
```

Since many application programs include overlay files, you must also be sure to copy those files to your new system disk. For instance, suppose your word processor requires a file called WP.OVL. You would need to have that file on the system disk containing your new AUTOEXEC.BAT file. Or, as I demonstrated above with QBASIC, you could use the CD command to change the current directory to the one that contains all the necessary files.

Changing the Default System Prompt

Changing your default system prompt is often so useful that you might want to have it set automatically when you turn on the computer. You can use the AUTOEXEC.BAT file to accomplish this, as DOS commands themselves can be executed automatically during startup. Normally, your system prompt consists of the drive identifier with a > sign, for example, C>. As you saw in Chapter 12's SETUP.BAT batch file, a typical system prompt consists of the current drive and directory with a greater-than sign. I activate it with the single command

```
PROMPT $p$g
```

➤ EXTRA!

AUTOEXEC.BAT Changes Do Not Have Immediate Effect!

After you've made any changes to your AUTOEXEC.BAT file, you can test whether the new setup will work as planned by restarting the computer from your system disk. The instructions within AUTOEXEC.BAT will naturally have no impact until you run the batch file itself. Since some instructions in AUTOEXEC.BAT cannot be run twice, you will be safest to restart DOS completely in order to achieve any new results from a modified AUTOEXEC.BAT file.

You can implement the changes in your AUTOEXEC.BAT file in two ways. First, you can turn off the computer, wait a few seconds, and then turn it on again. DOS should load and the AUTOEXEC.BAT batch file program should run automatically.

As an alternative, you can reboot your system by pressing the Ctrl+Alt+Del key combination. This will also restart the computer, and your AUTOEXEC.BAT will be executed. However, it will not perform the same internal hardware and memory checks that occur with an actual startup. Windows users should take note that there can also be dramatically different results. As a separate issue, Windows users will be safest by using a power down/up sequence to reinitiate your entire DOS system.

Using Ctrl+Alt+Del is called *warm booting* since the computer has already been turned on. A *cold boot* occurs when you first turn on the computer's power; the same sequence takes place then, with the addition of several internal hardware tests.

In all of this, however, take warning! You should never get too casual about the Ctrl+Alt+Del rebooting method. If you are in the middle of running a program like a word processor, a database manager, or a spreadsheet, rebooting may easily destroy your current working file.

Either of these rebooting procedures can be followed with most programs, and any main program can be run automatically at system startup. However, keep in mind that some copy-protected programs have their own instructions for automatic startup. In addition, some programs will themselves intercept the Ctrl+Alt+Del key combination, as does Windows, so it may not produce an immediate reboot on your system.

If this is all you need and want, you can create a one-line AUTO-EXEC.BAT that contains only this line. You could try this now and then reboot. (Remember that the code characters within a PROMPT command are case sensitive; that is, they must match for upper and lower case as shown in the examples you find in this section.)

TIP

Using the PROMPT command in the AUTOEXEC.BAT file changes all primary and secondary command prompts. (Remember that a secondary command prompt is what you obtain by pressing Shift+F9 or by selecting Command Prompt from the shell.) However, using PROMPT from a secondary prompt (i.e., when the shell is still resident in memory) will affect only that subordinate command prompt; the main DOS prompt will remain unchanged.

Take another look at Figure 14.1. The next to last line contains the one-line command

```
CALL SETUP
```

This line runs the SETUP.BAT file (see Chapter 12) which contains the following four lines to initialize the F11 and F12 keys, as well as the DOS command prompt:

```
Rem SETUP.BAT initializes function keys F11 and F12
PROMPT $e[0;133;"DOSSHELL";13p
PROMPT $e[0;134;"EXIT";13p
PROMPT $p$g
```

Note how the CALL subcommand is used to activate the SETUP batch file. Remember the discussion in Chapter 13 about chaining versus subroutines. Without the CALL subcommand, control would be passed to the SETUP.BAT file and would never return to AUTOEXEC.BAT. With the CALL subcommand, control returns to AUTOEXEC.BAT after the PROMPT commands execute and the DOSSHELL file executes.

Although notable only in its absence, this AUTOEXEC.BAT file contains no initial ECHO OFF instruction. Usually, you would suppress echoing during AUTOEXEC.BAT execution. However, when a batch file contains any PROMPT escape sequences (as does the SETUP.BAT file), you must have echoing enabled (ECHO ON) while these instructions execute.

Checking for Computer Viruses

The possibilities are limitless when it comes to adding useful instructions to your AUTOEXEC.BAT file. Just about anything you've already learned, from setting the prompt uniquely to initializing function keys, could be included in your startup AUTOEXEC.BAT file. Of course, everything else you'll read about in this chapter could be included in it as well.

WARNING

There is no limit to the number of command lines you can have in any batch file. However, you should not write batch files with too many commands in them. They become harder to understand, modify, and debug as they get larger.

Suppose you want to run a simple check for a computer virus every time you start your system. There are many kinds of computer viruses, and some of them can do immediate damage to your system. However, many viruses do not cause immediate damage; rather, they hide in your COMMAND.COM file and wait for some later time to wreak havoc, and even to replicate themselves on other disks.

Figure 14.2 shows the instructions contained within VIRUSTST.BAT. This batch file combines a number of techniques you've learned in earlier chapters. Its main purpose is to detect if your system's COMMAND.COM has been surreptitiously altered to store some form of computer virus.

FIGURE 14.2

VIRUSTST.BAT offers a quick and easy batch file example of checking COMMAND.COM for possible virus infiltration. It performs only one of the many type checks done by the Microsoft Anti-Virus (MSAV) program discussed earlier in Chapter 9.

```
@ECHO OFF
Rem VIRUSTST.BAT checks for possible virus infiltration.
Rem Assumes that COMMAND.COM's size and date do not change.
Rem Replace values in the FIND line for your version.
DIR C:\COMMAND.COM > VIRUS
FIND "COMMAND  COM     52925 02-12-93" VIRUS  /C > VIRUS.TXT
ECHO Virus Status: 1 for healthy, 0 for possible problem.
TYPE VIRUS.TXT
```

The basic assumption in this logic is that each version of DOS contains a fixed-size COMMAND.COM file, prepared on a specific date. If a virus has been injected into this COMMAND.COM file, then the file size or creation date has probably changed. Each time you run VIRUSTST.BAT, your system's COMMAND.COM is checked against its original date and size. You are informed, as shown in Figure 14.3, as to whether or not any changes have occurred that should make you suspicious.

The DIR instruction in VIRUSTST.BAT obtains a brief listing from DOS that includes name, file size, and creation date of the system's current COMMAND.COM file, and uses redirection to send this information into a file named VIRUS:

```
DIR C:\COMMAND.COM > VIRUS
```

FIGURE 14.3

Running the VIRUSTST batch file produces a simple output. A batch file can almost always be written to do a job more quickly than, if not as prettily as, a more complex application program.

```
C:\>VIRUSTST
Virus Status: 1 for healthy, 0 for possible problem.

---------- VIRUS: 1
C:\>
```

The FIND command subsequently interrogates this VIRUS file to locate a string of characters that matches the original COMMAND.COM data when you first installed DOS. I obtained these characters by performing a DIR command on my original DOS system disk.

```
FIND "COMMAND COM 52925 02-12-93" VIRUS /C > VIRUS.TXT
```

On my system, DOS 6 contains 52,925 bytes and was created on February 12, 1993. On your system, you will have to change the data within quotation marks to exactly replicate the results of a DIR command. Make sure that you exactly reproduce all characters, including blank spaces and leading zeros.

If the FIND command is successful in matching this character string with the current results of a DIR command (in the preceding instruction), you can feel reasonably confident that no changes have occurred in your COMMAND.COM file. Because the /C switch has been used with the FIND command, the result of the command is the target file name (VIRUS) and a count of how many occurrences of the specified string were found.

This resulting numeric count can only be one or zero. The ECHO command is used to interpret in English what the two numbers mean:

```
ECHO Virus Status: 1 for healthy, 0 for possible problem.
```

If the complete string of characters was found, it means that the current COMMAND.COM size and date are precisely the same as the original. In this case, the FIND command locates exactly one occurrence of the string. Your system is still healthy. However, if any changes occurred to COMMAND.COM, then the string of characters containing the original file size and date will not be found in this current directory listing; the occurrence count will be zero. This result can be seen by displaying the text file created by redirecting the FIND output to VIRUS.TXT:

```
TYPE VIRUS.TXT
```

Once you've written your own version of VIRUSTST.BAT, and tested it, you can include it in your system's AUTOEXEC.BAT. Do this in the same way as I ran SETUP in Figure 14.1, by running the batch file with the CALL command:

```
CALL VIRUSTST
```

Also remember to use date and time values for the FIND command that are correct for your original DOS system disk.

The rest of this chapter contains a host of additional tips, tricks, and techniques that can be used with batch files. You'll want to include some of these in your AUTOEXEC.BAT file. Others you'll wish to run at specific times of your own choosing. Use your own judgment and creativity in adding commands to your AUTOEXEC.BAT file.

Creating Your Own Menu System

In this section, I'll demonstrate how to use the tools built into DOS to create and customize your own application menuing system. The first step in creating your own menu system is to create a file that will contain a listing of the programs available on your system. Let's put this display menu into a text file called MENU.SCR, as shown in Figure 14.4.

As a personalized alternative to the shell, you can write a MYMENU.BAT file that displays this file of text each time your system boots up. All you must do to initiate this menu system is to:

```
CALL MYMENU
```

FIGURE 14.4

An entire file of text can be swiftly displayed with a single TYPE command. This is actually much faster than using a series of ECHO commands to produce the same effect.

```
********     MENU OF AVAILABLE PROGRAMS ********
To Select One, Type Its Number and Press <Enter>
A - Inventory Management System
B - Budget Analysis System
C - Word Processing
D - System Utilities
```

You can see the partially completed MYMENU.BAT file in Figure 14.5. The TYPE command displays the MENU.SCR file of choices, and the CHOICE command transfers control to the appropriate group of instructions to process a user's choice. The CHOICE command returns an ERRORLEVEL equal to the position of the selection in the /C group. In other words, ERRORLEVEL is set to four in MYMENU.BAT if the user selects the fourth alternative (i.e. choice D in this example). Similarly, choices A, B, or C would produce an ERRORLEVEL value of 1, 2, or 3, respectively.

FIGURE 14.5

The MYMENU.BAT batch file demonstrates how to use the CHOICE command to manage user selections and alternative actions in a batch file. CHOICE sets the ERRORLEVEL value, which can then be tested with an IF statement to transfer control to an appropriate location.

```
                    @ECHO OFF
        Rem MYMENU.BAT displays a customized menu.
        CLS
        TYPE MENU.SCR
        CHOICE "Enter Your Choice Now, Please: " /C:ABCD
        IF ERRORLEVEL 4 GOTO CHOICE_D
        IF ERRORLEVEL 3 GOTO CHOICE_C
        IF ERRORLEVEL 2 GOTO CHOICE_B

        :CHOICE_A
        rem CD \DBMS\INVNTORY
        rem DBASE INVENT
        rem CD \
        echo choice a
        GOTO :NEXT

        :CHOICE_B
        rem CD \LOTUS
        rem LOTUS
        rem CD \
        echo choice b
        GOTO :NEXT

        :CHOICE_C
        rem CD \WP
        rem WP
        rem CD \
        echo choice c
        GOTO :NEXT

        :CHOICE_D
        Rem System Utilities instructions
        echo choice d

        :NEXT
        CHOICE "Press C to Continue, or E to Exit the menu: " /C:CE
        IF ERRORLEVEL 2 Goto :END

        MYMENU
        :END
```

➤ EXTRA!

DOS 6 Makes Menuing System Creation a Snap!

It's always helpful to set up a mechanism that makes it easy for you and others to run programs. Hard-disk menu systems are designed to provide that very capability. Of course, you can always buy one; however, DOS's batch-file feature, along with the CHOICE command, provides an inexpensive way to set up a menu system on your own.

Naturally, you can take advantage of the shell's program groups, which are already in place. However, this does require that you conform to the rules set up by DOS. If you understand and apply the techniques shown in this section, you'll be able to set up a comparable menu structure. Your structure, however, will have unlimited flexibility. You can easily change both the appearance and the functionality of your own batch files.

The CHOICE command enables you to both display a message to a user, and simultaneously provide a series of single character choices. The CHOICE command will only accept one of the allowable choices, and will return an ERRORLEVEL equal to the position of the selection in the group of allowable choices. A /C switch is used to construct the group of valid choices. In other words, if your CHOICE statement looks like:

```
CHOICE "Choose One of These Programs" /C:ABCD
```

then DOS sets the ERRORLEVEL return code from the CHOICE command equal to four if the user selects the fourth alternative (i.e., choice D in this example). Similarly, choices A, B, or C would produce an ERRORLEVEL value of 1, 2, or 3, respectively.

To run the inventory management system, you only need to type A and press Enter. This executes the instructions in the :CHOICE_A section of the MYMENU.BAT file. These instructions control the following actions:

1. Changing to the correct directory (e.g., C:\DBMS\INVNTORY).

2. Running the program. In this case, the batch file runs dBASE IV and specifies a customized inventory program (written in the dBASE IV programming language) called INVENT.PRG:

```
DBASE INVENT
```

3. Returning to the root directory after the program has completed.

At this point, you should modify the MYMENU.BAT file to fill in the CHOICE_D section with your own desired fourth execution choice. Although you can use your imagination, start off by writing instructions to accomplish the following simple tasks:

1. Clear the screen, and display a file of new choices with DOS's TYPE command. Call this file UTIL.SCR, and give the user these options:

```
1. Display the current date and time
2. Format a new diskette in drive A
```

Use the CHOICE command again to pass control properly to one of two new sections of instructions that you write, called CHOICE_D1 and CHOICE_D2.

TIP

Remember to add REM statements to document all batch files that aren't transparently simple. Use them for your successor, for another programmer who uses your batch file, and for yourself—after all, *you* could be the one who, two months later, tries to figure out why a certain statement was included. You can also make your batch files more readable by inserting blank lines between groups of related commands. This helps to logically tie together some commands, while visually separating command groups. This is particularly valuable in batch files that perform several tasks during the course of their processing.

To test the entire menu system, run the MYMENU.BAT file. If you've called MYMENU.BAT from within your AUTOEXEC.BAT file, you can reboot your system to pass control to your customized menu system. You should test each option on the main menu, as well as each option you programmed into the submenu. Be careful to use a new disk or scratch disk when testing the FORMAT choice on your Utility menu.

Improving Performance with Batch Files

There are many ways to improve performance with batch files. Some of these are ridiculously easy—what's hard is thinking of them at all. In this section, you'll learn a host of simple possibilities for batch files. Since the lines of code are few, you can implement these approaches quickly if you choose.

NOTE   Remember that nearly everyone designs and programs differently, and that all of the batch files you see here are demonstrations. Feel free to add embellishments or to design the instruction sequences differently.

Simplifying Consistent Sequences

Most of us are not great typists. Even for those who can speed along, there is great value to be gained in reducing the number of keys to be pressed. In the music world, there is much debate on the value of pressing one button on a synthesizer and obtaining the sound of an entire rhythm section. No such debate rages in the PC world: Anything that gets the same result with fewer keypresses receives a broad welcome.

Abbreviating Commands

Any DOS command can be abbreviated to the ultimate in simplicity with a one-line batch file. For example, the CHKDSK command can be shortened to the letter C simply by creating a batch file called C.BAT, and including in it the one instruction

```
CHKDSK
```

When you type C and press Enter at the DOS prompt, the batch file C.BAT will be given control, and its one instruction will be executed as if you had typed it at the DOS prompt.

This technique can also be used for commands, programs, or batch files that normally take parameters, such as the XCOPY command or the KEYDEFS2 batch file we created in Chapter 12. You could just as easily create a batch file called K.BAT that only contains the one executable instruction

```
KEYDEFS2 %1 %2
```

When you want to use this command, you could type K instead of typing KEYDEFS2 along with the variables. For instance, if you wanted to assign the character string DOSSHELL to function key F11, you could now type

```
K F11 DOSSHELL
```

DOS would quickly discover that K is a batch file, and the job would be handled through the batch-file invocation of the KEYDEFS2 batch file, using the parameters represented as %1 and %2. Each time you run the K batch file, you've saved seven keystrokes compared to what you'd have to type if you entered KEYDEFS2 for each request line.

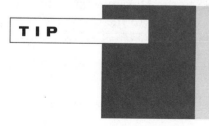

TIP If you run your batch files from the shell, do not bother to abbreviate commands with batch files. Since you do not have to type in the batch-file name to run if from the shell, you do not save time by reducing the keystrokes in the name.

Using Shorthand Notation for Commands

Certain commands that perform fixed chores can also be simplified with batch files. For instance, you learned in Chapter 8 how to use the MODE command to manage various aspects of different devices. If your system has both a color and a monochrome monitor, you could use a batch file to invoke the proper version of the MODE command. To switch output to the monochrome monitor, you could enter

```
MODE MONO
```

in a file called MONO.BAT. To switch output to the color monitor using 80 columns with color enabled, you could enter

```
MODE CO80
```

in a file called COLOR.BAT. Then, whenever you needed to switch, you would only have to enter the simple batch name, MONO or COLOR, to obtain the desired result. With this method a user doesn't have to remember (or even know) the actual DOS command or command/parameter sequence that produces a particular result.

Another good use of this technique is turning on the compressed printing mode for your Epson- or IBM-compatible printer, which you learned about in Chapter 7. You could create a batch file called COMPRESS.BAT that contains one line:

```
MODE LPT1: 132
```

You could create another batch file called NORMAL.BAT that would also contain only one line:

```
MODE LPT1: 80
```

You could now type COMPRESS at the DOS prompt before sending a wide spreadsheet or database information to the printer. When you are done, you could enter the command NORMAL to return the printer to its normal configuration.

Another benefit of this method appears when you acquire new printers at a later date. Only the inside portion of the batch file (the one containing any special printer codes) has to be changed, and only once, by one knowledgeable person. Everyone else using the system will still only have to remember to type COMPRESS or NORMAL.

➤ EXTRA!

You Can Easily Repeat Commands Automatically!

Any time you need to execute the same command repeatedly, the following technique can come in handy. Perhaps you need to find a text string in a series of files located in different directories; or perhaps you just need to obtain a directory listing of several diskettes successively. This method relies on the fact that %0, as a batch-file variable, represents the actual name of the batch file itself.

Take a look at the CONTENTS.BAT file shown in Figure 14.6. In this batch file, the PAUSE command prompts you to enter a new diskette into drive A and then waits for you to do so.

When you press the Enter key at this point, you will receive a directory listing of the diskette you placed in drive A. You can see the last portion of the previous diskette's listing in the top portion of Figure 14.7. At this point in the batch program, you can terminate this otherwise unending sequence by pressing Ctrl+Break (or Ctrl+C). DOS will display

```
Terminate batch job (Y/N)?
```

If you respond Y, DOS will discontinue processing the batch file instructions, returning you immediately to the DOS command prompt, as can be seen at the bottom of Figure 14.7. If you have changed your mind (maybe you just needed time to think about what was happening) and you respond N after first deciding to break, the batch file will retype its own name and the word "CONTENTS," and will begin to execute again. You will be prompted to enter another diskette, as can be seen in the lower portion of Figure 14.7.

The key to this repetitive behavior is in the last line of the listing. The variable parameter %0 acts as a substitute for the original batch file name typed at the DOS prompt.

Anything that saves keystrokes is a form of shorthand notation. Figures 14.6 and 14.7 demonstrate another means of saving time and keystrokes when you have to repetitively run the same batch file.

FIGURE 14.6

The CONTENTS.BAT file demonstrates how to program recursion in a DOS batch file. The %0 parameter represents the name of the batch file itself. Placing it by itself on the last line transfers control back to the start of CONTENTS.BAT each time the batch file is about to end.

```
Rem   CONTENTS.BAT

@ECHO OFF
PAUSE Load diskette into drive A:
DIR  A: /P
%0
```

FIGURE 14.7

Running the CONTENTS.BAT file produces the output shown here for successive diskettes placed in the A drive. The PAUSE command makes DOS wait until you've placed a new disk in drive A, or press Ctrl+Break to end this repetition.

```
C:\SIG1D\DOCS\DOS6>Rem   CONTENTS.BAT

C:\SIG1D\DOCS\DOS6>
Load diskette into drive A:
Press any key to continue . . .

  Volume in drive A is MSD
  Volume Serial Number is 0819-0315
  Directory of A:\

BEFCOMP  CHK       407 11-16-92   6:07p
BEFCOMP  DIR       590 11-16-92   6:07p
CHKAFT   BAT      3209 10-26-92   6:00a
CHKBEF   BAT      2639 10-26-92   6:00a
DSSNAP   EXE     10227 10-26-92   6:00a
MEMTEST  BAT      2752 10-26-92   6:00a
MSD      EXE    158489 10-26-92   6:00a
MSDTEST  BAT      3604 10-26-92   6:00a
T        EXE    288062 10-26-92   6:00a
        9 file(s)      469979 bytes
                       985088 bytes free
Load diskette into drive A:
Press any key to continue . . .
```

Program Setup and Restoration

This section offers different approaches for initiating your own programs. You've already seen a typical small application method in Figure 14.5. In that example, a main program was run (perhaps with initial parameters) after the proper directory was entered. Now let's look at two other times you'll want to consider using batch files.

Invoking the Same Sequence of Programs

You sometimes perform a recurring series of steps in the computing world. For instance, you may run your word processor (WP.EXE) to create a new document and then, as a matter of course, run your grammar and style checker (STYLE.COM). You may also run a specialized spelling checker (SPELL.EXE) before you rerun your word processor to implement any suggested changes. The sequence, then, is as follows:

1. word processor

2. style checker

3. spelling checker

4. word processor again

Using variable parameters (%0 to %9) to pass information to a program when you initiate it is called *parameter passing*. If the programs above do not allow parameter passing, you could write a batch file called WRITE.BAT, which would consist of the following lines:

```
WP
STYLE
SPELL
WP
```

On the other hand, many programs now allow you to specify a parameter to indicate the name of a file to be selected. If a program allows such a specification, then a batch file can be even more useful. Suppose you are working on a proposal called PROPOSAL.DOC. Your WRITE.BAT file could do more work if it contained these lines:

```
WP PROPOSAL.DOC
STYLE PROPOSAL.DOC
SPELL PROPOSAL.DOC
WP PROPOSAL.DOC
```

Simply typing WRITE at the DOS prompt would bring you successively through all four program invocations, each one bringing in the specified PROPOSAL file.

Here's another example. You may be working on the Great American Novel, and every chapter you write undergoes the same painstaking care and attention as the rest of your word-processed documents. You can take the simplifying process one step further by using the variable parameter technique. Look at the following batch file:

```
WP CHAPTER%1
STYLE CHAPTER%1
SPELL CHAPTER%1
WP CHAPTER%1
```

If you've named your files CHAPTER1, CHAPTER2, and so on, you can then invoke your four-program sequence by typing at the DOS prompt the chapter number as the parameter:

```
WRITE 5
```

Keep in mind that if your novel has more than nine chapters, you'll have to name them along the lines of CHAP01, CHAP02, and so on so that you don't exceed DOS's maximum limit of eight characters in a file name.

Setup and Restoration for Dual Diskettes

Some programs assume that the *data* they use is available on the default disk drive and directory. Since DOS allows you to run a *program* that isn't in the current drive and directory, you can first switch to the drive or directory containing your data and then still run a program in a different directory. After the program is done, you can change back to your original drive or directory. This is usually the root for hard-disk systems, and drive A for dual-diskette systems. The technique for returning to the root was shown in Figure 14.5:

```
CD \
```

On a dual-diskette system, you can perform a similar sequence of steps. Figure 14.8 shows a typical configuration, in which programs reside on drive A and data files reside on drive B. Suppose you want to run a main program called ESTATE.EXE, which is on your program disk, and which uses several real-estate data files on the data disk in drive B. The following batch file (SWITCH.BAT) will change the default drive to B for the duration of the execution of ESTATE.EXE, and then reset the default drive back to A. DOS will look on B for any files referenced by the ESTATE program.

```
REM SWITCH.BAT
B:
A:ESTATE
A:
```

This same technique can be used between directories on a hard disk. In fact, if you look closely at the CHOICE_A set of instructions in the MYMENU.BAT file above (see Figure 14.5), you will see this technique. In that instance, the data files are actually located in the C:\DBMS\INVNTORY directory, while the executable dBASE IV program is located in the C:\DBMS directory, which is actually found along the system PATH.

FIGURE 14.8

Typical configuration for a two-drive operation. Analogous to using two directories for programs and data, you can use two disk drives to separate the two.

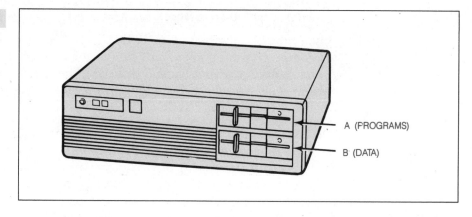

A (PROGRAMS)

B (DATA)

Chaining for Diskette-Switching Applications

As you know, any batch file can contain references to other batch files. Now you'll learn how those referenced batch files can also be on different drives. You can use this technique to develop sophisticated multidiskette applications. For example, you could have a batch file called INITIAL.BAT on drive A, which has a number of instructions in it, ending with an invocation of a CONTINUE.BAT file, located on drive B. A segment of the INITIAL.BAT file might look like this:

```
Rem INITIAL.BAT
Instruction 1
Instruction 2
   .
   .
   .
Last instruction in this batch file
B:
CONTINUE
```

The CONTINUE.BAT file, which might control for example the backing up of your files onto a clean diskette, could be located on your data disk. CONTINUE.BAT might look like this:

```
Rem CONTINUE.BAT
PAUSE Place a blank backup diskette into drive A:
XCOPY *.* A:
PAUSE Replace your original system diskette in drive A:
**** Final Instruction line in this batch file ****
```

When control transfers to CONTINUE.BAT, its first instruction pauses the computer, prompting you to remove the main program diskette from A and replace it with a backup diskette. After performing the XCOPY backup sequence, the batch file pauses again so you can reinsert your original system diskette in drive A.

The last statement in CONTINUE.BAT is your opportunity to continue the execution chain. This last line can contain the name of another batch file to execute on either A or B. You can even include a variable such as %1 in this last line. In this way, you can transfer the information originally passed via %1 to INITIAL.BAT to a completely different batch file. The

%1 could just as well be a command that would be executed as the last instruction of the CONTINUE.BAT file. In short, the last line in the CONTINUE.BAT file could contain any of the following possibilities:

A:INITIAL   This would rerun the original starting program.

%1   This would run a command passed as a parameter from INITIAL.BAT to CONTINUE.BAT. In this case, of course, INITIAL.BAT should be modified to include a parameter in its final line.

Another batch file name   This will continue the batch file chain.

Initializing Your Color Monitor

You learned in Chapter 9 how to use the PROMPT command to set up the foreground and background colors on a color monitor. Having to look up or remember the codes can be tedious. Just as you eventually used the KEYDEFS2 batch file to make key redefinition quick and easy, so can you do the same with screen-color definition. This is a perfect opportunity for a batch file that will remember all the necessary PROMPT codes.

➤ EXTRA!

Use a Batch File to Initialize Your RAM Disk

A batch file is an obvious place for the series of commands necessary to set up your RAM disk. If you use the appropriate command options in your CONFIG.SYS file, your RAM disk will already have been created at bootup. However, some memory boards (like AST boards) come with a program that can initialize a RAM disk whenever you choose. If this is the case on your system, you should invoke the program with a batch file.

Say you have created a RAM disk called D. The following RAM-INIT.BAT file could copy programs and files to it—for instance, commonly used batch files like KEYDEFS2.BAT and frequently used DOS programs like CHKDSK.COM, SORT.EXE, and the command processor COMMAND.COM.

```
COPY KEYDEFS2.BAT D:
COPY CHKDSK.COM D:
COPY SORT.EXE D:
COPY COMMAND.COM D:
```

You could also set the COMSPEC environmental variable here to tell DOS where to find the command processor. COMSPEC is a special DOS variable, designed to specify where a copy of COMMAND.COM can be found. You will learn more about this variable in Chapter 19.

Finally, you could reset the path to check the RAM disk for referenced files that are not in the default directory:

```
SET COMSPEC=D:\COMMAND.COM
PATH D:\;C:\LOTUS;C:\WP;C:\UTILITY;C:\DOS
```

If you use this RAM disk method for improving your system's performance, remember to put the RAM disk on your path *before* any other references to directories that may contain the original copies of the files. Then the fast-access RAM copy of the referenced file is located first, before the slower disk-resident version of the same file.

RGB.BAT will expect two parameters, each specifying what colors the monitor should use for the foreground and background. The calling sequence will be

```
RGB Foreground Background
```

When complete, you can enter the following sequence at the DOS prompt to cause all future output to appear in blue letters on a white background:

```
RGB BLUE WHITE
```

The completed batch file itself can be seen in Figure 14.9.

FIGURE 14.9

RGB.BAT sets foreground and background colors. Notice how the parameter itself is used to control the flow of control. For example, GOTO %1 might send control to the label :BLUE to set a foreground color, if %1 equals "BLUE".

```
@ECHO OFF
Rem  RGB.BAT
IF PARAM==PARAM%2 GOTO FOREGROUND
GOTO BK%2
:BKBLACK
PROMPT $e[40m
GOTO FOREGROUND
:BKWHITE
PROMPT $e[47m
GOTO FOREGROUND
:BKRED
PROMPT $e[41m
GOTO FOREGROUND
:BKGREEN
PROMPT $e[42m
GOTO FOREGROUND
:BKBLUE
PROMPT $e[44m
GOTO FOREGROUND
:BKMAGENTA
PROMPT $e[45m
GOTO FOREGROUND
:BKCYAN
PROMPT $e[46m
GOTO FOREGROUND
:BKYELLOW
PROMPT $e[43m

:FOREGROUND
ECHO ON
ECHO OFF
CLS
IF PARAM==PARAM%1 GOTO DONE
GOTO %1
:BLACK
PROMPT $p$g$e[30m
GOTO DONE
:WHITE
PROMPT $p$g$e[37m
GOTO DONE
:RED
PROMPT $p$g$e[31m
GOTO DONE
:GREEN
PROMPT $p$g$e[32m
GOTO DONE
:BLUE
PROMPT $p$g$e[34m
GOTO DONE
:MAGENTA
PROMPT $p$g$e[35m
```

FIGURE 14.9

(continued)

```
GOTO DONE
:CYAN
PROMPT $p$g$e[36m
GOTO DONE
:YELLOW
PROMPT $p$g$e[33m

:DONE
ECHO ON
CLS
```

Several interesting points are demonstrated in this file:

- There are two major sections in the logical flow. The first large group of instructions controls the setting of the foreground colors, according to the first color parameter specified after the batch-file name RGB. The second section controls the background color settings, based on the value of the second parameter on the batch-file line.

- This batch file is not case sensitive, as other batch programs that relied on the IF subcommand would be. In other words, each of the following commands would produce the same result:

```
RGB BLUE WHITE
rgb blue white
```

- You can use the IF PARAM==PARAM%2 technique to test for the absence of a variable parameter. This IF test will only be true if the variable is missing.

- ECHO ON and OFF, followed by a screen clearing, is necessary between the setting of the foreground and background colors. The foreground prompt must take effect while ECHO is off and before the background color is set.

The overall flow of this program can be seen in Figure 14.10.

FIGURE 14.10

Logical flow in the RGB.BAT file. You should always check the possibility that a user has forgotten to type a required parameter. If so, your batch file should either display an error message or assume a default value.

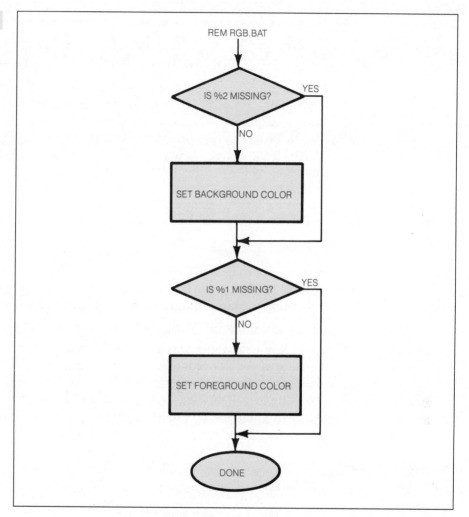

Take some time now to type in this program and test it out on your system. Or, you can use the order form at the end of this book, and move on to the next section to read about other advanced possible applications with batch files.

Sophisticated Batch Files

This section deals with some specific batch files used by experienced DOS users. People's perceptions of advanced subjects differ dramatically; what one person views as sophisticated, another views as old hat. The batch-file techniques presented here are beneficial. If they're new to you, that's all the better. If they're old hat, perhaps you'll learn some new approaches by the manner in which these batch programs are implemented.

Customized System Help Screens

Some systems are used by many people at different times. A desirable feature for such a system is customizable help screens. You can use the batch-file mechanism in DOS to easily set up this capability. All it takes is the INFO.BAT file, shown in Figure 14.11.

Once you've installed this batch file in your path, you can use it from any directory. All you need to do is write a text file with a .HLP extension. This file should contain the text information you'd like displayed for anyone requesting help. The user, in turn, will only need to run the INFO.BAT file, specifying the first parameter as the topic for which help is desired.

FIGURE 14.11

INFO.BAT demonstrates how to use text files (named with .HLP extensions) to prepare your own customized help mechanism. The IF test verifies that a file exists for the topic requested (in parameter one), and the TYPE command displays the file.

```
@ECHO OFF
Rem   INFO.BAT

IF EXIST %1.HLP  GOTO OK
ECHO Sorry.  No help available for %1
GOTO END

:OK
TYPE %1.HLP
PAUSE

:END
```

For example, if there is a subject named JUJUTSU for which you wish to provide users with helpful online information, you should place the information in a text file called JUJUTSU.HLP. Then the user need only enter

    INFO JUJUTSU

to display the predefined textual information (see Figure 14.12). If help is not available on your system (that is, a .HLP file does not exist for the subject), then a simple message to that effect is given (see Figure 14.13).

TIP

In this sample help file, no CLS instruction is executed. It was omitted so that Figures 14.12 and 14.13 could show the initiating command as well as the results. If you were to write a similar INFO system for yourself, you might want to insert CLS instructions before the output lines (TYPE statement) in the INFO.BAT file.

FIGURE 14.12

INFO.BAT makes online help readily available.

```
C>INFO JUJUTSU

JUJUTSU (or jujitsu) is one of the less well known, but most
deadly, martial arts. It builds on the familiar throws and
immobilizing holds seen in wrestling and judo. Adding a
variety of joint locks and pressure point techniques, it is
extremely effective in close fighting situations.

Press any key to continue . . .
```

FIGURE 14.13

When help is not available, a message to that effect is displayed.

```
C>INFO Zen
Sorry.  No help available for Zen
C>
```

The program in Figure 14.11 can be understood quickly by looking at the logic-flow diagram in Figure 14.14. The heart of the batch program begins with the IF EXIST statement. If a .HLP file exists for the subject (entered as %1), then the batch file continues executing at the OK statement. This is really the TYPE statement, since the label :OK is needed by the GOTO OK statement if the .HLP file exists. The PAUSE statement just after the TYPE instruction ensures that the user will have time to read the information before anything else appears on the screen or before the screen is cleared.

If no help file exists, the IF statement does not redirect the flow of control down to :OK. Instead, control flows directly to the ECHO statement on the next line. This ECHO statement displays a "Sorry" message indicating that no help text has been prepared for this particular subject. Immediately after this message is written, an unconditional GOTO statement sends control to the end of the batch file, skipping over the OK section of the code.

FIGURE 14.14

The flow of logic in the INFO.BAT batch file.

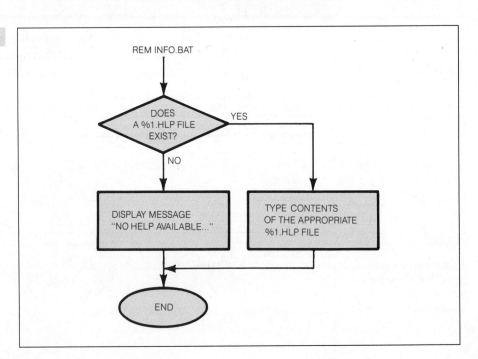

Appointment Reminder System

Some computer systems offer the luxury of automatic appointment reminders. In addition, some utility packages like SideKick permit the entry and retrieval of date-oriented information. However, this latter facility is not automatic. The following example can solve the problem of forgetting to check your message or appointment log.

Unless you're very self-disciplined, the easiest way to implement this method begins by including a couple of reminders in your AUTO-EXEC.BAT file. For instance, these three lines should jog your memory:

```
ECHO Remember to enter the following command to
ECHO get your messages for today (or any day).
ECHO TODAY mm-dd-yy
```

When you want to see the message or appointment file for, say, January 2, 1994, you only need to enter

```
TODAY 01-02-94
```

The results of this sequence can be seen in Figure 14.15.

FIGURE 14.15

Running the TODAY.BAT file is just another way of using named text files for informational purposes. This can serve as a reminder mechanism for yourself, or be the basis of information sharing with others who may also use your system.

```
C:\>TODAY 01-01-94

Happy New Year!

Now get back to work.

Lucky you...Only two more days 'til the weekend.

Remember to prepare the paperwork for the new programmer starting this monday.

Don't forget to write 1994 on all new checks you write!!!

C:\>
```

The actual batch file that manages this simple operation is shown in Figure 14.16. As you can see, it is only a variation on the help method of the preceding section. The date files are text files, differing only in name and content from the .HLP files.

The way in which these text files are used (via the TYPE command) also reflects a similar batch-file approach. With the INFO method, all the files were given a .HLP extension, and their base names reflected the actual topic for which help was desired. In this appointment reminder system, the actual file name is understood (via %1) to be the date itself, a simple enough naming convention. The batch file types out the text file by that precise name. Here, you cannot assume that the batch-file code has the intelligence of the DOS DATE command; in other words, 01-02-94 could not be replaced by 1/2/94 or any other variation.

WARNING

The naming convention for date files must be adhered to precisely. If you use dashes, slashes, or even leading zeros to create the text files, then you must also use them when you run the TODAY.BAT file.

One of many additions to this batch file could be the simple addition of the line

    DATE %1

FIGURE 14.16

TODAY.BAT uses GOTO statements to control the flow of execution in the batch file.

```
@ECHO OFF
Rem   TODAY.BAT

IF NOT EXIST %1 GOTO ERROR

TYPE %1
GOTO END

:ERROR
ECHO No messages for %1

:END
```

just before the TYPE instruction. In systems that do not have a battery-powered clock and calendar, the DATE command is usually run when you bring up the system. Since you must enter the date once for your appointment-making system, you can let the batch-parameter mechanism do the work of setting the date as well. Programmers are always looking for ways to reduce user intervention time, system program time, or both. Minor improvements like this will add up dramatically over time.

TIP

Remember to erase your older date files when you no longer need them, or they will proliferate quickly.

Broadcasting Messages to All Users

Yet another variation on the theme of this section can be seen in the simple ANNOUNCE.BAT file of Figure 14.17. This batch program uses an area in memory called the *DOS environment,* which contains a set of variables and the values assigned to them. The DOS environment always includes the COMSPEC variable and the values you assign to PATH and PROMPT variables, as well as other arbitrarily named variables used by some programs or by the batch files described here. Environmental variables are presented in greater detail in Chapter 19.

A little-known technique of referencing DOS environment variables from within batch files allows you to broadcast messages to your system's users. This technique is useful for systems that have a number of different users, with perhaps one primary user. The goal is to have a simple command like ANNOUNCE display any and all current system messages for a user (see Figure 14.18).

In this figure, the first line is the key to the technique. You initialize a DOS environment variable (MESSAGE) equal to the name of this week's message file. In this case, the primary user only has to assign the character

FIGURE 14.17

The ANNOUNCE.BAT batch file uses an environmental variable to store the filename containing the desired text. You must surround such a variable's name in single percentage symbols to identify it as an environmental variable, as opposed to a referenced filename itself.

```
@ECHO OFF
Rem ANNOUNCE.BAT

TYPE %message%
```

FIGURE 14.18

ANNOUNCE.BAT displays all current system messages, although you could have set the MESSAGE variable equal to the name of any desired text file. This is an example of a generic technique that can be adapted to your unique needs.

```
C:\>SET MESSAGE=C:\WEEK33.TXT

C:\>ANNOUNCE
                Messages for Week 33 of FY94
               --------------------------------
Jim Samuels is on vacation. Suzanne Powers will be filling in.

This Sunday is the company outing to Disneyland. Tickets can
be picked up at Personnel.

Computers will all be down for monthly Preventive Maintenance
this Wednesday. Please backup, backup, backup your files.

Time cards due one day early (Thursday) this week!
C:\>
```

string WEEK33.TXT to the variable MESSAGE once, usually at the beginning of the day. You would do this by typing

```
SET message=C:\WEEK33.TXT
```

at a command prompt.

For the rest of the time that the system is up, simply typing ANNOUNCE at the DOS prompt will display the current message file. Only the primary user needs to know the name of the actual message file. From week to week, everyone's procedure for displaying system messages remains the same. Even the naming conventions can change, and the primary user is the only one who needs to know it.

This batch program can be modified slightly to allow for recurring messages that don't change from week to week. For instance, you could insert the following instruction just before the TYPE line in ANNOUNCE.BAT:

```
TYPE ALWAYS.TXT
```

The ALWAYS.TXT file could contain any consistent set of messages that you always wished to display, regardless of the week. This could contain such things as the primary user's name and phone number, the service bureau's phone number, the security guard's extension, and so forth.

Using Batch-File Subroutines for Status Tracking

Programmers use a variety of techniques for debugging their code. One of those techniques places additional printing statements at critical points in the source code. These are like snapshots. When the execution flow reaches these points, various parameters and variable values are printed out. The current program status can then be assessed and the problem discovered.

Programmers using this technique quickly learned the value of sending these debugging snapshots to a disk file instead. In this way, their program is not slowed down, and normal screen output is not compromised by debugging output.

You can borrow a page from the programmer's book for your own batch-file programming. Your batch files may at times become complicated, especially if you use the multifile technique of chaining. In writing any batch file, consider writing your own SNAPSHOT.BAT file. In a simple implementation, it could consist solely of the following two commands:

```
DIR >> AUDIT.TXT
CHKDSK >> AUDIT.TXT
```

Whenever SNAPSHOP.BAT is invoked, the current directory and disk status are noted, and the >> redirection symbol ensures that the AUDIT.TXT file receives this information. (Remember that the > redirection symbol sends text to a file, erasing any existing data in that file.

The >> double symbol ensures that new text sent to a file is added on to any existing text.) You could later peruse the contents of this "tracking file" at your leisure.

The CALL subcommand is necessary to use the snapshot method. You may want to note the current disk directory and memory status at various points during the execution of one of your batch files.

The ANYOLD1.BAT file shown in Figure 14.19 represents any batch file you might write; the vertical dots just stand for your own instructions. The system snapshot can be taken whenever you like by inserting a CALL SNAPSHOT line that runs the SNAPSHOT.BAT file whenever the execution flow reaches that line.

In Figure 14.19, SNAPSHOT is CALLed twice. All of the snapshot results will be written into the AUDIT.TXT file. You can erase this file any time you'd like to clear it out, since the >> redirection parameter will recreate the AUDIT.TXT file if you run SNAPSHOT when AUDIT.TXT does not exist. After your batch file is complete and working just the way you want it to, you can remove all of the snapshot lines.

FIGURE 14.19

The ANYOLD1.BAT file is meant to represent any batch file that you are trying to debug. Insert CALLs to the SNAPSHOT batch file wherever you wish to capture system status information for later debugging analysis.

```
@ECHO OFF
Rem ANYOLD1.BAT

REM       .
REM       .        Preceding statements in the batch file
REM       .


CALL SNAPSHOT A

REM       .
REM       .        More statements and batch file activity
REM       .


CHOICE "OK? Continue or Debug " /C:CD
IF ERRORLEVEL 1 IF NOT ERRORLEVEL 2 GOTO END
CALL SNAPSHOT B
:END
```

Note the use of the CHOICE command in ANYOLD1.BAT. In this example, the user can decide at execution time whether or not to ask for additional debugging output to be added to the AUDIT.TXT file. If he types D (for Debug), then the extra:

```
CALL SNAPSHOT B
```

line will be executed. Otherwise, it will be skipped and the batch file will end. Naturally, you can get even fancier, incorporating additional choices that will pass control of the batch file execution to different places.

If you really want to get fancy, you can embed a number of calls to SNAPSHOT in your batch files, all based on the value of an environmental variable. See Chapter 19 for an explanation of how to use such a variable to turn on or off debugging throughout your code. For example, you could include a test for a variable DEBUGON, giving it the value "YES" at a command prompt:

```
SET DEBUGON=YES
```

Within your batch file, you can insert any number of lines that look something like this:

```
IF DEBUGON==YES CALL SNAPSHOT n
```

where n varies for each such line.

Several creative variations on this method are available to you. Look at the modified SNAPSHOT.BAT file in Figure 14.20. In this version, two additional lines have been added before the DIR and CHKDSK lines. In

The SNAPSHOT.BAT file currently captures only CHKDSK and DIR/W output for debugging analysis. The >> redirection operator is used to append each output group to the current contents of the AUDIT.TXT file.

```
@ECHO OFF
Rem  SNAPSHOT.BAT

ECHO Snapshot at point %1  >> AUDIT.TXT
DIR/W  A:  >> AUDIT.TXT
CHKDSK A:  >> AUDIT.TXT
DIR/W  C:  >> AUDIT.TXT
CHKDSK C:  >> AUDIT.TXT
```

fact, the DIR and CHKDSK commands are now being executed for both of the disks affected by commands in ANYOLD1.BAT.

You could, of course, use DOS's DATE and TIME commands instead of an additional utility, redirecting their output to the AUDIT.TXT file. However, doing this would require you to press the Enter key twice. This is because DOS will place its normal request for any date and time changes in the AUDIT.TXT file instead of on your video monitor. You won't see the requests, but DOS will wait for your response anyway. Elsewhere in this book, there are alternative batch files shown in EXTRA! sidebars that explain how to incorporate date and time stamping without any Enter key intervention required at all. See the order form at the end of this book for information on ordering a diskette that contains all the batch files discussed or shown throughout this book.

NOTE

Naturally, you can modify the snapshot examples presented here to include any other utility program lines or DOS commands that will provide you with useful information. For example, the SET and MEM commands provide helpful debugging information about system status.

The new ECHO line that has been added,

```
ECHO Snapshot at point %1 >> AUDIT.TXT
```

represents another useful debugging technique. The AUDIT.TXT file will often expand to include many entries, depending on the complexity of your batch file and how often you invoke the CALL instruction. Each entry can be tagged with this ECHO instruction so that it indicates where the snapshot was taken.

Figure 14.21 shows the beginning of the AUDIT.TXT file, seen after running the ANYOLD1.BAT file of Figure 14.19.

The first AUDIT entry sequence is labeled A. When SNAPSHOT runs, the first parameter (%1) is passed along. This ECHO statement accounts for the value of this parameter (A) appearing in the output file AUDIT.TXT. You need only type a different string of characters each

FIGURE 14.21

Sample contents of AUDIT.TXT after running ANYOLD1.BAT. You can send the entire AUDIT.TXT file to the printer, or you can use the MORE filter to display it one screenful at a time.

```
Snapshot at point A

 Volume in drive A is MSD
 Volume Serial Number is 0819-0315
 Directory of A:\

BEFCOMP.CHK     BEFCOMP.DIR     CHKAFT.BAT    CHKBEF.BAT      DSSNAP.EXE
MEMTEST.BAT     MSD.EXE         MSDTEST.BAT   T.EXE
        9 file(s)      469979 bytes
                       985088 bytes free

 Volume MSD           created 10-26-1992 6:00a
 Volume Serial Number is 0819-0315

    1457664 bytes total disk space
     472576 bytes in 9 user files
     985088 bytes available on disk

        512 bytes in each allocation unit
       2847 total allocation units on disk
       1924 available allocation units on disk

     651264 total bytes memory
     375680 bytes free
-- More --
```

time you make a CALL entry from any batch file you want to trace through. For example, at various points in the batch file you are tracing, you might insert each of the following:

```
CALL SNAPSHOT C
CALL SNAPSHOT D
CALL SNAPSHOT E
```

Controlling User Access

Entire books have been written on the subject of password protection. Even more advanced tomes discuss the subject of *resource allocation,* which involves usage as well as access. Resource allocation means controlling access to both the contents of data files and the running of program files. Let's look at a simple but subtle form of password protection that you can implement with DOS alone.

The DOS environment affords you a special password feature. You can initialize a PASSWORD variable at the DOS prompt or in another batch file. For instance, you can enter

```
SET PASSWORD=EELS
```

➤ **EXTRA**

Run Your Favorite Programs from a RAM Disk!

You can learn in Chapter 18 how to initialize a RAM disk. You only needed to include an appropriate DEVICE instruction in your CONFIG.SYS file. The RAM disk's size can vary according to what you intend to use it for. Once you've created it, you can proceed to transfer the most useful files to it. The following examples demonstrate how to successfully use a RAM disk for improved performance. They assume that you have previously transferred the correct main programs, help files, overlays, and so on, to your RAM disk.

As a first example, suppose that you want your RAM disk (e.g., D:) to run your word processor. You could write the following lines into a batch file named RAMWP.BAT:

```
REM RAMWP.BAT
CD\PROGRAMS\WORDPROC
D:
WP
C:
CD\
```

to create a file called RAMWP.BAT.

Before running your word processor from the RAM disk, you must have previously copied the main WP file and all required support files to D:. Storing the RAMWP.BAT file in your root directory, and assuming your root is on your path, you could switch to rapid RAM-based word processing easily and quickly by simply typing RAMWP.

You can use the same technique for your database management program, or for any other program that is slow because of normal disk-access speed. A variation of the RAMWP.BAT file for a database management system might contain these lines:

```
REM RAMDBMS.BAT
CD \PROGRAMS\DATABASE
D:
DBMS
C:
CD\
```

Again, the main program file (in this case DBMS) and its support files must first be copied to your RAM drive.

This batch file also makes the C:\PROGRAMS\DATABASE directory the one that presumably contains your document or data files. D, the RAM disk, is made the current drive so that the WP or DBMS program that executes is the one found on the RAM disk. Any references to C alone, with no directory path, will access the files in the current default directory on the C drive.

If you plan to locate and run more than one major program (for example, both a word processor and a DBMS) on the same RAM disk, you must have enough space reserved for both. If you do not, you may need to write a separate batch program to copy each group of required programs to the RAM drive. Each batch file can use the IF and EXIST subcommands to first check the RAM drive to determine what files are needed and whether any existing files need to be erased to make room for the new ones.

In this case, the following code segment must be contained in a batch file to restrict access to only those people who know the password:

```
IF %PASSWORD%==EELS GOTO RUN
IF %PASSWORD%==eels GOTO RUN
ECHO Sorry. That's an invalid password.
GOTO END
:RUN
PROGRAM
:END
```

If PASSWORD was set correctly to EELS before a batch file containing this code was run, then PROGRAM will run. Otherwise, the invalid password message will be echoed, and the batch file will terminate. In short, only those users who know that the password is EELS and set it correctly will be able to run the particular program. The desired program could be any .EXE or .COM file, and of course, the batch file could properly reset the directory if necessary in the :RUN section.

NOTE This password code uses IF statements to check for entry of the password in uppercase and in lowercase. You never know what case users will enter when they try to run your batch file or menu system.

The password feature can easily be extended by using several DOS environment variables (which will be presented in Chapter 19), each containing different passwords. Your batch programs can check for the proper values. For instance, you can have three passwords controlling access to the inventory, personnel, and accounting programs. Doing this might require several blocks of code like the code just seen, and three passwords, PASS1, PASS2, and PASS3, controlling access to INVENTRY.EXE, PRSONNEL.EXE, and ACCOUNTS.EXE.

You might have a menu system that passes control to three batch files instead of directly to the three main programs. For example:

```
IF %PASSWORD%==STORE GOTO RUN
IF %PASSWORD%==store GOTO RUN
ECHO Sorry. That's an invalid password.
GOTO END
:RUN
INVNTRY
:END


IF %PASSWORD%==JOSHUA GOTO RUN
IF %PASSWORD%==joshua GOTO RUN
ECHO Sorry. That's an invalid password.
GOTO END
:RUN
PRSONNEL
:END


IF %PASSWORD%==1812 GOTO RUN
ECHO Sorry. That's an invalid password.
GOTO END
:RUN
ACCOUNTS
:END
```

Only users who properly knew and set the appropriate DOS environment variable would be allowed access to the program they chose from the menu. Notice in this figure that the third password contains digits only, so IF tests for uppercase and lowercase do not have to be performed.

Summary

You've come a long way in this book. Not only have you learned a wide variety of commands and DOS features, but you've learned how to knit those features into seamless and sophisticated automatic batch files. This chapter presented the following examples:

- The AUTOEXEC.BAT file offers you the opportunity to automate your system's startup, including running any DOS command, running add-on utility software packages, and even running separately written batch files to check for computer viruses.

- Batch files can be used to create simple but functional menu systems to drive the most sophisticated application setup.

- Batch files can simplify consistent instruction sequences. Through the use of abbreviations and shorthand notation, you can reduce your typing burden while simultaneously speeding up your system processing.

- The variable parameters allowed in batch files can provide a valuable tool for repeating critical application tasks automatically.

- A batch file quickly and automatically invokes any application program that is nested in its own subdirectory structure. The current directory and DOS path can be set up before program execution and restored afterwards.

- Operations involving multiple disks and diskettes, as well as sophisticated modular batch systems, can easily be developed with batch-file chaining.

- You can make batch files that will prepare and initialize your RAM disk automatically. This increases system efficiency and improves response time.

- Color monitors can be controlled easily through judicious batch-file development. You saw how a single batch file can make short work of setting the foreground and background colors on color screens. You also saw how the KEYDEFS2 batch file facilitates quick and easy redefinition of any function key combination.

- With batch files, you can create customized help features, as well as an appointment reminder system. You can also broadcast messages to other users. These features can be very useful on systems that involve many people sharing the computer at different times.

- The CALL subcommand can be woven into sophisticated applications. You saw how to do this for capturing system-status "snapshots," which can help you debug and analyze your system.

- You also learned a couple of new tricks for dealing with RAM disks. Batch programs can load main word-processing, spreadsheet, or database programs onto a RAM disk, and then execute the RAM-resident version of the main program using data files from your hard disk.

- The DOS environment can be used with batch files to manage a password-control system.

Congratulations! Now that you are comfortable with batch-file techniques, you can consider yourself an advanced DOS user. However, keep reading. Chapter 15 offers you a chance to learn even more advanced DOS command techniques, including how to create fast in-memory macros.

CHAPTER

15

DOS Macros and the DOSKEY Utility

ALTHOUGH you'll probably spend most of your time at the shell, many of DOS's most unusual and sophisticated command capabilities can only be obtained while at a command prompt. You have already learned of a number of these features, such as maintaining print queues (Chapter 7) and redirecting the flow of information (Chapter 10).

In this chapter, you will learn how to enter and reenter commands from a command prompt more efficiently. You will learn about all the capabilities of the powerful DOSKEY utility program with which you can enter multiple commands on one line, as well as edit and reuse commands that were entered earlier in your command session. You will also learn how to use DOSKEY to create in-memory *macros*—a fast, albeit restricted, alternative to the batch file mechanism you've just studied. Whenever you can use a macro instead of a batch file, you should use the macro. It will speed up the responsiveness of DOS to your command requests.

You'll learn all about these command manipulation features of DOSKEY in this chapter. You'll also explore a series of example macros, demonstrative of how macros can replace batch files. You'll use some of the application examples from Chapter 14 that were used to demonstrate how batch files can make your system more efficient. Macros can take you one giant step further.

Initiating the DOSKEY Utility

DOSKEY.COM is an external DOS command that acts as a TSR, or terminate-and-stay-resident program. Since it becomes memory-resident, and maintains special memory areas for its command list and its macros, you should initiate it before you bring up the shell on your system. In that way, it will always be available whenever you later initiate (or exit from the shell to) a command prompt. Once installed, DOSKEY provides a powerful customization facility for DOS command lines. You can capture, edit, and reissue any commands. Also, you can quickly and easily create new batch files from the set of previously issued commands.

In order to install DOSKEY, you should run it from a command prompt, specifying any desired initiation switches. The formal syntax of the command, which includes all possible switches, is as follows:

```
{D:Path}DOSKEY {Macroname=macrotext}{/Bufsize=xxx}{/History}
{/Macros}{/Insert}{/Overstrike}{/Reinstall}
```

where the following explains each of the possible parameters:

D:Path is the drive and path where the DOSKEY utility program is located if it is not in the current directory.

Macroname is a text name you wish to assign to a macro you are defining with this run of DOSKEY. You can later run the macro by typing *macroname* at a command prompt.

Macrotext is any valid string of characters that make up the instructions executed when *macroname* is later executed.

/Bufsize lets you specify a memory buffer of *xxx* bytes in which to capture command-line keystrokes and to store keyboard macros.

/History displays a list of all previously captured commands.

/Macros displays a list of current macros.

/Insert sets the keyboard typing mode to Insert.

/Overstrike sets the keyboard typing mode to Overstrike.

/Reinstall enables you to install a new memory-resident copy of the DOSKEY program. Use this option only if you intend to use DOSKEY with a Microsoft Windows command prompt.

On average, DOSKEY consumes approximately 4K of memory, which includes the size of the default areas necessary for DOSKEY's own code, its command history list, and any macros you define. Figure 15.1 depicts this total usage, in the context of DOS and your application programs.

As Figure 15.1 suggests, DOSKEY loads its own code after DOS is loaded. It separately consumes an area of memory that is used to store macro definitions and a history list of typed commands. The /bufsize switch enables you to expand the size of this temporary memory (default size of 512 bytes). Use this switch if 512 bytes is insufficient for both the

FIGURE 15.1

DOSKEY uses some memory for its own code, some memory for its macro definitions, and still more memory to store its command history list. The macros and the recalled commands both share the same portion of memory, whose size you can define with the /BUFSIZE switch.

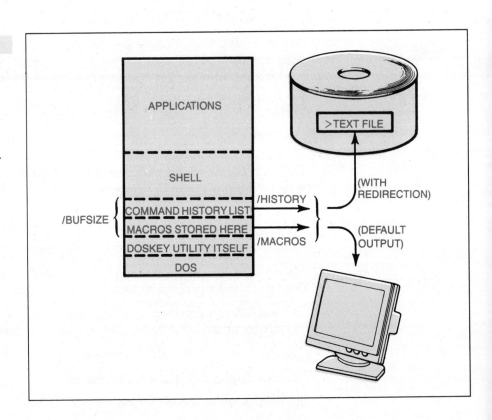

macros you write and the number of commands you wish to keep accessible in the historical command list. Also, if you wish to reduce DOSKEY's drain on memory, you can use /bufsize to reserve even less than 512 bytes.

As an example, you can initiate DOSKEY with a 2048 byte area of memory for macros and command lines by typing

```
DOSKEY /BUFSIZE=2048
```

I use this line in my AUTOEXEC.BAT file to ensure enough space to load the more than twenty-five useful macros that I've incorporated into a MACROS.BAT file, which I also run from my AUTOEXEC.BAT file (see the EXTRA! sidebar).

➤ EXTRA!

Extend the Power of DOS with These DOS Macros

Loading the DOSKEY utility enables you to write and incorporate your own customized new commands into DOS. Here is my personal set of thirty major time-savers when I work at a command prompt. In particular, note the SAVEMACS and LISTMACS macros for managing this list, especially after you customize it for your system:

```
@ECHO OFF
REM MACROS.BAT PREPARES A HOST OF USEFUL DOSKEY MACROS:
Rem ARRANGE sorts filename $1, writing sorted text into $2.
Rem CD... changes directory to parent's parent (i.e. two up).
Rem CDD changes to drive $1, then to dir $2 in root,
Rem CDD- then $3 in $2, $4 in $3, $5 in $4. All in one step!
Rem CHANGE makes a parallel-level directory ($1) current.
Rem CHKDSK2 automatically runs CHKDSK on drives C and D.
Rem CLUSTER displays the cluster (i.e. allocation unit) size.
Rem DEL ensures that an attempted deletion is always confirmed.
Rem DIRN displays the current directory sorted by name.
Rem DIRE displays the curr dir sorted by name within extension.
Rem DIRSIZES prints bytes consumed by each dir on current drive.
Rem DIRSIZES- ignores slack space at end of file's last cluster.
Rem DOS6 demonstrates how to set up a typographical shortcut to
Rem DOS6- quickly change directories deep into the disk tree.
Rem FF sends a Form Feed character to your printer.
```

```
Rem HIDDENS displays all filenames with the hidden attribute.
Rem HIDE makes the $1 file (or set of files) invisible.
Rem KEYFAST speeds up the keyboard to maximum settings.
Rem LINECNT counts the number of lines in a text file ($1).
Rem LISTMACS displays a sorted list of resident DOSKEY macros.
Rem LOCATE displays all filenames matching $1 on drive $2.
Rem LOCATE- If $2 is not specified, this uses the current drive.
Rem MCD creates the $1 directory, then switches to it.
Rem MULTDEL deletes multiple files or file specs ($1 $2 etc).
Rem PRINTDIR prints an alphabetized listing of directory $1.
Rem PRINTIT prints a specified text file ($1), then ejects paper.
Rem REMOVE deletes up to four filenames specified as parameters.
Rem SAVEMACS stores existing macro definitions to MYMACROS.BAT.
Rem SAVEMACS- You must type "DOSKEY" at beginning of each line.
Rem SHOWTEXT is a fancy TYPE replacement, allowing wild cards.
Rem SUBDIR lists all subdirectories in the $1 directory.
Rem UNHIDE makes a hidden file (or set of files) visible again.
Rem VGA resets the number of lines shown on your display adapter.
Rem VGA- $1 should be 25, 43, or 50.
Rem ZCOPY copies visible files/dirs from disk $1 to disk $2.
Rem ZCOPY- will copy between differently sized disks.
DOSKEY ADMIN=CD \XYWRITE\BOOKS\FRACTALS\ADMIN
DOSKEY ARRANGE=SORT $1 $1 $g $2
DOSKEY CD...=CD.. $t CD..
DOSKEY CDD=$1: $t CD \$2 $t CD $3 $t CD $4 $t CD $5
DOSKEY CHANGE=CD ..\$1
DOSKEY CHKDSK2=FOR %%i IN (C: D:) DO CHKDSK %%i
DOSKEY CLUSTER=CHKDSK $b FIND "each"
DOSKEY DEL=DEL $1 /P
DOSKEY DIRN=DIR /ON /P
DOSKEY DIRE=DIR /OEN /P
DOSKEY DIRSIZES=DIR \ /S $b FIND "i" $g PRN $t ECHO ♀ $g PRN
DOSKEY DOS6=CD \SIG1D\DOCS\DOS6
DOSKEY FF=ECHO ♀ $g PRN
DOSKEY HIDDENS=DIR \*.* /S /AH
DOSKEY HIDE=ATTRIB +H $1
DOSKEY KEYFAST=MODE CON RATE=32 DELAY=1
DOSKEY LINECNT=FIND "^&@*" $1 /V /C
DOSKEY LISTMACS=DOSKEY /macros $b SORT
DOSKEY LOCATE=DIR $2\$1 /B /S /P
DOSKEY MCD=MD $1 $t CD $1
DOSKEY MULTDEL=FOR %%j IN ($*) DO ERASE %%j
DOSKEY PRINTDIR=DIR $1 /ON $g PRN $t ECHO ♀ $g PRN
DOSKEY PRINTIT=TYPE $1 $g PRN $t ECHO ♀ $g PRN
DOSKEY REMOVE=FOR %%i IN ($1 $2 $3 $4) DO IF EXIST %%i DEL %%i
DOSKEY SAVEMACS=DOSKEY /macros $g MYMACROS.BAT
DOSKEY SHOWTEXT=FOR %%j IN ($*) DO TYPE %%j
DOSKEY SUBDIR=DIR $1 /AD /ON
DOSKEY UNHIDE=ATTRIB -H $1
DOSKEY VGA=MODE CON: LINES=$1
DOSKEY ZCOPY=XCOPY $1\*.* $2 /S /E
```

Since DOSKEY is such a useful and powerful assistant, running DOS-KEY each time you bring up DOS is a wise idea. Run the DOSKEY command line from your AUTOEXEC.BAT batch file, unless the 4K (the average cost in memory of loading DOSKEY) is too much for your applications to bear. Assuming that you probably end your AUTO-EXEC.BAT file with a DOSSHELL command line, insert the following line just prior to the shell request:

```
DOSKEY
```

You can always come back to edit this line to add any of the possible switch settings, if you later determine that they'll be valuable to you generally in the way you run your system. I prefer to work with this and all text modification programs in insertion mode rather than over-strike mode, so I recommend that you actually initiate the DOSKEY program with:

```
DOSKEY /INSERT
```

It seems to be less frustrating over the long haul to occasionally have to delete extra characters, because of being in insertion mode, than to have to remember characters that were accidentally erased because of being in overstrike mode.

As you'll see later in this chapter, the entire series of recorded command lines can be stored into a named file with the /HISTORY switch. In this way, you'll be able to test a series of instructions at a command prompt, then save them after the fact to a .BAT batch file. After some minor editing (if any is required), you'll have a permanent batch file to work with in the future.

In addition, you can specify the /MACROS switch to save (in an editable text disk file) *all* currently defined macros. In this way, you can first develop a set of macros while at a command prompt, then quickly restore them in the future when you start up your system again.

Managing the Command History

During any DOS session, you will often initiate a number of command, batch file, and utility program requests from a command prompt. Sometimes, the command prompt will be the initial DOS prompt, from which you first start up the shell. Other times, the command prompt may be one accessed from within the shell itself (by pressing the Shift+F9 key combination). No matter which way you reach a command prompt, DOSKEY will record each command line you enter, once it has been properly installed.

DOSKEY can only retain command lines until it runs out of space in its own memory buffer area. Remember that this area defaults to 512 bytes, unless you set it differently with the /bufsize switch when you initiate DOSKEY. As Figure 15.1 indicated, this memory buffer is used up for both macros and command lines, in that order. Space is always carved out of the area for new macros you may define. DOSKEY does this by erasing from the command-history list the oldest, presumably least important, command lines that were entered.

Other than making space for macros, DOSKEY must also make space for new command lines that you type. It does this, as suggested in Figure 15.2, by scrolling oldest command lines out of the memory area to free up space for the newest command you've typed.

Although Figure 15.2 depicts 14 commands, this number is quite variable. Exactly how many commands are stored in this command-history list depends on how much space is required to store the macros that are consuming space in the DOSKEY buffer. Also, since each command line can be as large as 127 characters, the number of commands actually stored depends on the actual number of characters in each command line.

For example, suppose that you've defined no macros, but you've specified /BUFSIZE=500. This would enable you to enter fifty 10-byte commands, or only ten 50-byte (more complex) command lines. You'll learn in this section how to manage this command-history list, discovering at any time how many commands are stored, what they are, and how to access any one of them.

FIGURE 15.2

DOSKEY maintains a command history. By pressing the right keystrokes, you can bring back to the command line any complete command that has been stored in DOSKEY's command history buffer.

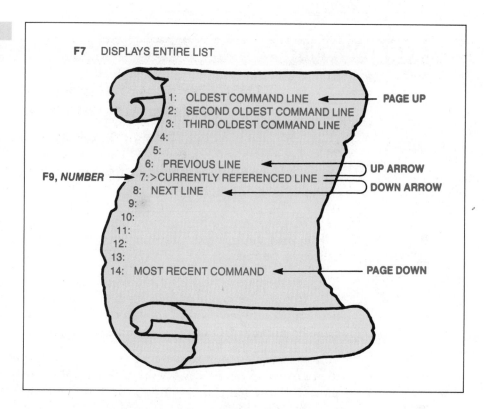

Accessing Previous Commands

DOS permits you to use function key F3 to recall to the command prompt your most recently entered command. If you wish to reissue that command again, you only need to press Enter after using F3. You might do this if you are running a particular program against different diskettes. For instance, you may have a program called LABELMKR.EXE which scans the disk in drive A in order to prepare a formatted label that lists the disk contents.

To run this program, you might have to type

```
LABELMKR A:
```

Without DOS's F3 command-line recall, you might have to type this command line over and over again, for each diskette that you successively

➤ EXTRA!

DOSKEY Has a Good Memory for Your Commands!

DOS itself maintains a small memory image of your entire command line. This memory image is a fixed 127 characters long, and is known as the *template*. Because of the template's fixed maximum size, DOS implicitly forces a maximum size of 127 characters on any command line. After you type a command, DOS usually erases the command line and redisplays its prompt for you. Although you can't directly see it happening, DOS writes your entire command-line entry into this special memory area called the template.

If you immediately press F3, DOS reads the current command-line entry back from the template and writes it onto your screen for you, as if you had completely retyped the command yourself. If you wish to rerun the same command, DOS has saved you the trouble of doing so.

You can make minor adjustments to this immediately preceding command by using the F1 key. By pressing F1, DOS reads one character at a time from the template, writing it back to your screen's new command prompt. With judicious use of the Ins key to toggle between insert and overtype mode, you can draw partial command-line information from the template and merge it with newly typed instructions or characters.

But what happens if the command you want to rerun without retyping was issued two or three, or thirty-seven command lines ago? The F1 and F3 keystrokes are useless for any command previous to the last one. But DOSKEY can do the job.

If you ran the DOSKEY command at the beginning of your session, it has been keeping a record of each typed command line, and with a few of its special keystrokes, you can quickly recall, edit, and reissue any one of these previously entered commands.

place in drive A. However, you can actually type the command just once: for the very first diskette to be tested. After that, you can place a new diskette into drive A, press F3 and Enter, and DOS will automatically rerun the program for you.

Table 15.1 summarizes the keystrokes that DOSKEY recognizes for managing its internal command history. Looking back at Figure 15.2, you can now see how each of these keystrokes affects the command history.

DOSKEY enables DOS to do a lot better than recalling the most recent single command. Typically, it can recall all your commands from a single session. Referring to Table 15.1, the most commonly used keystroke is the F7 function key. Whenever you depress this key, DOSKEY displays a numbered list of all remembered command lines. Figure 15.3 shows just such a list, after I'd been working on my system for a while.

TABLE 15.1: Command history–management keys

KEYSTROKE	EFFECT
F7	Display entire list of recorded commands, complete with identifying entry numbers
F8	When pressed alone, displays the previous command in the history list. When pressed after typing any sequence of characters, displays the preceding command that begins with those characters. You can then continue to press F8 to cycle backwards (and then around the list again) through all commands that begin with those same characters.
F9	Select a command by its entry number
Alt+F7	Erase the entire internal command history
Alt+F10	Erase all macros in memory
Page Up	Display the oldest command in the list
Page Down	Display the most recent command in the list
up arrow	Display the preceding command from the list
down arrow	Display the next command in the list
Escape	Erase the currently displayed command line

FIGURE 15.3

Press F7 for a numbered list of all previously typed commands. You can then press F9, followed by a line number, to quickly recall to the command line that particular command.

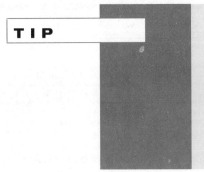

```
C:\>
 1: cls
 2: dir
 3: dir c:\sig1d
 4: chkdsk
 5: chkdsk d:
 6: vtsr
 7: norton
 8: qd3
 9: cls
10: dir d:\
11: cls
C:\>
```

TIP

You can avoid retyping the preceding command by simply pressing the up arrow key. DOSKEY, if installed, retypes the most recently entered command for you. Press Enter to then resubmit it to DOS, or first make any desired minor changes, then press Enter. Press the up arrow multiple times to ask DOSKEY to successively redisplay previously entered commands, one at a time.

Notice in Figure 15.3 that eleven commands have been entered and captured into DOSKEY's memory buffer. The most recently entered command (on line 11 in this figure) is the CLS request. The up and down arrow keys shown in Table 15.1 work with respect to this current command line. You can use any of the command history–management keys shown in Table 15.1 to influence which formerly entered command line would become the current one.

For example, Figure 15.4 depicts the DOSKEY command history after working on my system for a while longer. Although the most recently typed in command is the last one shown (CLS on line 23), I was able to reset the current command indicator to line 8. I did that by typing the letter *q* then pressing F8.

In response to F8, DOSKEY reset the current history line indicator to line 8. This is because F8 automatically finds the first command (looking backwards in the command list) that begins with the character(s) you type. I had to press F7 once again to see the location of the > symbol, which indicates which command in the history list has been made the current one.

FIGURE 15.4

Controlling the current command indicator. The > sign indicates your current position in DOSKEY's command buffer. Pressing up or down moves you to the command that precedes or follows this one.

```
 9: cls
10: dir d:\
11: cls
12: d:
13: show *.tif
14: norton
15: cls
16: cls
17: mem /c
18: mem /p
19: mem/
20: mem/?
21:>mem/f
22: set
23: cls
24: cd ..
-- More --
25: show *.tif
26: date
27: date 4/29/94
28: date
29: date 11/24/92
30: mem/c ¶ mem/f ¶ mem/p
31: cls
D:\>
```

Suppose that instead of resetting the current command indicator from line 23 to line 8, I had wanted to actually reset it to line 17, which runs the MEM command with the /C switch. If I typed *m*, then pressed F8, DOSKEY would first move the current line indicator to line 21. Successively pressing F8 would move the indicator back to each preceding line that began with the letter *m*.

Once you've displayed the numbered command history, the easiest way to reset to a particular entry is to press F9. DOSKEY then prompts you for

    Line number:

At this point, you can type the desired line number and press Enter. DOSKEY immediately resets its internal current line indicator to that line; furthermore, it reads that line's command, writing it to your screen at the command prompt. In this way, if you wish to rerun any command line from within the history, you only have to press F9 and type its line number. It's instantly displayed at the command prompt; you can rerun it by pressing Enter, or edit it with any of the key techniques explained in the next section.

Revising and Rerunning Previous Commands

You will not always wish to rerun a previously issued command exactly the way it was originally entered. For example, suppose that you've been working on drive D and you want to see a listing of the documents in the C:\SIG1D\DOCS directory. Rather than typing the entire required DIR command, you can let DOSKEY do most of the work for me. In this example, you can press F9, then type 3 and press Enter to display an earlier DIR command that is almost what is needed. Then you can use any of the command-editing keystrokes shown in Table 15.2 to modify the command before resubmitting it (by pressing Enter). In this example, you would simply tack on \DOCS to the existing command line that DOSKEY recalls to the command prompt for you.

Because DOSKEY is active, you can use the various command editing keystrokes with any command, whether you type it yourself, or whether DOSKEY types it for you by recalling an earlier command line. With this minor addition, your entire new command:

```
dir c:\sig1d\docs
```

is ready to resubmit. Pressing Enter is all you need to do to rerun the newly modified DIR command line.

In command lines that have several parameters or switch entries, the Ctrl+right arrow and Ctrl+left arrow keystrokes will quickly move the cursor from one parameter or switch entry to the next. A *word* in Table 15.2 refers to the sequence of characters located between separation spaces.

TABLE 15.2: DOSKEY's command-editing keys

KEYSTROKE	EFFECT
Backspace	Erase character preceding the cursor
Ctrl+End	Erase all characters through the end of the line, beginning with the character at the current cursor location
Ctrl+Home	Erase all characters from the beginning of the line up to, but not including, the current cursor location
Ctrl+left arrow	Move the cursor backward to the first character in the preceding word on the current command line
Ctrl+right arrow	Move the cursor forward to the first character in the next word on the current command line
Del	Erase the character at the current cursor location
End	Move the cursor to the end of the current command
Esc	Erase the currently displayed command
Home	Move the cursor to the first character in the displayed command
Ins	Toggle between insert and typeover mode for character insertions into a command
left arrow	Move the cursor one character to the left in the command line
right arrow	Move the cursor one character to the right in the command line

As another simple yet demonstrative example, suppose that you wanted to quickly find out what day of the week April 29, 1994 falls on. Perhaps it's a special birthday, or an anniversary. Since the DOS DATE command displays the current day of the week, you could conceivably change the system date momentarily, then use DOSKEY to help you to restore the correct date. For example, try the following sequence on your computer:

1. Type the command to display and change the system date:

   DATE 4/29/94

2. Press Enter to submit the command to DOS.

3. Press the up arrow key to redisplay the last entered command.

4. Press the Backspace key seven times to erase the 4/29/94.

5. Press Enter to resubmit DATE to DOS. You will learn that 4/29/94 is a Friday.

6. Press Enter again to redisplay the command prompt.

7. Press the up arrow key twice to redisplay the DATE command that included the 4/29/94 parameter (two commands ago).

8. Press Ctrl+left arrow to move the cursor back to the first digit (4) in the date (4/29/94).

9. Type over each digit as necessary in order to specify today's date.

10. Press Enter and DOSKEY resubmits the entire command to DOS again, this time restoring the system date to its correct setting.

This example and all the preceding ones show how to manipulate one command at a time. In fact, adding DOSKEY to your system enables you to manipulate more than a single command at once.

Writing Batch Files Automatically

As you learned in the preceding chapters, a batch file is nothing more than a text file that includes a group of individual DOS commands or acceptable command lines. You can create such a batch file in two ways. You can write a batch file's commands and test/revise the batch file until it works perfectly. Alternatively, a batch file can evolve after trying a series of commands at the command prompt until you find a sequence that works.

Take a Coffee Break. Submit Multiple Commands at One Time!

DOSKEY offers significant benefits that can save you time and make both you and your DOS system considerably more efficient. In particular, DOSKEY enables you to type more than one DOS command on a single command line. Because you only have to press Enter once, you save the time of having to wait until each command finishes before typing or submitting the next one. You can type several short commands on a single line, then submit them as a single group by pressing Enter. Altogether, however, the line cannot have more than 127 characters.

In one way, this is even more powerful than the batch-file facility. Remember that you can submit several commands from within a single batch file, but each command has to occupy its own line. DOSKEY accepts separate commands on a single command line if you separate each one with a Ctrl+T character. What DOSKEY actually displays on the screen in response to Ctrl+T is a ¶ character. Take a look at Figure 15.4 again. On line 30, I actually submitted three MEM requests on the same line. This one command line:

```
mem/c ¶ mem/f ¶ mem/p
```

is equivalent to first submitting mem/c and then, without any further waiting or intervention, submitting the /f and /p requests for the mem command. After each Ctrl+T keypress, you can actually submit any other command string you like.

The difference in these two techniques becomes apparent and important in an example like this one. As will be true with many commands that you may submit to DOS, some programs take a variable amount of time to complete. Consequently, you can't always be sure how much time will elapse before the first command will complete. If you submit the two or three (or more) commands on separate lines, you must wait around until the first completes before you can submit the second, and so on.

However, if you use DOSKEY, you can take a break immediately after submitting the multi-command line seen in line 30. DOSKEY will monitor the completion of the first command (mem/c). When that command completes, and control would otherwise return to a command prompt, DOSKEY will automatically submit the second command that you typed on the multiple-command line (in this case, mem/f). The same process will occur for the third command on that line. The commands submitted will take precisely the same amount of time, but the time spent by you waiting between commands can be dramatically reduced by using DOSKEY judiciously.

Only then do you write the .BAT file that will run the successful sequence of instructions.

DOSKEY can help you with the second of these two approaches. The /HISTORY switch displays all commands from the history list, but drops the entry line numbers. For example, typing the following line will display the entire history buffer:

```
DOSKEY /HISTORY
```

on your monitor. You can combine this switch with redirection to send an unnumbered copy of all recorded instruction lines to a disk file. For example, suppose that I wanted to prepare an MEMSTUFF.BAT file that contained a series of command lines that repeated the optimization instructions just seen. You could submit a modified DOSKEY request that sends its unnumbered history list to the MEMSTUFF.BAT file:

```
DOSKEY /HISTORY > MEMSTUFF.BAT
```

This creates the MEMSTUFF.BAT file with all the instructions just run at the command prompt. It only requires a few moments now to call up the .BAT file with the Editor to eliminate unnecessary lines, modify other lines, and insert additional instructions that you might not have thought of earlier. Presto. You've got a working batch file in a relatively short amount of time.

DOSKEY offers you the opportunity to group several commands into a named, executable entity that is memory-resident; this is then called a *macro*. Just as with a batch file, you can run all the instructions within a macro by typing its name at a command prompt. DOSKEY offers a powerful facility for creating, running, and editing these memory-resident control macros.

Understanding How Macros Differ from Batch Files

Before you go on to actually create and use any macros, let's compare the aspects of macros and batch files. Figure 15.5 depicts the most critical differences between the two techniques. First and foremost, macros are stored in memory rather than on disk. Remember that DOS must find a batch file and then read it into memory before it can run the instructions contained within it. This means that the batch file must reside in the current directory, or be found in one of the directories listed in the system PATH.

Sometimes, you can't even get a batch file to run at all because it can't be found by DOS. If the file has been written and tested, this problem is almost always because of a poorly constructed PATH. But even when the batch file *can* be found, it takes a certain amount of time first to locate it, and then to read its contents into memory. Only after that time has been spent can DOS begin to execute its instructions. When you type in a macro's name at a command prompt, it is immediately ready to execute its instructions.

On the other hand, the instructions within a batch file are always safely stored in a permanent disk file. In contrast, the instructions within a macro are resident in volatile memory. When you turn off your system, the

FIGURE 15.5

Macros are very similar to batch files. Each can execute one or more commands. But macros are memory resident, and are limited in size. Batch files are disk resident and have no inherent limit to the number of commands that can be executed.

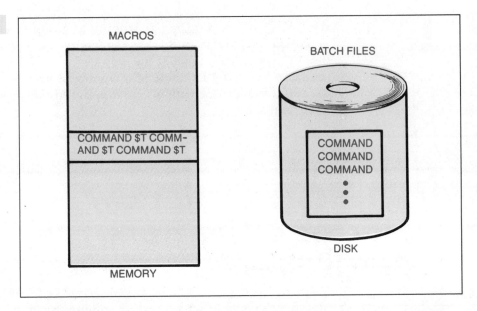

macros are lost along with whatever else resides in your system's memory. When you restart your system, you'll have to recreate or recover your macro definitions. You'll learn how to do this easily in a later section of this chapter.

As you've learned thus far, DOSKEY can manage multiple commands on one line, submitting each succeeding command to DOS after its predecessor completes execution. Similarly, in most cases a DOSKEY macro consists of multiple commands on one line. When you define macros with DOSKEY, it produces a very compact series of commands. In fact, a macro is *limited* to a single line; so you *must* fit all the necessary individual commands within the 127-character limit for a single DOS command line. These 127 characters must include not only the individual macro command instructions, but also the characters needed to define the macro name itself. You'll discover exactly what is entailed in this definition process in the next section.

Batch files are noticeably more flexible and powerful for more complex tasks. You can include limitless numbers of command lines in a batch file,

➤ **EXTRA**

Macros Are Usually Preferable to Batch Files

I invariably write macros now rather than batch files, if the size of the instruction sequence can fit within a macro. Macros are memory-resident. Batch files are disk-resident. Consequently, a macro is always faster to initiate than a batch file. You should always try to write macros for tasks that must initiate quickly.

Also, whenever possible, there is another powerful incentive for defining macros rather than batch files for all tasks small enough to fit within the 127-character limitation. Doing this will save you a considerable amount of disk space. This is because each batch file, no matter how small, consumes at least one complete cluster of disk space (usually 2048 bytes). Macros, which are stored completely in memory, consume no additional disk space at all.

To me, my most frequent decisions on any computer system are concerned with speed, space, and convenience. This section discusses the various tradeoffs between batch files and macros. However, when it is possible to use macros, you'll quickly discover how they enhance speed, take up less space, and are more convenient and easier to write and modify directly at a command prompt. Use them!

and you can use a variety of helpful batch-file commands and subcommands to control the processing. For example, you can use the GOTO command to change the executing instruction line. Since macros contain only one command line (perhaps containing multiple commands), the GOTO command is not allowed.

On the other hand, the IF and FOR subcommands are still functional since they can do all their required work in one line. The IF command works exactly as it did within a batch file, but the FOR command requires a slight modication. Specifically, when you include a FOR command in a macro definition, the special %% parameter discussed in Chapter 13 requires only a single % sign.

Note that this confusing adjustment is only required when you define a DOSKEY macro at a command prompt. If you define your macros in a batch file, as in the MACROS.BAT program (see the EXTRA! sidebar earlier in this Chapter, or order the Companion diskette to this book), you can once again use the double percent sign method. For example, the SHOWTEXT macro in the batch file looks like this:

```
DOSKEY SHOWTEXT=FOR %%j IN ($*) DO TYPE %%j
```

However, it would look like this if you defined it directly at a command prompt:

```
DOSKEY SHOWTEXT=FOR %j IN ($*) DO TYPE %j
```

Batch files are also designed for more complex system tasks. One batch file can depend on another, and batch files can readily pass execution control among themselves—one batch file can run another batch file, or it can transfer control irrevocably (by chaining) to another batch file. However, a batch file cannot execute a macro, whereas a macro can indeed run a batch file. Hence, you can use macros to initiate more complex, prewritten batch-file systems.

N O T E

Just as a batch file cannot execute a macro, a macro cannot execute a macro. Use macros for independent tasks that do not involve any of the complex intertwining that is possible with batch files.

You can create macros by means of commands within a batch file. As you'll learn in the next section, you can create a macro either at a command prompt or from within a batch file. Once you've determined which macros you will want to have in your system, you should in fact create a batch file that includes the necessary definition commands within it. Naturally, you can just as easily include these instructions within your opening AUTOEXEC.BAT file.

While macros and batch files execute their contained instructions, you can influence the processing in a couple of ways. First, you can control echoing in a batch file with the ECHO ON|OFF command. This command does not work in a macro, so you cannot control as effectively whether or not your macro commands will appear on your monitor. Macro commands will always be echoed to your monitor before they execute.

Furthermore, both batch files and macros are sensitive to your Ctrl+C, or Break, keypress. However, they respond in different ways:

- During a batch file, a single Break keypress is sufficient to interrupt the entire group of instructions in the batch file. You are asked if you wish to stop batch-file processing, or continue it from the next command in the batch file.

- Interrupting a macro with a Ctrl+C keypress only interrupts the individual command that is executing at that moment. In a macro that includes three separate commands, you must press Ctrl+C three times to completely terminate the macro. You are not asked to verify that you really want to stop processing. If you press Ctrl+C fewer times than there are commands in the macro, the next remaining command immediately begins to execute.

Lastly, just as with batch files, you can pass parameters to macros when you run them, using variable (or replaceable) parameters to defer execution decisions until you are ready to run the macro. To do this in batch files, you used variable parameters named %0 through %9. With macros the variable parameters are named with dollar signs: $* and $1 through $9. Redirection operators are also available within macros. They also have their own special $ symbol operators; you'll see examples of macro redirection in a later section of this chapter as well.

➤ **EXTRA**

Use DOSKEY to Create Your Own Keyboard Shortcuts!

The name of a DOSKEY macro is not as limited as a typical DOS filename. In fact, you can use quite a large number of special characters (like slashes, asterisks, and plus signs) and keystroke combinations (like Ctrl+A and Ctrl+K) in DOSKEY macro names that are otherwise illegal to use in a file name. For example, you can define Ctrl+Q to be a shortcut key to start up QBasic with this command line:

```
DOSKEY ^Q=QBASIC
```

Remember that ^Q is just what appears on the screen when you actually press the Ctrl+Q key combination. Only seventeen (ABDEGKLNOQ-RUVWXYZ) of the possible alphabetic characters can be defined by DOS-KEY as a shortcut keystroke in this way. In fact, if you really want to be obscure, you can even define Ctrl+\, Ctrl+_, Ctrl+^, and Ctrl+^] as well.

Using Memory-Resident Macros

In this section, you'll use some of the example batch files from the preceding chapter as models for macros. Now that you can see the benefits of macros, you'll want to consider using them in many situations where you previously might have considered a batch file as the only answer.

In the "Improving Performance" section of Chapter 14, you used command abbreviations as batch files; for example, C.BAT took the place of typing CHKDSK at a command prompt. Writing a macro to perform the same function can be an even better alternative, because macros are memory-resident.

Writing Simple, Fixed-Instruction Macros

To write your first macro, you must invoke the DOSKEY utility with the macro name followed by an equals sign (=) and the one or more command instructions that you wish to be automatically run when the macro name is typed. Remember that a single DOS line cannot exceed 127 characters. This definition line therefore includes the utility program's name (DOSKEY), then a space, then the macro name, then an equals sign, and finally the command(s) that will constitute the definition of the macro. Altogether, you are limited to 127 characters. You can make the macro name as many characters as you like, but this directly reduces the number of characters that remain for the command(s).

As an example, you can create a macro called C to replace your C batch file by typing

```
DOSKEY C=CHKDSK
```

TIP

To seemingly disable any DOS command, define a DOSKEY macro with the same name and make it a REM (Remark) instruction. For example, to make the ERASE command appear to be unavailable to a user, define the following macro after DOSKEY has been loaded:
```
DOSKEY ERASE=Rem ERASE is no longer allowed.
```

As you saw in the preceding chapter, the CHKDSK command works against whatever the current DOS disk drive happens to be. Suppose that you want to run CHKDSK against the C, D, and E drives. With a macro, you could place all three commands on one line, defining the macro with this single DOSKEY request:

```
DOSKEY C3=CHKDSK C: $T CHKDSK D: $T CHKDSK E:
```

With a batch file, you would have included three commands on three separate lines to do this chore:

```
* C3.BAT runs CHKDSK against drives C, D, and E.
*
CHKDSK C:
CHKDSK D:
CHKDSK E:
```

You learned earlier in this chapter how to run multiple commands on one line at a DOS command prompt. To do that, you actually separated the commands with a Ctrl+T keypress. This displayed ¶ on your video monitor. If you are going to include multiple commands in a macro definition, you must similarly separate each of the commands from one another. However, you must do so by typing the $T character sequence. As is usually the case in command-prompt or batch-file operations, you can type any of these command instructions in upper or lowercase.

Creating Flexible Macros with Replaceable Parameters

Just as you can do with batch files, you can define your macros in a more flexible way by using replaceable parameters. Each of the two preceding macros could be more useful as a shorthand notation for CHKDSK if they allowed for the same parameter and switch entries as the CHKDSK command itself does.

As the C macro is currently written, you could not type:

```
C G:
```

to run CHKDSK against a drive G. And you certainly could not add the /F switch to ask CHKDSK to fix any discovered disk allocation errors. But this is precisely what you probably would want to do with a truly useful abbreviation macro.

In macros, you can pass individual parameter values such as these by using $1 through $9. Remember that batch files conveyed parameter values by using the same stand-in expressions with a percent sign rather than a dollar sign. To define a macro with a replaceable parameter, just include a $ expression to signify the positional number of the parameter. The first parameter to a command is called $1, the second is called $2, and so on.

➤ EXTRA

Running Macros Is Usually a Snap!

To run any macro that you've created, you only need to enter its name at a command prompt. For instance, to run the CHKDSK command against the current disk drive, you could type

    C

Since you've also defined a C3 macro to include three separate CHKDSK commands, you can run CHKDSK against drives C, D, and E by simply typing

    C3

Each of these two macros is fixed in what it will do. As they stand now, you cannot pass a drive identifier, or any switch values, to the CHKDSK program that is the eventual target of the macro. But, as the text discusses, the DOSKEY macro facility does offer the same opportunity for flexible definitions that is offered by the batch-file mechanism.

DOSKEY macros take precedence over batch files or DOS commands with the same name. However, there may be times when you decide to create a macro with an existing program's name. On my system, one of the Norton Utilities is named FF.EXE, for FileFind. I didn't wish to change that name, because it might confuse other people who occasionally use my computer. However, I wrote the FF macro, which stands for the easily remembered Form Feed action on my printer. So, I've created a potential name conflict.

If you wish to truly execute a DOS command or batch file, avoiding the automatic execution of a memory-resident macro, you only need to press the spacebar before typing the command or batch-file name. For example, I have the Norton utility program FF.EXE (FileFind) on my PATH. I also have my frequently used DOSKEY macro named FF readily accessible. Usually I just type FF to eject the page in my printer. But when I occasionally want to run the FileFind program, I just type a space before typing the program name:

    _FF

Since the CHKDSK command can take one disk-drive identifier parameter, you could define the C macro more correctly by typing

```
DOSKEY C=CHKDSK $1
```

With this definition, you would only have to type

```
C G:
```

What about switches on a command? The CHKDSK command, like other DOS commands, can accept switches as well as a drive identifier. By defining the macro with only one replaceable parameter, $1, you are not allowing for the entry of any switch values later. This can be handled more generally with the special $* parameter.

In a macro, the $* parameter stands for all the text that follows the macro name itself when you type it in. You should use $* whenever you define a macro that invokes a variable number of parameters or switches—a number that will be unknown in advance. For example, depending on the situation, you might wish to run CHKDSK with no parameters, or with one drive identifier, or with a drive identifier and up to two switches. To ensure that the C macro works perfectly regardless of how many parameters are later typed in, you should define it with this command line:

```
DOSKEY C=CHKDSK $*
```

In this way, you can later type any of the following commands and they will pass all the parameters and switches through to the actual CHKDSK utility command:

```
C G:
C G: /V
C G: /F /V
```

Replaceable parameters can be used as parts of a more complex character sequence as well. In the last chapter, you saw how a batch file called WRITE.BAT could successively and automatically run a word processor, style checker, spell checker, and then the word processor again. You used replaceable parameters to run these programs against CHAP1, or CHAP6, or any chapter whose name was constructed out of the four letters C-H-A-P followed by the chapter number itself. In fact, during consistent operations, this sequence of programs may be repeated regularly:

```
WP CHAP%1
STYLE CHAP%1
SPELL CHAP%1
WP CHAP%1
```

A macro could do the job just as well, and more quickly. Just define it with the following command line:

```
DOSKEY WRITE=WP CHAP$1 $T STYLE CHAP$1 $T SPELL CHAP$1 $T WP
CHAP$1
```

In this way, you can initiate this macro for Chapter 5 by typing

```
WRITE 5
```

The result is that all four programs will execute in order, acting on the same file CHAP5:

```
WP CHAP5
STYLE CHAP5
SPELL CHAP5
WP CHAP5
```

Now that you know some example macro possibilities, it's almost time to begin creating and modifying some macros on your own system.

Manipulating Macro Instructions

Remember that as you develop macros, you can use DOSKEY's command history and its command-editing keys to simplify your work. You can type a DOSKEY macro-definition line, then test it by typing the macro name at the next command prompt. If it doesn't work exactly as you'd anticipated, don't retype it. Use the command-history manipulation keys to recall the earlier definition line (press F7 to see all commands in the history). Then use the command-editing keys to assist you in correcting this earlier definition. Finally, just press Enter to redefine the newly modified macro definition.

You can reissue any DOSKEY macro-definition line. This will be sufficient to completely replace the earlier definition of that macro. But suppose that you begin to create a number of macros and run out of space in the currently defined DOSKEY buffer. DOSKEY will display a notice on your monitor that you've run out of buffer space:

```
Insufficient memory to store macro.
Use the DOSKEY command with the /BUFSIZE switch to increase
available memory.
```

You can do one of several things at this point. You can always restart your system, this time initiating DOSKEY with a larger /BUFSIZE. This solution will require you to redefine all currently used macros that are necessary for your operations. Alternately, you can release some of the current buffer space by erasing some existing macro definitions. You can do this by calling DOSKEY again and specifying the macro name without a new definition after the equals sign. For instance, to release the memory space consumed by the C3 macro, type

```
DOSKEY C3=
```

Suppose you've run out of space and can't remember all the macro names that you've written. Perhaps some of them were used for temporary or testing purposes only. You can always display a list of all currently defined macros by using the /MACROS switch:

```
DOSKEY /MACROS
```

Figure 15.6 shows the results after a series of macro definition lines and one request for a display of the existing macros. Notice how the DOSKEY macro named D retains only the most recent definition assigned to it.

You can now decide which of the existing macros, if any, are no longer needed. Run DOSKEY with that macro's name followed by just an equals sign, and its memory buffer space will be freed up.

FIGURE 15.6

Macros are very similar to batch files. Each can execute one or more commands. But macros are memory resident, and are limited in size. Batch files are disk resident and have no inherent limit to the number of commands that can be executed.

```
C:\>doskey c=chkdsk

C:\>doskey c3=chkdsk c: $t chkdsk $t chkdsk d:

C:\>doskey write=wp chap$1 style chap$1 $t spell chap$1 $t wp chap$1

C:\>doskey d=dir /w d:

C:\>doskey r=rename $1 $2

C:\>doskey opt=vopt c: $t vopt d:

C:\>doskey d=dir /ah

C:\>doskey /macros
C=chkdsk
C3=chkdsk c: $t chkdsk $t chkdsk d:
WRITE=wp chap$1 style chap$1 $t spell chap$1 $t wp chap$1
R=rename $1 $2
OPT=vopt c: $t vopt d:
D=dir /ah

C:\>
```

TIP

Let DOSKEY relieve you from the anxiety of typographical errors. Just define a macro named after a common typo, and DOS will no longer complain about being unable to find the command you specified. For example, if your hand rests heavily on the keys and DIR often comes out FDIR, just define FDIR to run the DIR command:DOSKEY FDIR=DIR $1 $2 $3 $4

Suppose that you've written and tested several macros that you are now sure you'd like to retain for future use. If there were no way to save and recall them, you'd have to reenter them every time you bring up your system. But DOSKEY offers two mechanisms for saving your macros for future use, as discussed in the next section.

Advanced Macro Techniques

In Chapter 10, you learned about redirection techniques and some of the advanced applications of this DOS capability. In this section, you'll take a look at two uses of redirection in the context of macros. First, you'll use DOS redirection to save your macro instructions for later use. Second, you'll learn how to implement data redirection within macros themselves.

Saving Macros for Future Use

Figure 15.7 demonstrates the first method of capturing macro definitions for future use.

At the top of the figure, I pressed F7 to display the current command history. The list currently contains three DOSKEY definition lines:

```
doskey c=chkdsk
doskey c3= chkdsk c: $t chkdsk d: $t chkdsk e:
doskey write=wp chap$1 $t style chap$1 $t spell chap$1 $t wp
chap$1
```

FIGURE 15.7

You can save existing macro definitions in a text file by using the /HISTORY switch and the redirection operator. Of course, you'll have to edit the command lines that are saved to make use of these lines for later macro redefinitions.

```
C:\>
1: doskey c=chkdsk
2: doskey c3=chkdsk c: $t chkdsk d: $t chkdsk e:
3: doskey write=wp chap$1 $t style chap$1 $t spell chap$1 $t wp chap$1
4: doskey /macros
5: cls
C:\>DOSKEY /HISTORY > STARTUP.BAT

C:\>type startup.bat
doskey c=chkdsk
doskey c3=chkdsk c: $t chkdsk d: $t chkdsk e:
doskey write=wp chap$1 $t style chap$1 $t spell chap$1 $t wp chap$1
doskey /macros
cls
DOSKEY /HISTORY > STARTUP.BAT

C:\>
```

Since all needed macro definitions can be captured directly from the history, you can use DOS redirection to send the entire list (without the entry numbers) to an editable batch file. The instruction in the middle of Figure 15.7 does this:

```
DOSKEY /HISTORY > STARTUP.BAT
```

Rather than simply displaying the unnumbered command history on the screen, DOS interprets your redirection request and creates the STARTUP.BAT file. At the bottom of Figure 15.7, the TYPE command shows what has been placed in the STARTUP.BAT file: the contents of the history buffer, including the most recent DOSKEY command itself. By simply editing the STARTUP.BAT file, you can delete such extraneous command lines, leaving only the three macro-definition lines. The batch file is ready to go, and can be run automatically each time you bring up your system by including:

```
STARTUP
```

as one of the instructions in your system's AUTOEXEC.BAT file. You can conveniently store STARTUP.BAT in the root directory of the boot drive. Alternately, you can carefully store it in a directory that can be found on the system's path when the STARTUP command runs from within the AUTOEXEC.BAT file.

But what can you do if you've created quite a few macros, and done so much work at the command prompt that the command history no longer retains the original macro definitions? In this case, you can use the /MACROS switch that you learned about earlier. But rather than simply displaying macros on your video monitor, you can use redirection to send the existing macro definitions to a batch file as well.

Figure 15.8 depicts a sequence similar to the preceding one, except this shows how to use redirection to save macros directly from the DOSKEY macro buffer.

At the top of this figure, the /MACROS switch displays the three currently defined macros. In the middle of the figure, I used redirection to send these three definitions to a batch file named BEGIN.BAT:

```
doskey /macros > BEGIN.BAT
```

FIGURE 15.8

Storing macro
definitions directly to
disk. You can use the
saved output lines
from a /MACROS
switch by simply
prefacing each macro
line with the
executable DOSKEY
command. Later, if a
file like BEGIN.BAT
has been suitably
edited, it can be run to
restore your macro
definitions.

```
C:\>doskey /macros
C=chkdsk
C3=chkdsk c: $t chkdsk d: $t chkdsk e:
WRITE=wp chap$1 $t style chap$1 $t spell chap$1 $t wp chap$1

C:\>doskey /macros > BEGIN.BAT

C:\>type BEGIN.BAT
C=chkdsk
C3=chkdsk c: $t chkdsk d: $t chkdsk e:
WRITE=wp chap$1 $t style chap$1 $t spell chap$1 $t wp chap$1

C:\>
```

Lastly, the TYPE command shows that the BEGIN.BAT file contains the three macro definitions exactly as they exist in memory. However, while you do not have to delete extraneous lines, as you did with the /HISTORY switch technique, you will have to insert the word *DOSKEY* and a space before each of these three lines. Only then can you use this BEGIN.BAT batch file to successfully recreate the three macros during a later DOS session.

Using Redirection within Macros

You've been learning how to write macros and implement some features within them that parallel other features you've already learned about in DOS. You've seen how you must use special $ operators to signify macro operations. For instance, where you used Ctrl+T to separate commands when issued at a command prompt, you use $T to separate the same commands when written into the body of a macro.

In the same way as batch files use replaceable parameters %1 through %9, a DOSKEY macro can use replaceable parameters $1 through $9. And DOSKEY has the special $* key sequence to represent all replaceable parameters, beginning with $1 and including however many entries are typed on the macro execution line.

DOSKEY uses $ operators to signify redirection as well, so as not to confuse DOS by using the same operators within macros that it uses outside of macros. Table 15.3 summarizes the parallels between DOS redirection operators and DOSKEY macro redirection operators.

Suppose that you work with a text file containing a list of your business clients, as shown in Figure 15.9.

Although you may take pains to keep your list in alphabetical order by company name, there may be times when you need a printed list of clients

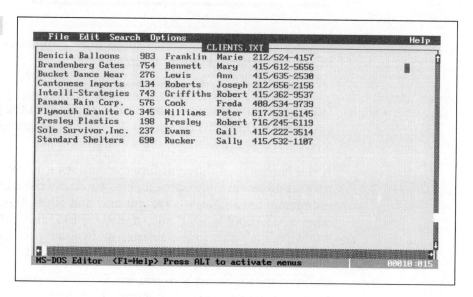

FIGURE 15.9

An example list of clients, in order by company name. A macro is easily written to resort this file by last name, displaying the results on the screen or printing them. The S macro uses redirection techniques to send the sorted output to the printer.

TABLE 15.3: DOSKEY's redirection operators

DOSKEY OPERATOR	DOS OPERATOR	EFFECT
$G	>	Redirect a command's output
$L	<	Redirect a command's intput
GG	>>	Append a command's output to an existing file
$B	¦	Pipe one command's output to another command's input

in last-name order. Remember that a SORT command can help you do this, using input and output redirection:

```
SORT /+26 < CLIENTS.TXT > PRN:
```

(Remember also that you'll have to manually eject the printed page from your printer since this command does not automatically include a form-feed character at the end of the sorting.)

If you have several different files that you want to sort by last name and they are all set up in the same format, you can write a macro that employs redirection techniques to save you time and effort. For instance, you may have a CLIENTS.TXT file, a PROSPECT.TXT file, and a CUS-TOMER.TXT file. In the absence of database management software to do this type of chore, DOSKEY can now help you.

Define a macro called S to run the SORT command, specifying a /+26 switch to sort beginning in column 26. Referring to Table 15.3, you can see that you would use $L to use input redirection to obtain the input file name from the first parameter ($1). Next, use $G to use output redirection to guide the sorted output to the printer (PRN:). Your definition command line should look like:

```
DOSKEY S=SORT /+26 $L $1 $G PRN:
```

Once you have defined this S macro, you can sort and print any of the files you have organized in fixed columns—simply type *S* and the name of the file. Try this now on any text file of your own. Be sure to change the number for the /+ switch to reflect the column to be sorted in your files.

To challenge yourself, modify the macro to send the sorted results to another file. Create an S2 macro using a second parameter ($2) to type the name of the desired file that should receive the sorted data.

To make this modification, you'll be replacing *PRN:* in the S definition line with *$2*. When you run this macro, of course, you'll be required then to specify a second parameter. For example, you might type

```
S2 CLIENTS.TXT LASTNAME.TXT
```

to create a new text file called LASTNAME.TXT that will contain the sorted results, as demonstrated in Figure 15.10.

You can now print or modify the text in this newly created file without fear of affecting the original CLIENTS.TXT file in any way.

FIGURE 15.10

Macro redirection can just as easily create new text files, as the S2 macro demonstrates by sorting the file named in the first parameter and sending the results to a new file named in the second parameter.

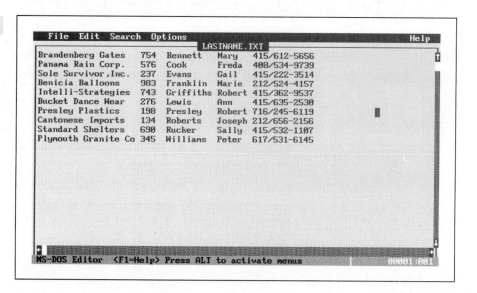

Summary

In this chapter, you've learned about the DOSKEY utility—a powerful and flexible alternative to the batch-file mechanism. You learned the following information about managing DOSKEY's command history and about its macro facility:

- The DOSKEY utility is memory-resident and occupies approximately 4K of memory in its default configuration.

- DOSKEY enables you to record, retrieve, edit, and reissue any previously submitted DOS command. Function keys F7, F8, F9, Alt+F7, and Alt+F10 serve to display, retrieve, and clear any previously entered commands.

- DOSKEY's command history also enables you to test and retest command-prompt instructions before you collect them into batch files.

- Macros are similar to batch files in grouping commands, but they are memory-resident rather than disk-resident, so they initiate faster. Macros allow multiple commands on a single line, but they allow only a single (127-character) command line. They are attractive for efficiently automating tasks that can be accomplished with a single line of commands.

- DOSKEY permits you to enter multiple commands at a DOS command prompt; you must separate each command by Ctrl+T. DOSKEY also permits you to define macros that contain multiple commands, each of which must be separated by a $T.

- DOSKEY supports the use of replaceable parameters with the codes $* and $1 through $9. It also allows redirection and piping facilities with $G, $L, $GG, and $B (which parallel DOS's >, <, >>, and ¦ symbols).

- Two switches on the DOSKEY command itself enable you to store all recorded command lines into a file (using the /HISTORY switch) or to store all defined macros in a file (using the /MACROS switch).

Now that you've learned about both disk-resident batch files and memory-resident macros, it's time to look at one of DOS's most advanced features—the QBasic programming language. With the limitless opportunity for creativity offered by QBasic, you can truly mold DOS to fit your system needs perfectly.

CHAPTER

16

QBasic:
Programming
for Any DOS User

THE QBASIC programming environment allows unlimited customization of your DOS system. QBasic is derived from the QuickBASIC language, which combines the simplicity of the original BASIC (**B**eginners **A**ll-Purpose **S**ymbolic **I**nstructional **C**ode) language with the power of more sophisticated languages like Pascal, C, and Fortran. The version of QBasic provided with DOS is easy to learn and use, yet offers dramatically more power than predecessor BASICs. The QBasic environment also includes an Editor that automatically performs a number of syntactical and structural tasks on your QBasic instructions. Furthermore, the environment offers several execution and debugging assists, and, finally, it comes free with DOS! If you have DOS 6, you have QBasic. All told, these attractive features will ensure that QBasic will become the first choice of many programmers.

Understanding QBasic

QBasic is primarily a computer programming language. Just as English facilitates conversations with Americans and Australians, or Italian is useful for speaking with Italians, so does QBasic enable you to communicate with your computer. Just as English and Italian include their own vocabulary and sets of grammatical rules, so does QBasic include its own vocabulary (known as *reserved words*) and its own rules for constructing complete sentences, or commands.

➤ **EXTRA!**

Learning QBasic Is Like Learning a Foreign Language

Each QBasic program is simply a text file that includes a group of commands. Each command (known as a *statement* or a *function*) instructs your computer to perform an individual task. The online hypertext help system includes a brief explanation of every command along with its *syntax* (its required grammatical construction). As you'll see in this section, you can access this help text while you write the individualized instructions in your customized QBasic programs.

In QBasic, you direct the computer to do things by creating a text file that includes a series of individual commands. When you ask the QBasic programming environment to *run* your program, QBasic interprets each command in your text file. As a result, the computer sequentially performs a series of instructions. Each QBasic program that you write is merely a collection of instructions designed to perform some overall chore.

When writing in other business or personal settings, you often organize your material into sentences, paragraphs, and chapters (just as I am doing for this book). A QBasic program can also be organized into similarly structured *modules*. This chapter will teach you about the individual instructions you can use in your programs. You will also learn techniques necessary to ensure that you effectively group these instructions into clearly written, easily understood, well-documented, and correctly working programs.

Getting Started with QBasic

This section will explain the main elements of the QBasic screen and how to perform essential programming work in the QBasic environment.

To start the QBasic program, you can select *MS-DOS QBasic* from the main DOS program group. This produces the dialog box seen in Figure 16.1. As you did with the Editor in Chapter 6, you can enter a file name here and press Enter, or you can simply press Enter. If you do not enter a name, you receive the opening screen seen in Figure 16.2, where the top portion of the screen is named *Untitled*. QBasic now awaits your instructions. You can press Enter to see a "Survival Guide" help screen which mimics closely the opening Survival Guide you saw in Chapter 6. Or, you can press Esc and immediately begin to type the series of instructions that will constitute your QBasic program.

FIGURE 16.1

Choose *MS-DOS QBasic* to run the QBasic program-language interpreter built into DOS. You will first be asked the name of a QBasic program file. You can ignore this and press OK if you do not have a particular file you wish to work with.

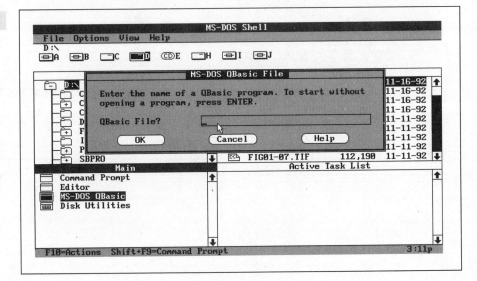

FIGURE 16.2

The QBasic opening screen allows you to move either into the help system (called the Survival Guide) or into the programming system (by pressing Esc). This screen only appears if you have not specified an opening file from the preceding figure.

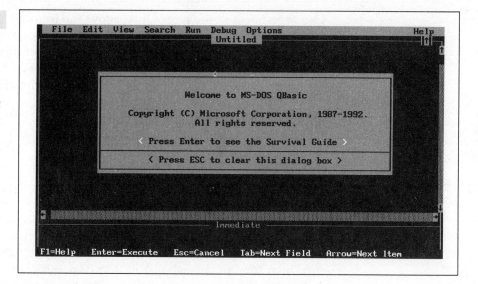

If you were to enter a specific name into the dialog box of Figure 16.1, then the opening screen of Figure 16.2 would not display the Survival Guide dialog box. The screen would be almost completely blank and your entered file name would replace the name *Untitled* at the top of this entry screen.

All aspects of this screen will remain visible during your development work, although both the contents and size of each screen section may change. The bottom line of the screen is called the *reference bar*. It provides information about which keys are active at any given moment, and what the results will be if you press them.

Just above the reference bar, you can see a short, wide rectangular area that is known as the *Immediate window*. In this expandable window, you can experiment with individual QBasic instructions. Each instruction that you type into this special window can be executed immediately, thereby enabling you to instantly see the effects of the instruction. When you've adjusted the instructions in the Immediate window to do exactly what you want, you can then incorporate them into your actual program. The remainder of the screen above the Immediate window is used to develop actual customized programs.

The largest area of the screen, just above the Immediate window, is called the *View window*. The bulk of your program development, debugging, and testing occurs here. The top line of your screen is of course called the *menu bar*. By now, you should be comfortable enough with both your keyboard and your mouse to effectively use any of the menu choices.

Exploring the Menus and Keyboard Shortcuts

Just as you learned with the DOS Shell and with the Editor, you can use a number of special keys on your keyboard. Some key names are displayed in the reference bar at the bottom of your screen. Sometimes, other keys and key combinations are also active, but you must pull down the appropriate menu to find them—they're listed next to the relevant menu option when they are available. You'll learn about many of these optionally available keystrokes at appropriate times throughout this chapter.

By exploring the menus, you will discover that many of the choices are quite familiar. In fact, they are often precisely the same as those you saw in the earlier chapter on the Editor. This is because the DOS Editor is actually contained within the QBasic programming environment itself. When you choose to run the Editor, you are actually running a stripped-down version of the QBasic programming environment, customized for text editing only. For example, the File menu is exactly the same. This is because each QBasic program that you write is simply a text file (whose contents are a series of instruction lines). These individual instructions will be interpreted and executed later by the QBasic programming environment.

NOTE On the one hand, QBasic is a computer *program* that you can run from a shell program group. On the other hand, the QBasic programming *environment* enables you to use its built-in language tools to write your own new programs, which themselves can be run under QBasic auspices. You'll soon see how to run these programs that you write.

In the next few sections we'll discuss most of the menus available for development work in QBasic. The Debug menu will be left for the end of the chapter.

Let's take a preliminary look at the menu bar possibilities now. The **File** menu is used to perform common actions on entire files. You learned how

➤ EXTRA!

Dress Up Your Screen with QBasic Screen Boxes

Use the WINDOW.BAT batch file below to create a double-walled box on the screen. You can have other batch file commands then place a choice of predetermined texts within the box. This demonstrates how to write a QBasic program and incorporate its potentially sophisticated capabilities into any batch file you then write. The essential technique is that each **ECHO** statement sends (via redirection) a validly constructed QBasic command into a W.BAS file, which is run with the **QBASIC /RUN** command from within the sample batch file.

```
@ECHO OFF
Rem WINDOW.BAT creates a double walled box on the screen.
Rem You must specify as parameters the following data:
Rem    1-2. The line/column for the box's upper left corner
Rem     3. The box width   (should be at least = 3)
Rem     4. The box height (should be at least = 3)
Rem
Rem Syntax: WINDOW UpperLeftRow UpperLeftColumn Width Height
Rem
ECHO ON ERROR GOTO ByeBye: > w.bas
ECHO CLS >> w.bas
ECHO FOR i=1 TO %1 >> w.bas
ECHO PRINT >> w.bas
ECHO NEXT i >> w.bas
ECHO PRINT STRING$(%2," ")+"╔"+STRING$(%3 -2,"=")+"╗" >> w.bas
ECHO FOR i=1 TO %4 -2 >> w.bas
ECHO PRINT STRING$(%2," ")+"║"+STRING$(%3 -2," ")+"║" >> w.bas
ECHO NEXT i >> w.bas
ECHO PRINT STRING$(%2," ")+"╚"+STRING$(%3 -2,"=")+"╝" >> w.bas
ECHO ByeBye: >> w.bas
ECHO SYSTEM >> w.bas

QBASIC /RUN w.bas
DEL w.bas
```

to use all of these choices in Chapter 6, so you'll skip over them here. The shortcut keystrokes recognized in QBasic are the same as those recognized in the Editor. You'll learn about additional shortcut keystrokes at the appropriate points in this chapter.

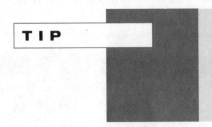

TIP As you develop QBasic programs, use the *Print* choice on the File menu to print all or selected portions of your program code to help you keep track of what you are doing and to give you something to jot your notes on.

The **Edit** menu also offers the same choices you saw in Chapter 6 for cutting, copying, pasting, and clearing text. However, there are two new possibilities offered now:

- *New SUB*
- *New FUNCTION*

These two extra choices offer you the opportunity to organize your text file into text groups. While the main text lines are interpreted as computer instructions, you can ask QBasic to treat some groups of instructions as *subroutines* and others as *functions*. Both enable you to write customized programs that are more structured, easier to read, and simpler to debug when problems arise.

Within the QBasic programming environment, you will often need to find the location in your program that contains specific instructions that you wish to modify, augment, or delete. The **Search** menu offers the same possibilities you saw with the Editor for finding and changing selected text. Refer to Chapter 6 for explanations of how to locate and replace specific text strings.

Viewing Your Modules, Routines, and Code Groups

You can structure your QBasic instructions with modular, organized groupings. However, QBasic does not normally display the submodules on the same screen with the main program. You must use the **View** menu (Figure 16.3) to change your screen view of the QBasic programming environment.

As you work with your programs, such as a main program and its referenced subroutines and functions, you can use the *SUBs* choice on the View menu to select among the current memory-resident instructions. A list of programs and subprograms will be displayed for you to select from; your choice then appears in the View window.

(Later in this chapter, you will learn more about the nature of subroutines and functions, including how to use them most effectively. For the moment, think of subroutines and functions as individual employees who are asked to perform specific tasks by the "supervisor," the main QBasic program.)

FIGURE 16.3

The View menu is most often used to switch between the programming screen and the program output screen.

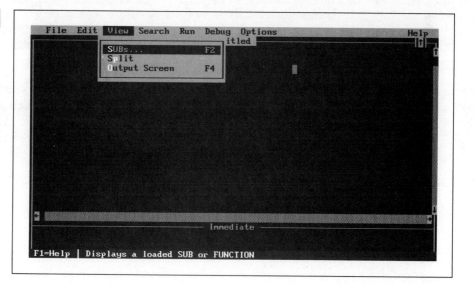

As you'll see below, you can also split the View window into two sections. In this way, you can work with two code groups at the same time. The *Split* choice on the View menu enables you to toggle between full-window and split-window operations.

➤ EXTRA!

QBasic Treats Your Video Monitor like Two Screens!

To understand the last choice on the View menu, *Output Screen*, it is necessary to understand how QBasic treats your video monitor.

If your system included two video monitors, it might be sensible to write your instructions on one monitor, then run the program and view the resulting program output on the other monitor. This is not how the QBasic programming environment works. Recognizing that most users have only one monitor, QBasic uses the one screen for your programming work as well as for the output results.

When you run your instructions, QBasic automatically switches to the mode in which you can see the output results. When you finish viewing your output, you can press any key to return to the development-environment screen. You can always return to view the last program output by switching back to the output-screen mode.

Selecting *Output Screen* from the View menu lets you visually switch between the QBasic development-environment screen and the program's output screen. Pressing the F4 shortcut key, instead of pulling down this menu and choosing *Output Screen*, achieves the same effect and is considerably more efficient.

Running Your QBasic Programs

The **Run** menu appears in Figure 16.4 and includes three commands for controlling the execution of your programs.

You can run all the text instructions in your entire program by pulling down the Run menu and selecting *Start*. Alternatively, you can press the shortcut key Shift+F5. This runs the currently loaded main program. Since your program may create some variables and then vary their values, running your program a second time may not necessarily produce exactly the same result as the first time. The *Restart* choice was designed to overcome this problem. Restart prepares your program for running with the same initial values. All numeric variables are reset to zero, all string expressions are set to zero-length (null) strings, and the program's first statement is set to execute next.

FIGURE 16.4

The Run menu offers three choices. Generally, pressing Shift+F5 to start or F5 to continue executing your program is much faster.

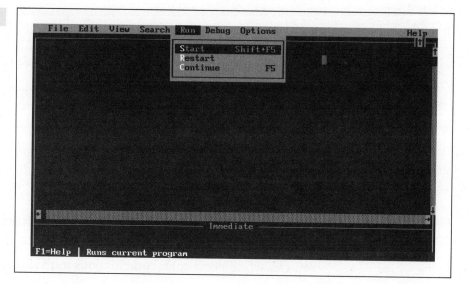

TIP

In order to run existing BASICA or GW-BASIC programs under DOS's QBASIC, you must convert those programs first. To do so, simply save them as ASCII files. You should also start QBASIC with the /MBF runtime switch. Finally, if your earlier programs contain any CALL statements, you should change them to CALL ABSOLUTE.

The *Continue* choice is typically used during debugging procedures to continue execution after some purposeful exploratory pauses. When a program does not work as expected, you must "debug" the program to figure out why. When debugging your code, you can stop the program's execution and explore the intermediate status of the program and any variables or files affected by the program. After each such break, you can continue the program's execution by pulling down the View menu and selecting *Continue*.

Customizing Your QBasic Development Environment

The **Options** menu offers three choices that enable you to customize your QBasic development environment:

- *Display*
- *Help Path*
- *Syntax Checking*

Choosing *Display* enables you to control your screen's color and display settings, as shown in Figure 16.5.

You can set different color combinations individually for:

- The normal text instructions you write.
- The currently executing statement. (This becomes important when you are "tracing" through the program as it executes.)

FIGURE 16.5

Control colors and display options from this screen. Use different color combinations for different statement types to make debugging easier.

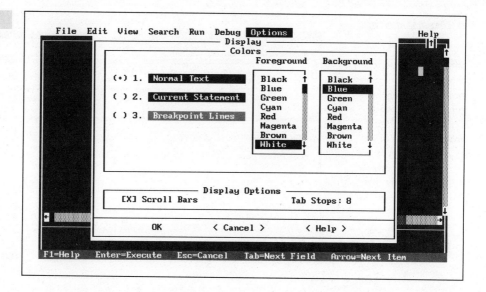

- Any line at which a *breakpoint* has been set. A breakpoint is a point in your program at which you have QBasic pause when the program actually runs. (Tracing and breakpoints are presented later in this chapter, in the sections concerning debugging.)

You can also control whether or not scroll bars appear at the right side and at the bottom of your View window. Lastly, you can set tab stops to some number other than the default value of *8*.

The second primary choice on the Options menu, *Help Path*, enables you to tell QBasic where to find the QBASIC.HLP file. This file contains the hypertext screens which contain all of the help information. This option exists mainly for those of you who for whatever reason are using a computer without a hard disk, in which case you will need to change this setting according to which diskette drive you wish to use for hypertext help. Figure 16.6 shows the initial help index screen.

The third choice on the Options menu, *Syntax Checking*, is a simple toggle switch: selecting it turns this special QBasic Editor function on or off. As you'll learn shortly, this applies a number of tests to your entries to ensure

FIGURE 16.6

The online help index offers rapid hypertext access to help information. Type any letter to jump to the beginning of that alphabetic group. Click on any highlighted term to immediately receive detailed help about it.

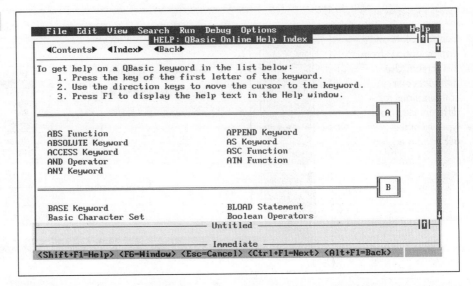

that your lines of code are correct. This reduces the number of simple errors that can creep into your instructions as you write your QBasic programs.

Introducing QBasic Windows

So far, you've seen that the QBasic programming environment contains many helpful development tools. All of these features are available either through the menu structure or through certain shortcut keystrokes. In this section you will explore further the graphic face of QBasic by studying the types of available screen windows. You'll learn how to efficiently use the contents of the View window, the Immediate window, and the Help window.

➤ EXTRA!

Context-Sensitive Online Help Is Readily Available!

Help is always only a keystroke away. The Help menu in QBasic contains five choices:

Index
Contents
Topic
Using Help
About

QBasic help is similar to the Editor's hypertext system. It is more extensive because it includes help text for commands, menu items, and programming keywords.

You can display an alphabetized list of all QBasic keywords by selecting *Index*. Select any individual keyword on the index screen (which is shown in Figure 16.6) to display the relevant help screen. You can move quickly to any alphabetical group of keywords by typing the first letter of the word. The screen instantly scrolls the index to the portion that includes words that begin with that letter.

If you're not sure of the keyword you're looking for, the *Contents* choice displays in plain English a list of general topics. Select any topic of interest in order to display a more detailed help screen about that topic, often including any relevant keywords.

If the topic for which you want help is already included in the text displayed in your Immediate or View window, you can highlight the word of the line and then select *Topic* to obtain the help text (or just press F1).

The *Using Help* choice displays some text which explains how to use the help facility itself. This is the simplest introduction to accessing the hypertext system itself, and includes some additional shortcut keys. Lastly, the *About* choice merely displays the version number of the QBasic program you are using.

➤ EXTRA!

Check Out the Free Sample Programs!

Your QBasic system comes with a variety of example programs, usually found in the C:\DOS directory. Pull down the File menu and select *Open*, then use the File Name area in the Open dialog box to request the *.BAS files in the C:\DOS directory. Select one of these programs in the Files area now. The former label for the View window, "Untitled," will be replaced with the actual name of the program you have opened and can now use. To become familiar with the structure and appearance of programs you may want to use in QBasic, you should investigate all the .BAS programs that came with DOS as you read the following sections.

Controlling Window Relationships

You can run any QBasic program by pulling down the Run menu (or by pressing Alt+R) and selecting *Start*. The program you run may be one that you've just been writing, and appears on the screen in front of you, or it may be one that already exists on the disk. The program I'll be using for illustration purposes in this section, PHONE.BAS—which may or may not have been included with your DOS package—is a simple program for building, maintaining, sorting, and printing a simple database of people you frequently need to contact. Once you've loaded a program into memory in this way, the View window immediately displays the QBasic-language instructions that make up the program, as seen in Figure 16.7.

Once you load a program into a View window, or write a new program, you can run the instructions by simply pressing Shift+F5. (F5 by itself is for when you want to *continue* running the program after interrupting or pausing it, in which case it continues from the last executed step.) QBasic

FIGURE 16.7

The View window shows the current program or code module you are working on. Scroll bars enable you to move up, down, or sideways in the program text.

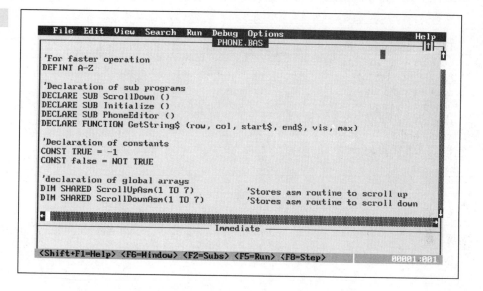

```
   File  Edit  View  Search  Run  Debug  Options                    Help
                              PHONE.BAS
  'For faster operation
  DEFINT A-Z

  'Declaration of sub programs
  DECLARE SUB ScrollDown ()
  DECLARE SUB Initialize ()
  DECLARE SUB PhoneEditor ()
  DECLARE FUNCTION GetString$ (row, col, start$, end$, vis, max)

  'Declaration of constants
  CONST TRUE = -1
  CONST false = NOT TRUE

  'declaration of global arrays
  DIM SHARED ScrollUpAsm(1 TO 7)        'Stores asm routine to scroll up
  DIM SHARED ScrollDownAsm(1 TO 7)      'Stores asm routine to scroll down

  ─────────────────────────── Immediate ───────────────────────────

  <Shift+F1=Help>  <F6=Window>  <F2=Subs>  <F5=Run>  <F8=Step>       00001:001
```

instantly runs the program, switching your video monitor to what is known as the output screen. The output of the PHONE.BAS program can be seen in Figure 16.8.

This program allows you to enter your contacts in separate lines on the screen. When the program is running, QBasic displays only the output screen. At the top of the screen, you can now type the information into the six screen fields (Name, Phone, Address, City, State, and Zip) for each contact. At the bottom of the screen, the five applicable function keys are identified. You can press F2 to return to the QBasic programming environment's View window, F5 to sort all the contact names you enter, F6 to print the lines of names, F9 to insert new blank lines for new contacts, or F10 to delete an entire line of data (the one containing the reverse-video cursor).

To manage these distinct chores, the actual program is organized into a main module and several smaller modules. Once the View window is showing, F2 changes its function to "SUBs," to display the names of all

FIGURE 16.8

The output screen appears when you run the program that appears in the View window. This figure displays the initial output of the PHONE.BAS program.

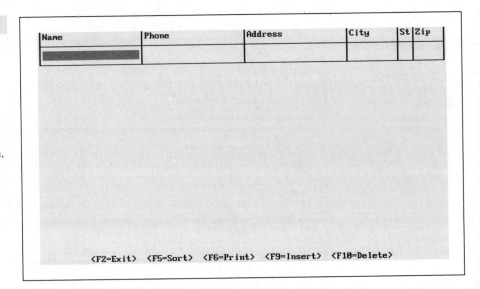

portions of the currently loaded QBasic program file. The result for PHONE.BAS is illustrated in Figure 16.9.

The SUBs dialog box enables you to edit or delete one of the named blocks of text (i.e., modules). QBasic actually stores a main program and

FIGURE 16.9

From the View window, press F2 to display the names of all subordinate modules currently resident in memory. You can see here that PHONE.BAS is the main module, and makes use of five individually named support modules.

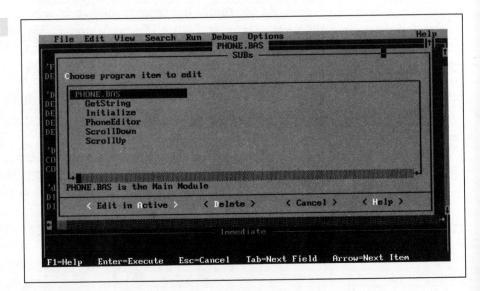

all its submodules in the same physical disk file. The SUBs dialog box is your mechanism for accessing and editing any one of the modules.

Generally, it can be quite effective to view and edit a main program module at the same time as one of the subprograms. To view both, you must first select the *Split* choice from the View menu. Then, bring up this SUBs dialog box by pressing F2 (or select *SUBs* on the View menu), and select one of the displayed subprogram names. The selected program item will be read into the active half of the View window. You will then be able to switch between your screen windows to edit either module. If you have not selected Split when you display this dialog box and select a program item to edit, the program item will replace the current module in the full-screen View window.

Try splitting the screen and then selecting one of the SUBs listed—in Figure 16.9 I chose PhoneEditor—and then choose <Edit in Active>. You should then have three separate windows visible, as can be seen in Figure 16.10.

When multiple windows appear on your screen, you can change the active window from one to the other by pressing F6. Do that now several times in succession. When the input focus shifts from one window to another, the title of the window becomes highlighted and the cursor shifts to that

FIGURE 16.10

Choose View➤Split to divide the View window into two programming sections. You can then view and edit two modules at the same time. Press F6 to switch between screen windows.

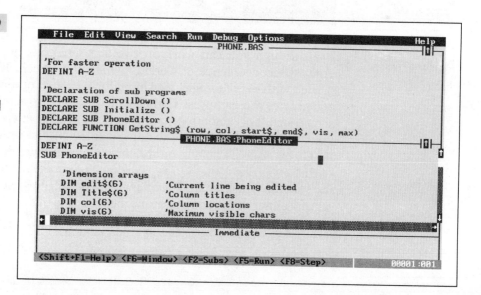

window. If you move the cursor to one of the two View windows, scroll bars will appear in that window as well. Subsequent keystrokes act on the text in the active window only, or control the actions taken on the text in that window only.

You can cycle through the text in each of the loaded code modules by repeatedly pressing Shift+F2. Each time you press this key combination, QBasic shows the instructions contained within the next named entry in the SUBs list.

T I P

Although it is often advantageous to view multiple windows simultaneously, it is also often more advantageous to work with as many lines of text in a file as possible. QBasic recognizes certain key combinations that allow you to adjust your environment to suit your particular needs. Remember that pressing Alt and the plus key from the numeric keypad (remember that NumLock must be toggled *off*) will enlarge the size of the active window by one line; pressing Alt and the minus key will shrink the active window by one line each time you press that key combination.

Even though you can work on two separate code groups, you can still enjoy the convenience of working with a full screen. If you are not concerned with *simultaneously* viewing information in other windows than the active one, you can press Ctrl+F10 to enlarge the active window to full-screen size. This key combination acts as a toggle between a full-screen active window and a multiple-window display. Mouse users can activate this toggle by double-clicking on the title line of any window. The advantage of this keystroke is that QBasic continues to manage the split-screen editing process. You can then decide when you want to use the full screen for editing either of the two code modules residing in the two editing sections.

Previewing Output Results in the Immediate Window

The Immediate window enables you to experiment individually with QBasic commands. Serving a utility role, QBasic executes each command in the Immediate window as soon as you type it and press Enter. When trying out particular variations of a single command, you can quickly determine the correct syntax, as well as try out a set of different parameter values. You can even type a series of separate instructions in the Immediate window and then test them one at a time by moving the cursor to each instruction and pressing Enter.

Take a moment now to try this facility. Press F6 until the title line of the Immediate window becomes highlighted. It is now the active window. You can expand the Immediate window to a maximum of ten screen lines, even though you can enter more than ten lines of instructions. You can scroll up or down through all the lines of code you enter in this Immediate window. Once you've figured out a series of instructions that work in the Immediate window, you can use the cut-and-paste technique to avoid retyping them into the actual code module in the View window.

Suppose you wanted to write a graphic program that displayed some data as a proportional pie chart. Just to become sure of the required parameters, you might have to spend a good deal of time studying QBasic documentation or the hypertext screens. In either case, you could experiment quickly with the **CIRCLE** command by using the Immediate window. If the result is not what you want or expect, just adjust the command instruction slightly in the Immediate window and press Enter again.

For the moment, just type the following three commands in the Immediate window:

```
CLS
SCREEN 12
CIRCLE (320,240),160,,-3.00,-2.00
```

After typing each instruction, QBasic verifies the entire line for correct syntax. If the line passes the tests, it is immediately executed. If anything is wrong, you will receive a *message box* in the center of your screen explaining what seems to be wrong. This is the simplest possible dialog box;

its role is to inform you of a problem. It also asks you to confirm that you understand the problem or to request additional help.

After each instruction executes, QBasic switches your video monitor from the development environment screen to the output screen so that you can see the results of the instruction. To return to the development screen, you only need to "Press any key to continue"—as is noted at the bottom of the output screen.

Figure 16.11 demonstrates this situation after the three lines above have been entered successfully into the Immediate window.

Try this sequence yourself for a few minutes. Use these three instructions to begin with, varying the parameters to explore how the **CIRCLE** command works. Basically, **CLS** clears the output screen once, while **SCREEN 12** sets the monitor into the common 640×480, VGA graphic mode. If your monitor is capable of other resolutions, so you can use one of the other mode values (see Table 16.4 later in the chapter) in the SCREEN command. The CIRCLE command itself draws the primary circle with the missing wedge.

Remember that you can always press F4 to switch back and forth between the QBasic development screen and the last output screen. Since this key

FIGURE 16.11

Executing Immediate instructions switches to the output screen. To do this, just switch to the Immediate window at the bottom of a QBasic screen, type any command, and press Enter. Use this to test an individual instruction for syntax or effect.

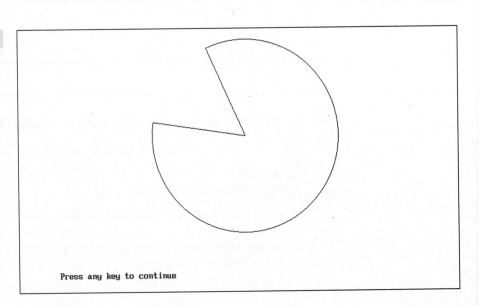

Press any key to continue

works at all times, you can use it from the Immediate window and, during program development later, from the View window(s) as well.

As you develop instructions that work correctly in the Immediate window, you will discover several things. First, an instruction line is executed whenever you press Enter after placing the cursor on that instruction line. Second, after returning from the output screen, QBasic automatically moves the cursor to the next instruction line in the Immediate window. This is helpful when you wish to execute several lines of code in the Immediate window.

No line is erased from the Immediate window unless you reuse the line by typing a new instruction over an old one, or press Ctrl+Y when the cursor is on the line; doing so will erase the line completely. In addition, remember that pressing Ctrl+Home always moves the cursor back to the first position of the first line in an active window. When using the Immediate window, you will probably use Ctrl+Home often in order to re-execute all your test lines successively, starting with the first.

Once you've successfully constructed one or more instructions in the Immediate window, you may wish to include them in a program that you are developing in one of your View windows. Remembering the cut-and-paste procedure you learned about in Chapter 6, you can move any desired lines from the Immediate window to the appropriate place in the View window.

Use standard selection techniques to highlight, then cut, the desired text from the Immediate window. Then, switch your active window to the appropriate View window. Move the cursor to the point where you'd like to position the text that was cut from the Immediate window, and then paste the text at that point. Remember that the Edit menu controls both cut and paste operations.

You can write much of your program in the Immediate window. After the statements have been written, corrected, and seen to produce successful results, you can move them all into the actual program area. After you consolidate larger and larger groups of instructions in the View window, you can eventually save the code to a named disk file.

➤ EXTRA!

Include Timed Pauses in Your Batch Files!

Use the WAIT.BAT batch file below to create a double-walled box on the screen. Other batch file commands can then place desired text within the box. This demonstrates how to write a QBasic program and incorporate its potentially sophisticated capabilities into any batch file you then write.

The essential technique is that each **ECHO** statement sends (via redirection) a validly constructed QBasic command into a WAIT.BAS file, which is run with the **QBASIC /RUN** command from within the sample batch file. Once you've constructed this batch file, you can incorporate a pause of *xx* seconds into any other batch file by simply including the command line **WAIT** *xx* at the point you wish the pause to occur.

```
@ECHO OFF
Rem WAIT.BAT
Rem Syntax: WAIT NumSeconds
Rem where NumSeconds is the number of seconds to pause.
ECHO 10 ON ERROR GOTO 300 > WAIT.BAS
ECHO 30 LET Counter = %1 >> WAIT.BAS
ECHO 50 IF Counter = 0 GOTO 300 >> WAIT.BAS
ECHO 70 LET BeginTime = TIMER >> WAIT.BAS
ECHO 90 LET EndTime = TIMER >> WAIT.BAS
ECHO 200 WHILE INT(EndTime) = INT(BeginTime) >> WAIT.BAS
ECHO 210 EndTime = TIMER >> WAIT.BAS
ECHO 230 WEND >> WAIT.BAS
ECHO 250 LET Counter = Counter - 1 >> WAIT.BAS
ECHO 260 PRINT "Counting Down: "+STR$(Counter) >> WAIT.BAS
ECHO 270 Goto 50 >> WAIT.BAS
ECHO 300 SYSTEM >> WAIT.BAS

QBASIC /RUN WAIT.BAS
DEL WAIT.BAS
```

Developing Programs

There is a pattern that becomes apparent when developing computer programs. At some point, you decide on a task that the computer will help you to accomplish. Then, you type in a series of QBasic instructions that you believe will accomplish this task. Next, you test the instructions by running the program from the Run menu, or by pressing Shift+F5. If the code doesn't work as you expect or as you want, you figure out what to change (i.e., *debug*), then rewrite some of the instructions until you are satisfied.

If you are so inclined during this process, you may document your work for your own benefit later, or for the benefit of others who will work with your program. You may also change some instructions to make the program work faster, or the instructions themselves easier to read, or the output more attractive to view. If the program is intended for someone else's use, that user may request certain other improvements, corrections, or additions.

All in all, the development phase of a computer program can be somewhat circular, as illustrated in Figure 16.12.

Most of the time you spend writing a computer program will probably be spent in the cyclic development portion. In this chapter, you will exercise your skills in all areas. However, pay particular attention to the tips and techniques offered for debugging. To ensure the fastest and smoothest development of QBasic programs, you will have to become more skilled in correcting errors than in simply writing instructions.

Writing and Running a New Program

If you've brought up your QBasic programming environment, and the View window is now empty, you can begin typing in QBasic instructions. Type in the series of instructions shown in Figure 16.13. I'll be using this

Life cycle of a computer program. Very few programs work correctly the first time you run them. Even if they don't require debugging, you'll usually still edit them to modify the appearance of the results.

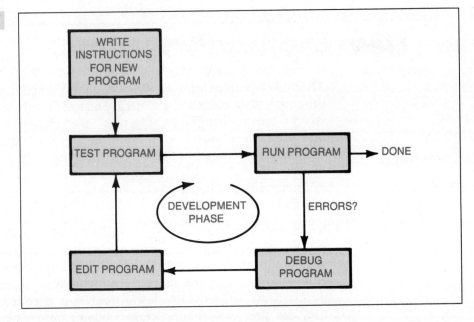

The CLARITY.BAS text file is a working program that analyzes the clarity of your writing. Run this program and specify a text file you've written to assess how simple or complex your prose appears to be.

```
'* CLARITY.BAS judges how well you write.
CLS
INPUT "Enter filename: "; name$
OPEN name$ FOR INPUT AS #1
    length% = 0
    words% = 0
    sentences% = 0
    fogcount% = 0
DO
    onechar$ = INPUT$(1, #1)
    SELECT CASE onechar$
        CASE ";", ",", ":", CHR$(10)
        CASE "."
            sentences% = sentences% + 1
        CASE " ", CHR$(13)
            words% = words% + 1
            IF length% > 7 THEN
                fogcount% = fogcount% + 3
            ELSE
                fogcount% = fogcount% + 1
            END IF
            length% = 0
        CASE ELSE
            length% = length% + 1
    END SELECT
LOOP UNTIL EOF(1)
averagefogcount% = fogcount% / sentences%
PRINT words%; "words in"; sentences%; "sentences"
PRINT "Average fog count is "; averagefogcount%
END
```

program to explain fundamental characteristics of the QBasic programming language. Pay particular attention to punctuation, special characters, and indentation. You'll learn what everything means as you continue reading through this chapter. When you finish entering these instructions, use the *Save* choice on the File menu to back up your typing work to a text file named CLARITY.BAS.

T I P

As you continue to work on any QBasic programs, remember to use the File➤Save to periodically back up your work. This will minimize the possible loss that would otherwise result from a power failure on your computer system.

CLARITY.BAS performs a useful example task. It will read any ASCII text file (without formatting and control codes) to count the number of words and sentences in that file. At the same time, the program computes a *Fog Count*. The Fog Count of any piece of writing is a numerical measure of the document's readability. It is used by the U.S. Air Force and a number of large corporations to assess the quality of various documents. If your file's Fog Count is 25 or less, you've met the Air Force's specification for a readable piece of writing.

When CLARITY runs, it first expects you to type the name of the text file that you wish to analyze. The program then reads the file, one character at a time, and computes the number of words and sentences, as well as the Fog Count. Have some fun by trying out this program on some text documents that you've written.

T I P

To run multiple QBasic programs from within a batch file, be sure to end each QBasic program with a SYSTEM statement. This returns control to DOS and the batch file that is executing, rather than returning directly to QBasic for further instructions.

Automatic Editing Benefits

QBasic contains its own built-in text editor, which is actually a slight variation on the EDIT program you learned about in Chapter 6. While you type in each instruction line, and press Enter, the Editor automatically performs several chores:

1. Reformatting
2. Syntax checking
3. Text insertions

First, each line is reformatted according to several rules of appearance. Second, QBasic checks the syntax of each line. Lastly, if necessary, it inserts extra declaration lines to assist with modularization (i.e., subprograms).

Reformatting Makes Instructions Easier to Understand

The Editor automatically capitalizes each QBasic keyword. Notice in Figure 16.13 how reserved words such as **CLS, INPUT,** and **OPEN** are capitalized. When I typed those words, I didn't have to capitalize them myself. QBasic did that for me as soon as I pressed Enter.

QBasic also inserts spaces between operators (such as **>** and **=**) and after punctuation marks (such as commas and semicolons). In addition, the Editor capitalizes the names of variables, procedures, and symbolic constants in the same way throughout your program. Take a close look at the program in Figure 16.13. In the tenth line, the spaces on either side of the equals sign, and just after the comma, were all added by QBasic after I pressed Enter. Obviously this helps you to type program lines more rapidly, since you do not have to remember whether you need to put spaces for readability. This results in neater, more attractive, and more readable instruction lines, even if you didn't think to include such spacing.

Notice also the indentation I used for compound statements like **SELECT CASE** and **IF...ELSE...END IF**. I'll explain those statements further later in this chapter. For now, simply be aware that if you indent a line, the Editor maintains that indentation for subsequent lines. (You can backspace to return to a previous "left margin.") When you include several instructions within a single compound statement (such as the **CASE** statement), the *nesting* of instruction groups becomes visually apparent. This enhances the readability of your code.

The Editor offers one other unusual formatting feature. Although typically you should write code that consistently contains all uppercase or all lowercase entries for all variable names, procedure names, and symbolic constants, you may wish to use a mixed convention of your own—e.g., *fogcount%* becoming *FogCount%*. To do this, you only need to change the spelling of the name in one place in your program. The Editor would immediately change all other instances of *fogcount%* to *FogCount%*.

The net effect of all of these formatting adjustments is only cosmetic. However, when you improve the organization, the consistency, and the visual clarity of your code, you are also producing a program which is easier to read, debug, maintain, and understand. Since most of the development phase of a computer program concentrates in these arenas, you gain a constant benefit from the automatic reformatting.

Validating Your Instruction Syntax

When you press Enter to complete a new instruction line, the Editor verifies the correctness of each line. Although it can't check completely for your intended meaning (i.e., the *semantics* of your instruction), it can check that the entire line adheres to QBasic's rules (i.e., the *syntax* of the instruction).

For example, take a look at Figure 16.14. In the **PRINT** statement just typed, a colon was erroneously typed instead of the proper separator, a semicolon. The Editor highlights the portion of the line which, because of the error, does not make sense. It also displays a dialog box that contains an explanatory error message. In Figure 16.14, the dialog box offers a

QBasic provides automatic syntax checking. If a statement does not work, you'll receive an immediate message box such as this one. Additionally, you can see that the location in the program code of the offending statement is highlighted for your debugging convenience.

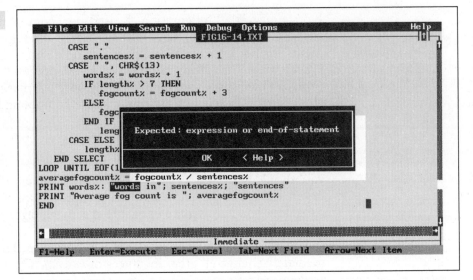

brief message, and the option for an additional help screen with further details if you need them. If you already recognize what needs to be done (for example, you realize that the colon needs to be replaced with a semicolon), select *OK* and correct the line. If you're not sure what's wrong, select *Help* and read the additional information that will be displayed.

TIP The actual error in an instruction is usually located just to the left of the highlighted portion of the line.

This dialog box is informative only. It doesn't prevent you from continuing with your coding; it doesn't even require you to fix the error immediately. You can correct it now or you can correct it later. If you choose not to correct the problem now, the error will be caught again when you run the program later. It is often easiest, however, to correct a simple syntactical error at the moment it is typed, when your mind is still concentrating on the statement and its context.

Inserting Procedure Declarations

The Editor performs one last automatic chore, but only occasionally: it offers a special form of support for using procedures. As you've learned already, groups of instructions are sometimes grouped into separately named and easily invoked support modules known as functions or subs. When you reference such procedures in your programs, you must also notify QBasic of their use and appearance.

The Editor relieves you of this burden by automatically inserting the required **DECLARE** statements at the beginning of your program file. If you haven't written the necessary DECLARE statements by the time you save your file, QBasic does so for you. At that point, all procedures are stored at the physical end of the program file (see Figure 16.15).

A **DECLARE** statement must appear at the beginning of the main code module. This special statement enables QBasic to distinguish between instruction references to procedure names and those made to simple variable names. In addition, for those of you already familiar with the concept of procedures, a DECLARE statement also defines all parameters that may be used by the procedure. When you later run the procedure, QBasic can verify that you have correctly specified the number and type of these parameters.

FIGURE 16.15

All program modules are stored in one .BAS file. The file is easily readable, so you can explore exactly how QBasic stores your programs after you've written them. For that matter, you can use your own preferred word processor to write or edit your programs.

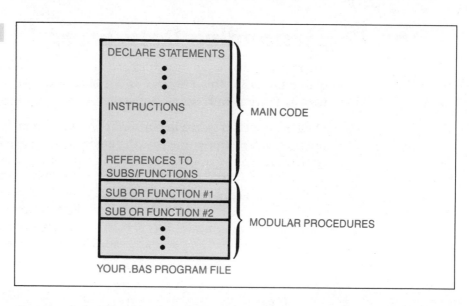

Designing Programs

In this section, you will learn more about the contents and construction of the conventional QBasic program.

In general, any computer program must do three things:

1. Obtain data to work with, or directions to follow.

2. Process that data, or follow those instructions.

3. Output results in some fashion.

QBasic provides many commands which facilitate these three steps. For Step 1, this section will concentrate on the two most important input commands, **INPUT** and **READ**. For Step 2, you'll learn about a number of example commands, as shown in the CLARITY.BAS program. For Step 3, you'll focus on the **PRINT** command. As you'll soon realize, QBasic programs offer a flexible way of getting various tasks accomplished. Some program aspects are required, while others are optional. As you learn about different commands, you can draw upon this knowledge to write your own successful QBasic programs.

Understanding Data Types

All interactive programs establish a dialog with a user. The DOS shell uses dialog boxes for this purpose. In QBasic, you can communicate with a user by writing an **INPUT** statement.

Data of all sorts is stored in portions of memory managed by QBasic. Your program will reference the data during its processing. In order to establish consistency in the storage and handling of your data, QBasic must assign a *type* to each item of data. Some data is used in calculations; other data is used as straightforward text. QBasic calls these two types of data *numbers* and *strings*. As an example, 23 could be a number, to be used in a calculation. Or it could be the first two characters in the expression "23 Sherman Road"; in this second case, 23 represents a character string.

You can explicitly specify the type of your data in a number of ways. The easiest way is to assign a name to the storage location for the data, then to append a special suffix character to the assigned name. This assigned name is called a *variable* because it can later house different data at different times. When you eventually store a particular piece of data in that

---

➤ EXTRA!

You Can Never Document Too Much!

Although user documentation usually accompanies your software, it is also advisable to incorporate some amount of *programmer documentation* within the program code itself. This can help you, or other programmers, to work with the program instructions themselves.

There is no limit to the amount of explanatory text lines you may include in your program file itself. To mark a line of text as a comment or explanation, just begin the line by typing an apostrophe. For example, the first line of the CLARITY.BAS program demonstrates this in a simple way:

```
'* CLARITY.BAS judges how well you write.
```

In one line, I've ensured that a reader knows the name of the text file that this listing represents, as well as the logical task that it performs. It's always a good idea to begin programs with several lines like this that explain the program's name, purpose, and any special requirements. If the program includes procedures, these opening lines should also include a brief explanation of any necessary parameters.

You can add commentary lines like this anywhere you like in a program. Do this to explain the purpose of instructions at a point where they are not immediately obvious. For example, at a point where your program includes any unusual or complicated instructions, add a note to explain them.

Incorporating documentation like this into your programs is easier when you are writing the program than later. If you get into the habit now, the textual comments will make it much easier to come back to the code later and make any desired changes.

location, you are said to be assigning a *value* to the variable. Table 16.1 shows some QBasic variable types, with example values.

TABLE 16.1: Sample variable types with example values

VARIABLE	VALUE
STATE$	California
STUDENTS%	32
TAXES&	1,312,125
INTEREST!	14.34976
ORBIT#	$21.238 \star e^7$

Variable names (such as STUDENTS%) that end with a percent sign (**%**) are typically used to store simple integers, which can be any number between −32,768 and +32,767. Other numeric variables consume a specific amount of computer memory, depending on which type of suffix is used. The suffix also defines how large or small a number can be stored in that variable location. String variables, denoted by a dollar sign ($) suffix, consume a differing amount of memory, depending on how many characters are contained in the string.

For example, all % numbers are stored in 16 bits (two computer bytes). While this consumes the least amount of space, it is also the most restrictive. You cannot store decimal numbers in such a variable, and the allowable range is constrained. Larger integers require an ampersand (**&**) suffix, and can store numbers from approximately −2 billion to +2 billion. Such **&** variables are called *long integers*. QBasic uses twice as much storage space (32 bits versus 16) to afford you this greater range of numeric values.

Both remaining data types are called *floating-point* numbers. You must use one of these other two suffixes for variables that are intended to store numbers that contain fractional or decimal parts. An exclamation point (!) suffix denotes a *single-precision* number whose value can range from approximately $-(3.4 \times 10^{38})$ to $+3.4 \times 10^{38}$. You can employ the number sign (#) suffix whenever your data values require even greater magnitude or range; such a variable is called *double-precision*. Single-precision variables consume 32 bits of memory, while double-precisions consume 64 bits of memory. The extra bits, and the special algebraic format that is used, enable QBasic to store numeric values in double-precision variables that exceed 10^{38}.

Finally, you will always use strings of characters in your formatted output. Typically, you will use them as labels, or as interspersed text to clarify numeric output, such as is done at the end of the CLARITY.BAS program. QBasic stores character strings in *string variables*, denoted by a dollar sign ($) suffix. The variable named STATE$ in Table 16.1 contains the character string "California", which requires as many bytes (8 bits each) as there are characters stored in the string. The 10 characters in the example shown—California—require 10 bytes of storage.

You can name variables with up to 40 characters. Although you can use a variety of characters in a variable name, the very first character must be a letter.

It can be quite helpful to assign meaningful names to variables. These names are then known as *self-documenting variable names*. Using such names, as has been done in the CLARITY.BAS program, makes a program easier to read and understand. The only weakness to this naming convention is the extra time required to type longer variable names. But do it anyway; the benefit of added readability will be worth the effort.

Inputting Data into Your Program

The third line of the CLARITY.BAS program shows the primary command necessary for obtaining values to store into variable locations:

```
INPUT "Enter filename: "; name$
```

The **INPUT** statement causes QBasic to display the prompting message that appears within quotation marks, followed by a question mark:

```
Enter filename: ?
```

QBasic displays a question mark because of the semicolon in the instruction line. If you do not wish a question mark to appear after your prompting message, use a comma instead of the semicolon. In either case the program then waits until a user types a file name; it can be any valid path name to a desired text file the user wishes this program to analyze. The string of characters the user types in is stored in the string variable *name$* and is later used by other instructions in the CLARITY.BAS program.

You can prompt a user for several values on the same line by listing the variable names on a single INPUT line. For example, if your program contains this statement:

```
INPUT "Please type ID and salary: ", ID%, SAL!
```

then the INPUT statement waits for two numbers to be entered, separated by a comma. If the user fails to enter the correct sequence of data items (corresponding in both number and type to the variable names in the INPUT statement), then QBasic displays the message

```
Redo from start
```

The same prompting string is redisplayed and you get another chance to enter the expected input values. The program will continue to the next instruction line only when you have correctly entered values for each variable name contained in the INPUT statement.

Exploring Other Input Techniques

There are other techniques for storing values into QBasic variables. In this section, you'll look briefly at these alternatives to discover if any of them are more appropriate to your specific applications.

Initializing Variables

Some data values are known before you begin a program. For example, a table of constant values may be used repeatedly in a series of calculations.

You can preset the entire series of data values into a program with **DATA** statements. After creating a list of values with one or more DATA statements, you can use a QBasic **READ** statement to read values from the list. In effect, you can store known values into specific variable names whenever you like; you don't have to use an **INPUT** statement to obtain the value from a user.

For example, suppose that your program is designed to compute employee vacation-time accrual. You will need the INPUT statement to acquire an employee's ID and the hours worked. But you can rely on the DATA statement to preset a fixed set of vacation accrual rates. Assuming that your company offers three different rates (i.e., two, three, or four weeks per year, according to seniority), you could use the DATA and READ statements in combination to initialize several variables such as *vacation1%*, *vacation2%*, and *vacation3%* with the appropriate rates.

You can insert DATA statements anywhere in a program, although the best place to write them is just ahead of the READ statement(s) that will reference them. For example, this DATA statement prepares the three data values in terms of hours (at 40 hours per week):

```
DATA 80, 120, 160
```

Your program would then require one READ statement to initialize the three variables, with no need to pause for intervention by you to type in values:

```
READ vacation1%, vacation2%, vacation3%
```

If the accrual table changes at some point in the future, you only need to change the DATA statement but none of the remaining program instructions. These three variables are called *symbolic constants*, because they stand for constant values that will not change during the execution of the program.

Sometimes your program may require a large table of preset values. For these times, QBasic offers another special feature called *arrays*.

Using Groups of Variables in Arrays

An *array* is a group of similarly named variables that are to be used for almost the same purpose. Each variable can be uniquely identified by a position number (rather than a unique name). This identifying number is called a *subscript*. Suppose you ran a European company that hired American, Dutch, and Austrian employees. Vacation time might involve a range of accrual rates, from two weeks (80 hours) per year to nine weeks (360 hours) per year, with some rates involving half-weeks.

To handle the rates that contain fractional amounts, you will have to use a single-precision **!** suffix. You can create a *vacation!* array, containing enough memory space for all the rates, by including a **DIM** (dimension) statement at the beginning of your program:

```
DIM vacation!(15)
```

The following list shows how the array of possible accrual rates is stored in the variables whose names are *vacation!(1)*, *vacation!(2)*, *vacation!(3)*, and so on:

NAME OF VARIABLE	STORED VALUE
vacation!(1)	2.0
vacation!(2)	2.5
vacation!(3)	3.0
vacation!(4)	3.5
vacation!(5)	4.0
vacation!(6)	4.5
vacation!(7)	5.0
vacation!(8)	5.5
vacation!(9)	6.0
vacation!(10)	6.5
vacation!(11)	7.0
vacation!(12)	7.5
vacation!(13)	8.0
vacation!(14)	8.5
vacation!(15)	9.0

Your program might include multiple **DATA** statements which look like:

```
DATA 2.0, 2.5, 3.0, 3.5, 4.0, 4.5, 5.0
DATA 5.5, 6.0, 6.5, 7.0, 7.5, 8.0, 9.0
```

You can then use several **READ** statements to move the values into the vacation! array:

```
READ vacation!(1), vacation!(2), vacation!(3)
READ vacation!(4), vacation!(5), vacation!(6)
READ vacation!(7), vacation!(8), vacation!(9)
READ vacation!(10), vacation!(11), vacation!(12)
READ vacation!(13), vacation!(14), vacation!(15)
```

Then, at any subsequent point in your program, you can reference individual array values by using the array name followed by the subscript contained within parentheses. Whenever your program contains multiple DATA statements, each of the values listed can be quickly read in order by successive READ statements.

Inputting Characters

In cases where a fixed number of characters is required, you can use the **INPUT$** function such as you see in CLARITY.BAS for reading one character at a time from a file.

```
onechar$ = INPUT$(1, #1)
```

Many applications require typed input from a user. Without the second (**#1**) parameter above, the INPUT$ function would accept input directly from the keyboard. If your program wanted to accept keyboard input of exactly four characters for a *PASSWORD$* variable, you would write this instruction:

```
password$ = INPUT$(4)
```

At other times, you may need to read an unknown number of characters, such as the short or long name of a file. For this, you'll use the **INPUT** command with a string variable, which is also seen in CLARITY.BAS:

```
INPUT "Enter filename: "; name$
```

All characters typed in response to the prompt are stored in the *name$* string variable, however many there are until the Enter key is pressed. But remember that an INPUT statement can also accept several separate values on a single line by simply including punctuation separators between the values.

A comma is the most common punctuation mark used to separate multiple entries on a single line. However, you should only use it when you have instructed QBasic to accept multiple values with a single INPUT command. Otherwise, QBasic will redisplay the prompt string that is in quotation marks in the command, and instruct you to

```
Redo from start
```

Yet another input mechanism is the **LINE INPUT** statement. Use this whenever your program must accept an entire line of input characters, without regard to the meaning or placement of the characters or punctuation. With this command, you name a single string variable to receive all typed characters leading up to the Enter key.

Using Variables during Processing

In general, a computer program takes data in, applies some sort of logic to it, and outputs meaningful results. In this section, you'll explore the most common methods used for processing your data.

Performing Arithmetic Calculations

A QBasic *operator* is any symbol that stands for a particular action. For example, division is an action, and the QBasic operator for it is a slash (*/*). If you place the */* between two variable names, you have defined each of those two variables as *operands*. An *expression* is a group of operators and operands in one instruction line that produces a single resulting value. The following are examples of expressions:

```
length% = 0
answer& = 5 * A + 67
words% = words% + 1
months% = 12 * (years2 - years1)
averagefogcount% = fogcount% / sentences%
```

Each of these lines is called an *assignment* statement. On the right side of the equals sign are different numeric expressions that result in single numeric value. After the right side of the expression is computed by QBasic, the resulting value is stored into the variable name specified on the left side of the statement.

In the first expression, the variable *length%* is assigned the value *0*. There are four such statements near the beginning of the CLARITY.BAS program; they are sometimes called *initialization statements*, because they explicitly initialize variables to startup values.

In the second statement above, the variable *answer&* is assigned the value that results when QBasic multiplies by 5 the value stored in a variable named *A*, then adds 67. In the third statement, the current value found in *words%* is incremented by 1. This computed sum is then stored into the very same variable location known as *word%*, replacing the previous value.

The fourth expression demonstrates the importance of parentheses in arranging the order, or *precedence*, of calculation. In complex expressions, there are sometimes subexpressions contained within parentheses. These subexpressions are always calculated first. In this example, *years2—years1* is calculated first, then that intermediate result is multiplied by 12 to obtain the final value, which will be stored in the variable *months%*.

The last expression shows how intermediate program results (such as the values for *fogcount%* and *sentences%*) can be used in other computations (such as this division) to produce the main program's resulting number.

QBasic includes the standard as well as some special operators. Table 16.2 lists all the allowable arithmetic operators.

TABLE 16.2: Arithmetic operators in order of precedence

OPERATOR	PROCESSING TASK
()	Grouping
^	Exponentiation
–	Negation
* or /	Multiplication or Division
\	Integer Division
MOD	Modulo Calculation (returns the remainder of an Integer Division)
+ or –	Addition or Subtraction

When expressions become complicated, it is crucial to understand the order in which the operations are performed. The order (sometimes called hierarchy or precedence), determines which possible answer is really correct. For example, what value will be stored in *answer* after the following statement is interpreted by QBasic?

```
answer = 2 * 3 + 2 ^ 3
```

There are a number of possible answers, depending on the order you apply the arithmetic operators (multiplication, addition, and exponentiation) but QBasic would calculate an answer of 14. If you do not include any parentheses to separate subexpressions, forcing QBasic to evaluate them first, QBasic performs operations in the order suggested by Table 16.2. Operators found at a higher position in this table are computed first. In this simple example, the final value of 14 results because the exponentiation is performed first (2^3=8), the multiplication is performed next (2*3=6), and the addition is performed last (6+8=14).

Using Logical Expressions

As you will discover later in this chapter, QBasic programs do not always process each statement in the order it appears in the program. The actual order in which program statements are executed is called the *flow of control*. In order to set or determine this order, you will use special logical and relational operators. With these, you can construct special expressions that manage decision-making, looping, and multiple-choice program actions such as selection from menus.

A *logical expression* is one that evaluates to a TRUE or FALSE value. Using such expressions, you can control whether certain program statements execute. For example, you might want to produce a special message if an employee's vacation accrual exceeds 600 hours. You might construct the following logical expression:

```
accrued! > 600
```

This expression has a value of TRUE if *accrued!* is greater than 600, or FALSE if *accrued!* is less than or equal to 600. Each operand is numeric, but the net effect is logical. This happens because the two operands are connected by a *relational operator* (the *greater than* symbol, >). This type of operator (and the other relational operators listed in Table 16.3) enables you to relate or compare two variables, values, or expressions.

In a single expression, relational operators are processed after arithmetic operators. Consequently, arithmetic computations are performed first, followed by any relational operators to compare the intermediate arithmetic values. One final logical value results, which is then used to control the next execution step to be taken by the program. You'll see shortly how CLARITY.BAS uses these logical techniques to control the calculation of the Fog Count.

TABLE 16.3: Relational operators

OPERATOR	PROCESSING TASK
=	Equal To
>	Greater Than
<	Less Than
<>	Not Equal To
>=	Greater Than or Equal To
<=	Less Than or Equal To

► **EXTRA!**

Formatting Your Screen and Your Printed Output

Once your program completes its processing tasks, it is typically up to the **PRINT** command to output the results. This command can direct output to the screen, to a printer, to a file, or even out through one of your hardware ports. Let's take a look at the most common procedure of sending output to your video monitor.

PRINT will display on the screen the values contained in any variable names you specify. For example, if *words%* contains the number of words found in a text file, you could display this number on the next available output-screen line by executing:

```
PRINT words%
```

It's common to erase the screen first with a **CLS** statement prior to outputting any information with one or more PRINT commands. The output will then appear on successive screen lines.

Your video monitor is organized into rows and columns, with rows numbered from top to bottom and columns numbered from left to right. The exact number of rows and columns depends on the resolution of your monitor and display adapter, as well as on what **SCREEN** mode you've selected.

If you wish to print your output results in a highly formatted way, you can use the **LOCATE** command for precise row and column position control. This statement enables you to place the cursor at a specific screen position. Output from the next PRINT statement will begin at that position. For example, if you wanted to position the final output information on line 15 of the screen, beginning at column 30, you would insert a LOCATE command before the final PRINT statement:

```
LOCATE 15, 30
PRINT "Average fog count is "; averagefogcount%
```

Managing the Flow of Control

Most non-trivial computer programs do not follow the same series of steps each time the program is run. Even though the instruction lines are written one after the other, the order in which those lines are executed (i.e., the *flow of control*) is often different.

Most textual QBasic statements fit on one program line. However, other statements exist that take up multiple lines; they are called *compound statements*. When used in your programs, as you'll now discover, these compound statements enable your code to manage unattended decision-making and repetition of instructions. All compound statements control the flow of execution after evaluating the value of some expression, usually a logical one.

IF statements and **CASE** statements enable your program to decide which of several groups of statements, called *statement blocks*, should execute. The IF statement is the most common and popular of these; IF statements manage simple decision-making in a program. The CASE statement offers a concise mechanism for managing multiple-choice decisions in a program. Lastly, when a block of statements must be repeated a number of times, the **DO** command is usually called upon.

Making Decisions Automatically

An **IF** statement enables you to change the normal line-by-line order of instruction execution. For example, in the middle of the CLARITY.BAS program, you'll find this example of an IF statement:

```
IF length% > 7 THEN
   fogcount% = fogcount% +3
ELSE
   fogcount% = fogcount% +1
END IF
```

This is known as an *either/or* decision. The general form of such a statement is:

```
IF condition THEN
    StatementBlock1
ELSE
    StatementBlock2
END IF
```

This compound statement first evaluates the condition. If it is true, then all statements following the word **THEN** and preceding the word **ELSE** are executed. If the condition is false, then all statements following the word ELSE and preceding the word **END** are executed. In this example, the condition determines whether the length of a word in a sentence exceeds seven characters (*length% > 7*).

The program builds up a Fog Count for each sentence by adding a value of 1 for each word, unless the word is too big. Long words (those with more than seven letters) add a value of three units to the overall Fog Count. The **IF** statement controls which assignment statement the program actually executes. For small words, the program executes the assignment statement that adds 1 to the running Fog Count. For long words, the program executes the assignment statement that adds 3 to the running Fog Count. The assumption here is that long words make your writing "foggier" and more difficult for an average reader to understand.

QBasic does not require you to indent statement blocks within compound statements, but it is good programming practice. Because it calls attention to the changing flow of control, it becomes easier to see the compound statement and to see which statements make up each statement block. It is, furthermore, easier to understand the statement block's effects since the key words appear one above the other.

Indentation becomes even more important when blocks contain multiple statements, or when one compound statement appears within another. Looking closely at CLARITY.BAS, you can see that the **IF** statement is actually contained within a **CASE** statement, which itself is contained within a **DO** statement. Let's take a look at these other flow-of-control statements now.

Controlling Multi-Way Decision-Making

A **CASE** statement is quite useful in situations where a condition takes on multiple values. Just as an **IF** statement begins with the word IF and ends with the line **END IF**, so does a CASE statement begin with the two-word phrase **SELECT CASE** and end with the line **END SELECT**. Although you can construct a series of IF statements, sometimes one within another, to perform the same overall processing chore as a CASE statement, the SELECT CASE is usually simpler to construct and easier to read.

In CLARITY.BAS, you can see an example of this type of compound statement:

```
SELECT CASE onechar$
   CASE ";", ",", ":", CHR$(10)
   CASE "."
      sentences% = sentences% + 1
   CASE " ", CHR$(13)
      words% = words% + 1
      IF length% > 7 THEN
         fogcount% = fogcount% + 3
      ELSE
         fogcount% = fogcount% + 1
      END IF
      length% = 0
   CASE ELSE
      length% = length% + 1
END SELECT
```

The first statement defines how and when each specific CASE will be selected and executed. There is no limit to how many separate blocks of instructions can be selected with this type of compound statement. The value of the variable *onechar$* determines which of the four CASE blocks in this example will be executed. If the character input into the program is a semicolon, a comma, a colon, or a line feed—the CHR$(10) code—then no action is taken at all: as you can see, there are no statements to execute between the first CASE line and the next. If the character read from the target file is not one of these first four listed, then the next CASE statement is checked. If the character read is a period, then the statements within the next CASE are activated. As it turns out, this amounts to the single instruction

```
sentences% = sentences% + 1
```

and this instruction is executed.

If the *onechar$* variable contains a blank space or a carriage return—the CHR$(13) code—then the third CASE is activated and the statements within it are executed. When this occurs, the program assumes that a word is complete. The subsequent three-statement block executes:

```
words% = words% + 1            (Statement 1)

If length% > 7 THEN            (Statement 2)

   fogcount% = fogcount% + 3

ELSE

   fogcount% = fogcount % + 1

END IF

length% = 0                    (Statement 3)
```

The first and third statements in this statement block are assignment statements (to the variables *words%* and *length%*), while the second statement is the compound IF statement that you just studied.

The final CASE is unique; the last statement block begins with a **CASE ELSE** clause designed to handle all other possibilities. You should always write such a clause so that your program proceeds under your control, no matter what conditions exist. Any other character is assumed to be part of the word that is being processed, so the word's length is incremented by 1 before the next character from the file is read.

Repeating Blocks of Code

QBasic offers the **DO** command for repeating groups of instructions. With minor variations, it can be used to construct several different kinds of *loops* that repeat one or more instructions. First, you can determine beforehand the number of times it will repeat a block of statements. Second, you can use it to access data in a file, then execute a block of instructions a varying number of times depending on the size of the file. Third, in the most general case, you can repeat the loop a varying number of times, the number of repetitions depending on a repeatedly evaluated logical expression that is based on the data itself.

CLARITY.BAS demonstrates one of these uses of the DO instruction. Figure 16.16 shows the complete extent of the loop in the program code.

The general form of this version of the DO loop is

```
DO
    StatementBlock
LOOP UNTIL condition
```

Although there are several variations on the DO command in QBasic, I'll explain only this one technique. You can refer to your QBasic documentation for further details on the other versions of the DO command. As you can see in Figure 16.16, there are two principal statements contained within the DO statement:

1. The **INPUT$** line in which a character is read from the file and stored in the *onechar%* variable

FIGURE 16.16

You should use the **DO LOOP UNTIL** construction seen here to repeat code until a condition becomes TRUE. The condition used here is a special one which only becomes true when the processing reaches the end of the data file.

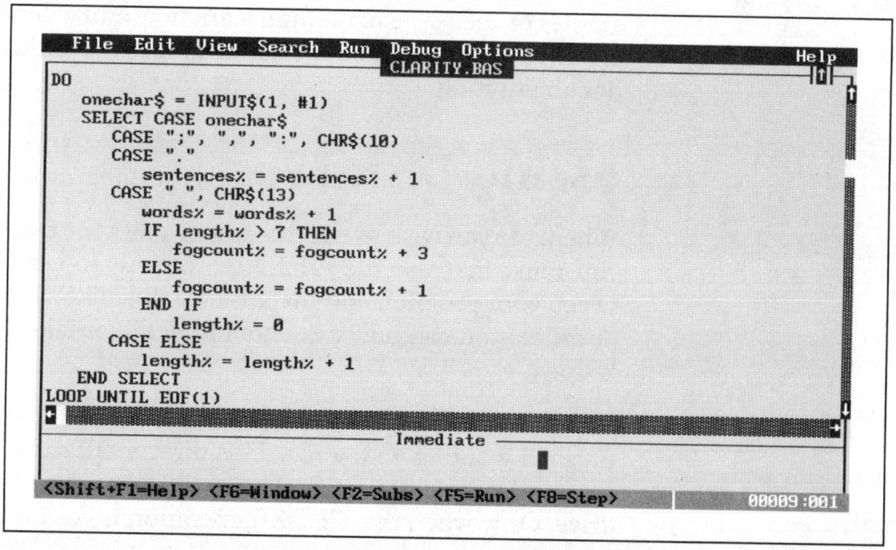

```
 File  Edit  View  Search  Run  Debug  Options                    Help
                              CLARITY.BAS
 DO
     onechar$ = INPUT$(1, #1)
     SELECT CASE onechar$
         CASE ";", ",", ":", CHR$(10)
         CASE "."
             sentences% = sentences% + 1
         CASE " ", CHR$(13)
             words% = words% + 1
             IF length% > 7 THEN
                 fogcount% = fogcount% + 3
             ELSE
                 fogcount% = fogcount% + 1
             END IF
             length% = 0
         CASE ELSE
             length% = length% + 1
     END SELECT
 LOOP UNTIL EOF(1)

                              Immediate

 <Shift+F1=Help> <F6=Window> <F2=Subs> <F5=Run> <F8=Step>          00009:001
```

2. The **SELECT CASE** statement in which the word length, number of sentences, and Fog Count are computed

Each of these two statements (one simple assignment and one compound selection) is repeated as many times as there are characters to interpret from the specified text file. The condition that terminates the looping is **EOF(1)**, which is a special function that becomes TRUE when the end-of-file marker is reached on the file that had been **OPEN**ed as #1 earlier in the program. Each time the INPUT$ line reads another character from the file, QBasic automatically adjusts a file-position pointer, moving it closer to the end of the file.

Controlling Input and Output for Files and Devices

QBasic can treat three specific types of data files: unstructured sequential, structured sequential, and random access. In this section, you'll see examples of each type of file, and learn how and when to use them. For more extensive instruction on file applications, you should refer to your QBasic documentation.

Accessing Disk Files

Whenever you wish to use the data in a disk file from within your program, you must first use the **OPEN** command to establish a connection between your program and that disk file. Just like a storage box in your home or office, you can only put data into a file or take data from a file when it is open.

For the same reason, you must use the **CLOSE** command when you have finished working with a file. This directs QBasic to put the text lines still in memory into a specifically named "box," or file, on a specified disk drive. Only when this CLOSE operation is complete can you be sure that intermediate instructions still in memory have been copied, or *flushed*, to the disk.

The OPEN command has this formal syntax:

```
OPEN "filename.ext" FOR OperationType AS #IDnumber
```

As you can see, the command not only opens a file, it assigns it a number. When you use this command in a program (or in the Immediate window), you should of course replace *filename.ext* with the actual name of the file you plan to read from or write to. The *IDnumber* value can be a number of your choosing (from 1 to 255) that has not already been specified to identify another file. The number symbol or pound sign (#) is a required prefix.

You can tell QBasic in advance how you are going to use the file by replacing *OperationType* with one of the following words: **INPUT**, **OUTPUT**, **RANDOM**, **APPEND**, or **BINARY**. For example, you can open the EMPLOYEE.TXT file for the express purpose of reading its textual contents:

```
OPEN "employee.txt" FOR INPUT AS #1
```

INPUT means you only intend to read data from the file; QBasic has less responsibility for setup if it knows it will never have to write any changes out to the file. Similarly, **OUTPUT** means you will be writing data from your program out to the disk and into that file. Both operations treat the data items in the referenced file in successive order. When the file is read or written in this manner, it is known as a *sequential file*.

A sequential file is analogous to an audio tape. When there are several individual songs on the tape, they are recorded one after the other. To listen to the fourth song, you must pass sequentially through each of the first three songs. Similarly, to write or read the fourth data item in a sequential file, you must first write or read the preceding three records.

To understand what it means to open a file for **OUTPUT**, you must extend the tape analogy. If a file that you open for OUTPUT does not already exist on the disk, QBasic creates the file. If it does exist, it "rewinds" the file to the beginning storage position (like the first song on an audio tape). In this way, writing data into a file opened for OUTPUT erases any existing data in the file, just as recording on an audio tape from the beginning records over any existing music.

Sometimes, you will wish to retain existing data in a file, yet add new data to it; at these times, you must open the file with the **APPEND** operation type. This is analogous to fast-forwarding your audio tape to a position just beyond the last song. APPEND essentially fast-forwards a disk file to just beyond whatever data is currently in it. New data can then be written to extend the total amount of file information without erasing any current data; new data is effectively *appended* to the old.

Reading sequentially is not satisfactory for many applications. It can be a slow process, having to wade through predecessor data just to get to the specific piece you want. Many online applications require instant access to individual groups of data (often called *records*). For these types of database management tasks, you need the special operation type of **RANDOM**. This tells QBasic in advance that you intend to access records anywhere in the file for both reading and writing without having to pass through any intermediate records.

The preceding methods are used for text files. The last operation type, **BINARY**, is used for non-ASCII files such as .EXE or .COM files. BINARY permits your program to read or write individual bytes of the file.

When your program is finished accessing a file, it should quickly issue a command to close the file, using the same ID number with which the file was opened:

```
CLOSE #IDnumber
```

As soon as you close a file (particularly one that was opened for writing to), you are assured that intermediate data in memory is successfully written out to the file. The longer your program waits to close a file, the more likely it is that a power failure will cause you to lose a portion of your data. The CLARITY.BAS program does not update the file it opens; it only reads the text within the file and analyzes it, so closing the file immediately after working with it is not overly important. Indeed, QBasic automatically closes any open file when your program completes.

Using QBasic's File Types

QBasic offers three common types of files for your application purposes. In this section, you'll learn which one to use for your particular applications.

Using Unstructured Sequential Files

The CLARITY.BAS program analyzes text files by counting words and sentences, then computing a Fog Count based on the readability of your writing. In this particular program, the **INPUT$** function reads one character at a time. A space character denotes the end of a word, and a period character denotes the end of a sentence.

You can process any ASCII text file with this technique. In fact, by using a type of interpretation called *parsing*, QBasic interprets your instruction lines in a manner similar to the way CLARITY.BAS interprets your text lines. Naturally, QBasic interprets your characters quite differently than CLARITY.BAS does, assessing each specific word in your text file to determine what action is to be taken (based on whether it is a keyword, a variable, a function, and so on).

The disk file for this book is an example of an *unstructured sequential file*. There is a series of consecutive chapters of no specific length, themselves made up of a series of paragraphs of no specific length, each of which is ended by the control characters for a carriage return and line feed (CR-LF). If there is a space (an extra line feed) between paragraphs, CLARITY.BAS considers it to be a paragraph that contains no sentences. A section title is considered a paragraph that contains one sentence.

In programming language, each group of characters leading up to a CR-LF pair is formally called a *record*. In the files we have worked with so far in this chapter, the records could be any length, even zero. (A blank paragraph between normal paragraphs is called an *empty string*, or a *null record*.) Text files with variable-length records are called *unstructured*, or *free-form*. An even more common example of an unstructured file is the MAIL.LST file seen in Figure 16.17.

FIGURE 16.17

An unstructured
sequential file contains
data fields that are
usually separated by
commas and
character strings that
are surrounded by
quotation marks.
There is no columnar
alignment, the
distinction between
fields being made by
the commas and
quotes, which are
examples of field
delimiters or
separators.

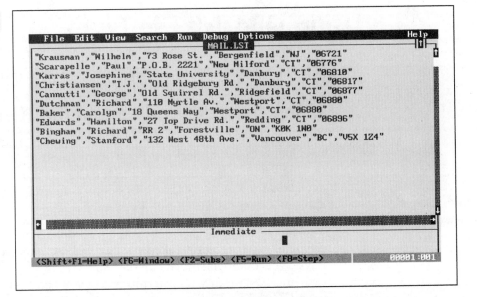

This file contains a series of unstructured records containing name and address information. Since the entries are all of variable length, the overall width of each record line is different. In this type of unstructured file, individual data items, or *fields*, are made distinct from one another by using delimiter characters. For instance, a comma delimits each field from its neighbor, while quotation marks distinguish string values.

QBasic's **INPUT** statement is appropriate to use for *reading* simple data files like the MAIL.LST file. INPUT allows you to specify individual field names to read; it then scans each line for punctuation and extracts each numeric or string value. To *create* an unstructured sequential file from QBasic, you can use the **PRINT** or **WRITE** statements. With PRINT, the output data is *zoned*; that is, each output value is stored in fixed-width portions of the output line. While this creates output that looks neat, you may actually want your output to contain commas between each field, with quotation marks around each string value. To do this, simply use WRITE instead of PRINT as your output statement. Many word-processing mail-merge applications require data to be written in this latter format.

Using Structured Sequential Files

A structured file, such as the one in Figure 16.18, contains fixed-width records that each contain the same number of characters. In such a file, each field in each record occupies a known position and has a known width. The **LINE INPUT** command can easily read an entire record at once, reading all the characters up to the CR-LF. Because all individual fields are assumed to be strings of characters, even fields that are intended to be used as numbers, you must use QBasic's **MID$** function to extract individual field values, and, when necessary, the **VAL** function to convert any desired strings to numeric values.

Relational database management systems store data in precisely this type of easily understood columnar format. However, you can still only read or write a QBasic sequential file in sequence. As with the audio tape analogy, records can only be accessed by passing over each preceding record in the file.

Using Random-Access Files

When you open a file for **RANDOM** access, you are using QBasic's most flexible and powerful form of file access. You can read or write any record

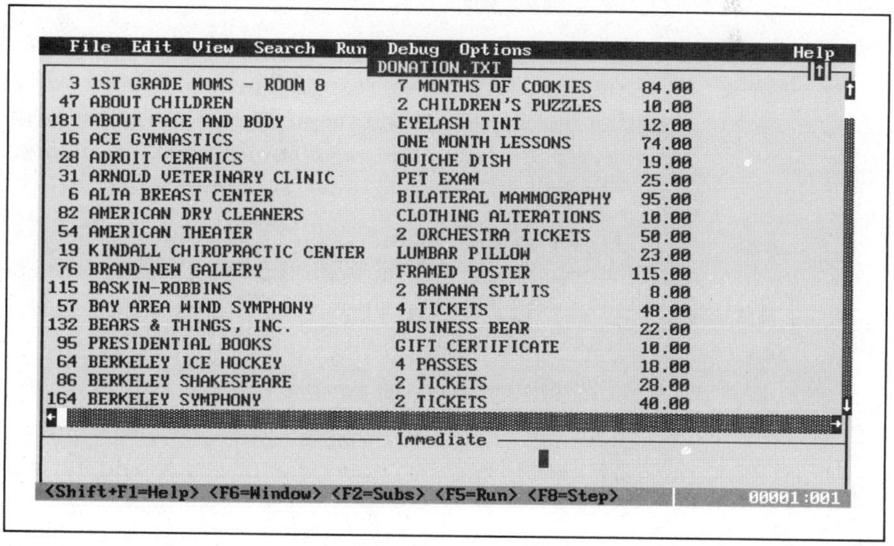

FIGURE 16.18

A structured sequential file displays an easy-to-understand columnar alignment. Separate fields are defined by position in each row, or record. All sequential files contain data that is read or written in order, one after the other.

```
 File  Edit  View  Search  Run  Debug  Options                    Help
                           DONATION.TXT
    3 1ST GRADE MOMS - ROOM 8        7 MONTHS OF COOKIES    84.00
   47 ABOUT CHILDREN                 2 CHILDREN'S PUZZLES    10.00
  181 ABOUT FACE AND BODY            EYELASH TINT            12.00
   16 ACE GYMNASTICS                 ONE MONTH LESSONS       74.00
   28 ADROIT CERAMICS                QUICHE DISH             19.00
   31 ARNOLD VETERINARY CLINIC       PET EXAM                25.00
    6 ALTA BREAST CENTER             BILATERAL MAMMOGRAPHY   95.00
   82 AMERICAN DRY CLEANERS          CLOTHING ALTERATIONS    10.00
   54 AMERICAN THEATER               2 ORCHESTRA TICKETS     50.00
   19 KINDALL CHIROPRACTIC CENTER    LUMBAR PILLOW           23.00
   76 BRAND-NEW GALLERY              FRAMED POSTER          115.00
  115 BASKIN-ROBBINS                 2 BANANA SPLITS          8.00
   57 BAY AREA WIND SYMPHONY         4 TICKETS               48.00
  132 BEARS & THINGS, INC.           BUSINESS BEAR           22.00
   95 PRESIDENTIAL BOOKS             GIFT CERTIFICATE        10.00
   64 BERKELEY ICE HOCKEY            4 PASSES                10.00
   86 BERKELEY SHAKESPEARE           2 TICKETS               28.00
  164 BERKELEY SYMPHONY              2 TICKETS               40.00
                                  Immediate

 <Shift+F1=Help> <F6=Window> <F2=Subs> <F5=Run> <F8=Step>        00001:001
```

in the file, and you can do so in whatever order you need. Furthermore, with a few advanced techniques, you can address specific fields within each record. From the user's point of view, a random-access file might look exactly like the DONATION.TXT file seen in Figure 16.18. However, the storage mechanism and the access commands are different.

When you set up a random-access file, each record is made up of a group of named field values. In this example, a single record has values for the donor's ID, the donor's name, the donation, and the value. Each record consumes one row in this file, and QBasic assigns each row a number based on its relative position in the file. For instance, the assigned number for Ace Gymnastics is 4.

QBasic provides a special command mechanism for referencing individual field values in random-access file rows. It is called a *user-defined type*. Unlike simple data types like **INTEGER** or **STRING**, a user-defined type is a complex grouping of simpler types. For instance, the following TYPE command precisely defines the record seen in the DONATION.TXT file as a *Donate* type, comprising various field types:

```
TYPE Donate
ID AS INTEGER
Donor AS STRING * 30
Donation AS STRING * 24
Cost AS SINGLE
END TYPE
```

A **TYPE** statement only defines the nature of the data to be stored in a random-access file's record. The first field (the *ID*) in every record of this file is defined as a simple integer. The last field (the *Cost*) is defined as a single-precision floating-point number. The two text columns in between are defined as string values of different lengths.

So far in this chapter, you've seen how variables are used to reference simple types of data. With the more complex user-defined types that are necessary for random-access file data, you must use a **DIM** statement, which defines a special program variable. For example,

```
DIM Eachline AS Donate
```

specifies that your program will use a variable named *Eachline* of type *Donate*. In order to now reference each field in a particular *Donate* record, you must combine the variable name, a period, and the field name. For example, after randomly reading an entire row from the file into the program variable *Eachline*, you can reference individual fields with these expressions:

```
Eachline.ID
Eachline.Donor
Eachline.Donation
Eachline.Cost
```

Figure 16.19 demonstrates how complex variables and user-defined types relate to one another.

The user-defined type (*Donate*) represents the structure of every record in the file. The TYPE statement specifies that the name *Donate* is to be used when defining new complex variables of this user-defined type. The *Donate* data type contains the field names themselves, as well as the size of each field. Each variable in your program that you DIMension to be of this type will actually contain the data that will be manipulated by the program. What all this means is that you do not use a *type* as a storage variable. You must create your own special variables by using the DIM statement. Each new variable has parts, and is created in the image of the TYPE you select. Only after defining a TYPE, then creating (with DIM) a variable of that type can you begin to store and manipulate data in the variables created with DIM.

With random-access files in QBasic, you can write programs that perform the standard chores of any database management system.

FIGURE 16.19

User-defined types are constructed from groups of simpler variables. This allows a simple reference to the special type, which is itself seen as complex because it contains several distinct and separate variables.

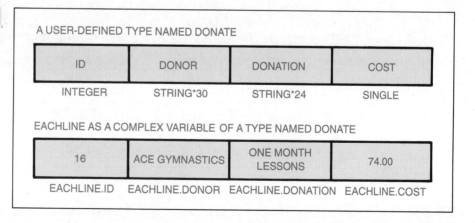

➤ EXTRA!

What Are the Trade-offs between File Types?

Both sequential and random files enjoy their own advantages and disadvantages. You must first understand your application to decide the file type that is best to use. Sequential-access files are best when your data consists of variable-length records. Such files make more efficient use of disk space, since no unnecessary trailing blanks appear after any field values. Sequential files are also useful for historical-type data, data that is rarely changed and infrequently accessed.

Since sequential files are easier and quicker to deal with, not requiring **TYPE**s and **DIM**ensions as do random-access files, you should use them for "quick and dirty" applications that demand fast answers, and that do not require frequent reuse of the program that you write. Using a sequential file saves the time normally required to design and prepare the field structure of a random-access file, and to write the code that references the more complex variable references.

By contrast, you should use random-access techniques for applications that require rapid access to any record in the file. This includes frequent deletions, insertions, or even just simple accesses for display purposes. QBasic accesses random-access files in a manner that consumes less system time than that required by a sequential file.

In addition, if your application requires frequent updating of records, you should use **RANDOM** to provide both reading and writing support. In particular, if you must sort the stored records frequently, a random-access technique will save considerable system time.

Creating Graphic Output

Graphic output is a powerful alternative way to provide the information you might otherwise output with a **PRINT** statement. QBasic provides commands ranging from instructions for drawing individual points to sequences for animating figures for games. We'll concentrate here on the more common techniques of line, circle, and bar drawing.

In text mode on your video monitor, you are(usually) limited to a grid of 25 rows by 80 lines. Graphic output can be much more precise than this, since a graphic image can use all of the possible dots on your screen. Each screen dot is called a *pixel*, and unique graphic shapes are created by turning on or off a different set of these pixels. Some of the commands to turn on a particular screen pixel can also have a color associated with them. Consequently, you can control both the color and the shape of graphic images from QBasic.

The number of pixels on each screen differs, depending on both your monitor and your computer system's video adapter. Before executing any graphic instructions, you must use the **SCREEN** command to tell QBasic your computer's combination of monitor and adapter:

SCREEN *mode*

The *mode* parameter (you type a number to replace *mode*) specifies one of several adapter/monitor alternatives. The default, mode **0**, supports only text output; consequently, none of the graphic commands presented in this chapter will work unless you precede them with a SCREEN statement. Table 16.4 summarizes the more common possibilities.

Screen mode 12 (VGA) is one of the most common graphic modes, since it supports both the 25x80 text format and the common 640x480 graphic layout. Virtually all programs that provide any graphic output at all support these formats, so you can probably use screen mode 12 no matter what type of graphic monitor/adapter you have on your system.

TABLE 16.4: Mode values for video screen/adapter combinations

MODE	GRAPHICS	TEXT
0 (the default)	None	{40 or 80} x {25, 43, or 50}
1	320x200 CGA, EGA, VGA, or MCGA	40x25
2	640x200 CGA, EGA, VGA, or MCGA	80x25
3	720x348 monochrome, Hercules graphics	80x25
4	640x400 graphics	80x25
7	320x200 EGA or VGA	40x25
8	640x200 EGA or VGA	80x25
9	640x350 EGA or VGA	80x{25 or 43} text
10	640x350 EGA or VGA, monochrome only	80x{25 or 43} text
11	640x480 VGA or MCGA	80x{30 or 60}
12	640x480 VGA only (increased color control)	80x{30 or 60}
13	320x200 VGA or MCGA	40x25

Graphic output assumes a coordinate grid. Points on a graphic screen are located by a pair of values, known as an *(x,y) pair*. As you can see in Figure 16.20, the first value in the pair specifies how many pixels across the screen, and the second value specifies how many pixels down the screen. Regardless of which video mode you select, the starting position for the upper left corner of the screen is always (0,0). A given (x,y) pair identifies a unique screen pixel (which, depending on the resolution of your screen, might appear to be at a different place on the screen).

FIGURE 16.20

QBasic's graphic coordinate grid can individually access each pixel on your screen. Depending on your video mode, controlled by the **SCREEN** command, the number of horizontal and vertical pixels differs. Seen here are the values for the common 640x480 VGA display.

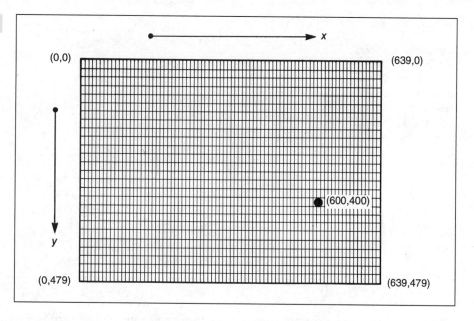

Drawing Lines and Rectangles

Line graphs and bar charts are common mechanisms for presenting business and scientific data. The **LINE** command enables you to quickly draw a single line or a solid rectangle between any two points on your screen. The simplest form of the command is

```
LINE (x1, y1) - (x2, y2)
```

The first (*x1,y1*) pair of values represents the grid position of the starting point of the line segment, while the second (*x2,y2*) pair of values represents the ending point of the line segment. For example, the following LINE command draws a line (as seen at the left side of Figure 16.21) on the screen from point (50,50) to point (150,150), which is located 100 pixels to the right and 100 pixels below the starting point.

```
LINE (50, 50) - (150, 150)
```

To draw a line graph, you only need to draw a continuous sequence of lines with multiple LINE statements. Each succeeding LINE statement

FIGURE 16.21

Generating graphics in QBasic is simple. The **LINE** and **CIRCLE** commands are your means to create more complex and colorful screen effects and images.

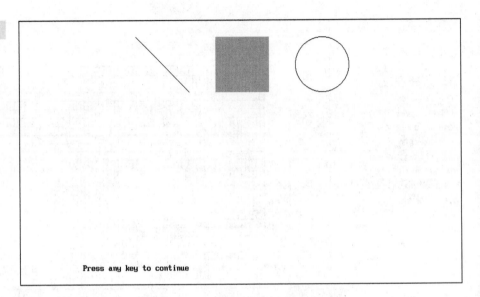

```
Press any key to continue
```

should have its starting (x,y) pair be the same as the ending (x,y) pair of the preceding line segment.

A LINE statement can do more than just draw simple lines. The LINE statement has an additional form:

```
LINE (x1, y1) - (x2, y2), color, {B|BF}, style
```

This version of LINE creates filled or unfilled screen boxes—**B** for a simple box, **BF** for a box filled in color. (The vertical bar in the brackets shows that you can use either B or BF but not both.) The command creates the box using any color supported by your monitor, and any of several styles (i.e., dashed, dotted, and combinations of both) for the lines.

The following version of LINE creates a rectangle on the screen, using the two (x,y) pairs as opposite corners of the rectangle. For example, you can generate the solid rectangle seen in the center of Figure 16.21 with this statement:

```
LINE (250, 50) - (350, 150), 3, BF
```

In this example rectangle, **BF** was specified to direct QBasic to create a box filled with color 3 on my monitor.

TIP

You can now create bar charts with QBasic data by constructing a series of LINE commands with the proper rectangular corner values.

By switching from text to graphic mode and back again, you can output text as well as graphics on the same screen. By using colors within boxes before outputting actual graphic or text data to the screen, you can visually highlight individual screen "windows" prior to putting information (graphic or text) into the box.

Drawing Circles

Circles are another common graphic output. The most common use of circles is in creating pie charts for representing numerical data. To draw a circle on your screen, you must first define an (x,y) point to serve as the center of the circle. Next, you can specify the radius of the circle, which represents all the points on the screen located at a fixed distance from the center. For simple circles, that's all you need:

```
CIRCLE (x, y), radius
```

For example, the circle in Figure 16.22 was centered at position (450,100) and has a radius of 50 units. It was drawn using this command:

```
CIRCLE (450, 100), 50
```

An *arc* is any portion of a circle's periphery. From basic geometry, we know that a circular arc can be precisely represented by first noting the center and radius of the circle on which it is located, then identifying a starting and ending angle. Figure 16.22 depicts this aspect of circles.

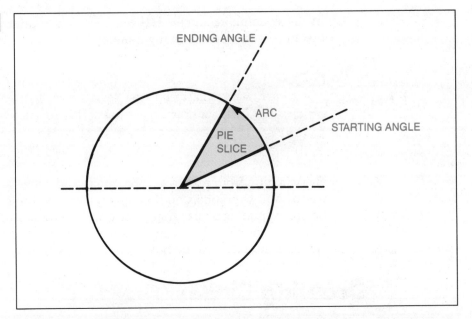

Understanding arcs is necessary when you wish to represent data as slices in a circular pie. A pie slice, or wedge, is usually quite obvious: graphically, it consists of the screened area in Figure 16.22, which is bordered by two radius lines and the arc connecting them. The radius lines are drawn from the center of the circle to the beginning and ending points of the arc.

The **CIRCLE** command allows additional parameters with which you can specify color for the circle and whether to draw just the arcs or pie slices rather than the entire circle. The syntax for drawing arcs is:

```
CIRCLE (x, y), radius, {color}, start, end
```

The *color* parameter is optional; if you do not set it, you must still include its comma to denote a missing optional parameter. The *start* and *end* angle values require values given in geometric radians. (2 pi radians equals 360 degrees.) In order to draw a pie slice, you simply add a minus sign (or hyphen) before start or end angle. This asks QBasic to draw the radius from the center of the circle to that start or end point. To draw a solid slice, add a minus sign before both the start and the end angles.

Debugging Your Programs

Bugs in QBasic programs are not cute little creatures that creep into your code when you're not looking. They are mistakes which deserve extra effort on your part to avoid. As you debug your programs, you will be part detective and part artist; it is a chore that is partly mechanical and partly creative. But you will find it to be extremely satisfying to make a computer program do what you want, and to figure out exactly how to correct a program that is not working in just the desired way. In this section, you'll first learn some general debugging techniques, then explore specific QBasic tools that are at your disposal.

In general, you can apply these basic debugging techniques immediately:

1. *Think.* Yes, this is the same advice you've heard for years. Think before you go off half-cocked, and spend a moment thinking before you use any of the following debugging techniques. What recent changes have you made to your modules? What is the flow of your program's logic (or illogic)?

2. *Isolate.* Test the program a number of times to determine if the error is consistent (occurring in the same way, given the same inputs). Errors that repeat are easily isolated in your code; intermittent errors are much more difficult. Identify the portions of your program that worked before the bug showed up. By eliminating from consideration all parts of your program that still seem to work correctly, you can focus on a more limited body of instructions.

3. *Desk check.* Read through your program modules, line by line, and interpret for yourself exactly what the program should do when it runs. By understanding each command, and knowing the input data, you can predict the result of each successive instruction. When you run the program, you can more easily identify where the actual result deviates from the predicted one. Setting *Trace On* from the Debug menu can help you to visualize the same process dynamically.

4. *Get help.* A colleague can often identify errors that you repeatedly overlook. Furthermore, when you are forced to explain your instructions to someone else, you will often discover the error yourself, because you have in fact just forced yourself to desk check it again.

5. *Study intermediate results.* During your program's execution, you can look at the values of variables and the intermediate contents of data files. To do this, you can pull down the Debug menu and set breakpoints at critical junctures of your code.

6. *Validate your tests.* Your program may in fact work correctly, but you may be testing it with invalid values.

7. *Go home.* Take a break. Do something else. Give up ... but only until tomorrow. Come back fresh.

In my opinion, debugging is the single most important factor in rapid and effective computer programming. You learn best by actually doing, and when you do something wrong, you usually try to not make the same mistake twice. Learning the **DEBUG** commands and using the choices on the Debug menu are your best ways to gain the most advantage from the natural mistakes you will make while learning QBasic.

Using Debug

The **DEBUG** command utility enables you to write and modify assembly-language programs. It provides a way to run and test any program in a controlled environment: you can change any part of the program and immediately execute the program without having to reassemble it. You can also run machine-language (object) files directly. Programmers often use this DOS tool to make quick program changes, to test variations, and to rapidly isolate errors in assembly-language code.

Once DEBUG begins, you can type a question mark to display a list of all the debugging commands, along with the required command syntax. For your convenience, Table 16.5 provides a brief explanation for each command.

TABLE 16.5: DEBUG commands

COMMAND	EXPLANATION
A	Assembles the instructions at a particular address
C	Compares two memory ranges
D	Displays contents of memory
E	Enters new or modifies old memory contents
F	Fills in a range of memory
G	Executes a program in memory
H	Adds and subtracts two hex values
I	Inputs and displays a byte from a port
L	Loads disk data into memory
M	Copies a range of memory values
N	Names a file to load or create
O	Outputs a byte to a port
P	Proceeds with execution to the next memory instruction
Q	Quits from DEBUG back to DOS
R	Displays (and changes) contents of registers and flags
S	Searches for characters
T	Traces execution of memory code
U	Unassembles hex bytes into assembler instructions
W	Writes memory data to disk
XA	Allocates expanded memory
XD	Deallocates expanded memory
XM	Maps logical pages onto physical ones
XS	Displays expanded memory status

As you'll discover in this section, the DEBUG utility can enable you to powerfully augment your DOS system by writing completely new and uniquely customized commands. The required format is:

[*Drive:Path*]DEBUG < [*FileSpec*] [*Parameters*]

Drive:Path is the drive and path where the command file is located if it is not in the current directory. *FileSpec* is an optional drive and path, including the file name and extension, of the file that is the object of the command. *Parameters* are any optional arguments that are needed in order to run the file indicated by *FileSpec*.

Working with the Debug Menu

The Debug menu (Figure 16.23) contains six choices that can help you to identify and correct program errors.

Choice 1, *Step*, asks QBasic to execute your instructions one at a time, including any instructions grouped into a support procedure, such as a SUB or a FUNCTION. The second choice, *Procedure Step*, enables you to step through main program instructions, but skips over instructions contained

FIGURE 16.23

The Debug menu offers valuable assistance in debugging your programs. Use stepping to slow down execution into understandable chunks. Use tracing to follow the flow of execution. Use breakpoints to temporarily pause execution at key program points in order to explore variable values.

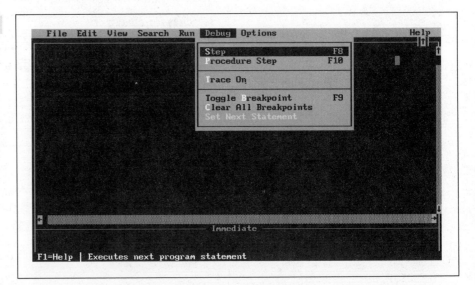

within procedures. This saves you the delay of wading through the instructions of a subordinate procedure once you are sure that it works properly.

Choice 3, *Trace On*, highlights each instruction line as it executes. This enables you to visually follow through your program text and identify the flow of logic as QBasic is actually interpreting it.

The next group of options deal with *breakpoints*. A breakpoint is a point in your program at which you have QBasic pause when the program actually runs. The *Toggle Breakpoint* choice places or removes a breakpoint at the line containing the cursor. When viewing your program text later, a line at which a breakpoint has been set is displayed in reverse video or in a different color combination. The *Clear All Breakpoints* choice is only used after you no longer need any of the currently defined breakpoints.

The final choice, *Set Next Statement*, offers you the option to continue program execution from the current position of the cursor. (Each instruction line is typically called a *statement*.) When you next *Continue* the program's execution, it will begin from the statement you set with this option rather from the point where it was last paused.

Writing .COM Programs with the Debug Utility

This section will provide an introductory glimpse into a valuable special aspect of **DEBUG**—its ability to enable you to produce short, customized, executable .COM files. In particular, I'll show you how to use DEBUG to create a CODESCAN.COM program that will read any keystroke and make it easy for you to test whether or not that key was typed during a batch file's execution.

By common convention, people write short script files (with a .SCR extension) that include all the desired assembler instructions for DEBUG to process. The commands available for DEBUG are shown in Table 16.5.

One of the instructions you include in your script file will usually name the desired .COM file to create. For example, here is my CODE-SCAN.SCR script file:

```
A 100
MOV AH,0
INT 16
MOV AL, AH
MOV AH,4C
INT 21

RCX
A
N CODESCAN.COM
W
Q
```

You can create this text file with any word processor, then specify it as the first parameter in your DEBUG command line:

```
DEBUG < CODESCAN.SCR
```

That's all it takes to instruct the DEBUG utility to create the CODE-SCAN.COM executable file. Let's see how it all happens. Don't be concerned if you don't understand each of the individual instructions in the CODESCAN script file. Most of them are assembler instructions, and some of them are direct DEBUG instructions.

Referring to the script file above, the first instruction is the **A** command, which directs DEBUG to start the created .COM file at address 100H. The next several assembler instructions perform various operating system chores. The **MOV AH,0** instruction prepares for a BIOS read of a single character. The **INT 16** instruction makes the actual operating system request for the byte read. The next **MOV AL,AH** instruction makes the exit code from the program equal to the keyboard hardware-scan code. The **MOV AH,4C** requests an exit from CODESCAN.COM back to the operating system. The **INT 21** call uses the function **4C** that was set up in the preceding MOV command.

There is an intended and required blank line after the INT 21 command and the **RCX** instruction. Be sure to place a blank line in your text file at this point. The RCX instruction obtains the contents of the CX register, and the following **A** represents the length (10 bytes, or A bytes in hexadecimal notation) of this program. The **N** instruction names the

.COM file to create, and the **W** command writes the assembler instructions to that file. Finally, the **Q** command exits from DEBUG.

To see several useful examples of how the CODESCAN.COM program can be incorporated into batch files, you can take a look at some of the sample batch files I've placed in the *EXTRA!* sidebars throughout this book. For example, you can read the PASSWORD.BAT file in a Chapter 1 *EXTRA!* to see how CODESCAN enables you to password-protect your system from anyone who does not know the required key combination.

In Chapter 9, you can take a look at the HELP-F1.BAT file in an *EXTRA!* sidebar. It demonstrates how to incorporate your own help text into a batch file, at the press of the F1 key. Finally, in Chapter 12, the TESTSCAN.BAT file demonstrates how to recognize any of the ten standard function keys. That batch file merely displays an echoed statement of which key was pressed, but you could substitute other code to control execution as you like, based on which key was pressed (i.e., which ERRORLEVEL is set by the CODESCAN.COM program).

Programming Tips and Techniques

Now that you know the major commands and methods for constructing QBasic programs, you should pause for some advice on how to combine these tools.

Don't be concerned about mistakes while you are learning how to program in QBasic. The more mistakes you make, the faster you'll learn what works and what doesn't work. Because mistakes are common, even for experienced programmers, debugging techniques become quite valuable. The information in this section can minimize the amount of debugging, so pay careful attention here.

Develop Your Programs in Steps

Here are the three steps for developing great QBasic programs:

1. Make it work.

2. Make it look good.

3. Make it efficient.

Step 1 is crucial. Information that looks pretty but is wrong is useless. Programs that execute faster than a speeding bullet are also useless if they obtain the wrong answers. Just get the program logic to work correctly. Only then should you spend time prettying up the screens or the reports. And only at the end, if there's any time left, should you bother with improvements to the processing efficiency.

➤ EXTRA!

Write Friendly Programs!

Approach your applications with techniques that will ensure that your programs are both user-friendly and programmer-friendly:

- *A user-friendly program* offers well-designed screens, flexible methods for data entry and retrieval, and helpful reports. Such a program also handles errors smoothly and offers clear documentation on how the application should be used.

- *A programmer-friendly program* uses professional development methods and demonstrates good programming habits. Such programs also provide accurate and detailed documentation about the system design and the internal programming logic.

Learn Good Programming Habits

QBasic's Editor automatically adds spaces between operators and operands as you type; you can do still more to ensure a consistent appearance. As often as you can, use indentation, blank spaces, and blank lines to improve program readability. As you saw in CLARITY.BAS, indentation should be used consistently for all instructions that appear within compound statements. In fact, when any compound statement appears within another compound statement, you should increase the indentation level again. Since the number of blank spaces at the beginning of a command line has no effect on QBasic, this indentation is for *your* benefit, not QBasic's.

Indentation reveals a program's structure, enabling you to understand the flow of control more readily. You can make portions of your program stand out even more by setting them off with blank lines. (Blank lines are also ignored by QBasic.)

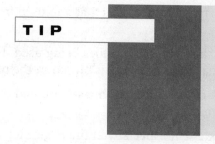

TIP

You can run any QBasic program you like from within a batch file. To do this, and ensure that control returns to the batch file after the QBasic program runs, you should use the QBASIC /RUN format. Also, be sure that the last statement in your QBasic program is a SYSTEM command.

Document Your Work

Three types of documentation are important before, during, and after your programs are developed. Write *system documentation* to explain the overall chores to be accomplished by your set of programs. Write *program documentation* to explain how each module does its work. And finally, write *user documentation* to explain how to use the system.

System Documentation

You can develop system documentation when first designing the programs you will need to write. It should include the following:

1. *System purpose* in a couple of sentences

2. *System structure* to explain the tasks performed by each separate code module

3. *Interface definition* to explain the parameters required by all SUB and FUNCTION procedures

4. *Validation criteria* to clarify what tests should be performed to verify that your logic works

Program Documentation

You should explain each program you write for the benefit of any programmer who may work with it in the future (including, incidentally, yourself). Include the following information:

1. *The versions* of the QBasic instruction modules that you used in developing your program

2. *File structures*, which explain the types of data files being used. Explain each field, and include samples of the data stored in the file

3. *Logic descriptions* to explain the purpose of each task-oriented block of instruction statements

4. *Comments* throughout the code, but especially at the beginning of each module

User Documentation

Let's not forget the people who will actually use the software. You need to think of writing user documentation as an ongoing process. When you initially write instructions, you may not anticipate every problem or question your intended users might have. Write a simple description of the purpose of your program, include instructions for using it, and plan on being available to assist your first users. In particular, the most important things you can do to improve your programs are:

1. *Watch others use your programs,* paying attention to any questions asked, mistakes made, difficulties encountered, and erroneous assumptions made. Change your documentation or your code accordingly.

2. *Anticipate mistakes* and include instructions to handle expected error situations.

Summary

In this chapter, you learned about the powerful QBasic programming environment that is included in DOS. You learned that:

- You can immediately execute individual QBasic program statements in the Immediate window, or you can group many statements into a program using the View window.

- Programs are typically written in the View window, which can be split into two smaller windows (through the *Split* choice on the View menu) to work with two text modules at the same time.

- You can use *Cut* and *Paste* from the Edit menu to save retyping code by moving it from the Immediate window to a View window.

- QBasic's editor understands the programming language and can automatically perform several chores: automatic syntax checking of each line as you enter it, reformatting of each line to improve readability, and insertion of necessary procedure declarations.

- QBasic programs consist of input, processing, and output statements. All text lines that begin with apostrophes are treated as program documentation.

- Named memory locations that store data values are called *variables*. You can tell QBasic the type of data you will be using, and how much space it will need, by suffixing a special symbol to each variable's name: strings (**$**), simple integers (**%**), long integers (**&**), single-precision floating-point numbers (**!**), and double-precision floating-point numbers (**#**).

- An *array* of variables permits you to define one variable name for a group of similar variables, using a unique number called the *subscript* to individually identify each separate variable.

- The **INPUT** command accepts keyboard data, while the **DATA** and **READ** statements allow you to initialize a series of values for consecutive use in your program.

- The **LINE INPUT** statement reads entire lines of character data into your program, and the **INPUT$** function can read individual characters one at a time. The **PRINT** command is the simplest statement for outputting program results.

- *Operators* indicate the action to be performed, and *operands* are the QBasic expressions to be acted upon. All arithmetic operations are performed first in a complex expression, prior to evaluating any relational comparisons. Logical operations are done last. When multiple operators appear in an expression, a precedence hierarchy determines the order in which each operator is evaluated.

- QBasic includes a number of compound statements that require multiple lines in your programs. These types of statements control sophisticated execution flow, and, subject to logical tests, can execute groups of other QBasic statements at one time.

- **IF** statements control simple decision-making within your programs. The **CASE** statement manages multiple-choice decisions. Use the **DO** statement to repeat any block of instructions.

- You can **OPEN** a file for **INPUT** or **OUTPUT** (both modes offer simple sequential access), for **RANDOM** access (for both input and output), for **BINARY** (byte-level) access, or in **APPEND** mode (to add new records to an existing sequential file).

- Use the **INPUT** or **LINE INPUT** commands to read data from a *sequential file*. Use the **WRITE** and **PRINT** commands to write data into a sequential file.

- Use sequential files to manage variable-length record data, or in systems short on disk space, or for infrequently accessed historical data.

- You can use *random-access files* to manage your own database with QBasic. Define each record with a **TYPE** statement; create individual variables of each type with a **DIM** statement.

- Use random-access files for online applications which require fast access, frequent deletions, insertions, or in-place record updating.

- The number of screen pixels you can work with depends on both your video monitor and your graphics adapter; use the **SCREEN** command to specify the graphic mode to use on your system.

- After using **SCREEN** to specify a graphics mode, you can use the **LINE** command to draw graphic lines or rectangles, and the **CIRCLE** command to draw circles, arcs, and pie slices.

- You learned many tips and techniques for designing, writing, testing, and debugging your QBasic programs.

Now that you have learned about the highly sophisticated program-language environment included with DOS, you'll learn a host of advanced techniques for optimizing all aspects of your DOS system.

Part

FIVE

Optimizing Your DOS
or Windows System

CHAPTERS

CHAPTER

17

Fine-Tuning Your System Memory

TUNING your car involves a number of factors, from spark plugs to engine timing. Tuning your computer system likewise involves many different factors, from specifying your individual application's priorities to optimizing your hard disk's caching parameters. This is especially important if you run Windows. In this chapter, I'll focus on those aspects of DOS that specifically affect memory availability and usage for both Windows and non-Windows systems.

First, you'll learn how to use the HIMEM.SYS driver to manage extended memory. You'll also learn how the EMM386.EXE program can manage reserved memory and emulate expanded memory. *Extended* memory is additional physical memory above the one megabyte level that is directly addressable in protected mode on 80286 microprocessors and above. By contrast, physical memory known as *expanded* memory is available on all processors. However, it requires a special device driver that uses a predefined block of conventional memory as an access window. The driver makes available to your programs one portion at a time of the total pool of expanded memory addresses.

Then you'll learn how to free up as much memory as possible before even starting any applications. Since Windows is becoming increasingly important and popular as an environment within which DOS applications are run, I'll provide specific information about Windows issues.

> ## ➤ EXTRA!

Use DOS 6 for Maximum Memory Utilization

DOS 6 offers a number of significant memory- and performance-oriented enhancement possibilities that are simply not available in earlier versions of DOS. To begin with, it offers these same improvements as DOS 5 over even earlier versions of DOS:

- It requires less conventional memory to run.

- It permits part of DOS to be placed in extended memory.

- It can manage extended memory, emulate expanded memory, and load device drivers and TSRs in upper reserved memory blocks (between 640K and 1MB).

Next, it offers a number of additional memory-related advantages to justify upgrading even if you are currently still using DOS 5:

- The MemMaker utility can automatically make decisions about which device drivers and memory-resident programs can fit in upper-memory blocks. This makes memory optimization even easier, often removing the mental effort needed to figure out what programs can and should go where in the UMB region.

- The EMM386 driver is further enhanced to make UMB access even more efficient.

- The LOADHIGH and DEVICEHIGH commands are enhanced to enable control over memory regions into which programs and drivers are to be loaded.

- The MEM command is also improved to provide more details about program usage of memory.

- An integrated anti-virus facility to protect your system and memory from the intrusive effects of over 1000 computer viruses.

- The Microsoft Diagnostics utility (MSD) is now part of DOS. It obtains and displays information about your entire computer system.

Freeing Up Memory at Bootup Time

You can increase the amount of memory that Windows can use by making some good decisions prior to even receiving your first DOS prompt or shell screen. You can optimize your DOS environment in several ways. DOS itself has many options for configuring memory efficiently. The more you do before you ever run an application, the better your overall system will perform.

Extended memory is essential for running some applications. Windows in particular relies heavily on available extended memory. To optimize your use of extended memory under Windows, you must begin by optimizing DOS's management of memory prior to starting Windows. The 80286, 80386, and 80486 models provide hardware access to that memory, but you must configure your DOS system properly to actually use it. The HIMEM.SYS device driver offers system support to manage extended memory.

In addition to extended memory, DOS and Windows each provide a version of the EMM386.EXE program. This driver can perform two chores. First, it can manage the region of memory located between 640K and 1Mb, which is called *reserved* memory (or the *upper memory blocks*, or *UMB*, region). Second, this program can emulate expanded memory for DOS applications that run in 386 Enhanced mode. I'll discuss these two services in this section as well.

Use DOS to Maximize Available Windows Memory

Pay careful attention to how you configure your entire system. Using the latest version of DOS invariably means that you gain the benefits of the latest memory-enhancement techniques. The first *EXTRA!* in this chapter discussed the specific advantages of DOS 6.

Various entries in CONFIG.SYS can greatly affect the amount of memory that remains when you start Windows. This in turn can impact the overall performance of Windows. See the CONFIG.SYS *EXTRA!* for a summary of applicable techniques.

➤ EXTRA!

Optimize Windows by Optimizing DOS's CONFIG.SYS

DOS and Windows are becoming more closely entwined on many systems. Because Windows depends greatly on DOS for support and an overall context, there are ways in which to enhance Windows performance by carefully configuring your DOS. There is no better place to start than with your DOS configuration module, CONFIG.SYS.

- Install the high memory manager, like HIMEM.SYS.

- Include the EMM386.EXE upper reserved blocks in order to actually manage access to the reserved memory portion of RAM.

- Include a DOS=HIGH line to load portions of DOS in the high memory area (HMA).

- Include a DOS=HIGH,UMB line if you wish to load portions of DOS in the high memory area (HMA), as well as to be able to load device drivers and TSRs in upper memory.

- Use SMARTDRV.EXE to establish disk caching.

- Use RAMDRIVE.SYS to create a RAM disk.

- Set BUFFERS=10 and FILES=30, unless one of your application programs requires that they be set higher.

- Use DEVICEHIGH commands to load device drivers into upper reserved memory blocks.

- Remove any drivers that will be unnecessary to Windows, like MOUSE.SYS, unless you plan to run applications under DOS after exiting or before starting Windows.

You can effectively start (or refrain from starting) many programs and environment variables in your AUTOEXEC.BAT file. These in turn can have notable impacts on your overall system's efficiency. For instance, follow these guidelines to improve your existing system:

- Remove any TSRs that can be run from within a DOS session under Windows.

- Remove any TSRs whose graphics-handling techniques are incompatible with Windows. Run these separately after exiting Windows if you still need to run them.

- Use LOADHIGH commands to load TSRs or small application programs into upper reserved memory blocks.

Remember to reboot your system after making any changes to CONFIG.SYS and AUTOEXEC.BAT.

Managing Extended Memory with HIMEM.SYS

The HIMEM.SYS extended memory manager must be loaded in your CONFIG.SYS before any applications or other device drivers that may access extended memory.

To install HIMEM.SYS (which comes with Windows as well as with DOS), you must include a DEVICE line in CONFIG.SYS:

```
Device=[path]HIMEM.SYS [options]
```

where [options] can be any or all of the optional settings summarized in Table 17.1. Refer to your online system documentation for more extensive details about each option. Be sure to use the latest version of HIMEM.SYS that comes with the version of DOS that you are using.

TABLE 17.1: Optional parameters for HIMEM.SYS

PARAMETER	EXPLANATION
/a20control:*on|off*	Toggles control by HIMEM.SYS of the HMA A20 line
/cpuclock:*on|off*	Toggles clock-speed management by HIMEM.SYS
/eisa	Explicitly allocates all available extended memory
/hmamin=*m*	Sets *m* kilobytes as the requirement for access to HMA
/int15=*xxxxx*	Defines how many kilobytes are reserved for Interrupt 15 handling
/machine:*name*	Explicitly defines the computer type
/numhandles=*n*	Specifies *n* as the maximum number of simultaneous extended memory block handles
/shadowram:*on|off*	Toggles shadow RAM on or off
/verbose	Displays status and error messages while loading

Maximizing Memory Settings in the CONFIG.SYS File

DOS 6 offers a number of CONFIG.SYS settings that impact memory usage. This section will offer specific advice for using these settings to maximize the conventional memory prior to starting Windows.

Loading DOS Itself into Extended Memory

Once you've started HIMEM.SYS from your CONFIG.SYS file, you can improve the efficiency of your system by using the extended memory that HIMEM.SYS now manages. Start by including the following command line in your CONFIG.SYS file:

```
DOS=HIGH
```

This enables DOS to place a number of its own internal tables and buffers in memory areas beyond 1MB, thereby freeing up additional conventional memory. This one line directs most of the command processor itself

(COMMAND.COM), the DOS kernel, all buffers, and all code-page information to use space from the 64K HMA, or High Memory Area. This is the first 64K of your system's available extended memory.

TIP

Use the DOS=HIGH command in your CONFIG.SYS file. After using this command, the conventional-memory burden of DOS 6 itself is less than 20K.

More available conventional memory means faster processing by applications that may swap to disk. This is because the extra memory will be used by Windows to minimize the need for swapping.

By retaining more low memory for programs, you enable your system to use overall memory more efficiently. In many cases, this technique even lets you consider running programs that couldn't run before because they required more physical memory to run than was available in your system. Remember also that the greater the conventional memory that remains available when Windows starts, the more the overall memory that will be available to each non-Windows application that you run in a 386 Enhanced–mode virtual machine.

Best Settings for CONFIG.SYS Values

The FILES command in your CONFIG.SYS determines how many file handles (essentially equivalent to the number of files used by your applications) will be allocated for DOS to manage. To initially run Windows well, you should usually set this value to at least 30:

    FILES=30

However, any one of your applications may require access to more file handles. This depends on the application. Use a number equal to the largest suggestion in your applications' documentation.

The BUFFERS command can be a problem if you're not careful. To run Windows without a disk cache, you need at least 30 buffers. However, if you install a disk cache (with DOS's SMARTDRV, as I'll explain in the next chapter), you do not need that many buffers. The disk cache takes care of the same buffering chore to a large extent, so Windows users can reduce the buffers consumed to 15:

```
BUFFERS=15
```

Configure your SHELL command to use only as much environment space as you actually need. Many writers suggest that you blindly specify a SHELL command with a /E switch that allocates a 1024-byte environment. While some systems need this, most don't—in which case it costs you one kilobyte of conventional memory.

The default environment space is usually enough. Unless you determine that you need extra space, don't bother to use the /E switch. If you discover that you do need extra space, refer to the section "Giving DOS Applications What They Need" near the end of this chapter for an explanation of how to provide it.

Managing Reserved Memory with EMM386.EXE

You load HIMEM.SYS to manage extended memory, and you use the DOS=HIGH configuration command to direct DOS to use some of this memory for its own internal needs. But there is still the problem of TSRs and drivers consuming conventional memory, leaving less memory available to Windows or other applications you may run.

If you could load one or more TSRs or device drivers somewhere other than conventional memory, you would have more conventional memory remaining available when you start Windows. The EMM386.EXE program enables you to do this. This program lets you use any available space in the reserved memory area between 640K and 1MB. Rather than consuming precious conventional memory, you will be able to load some or all of your system's device drivers and TSRs into upper memory blocks.

Whatever device drivers or applications you load in the UMB region will still be available to your system. However, there are some operating concerns that you must have in loading drivers and programs in this High Memory Area. The biggest issue is whether or not the device driver or TSR operates correctly when placed in the formerly unavailable reserved memory (640K–1MB) addresses. You'll have to carefully test the program to determine this.

Installing the Reserved Memory Manager

You should first direct DOS to use reserved memory areas by including

```
DOS=UMB
```

in your CONFIG.SYS file. The UMB parameter stands for upper memory blocks, which is what the addressable portions of this reserved system memory area are called. If you already have included a DOS=HIGH line, you can combine these two lines into one command that both loads DOS into the HMA and connects low memory with the upper memory blocks:

```
DOS=HIGH,UMB
```

To be more precise, the UMB parameter in this command directs DOS to include in the total free-memory pool all the available upper memory blocks that EMM386.EXE now provides. The pool is now enlarged to include both conventional memory and reserved memory. The DOS program loader now has a larger total memory space within which to load programs.

Once you've included the DOS=UMB command line, you can then load the special UMB manager by including the line

```
DEVICE=EMM386.EXE [options]
```

in your CONFIG.SYS.

This assumes that the EMM386.EXE file is in the root directory of your boot drive. If it is not, you must enter the complete path and file name, including the extension.

TIP

To maximize the amount of conventional memory available to DOS sessions under Windows in 386 Enhanced mode, you must be sure to *include* a DEVICE=EMM386.EXE line in your CONFIG.SYS file. This gains for you the ability to load TSRs and device drivers in the UMB region (i.e., to load them *high*).

There are many options available for customizing your installation of EMM386.EXE. They are summarized in Table 17.2 and are explained in more detail below and in your system documentation. The most common option to specify is either RAM or NOEMS.

TABLE 17.2: Optional parameters for EMM386.EXE

PARAMETER	EXPLANATION
/p*mmmm*	Defines page frame address explicitly
/p*n*=*address*	Defines segment *address* for a specific page *n*
a=*altregs*	Allocates a number of fast alternate register sets to EMM386.EXE
altboot	Directs DOS to use a different method for handling Ctrl+Alt+Del requests for warm booting. Use this if your computer freezes up during warm boots.
b=*address*	Defines the lowest address to use for EMS bank switching
d=*nnn*	Reserves *nnn* kilobytes for buffered DMA
frame=*address*	Defines starting address of 64K page frame
h=*handles*	Defines number of handles usable by EMM386.EXE
i=*mmmm-nnnn*	Includes the specified range as allowable memory addresses
l=*minXMS*	Defines how much extended memory to leave available after loading EMM386.EXE
memory	Defines how much extended memory EMM386.EXE is to use for emulating expanded memory
min=*Size*	Specifies minimum EMS/VCPI memory that EMM386 will provide
m*x*	Specifies one of 14 possible predefined page-frame addresses

TABLE 17.2: Optional parameters for EMM386.EXE (continued)

PARAMETER	EXPLANATION
noems	Enables UMB access but disables LIM3.2 expanded memory
novcpi	Disables VCPI application support
nohi	Disallows any portion of EMM386 itself from loading into upper memory area
highscan	Limits scanning of the upper memory area
nomovexbda	Keeps EMM386 from relocating extended BIOS area into upper memory
*on	off	auto*	Toggles EMM386 status *on*, *off*, or *auto*
ram=*mmmm-nnnn*	Enables both UMB access and expanded memory, and specifies a range of segment addresses to use for UMBs
rom=*mmmm-nnnn*	Reserves address range for EMM386 shadow ram
verbose	Displays informational messages when EMM386 starts
w=*on\off*	Toggles Weitek Coprocessor support on or off
win=*mmmm-nnnn*	Reserves address range for Windows rather than EMM386
x=*mmmm-nnnn*	Excludes an address range from use by EMM386.EXE

If you have no need for expanded memory in your non-Windows applications, use the NOEMS parameter:

```
Device=EMM386.EXE NOEMS
```

In this way, your system will have access to the UMB region, but will not need or reserve a 64K EMS page frame. This 64K region will thus be available to your memory managers from the UMB region.

If you specify RAM instead of NOEMS, the EMM386.EXE memory manager will provide both UMB management and a 64K EMS page frame.

Loading Device Drivers and TSRs in Upper Memory Blocks

Normally, device drivers as well as applications load into low memory. However, with EMM386.EXE, you can now load most device drivers in UMB. After EMM386.EXE has been installed, you can include a DEVICE-HIGH command in your configuration file to load a device driver into this reserved memory area. (First, though, you might check to make sure the device driver is recent enough to work in the UMB region.)

WARNING   Some application programs cannot run properly if EMM386 is active, largely because of the way in which EMM386 runs DOS in a special Virtual 86 mode. To run this kind of a program, you must disable EMM386 just prior to running the application. Use the command EMM386 OFF at the command prompt, or in a batch file that runs your application. Unfortunately, you cannot do this if EMM386 is either providing expanded memory to another application, or if you have used EMM386 to support upper memory block loading of TSRs or device drivers.

Generally, all that you must do is change existing DEVICE statements to DEVICEHIGH statements, but I suggest that you take a little extra time to do this one statement at a time. Naturally, you can change all DEVICE statements at once and only follow a more cautious procedure if something doesn't work. The more cautious procedure is to change one statement at a time and then reboot your system and verify that everything is working as before. If there is a problem, you may have to run the driver in low memory, or you may have to obtain a different version that can work in upper memory.

Once you've configured your system to use the upper memory blocks in the reserved area, you can even load applications into that area as well. Assuming that they are small enough and will fit there, you can load an application into reserved memory with the LOADHIGH command at a command prompt. For example, suppose that your scanner device comes with a special Optical Character Recognition (OCR) software program. If it fits, you can request that DOS load it into reserved memory with this command:

```
LOADHIGH OCR.EXE
```

As you'll learn later in this chapter, you can avoid all decision making by simply running the MemMaker utility program. It will decide which of your memory-resident programs and device drivers can or should be loaded in upper memory. MemMaker will run the LH (or LOADHIGH) command for each appropriate memory-resident program in your AUTOEXEC.BAT file.

Figure 17.1 demonstrates how to use the MEM/C command to display the results of any LH commands you include.

➤ EXTRA!

Discover Where Programs and Drivers Are Loaded

If a program that you try to load high requires more reserved memory than is available, DOS will automatically load it into conventional memory without informing you. However, DOS includes a MEM command that will display the names and locations of all loaded drivers and programs. To display this information on screen, type

```
MEM/C. /P | MORE
```

at a command prompt prior to starting Windows. This will display useful information, one screenful at a time, that will enable you to learn not only what is loaded where, but what amount of memory remains (and where it is) for possible optimization. To obtain a printout of the same information, such as the example shown in Figure 17.1, just send the results of

> ➤ **EXTRA!**

the MEM command (without the /P switch) on your system to the printer:

```
MEM/C > PRN:
```

Use LOADHIGH in your AUTOEXEC.BAT file to load short, memory-resident programs or TSRs into upper memory blocks. Use DEVICE-HIGH in your CONFIG.SYS file to load device drivers into available UMB space. If DOS cannot fit a program in upper memory blocks, it will load it in conventional memory without notifying you. Use MEM/C to discover where individual programs have been loaded by DOS.

FIGURE 17.1

Run the MEM/C command to display the DOS memory load map. This useful display informs you as to the current use of the various types of memory on your system. Use the top portion particularly when seeking to maximize conventional memory and to use upper memory effectively.

```
Modules using memory below 1 MB:

  Name          Total      =   Conventional   +   Upper Memory
  --------    ----------------     ----------------     ----------------
  MSDOS        19917   (19K)      19917   (19K)         0   (0K)
  SETVER         624    (1K)        624    (1K)         0   (0K)
  HIMEM         1104    (1K)       1104    (1K)         0   (0K)
  EMM386        3072    (3K)       3072    (3K)         0   (0K)
  ATDOSXL       9536    (9K)       9536    (9K)         0   (0K)
  ANSI          4208    (4K)       4208    (4K)         0   (0K)
  RCD          13040   (13K)      13040   (13K)         0   (0K)
  SMARTDRV     30832   (30K)       2480    (2K)     28352  (28K)
  COMMAND       3760    (4K)       3760    (4K)         0   (0K)
  MOUSE        16864   (16K)      16864   (16K)         0   (0K)
  UNDELETE     13616   (13K)      13616   (13K)         0   (0K)
  DOSKEY        5680    (6K)       5680    (6K)         0   (0K)
  DBLSPACE     52512   (51K)          0    (0K)     52512  (51K)
  Free        630288  (616K)     560528  (547K)     69760  (68K)

Memory Summary:

  Type of Memory      Size       =      Used       +       Free
  ----------------    ----------------     ----------------     ----------------
  Conventional        654336   (639K)      93808   (92K)     560528   (547K)
  Upper               150624   (147K)      80864   (79K)      69760    (68K)
  Adapter RAM/ROM     243616   (238K)     243616  (238K)          0     (0K)
  Extended (XMS)     7340032  (7168K)    2457600 (2400K)    4882432  (4768K)
  Expanded (EMS)           0     (0K)          0    (0K)          0     (0K)
  ----------------    ----------------     ----------------     ----------------
  Total memory       8388608  (8192K)    2875888 (2808K)    5512720  (5384K)

  Total under 1 MB    804960   (786K)     174672  (171K)     630288   (616K)

  Largest executable program size           560352  (547K)
  Largest free upper memory block            69712   (68K)
  MS-DOS is resident in the high memory area.
```

Optimizing the Use of Your Upper Memory Blocks

The UMB region can at first appear to be a confusing collection of different things, from video adapter buffers to EMS page frames to BIOS buffers. To be able to use the available chunks of memory in this region will mean savings in conventional memory space. This will translate directly into extra memory for Windows to use, both in multitasking and in enlarging each DOS virtual machine in 386 Enhanced mode. To gain the most from the management services of EMM386.EXE, you should consider a number of optimization factors.

TIP

Before running the MEMMAKER utility, be sure to have a boot diskette prepared for your system. Memory optimization is a complex process, and your system may have a difficult combination of hardware, device drivers, and memory-resident programs. If your system does not reestablish itself properly after running MEMMAKER, you may need a previously prepared boot diskette in order to reboot your system. In addition, be sure to make copies of your AUTOEXEC.BAT and CONFIG.SYS files prior to running MEMMAKER. If the MEMMAKER utility fails, you can then reboot from a diskette, erase any newly modified versions of AUTOEXEC.BAT and CONFIG.SYS, then rename your backed-up copies (e.g., AUTOEXEC.BAK and CONFIG.BAK) to the normal names (e.g., AUTOEXEC.BAT and CONFIG.SYS). Then, you can safely reboot your system, reestablishing the configuration that existed prior to attempting to run MEMMAKER.

Alternatively, you can ignore all optimization considerations and ask the DOS 6 MemMaker utility to do it all for you. In this section, I'll discuss what MemMaker does as well as some of the decisions that either MemMaker can do, or you can do for yourself, in order to more directly manage how your system is optimized.

The MemMaker Utility Does It All Automatically

DOS 6 includes a formidable utility program called MEMMAKER.EXE, which can automatically make decisions about how best to use existing memory. You can run the MemMaker program by simply typing:

MEMMAKER

at a command prompt. MemMaker makes more conventional memory available by modifying your CONFIG.SYS and AUTOEXEC.BAT files to use the upper memory blocks more efficiently. After MemMaker is through performing its magic, you will discover more LH (or LOAD-HIGH) and DEVICEHIGH commands in these system startup files. In this way, MemMaker moves some or all device drivers and memory-resident programs into the UMB region.

After MemMaker begins, a sequence of screens will appear. Each screen will list various highlighted choices for you. You only need press Enter to accept a highlighted choice. Alternatively, you can press the spacebar to display other options. When the one you prefer is highlighted, pressing Enter will select it for you. As with most programs, you can always press F1 at any time for additional help text about a highlighted option.

MemMaker offers two principal ways to optimize your memory. You select from these two alternatives on the second screen that appears once you've initiated MemMaker. If you select *Express Setup*, MemMaker will analyze your system and automatically makes its own decisions about how to adjust your system files. If you select *Custom Setup*, MemMaker will allow you to make the final decisions about exactly how and what changes are to be made to your key system files.

In both cases, MemMaker will analyze the potentially hundreds of possible scenarios with the device drivers and memory-resident programs on your system. You will be asked more customizing questions if you select

Custom Setup. For example, Figure 17.2 shows the screen of Advanced Options that appear if you select a custom setup.

FIGURE 17.2

Advanced MemMaker options control how the MemMaker utility will execute. Few current machines require the mono- chrome region, so you may be able to answer Yes here. Windows users may not need any EMS memory, so the page frame may not need to be set aside.

```
 Microsoft(R) MemMaker
 _____

                        Advanced Options

 Specify which drivers and TSRs to include during optimization?   No
 Set aside upper memory for EMS page frame?                        Yes
 Scan the upper memory area aggressively?                          Yes
 Optimize upper memory for use with Windows?                       Yes
 Create upper memory in the monochrome region (B000-B7FF)?         No
 Keep current EMM386 memory exclusions and inclusions?             Yes
 Move Extended BIOS Data Area from conventional to upper memory?   Yes
 _____


 To move to a different option, press the UP ARROW or DOWN ARROW key.
 To accept all the settings and continue, press ENTER.




 ENTER=Accept All  SPACEBAR=Change Selection   F1=Help  F3=Exit
```

After you've ansered Yes or No to each of the customizing advanced options, MemMaker may ask further questions. Specifically, if you answer Yes to the first option, MemMaker will then ask you to separately specify whether or not to include each possible program and driver in its upcoming analysis. When you've completed these preliminary screen inputs, MemMaker will direct you to remove any floppy diskettes from your drives, because it will then automatically reboot your computer. This reboot procedure is necessary to complete a sizing analysis of each of the drivers and programs to be included in the possible optimization.

Rebooting will actually occur twice. MemMaker reboots a first time, using a special SIZER utility program to assess the memory requirements of each program and device driver. MemMaker will then analyze all possible configurations of these programs. Once MemMaker decides on the best startup scenario, your CONFIG.SYS and AUTOEXEC.BAT files are adjusted and the second rebooting will take place.

TIP

If your system includes a menu program at bootup time, you must exit from the menu program during MemMaker's automatic optimization sequence. Only then can MemMaker continue its optimization properly. In a similar vein, you should understand that MemMaker performs its chores over the course of several boots by adding a command line at the end of your AUTOEXEC.BAT file. If your AUTOEXEC.BAT transfers control to any other batch file, which sometimes occurs on the last line, you should either REM it out or change it temporarily to a CALL command. This ensures that control flows through AUTOEXEC.BAT all the way to the end, where MemMaker has placed its control command.

Under normal conditions, MemMaker will complete its optimization procedures without any problems. Once the rebooting and adjustment steps are complete, your system will be successfully running with some device drivers and programs running in upper memory. More conventional memory will then be available to application programs that you run.

The final steps of the MemMaker process include a query as to whether or not your system seems to be working successfully. If you received no adverse messages during this final booting, you can answer Yes. Mem-Maker will display an optimization summary screen, such as the one seen in Figure 17.3.

If, on the other hand, your system does not appear to be working normally, or if you received any unusual messages during the new bootup, you should answer No to MemMaker's query. MemMaker will then automatically reverse its changes and restore your system to the state it was in prior to MemMaker's optimization processing.

You can always run MemMaker more than once, especially if your system changes or if you decide to add or delete one or more programs or device drivers. As you can see from Figure 17.2, some of the optimization criteria deal with Windows. Feel free to rerun MemMaker if changes in your system make you suspect that further optimization gains can be had. By

MemMaker's optimization summary screen. Check this screen carefully, especially if you had previously optimized your upper memory area yourself. MemMaker may not gain anything more than you already had done for yourself.

```
Microsoft(R) MemMaker
_____

MemMaker has finished optimizing your system's memory. The following
table summarizes the memory use (in bytes) on your system:

                                  Before       After
      Memory Type                 MemMaker     MemMaker     Change
                                  _____     _____     _____

   Conventional memory:
      Used by programs            136,064      136,064         0
      Free                        518,256      518,256         0
   Upper memory:
      Used by programs            144,400      144,400         0
      Reserved for Windows              0       24,576      24,576
      Reserved for EMS                  0            0         0
      Free                         38,848       14,272     -24,576
   Expanded memory:              Disabled     Disabled

Your original CONFIG.SYS and AUTOEXEC.BAT files have been saved
as CONFIG.UMB and AUTOEXEC.UMB.  If MemMaker changed your Windows
SYSTEM.INI file, the original file was saved as SYSTEM.UMB.

ENTER=Exit  ESC=Undo changes
```

looking closely at Figure 17.3, you'll see that this particular run of Mem-Maker was in fact done later than my initial optimization sequencing. This last MemMaker run did not free up any additional conventional memory; in fact, it consumed some additional portions of upper memory in order to reserve their use by Windows.

When I first ran MemMaker on my test system, the only item that was loaded high was the DBLSPACE disk-compression manager. In Figure 17.1, you can see in the rightmost column that only DBLSPACE (51K) and SMARTDRV (28K) are loaded high. After running MEM-MAKER on this system, MemMaker made a number of changes to my AUTOEXEC.BAT and CONFIG.SYS files. Figure 17.4 shows the resulting memory usage after MemMaker completed its adjustments.

Specifically, MemMaker changed these three lines in my AUTOEXEC.BAT:

```
C:\DOS\UNDELETE /LOAD
C:\DOS\SMARTDRV
C:\DOS\DOSKEY /BUFSIZE=2048
```

to the following:

```
LH /L:1,53904 C:\DOS\UNDELETE /LOAD
LH /L:0;1,44448 /S C:\DOS\SMARTDRV
LH /L:1,6400 C:\DOS\DOSKEY /BUFSIZE=2048
```

FIGURE 17.4

Memory configuration after MemMaker executes. If you haven't done any upper memory optimization, MemMaker will provide a tremendous boost in available conventional memory.

```
Modules using memory below 1 MB:

  Name          Total      =  Conventional   +  Upper Memory
  --------    -------------    --------------    --------------
  MSDOS        19853  (19K)     19853  (19K)         0   (0K)
  HIMEM         1104   (1K)      1104   (1K)         0   (0K)
  EMM386        3072   (3K)      3072   (3K)         0   (0K)
  SMARTDRV     30832  (30K)      2480   (2K)     28352  (28K)
  COMMAND       3760   (4K)      3760   (4K)         0   (0K)
  MOUSE        16864  (16K)     16864  (16K)         0   (0K)
  SETVER         656   (1K)         0   (0K)       656   (1K)
  ATDOSXL       9568   (9K)         0   (0K)      9568   (9K)
  ANSI          4240   (4K)         0   (0K)      4240   (4K)
  RCD          13072  (13K)         0   (0K)     13072  (13K)
  DBLSPACE     52512  (51K)         0   (0K)     52512  (51K)
  UNDELETE     13616  (13K)         0   (0K)     13616  (13K)
  DOSKEY        5680   (6K)         0   (0K)      5680   (6K)
  Free        617936 (603K)    607232 (593K)     10704  (10K)

Memory Summary:

  Type of Memory       Size     =     Used      +     Free
  ----------------  -------------    -------------    -------------
  Conventional        654336 (639K)     47104  (46K)    607232 (593K)
  Upper               138400 (135K)    127696 (125K)     10704  (10K)
  Adapter RAM/ROM     255840 (250K)    255840 (250K)         0   (0K)
  Extended (XMS)     7340032 (7168K)  2445312 (2388K)  4894720 (4780K)
  Expanded (EMS)           0   (0K)         0   (0K)         0   (0K)
  ----------------  -------------    -------------    -------------
  Total memory       8388608 (8192K)  2875952 (2809K)  5512656 (5383K)

  Total under 1 MB    792736 (774K)    174800 (171K)    617936 (603K)

  Largest executable program size    607056 (593K)
  Largest free upper memory block     10624  (10K)
  MS-DOS is resident in the high memory area.
```

Each program was explicitly loaded high, using the /L switch. The UNDELETE and DOSKEY programs were loaded into region 1, unlike previously when they both loaded into conventional memory. As before, 2K of the SMARTDRV program was loaded partially into region zero (conventional memory) and the remaining 28K was loaded into region one. SMARTDRV formerly made this split by itself, but the loadhigh command now makes it explicitly, using the complete /L switch. After a complete analysis, MemMaker decided that this was in fact the best split and location of the pieces of SMARTDRV.

In addition, these six lines in CONFIG.SYS were modified:

```
DEVICE=C:\DOS\SETVER.EXE
DEVICE=C:\DOS\EMM386.EXE NOEMS
DEVICE = C:\ATDOSXL.SYS
DEVICE=C:\DOS\ANSI.SYS
DEVICE = C:\BERNOULI\RCD.SYS /FO /P4
DEVICEHIGH=C:\DOS\DBLSPACE.SYS
```

to become the following:

```
DEVICE=C:\DOS\EMM386.EXE NOEMS X=C900-C9FF WIN=ED00-EFFF
WIN=EA00-ECFF
DEVICEHIGH /L:1,12048 =C:\DOS\SEVER.EXE
DEVICEHIGH /L:1,22592 =C:\ATDOSXL.SYS
DEVICEHIGH /L:1,9040 =C:\DOS\ANSI.SYS
DEVICEHIGH /L:1,30272 =C:\BERNOULI\RCD.SYS /FO /P4
DEVICEHIGH /L:1,52528 =C:\DOS\DBLSPACE.SYS
```

Several things have happened here. First, the load ordering has changed. EMM386.EXE is loaded before the SETVER.EXE program. Second, the WIN switch on the EMM386 line is used twice to reserve portions of upper memory for the Windows system that MemMaker discovered on my disk. Third, four programs or device drivers (SETVER, AT-DOSXL, ANSI, and RCD) that were formerly loaded in low memory are now loaded in region one of upper memory. Finally, a device driver (DBLSPACE.SYS) that was formerly loaded high is now explicitly loaded into region one with a size cap of 52528 imposed.

All in all, MemMaker has sized, placed, and constrained various device drivers and memory-resident programs into the most efficient locations and ordering. As the rightmost column of Figure 17.4 demonstrates, only 10K now remains free in upper memory. This was essentially wasted space before. The valuable result from using more of this upper memory is that free conventional memory has been increased from 547K (as seen in Figure 17.1) to 593K (as seen in Figure 17.4). Every application program you choose to run now has this larger address space to use.

In the next sections, you'll see how I personally like to use the MEM/C command to determine exactly how much improvement occurred after a run by MemMaker. The MEM command can also provide a detailed answer to the question of exactly how MemMaker achieved its gains.

The Order of Loading High Makes a Big Difference

Available UMBs are not usually contiguous. This is why the available upper memory is treated as blocks with separate memory ranges. Remember that this reserved memory area is also known as the adapter segment, a name that derives from its use by different hardware device adapters. The address ranges used by the separate devices are independent of one another and rarely occupy contiguous blocks.

Programs and drivers that load high must fit into one or more available blocks of memory, and each will probably be a different length. Since the programs that you load high are themselves different in length, it's a little like packing a suitcase or the trunk of a car. Items can sometimes fit in one way and not another. You would typically load the largest item into your trunk first, then fit smaller remaining items around it. In fact, this is precisely the technique used by DOS.

As each LOADHIGH or DEVICEHIGH is processed, DOS looks at the remaining blocks and tries to place the new program or driver into the largest remaining block. This normally works out best for fitting all your requests successfully into UMBs. Especially if you use MemMaker, you can probably assume that the order of loading is best. However, this is not always true. Understanding exactly why can help you to use MemMaker most efficiently, or even make your own later adjustments to your CONFIG.SYS and AUTOEXEC.BAT files.

A problem sometimes arises because the memory initially required to load some drivers or programs is greater than that required to actually run them after loading. For example, on my system, the Microsoft MOUSE driver can be loaded high and only requires about 16K of space. However, during loading it consumes approximately 25K. This means that in order to successfully load it in reserved memory, there must be at least one block of 25K or more available when its LOADHIGH command is processed. MemMaker uses the SIZER program to help determine this information while it analyzes the optimum arrangement of drivers and programs.

Because the loading burden of some programs is greater than others, the order in which you submit LOADHIGH or DEVICEHIGH can sometimes affect your success in fitting your requests into the UMB region. As an example, take a look at Figure 17.5. In this example, I'll try to load DOSKEY.EXE and MOUSE.COM into a single UMB that consists of 30K. Your MOUSE driver may consume more or less memory, since individual manufacturers create their own sometimes different device drivers.

FIGURE 17.5

The order of loading high often affects the final results. Some drivers, like MOUSE.COM, require much more memory during the loading process than they eventually require during the more stable, system execution phase.

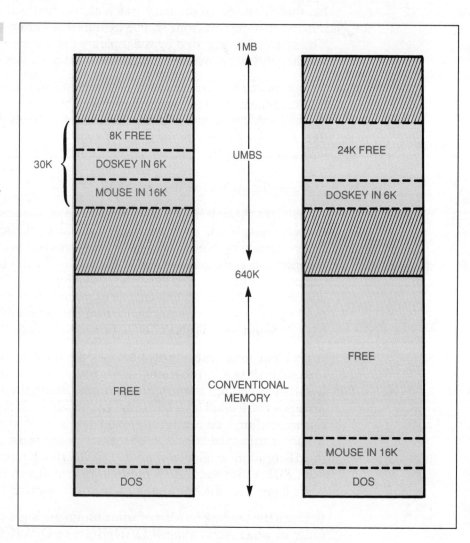

On the left side of the figure, I've loaded the MOUSE driver first. This represents Case 1:

```
LOADHIGH MOUSE.COM
LOADHIGH DOSKEY.EXE
```

After MOUSE.COM completes loading, it consumes 16K, leaving 24K in the UMB. This is more than enough to load DOSKEY.EXE, which after loading consumes only 6K. Both programs have loaded high, avoiding any impact on conventional memory. But suppose you tried to load these two programs in the reverse order. This would represent Case 2 in Figure 17.5:

```
LOADHIGH DOSKEY.EXE
LOADHIGH MOUSE.COM
```

In this case, the DOSKEY program loads and consumes 6K. However, when it's finished loading, only 24K remains. While this might be enough for MOUSE.COM after it's loaded (i.e., only 16K is needed), it is insufficient for MOUSE's initial memory requirements (25K). Consequently, DOS just loads it into conventional memory without giving you any indication. You only discover it later when you run the MEM/C command. Windows users would later realize that every virtual machine under Windows has 16K less memory available.

Use Video Adapter Space

Video adapter ROM consumes a large initial memory area in the upper memory region. In fact, unless you request it via the Advanced Options screen of MemMaker, the EMM386.EXE program does not automatically look in the area below hexadecimal address C800 for available memory in which to load TSRs and drivers.

However, suppose that you know exactly which video modes your system uses and doesn't use. You can direct EMM386.EXE to explicitly include specific addresses in memory space that is otherwise ignored. The I, or Include, parameter on the EMM386.EXE device line in your CONFIG.SYS file will give you this facility.

For example, a monochrome display adapter uses only the addresses from B000 to B7FF (ROM hexadecimal). The same goes for a Hercules adapter's Video Page 1, or it might be used by a VGA adapter that is using 256 colors. If you are not using any of these, you can direct EMM386.EXE yourself to gain that 32K by adding the explicit address range with the I, or Include, switch:

```
DEVICE=D:\WINDOWS\EMM386.EXE NOEMS I=B000-B7FF
```

To discover the address ranges your system's adapter uses, and under what application circumstances those ranges are used, you can always call your video board manufacturer. On my system, I added the I switch myself. Alternatively, I could have answered Yes to the Advanced Option question (see Figure 17.2 above) that asks about using the monochrome region.

The results on my test system of adding in the I=B000-B7FF switch can be seen in Figure 17.6.

FIGURE 17.6

EMM386's I= switch includes extra upper memory. Including the monochrome video region adds 32K of upper memory to MemMaker's analysis.

```
Modules using memory below 1 MB:

Name          Total      =    Conventional   +   Upper Memory
--------   ----------------    ----------------   ----------------
MSDOS         19853   (19K)       19853   (19K)          0   (0K)
HIMEM          1104    (1K)        1104    (1K)          0   (0K)
EMM386         3072    (3K)        3072    (3K)          0   (0K)
SMARTDRV      30832   (30K)        2480    (2K)      28352  (28K)
COMMAND        3760    (4K)        3760    (4K)          0   (0K)
SETVER          656    (1K)           0    (0K)        656   (1K)
ATDOSXL        9568    (9K)           0    (0K)       9568   (9K)
ANSI           4240    (4K)           0    (0K)       4240   (4K)
RCD           13072   (13K)           0    (0K)      13072  (13K)
DBLSPACE      52512   (51K)           0    (0K)      52512  (51K)
MOUSE         16864   (16K)           0    (0K)      16864  (16K)
UNDELETE      13616   (13K)           0    (0K)      13616  (13K)
DOSKEY         5680    (6K)           0    (0K)       5680   (6K)
Free         638368  (623K)      624096  (609K)      14272  (14K)

Memory Summary:

Type of Memory        Size      =      Used       +      Free
----------------   ----------------    ----------------   ----------------
Conventional        654336  (639K)       30240   (30K)     624096  (609K)
Upper               158832  (155K)      144560  (141K)      14272   (14K)
Adapter RAM/ROM     235408  (230K)      235408  (230K)          0    (0K)
Extended (XMS)     7340032 (7168K)     2465792 (2408K)    4874240 (4760K)
Expanded (EMS)           0    (0K)           0    (0K)          0    (0K)
----------------   ----------------    ----------------   ----------------
Total memory       8388608 (8192K)     2876000 (2809K)    5512608 (5383K)

Total under 1 MB    813168  (794K)      174800  (171K)     638368  (623K)

Largest executable program size        624000  (609K)
Largest free upper memory block         11024   (11K)
MS-DOS is resident in the high memory area.
```

As you can see, making available the additional upper memory space in this monochrome region was enough to load and fit the MOUSE driver. Formerly occupying 16K in conventional memory, MOUSE.COM now fits comfortably in upper memory. The net effect is that application programs now see a total of 609K of free memory (as compared to only 593K in Figure 17.4).

If you make this kind of setting adjustment, be cautious for a while until you verify that your system continues to work reliably. When you run your applications, back up your work even more frequently than usual to be sure of minimizing any data loss. If you were wrong in the address range you specified, and your video adapter does in fact use certain addresses (that you have now loaded another driver or TSR into), your system will be very likely to crash.

EMM386.EXE also ignores all memory above the hexadecimal address DFFF. Thus, if you are sure that no program, driver, or system function uses some portion of these highest UMB addresses, you can also use the I switch to enlarge the usable UMB ranges even further. Be even more cautious up here. Since the system BIOS is located at the top of the UMB area, you must really know what is going on up there before you make use of address ranges.

Increase UMB Space by up to 64K

On my system, and perhaps on yours, the amount of free UMB memory can be increased by up to 64K by simply adding the M9 parameter to the DEVICE=EMM386.EXE command line in your AUTOEXEC.BAT file. If MemMaker determines that some of the additional space should be reserved for Windows, you will gain some but not all of the possible additional 64K of upper memory space.

Although this technique works on most AT-compatible systems, it doesn't work on all machines. In particular, it doesn't work on IBM's PS/2 computer systems. If you add M9 to your EMM386.EXE line on a PS/2 machine, you'll receive a warning message about optional ROM or RAM being detected in the page frame area. If you also receive that message on your computer after adding the M9 parameter, you should immediately remove the parameter from the CONFIG.SYS line and reboot.

On my AT system, I changed the initiation line in my CONFIG.SYS to the following:

```
DEVICE=D:\WINDOWS\EMM386.EXE NOEMS X=A000-CFFF M9
```

Even though I'm running EMM386.EXE with the NOEMS parameter and didn't wish to reserve any EMS memory, you'll see that this technique still made 24K of extra memory available on my system. For Windows users, the NOEMS parameter disables access only to LIM 3.2 expanded memory. LIM *4.0* expanded memory is still available in 386 Enhanced mode, so the page frame is still initially reserved.

By convention, the upper memory block that begins at hexadecimal address D000 is used for the normal page frame. The M9 parameter moves the starting address up to E000, extending whatever UMB ended at D000 by this now freed-up 64K of extra space. Of course, MemMaker analyzes whether or not some of this 64K should still be reserved. If so, it adds one or more WIN= switch entries to the EMM386 line.

Running the MEM/C command after making this simple change produced the results seen in Figure 17.7. As you can now see, there are several visible results. Formerly (in Figure 17.6), there was 609K available in conventional memory, and only 14K seemingly left free in the UMB region. This adjustment added nothing to the free conventional memory, but it did increase upper memory from 14K to 38K. This extra memory will be available to me if I later add other memory-resident programs or device drivers that can run in the upper memory area.

The final result in Figure 17.7, when compared to the starting point in Figure 17.1, demonstrates an important principle. Note that back in Figure 17.1, before any of this chapter's techniques were applied, there was 68K of unused upper memory, and only 547K of free conventional memory.

FIGURE 17.7

Adding the M9
parameter to the
EMM386.EXE device
driver line in CON-
FIG.SYS can gain up
to 64K of additional
UMB space.

```
Modules using memory below 1 MB:

Name        Total      =   Conventional  +  Upper Memory
--------    ----------     ------------     ------------
MSDOS       19853 (19K)     19853 (19K)         0  (0K)
HIMEM        1104  (1K)      1104  (1K)         0  (0K)
EMM386       3072  (3K)      3072  (3K)         0  (0K)
SMARTDRV    30832 (30K)      2480  (2K)     28352 (28K)
COMMAND      3760  (4K)      3760  (4K)         0  (0K)
SETVER        656  (1K)         0  (0K)       656  (1K)
ATDOSXL      9568  (9K)         0  (0K)      9568  (9K)
ANSI         4240  (4K)         0  (0K)      4240  (4K)
RCD         13072 (13K)         0  (0K)     13072 (13K)
DBLSPACE    52512 (51K)         0  (0K)     52512 (51K)
MOUSE       16864 (16K)         0  (0K)     16864 (16K)
UNDELETE    13616 (13K)         0  (0K)     13616 (13K)
DOSKEY       5680  (6K)         0  (0K)      5680  (6K)
Free       662944 (647K)   624096 (609K)    38848 (38K)

Memory Summary:

Type of Memory       Size      =     Used     +     Free
---------------    ------------     ------------     ------------
Conventional       654336 (639K)     30240  (30K)    624096 (609K)
Upper              183408 (179K)    144560 (141K)     38848  (38K)
Adapter RAM/ROM    210832 (206K)    210832 (206K)         0   (0K)
Extended (XMS)    7340032 (7168K)  2490368 (2432K)  4849664 (4736K)
Expanded (EMS)          0   (0K)         0   (0K)         0   (0K)
                  ------------     ------------     ------------
Total memory      8388608 (8192K)  2876000 (2809K)  5512608 (5383K)

Total under 1 MB   837744 (818K)   174800 (171K)    662944 (647K)

Largest executable program size           624000 (609K)
Largest free upper memory block            27696  (27K)
MS-DOS is resident in the high memory area.
```

By judiciously manipulating the ordering of drivers, and by judiciously
controlling the initial EMM386.EXE device settings, MemMaker and I
were able to accomplish a significant memory enhancement. First, my
system now has 609K of available free conventional memory. This represents a gain of 62K for each application program that now runs. If you're
a Windows user, that 62K of additional low memory is available for each
separate DOS program that is run in its own session. Second, to gain this
62K of low memory, I only had to use 30K of upper memory, since the
originally available 68K of UMB space is only down to 38K in Figure 17.7. And this 68K of upper memory blocks was not previously used
for any purpose.

Maximizing the Benefit of Available Memory

In the preceding sections you've learned how to maximize conventional memory most effectively and how to use upper reserved memory most efficiently. In this section, you'll learn a number of techniques for taking full advantage of whatever memory you actually end up with.

Using a RAM Disk

DOS and Windows include a device driver that can create a *RAM disk* (sometimes called a *virtual disk*). The RAM disk is not really a disk; it is an area in memory that simulates an additional disk drive. If your system has enough memory to assign to this purpose, and you use the resulting RAM disk effectively, it can be one of the best ways to trade memory for system performance.

Although the technique makes very different use of memory space than a disk cache, you can potentially gain more in terms of enhanced system performance. However, a RAM disk will improve efficiency only if it is used appropriately. If you have limited memory on your system, establishing a disk cache instead of a RAM disk will improve system efficiency more easily and for more of the time, since so much of a system's operation depends on disk reads and writes.

It takes more effort and understanding to make sure that a RAM disk contains the right programs, that the applications use those versions, and, when necessary, that the information on the RAM disk is properly copied elsewhere. The bottom line here is that I suggest you establish a disk cache first, and only then consider whether or not you have sufficient extra memory to use for a RAM disk.

The critical aspect of the RAM disk concept is that any files placed on the RAM disk are really memory-resident. They can therefore be retrieved at the speed of memory, which is usually microseconds or nanoseconds. File access on mechanical disk drives is slower, usually in the millisecond range. First, I'll briefly review how to create a RAM disk. Then, more importantly, I'll discuss the best ways to use it.

Creating a RAM Disk

Usually, you allocate some of your *extended* memory for RAM disk space, thereby reserving as much low memory as possible for your programs while gaining the performance benefits of a RAM disk. If you do not have extended memory to spare, forget about using a RAM disk. Although the driver can create a RAM disk in conventional memory, it would affect Windows' performance so adversely that it would be counterproductive.

As to the size of the RAM disk, that depends on too many factors. If you have lots of memory, and you've already established a disk cache, start out with a RAM drive equal to one-fourth of your total memory. As you use your system, pay attention to how you use the RAM disk (see next section) and whether you actually need this much space. If you don't need the space, reduce the size and allow Windows to use the memory for other purposes. If you find that you can profitably use a larger RAM disk, and your Windows performance hasn't suffered, then expand the size and see what happens.

TIP

RAM disks are counterproductive in limited-memory situations. Memory reserved for use as a RAM disk is no longer available for use by Windows. If you use too much space for a RAM disk, there may not be enough remaining memory for Windows to work efficiently. Windows users should remember that swapping only occurs when Windows runs out of physical memory. If you create a RAM disk to enhance performance, but force time-consuming swapping operations that otherwise would not have occurred, the overall effect will be slower Windows operations.

The RAM disk seen in Figure 17.8 can be implemented simply by including the following DEVICE line in your CONFIG.SYS:

```
DEVICE=C:\WINDOWS\RAMDRIVE.SYS 1024 /E
```

This statement first loads the RAM disk driver into memory. In this example, the RAMDRIVE.SYS file itself is located on drive C in the WINDOWS directory. The parameter value of 1024 in this example indicates that a total simulated disk of 1024K, or 1MB, should be created from the available extended memory. See the next section for advice on determining the size of your RAM disk, and on how to use it most efficiently.

FIGURE 17.8

A RAM disk uses physical memory to simulate a very fast real disk. A portion of physical memory replicates the emulated disk drive's directory table, while another portion emulates the file allocation table. Remaining RAM disk space emulates track and sector storage of files.

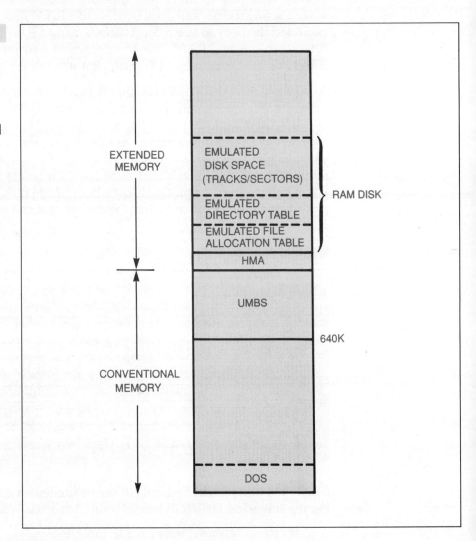

You can use two switches with this device driver command, depending on whether you wish to use extended or expanded memory for the RAM disk created. I've used the /E switch to use extended memory. For this command to work properly, you must have preceded this line with a DEVICE line for an extended memory manager, like HIMEM.SYS.

If you were to use the /A switch instead of /E, you could install your RAM disk in expanded memory. In this case, of course, you must precede the RAMDRIVE.SYS line with an appropriate DEVICE command for an expanded memory manager. If your system has an expanded memory board installed, and you must use the memory *as* expanded memory (as opposed to configuring it as extended memory), remember to use the driver that accompanied the physical expanded memory board.

You should usually install a RAM drive in extended memory (using the /E switch). If you do not specify either /A or /E, RAMDRIVE.SYS will attempt to install your RAM disk in conventional memory, which isn't recommended; use one of the two switches. For those of you who wish to exercise even greater control over the creation of a RAM disk on your system, use the following detailed syntax:

```
Device=[path]ramdrive.sys [Size [SectorSize [Entries]]] [/E|/A]
```

[Path] defines the full path to the RAMDRIVE.SYS file. The other parameter/switch possibilities are explained briefly in Table 17.3.

TABLE 17.3: Optional parameters for RAMDRIVE.SYS

PARAMETER	EXPLANATION
/a	Uses expanded memory for the RAM drive
DiskSize	Sets the number of kilobytes to allocate for the RAM drive
/e	Uses extended memory for the RAM drive
NumEntries	Sets maximum number of file and directory entries in the RAM drive's root directory
SectorSize	Sets the size of each emulated disk sector

FINE-TUNING YOUR SYSTEM MEMORY

Although you can use an expanded memory emulator, such as EMM-386.EXE, to obtain expanded memory for a RAM disk, it is inadvisable because of the inefficiencies associated with emulating expanded memory. Windows includes the emulation program to work with any 386 or 486 computer system; however, it does so mainly to enable you to run older applications that require expanded memory.

If you intend to use disk drives with drive identifiers beyond the letter E, DOS requires a LASTDRIVE statement to be included in your configuration file. This additional statement must be of the form

```
LASTDRIVE=x
```

where x is the last valid alphabetic character that DOS will use for a drive identifier.

Don't forget that changes you make to the CONFIG.SYS file don't take effect until the DOS system is rebooted.

Advice for Efficient Use of a RAM Disk

Now that you know how to create a RAM disk, you need to know how to use it to its best advantage. Here are some suggestions for using your RAM disk.

Place a copy of COMMAND.COM on your RAM disk. Then perform the following to inform DOS that COMMAND.COM is located on the RAM disk. Assuming your RAM disk is on drive E (substitute the appropriate letter on your system), include the following command in your system's AUTOEXEC.BAT file:

```
SET COMSPEC=E:\COMMAND.COM
```

This will speed up all programs that execute DOS commands from within themselves, such as Framework IV or QDOS III. These programs work by loading a second copy of the command processor (COMMAND.COM). This command will also speed up application software that overwrites the command-processor portion of DOS.

Before you follow the above suggestions for using your RAM disk effectively, you should learn how to use it safely. As you know, using a RAM

➤ **EXTRA!**

Take Advantage of Your System's RAM Disk

Follow any or all of these guidelines for the most efficient use of space reserved for a RAM disk on your system:

- Place a copy of COMMAND.COM on your RAM disk.

- Place frequently used DOS commands (such as EDIT.COM if you use the DOS editor often) onto your RAM disk.

- Place frequently used batch files and disk-resident utility programs on the RAM disk.

- Load any text files that are used frequently but are not changed.

- Load any large support files (like spelling dictionaries or a thesaurus file) that your word processor or integrated software may need.

- Place index-type files (generated by many database management systems) on the RAM disk for faster data access to records in large data files.

- Place overlay files on your RAM disk to speed up execution of software that references such overlay modules.

- Remember to set your PATH properly so DOS can find your main applications.

disk is much faster than using real disks. Programs that formerly took hours to run may take minutes, minutes can become seconds, and waiting time can disappear. When RAM disks are used improperly, however, hours of work can also disappear in seconds.

Since a RAM disk exists in memory, any information stored on it will vanish when the computer is turned off. You gain great advantage by storing and accessing the right files on a RAM disk, but you must remember that these files are destroyed when any of the following events occur: you turn off the power, a power failure or brownout occurs, your computer plug comes out of the wall, or you simply reboot your system with Ctrl+Alt+Del.

If you place and update important data files on a RAM disk for the sake of rapid access, save copies of them to a real disk before you turn off the power. Also back up copies of them to a real disk at frequent intervals to avoid losing all your work.

WARNING

If you use a RAM disk to work more efficiently with permanent files, remember to back up these files to a real disk frequently.

► EXTRA!

Improve Application Performance with the TEMP Variable

Many DOS (and Windows) applications create temporary files during their operations. For example, compiling and print spooling are notorious for generating temp files—I say "notorious" because they are a burden on your system. You can speed up operations greatly by first creating a RAM disk and then setting the TEMP variable to point to a directory on the RAM disk.

Because there is a design limit on the number of file names a root directory can hold, use a subdirectory (like E:\TEMP if your RAM disk is known as drive E:). You can't easily know in advance how many files will be temporarily created by your applications. If you choose to gain speed by setting TEMP to a RAM disk, you must also be sure to have created a sufficiently large RAM disk. Some programs will fail if they try to write to a disk that is out of space.

RAM disks are usually much smaller than the space available on a hard disk, so you are more likely to encounter problems if your RAM disk is not large enough. Because many printing jobs consume large amounts of space, you should not assign the TEMP variable to a RAM disk location unless you have at least 2MB to spare for this RAM disk. If you do not use a RAM disk location, you can and should still use the TEMP variable to enhance system performance by pointing it to a fast hard disk.

Set up a connection between your RAM disk and the TEMP variable with these commands in your AUTOEXEC.BAT file (replace E: with your RAM disk's drive identifier):

```
MD E:\TEMP
SET TEMP=E:\TEMP
```

Note that some programs (like a C compiler) may use a different environment variable (like TMP) for the same purpose as the more common TEMP. Read your application's documentation to discover the name of any environment variables used for this purpose. In these cases, you would simply include an additional SET command in your AUTOEXEC.BAT to point the application's environment variable to your RAM disk location.

Windows Users: Save Memory by Trimming System Fat

Several features of Windows consume variable amounts of memory. It is not even obvious in some cases that the memory is being consumed. This section will point out some of the areas that, once managed, can yield surprising gains for Windows users.

> ➤ **EXTRA!**

Wallpaper Is Not Free

The more detailed your wallpaper bit map is, the more memory it consumes. In order to redisplay your desktop, including the background wallpaper, Windows makes a copy in memory of your entire wallpaper file. I occasionally use a beautiful, peaceful mountain scene for wallpaper background on my 8MB system. When I do, I also occasionally receive an "Out of Memory" message.

If Windows sends you this message too often, try a less detailed .BMP image. Or eliminate wallpaper completely by setting Wallpaper to None in the Desktop section of the Control Panel. Remember that wallpaper images consume memory equivalent to their bitmap size, which in the case of graphics can be several hundred kilobytes.

Don't Load Unnecessary Drivers

There is a temptation to load small device drivers (of the .COM or .EXE file type) and TSRs prior to starting Windows. Even though it is clearly less efficient, and uses extra conventional memory, it is easier to load them once in an AUTOEXEC.BAT file. The alternative is to run DOS applications under Windows from customized batch files run from PIFs. This may be the most efficient way to do it, but it is still an extra effort.

If you are just running Windows applications, you needn't load a mouse driver at all. Only if you run DOS applications that require a mouse must you even consider loading a mouse driver in addition to the one that Windows includes. That is because Windows manages your mouse during all Windows operations, except when running full-screen DOS applications.

Similarly, although it may be tempting to use DOS's ability to load drivers and TSRs in upper memory blocks, don't do it just as a matter of course. After all, small TSRs from DOS itself, like DOSKEY, are useful and don't take up much room, right? Wrong. This whole chapter is about getting 5K here, 10K there, 32K another place. Every conventional memory program that can be placed in UMBs, and every buffer that can be moved into extended memory, frees up more conventional memory. This in turn improves the overall efficiency of your entire system.

Reduce the Size of WIN.INI

Reducing the size of WIN.INI can not only reclaim memory for your system but can also improve overall performance. While Windows is executing, a portion of memory is reserved to hold a copy of the WIN.INI configuration settings. By making WIN.INI smaller, you reduce the necessary amount of memory that must be reserved. This will make extra memory available to Windows for other uses, not to mention reducing the time it takes to load and later update the WIN.INI file itself. Try any or all of these techniques to reduce WIN.INI file size:

- First make a backup copy elsewhere for safety, readability, and ease of restoration.

- Remove all comment lines. (These all begin with a semicolon.)

- Remove all blank lines.

- Remove all initialization sections for applications you no longer need or use.

- Remove all lines in the [ports] section for any ports your hardware does not have, or that your software will not use.

- Remove lines in the [fonts] and [TrueType] sections for fonts you do not expect to use.

- Remove lines in the [extensions] section for associated programs that you do not typically expect to run via the associated data file.

- Remove all entries from the [intl] section except those that override (are not equal to) the default values.

- If you don't expect to print from multiple programs at once, you may not need the Print Manager. Setting Spooler=False in the [Windows] section will retain memory otherwise assigned to the Print Manager.

➤ EXTRA!

Windows Users Can Save Memory by Eliminating Fonts

Font files are stored in the SYSTEM directory. If you eliminate access to fonts from within Windows, you are not necessarily erasing them from the disk. You are merely freeing up the memory used by Windows as a means of providing font selections to your applications.

Select the Fonts icon in the Control Panel in order to display the Fonts dialog box. You can save memory in three ways from this box:

1. Remove the mark beside the Use TrueType checkbox, but only if one of your applications uses TrueType fonts.

2. Turn on the mark beside the TrueType Only checkbox, but only if all of your applications use TrueType fonts.

3. Remove any fonts that you know are not used by Windows or any of your applications. You can always restore them by later selecting Add from this same screen and telling Windows to add from the list of fonts found in the SYSTEM directory.

Giving DOS Applications in Windows What They Need

DOS applications that run under Windows are sometimes a demanding lot. They expect to have an entire system's resources available to them. This section deals with providing memory-related resources, like expanded memory and environment space, that they occasionally need in order to run successfully in the Windows environment.

Managing Environment Space

Do you use up most of the space in your DOS's default environment? If you've changed your DOS Shell command (in CONFIG.SYS), you may think that you've increased the environment size—and in fact, you have—but only in DOS, not in Windows.

TIP

Some TSRs make a copy of the DOS environment when they first load. The fewer environmental variables that exist when you first load the TSR, the smaller the memory drain. Consequently, you can save small amounts of memory in your AUTO-EXEC.BAT file by loading needed TSRs first, prior to running any commands that set environmental variables (such as PATH, COMSPEC, and PROMPT).

To enlarge the environment space, you added the /e:*nnnn* switch to increase the available environment to *nnnn* bytes. But once you start Windows, each DOS session you start (i.e., each DOS shell that you spawn), and each DOS PIF that you use to launch a DOS application, consumes an additional *nnnn* bytes of environment space.

Some DOS applications require additional environmental variable space beyond what is initially used. If the available space is exceeded, the application may erroneously attempt to use addressable locations that it should not or can not, and the application may freeze up, or worse.

You must use one of the following techniques to ensure that your non-Windows applications receive a larger environment. There are two ways to launch a DOS application with more than the default number of environment bytes:

- *To launch DOS applications from a DOS prompt that you bring up via the DOS Prompt icon in the Main group of the Program Manager:* Open up the Main subgroup in the Program Manager. Highlight the DOS Prompt icon. Then pull down the File menu, and select Properties. Change the Command Line field entry from COM-MAND.COM to

```
COMMAND.COM /e:1024
```

or any other size that you'd like.

- *To launch DOS applications from their own customized .PIF files:* Run the PIF Editor from the Accessories subgroup in the Program Manager. In the Program Filename field, enter COMMAND.COM. In the Optional Parameters field, type the environment size specification (e.g., /e:1024), followed by a /C and the name of the program you actually wish to run. For example, to run 123.EXE, you might enter in this field

```
/e:1024 /c c:\123r23\123.exe
```

In either of these two cases, the extra environment size will ensure more successful execution of your program. And the memory consumed is only a temporary burden on that particular DOS session under Windows. When the DOS application ends, the environment memory is freed up along with all other memory that was specific to this single DOS session under Windows.

Providing Expanded Memory

As a rule, Windows users should configure any expanded memory in your system as extended memory. Follow the instructions that accompanied your expanded memory board for doing this. DOS users only should make decisions about expanded memory based on the programs you are using. 1-2-3, for instance, uses expanded memory efficiently for large worksheets.

Windows can use the EMM386.EXE device driver, when running in 386 Enhanced mode, to emulate expanded memory whenever necessary for your non-Windows applications. Consequently, your system needs no actual expanded memory in order to satisfy the occasional expanded-memory needs of a non-Windows application. Maximizing the available extended memory is the best use of any physical expanded memory in your system.

If you run non-Windows applications in 386 Enhanced mode, but none of those applications requires expanded memory support, you should enter or modify the following line in the [386Enh] section of your SYS-TEM.INI file:

```
ReservePageFrame=No
```

Turning this setting off frees up conventional memory. Since the page frame in upper reserved blocks (between 640K and 1MB) is no longer reserved for EMS support, Windows can now use this space for other purposes, such as allocating DOS transfer buffers when necessary.

When running in standard mode, configure your expanded memory board to provide as expanded memory only as much of its memory as is needed by your non-Windows applications. For most efficient Windows operations, the remainder of the board's memory should be configured as extended memory.

Summary

In this chapter, you've learned some very powerful methods in DOS to optimize the availability and usage of memory:

- The MemMaker utility can automatically make changes in your AUTOEXEC.BAT and CONFIG.SYS files to optimize the use of upper memory and maximize the amount of free conventional memory for applications.

- The CONFIG.SYS file permits you to initialize several internal DOS system variables at bootup time.

- The BUFFERS command defines precisely how many internal buffers DOS will use.

- The FILES command specifies the maximum allowable number of open files that DOS will understand and support while DOS and your application programs run.

- The DEVICE command allows you to incorporate any number of specialized peripheral device drivers into your DOS configuration.

- The DEVICEHIGH command loads device driver files into upper memory blocks (640K–1Mb), assuming that your CONFIG.SYS file contained an earlier DOS= command that specified the UMB parameter. The LOADHIGH can also load memory-resident programs into available upper memory blocks.

- A RAM disk is a memory-resident simulation of a typical mechanical disk. The RAMDRIVE.SYS device driver offers flexibility, because you can specify which files are stored in the RAM disk. It also offers you increased system performance and speed.

- Many Windows specific techniques are discussed to help optimize memory usage in DOS systems that run Windows.

CHAPTER

18

Optimizing
Performance for DOS
and Windows Applications

THIS chapter focuses on specific techniques for enhancing your overall system performance. Although this book is primarily about DOS, the information in this chapter is aimed at both DOS and Windows users. Many of the methods discussed work effectively for improving the performance of both Windows and non-Windows (or strictly DOS) applications; others are useful for running non-Windows applications in Windows.

You will learn techniques for making more efficient use of your system's hard disk and CPU. I'll start with hardware and software methods for implementing *disk caches*, then I'll move on to explain how *swapping* helps both multitasking and throughput (especially important for Windows users). I'll also discuss how you can customize swapping to suit your own particular needs.

Beyond using a caching scheme, you can also increase performance dramatically by simply improving file layout and access techniques. Later in the chapter I'll present the information you need for making these improvements.

I'll also show you how to tweak Windows settings, such as those in the WIN.INI and SYSTEM.INI files, to have Windows manage hard-disk data more efficiently. Some of these settings enhance hard-disk access, while others enhance the distribution of CPU cycles among executing applications. Throughout the chapter I'll present a wide range of techniques for enhancing performance of both DOS and Windows applications through improved use of your CPU and your system's hard disks.

➤ **EXTRA!**

Control Paging on Your Machine

You can disable swapping in Windows 386 Enhanced mode by specifying a swap-file type of *None* in the Virtual Memory dialog box. Alternatively, in the [386Enh] section of SYSTEM.INI, you can set Paging=**No** to disable demand paging completely.

When might you want to disable paging?

- When you are tight on disk space and don't want Windows to use any space at all for paging activities.

- When you want to improve the performance of active applications at the expense of new applications. Newer applications may not be able to run at all if existing applications cannot be swapped to disk. However, currently running applications will run and switch faster because all switching will be memory-based, involving no disk swapping of any application memory segments.

- When your system has more memory than it needs for your mix of applications.

By disabling paging, you gain:

- More memory for applications, because no memory is consumed by the swap file and associated tables.

- More disk space for applications, because no swap space is allocated on the disk.

- Faster processing, because the internal Windows overhead for managing the swapping process is eliminated.

Boosting System Performance with Disk Caching

It's simple. I've said it before, and you'll probably hear it again: The more memory your system has, the better it will perform. DOS can access memory in a matter of nanoseconds. This is a lot faster than accessing data from disk, which typically takes milliseconds (which is fast, but clearly not as fast as the CPU). If you have enough RAM, you can configure DOS (and Windows, for that matter) to do much if not most of its application work in RAM, and the disk will rarely need to be accessed.

Windows will from time to time read different parts of a program's code or data into memory. From time to time, Windows also makes room in memory for a new program by moving portions of executing programs out to specially designed files on the disk. And from time to time, Windows will read new information for its own purposes into memory. Every disk read or disk write reduces overall system performance. Any technique that reduces the average time necessary for disk reads or writes will make Windows and your applications run faster. This section begins the discussion on disk improvements by explaining how to use a technique called *disk caching* to speed up overall disk input and output.

Understanding the Concepts behind Disk Caching

Disk caching is the best direct improvement you can make to a hard disk's performance. A *disk cache* is simply an area of memory that replicates disk data. By using the data in memory instead of on disk, programs can access the data at RAM speeds instead of at disk speeds.

As Figure 18.1 depicts, a disk cache can be constructed in hardware or in software. Both methods offer improvements in performance. Software

Disk caches come in hardware and software versions. A caching disk controller is the fastest and best solution, but also costs the most. DOS comes with the SMARTDRV disk-caching program, which improves performance at the cost of only some extended memory.

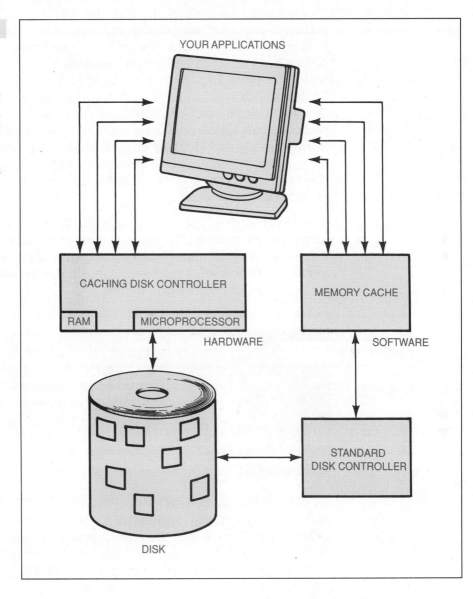

YOUR APPLICATIONS

CACHING DISK CONTROLLER

RAM   MICROPROCESSOR

HARDWARE

MEMORY CACHE

SOFTWARE

DISK

STANDARD DISK CONTROLLER

cache programs are inexpensive and use memory that already exists in your system. They result in a significant speed boost. Hardware caching controllers are significantly more expensive, but offer an even more noticeable jump in performance. In large part, this results because the hardware board provides its own cache memory. Because of this, the cache does not reduce available memory, thereby reducing the performance impact on all remaining activities. Additionally, hardware cache boards usually include their own processor chip to manage the cache. Consequently, your system's processor chip is freed up from caching chores to concentrate on other tasks, thereby improving your system's performance even more.

In both types of caches, there is additional overhead involved in creating, filling, and maintaining the cache. If data were read or written only once, a disk cache would not provide any speedup. But disk caching provides significant performance improvements; I'll discuss why this is invariably true as I explain both types of caches.

N O T E

If you're not careful, you may find that you have installed both a hardware caching controller board and a software caching program. In this instance, you may be asking your system to maintain two copies of all cached data. This is wasteful. If your hardware supports its own caching, discontinue software caching.

DOS includes the SMARTDrive utility (SMARTDRV.EXE), a disk-caching program that significantly improves system response. It is software-based, so to gain the performance improvement possible with a cache, you must allocate some of your extended memory to the cache. If your system is short on memory, you should allocate a proportionally smaller amount of memory to the cache, or you should add more memory.

All software caches work in roughly the same way. The disk cache program intercepts all disk read and write requests, which come from applications and from Windows itself. The cache program attempts to satisfy the disk requests by locating a copy of the disk data in the RAM-based cache. If the disk data has already been read from the disk once, for instance, the data will be found in the cache. If the same data is requested more than once, it can be provided to your application or to Windows much more quickly from the RAM cache in which it is held than it can by rereading it from its disk location over and over again.

On the one hand, some competitive software cache programs are more efficient than Microsoft's SMARTDRV program. These programs have more effective algorithms for managing the memory assigned to the cache and for reading data from and writing data to a disk. If all other things were equal, I'd suggest getting the smartest and most effective cache program on the market. On the other hand, SMARTDRV comes with DOS and with Windows, and is therefore always compatible with the current version of Windows. Nearly every other competitive cache program is potentially incompatible with each new DOS or Windows release. Typically, the cache vendors must release new versions of their programs each time Microsoft releases a new version.

At the very least, using a third-party cache program entails a time lag during which you may have to spend time without a disk cache (or go to the trouble of installing SMARTDRV). It typically necessitates an additional expense because upgrades cost money. And there might be more: I always have a nagging suspicion that the competitive program has additional incompatibilities that may put my hard disk's data at risk.

I may be somewhat conservative, but I strongly recommend installing SMARTDRV. Read the next two sections, however, to learn what other possibilities there are for improving on SMARTDRV. You can then decide for yourself whether or not to buy into the possible improvements in exchange for the additional cost, possible incompatibilities, and extra effort of learning and installing the competitive program.

Using a Software-Based Disk-Caching Program

You must load software cache programs at the time you start your system. You load some disk caches as device drivers in your CONFIG.SYS file, and you load others, like Windows' SMARTDRV.EXE program, from the command prompt, perhaps in AUTOEXEC.BAT. When a disk-caching program is first loaded, it reserves for itself a portion of available memory. SMARTDRV starts out by allocating a portion of extended memory, although Windows and SMARTDRV work in tandem to increase or decrease this amount dynamically as Windows' needs for memory vary.

This technique can be quite efficient. Some other cache programs allocate a fixed amount of memory. Still others allocate all available memory, releasing it only when applications request it for other purposes.

Caching Disk-Read Requests

Once installed, a disk-caching program is activated each time that any executing program makes a disk request. The cache program intercepts the read request and checks to see whether the requested data already resides in the cache. If so, the request is satisfied from the data in the cache. If not, the data is read from the disk and placed in the cache. Again the request is satisfied from data in the cache. Note that the next time the data is requested, it is returned from the cache and no disk read is necessary.

Typically, each time data is requested, more data is read from the disk than was requested. The portion of the cache that holds this extra information is sometimes called a *read-ahead*, or *look-ahead*, buffer. Figure 18.2 depicts this caching scenario. This constitutes intelligent guessing by the disk cache program about upcoming read requests.

The extra information that is read is simply data from adjacent sectors on the same track. This will be helpful only if your disk is unfragmented (see later in this chapter) and if adjacent sectors do in fact contain related portions of the same file.

When your application next makes disk requests, the cache program intercepts the requests again, and if the requested data can be found within the read-ahead buffer, the read request is satisfied, saving time when compared to a disk read. If it is not already in the cache, it is read into the cache from disk (once again along with some extra sectors to increase the possibility of satisfying subsequent read requests).

Disk caching anticipates upcoming read requests. A read-ahead buffer stores more data than was required by the previous request. Once the data is in memory, subsequent requests can be satisfied from this cache much faster than by additional disk accesses.

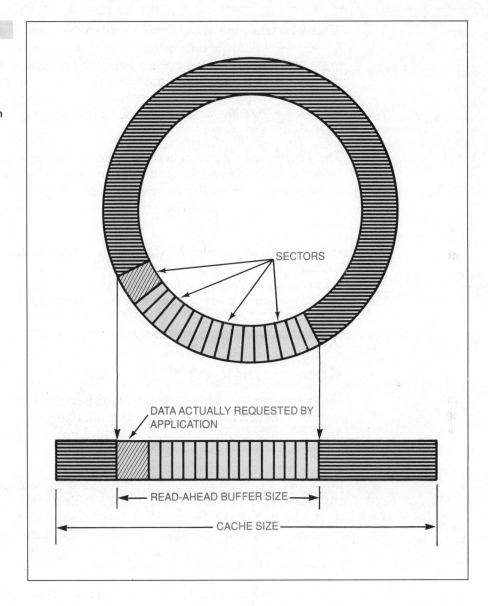

SECTORS

DATA ACTUALLY REQUESTED BY APPLICATION

READ-AHEAD BUFFER SIZE

CACHE SIZE

After a certain time, the disk cache will fill up with copies of disk data. Some of this information will be from earlier application requests. To make room in the cache for new data, some portions of the cache holding the data least recently used are freed up. The assumption here is that whatever data has been stored in the cache for the longest amount of time, without having been accessed, is the least likely to be needed in the immediate future.

The smarter the algorithm in the disk cache program, the more likely the memory cache will actually contain sectors that will satisfy upcoming disk information requests. The more often that disk requests are satisfied from the cache rather than from new physical disk reads, the faster your system will be.

In addition, an intelligent disk cache program can intercept CPU memory-management requests as well as disk requests. If disk requests are not a bottleneck, the software will recognize this and can free up some of its temporarily underutilized disk cache memory. This gives Windows more memory for improving the performance of tasks such as spreadsheet recalculations or database sorting.

Caching Disk-Write Requests

The preceding section explains how disk caching can improve performance by reducing disk reads. But what about disk *writes*? Once again, the disk-caching software can have a dramatic impact on performance. However, there is a certain risk to be run when using disk-write caching. If physical disk writes are not done immediately when requested by applications, there is the possibility that the file itself will not always contain the changes made to it. If power is lost, your file's integrity could be compromised. Because of this, some caching programs do not intercept write requests at all. Theoretically, this ensures that all requested writes are made directly to your disk. This way, if you have a power outage, you can be sure that all requested disk writes were done.

Under normal, uncached, conditions, multiple write requests will result in multiple disk writes. If those writes are made to adjacent sectors in the same file, located in the same unfragmented track, an obvious optimization is possible with caching. A smart caching program can collect all the writes in adjacent cache memory locations. Periodically, a group of updates to the file could then be made with a single physical disk write.

Some reviewers claim that the period of time during which a loss can occur between cache writes is so small that it's not worth worrying about. The performance improvement can be substantial, so go with it, they say. But power brownouts and blackouts happen often enough that I'm leery about relying on delayed write-backs to a disk, unless my system is plugged into a battery backup device.

I have to marvel, however, at the ingenuity demonstrated by caching techniques. Because the overall time savings can be substantial, you should weigh the trade-offs in using disk caches for both reading and writing.

Depending on the caching technique used, pending writes can be done at fixed, periodic times or when a certain number of sectors' worth of data to be written from the cache accumulates. Or they can be done a certain amount of time after an application actually writes the data into the cache. Or they can be done at times when the cache program determines that the CPU is idle. Each program makes its own decisions about trade-offs in CPU usage and disk/memory efficiency.

There are also advanced techniques that defer writing of data until certain *percentages* of individual tracks must be updated and rewritten. Some caching programs even analyze the pending writes and reorder them according to the type of disk you have. If the movement of the disk heads is considered when the writes are performed, this overhead can also be minimized. Reducing disk write time will eventually result in a more efficient Windows system.

Smart caching logic also compares write requests from applications to existing sector data currently in the cache. There are a couple of powerful algorithms that can be employed here. First, suppose that the caching program determines that a new write request does not change data that has already been written to the disk. In this case, the new write request will simply be ignored.

WARNING   If you warm boot your system (perhaps via a batch file), be careful to ensure that cached writes are actually performed by SMARTDRV. Execute a SMARTDRV /C command to flush the Smart Drive buffer to disk. If you are executing in a multitasking environment, such as Windows, you should also turn off the write-caching feature with SMARTDRV /C prior to performing the warm boot.

Next, suppose that a new write request causes changes to occur to data that is still being held in the cache (i.e., it has not yet undergone its delayed, or *staged*, write). The caching program can simply throw away the earlier request to the affected data sector, replacing it with this more current write request. This means that multiple application requests to write the same data will take dramatically less time because only the final write request has to be written to the disk.

All these techniques can further reduce the overhead of disk accessing. Since no one caching program implements all of them, you really have no way of knowing which program to buy, but you now know why there are differences among the programs. Most differences lie in the degree of intelligence in each program's caching logic.

Using the SMARTDRV.EXE Disk-Caching Program

Both DOS and Windows include a version of SMARTDRV. You should always use whichever version is most recent. In addition, you should use the version of HIMEM.SYS that came with the SMARTDRV.EXE that you choose to use.

Because SMARTDRV almost always improves performance, you should make sure that the SMARTDRV command line is in your AUTO-EXEC.BAT file. When you first install Windows 3.1, Setup includes a single line at the beginning of AUTOEXEC.BAT that specifies the SMARTDRV.EXE program:

```
C:\WINDOWS\SMARTDRV.EXE
```

This line accepts all the default settings, which typically work just fine for your system. However, this version of SMARTDRV has a number of optional settings that you can use to optimize your particular environment.

➤ EXTRA!

Fragmentation Affects Directory and File Entries!

Large files usually exceed the size of a single DOS allocation unit (i.e., a cluster). If the immediately following allocation unit on the disk happens to already be in use, DOS must allocate space from elsewhere on the disk. This means your file becomes fragmented.

The same concept applies to the more subtle storage of directory entries for other subdirectories, and not just for data or program files. Each entry in a directory forces DOS to create a 32-byte entry that includes the file's name, length in bytes, attributes, and starting disk location. There are only so many of these 32-byte entries that can fit into a single cluster.

If the number of directory entries exceeds this particular number (which depends on your drive's cluster size), then DOS must allocate additional space just to store the data about the directory's entries. In other words, directory entries can become fragmented, just as can file entries.

Use the **DEFRAG** utility to reduce fragmentation after it occurs, or be careful not to have too many entries in any one directory. The greater the number of entries, the more likely it is that the directory will become fragmented. Until you actually do use DEFRAG to eliminate fragmentation, all file accesses into that affected directory will incur the higher overhead involved with getting past the directory fragmentation.

Customizing Your Version of SMARTDRV

To install SMARTDRV with customized settings, you can issue the following command line:

```
[pathname]SMARTDRV.EXE options
```

where *pathname* indicates where the SMARTDRV.EXE program resides. The *options* can be any or all of the following:

Drive[+ | −]   Each *drive* entry specifies a disk drive to be cached. You can specify multiple drives, separated by spaces. If you do not specify a particular drive, SMARTDRV will automatically set its own level of caching for drives not indicated. It will cache read requests only for floppy disks, will cache read and write requests for hard disks, and will ignore both read and write requests for CD-ROM and network drives. You can follow each drive identifier with a plus or a minus sign. Appending a plus sign enables read and write caching on that drive. Appending a minus sign disables read and write caching. Entering a drive letter but not appending either a plus or a minus sign enables read caching but disables write caching.

InitCacheSize WinCacheSize   This option consists of either a single kilobyte value, which represents the initial DOS cache size, or a pair of kilobyte values, which represent the initial DOS cache size and a smaller Windows cache size, as explained below:

InitCacheSize   Defines how many kilobytes are to be initially reserved for a SMARTDRV cache. Because the cache is actually set up when DOS alone is active, the amount of the cache may drop when Windows runs. The difference between *InitCacheSize* and *WinCacheSize* (below) represents the amount of memory reduction that Windows will be allowed if it needs to reduce cache usage to satisfy other memory needs. Table 18.1 summarizes the default values used by SMARTDRV for this initial cache size.

TABLE 18.1: Default SMARTDRV settings

EXTENDED MEMORY (X)	INITCACHESIZE	WINCACHESIZE
Less than 1Mb	Uses all extended memory	0
At least 1Mb, but less than 2Mb	1Mb	256K
At least 2Mb, but less than 4Mb	1Mb	512K
At least 4Mb, but less than 6Mb	2Mb	1Mb
6Mb or more	2Mb	2Mb

WinCacheSize   Defines the minimum size that Windows must retain for SMARTDRV if it decides to reduce the memory allocation to enhance Windows operations. In general, Windows and SMARTDRV cooperatively expand and contract the cache during multitasking. *WinCacheSize* controls the minimum cache size, just as *InitCacheSize* controls the maximum cache size. When you exit Windows, the cache is restored to the *InitCacheSize* amount.

/E:*elementsize*   Each *element* defines how many bytes of memory will constitute the smallest amount of information to be processed at a single time by SMARTDRV. By default, an 8K element is used, although you could also select one of the following smaller values: 1024, 2048, or 4096.

/B:*buffersize*   *Buffersize* defines how many bytes are to be in SMARTDRV's look-ahead buffer. Regardless of how many bytes are actually requested during a disk read request, SMARTDRV will read the specified number of bytes into its memory cache. The default buffersize is 16K, but it can be any multiple of *elementsize*.

/C   Clears all delayed-write data from the cache out to disk. Normally, SMARTDRV delays writing data from the cache memory until other disk activity has been completed.

/L Forces SMARTDRV to load itself into low memory (below 640K). This option is meaningful only if you have enabled the upper memory blocks (UMB) region with the EMM386.EXE program.

/Q Prevents the display of SMARTDRV information messages on your monitor.

➤ EXTRA!

Should You Opt for Permanent or for Temporary Swapping?

In Windows 386 Enhanced mode, you have the option of using a permanent swap file or allowing Windows to create and maintain a temporary file as necessary. Windows only creates a temporary file if you have not explicitly created a permanent one, and if sufficient disk space remains available.

Advantages of a permanent swap file:

- Windows runs faster because it reads the reserved disk clusters directly, rather than going through the DOS file-management system.

- Windows starts up faster because it doesn't have to create a temporary swap file.

- Multitasking can proceed more smoothly because of the guaranteed disk space that is available for virtual memory if your system runs out of actual physical memory.

Disadvantage of a permanent swap file:

- Free disk space is reduced because of the guaranteed swap-file space that Windows reserves. Even when Windows is not running, this space is unavailable to other programs.

/R   Restarts SMARTDRV, after first taking care of any delayed writes out to disk.

/S   Displays extra status information about SMARTDRV.

/?   Displays help text about the SMARTDRV utility and its command options.

Setting the SMARTDRV options to their optimum values is not a precise science. As Table 18.1 suggests, there is no specific percentage of available extended memory that works all the time. Under Windows, the defaults used by SMARTDRV use a larger proportion of extended memory as the amount of available extended memory increases. This is reasonable because once the memory needed by applications is satisfied, the remaining memory can be used by SMARTDRV to satisfy disk requests more efficiently.

Analyzing the Performance of SMARTDRV

At first glance, you would think that the larger the cache, the more frequently the requested data would be found in the cache. In fact, on my system approximately 84 percent of all disk data requests were satisfied from the cache. I calculated this percentage from the information in Figure 18.3: SMARTDrive gave me 11,531 cache hits out of 13,646 (that is, 11,531 + 2,115) possibilities. (A *cache hit* is when SMARTDrive finds the desired data in the memory cache; having to access the disk is called a *cache miss*.)

Although you should adjust your cache-size values according to your particular mix of applications, my 84 percent hit rate was obtained using a cache size of 2Mb. This was my starting cache size; Figure 18.3 shows that the cache size while running Windows is still equal to 2Mb. My own rule of thumb is to specify a starting cache of one-fourth of available memory. I let Windows work that size down as necessary in response to application demands.

As you can also see in Figure 18.3, the entire 2Mb is still available. This confirms that Windows is not feeling pressed to reduce cache size to

Use the **/S** switch to obtain SMARTDRV status information online. You can discover whether reads or writes are cached for each of your drives. Use the **/?** switch to learn about more detailed switch settings for SMARTDRV.

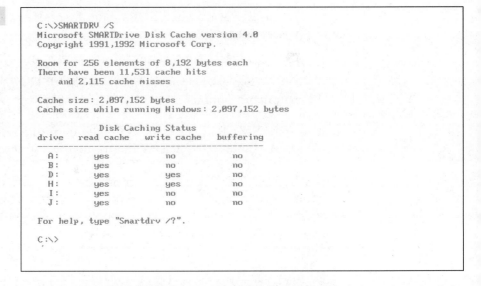

```
C:\>SMARTDRV /S
Microsoft SMARTDrive Disk Cache version 4.0
Copyright 1991,1992 Microsoft Corp.

Room for 256 elements of 8,192 bytes each
There have been 11,531 cache hits
     and 2,115 cache misses

Cache size: 2,097,152 bytes
Cache size while running Windows: 2,097,152 bytes

               Disk Caching Status
drive    read cache    write cache    buffering
-------------------------------------------------
  A:        yes            no            no
  B:        yes            no            no
  D:        yes            yes           no
  H:        yes            yes           no
  I:        yes            no            no
  J:        yes            no            no

For help, type "Smartdrv /?".

C:\>
```

satisfy other applications' needs. This even suggests that, for my particular mix of multitasking programs, I should be able to improve the percentage of cache hits by enlarging the initial size of the cache.

There is almost no end to the number of suggestions that I could make about specifying cache sizes. What sizes to use depend greatly on your mix of applications and how you use them. For example, suppose that you open and run new applications frequently and open and close documents frequently. In both cases, your disk is accessed frequently. A disk cache will be very helpful. In this case, you will probably want to increase your cache's size.

On the other hand, suppose that you run certain applications regularly, leaving them open on the desktop once you've started them. Particularly if you use certain documents repeatedly, Windows will be better able to use the cache memory if it can assign it to the applications. In this case, a smaller disk cache will probably be better for your system.

Is Unnecessary Buffering Occurring in Your System?

At the bottom of the window in Figure 18.3, you can see a column of information that indicates that no buffering is being done for any of my drives (A, B, D, H, I, and J). This means that my particular computer is relatively new, has a correct BIOS, and can work with virtual memory. If your equipment is older and cannot handle the requirements of the SMARTDRV program, Setup inserts the following line in your CONFIG.SYS file:

```
Device=smartdrv.exe /double_buffer
```

This implements an extra level of *buffering*, which may be necessary for some equipment. However, Setup may not always be able to assess the capabilities of your equipment correctly. If you run SMARTDRV at the command prompt with the **/S** option, and all the entries in the "buffering" column are *NO*, then you do not need this extra buffering. If the Device=smartdrv.exe line appears in CONFIG.SYS, you should exit Windows, remove the line from CONFIG.SYS, and reboot. Your system will perform more efficiently without double buffering.

Using a Hardware Cache Controller

Using a hardware disk cache is more efficient but much more costly than using a software disk cache. A disk controller that has caching capabilities includes a microprocessor and RAM on the board. The microprocessor manages the cache reads and writes, and the RAM on the controller card handles the job formerly done by a part of your system's extended memory.

If your system includes a hardware cache controller, you can remove the software cache program to free up memory. You will have more UMB space available for other TSRs or device drivers, or more low memory available for virtual machines when running DOS applications under Windows.

Because a hardware controller contains a separate microprocessor, it can perform its disk-sector caching duties while your system's CPU carries out other chores. Consequently, your CPU is used more efficiently, and Windows can use the freed-up RAM more efficiently—your entire system benefits. Particularly in multitasking environments and in heavily burdened network environments, a hard-disk cache controller will frequently account for noticeable improvements in overall system performance.

➤ **EXTRA!**

What Are the Best Performance Settings?

There is no "best" size for any of the key performance facilities: swap files, RAM disks, or disk caches. Each of them depends on a number of variables, and will be different for many people's systems. All of the following factors may influence your decisions:

1. Amount of installed memory
2. Amount of free disk space
3. Number and type of running applications
4. Size of running applications
5. Mix of DOS and Windows applications

Many adjustments require that you experiment on your own system to determine the best mix of settings for your particular combination of hardware, software, and execution environment. Here's a thumbnail guideline for settings to get you started:

1. RAM Disk (e.g., RAMDRIVE.SYS): One fourth of your total physical memory.
2. Disk Cache (e.g., SMARTDRV.EXE): One fourth of your total physical memory.
3. Permanent swap file: One fourth of your available hard-disk space.

Because of their expense, hardware cache controllers are probably most worthwhile in networking environments, where the speed improvements can benefit many users. In addition, realize that the RAM on a cache controller card cannot be used for other system purposes if, for instance, your applications are CPU-intensive and disk efficiencies are not your system's bottleneck area.

Speeding Up Multitasking for DOS and Windows Users

Windows uses disk space to support the efficient use of memory. My *Supercharging Windows* (SYBEX, 1992) offers more extensive details on the implementation of swapping in both operating modes of Windows. This section concentrates on some of the performance-oriented implications of the swapping facility. You will learn methods to improve swapping speed, which will improve the performance of your DOS and Windows system.

When memory must be reassigned from one application to another, Windows temporarily makes a copy of the memory to be swapped before freeing it up for a different application's use. If your system is running in 386 Enhanced mode, these memory images are stored on disk in a file known as the *swap file*. If your system is running in Standard mode, these images are stored for non-Windows applications only in individual *application swap files*. Windows applications in Standard mode are not swapped, so when you run out of physical memory, you simply cannot start another application until memory is freed up.

TIP

Windows Users: If you run out of space on your
swap disk, Windows will be unable to swap out an
application. Your overall system performance will
suffer in a number of ways. Perhaps a new application will be unable to begin or a current
application will be unable to continue. Make sure
that you're not tight on disk space for swapping.
Specify a different disk, if necessary, that has plenty
of free space.

Improving Swapping in 386 Enhanced Mode

In 386 Enhanced mode, Windows uses a single file for memory copied
(i.e., swapped) to disk during multitasking. If you have established a permanent swap file, this file's name is 386SPART.PAR. It is a hidden file and
is usually stored in the root directory of your system's boot drive. If there
is no permanent swap file, Windows will create a temporary one in your
WINDOWS directory as necessary, named WIN386.SWP. Figure 18.4
depicts this situation.

Should You Use a Permanent or a Temporary Swap File?

When you first install Windows, the Setup program decides whether or
not to set up a permanent swap file, a temporary one, or none at all. If it
can, it will always attempt to carve out a permanent swap file. For several
reasons, it is always more efficient to use a permanent swap file because
Windows will run faster.

- First, Windows can use direct disk reads and writes to a permanent swap file (i.e., specific track and sector addresses are
  used), because it will know exactly where on the disk the permanent file is located. Windows will have exclusive use of this disk
  space. Windows will not then incur the overhead of standard DOS
  file-system requests to access the contents of the swap file.

FIGURE 18.4

Windows users can use 386 Enhanced Mode with sufficient hardware. In this mode, Windows uses a single swap file. A permanent swap file (386SPART.PAR) is preferable because it enhances performance more than the slower temporary swap file (WIN386.SWP).

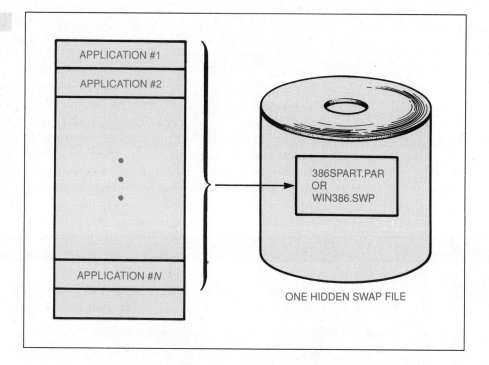

APPLICATION #1

APPLICATION #2

APPLICATION #N

386SPART.PAR
OR
WIN386.SWP

ONE HIDDEN SWAP FILE

- Second, if a temporary swap file is created each time you start Windows, you must incur a certain amount of extra overhead each time Windows starts. If you start Windows in 386 Enhanced mode, you don't have this burden.

- Third, a temporary swap file might be located anywhere on the disk, so it might consist of a number of separate, or fragmented, parts. (See the discussion later in this chapter on fragmentation.) This fragmentation is not possible with a permanent swap file, because Windows ensures that such a file is created only from contiguous sectors. Because of the way caching works, a permanent swap file results in a higher percentage of cache hits and a more efficient system.

- Fourth, a permanent swap file is always the same size unless you change it yourself. This means that your system has a consistent amount of virtual memory, guaranteeing that Windows will have enough disk space to create virtual memory if your system runs out of physical memory.

With a temporary swap file, the amount of virtual memory varies according to how much disk space remains available at any given time. Windows can only allocate temporary swap space out of available disk space. This may translate into an ability to run varying numbers of programs in each Windows session. One time, you may be able to run a particular group of applications simultaneously; the next time, you may not be able to do so because there is less disk space available for swapping.

➤ EXTRA!

Don't Blindly Accept Background Multitasking!

Some non-Windows applications needn't run concurrently in the background while you are running a different application in the foreground. For example, a TSR in its own session or your favorite DOS hard-disk manager will typically have no need for processing time except when you've switched them to the foreground.

Save time, save memory, and make Windows operations smoother by turning off the checkbox beside *Background Execution* in the specific PIF file. You can also turn off this checkbox setting in _DEFAULT.PIF, which applies to all non-Windows applications that do not have their own PIF file. In this case, you get the time and memory benefits for all non-Windows applications.

Occasionally, you may wish to activate background processing for a particular program. Do this in 386 Enhanced mode by running the program in a window (press Alt-spacebar), opening up the control menu, and clicking the *Background* checkbox from the Settings dialog box.

The only advantage of a temporary swap file is that a large portion of your hard disk is not made permanently unavailable. For example, if your hard disk has 20Mb of available contiguous storage when you run Setup, roughly 10Mb will be reserved for a hidden 386SPART.PAR permanent swap file. Even when Windows is not running, this space will be unavailable to you for any other purposes.

Even if Setup can create a permanent swap file on your system, you may choose to create a temporary swap file to reclaim the otherwise unusable 10Mb of disk space. Windows will then only consume as much disk space as it needs to support swapping for your particular mix of applications.

Modifying the Default Swap File Settings

Then again, you may decide that you don't want to use swapping at all. First, you may have more than enough physical memory to run all your applications. Disabling swapping will not affect your applications, and you will not even incur the internal Windows overhead relating to swapping.

Second, you may be limited in available disk space. Rather than allow Windows to consume any of it, you can disable both temporary and permanent swapping, but you will be able to run fewer applications. This runs counter to the benefits of 386 Enhanced mode, but the applications that do run will have more available disk space to use.

Regardless of whether you want to disable swapping, specify a temporary swap file, or define the precise size of a permanent swap file, the 386 Enhanced icon in the Windows **Control Panel** is your ticket. After selecting the icon, you should click on the *Virtual Memory* button to bring up the dialog box shown in Figure 18.5.

Your system's current settings appear in the upper left box. They indicate the drive on which the swap file, if any, resides, as well as the size and type of the file. If you have a permanent swap file, the size represents the actual amount of reserved disk space that is unavailable for any other purposes. As a reminder to you, Windows indicates that a permanent swap file uses

FIGURE 18.5

The Virtual Memory dialog box controls the specification of virtual memory in 386 Enhanced mode. You can define both the size and type of the swap file used for virtual memory in this increasingly popular Windows mode.

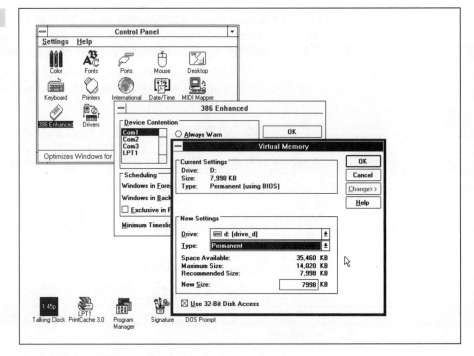

fast and direct 32-bit disk access. If the swap file were temporary, Windows would remind you that the slower accessing technique would be through the MS-DOS file system.

If you have specified a temporary swap file, the size value only represents the maximum space that Windows might possibly use, depending on need, during multitasking. A temporary swap file can expand during multitasking operations. If Windows does not need this much space for your application mix, the temporary WIN386.SWP file will not grow and the extra disk space will remain available for other purposes.

To change the type of swapping on your system, click on the down arrow beside the *Type:* list box in the New Settings section of the dialog box and select *Permanent, Temporary,* or *None.* In each case, Windows displays the current space available on your chosen drive. If there is not enough space on one drive, just click on the down arrow beside the *Drive:* list box to select a different drive for your swap file.

➤ EXTRA!

Increasing Priority Increases Speed!

You can specify two relative priority values for any non-Windows application: one to control its priority when it runs in the background, and the other for when it runs in the foreground.

Knowing exactly what value to set the foreground and background priority is not a precise science.

Guidelines:

1. Set initial foreground priority to 100, background priority to 50.

2. If you want an application to proceed faster than others, adjust these values, retaining the ratio by keeping the foreground priority equal to double the background priority (e.g., background=100, foreground=200).

3. If you want more visible progress in your application when you switch to it, triple or quadruple the foreground value as compared to the background value (e.g., background=50, foreground=200).

4. If your application is very computationally bound, as in engineering, mathematical, and compiling applications, increase both background and foreground values dramatically (e.g., background=1000, foreground=4000). However, you should typically run these types of applications in the background and do something else in the foreground.

Naturally, you can also apply many of these same considerations to setting the Windows priority values in 386 Enhanced mode. Make adjustments to the Scheduling settings in the 386 Enhanced dialog box, when you are trying to improve the performance of Windows applications in an environment which mixes Windows and non-Windows applications.

If you disable swapping completely by choosing *None* in the *Type:* box, the *New Size:* field is grayed. You can only view the amount of space available on the drive. Choose OK to accept the disabling of virtual memory on your system.

If you specify a temporary swap file by choosing *Temporary* in the *Type:* box, Windows displays a line below *Space Available:* that defines the recommended Maximum Size. This will be roughly half of your available disk space. You can constrain the amount of virtual memory by typing in a smaller number in the *New Size:* field.

If you specify a permanent swap file by choosing *Permanent* in the *Type:* box, Windows will display the maximum possible size of that swap file, as shown in Figure 18.5. This represents the largest contiguous block of disk space that can be found on the selected drive.

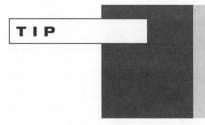

TIP

Be sure to defragment your disk before attempting to create a new or larger permanent swap file. When defragmented, Windows will offer you the largest possible contiguous block of disk space from which to allocate your permanent swap file.

Improving Swapping in Standard Mode

When you run Windows in Standard mode, there is no 386 Enhanced icon in the Control Panel. Swapping in Standard mode affects only non-Windows or straight DOS applications. As Figure 18.6 indicates, Windows will create a separate hidden swap file for each non-Windows application that you start. These files all begin with the four characters ~WOA and end with the extension .TMP.

When you switch away from a non-Windows application, Windows writes all or part of the application's memory out to its private swap file. Later, when you switch back to the application, Windows rereads the data from the swap file back into memory, restoring the application. When the application ends, Windows erases the swap file completely.

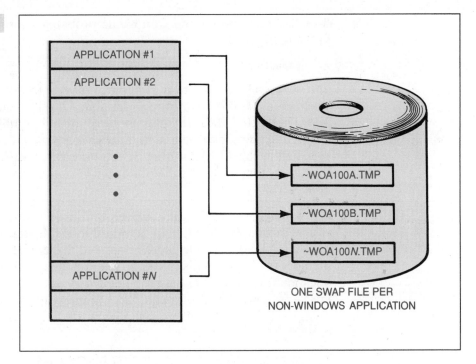

Controlling virtual memory in Standard mode. Windows creates a separate swapping file for each older DOS application that runs in its own session.

You can control swapping speed in your Standard-mode system by maximizing the rate at which Windows accesses swap files. The best way to do this is to ensure that Windows swaps occur to your system's fastest hard disk. In addition, you can gain slightly by making sure that the swap file is in the root directory of this disk.

If a second, slower disk drive has a much larger amount of free space, it will usually be better to use this drive. Because of the free space, the swap files will be more likely to reside in contiguous disk addresses (i.e., they will be less fragmented). This will minimize disk head movement during swapping and will make for faster switching to and from non-Windows applications.

To specify a particular disk and directory for application swap files in Standard mode, include a **Swapdisk=** entry in the [NonWindowsApp] section of SYSTEM.INI. For example, suppose that your C drive has a 28-millisecond access time, but your D drive is a Plus Hard Card with a

9-millisecond access time. You would probably want to include this line in SYSTEM.INI:

```
Swapdisk=D:\
```

You may still benefit from swapping to your fastest drive if you have specified a **TEMP** environment variable. Usually, you place this setting in AUTOEXEC.BAT. If you do not include a **Swapdisk=** entry in SYSTEM.INI, Windows sends its application swap files out to the disk specified in the TEMP setting. If you haven't set TEMP before running Windows, that's still okay; Windows will use the root directory of your boot drive.

There may be a problem, however, if you don't explicitly specify your system's swapping location in Standard mode. If your system has a RAM disk, the TEMP variable usually points to that disk. Using one portion of memory (i.e., a RAM disk) to swap memory images from an executing application is inefficient and a mistake. You incur the overhead of swapping, but because the RAM disk consumes memory itself, you do not gain any memory for other applications. Figure 18.7 depicts this self-defeating process.

To create the RAM disk in the first place, you have to allocate some of your system's extended memory, which reduces the amount of memory available for other applications. Consequently, when Windows swaps a DOS application out to its swapping drive, it only regains the memory formerly given up to create the RAM disk. The net gain is zero, and the net cost is the overall burden of swapping.

TIP

There is one situation in which you can benefit from setting a RAM disk to be your standard-mode swap disk: If your system has more memory than is necessary for your Windows applications. If there is enough excess memory to create a RAM disk without taking away from memory that would better be left for Windows, you can improve switching time to and from a DOS application. But this is a special, and relatively rare, case.

Windows users should not use a RAM disk for a swap disk. The extended memory that is consumed for the RAM disk could be better used by Windows for overall system multitasking chores. Also, swapping has an associated overhead that only sees a gain if memory is freed up.

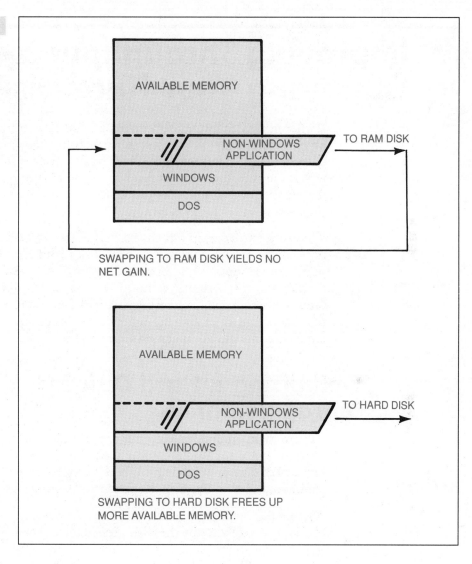

SWAPPING TO RAM DISK YIELDS NO NET GAIN.

SWAPPING TO HARD DISK FREES UP MORE AVAILABLE MEMORY.

Improving Throughput by Enhancing Your Hard Disk

Earlier in this chapter, you learned a good deal about disk caching and about swapping. In both cases, the techniques are aimed at improving the speed at which information is stored on or retrieved from your disks. Both techniques enhance system facilities that use your hard disk. In a sense, they make hard-disk access more efficient, but they do not directly improve your hard disk's efficiency.

There are two areas in which you can make adjustments that result in a noticeable improvement in your hard disk's (and consequently Windows') performance. First, I'll discuss the concept of *defragmentation*. Even though it is only a single technique for enhancing disk performance, it is often called *disk optimization* because it can have such a powerful and positive impact on your system. Second, I'll discuss methods for freeing up large amounts of disk space on your system.

Optimizing a Hard Disk by Defragmentation

As hard disks fill up, you and your applications will often delete older files to make space for the latest files. DOS manages the actual storage and retrieval of files on your disks. When it cannot store a large file in a single contiguous area of the disk, it stores the file in pieces around the disk.

When a file is split up in this way, it is said to be *fragmented*. All the file's contents are intact, but the disk's mechanical heads must move to multiple disk locations to read or write the contents of the file. The more fragmented the file, the longer the time spent accessing its contents. Take a look at Figure 18.8.

Programs that can reduce fragmentation will carefully move pieces of files around the disk to combine the parts into contiguous areas. Such programs are sometimes called *disk optimizers*, *disk compaction utilities*, *disk organizers*, or *defragmentation utilities*.

FIGURE 18.8

A fragmented disk before defragmentation. There are clusters between files that are unused, and many files are stored in noncontiguous clusters. This spreads out the disk data, forcing additional disk head motion which slows your system down.

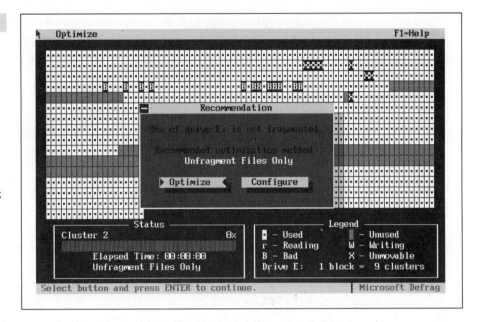

The graphic in Figure 18.8 depicts the existing, partially fragmented status of one of my Bernoulli removable disk cartridges in the E: drive. This screen results from my running the DEFRAG.EXE utility and specifying the E: drive:

```
DEFRAG E:
```

DEFRAG analyzes the hard drive and suggests that, while it does have some degree (96%) of fragmentation, it is probably most time-effective to simply unfragment the files on the disk. This choice is suggested in Figure 18.8 as the choice *Unfragment Files Only*. Pressing Enter at Figure 18.8 would proceed with this file-only defragmentation. This procedure would simply combine the pieces of all files that are currently fragmented, leaving alone any resulting gaps between files on the disk. Directories would be ignored, and the unfragmented files would then reside around the disk. Each file would be defragmented, resulting in contiguous clusters, although the files themselves may not all be contiguous with one another.

Personally, I prefer the alternative optimization method, which is called *Full Optimization*. This condenses directories as well as files, and removes all gaps between the files. Choosing *Configure* at Figure 18.8, and subsequently selecting the *Full Optimization* choice, would result in the completely defragmented disk shown in Figure 18.9.

If a disk can be made to contain no fragmented files, the mechanical overhead caused by fragmentation is eliminated. In a Windows multitasking environment, where the disk is accessed constantly, having an unfragmented disk means you will have faster response from your applications. This is true because all files are contiguous and can be read or written with fewer mechanical disk head movements. You enjoy the following benefits:

- The information in individual files can be retrieved more quickly.

- New files can be written to more quickly.

- Swap files in Standard mode can be written to and read from more quickly.

FIGURE 18.9

The optimized disk after defragmentation spreads your file information over fewer disk clusters. There is less travel time for the disk heads to access data, resulting in speedier performance.

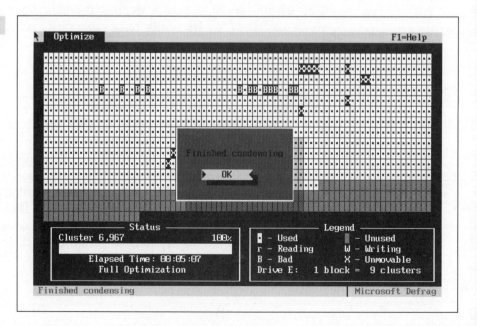

- A temporary swap file in 386 Enhanced mode can be written to and read from more quickly.

- Your disk-caching utility performs even more efficiently because the cache is used more effectively. When you access the tracks on an optimized disk, the cache is more likely to be able to fulfill upcoming disk requests. This is because nearby sectors are more likely to contain data from the same file as the preceding sectors.

➤ EXTRA!

Thumbnail Summary of Key Optimization Techniques

Enhance the Hard Disk:

1. Adjust the controller's interleave.

2. Defragment the files and directories.

3. Allocate space for a permanent swap file.

Enhance the Configuration:

1. Install a RAM disk.

2. Install a disk cache.

3. Set the **TEMP** variable to a RAM disk or to a fast hard disk.

Enhance Memory (See Chapter 17):

1. Install more extended memory.

2. Minimize the use of expanded memory.

3. Maximize available memory prior to starting Windows.

Optimizing Performance for DOS and Windows Applications

If you use a defragmentation utility like DEFRAG.EXE under Windows, you should follow these important steps:

1. Exit Windows first!

2. Run the **CHKDSK /F** utility at the DOS prompt (but not from within Windows!).

3. Remove any TSR that may attempt to use your hard disk during optimization.

4. Execute the compaction program.

You can customize the operation of the DEFRAG.EXE utility by pulling down the the Optimize menu seen at the top left of the screen (as shown in Figure 18.10). If you run the DEFRAG utility by typing its name at a DOS command prompt without specifying a disk drive identifier, the program opens up with a dialog box that requests you to select one of the existing disk drives. That dialog box is available by choosing *Drive* on the Optimize menu.

FIGURE 18.10

The DEFRAG Optimize menu provides all the facilities of the DOS defragmentation program. You can prepare for the optimization by choosing *Drive*, *Method*, and *Sort* before beginning the actual defragmentation with the *Begin* choice.

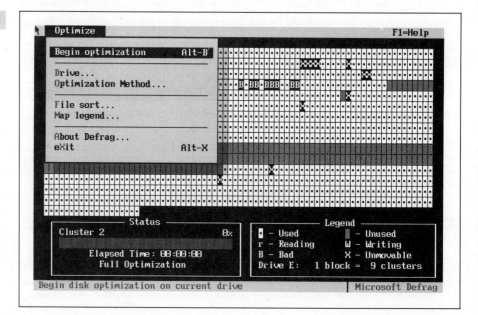

Choosing *Optimization Method* on the pull down menu displays a dialog box that offers two choices: *Full Optimization* or *Unfragment Files Only*. Continue your customized configuration by highlighting the desired choice, then press OK.

The *File Sort* choice is a nice customization feature. The dialog box that appears enables you to select the ordering that DEFRAG will impose on the defragmented files when it rewrites all directory entries. You can order files according to name, extension, date and time, or size. Additionally, you can specify ascending or descending sorts. These are the same choices that you can make when you use the **DIR** command. Naturally, the difference is that you needn't specify any switches on DIR at all if the files are already sorted in their directories in a desired way.

The *Map* legend choice on the Optimize menu merely explains each of the Legend entries seen at the bottom right of the standard DEFRAG screen. These entries represent DEFRAG's shorthand graphic notation for your disk. The Disk Map Legend dialog box offers a sentence explanation for each possible graphic symbol that may appear in your DEFRAG screen.

For example, the disk being analyzed in Figure 18.10 is represented by DEFRAG with a series of blocks, each of which stands for 9 clusters. A solid rectangle means that the block of clusters is unused. A letter *B* means that the disk area represented by this block has been declared Bad, and will be unaffected by DEFRAG's operations.

More experienced DOS users may wish to know about the possible command line switches that bypass the full-screen customization procedures just discussed. Each option has its own switch. For example, to load and run DEFRAG, specifying a Full Optimization on drive I:, you would type:

```
DEFRAG I: /F
```

Use the **/U** switch rather than **/F** if you wish to defragment files only. To further specify that all data be verified after being moved, you could add the **/V** switch (I always do). To restart your computer automatically when the optimization is complete, just add the **/B** switch. Finally, to ask DEFRAG to sort the files in their directories, just add the **/S** switch. Table 18.2 summarizes all of the possible command-line switches for the DEFRAG command.

TABLE 18.2: Switches for the DEFRAG utility

SWITCH	OPTIMIZATION EFFECT
/B	Reboots after defragmentation
/F	Full Optimization
/SKIPHIGH	Runs DEFRAG from conventional memory
/SD	Sorts chronologically by date and time
/SD-	Sorts reverse-chronologically by date and time
/SE	Sorts alphabetically by extension from A to Z
/SE-	Sorts reverse-alphabetically by extension from Z to A
/SN	Sorts alphabetically by name from A to Z
/SN-	Sorts reverse-alphabetically by name from Z to A
/SS	Sorts by size in increasing order
/SS-	Sorts by size in decreasing order
/U	Unfragment files only
/V	Verify data after moves

My favorite combination of switches is:

```
DEFRAG I: /V /SN /F
```

With this switch, my Bernoulli cartidge is defragmented fully. All moves are verified and all files are rearranged by file name for easy directory listings later.

Maximizing Hard-Disk Space

In the course of my work with computers, as I became more and more involved with Windows applications, I have been astonished at the growth in the size and number of my disk's files. I first outgrew a 40Mb hard disk and replaced it with an 80Mb disk. Next, I added a 105Mb Hard Card. Finally, I bought a Bernoulli transportable drive with 90Mb removable cartridges. That ought to take care of all my needs for a while.

However, that also took care of a lot of money that I can't use for other purposes. You may decide to save some money and make more effective use of your available hard-disk space. Naturally, you can use available disk space for new programs. I have to admit that when I install new programs, I install everything from text files to optional modules. But as I've discussed in this chapter, Windows can also use available disk space for swapping. Everyone goes through the agony from time to time of having to decide whether to delete files from a hard disk in order to free up space for other files.

Of course, it's up to you to decide which applications and which directories to eliminate. But this section can help you by giving you some guidance about how to reduce the burden on your disk imposed by the many optional modules installed by Windows.

Installing and Removing Optional Windows Components

To control the installation and removal of the many optional Windows file modules, select the Windows *Setup* icon in the Main group of the Program Manager. Then pull down the Options menu and choose *Add/Remove Windows Components*. You see the Windows Setup dialog box, shown in Figure 18.11.

This dialog box provides easy access to the megabytes of disk space that are consumed by optional files under Windows. As you can see, my disk is burdened with more than 2Mb of optional components. By removing the x beside any component name, I can free up the amount of space indicated. For example, by removing the x beside the *Readme Files* and *Games* entries, I would free up more than half a megabyte. If I never use the optional Windows accessory programs, like Notepad and Write, I could free up more than a megabyte by removing the x beside the *Accessories* choice.

You can be even more precise by removing some, but not all, of the files within a Windows optional category. Just click on the *Files* button on the right side of each component line. For example, clicking on *Files* to the right of *Wallpapers, Misc.* brings up the dialog box shown in Figure 18.12. To

FIGURE 18.11

The Windows Setup dialog box, which you use to remove or install optional Windows components. The primary value of the checkboxes seen here is to save disk space when installing Windows. Some or all of these file groups may be unnecessary for the way you'll use your system.

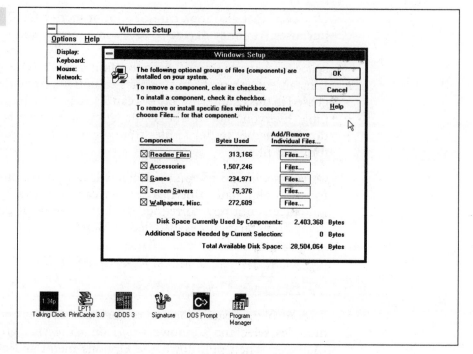

FIGURE 18.12

The Wallpapers, Misc. dialog box, which allows you to indicate which files are to be installed, removed, or added to an existing installation. Use this when first installing Windows to minimize disk usage, or use it later to add files that were earlier ignored.

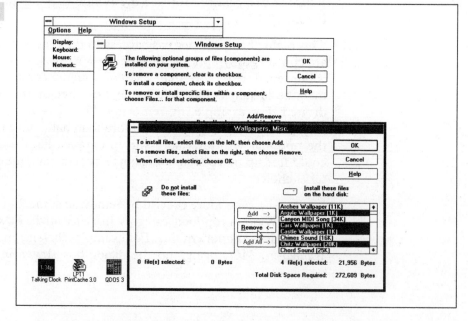

eliminate only some of the files (e.g., certain wallpaper bitmaps that are never used), just click on their names, choose *Remove*, and choose *OK*. This returns you to the Windows Setup dialog box. Choose *OK* to complete this procedure.

Cleaning Up Unnecessary Disk Files

There are some files that can be removed that are not so obvious. The safest way to determine which files these are is to exit Windows first.

When you are at the DOS prompt, change to the TEMP directory. (If you use a RAM disk for a TEMP directory, ignore this step.) All unnecessary files located there will disappear the next time you turn off your system. But if you use a hard-disk directory for a TEMP directory, you can probably delete all files in this directory now—You have left Windows to ensure that no TEMP directory files are still in use. If you have active TSR programs, however, be sure not to erase any TEMP files required by them.

A temporary swap file in 386 Enhanced mode is usually deleted when Windows shuts down. Similarly, application swap files are usually deleted when you exit from non-Windows applications in Standard mode. However, sometimes your system crashes and sometimes your computer loses power and you must reboot. In these situations, a temporary swap file may be left taking up space on your disk. You can erase any of these files if you're no longer in Windows.

Rearranging Information on Your Disk

I recommended earlier that, before defragmenting your disk, you run the DOS utility **CHKDSK** with the **/F** option. At the time, I didn't give a reason for doing this. The real purpose of this command is to locate and fix any disk clusters that have somehow become disassociated from real disk files.

Disassociated disk clusters waste space. By running the CHKDSK /F command, you can reclaim this space on your disk. By running this command before defragmenting your disk, the disassociated clusters become part of the freed-up contiguous space.

The CHKDSK command can collect lost clusters. But you can control a certain degree of file organization yourself. The fewer unnecessary files that you have in your WINDOWS directory, the faster DOS will be able to access any individual files in the directory, and the faster Windows will execute.

After installation of many Windows applications, some programs leave files in the WINDOWS directory. You can speed up disk access by re-organizing these files. Once they are reorganized, you may have to adjust the directory locations in the applications themselves.

For example, you might be keeping .BMP files in the WINDOWS directory itself. Instead, you could create a subdirectory that contains only these occasionally used files. As a second example, if you use Microsoft Excel, you might be permitting it to allow your .XL and macro files to accumulate within the WINDOWS directory. Instead, you can have it place them in a new subdirectory, called FILES or DATA.

Understanding the Impact of Your Hard Disk's Interleave

So far, I've talked about disk efficiencies that result from optimized organization of files on a disk. If all the sectors for a particular file are defragmented and on the same track, for instance, you should be able to access the information faster. The disk heads don't have to spend any additional time moving to tracks and sectors elsewhere on the disk.

But there is another facet of disk information retrieval that has nothing to do with DOS or Windows. It's called *interleaving*. In fact, without buying a third-party interleaving utility, you usually have no control over it at all. This section explains the concept to you and gives you enough information to discover whether you can change it to make additional big gains in performance.

On each track of a disk, there are a number of sectors of data (the exact number depends on your disk). Take a look at Figure 18.13. On the left it depicts a typical file as containing a series of sectors that logically follow one another.

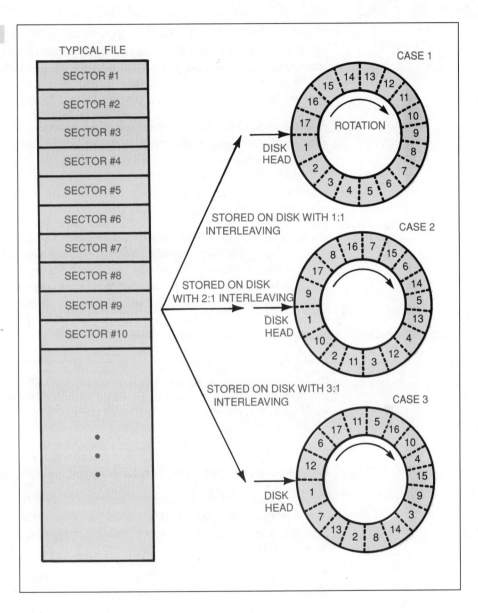

FIGURE 18.13

Interleaving greatly affects hard-disk performance. This diagram illustrates different interleaves for the same file: with sectors sequenced contiguously (1:1), sequenced every other sector (2:1), and sequenced every third sector (3:1).

When the file is stored on a disk, you might think that it is stored as you see it in Case 1 in the figure. This arrangement places each logical sector from a file in consecutive physical sectors on a disk track. (It's true that on fragmented disks, the physical sectors of a track often contain interspersed pieces of more than a single file, but I won't consider that here.)

Actually, the file system keeps track of which sectors belong to which files. The hard-disk controller merely stores and retrieves information on tracks and sectors, not caring what you place there. The issue of interleaving arises from the speed with which a hard disk's controller can actually respond to a system request for information on a certain track as the disk is spinning underneath it.

Imagine for a moment some highway workers at the end of a day of working on the road. One worker drives a pickup truck slowly down a lane while another worker reaches down to pick up an orange cone. While the truck continues to move forward, the worker who picked up the cone has to control the cone, reach back into the truck, carefully stack the cone over others that he has picked up, then reach back outside the truck to ready himself to pick up the next cone.

In the same way, a disk head has to read data from a sector while the disk platter is rotating. The disk controller is responsible for storing the data, transferring it back to a requester (e.g., DOS or Windows), then readying itself to get the next sector's worth of data.

What if the truck is moving too fast for the physical skills of the worker in the rear? By the time the worker has stacked the first cone and leaned out for the next one, the truck may have driven by a second cone.

One solution is to slow down the truck to match the physical capabilities of the worker who picks up the cones (the equivalent of slowing down the disk drive to match a slow controller's capabilities). This wastes time. There are better ways.

Another solution is to hire a faster, more agile worker to pick up the cones while the truck maintains a faster pace. This is a more efficient use of personnel and resources. Similarly, a faster disk controller should be able to keep up with today's faster hard-disk drive rotation. I'll use the sample layout shown in the cases in Figure 18.13, which have 17 sectors per track. The principle will hold for any disk, however.

Ideally, Case 1 in Figure 18.13 would match a drive with a controller that would be able to read sector 1, process the information within the sector, and be ready to read sector 2 before the start of the sector reaches the read/write head. There is a small intersector gap on each track, which accounts for a small amount of time during which the preceding sector's data can be dealt with.

As you have no doubt guessed, not all disk controllers can keep up with rotational speed. If the sequential sector numbering seen in Case 1 were maintained, a slower disk controller that misses sector 2 after reading sector 1 would have to wait until the entire platter rotated again completely in order to read sector 2. In this mismatched drive/controller environment, it would require 17 rotations to read all 17 sectors on a single track.

Interleaving is a solution to this problem—it physically reorders sectors on a track. In a 2:1 interleaving pattern, each successively numbered sector is actually placed two sectors away from its predecessor, as shown in Case 2 in Figure 18.13, rather than right next to it, as shown in Case 1. In a 3:1 interleaving pattern, each successively numbered sector is actually placed three sectors away from its predecessor, as shown in Case 3.

If your drive/controller combination cannot handle 1:1 interleaving, 2:1 interleaving will require only one extra disk rotation to read all sectors on the track. This is not as bad as 17 rotations, so interleaving is an intelligent solution to the problem of mismatched capabilities.

As an example, take a look at Case 2 in Figure 18.13. After sector 1 is read, it is processed by the controller while the disk continues to rotate. An entire sector (number 10 out of 17) is ignored. When the controller is ready to read another sector, it is labeled number 2. While this is being processed, sector 11 passes the disk head and is ignored. The next sector is number 3, and so on. In two complete rotations, the disk controller will process sectors numbered from 1 to 17. During the first rotation, sectors 1 to 9 are read; during the second rotation, sectors 10 to 17 are read. Even though the sectors are not physically contiguous, they are numbered and read (and data is stored in them) in logically contiguous order.

Naturally, slower and less capable controllers that are matched with faster disk drives may require 3:1 or even 4:1 interleaving. If your disk's interleave is not set accurately, you may be doubling or tripling the disk access time for all operations.

On the one hand, using an incorrect interleave can completely negate everything else that you do to enhance performance. On the other hand, it is possible to obtain a fantastic boost to your entire computer system by simply improving your hard disk's interleave. Interleaving is a low-level facility and is set by the hard-disk manufacturer. By the time the disk finds its way into your computer and is matched with a controller card, the original interleaving may not be optimum.

WARNING

Changing your disk's interleave can be hazardous to your system's health! While it is almost always worth exploring whether your disk's interleave is set properly, you should not undertake changing it lightly. Performing this chore incorrectly, or on the wrong type disk, can damage your disk and its data. If you have a third-party utility that can test for and optimize the interleave, make sure that your disk is listed *specifically* as one of the ones for which the program is designed. Otherwise, leave this sophisticated task to your dealer!

Enhancing Operational Speed

All the techniques presented so far aim at improving the efficiency of the Windows environment. A technique that improves hard-disk efficiency will improve any application that uses the hard disk. A technique that improves virtual memory usage will improve the speed of all applications. In this section, I'll present some techniques that can enhance specific operations more directly.

Speeding Up Your Backups

Do you use a permanent swap file in Windows? Do you run a backup program (like MSBACKUP or MWBACKUP) from time to time? If so, you may also be making a copy of the swap file, which can be a waste of time.

Many backup programs offer a way to ignore files during the backup process. Some backup programs do not automatically copy hidden files. Others contain configurations that you can set up once to ensure that certain files or directories are copied or ignored, according to your instructions.

To save time, run your backup program so that your Windows swap file is not copied. See earlier in this chapter for the names of the affected swap files.

➤ EXTRA!

Defragmenting Your Hard Disk: Basics

Disk optimizing programs reduce disk fragmentation, and are consequently called "defraggers" by many people. You should defragment your hard disk on a regular basis; Windows can run noticeably faster if your file structure is optimized by a defragmenting program like DOS 6's DEFRAG.EXE. How often should you defragment a disk? Monthly at worst. Weekly is a good plan. But also any time just after you've deleted a large number of files on your disk.

Remember to back up your disk just prior to initiating a defragmentation operation. To speed up the backup process itself, delete all temporary and unnecessary files from your disk.

Also, prior to compacting your disk, you should fix or delete lost clusters (*but not from within Windows*). Use the **CHKDSK /F** command to reclaim wasted clusters that are taking up valuable disk space. Then use the **DEFRAG** command in DOS to defragment and reorganize the information on your hard disk.

Accessing Required Files More Quickly

Windows currently performs nearly all disk requests through DOS. Remember that Windows reads and writes disk tracks and sectors for a permanent swap file in 386 Enhanced mode. For all file searches, DOS checks the current directory first, then checks each directory in your **PATH** statement in order. If the files you use frequently are found in a directory that appears late in the path, Windows will seem to slow down. This is part of a deficiency in the layered design of Windows (i.e., Windows runs on top of and depends on DOS).

Here are some guidelines on the best use of the PATH statement in DOS when you are running Windows:

* After creating a RAM disk and storing important files in its root directory, make the RAM disk's root directory the first directory in the PATH.

* Make the WINDOWS directory the second directory in the PATH, since WINDOWS is constantly accessing its own files.

* Make the DOS directory the third directory in the PATH.

* Make the UTILITY directory the next directory if you have grouped your most common utilities in one directory.

* Order the remaining directories according to how frequently you run applications that access the files within those directories.

* Remember that only one PATH statement is used: the last one executed. Your AUTOEXEC.BAT file's PATH statement is overridden if you execute a new PATH statement within a DOS session under Windows.

* Remember that the PATH environment variable is limited to 128 characters. You cannot include directories in the PATH that will force the variable to exceed this length. All characters after the 128th will be ignored. If you must include a large number of directories in the path, try renaming these directories with smaller names so that fewer characters will be required.

Don't Run Unnecessary Applications

There is only a finite amount of CPU time to go around. The fewer applications that are running at the same time under Windows, the more time for each one, and the faster each one will complete its tasks.

Make more time available for your important and necessary applications by running only them. Don't run frivolous applications (like fish that swim around on your screen) all the time. And don't leave useful applications running all the time when you only need the information from them once in a while (like mail programs or system monitoring programs). Run such programs when you specifically need them. Remember that besides the potential slowdown, each program consumes a certain amount of memory resources that are no longer available to the rest of your Windows system.

Improving Performance of Non-Windows Applications

Everything you've learned in this chapter so far can improve the performance of Windows overall. This section specifically discusses performance enhancement for non-Windows applications. Let's look now at some of the specific PIF settings that bear directly on performance.

There are a myriad of possible customization options that exist in the WIN.INI and SYSTEM.INI files. Many of these special settings have important effects on your system's performance. In this section, I'll also selectively organize and briefly discuss the most important of these settings.

If you have a non-Windows application that is running slowly, open its control menu and boost its priority setting. If it is running in the foreground, boost the foreground priority. If it is running in the background, and you want it to proceed relatively faster, boost its background priority.

If you want to maximize its speed when it isn't necessary to have any other programs continue running (such as a communications program in the background), you can check the *Exclusive* box. If these adjustments work effectively for your environment, you can make them permanent by using Windows' PIF Editor.

Don't forget that any DOS program runs noticeably faster if you run it in full-screen mode. You can always press Alt+Enter (in 386 Enhanced mode) to switch it back to windowed mode if you wish, or you can press Alt+spacebar to open up the control menu and switch a full-screen DOS application to windowed mode at the same time.

T I P

Running DOS applications under Windows in full-screen mode will speed up their execution. In 386 Enhanced mode, you can choose to run a non-Windows applications in full-screen mode or to run it in a window. Running in a window offers a number of advantages, such as the ability to move and size the window or cut and paste text through the Clipboard. However, if these considerations are not important, you can boost speed immediately by switching the application to full-screen mode. You will notice an instant improvement in just the processing of keystrokes, but in fact all processing requirements of your application will receive more CPU time.

The *Monitor Ports* checkboxes in the Advanced section of a 386 Enhanced mode PIF can slow down your application. When any one of these options is checked, Windows checks for consistency between your display adapter and your application. This takes time and is typically only necessary if you are using older-style video monitors and adapters. If your application works fine with these checkboxes cleared (especially when switching to it and from it), leave them cleared to boost a DOS application's performance.

In the Memory Options section of a PIF, be sure to carefully specify maximum values. They should be no more than you really need for the application, otherwise you may be consuming memory that could better be used by other applications. Any time that you waste memory, you increase the likelihood that Windows performance will be slowed.

Although it biases Windows toward your particular DOS application, you can clear the *Detect Idle Time* option in the Advanced Options dialog box in 386 Enhanced mode. This ensures that your DOS application receives its complete time allotment, even if it does not use it all. There is usually some time wasted, but your individual application keeps the CPU's attention, thereby increasing its own throughput.

Lastly, in the Display Options section, you can clear the *Retain Video Memory* option. This releases video memory to the system when you switch away from the application, making Windows more efficient. In theory, this will make your application and every other application work that much better. In practice, this can occasionally have a negative impact on your application if it is unable to obtain the video memory when eventually switching back to it.

Summary

In this chapter, you've learned some very powerful methods in DOS to boost performance in your system:

- A disk cache can be set up with the SMARTDRV.EXE device driver. DOS uses this portion of memory to store copies of recently referenced disk sectors, thereby enabling fast access to frequently used data.

- DOS and Windows users can benefit from using a permanent swap file in 386 Enhanced Mode. You learned techniques for improving the performance of swapping in general.

- You can defragment your hard disks with the DEFRAG utility, and you learned a range of techniques for maximizing the performance of any hard disk.

- You were shown methods for running software and managing your system that in themselves improve the overall operational speed of DOS and Windows, as well as the applications you run under either environment.

CHAPTER

19

Using Advanced DOS Commands

YOU HAVE now learned all the commands necessary for using your DOS system effectively. In this chapter, you'll extend your knowledge to include a special advanced set of commands. None of the standard uses of DOS require these commands, but they can help you immeasurably in dealing with special situations. With their help, you can tailor your system to your specific needs and increase the overall efficiency of your applications.

The commands presented in this chapter will allow you to expand the range of ways in which you manage, manipulate, and protect your files. Other commands will enable you to use, traverse, and protect your directory and disk structures more easily, quickly, and completely. A final group of commands will help you to run programs more efficiently by getting more mileage from both the shell and the main DOS controlling program, COMMAND.COM. You'll also learn about a special group of DOS commands designed to help those of you on the go to make your laptops work better and coordinate more easily with your desktop computer.

Improving Disk and Directory Management

The following commands influence the way that DOS looks at its disk drives and disk directory structures. These commands can be very useful when you are running older programs that make fixed assumptions about drives, or when your disk accesses seem to be too slow. These commands will also make your DOS application references easier and faster.

Treating Directories as Disks

The SUBST (Substitute) command enables you to treat any existing directory as a separate disk drive. To do this, DOS permits you to assign an available drive identifier to this subdirectory. This can dramatically reduce your typing burden. You can redefine any directory, no matter how deep in your hierarchical structure, as a single-letter drive identifier. All future command references will be shorter, and less liable to contain typing errors.

This command is also frequently used for running older software packages that cannot reference files in a hierarchical directory structure. By fooling these packages into thinking they are only addressing files on a disk drive, you can still make use of the DOS directory structure for file storage.

T I P

The SUBST command comes in handy in another common situation. If you have a hard disk with a directory structure containing many levels of subdirectories, this command allows you to avoid typing long path names. For the same reason, it is useful when you have a program that requests a file name and path but only allows a certain amount of characters to be entered.

SUBST has three possible syntaxes. The first actually performs the substitution, the second displays all current substitutions, and the third cancels a previous substitution.

Let's look at an example. Suppose that your disk contains the directory structure shown in Figure 19.1. Then suppose you need to run an older general-ledger program that needs the files in H:\ACCOUNT\GL, but the older program does not support paths. If you had included a LASTDRIVE command in your CONFIG.SYS (to enlarge the range of allowable drive identifiers), you could issue the following command:

```
SUBST J: H:\ACCOUNT\GL
```

FIGURE 19.1

A typical directory structure includes subdirectories within directories, making full pathnames often very long and cumbersome.

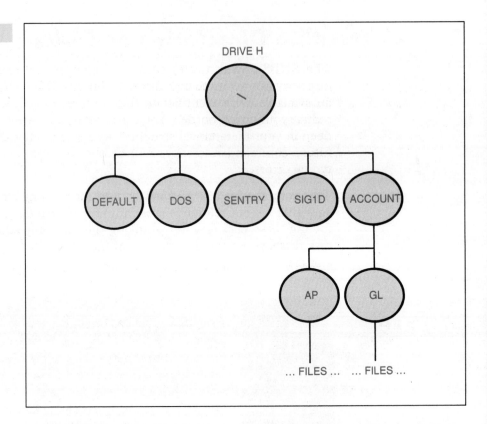

This command makes DOS believe there is a disk drive J, and that the files on this drive are the files in the ACCOUNT\GL subdirectory on drive H.

N O T E

DOS supports drives A through E by default, but it has the ability to support drives through M. In order to create and access drives lettered beyond E, you must first include in your CONFIG.SYS file the command LASTDRIVE=*n*, where *n* is the last letter allowed for a drive. For example, LASTDRIVE=J allows drives labeled A through J.

SUBST does not prevent you from accessing the specified subdirectory directly while the command is current. If you save a file to drive J, it will actually be saved in the substituted subdirectory (H:\ACCOUNT\GL), and if you save a file directly to H:\ACCOUNT\GL, it will appear in a listing of drive J, because both references actually access the same part of the disk (see Figure 19.2). In effect, this command opens up another "window" into a directory, and you can access that directory's contents through the window simply by using a drive specifier.

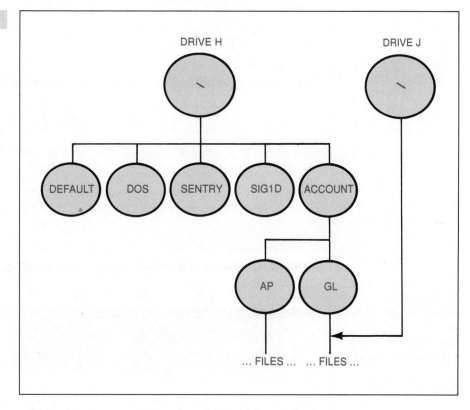

Let's use this first version of the SUBST command. In Figure 19.3, you can see drive H's directory structure, as well as the four files currently

FIGURE 19.3

Use the shell's File List capability to view a directory and its contained files. This figure shows the beginning directory structure prior to using the SUBST command.

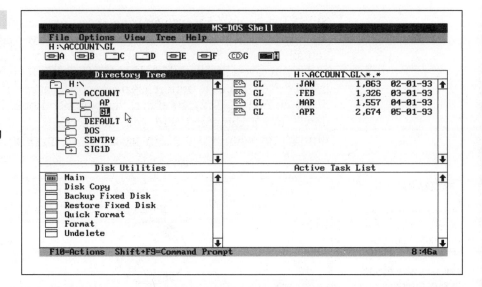

found in the GL directory. Notice that there are eight accessible drives in this example, identified by the letters A through H.

At this point, you can run the SUBST.EXE command, as seen in Figure 19.4. The first parameter, J:, is the new drive identifier for the second

FIGURE 19.4

Use the Run choice on the File pulldown menu to run any DOS command. The Command Line field will scroll to the right for long commands with many possible parameters, such as the SUBST command seen here.

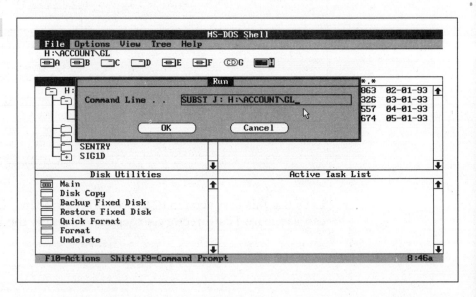

parameter, H:\ACCOUNT\GL.

Once the substitution has taken effect, as seen in the Dual File Lists view of Figure 19.5, you can access the four GL files in two ways. If you look at the file listing in drive J, you will see the same contents as in the H:\AC-COUNT\GL directory. These files do not actually exist twice. DOS is merely providing two methods for referencing the same files.

The second version of SUBST causes all currently active substitutions to be displayed. DOS will show you the created drive identifier and the drive and directory to which it is linked. For example, running SUBST with no parameters displays the following message to show you that drive J is currently being used as a substitute for directory ACCOUNT\GL on drive H:

```
J: => H:\ACCOUNT\GL
```

If you were not the primary user on this computer, you could use this version of SUBST to learn how someone else has set things up to save time. For example, you would find in this case that the ACCOUNT\GL directory can be accessed normally (on drive H) or, more quickly, through its substitute (on drive J).

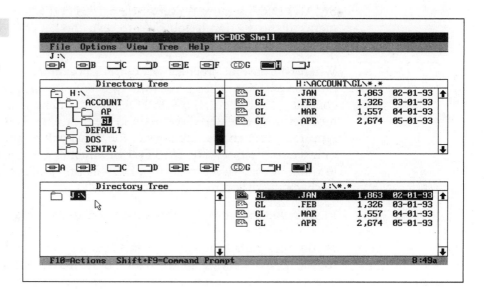

N O T E

SUBST offers convenience, not increased performance. A substituted drive is really only a portion of another drive; it is not a RAM drive.

The final version of SUBST is used to undo a substitution. To undo the SUBST command shown in the previous example, you would type

```
SUBST J: /D
```

The /D switch disassociates the directory from the fictitious drive J. After disassociating a drive, any continued attempts to use the drive would result in an invalid drive message.

Speeding Up Disk Access

The following command is most helpful if you are not taking advantage of SMARTDRV's disk caching (see Chapter 18). There is a good deal of functional overlap between what SMARTDRV does, and what the FASTOPEN command offers you. However, SMARTDRV requires the commitment of extra system memory. If you can afford this commitment, SMARTDRV is more powerful than FASTOPEN, so ignore the command in this section if you plan to reap the benefits of SMARTDRV's caching mechanism.

When you have a directory structure that contains many levels of subdirectories, DOS takes extra time to search for files and directories. To combat this problem, the FASTOPEN command maintains a list of the most recently accessed directory and file locations. This means that if you repeatedly reference a directory or file, DOS will be able to locate it more quickly on the disk. The FASTOPEN memory buffer contains the disk location of that directory or file; DOS can then access it without having to check the disk directory structure itself.

In fact, you can also use this command to set up a number of special memory buffers in DOS for the express purpose of holding the contents of your files, rather than just file and directory locations. In this way, when the file is referenced again, the data is retrieved from this so-called *memory cache.* Reading the data from this memory cache at the speed of memory chips is much faster than reading the data from the original sectors on the disk drives.

WARNING

Do not use the FASTOPEN command after starting Windows. Also, do not use any defragmentation utility like DEFRAG once FASTOPEN is active. Furthermore, FASTOPEN cannot be used on any network drive, or on any drive defined by the SUBST command.

The general format of this command is

    FASTOPEN *Drive:=Size*

Drive is the drive you want FASTOPEN to work for. You must repeat the *Drive:* and *=Size* parts of the command for each drive you want FAST-OPEN to affect. *Size,* an optional parameter, represents the number of directory or file *entries* that FASTOPEN will remember. If your system includes expanded memory, you can request that DOS install the FAST-OPEN storage area in expanded memory by simply adding a /X switch when you run the command. Using this switch will free up additional low (conventional) memory for program use.

Make sure that the FASTOPEN command file is available on the current directory or path. As with all DOS commands, you can precede the command name with the full path name leading to it.

The most common use of the FASTOPEN command is simply to specify the disk drive whose performance you want to improve. For example, entering

    FASTOPEN C:

will enable DOS to remember the last ten directories and files accessed (ten is the default), and thus be able to go right to them on the disk.

FASTOPEN can only be used once per boot session. It reserves 48 bytes per entry. A buffer size of 100 (FASTOPEN C:=100) would therefore consume about 4800 bytes of memory. It is recommended that *Size* be at least as great as the highest number of levels in the directory structure. In this way, there will be one FASTOPEN entry for each directory, so DOS can quickly obtain the directory's list of contained file names. Consequently, the contents of the individual file can be more quickly accessed on the disk. In fact, unless you are only working with one file, *Size* should be much larger. The default is reasonable, unless you have performed specialized timing tests on your system to determine that your system has special usage requirements.

Copying Files Faster

A special command called XCOPY allows sophisticated file transfers between disks and directories. You should consider using it for transferring groups of files, because it is usually faster than COPY, which is the command the shell would otherwise use behind the scenes. I also recommend it for transferring files from many different directories, because XCOPY understands better than COPY how to select files located in remote sections of the disk.

However, this is true only if the files can be described by a wild-card specification within the same portion of the disk hierarchy. If the files are dispersed around one or more disks, or if they do not fit any one wild-card specification, you will be better off using the multiple tagging and copying capability of the shell.

N O T E   You cannot use XCOPY to transfer multiple files to a printer. It is designed for disk transfers only.

The general format of the XCOPY command is

```
XCOPY Source Destination Switches
```

where *Source* and *Destination* are specified as they are with the COPY command. Using the *Switches* parameter, which represents one or more switches, can greatly expand the range of files to be copied. A simple example of using the XCOPY command is the following:

```
XCOPY C:\GLOSSARY\*.* A:
```

This command will copy all files in the GLOSSARY directory on drive C to the disk in drive A. As DOS copies the files, it displays the file names on the screen (see Figure 19.6). The unique aspect of this command is revealed by the message

```
Reading source file(s)…
```

which appears immediately after you enter the command. Unlike the COPY command, which reads a single source file and then writes a destination file, the XCOPY command reads a group of files from the source disk at one time. Similarly, it writes files to the target disk as a group, instead of one at a time.

XCOPY reads files into available memory before writing to the destination drive. Filenames are displayed as they are written out of memory and onto the target drive.

```
C:\>XCOPY C:\GLOSSARY\*.* A:
Reading source file(s)...
C:\GLOSSARY\FILE_ID.DIZ
C:\GLOSSARY\GL-READ.ME
C:\GLOSSARY\GLCFG.DAT
C:\GLOSSARY\GLOSRY.DAT
C:\GLOSSARY\GLOSRY.DBV
Reading source file(s)...
C:\GLOSSARY\GLOSRY.EXE
C:\GLOSSARY\GLOSRY.ICO
C:\GLOSSARY\GLOSSARY.REG
C:\GLOSSARY\GLTBLS.DAT
C:\GLOSSARY\GLTBLS.DBV
C:\GLOSSARY\CHKLIST.MS
        11 File(s) copied

C:\>
```

XCOPY uses available memory to set up a buffering scheme which allows the files already read into memory to be moved out of the buffer to the target drive, thereby freeing up more space for new files to be read into the buffer (see Figure 19.7). This helps the XCOPY command to use both time and space more efficiently than the COPY command. Since memory operations occur much more rapidly than disk operations, XCOPY can transfer a group of files faster.

XCOPY uses a memory-based buffering scheme to manage this very efficient reading and writing mechanism. XCOPY can often read several files in a single disk request, thereby using less time than the COPY command to read the same disk files.

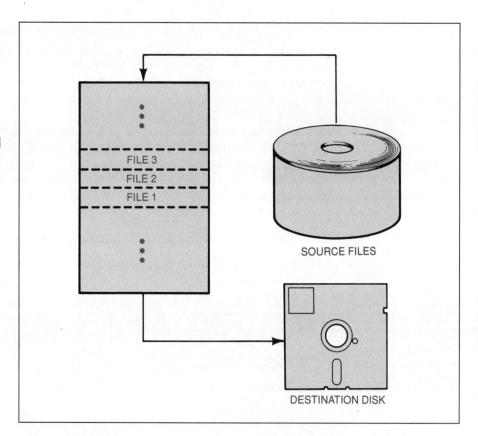

SOURCE FILES

DESTINATION DISK

T I P

The XCOPY command in DOS 6 does not copy hidden or system files, as it did in earlier versions of DOS. If you wish to copy these kinds of files, you should first use the ATTRIB command to turn off the hidden or system attributes from these types of files.

More specifically, XCOPY reduces the total time spent copying because there are fewer individual startups (i.e., for each file) for the disk drive heads. Notice also in Figure 19.6 that the available memory on my system was insufficient to read at one time all the files in the C:\GLOSSARY directory. After reading the first five files, available memory was filled and

XCOPY proceeded to write those files to the A:\ directory. Only then did it take the necessary time to read the remaining six files in order to write *them* to the A:\ directory.

You should now take a look at the XCOPY command's switches, in the order of their importance. The most powerful switch is /S, which lets you select files that are located within the subdirectory structure. As you can see in Figure 19.8, the /S switch—

```
XCOPY *.DAT A: /S
```

—directs DOS to look in all subdirectories of the source directory for file names that match your file specification, in this case *.DAT. Using the /S switch with *.DAT enables DOS to copy three files from the GLOSSARY directory, one file from the 123R24 directory, three more files from the MTEZ directory, and two remaining .DAT files in the CPBACK-UP\DATA and COMPANIO\COMPANIO.D5 directories.

If the respective directories containing the copied files do not already exist on the destination disk, DOS automatically creates them for you and then copies the files to them. The /S switch, therefore, directs XCOPY to do double duty. First, it enables XCOPY to search through the directory

FIGURE 19.8

XCOPY can search subdirectories with the /S switch to copy files from within a directory structure. The full pathname to the file appears on your screen when the /S switch delves into the directory hierarchy to obtain files.

```
C:\>XCOPY *.DAT A: /S
Reading source file(s)...
GLOSSARY\GLCFG.DAT
GLOSSARY\GLOSRY.DAT
GLOSSARY\GLTBLS.DAT
123R24\ICONS.DAT
MTEZ\NMODEMS.DAT
MTEZ\EDITORS.DAT
MTEZ\PRINTERS.DAT
CPBACKUP\DATA\CPSCOLOR.DAT
COMPANIO\COMPANIO.D5\CKSUMS.DAT
        9 File(s) copied

C:\>
```

structures on both source and target drives. Second, if the target drive hierarchy does not properly exist to match the files and structure from the source drive, XCOPY first creates directories, then copies files to them. In this way, files with identical names, but in different directories, will not be overwritten by each other.

You can also control the copying operation by employing the /P switch, which tells XCOPY to ask you, with each file name that matches the wildcard specification, if you want to carry out the operation for that file. You can then decide whether each file will be copied.

Look at the sample XCOPY transfer in Figure 19.9, which uses both the /S and the /P switches. In this example, I answered affirmatively (Y) only four times when prompted. XCOPY then copied only the four selected files to the destination drive. These files were

> C:\GLOSSARY\GLCFG.DAT
>
> C:\GLOSSARY\GLOSRY.DAT
>
> C:\GLOSSARY\GLTBLS.DAT
>
> C:\MTEZ\EDITORS.DAT

FIGURE 19.9

Use XCOPY's /P switch to prompt you for a decision about whether or not to copy each file. Use this switch when you are being very selective about which files to copy and which not to copy.

```
C:\>XCOPY *.DAT A: /S /P
GLOSSARY\GLCFG.DAT (Y/N)?Y
GLOSSARY\GLOSRY.DAT (Y/N)?Y
GLOSSARY\GLTBLS.DAT (Y/N)?Y
123R24\ICONS.DAT (Y/N)?N
MTEZ\MODEMS.DAT (Y/N)?N
MTEZ\EDITORS.DAT (Y/N)?Y
MTEZ\PRINTERS.DAT (Y/N)?N
CPBACKUP\DATA\CPSCOLOR.DAT (Y/N)?N
COMPANIO\COMPANIO.D5\CKSUMS.DAT (Y/N)?N
        4 File(s) copied

C:\>
```

TIP

You can write a DOSKEY macro to copy all the files from one disk to another, even if the disks are differently sized. Just write the following macro: DOSKEY ZCOPY=XCOPY $1*.* $2 /S /E. The new ZCOPY command copies all visible files and directories from disk $1 to disk $2. ZCOPY requires only the drive identifiers as parameters. The first parameter specifies the source drive and the second parameter specifies the destination drive. The /E switch causes subdirectories to be copied even though they are empty.

Another important switch, /D, allows you to specify that all files should be copied if their creation dates are the same as or later than the date you give. The form required is /D:*mm-dd-yy* unless you have installed a DOS version with a different date format.

The remaining switches are of less practical importance:

/A   Only files that are marked for backup are copied. The files' archive attributes are not changed by this switch.

/M   Copies the files marked for backup (i.e., the archive bit is turned on). Then turns off the archive bit to indicate that the files have been backed up.

/V   Requests the extra read-after-write verification step.

/W   This switch's only job is to pause briefly and ask you to press any key to begin copying files.

Advanced File Manipulation

A file attribute is something that describes that file. Height is an attribute of a person; disk storage space is an attribute of a file. Another attribute of a file is its archive status, indicated by the archive bit, which indicates whether the file has been changed since the last time it was backed up. Yet another attribute, indicated by the read/write bit, tells you whether you are allowed to make or delete permanent changes. You can use the AT-TRIB command to set this attribute to *read-only* for any file that you want to protect from accidental overwriting. Several advanced DOS commands have been designed to work specifically with files and attributes such as these.

Recovering Deleted Files

The UNDELETE and UNFORMAT commands exist to help you restore files, directories, and entire disks that have been corrupted, accidentally formatted, or deleted in error. Use the UNFORMAT command (see the *EXTRA!* page) for a large-scale loss of an entire disk, due to accidental erasure or directory-table corruption.

In Chapter 11, you learned how to make backup copies of your important program and data files using the Backup option of the MSBACKUP command. If you later needed to restore those backup copies to your main hard disk, you used the Restore option of the same command. Sometimes, however, you will find that you need a copy of a deleted file that has not been protected with an MSBACKUP copy. That's the time to use the UNDELETE command.

When a file is deleted from a DOS directory, DOS does not truly erase the contents of the file. This would take quite some time for some files, depending on the size of the file being erased. Instead, DOS actually makes only a minor adjustment to the directory table that contains the names of the files and subdirectories. By erasing only the first character

➤ EXTRA!

Rescuing an Accidentally Formatted Disk

Sometimes, you may lose quite a bit more than just one or two individual files. You may have lost your entire disk because of an accidental FORMAT. The UNFORMAT command can restore your entire hard disk after an inadvertent erasure through reformatting.

Keep your disks unfragmented with the DEFRAG utility. If you ever have to use UNFORMAT to rebuild an accidentally formatted disk, this command will be more successful at recovering files. Fragmented files are only partially recovered by UNFORMAT.

UNFORMAT has the following syntax:

```
UNFORMAT Drive: [Switches]
```

This command will restore the disk identified by *Drive:*. For example, UNFORMAT C: will attempt to restore your C drive to its status prior to its last format. It will attempt to hunt for and then use the disk's file allocation table and root directory. Finding this remnant information, UNFORMAT will use it to recreate the remainder of the disk hierarchical structure.

You can specify three possible switches when running this unformatting command. Using /L forces UNFORMAT to display each file and directory name that it discovers during unformatting. Without the /L switch, only fragmented files and directories are displayed. Using a /TEST switch turns on a test mode that only displays what the disk would look like if you actually performed unformatted the disk by running UNFORMAT without the /TEST switch. Finally, the /P switch would send output messages to the LPT1 port. Use this to record the unformatting process for later analysis.

UNFORMAT is only designed to work properly on local hard disk drives. Disengage a disk completely from any network before you try to recover files with this command.

of a file name, DOS signals itself that the entire file represented by that name is to be treated as unavailable, or "erased." Because of this simplified technique, it is possible to reclaim, or *undelete*, such a file.

The UNDELETE command offers several different mechanisms for providing protection against file deletion. Each method has advantages and disadvantages. My preference is the most comprehensive (and costly in terms of space) method known as *sentry* protection. But the simplest method, known as *standard* protection, requires no special preparation or setup. Let's look at that one first. I'll also explain the intermediate form of protection, known as deletion *tracking*.

NOTE If you simply run UNDELETE without specifying the mechanism to use, sentry protection is assumed. If no sentry protection was ever established, UNDELETE tries to use the deletion tracker method. If this method was also not ever established, then the simple DOS directory-table method is attempted.

If no other file creations or modifications have occurred on your disk since you "erased" the file in question, then a complete restoration of the file requires only that you somehow restore the first character of the file name to the directory table. The UNDELETE command enables you to do this, in its simplest form known as *standard* protection. To undelete a file by this method, you only need to type the following command:

    UNDELETE *Filename* /DOS

Filename is the full path name to the file whose name has been deleted. The /DOS switch forces UNDELETE to use the first-letter–erased technique in the DOS directory table for recovery purposes. You can use a wild card in this file name. As shown in Figure 19.10, UNDELETE will prompt you to enter a new first character for each file you specify that is found in the directory table.

In this figure, UNDELETE has found 49 deleted files using the Delete Sentry control file (see below). Using the simplest DOS directory table method, it only found three deleted files, but can successfully recover only

Standard undeletion uses the DOS directory table entries, if they still exist, and if the associated file space has not been used. Doing the simplest chore on a disk after a deletion will usually preclude undeletion by this simplistic technique.

```
UNDELETE - A delete protection facility
Copyright (C) 1987-1993 Central Point Software, Inc.
All rights reserved.

Directory: C:\DOS
File Specifications: *.*

    Delete Sentry control file contains   49 deleted files.

    Deletion-tracking file not found.

    MS-DOS directory contains    3 deleted files.
    Of those,    1 files may be recovered.
Using the MS-DOS directory method.

    ?NAPTEMP TMP    24000 12-29-92  3:39p  ...A  Undelete (Y/N)?Y
    Please type the first character for ?NAPTEMP.TMP: S

File successfully undeleted.

    ** ?AT_FIL2 TMP    2784 12-24-92  8:21a  ...A
Starting cluster is unavailable. This file cannot be recovered
with the UNDELETE command.  Press any key to continue.
```

one of them with the first-letter–replacement technique. Each file name found in the directory table is shown with a ? in the first character position. If you respond with a Y to the question

```
Undelete (Y/N)?
```

then UNDELETE asks you to

```
Please type the first character for <FileName>:
```

The UNDELETE command then proceeds to display each other file-name in the table, informing you about whether or not you can attempt to recover it.

WARNING

UNDELETE is sure to work perfectly only if you have done no other disk and file manipulations since the accidental erasure of the file you are trying to recover.

It is still possible that the directory-table entry for a deleted file may be itself have been reused by DOS even if you have not created new files or made changes to existing files on your disk. In this case, the /DOS switch on the UNDELETE command will be unable to find the former file name with the modified first character. However, you may still be in luck if you had used the deletion tracking facility (/DT switch) or the deletion sentry (/DS switch) when you first installed UNDELETE on your system.

To install undeletion protection, using either the sentry or tracker method, you must run UNDELETE at a command prompt (or place the line in your AUTOEXEC.BAT file), using the correct switch. For example, to load the memory resident portion of UNDELETE that manages a sentry file for the D drive, you would type:

```
UNDELETE /SD
```

If you choose to install deletion tracker protection, you would simply add a /T switch for the drive you wish to protect. For example, type:

```
UNDELETE /TC
```

to establish a deletion tracker file for deleted files on drive C. The sentry mechanism offers broader protection, so I suggest that you use it. If you want to establish sentry protection for more than one drive, or customize the protection still further, you can edit the UNDELETE.INI file that comes with DOS. My system's UNDELETE.INI file contains the following lines:

```
[configuration]
archive=FALSE
days=7
percentage=10
[sentry.drives]
C=
D=
[mirror.drives]
C=
[sentry.files]
s_files=*.* -*.tmp -*.vm? -*.woa -*.swp -*.spl -*.bak -*.img
[defaults]
d.sentry=TRUE
d.tracker=FALSE
```

NOTE If an UNDELETE.INI file exists, its contents override any parameters or switches set on a command line when you install the program.

As you can see, I've simply added a C= line and a D= line in the [sentry.drives] section of this UNDELETE.INI file. Refer to the online help for the UNDELETE command for a detailed explanation of all the possibilities for settings in this initialization file.

Once you've activated one or the other of these deletion protection levels, you have established an ability to restore deleted files. However, be aware that no mechanism is completely foolproof. If you wish to recover a deleted file, you are most likely to be successful if you do nothing else on the drive before attempting the file recovery.

In the case of the standard DOS deletion technique described above, the former disk space used by a file may have been reused by a new file. Or, even worse, a new file in the same directory may have reused the directory table entry for the original file name. In the first case, you can replace the ? mark with a character, but the data on the disk sectors no longer constitute the original file. In the second case, the file name is not even visible any longer in the directory table, and you can't even get started attempting to recover the original file.

Sentry protection is better than either standard or tracking protection. It establishes a special hidden directory called SENTRY on the protected drive. Each time you delete a file from that drive, UNDELETE moves the file to the hidden SENTRY directory, assigning it a temporary name. If you undelete the file, it can be easily moved back from the SENTRY directory to its original directory and disk location.

As Figure 19.11 depicts, you can undelete one or more files that have been deleted by running the UNDELETE command with this syntax:

```
UNDELETE FileSpec /DS
```

FIGURE 19.11

Sentry tracking offers the greatest probability of successful file undeletion. In this example, you can probably use the sentry method to undelete 67 out of 67 deletions, while only 2 out of 50 MS-DOS deletions can be recovered.

```
C:\>undelete *.* /ds

UNDELETE - A delete protection facility
Copyright (C) 1987-1993 Central Point Software, Inc.
All rights reserved.

Directory: C:\
File Specifications: *.*

    Delete Sentry control file contains   67 deleted files.

    Deletion-tracking file not found.

    MS-DOS directory contains   50 deleted files.
    Of those,   2 files may be recovered.

Using the Delete Sentry method.

     $MONOTMP PCX     6866 12-22-92  8:41a  ...A  Deleted: 12-22-92  8:44a
This file can be 100% undeleted. Undelete (Y/N)?y

File successfully undeleted.

     $MONOTMP PCX     7578 12-22-92  9:02a  ...A  Deleted: 12-22-92  9:02a
This file can be 100% undeleted. Undelete (Y/N)?
```

TIP

Use the UNDELETE.INI file to set limits on the percentage of disk space to be consumed by deletion sentry files, as well as the number of days to retain access to deleted files. To do this, specify the *percentage* and *days* entries in the [Configuration] section of the UNDELETE.INI file.

Each file found in the SENTRY directory is displayed, and you are informed whether or not the file can be successfully undeleted. Since you may have deleted various versions of the same file over time, this mechanism displays the time and date of the deletion. If you choose to undelete more than one version of a file, you will have to change the name of all but one of the file versions.

The deletion-tracking file is less powerful than deletion sentry because it only retains the name and disk location of the most recently deleted disk files. If a particular file name is one of the entries in the deletion-tracking file, you can still recover it even if the DOS directory table no longer lists it.

Table 19.1 shows in kilobytes the space required by UNDELETE to maintain a deletion-tracking file. The space taken up dictates how many filenames can be retained, and how much disk space is consumed by the tracking file itself. However, since deletion tracking only keeps track of information about deleted files, and deletion sentry actually manages the deleted files themselves, the tracking mechanism uses considerably less disk space than the sentry mechanism.

TABLE 19.1: Default PCTRACKR.DEL specifications

SIZE OF DISK	DELETION ENTRIES	RESULTING FILE SIZE
360K	25	5K
720K	50	9K
1.2Mb	75	14K
1.44Mb	75	14K
20Mb	101	18K
32Mb	202	36K
Larger	303	55K

A /DT switch directs UNDELETE to ignore both the DOS directory table and the sentry control file. Tracking only uses the entries found in the deletion-tracking file:

```
UNDELETE FileSpec /DT
```

Once again, you can use a wild-card specification for *FileSpec*. UNDELETE will check each file name in the deletion-tracking file and determine whether the former clusters occupied by the file are still available. Even though the name no longer appears in the DOS directory, the fact that the name and location information appear in the tracking file can still be enough, as Figure 19.12 shows. The MS-DOS directory table only has seven deleted entries that remain accessible, while the deletion-tracking file remembers information about twelve formerly deleted files.

FIGURE 19.12

Undeleting files with deletion-tracking data offers the middle ground for file deletion protection. This mechanism permits partial undeletion of data files, some of whose clusters may have already been reused by DOS for other files.

```
C:\>UNDELETE C:\MANAGER\*.* /DT

UNDELETE - A delete protection facility
Copyright (C) 1987-1993 Central Point Software, Inc.
All rights reserved.

Directory: C:\MANAGER
File Specifications: *.*

    Delete Sentry control file contains    0 deleted files.

    Deletion-tracking file contains    12 deleted files.
    Of those,   12 files have all clusters available,
                 0 files have some clusters available,
                 0 files have no clusters available.

    MS-DOS directory contains    7 deleted files.
    Of those,    7 files may be recovered.

Using the Deletion-tracking method.

      README   TXT    11932  3-14-91  1:01p  ...A  Deleted: 12-29-92  5:34p
All of the clusters for this file are available. Undelete (Y/N)?
```

In this figure, UNDELETE knows the complete name for the file. If DOS has reused the disk space formerly occupied by the file's data, UNDELETE displays

```
None of the clusters for this file are available.
The file cannot be recovered. Press any key to continue
```

and moves on to the next entry in the tracking file. If the clusters formerly used by the file have not been reused by any other file, UNDELETE displays

```
All of the clusters for this file are available.
Undelete (Y/N)?
```

Answer Y at this point, and UNDELETE recovers the file completely, ensuring that a new entry is made in the DOS directory table.

Notice in Figure 19.12 that deletion tracking can also determine if only some file clusters are available. In this case, you may recover a portion but not all of your deleted file. This is useless for program files, because they will no longer work correctly. But it may save you a good deal of reentry time if you can recover a portion of a data file. UNDELETE will prompt you to tell it whether you wish to recapture the available portion of the file.

➤ EXTRA!

Manipulating Hidden Files Is a Snap with DOS Macros

The DOSKEY utility (see Chapter 15) enables you to write and incorporate your own customized new commands into DOS. Here are three simple ones to demonstrate how easy it can be. To create any of these macros, you must have first loaded the DOSKEY utility.

HIDDENS displays all filenames on the current drive that have the hidden attribute. You only need to type HIDDENS at any command prompt. HIDE makes the $1 file (or set of files) invisible. Just type HIDE with one parameter, which specifies a file specification. UNHIDE makes a hidden file (or set of files) visible again. Use the first parameter to specify the filename or path.

These new commands can be created by typing these three lines at a command prompt:

```
DOSKEY HIDDENS=DIR \*.* /S /AH
DOSKEY HIDE=ATTRIB +H $1
DOSKEY UNHIDE=ATTRIB -H $1
```

Changing a File's Attributes

You can change a variety of attributes (characteristics) of any file on any disk. The actual external command that manages this chore is ATTRIB, although you can effect these changes by pulling down the File menu and selecting Change Attributes. This command can be very useful for setting or resetting any of four file attributes, as shown in Figure 19.13.

NOTE Copies of read-only files created with COPY will not be read-only.

FIGURE 19.13

Pull down the File menu and select Change Attributes to 1) make a file Hidden (or unhide it), 2) define it as a System (or user) file, 3) turn on its Archive bit (to identify it as needing backup), or 4) make it read only (or allow writing).

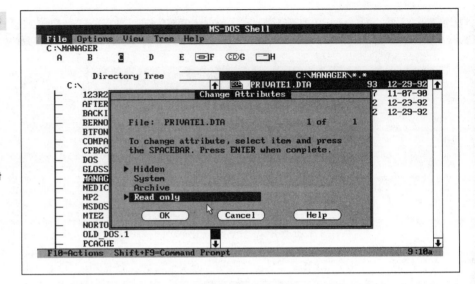

As with other File menu operations, you can change the attributes on more than one file at once. As Figure 19.13 suggests, you can also change more than one of the attribute settings at the same time. If you have selected more than one file prior to initiating the Change Attributes operation, you will be prompted to specify file-by-file adjustment or global adjustment:

```
1. Change selected files one at a time
2. Change all selected files at once
```

In this figure, you can see the names of the four file characteristics that you can control: Hidden, System, Archive, and Read only. You can highlight an attribute name and press the spacebar to toggle its setting between on and off. Alternatively, mouse users can highlight the attribute name and click button 1 to achieve the same result.

The Hidden attribute can be set on to protect a file from even being seen by users. A file whose Hidden attribute is on does not appear in a directory listing. Neither can it be deleted, run, or impacted in any way by commands that use the DOS directory for normal access. The System file attribute denotes whether or not a file contains special information that is used by DOS itself. For example, the hidden DOS system files fall into this attribute category.

TIP

You can hide an entire directory by explicitly typing the directory's name with the ATTRIB command. For example, to effectively hide the PERSONAL directory and all files within it, located within the SIG directory, you would type ATTRIB +H C:\SIG\PERSONAL

Influencing the Archive attribute allows you to control which files will be backed up. If you are using many temporary files, for example, you can reset their archive bits to 0 (off). Those files will then be ignored by all commands (such as MSBACKUP or the XCOPY /M command) that check for an ON archive bit. No backup or copy will take place, so the backup and copy operations for the rest of your files will be faster, and less disk space will be required.

You can turn on the Read Only attribute to block the deletion of a file. This helps to prevent a file or group of files from being erased or changed accidentally.

The Read Only and Archive attributes do not affect whether or not a file name is displayed in the Files area of the shell screen. Remember, however, that in order to see hidden or system files, you must turn on the shell viewing toggle. This particular toggle switch—*Display hidden/system files*—is available on the Display Options dialog box that appears when you pull down the Options menu and select File Display Options.

NOTE

If read-only status is set, it may not always be obvious why later operations become difficult. Programs that automatically save your work after a fixed time period may fail when trying to update a read-only file on the disk.

Updating Sets of Files

If you work mainly with one specific application program, you might want your backup disk to contain copies of only the most recently modified files. REPLACE allows you to make selective backups of files without using the BACKUP command. It can update the files on the backup disk that were recently changed or newly created on your working disk. It can also ignore any of your older and unchanged files.

WARNING

If you run REPLACE or other file management commands from the shell, remember that any file updates or directory adjustments do not become immediately visible on the subsequent shell display. However, you can always force DOS to update its shell screen and all file/directory information by double-clicking on the appropriate drive icon. Keyboard users can move the cursor highlight to the drive area, highlight the appropriate drive icon, and press Enter.

The REPLACE command is simply an advanced, selective, version of the COPY command. It is most commonly used when you change versions of DOS and need to update various system files or even an entire DOS directory on your hard disk. You can also use REPLACE to back up your new or modified files at the end of a work day.

The command-prompt format of this command is

REPLACE *Source File(s) Destination Switches*

As always, the command may be prefixed by an optional drive and path name indicating where the REPLACE command file is located. *Source* represents the changed or newly created files that are to be written to the destination disk. *Destination* is optional; it specifies the destination drive and path to receive the copies of the specified files. If no destination path is given, the default is the current directory.

The *Switches* parameter represents one or more switches: /A, /P, /R, /S, /U, or /W. Some of these switches cannot be used together. Let's use the two directories that I've named SOURCE and DEST in Figure 19.14 to demonstrate the behavior of the REPLACE command with its most important switches.

You can see in Figure 19.14 that the SOURCE directory contains three files, while DEST contains only two. These two files in DEST have the same names as two files in SOURCE but FILE1.TXT in DEST has a different date, and FILE3.TXT is obviously completely different in both directories.

The /A switch tells DOS to add files to the destination directory. DOS will only copy source files that are not in the destination directory. The /P (Prompt) switch instructs DOS to pause and ask you if it is all right to copy each file that meets the criteria of *any other* switch that is used.

Let's use the /A and /P switches together. If you issue the command

```
REPLACE C:\REPLACE\SOURCE\*.* C:\REPLACE\DEST /A /P
```

for the files shown in Figure 19.14, you will be asked if you wish to

```
Add C:\REPLACE\DEST\FILE2.TXT? (Y/N)
```

FIGURE 19.14

Use the Dual File List display in the shell to simultaneously view both the source and the destination directories for a REPLACE command.

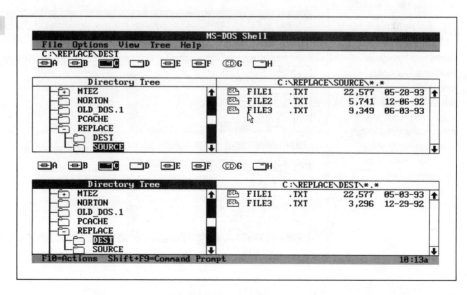

Respond with Y and DOS will copy the specified file and notify you:

```
Adding C:\REPLACE\DEST\FILE2.TXT
1 file(s) added
```

The one file in the source directory (FILE2.TXT) that did not already exist by name in the destination directory was selected for replacement. In this case, FILE2.TXT is added to the DEST directory; FILE1.TXT and FILE3.TXT are left as they were.

The /R switch overrides any read-only attributes of files in the destination directory. It allows you to replace those read-only files without generating an error message, even though a read-only setting would normally inhibit any attempt at overwriting the file. This switch should be used with caution, since you or someone else may have turned on the read-only attribute for a good reason.

The /S switch will only replace or update files, not add new ones. Therefore, it cannot be used with the /A switch. Be careful when you use the /S switch with a wild-card character—it will replace *all* files matching the source specification, including those in any subdirectories of the destination directory. Figure 19.15 shows the results of using the /S switch to

FIGURE 19.15

Use the /S switch with REPLACE to update all matching filenames. Note the file dates and sizes are updated when this switch is used. The final result reflects the data in the source directory for each file name that appears in both source and destination directories.

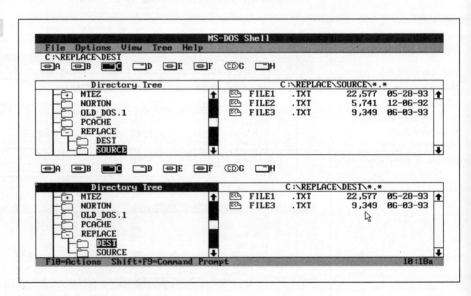

update the files in the DEST directory with the files found in the SOURCE directory. Entering

```
REPLACE C:\REPLACE\SOURCE\*.* C:\REPLACE\DEST /S
```

tells the computer to use the files in the SOURCE directory to replace any files they match in the DEST directory. Since only FILE1.TXT and FILE3.TXT are common to both directories, only they are replaced in the DEST directory. Notice that in this example I replaced the FILE3.TXT file that was originally in the DEST directory with a version from the SOURCE directory that was newer and larger.

True, the replacement file could just as well have been older and smaller. You can protect yourself from performing this type of replacement in error by using the /U switch. This switch ensures that no replacement will occur unless the source file has a newer date and time than the file to be replaced.

WARNING

Be careful to enter the source and destination directories in the correct order in your command. Performing a REPLACE backwards could copy your old data over your new versions.

The /W switch tells DOS to wait while you insert a new source diskette in a drive before the replacement process begins. For example, you can execute the REPLACE command from your C drive, specifying that the source files will come from a diskette in the A drive. DOS will then wait for you to insert the correct source disk before beginning the replacement procedure.

Running Programs Efficiently

The shell offers you an opportunity to customize its very appearance and functionality. You learned in Part Two of this book how to adjust screen colors, screen mode, and even the content and organization of the program groups. But you can do even more. In this section, you'll first learn how to get certain older programs to work at all under DOS 6. Then you'll learn how to use the DOS diagnostic utility command to discover what may be causing problems with one or more of your programs.

➤ EXTRA!

Discover What Your DOS Environment Uses!

The following batch program will tell you how much memory your current environment uses. Use it to quickly discover if you've run out of environment memory, or to determine if your environmental variable space is reaching its maximum. It may be time to expand your environment space with the SHELL command in CONFIG.SYS, or by running a secondary COMMAND processor with a larger /E switch setting.

To use this batch file, just type SIZENVIR with no arguments at any command prompt:

```
@ECHO OFF
Rem SIZENVIR.BAT obtains size of current environment memory.
Rem You must run SIZENVIR without any arguments!
CLS
IF NOT '%1'=='' Goto OK
SET > SIZENVIR.DTA
DIR SIZENVIR.DTA | FIND "SIZENVIR DTA" > TEMP.BAT
TEMP.BAT
:OK
ECHO Your environment requires %2 bytes.
ERASE TEMP.BAT
ERASE SIZENVIR.DTA
```

You'll also learn how to influence the command processor's working environment with two special commands. The internal SET command works by setting up values to be used to control DOS later. The COMMAND.COM file itself can be run more than once to create a secondary shell or command prompt with different characteristics.

The command processor on your system disk, COMMAND.COM, is the program that interprets all of the commands submitted from the shell or typed in from the keyboard. It has been primarily responsible for interpreting all the commands you've learned so far. It takes your command and first scans its own internal command list to see if it can handle your request without going to the disk.

If the command is a memory-resident, internal command, then COMMAND.COM contains instructions that define the way in which that command will work. If it is an external command, COMMAND.COM checks the directory to see if the command file is present. If it is not, and your command is not in a batch file, you will get an error message. If it does find the command file, control will be transferred to that file.

Let's look at some examples. TYPE is a resident command used to display the contents of ASCII files. When COMMAND.COM is ready to accept a command, it displays the DOS prompt. Say you type the command TYPE OUTLINE.TXT. First, COMMAND.COM determines that TYPE is a resident command. Then it looks internally for the instructions that tell it what to do when the TYPE command is used. Following these instructions, it reads the file name you typed and displays the file.

External commands are not really commands at all—each external command request actually runs a *program* contained in a separate file. These files are called COM or EXE files. For example, a file named CHKDSK.EXE contains the program that performs a CHKDSK command. Suppose that you issue the command

    CHKDSK D:

COMMAND.COM first checks to see if CHKDSK is a resident command. After first checking the current working directory, it will then find the file called CHKDSK.EXE somewhere along the specified path (probably in C:\DOS) and transfer control of the system to that file. When

CHKDSK is done checking drive D, control passes back to COMMAND.COM.

When COMMAND.COM is doing all of this, it must not only access those parts of itself that contain definitions and instructions, but it also must access an area of special values known as the DOS *environment*. The environment is a reserved portion of memory that contains user-defined definitions, such as the current path and the last available drive (LASTDRIVE in CONFIG.SYS). The SET command gives you direct control over the contents of these DOS environmental variables.

Dealing with Program Problems

DOS provides two special external commands for helping you to sort out some problems that may occur on your system. The first command, SET-VER, enables you to run older programs under DOS 6 that may otherwise fail to run just because the version number of DOS was unknown when the program was originally released. The second command, MSD, permits you to explore both the status and inner workings of your hardware. This information can be both revealing and essential to the diagnosis and treatment of otherwise difficult system problems.

Making Older Programs Work Properly

So you installed DOS 6 and suddenly your favorite disk-management program no longer works. What happened? Well, there are two possibilities. First, the program may simply be incompatible with DOS 6. In that case, you will not be able to run it at all. If the suggestion in this section doesn't work, you can probably confirm this by calling your software vendor's technical support line. If that is the case, you'll have to get an updated version.

The other possibility is something that can be circumvented. It is possible that your older program checks for your version of DOS and won't run with this previously unknown number version 6. If the program itself is actually compatible with DOS 6, but erroneously stops its own execution when it discovers an unknown version of DOS, you can fool the program into continuing. The SETVER command enables you to specify an earlier version of DOS that will then be fed to your software program when it attempts to run.

To take advantage of this version-setting workaround, you must first install SETVER in your CONFIG.SYS file. Under normal conditions, this is done automatically for you during DOS 6 setup. The following line is placed at the beginning of your CONFIG.SYS file:

```
DEVICE=C:\DOS\SETVER.EXE
```

If this device driver line is not currently in your CONFIG.SYS file, you can add it yourself. This memory-resident code intercepts all program calls that request from DOS the version number. Once resident, SETVER can return a version number other than DOS 6 to your program, thus fooling it into thinking that it is still running on an earlier DOS version.

DOS 6 comes with a list of application programs predefined in the SETVER internal table. You can see this list by typing the following command at any prompt:

```
SETVER | MORE
```

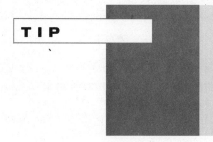

TIP

Take a look at the SETVER internal table list by typing SETVER at any command prompt. If you use none of the programs listed, you don't need to load the SETVER device driver. Remove this CONFIG.SYS command line and save about seven hundred bytes of conventional memory.

Since the list is quite long, you may shorten it by deleting entries. To remove a list entry, just run the command-prompt version of SETVER, specifying the filename as a single parameter. For example, if you do not use the NET.COM program, you can remove it from the SETVER table with this command:

```
SETVER NET.COM /D
```

If you want to try to fool a program into thinking it is running under an earlier version of DOS, you can add a new entry to the SETVER table. To do so, you should specify two parameters to the SETVER command. The first is the application filename itself, and the second is the version number of DOS under which it was originally programmed to run (or the last version of DOS under which you successfully ran it). For example, to add the ANALYSIS.EXE program to the SETVER table, specifying that it runs successfully under DOS 5, you would type the following at a command prompt:

```
SETVER ANALYSIS.EXE 5.00
```

Remember that this solution will only enable the ANALYSIS.EXE program to successfully run if it was really compatible in the first place. If the version-number check is circumvented, it is still possible that the program just won't work with DOS 6. In this case, SETVER won't help you at all. You should also understand that the SETVER table is read in from disk when you boot. If you add a table entry, it will not affect the execution of the application program in question until after you reboot your computer.

WARNING

SETVER can actually make matters worse for you. The version-number check may have been programmed in the first place to protect you and your program from misinterpreting internal system-level data. This suggests that if your program does not work, you should call the software vendor first to discover from them whether the SETVER command or a new software version from them is the best solution to the problem.

Diagnosing System Problems

DOS includes a very useful external command utility called MSD.EXE. This program provides a wide range of system information, covering everything from a hardware analysis of your computer, memory, and connection adapters, to a thorough listing of installed device drivers and interrupt lines in use.

Some portions of this information are simply interesting, while other portions are simply essential for figuring out what may be wrong with your system. To run this program, just type MSD at a command prompt. If you are running the diagnostic program on an LCD or a monochrome screen, type MSD /B instead.

Figure 19.16 shows the main screen that appears when you run the MSD utility.

Since MSD is a complete diagnostic tool, you can actually run it any time you like. You needn't wait till disaster strikes. If you are investigating your system, you can even run it from within Windows at a virtual machine prompt. By running it inside Windows, it can provide useful information about memory usage by both your applications and Windows itself. Furthermore, it can provide information about IRQ usage within Windows that can help to isolate the cause of the problem.

However, you should realize that you'll obtain the most accurate and complete MSD results if you run it outside of Windows. Within Windows, the MSD display will only show memory usage and memory types that are provided by Windows via the DOS session's PIF (Program Information File). Some other information, such as COM port usage and video

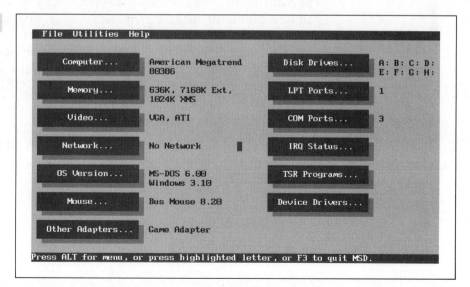

The main menu screen of the Microsoft Diagnostics command utility provides access to a wide range of system information displays. Use this tool to learn more about the inner workings of your system, or use it to identify the cause of complex hardware-oriented system bugs.

configuration may also be modified when seen through Windows. When you run MSD from within Windows, MSD will display a reminder about these possible variations, and then will ask whether or not you really wish to run it.

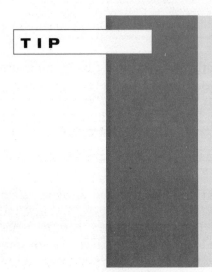

T I P

Plain vanilla systems don't have problems with IRQ conflicts. But those of you with lots of extra equipment in your computer can easily run afoul of IRQ interrupt-processing conflicts. Say your computer has a scanner card that uses IRQ 3. Then you go out and buy a fax card that also uses IRQ 3. At some point, you'll be scanning and a fax will arrive in the background. What can you do? Read the manuals to determine how to change the IRQ level used by one of the cards...and make sure not to assign any IRQ to one device that may simultaneously be used by yet another device in your system (e.g., a hard card, a Bernoulli box, etc.).

The main menu screen of the MSD utility (see Figure 19.16) includes the standard pulldown menu bar for file, utility, and help possibilities. I'll leave those to you to explore on your own. The primary menu choices appear in the center work space, with brief summary information provided as well. You can see that my computer, for example, is an 80386 with an AMI (American Megatrend) BIOS. It has three COM ports and one LPT parallel port.

When you press the highlighted or shortcut key (i.e., p for the Computer choice, or C for COM Ports), MSD will display additional screen(s) of more detailed information about your selection. Table 19.2 summarizes the information provided by each of these subordinate information–screen displays.

TABLE 19.2: MSD information categories

CATEGORY	INFORMATION PROVIDED ABOUT
Computer	BIOS, CPU, coprocessor, DMA, keyboard, and bus
Memory	RAM, ROM, and memory usage (640K–1Mb)
Video	Video board's BIOS, adapter, type, manufacturer, and mode
Network	Network type
OS Version	OS/Windows version IDs, serial numbers, location of DOS, and current environment variable contents
Mouse	Mouse driver, type, version information
Other Adapters	Connection, status, version information
Disk Drives	Type, free space, total size for local and logical drives
LPT Ports	Status and port information for all parallel ports
COM Ports	Status and configuration information for all serial ports
IRQ Status	Address, description, detection, and handling information
TSR Programs	Name, address, and size of memory resident software
Device Drivers	Installed hardware devices and filenames

You can also create a log of any or all of this diagnostic information. Pull down the File menu and select Print Report. This displays Figure 19.17.

From this screen, you can place an X beside any or all possible information entries. These include the choices available from the main screen (Figure 19.17) as well as useful other system aspects, available from the pulldown menus. These include such things as information about specific memory regions, your system's CONFIG.SYS and AUTOEXEC.BAT files, and your Windows initialization files.

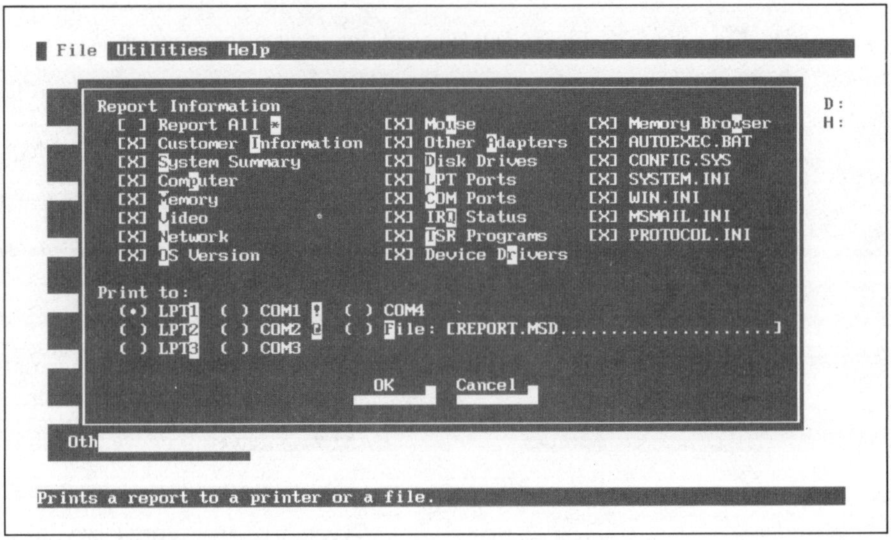

FIGURE 19.17

MSD can send all or some of its diagnostic information to a file, or to any parallel or serial port. Use this method to provide hard copy to an expert who may be debugging your system problems, or just to read through yourself at a more convenient time.

```
    File  Utilities  Help                                              D:
                                                                       H:
        Report Information
        [ ] Report All                [X] Mouse           [X] Memory Browser
        [X] Customer Information       [X] Other Adapters  [X] AUTOEXEC.BAT
        [X] System Summary            [X] Disk Drives     [X] CONFIG.SYS
        [X] Computer                  [X] LPT Ports       [X] SYSTEM.INI
        [X] Memory                    [X] COM Ports       [X] WIN.INI
        [X] Video              .      [X] IRQ Status      [X] MSMAIL.INI
        [X] Network                   [X] TSR Programs    [X] PROTOCOL.INI
        [X] DS Version                [X] Device Drivers

        Print to:
        (.) LPT1   ( ) COM1      ( ) COM4
        ( ) LPT2   ( ) COM2      ( ) File: [REPORT.MSD.................]
        ( ) LPT3   ( ) COM3

                              OK          Cancel

    Oth

    Prints a report to a printer or a file.
```

You can send the report directly to your printer port, as I've done in Figure 19.17. Alternatively, you can send a copy of the report to a file. The default filename used is REPORT.MSD, although you can change that to a different name, such as JUL14.MSD, by simply overtyping the default name on Figure 19.17 before clicking on OK.

Setting Environmental Variables

The SET command is used to change character strings and definitions within the DOS environment. Both you and DOS can set aside named areas of this environment for character strings. You can use them for anything you like—for example, individual path names for future commands, file names for later DOS operations, or variable values used by several batch files. You first saw some advanced applications of this special DOS feature in Chapter 14 when you created batch files to manage password protection and system announcements.

Use a Professional Technique to Debug Your Batch Files.

The batch files in this book typically start with an @ECHO OFF line. This suppresses the display of each command line in the batch file as it executes. This is a good technique once your batch file works properly. While you are developing your own batch files, you may need to debug them by observing these command lines as they execute.

There is a neat alternative to editing the first line from @ECHO OFF to @ECHO ON and back again. You can make the first line of your batch files:

```
@ECHO %DEBUG%
```

Then, you only need to set the environmental variable DEBUG equal to ON or OFF prior to executing your batch file. In fact, you can use this technique most effectively by placing this command in your AUTOEXEC.BAT file:

```
SET DEBUG=OFF
```

In this way, you only need to turn the DEBUG variable ON:

```
SET DEBUG=ON
```

at a command prompt whenever you run and test a batch file. If the DEBUG variable is ON when you run the batch file, you will be able to see the workings of each internal command. If the DEBUG variable is OFF, as will typically be the case, then the @ECHO %DEBUG% line will be treated as if it were @ECHO OFF and each internal command line display will be suppressed.

You are limited by default to 256 bytes of total available DOS environment space, although this default can be increased. To increase the total available environmental space, use the /E switch when submitting the following command in your CONFIG.SYS file:

```
SHELL=COMMAND /E:2048
```

In this example, you are requesting DOS to use a specially expanded version of COMMAND.COM as the new command interpreter. This new DOS shell is initiated with a total of 2048 bytes available for environmental variables.

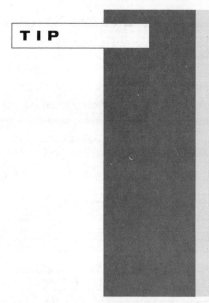

TIP

A simple DIR command at a system prompt displays files in the order in which they were created in the current directory. Although the shell permits you to arrange the listing, and switches on the DIR command also permit arrangement of the filenames, you can simplify things still more. You can set a particular environmental variable (DIRCMD) to contain the default ordering of your filenames. For example, to request ordering by filename rather than the default date/time, you can include the statement SET DIRCMD=/ON /P in your AUTOEXEC.BAT file. Whenever you later type DIR at any command prompt, your listing will appear in name order. Furthermore, the /P switch ensures that you will see large directories a screenful at a time.

The SET command with no parameters can display the current DOS environment settings:

```
COMSPEC=F:\COMMAND.COM
PATH=C:\;C:\DOS;C:\UTILITY
PROMPT=$p$g
LASTDRIVE=Z
FILES=\wordproc\wordperf\stuff\
```

The first four of these environment names (COMSPEC, PATH, PROMPT, LASTDRIVE) are predefined and have special meaning to the system. You've seen all of these except for COMSPEC. The COMSPEC variable is modified infrequently, and only when you want to relocate your command processor to some drive or directory other than the root of the boot disk. COMSPEC is most commonly used when you place COMMAND.COM on a RAM disk to speed up applications that invoke the command processor frequently.

A modified version of the SET command can erase any existing entry:

```
SET VariableName=
```

For example, if you enter the following at a command prompt:

```
SET PATH=
```

DOS will clear the existing value currently stored in the PATH variable. If you then execute the SET command, you will see that the PATH variable is no longer defined:

```
COMSPEC=F:\COMMAND.COM
PROMPT=$p$g
LASTDRIVE=Z
FILES=\wordproc\wordperf\stuff\
```

The entire path definition has been removed. Asking for the current PATH at the DOS prompt now will result in a "No Path" message.

The last version of SET will define or modify a DOS environment string. To create a completely new DOS environment string or to change one that already exists, use the format

```
SET Name=String
```

where *Name* is either a variable name defined by you, or one of the system's predefined names like PROMPT, PATH, LASTDRIVE, or COMSPEC. For example, you might want to define a different PATH. You can do it in one of two ways: by using the PATH command (see Chapter 5), or by using the SET command. Using the command

```
SET path=F:\;C:\;C:\DOS;C:\norton
```

would change or create the path definition, as shown here:

```
COMSPEC=A:\COMMAND.COM
PATH=F:\;C:\;C:\DOS;C:\norton
```

```
PROMPT=$p$g
LASTDRIVE=Z
FILES=\wordproc\wordperf\stuff\
```

Notice that the variable name "path" was changed to "PATH", but "norton" stayed in the same case. DOS does not change anything within the string, because the case of the string character's may have meaning to you and affect how you intend to use it.

Definitions contained in the DOS environment can be used (that is, actually referred to) only by programs or batch files. For example, typing CD FILES at the DOS prompt will not work. You can, however, create a batch file that accesses the DOS environment string FILES, by including a reference to FILES within percent symbols. For example:

```
dir %FILES%
```

would cause the command processor to look up FILES in the DOS environment and, when found, substitute its definition (in this case, \wordperf\wordproc\stuff\) for %FILES%. Remember, this is *not* available directly from the DOS prompt.

NOTE As you learned in Chapter 14, a leading percent sign (%0 to %9) indicates a batch-file variable. Leading and trailing percent signs together indicate a DOS environment string, and both percent signs must be used when referencing environmental variables.

As you can see, the DOS environment can be used by programs and batch files and is a convenient way to pass information to these programs. For example, suppose a program needs a certain file name or path, but for some reason (perhaps security considerations) the program does not ask the user directly for this information. The path information can be put into the DOS environment, which then can be made inaccessible to the user but readily obtainable from the program.

Using a Secondary Command Processor

There will be times when it may be useful to create or invoke a second command processor. COMMAND.COM, the first command processor, is invoked when the computer is turned on. It is the part of DOS that takes in, translates, and executes your standard commands. A typical startup command, DOSSHELL, brings up the application program known as the DOS Shell. Once that program is active, it can initiate another, completely new DOS command processor.

➤ EXTRA!

System Halted, Cannot Load COMMAND.COM

The first time I got this message, it was annoying because I had to reboot my entire system. The fifth time I got this message, it was frustrating because I couldn't figure out what was wrong. It happens just after you exit an application program—but only sometimes, it seems.

In fact, it will happen every time after certain application programs terminate. The solution is to either completely and correctly include a SHELL statement in your CONFIG.SYS file, or include a SET COMSPEC command in your AUTOEXEC.BAT file. The reason for this is that some applications use the same memory that is used by the transient, disk-resident portion of COMMAND.COM.

When this type of application ends, the memory resident portion of COMMAND.COM attempts to reload its transient portion from disk. DOS needs this transient portion of COMMAND.COM in order to successfully interpret your command prompt requests. The COMSPEC variable, either SET directly in AUTOEXEC.BAT, or set indirectly by the SHELL command in CONFIG.SYS, tells DOS where on disk to find the COMMAND.COM file. If COMSPEC is not set, or is set incorrectly, then your system cannot continue to function at all.

Invoking a second command processor by running the COM-MAND.COM utility program itself then gives you the ability to execute DOS commands from inside a program written in BASIC, Pascal, or whatever, and then return to that program. This is precisely what DOS does when you press Shift+F9; it runs the COMMAND.COM program to create a secondary command processor to interpret your commands.

Although the shell doesn't do this itself, the COMMAND utility does enable you to load and customize a command processor of your own that has special functions and abilities, or even altered command definitions. You can do this by running COMMAND at a DOS prompt. The COMMAND command has several switches: one to specify the memory residency status of the new command processor, one to name a file to be run on invocation, and one to change the size of the DOS environment.

The general format of this command is

COMMAND *Location Switches*

Location is the optional drive and path where the command processor to be invoked is located. This parameter gives you the ability to prepare and then use a nonstandard or restricted version of a command processor. The *Switches* parameter represents any or all of the optional switches /P, /C *String*, /E:*xxxxx*, or /K:*filename*.

The new command processor must be named COMMAND.COM as well. Once the new processor is invoked, however, the directory containing the new processor will not become the new root directory. Everything will run as it did before you reassigned the processor, but the processing rules of the new processor will be in effect.

The optional switches define the new processor's environment. The /P (Permanent) switch causes the new command processor to become the primary processor. DOS will assume as initial values all the existing DOS environment variables defined by the prior command processor. You may change any of them, but you will not be able to exit to the previous DOS environment. Without /P, the new DOS environment exists only temporarily, and you can exit from it only by using DOS's EXIT command.

This comes in handy if you are using a modified command processor for security reasons.

The /C *String* parameter tells the new processor to execute the command in *String* when it is invoked. If this is left out, the new command processor will be invoked and prompt you for commands. For example, the normal processor that is run every time you start the computer, COMMAND.COM, has a built-in *String* value of AUTOEXEC.BAT, which causes the AUTOEXEC.BAT file to be run when the system starts.

The /E:*xxxxx* parameter can define a new (and usually larger) DOS environment size, so that extensive use of the SET command will be permitted. This is only necessary when you begin doing fancy things with your batch files or your application programs.

For example, suppose you have a command processor in the UTILITY directory, in which the ERASE and FORMAT commands are disallowed. You would also like to have 512 bytes of DOS environment, and you would like this processor to supplant the COMMAND.COM processor permanently. The following command will do all of this:

```
COMMAND \UTILITY /P /E:512
```

COMMAND is the command name, and UTILITY is the directory containing the new command processor. The /P switch makes the newly active command processor (the secondary command processor) the permanent primary processor, and /E:512 tells the computer to allow half a kilobyte of DOS environmental memory.

Invoking a secondary processor without the /P parameter will cause the DOS environment to appear as in Figure 19.18. You may terminate the secondary processor invoked without /P by using the DOS EXIT command. This will deactivate the secondary DOS environment and reactivate the main processor. On exiting from the secondary processor, the computer will reenter the DOS environment of the first processor. Therefore, any changes you made to the DOS environment variables of the secondary command processor will be lost when you exit to the primary DOS environment.

FIGURE 19.18

Use a secondary command processor to work with a separate (and often larger) set of environmental variables. You can also use a different command processor to apply a redefined set of available commands for your users.

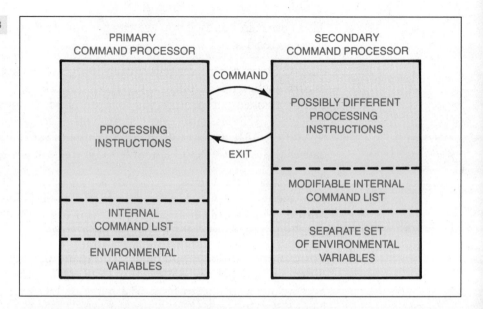

Any changes you make to the DOS environment while you are running the secondary processor will be lost when you exit to the primary processor. However, anything else you have done—such as changing drives and deleting files—will be permanent.

This can come in handy in a number of instances. If necessary, you could use this command to increase the available DOS environment. Simply reinvoking the original command processor with

```
COMMAND \ /P /E:2048
```

would activate the same processor, but expand the new usable DOS environment to 2048 bytes and make the new processor the primary processor.

You should not invoke a secondary command processor lightly, since each new invocation of COMMAND.COM consumes an additional amount of finite physical memory. Permanently attaching a secondary processor is better used as a technique for customization or security, rather than for simply expanding the DOS environment.

TIP

Some programs will not work correctly if loaded in the very first 64K of memory. Since you may have used upper memory successfully to free up part of the first 64K of memory, a program that previously ran may now fail. If any program displays a "Packed file corrupt" message, you should run the program with the LOADFIX command. For example, if your ANALYSIS.EXE program fails in this manner, after starting it by typing ANALYSIS at a command prompt, you should now start it by typing LOADFIX ANALYSIS.EXE

Making Laptops Work for You

One of the most inconvenient aspects of having more than one computer has always been the issue of accessing data and programs on all the computers you use. It's rarely realistic to keep copies of all your programs on each computer you use. It's almost never realistic to create matching data files on each computer.

Most of us either use 'sneaker power' to walk the programs between computers, using compatible diskettes. This is not always easy, since some computers only have 5.25" diskettes while others only have 3.5" diskettes. Some of you may have access to expensive and sometimes complicated network connections between computers. DOS 6 includes special utilities that make it easy to connect MS-DOS computers for accessing files for both data and execution.

Connecting Laptops to Desktops

In this section, I'll explain how MS-DOS enables you to both transfer files between connected computers and execute programs on the other computer. This can open up a number of possibilities. For example, you may collect data at customer sites on your laptop, connect your laptop to your office desktop, and run an analysis program located on the desktop that processes the data in a file on the laptop.

Of course, you can also use the simple approach of using the connection to move a copy of the laptop data file to the desktop. It could then be consolidated on the desktop with other files from other laptops. This approach lends itself to consolidation when multiple laptop users all use a home office computer system, or a common network at the home office. The fundamental concept here is that simple coordination among two or more computers no longer requires expensive or complicated network connections.

Take a look at Figure 19.19. It depicts how the MS-DOS connection takes place. This connection can be between a laptop and a desktop, or even between two desktops that have incompatible diskettes.

Once you establish a connection, such as the sample one in Figure 19.19, the server computer (typically the desktop) is temporarily unavailable but

FIGURE 19.19

Connecting computers only requires a single cable connecting a serial port on both machines, or a parallel port. INTERSVR establishes a connection between the machines, while the INTERLNK program enables one computer to use data and programs on the drives of the other computer.

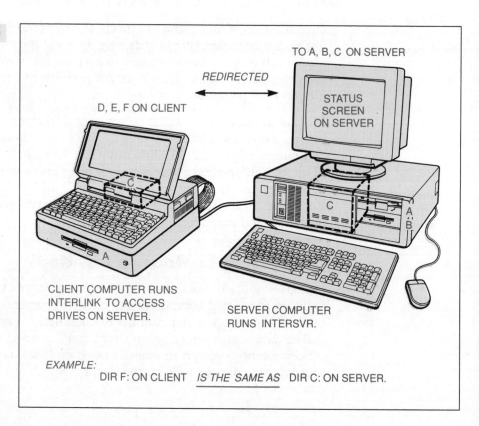

TO A, B, C ON SERVER

REDIRECTED

D, E, F ON CLIENT

STATUS SCREEN ON SERVER

CLIENT COMPUTER RUNS INTERLINK TO ACCESS DRIVES ON SERVER.

SERVER COMPUTER RUNS INTERSVR.

EXAMPLE:

DIR F: ON CLIENT   *IS THE SAME AS*   DIR C: ON SERVER.

the client computer (typically the laptop) can access the physical disk drives of the server. In Figure 19.19, for example, a directory listing of drive F: would actually display the files in the current directory of drive C: on the desktop server. Similarly, you could run from the laptop client any program found on drives A, B, or C of the desktop computer.

In essence, then, it is as if your laptop computer had five drives: its own physical drives A and C, and three extra drives D, E, and F. As you'll see shortly, you use the INTERLNK program to *redirect* these pseudo-drives to three real drives that just happen to be physically located on another computer.

To set up the connection between two computers, you must have the following:

- A free serial port on each computer, or a free parallel port

- An appropriate cable to connect the two available ports. This may be a bidirectional parallel cable, a standard three-wire serial cable, or a seven-wire null-modem serial cable. You will only use a null modem cable for simple copying of files, with the /RCOPY switch on the INTERSVR command. Since this procedure is significantly more limited than the procedure that this section covers, you should refer to your MS-DOS documentation if you plan to use this more limited connection capability.

- MS-DOS version 3.0 or higher

- At least 130K of free memory on the server computer, and at least 16K of free memory on the client computer

You should plug in the appropriate cable to both matching ports on your two computers. The computer that you plan to use as a server should have the INTERSVR.EXE program available to it. The computer that you plan to use as a client should have the INTERLNK.EXE program available to it. To establish the software connection between two computers, you should type INTERSVR at a command prompt on the server.

This displays a status screen lists drive identifiers on the server machine. If the connected client computer has redirected some drive identifiers (using the INTERLNK program as described below) then these drive identifiers are also displayed. If the connection does not yet exist, the right column here will be blank. The server screen will automatically update itself when you establish the connection from your client machine.

For example, the display that would appear on a server machine, set up as in Figure 19.19, might list this information:

```
This Computer            Other Computer
  (Server)                 (Client)
_____            _____
        A:      equals        D:
        B:      equals        E:
        C:      equals        F:
```

While actual data is transferred across the computer connection, a status line at the bottom of this screen describes the port being used, as well as information about the transfer speed. This INTERSVR screen monopolizes your server computer while the connection exists. Although you can establish a server from within a DOS session under Windows, you cannot switch to another task or use shortcut keys until you exit the server by press Alt+F4.

Most of the real work will be going on at your laptop command prompt. Whatever your client machine is, you must first set it up properly before this useful software connection can be successfully used. This requires a two-step procedure. First, you must install the INTERLNK.EXE device driver in your CONFIG.SYS and reboot your machine. Using appropriate switches on the device-driver line, you can influence which drive identifiers are to be used on the client machine to represent physical drive identifiers on the server machine.

In most situations, you can accept the device driver's defaults. Include this line in your CONFIG.SYS file:

```
DEVICE=C:\DOS\INTERLNK.EXE [Optional Switches]
```

You can type use the HELP system to discover details of the device driver's switches. On my systems, the defaults work fine, but Table 19.3 summarizes the optional switches that are possible for the INTERLNK.EXE driver command line in CONFIG.SYS.

TABLE 19.3: Optional INTERLNK.EXE device driver switches

SWITCH	EXPLANATION
/AUTO	Only installs INTERLNK if client-server connection can be established at client bootup.
/BAUD:rate	Sets a maximum serial communications baud rate. Default is 115200.
/COM	Specifies a serial port to use for connection.
/DRIVES:nC	Specifies the number of drives to be redirected (default is 3).
/LOW	Forces INTERLNK to be loaded in conventional memory.
/LPT	Specifies a parallel port to use for connection.
/NOPRINTER	Inhibits printer port redirection. Default is all printer ports are redirected.
/NOSCAN	Installs INTERLNK driver but explicitly prevents establishing connection.
/V	Prevents timer conflicts. Only required if one computer freezes when making connection.

The default number of drives redirected is three, which means that the next three drive-identifier letters on your client computer are used by IN-TERLNK.EXE for connection drives. Since drives A through C are used by the laptop in Figure 19.19, the INTERLNK.EXE driver consumes D, E, and F as pseudo drives. The message that appears during boot up is the following:

```
Drive letters redirected: 3 (D: through F:)
```

Later requests from the client computer for files on these drives will be redirected over the INTERLNK-INTERSVR connection to drives on the server computer.

Once the INTERLNK.EXE device driver has been installed, you can then use the INTERLNK program at a command prompt. Alternatively, you can include one or more INTERLNK lines in your AUTO-EXEC.BAT file to establish the actual connection between redirected client and actual server drives. You can only run the INTERLNK program at a command prompt if it was successfully installed as a device driver during power up. For example, to redirect client requests for drive F: to server drive C:, you would type the following at a command prompt on the client machine:

```
INTERLNK F:=C:
```

You can now switch to drive F: on the client, and you will be making drive C: on the server machine your actual current drive. You can also use any of DOS's usual commands, such as COPY or MOVE, to open or run files on any server drive that has been properly redirected.

Once you've completed any desired program accesses over the connection, you can regain control of your server machine while disconnecting the two machines by pressing Alt+F4 at the keyboard of the server. You can reestablish connection at any time thereafter by simply typing IN-TERSVR once again.

Saving Power on Your Laptop Computer

There is one more facility in DOS that works particularly for laptop owners. That is the power management feature, embodied in the POWER.EXE device driver and application program. It is similar to IN-TERLNK.EXE in that a single .EXE contains device-driver code as well as program code that you can access from a command prompt. This program is important for conserving battery power when you are using your laptop away from AC power.

In particular, the POWER program can enable you to reduce power requirements when applications and peripherals are idle on your laptop machine. To gain this savings, you must first install the driver in your CONFIG.SYS:

```
DEVICE=C:\DOS\POWER.EXE
```

If your laptop conforms to the industry standard Advanced Power Management (APM) specification, then you may be able to extend your battery life by as much as twenty-five percent. This varies according to your individual laptop, and the hardware contained within it. Even if your machine does not conform to this specification, the POWER program can still gain approximately five percent battery savings.

Once installed, you can display the current Power Management Status by simply typing POWER at any command prompt. You'll receive a display similar to this:

```
Power Management Status
_____

Setting = ADV: REG
CPU: idle 58% of time.
```

This display is the default display on a laptop that does not conform to the APM specification. You can use parameters to the POWER command to change the power management settings. The syntax is:

```
POWER [ADV [:MAX|REG|MIN] | STD | OFF]
```

where ADV: followed by MAX, REG, or MIN sets power savings to maximal. This actually reduces the amount of CPU time and battery power allocated, and may slow your applications down. If application or device performance becomes unacceptable when using this maximal setting, change it back to the default REG value, or to a minimal setting, which gives the applications what they want and reduces power savings down to virtually nothing.

If you want to shut down the management facility completely, just type POWER OFF. But the best gains are had when your hardware contains special power-management facilities that conform to the APM specification. In that case, just type POWER STD to gain the most significant savings when your applications and hardware are idle. If your system does not conform to APM, the STD setting will be treated as OFF.

Summary

You have now mastered some of the most advanced features of DOS. The sophisticated capabilities you've seen in this chapter often lie buried under unreadable documentation. In this chapter, however, you've seen how to use these advanced features to your advantage, when managing disks, directories, files, programs, and even entire computers.

- You can connect any two computers for easy access of data or program files with the powerful INTERLNK and INTERSVR commands.

- Laptop owners with the right hardware can reduce battery power consumption by up to twenty-five percent of by using the POWER command.

- You can successfully run some older programs that initially do not understand DOS 6 by using the SETVER command to trick the application into thinking it is running under an earlier version of DOS.

- You can use the Microsoft Diagnostics (MSD) command to discover internal hardware and system configuration information, which can then enable you to analyze and solve system problems.

- The UNDELETE commands can use three techniques for recovering lost, erased, or corrupted files and disks.

- Entire disks that have become entirely erased can often be recovered with the UNFORMAT command.

- The SUBST command allows you to treat an entire directory branch as a separate and unique (but fictitious) disk drive.

- Speedier disk access, for those not using DOS's SMARTDRV disk-caching facility, can be obtained with the FASTOPEN command, which keeps the disk locations of recently used files and directories in memory.

- The ATTRIB command gives you complete control over the file attributes that govern whether the file can be hidden, erased, modified, backed up, or designated as a system file.

- You can upgrade backups and software easily and quickly by using the REPLACE command.

- You can create sophisticated application environments with the SET command, which controls the creation and modification of DOS environment string variables.

- You can control the command processor itself by invoking a secondary processor with the COMMAND command. This allows unique security and customization possibilities.

You now have an almost complete picture of DOS, and you can see just how powerful it really is. Software developers continue to create new software designed to extend and enhance the power of DOS. In the next chapter, you'll learn how DOS itself now includes programs that can blend into and add new capabilities to Windows.

CHAPTER

20

Using DOS's Special
Windows Facilities

IN THE earlier chapters of this book, you learned many of the features of DOS that make it a powerful stand-alone operating system. It provides the setting within which your application programs can run. In this chapter, you'll explore how to similarly expand the power of the Windows environment by using some special Windows-oriented programs that are included with DOS. These are useful graphic programs that work only within the context of Windows—that is, you must have Windows on your machine to take advantage of these facilities. The programs available offer facilities for virus protection, backup, un-deletion, and disk-cache monitoring.

Figure 20.1 depicts the Windows program group that contains these four special programs.

The procedure for installing the Windows versions of the *Anti-Virus*, *Backup*, and *Undelete* programs and making them available in this "Microsoft Tools" program group in the Windows Program Manager is explained in Appendix A. You must use the Program Manager's File➤ New menu choice to add the *SmartMon* program (SMARTMON.EXE) to the program group.

NOTE   Except for the SmartMon program, all of these Windows programs are also available in the DOS environment. Their basic features and the options they share with the Windows versions have already been covered in Chapters 9 and 11. You should read through the discussions of the DOS versions of these programs first to familiarize yourself with them before you read about the Windows versions in this chapter.

FIGURE 20.1

The DOS 6 SETUP program (see Appendix A) can automatically install a program group named Microsoft Tools. It will usually include special icons for the Windows versions of Anti-Virus, Backup, and Undelete. As you can see, a disk caching monitor (SMARTMON.EXE) is also available.

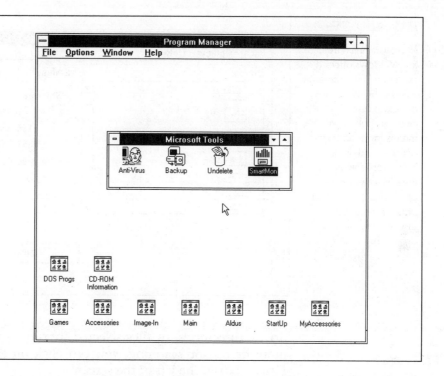

Using the Windows Anti-Virus Facility

Chapter 9 explained the DOS version of the Microsoft Anti-Virus software. It also explains the nature of viruses, including the different types that can gain access to your system. The Windows version of Anti-Virus offers exactly the same features as the DOS version, but does so using the standard Windows GUI (Graphical User Interface). Under Windows, you can run the Anti-Virus software by double-clicking on the Anti-Virus icon seen in the Microsoft Tools group of Figure 20.1. This displays a screen similar to Figure 20.2, although initially there are no

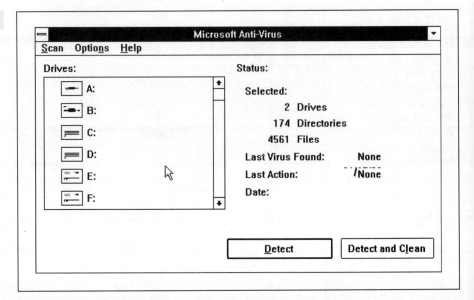

drives, directories, or files selected for virus scanning. To select one or more drives for scanning, you can click on the drive identifier in the Drives: box at the left of the screen.

TIP

To automatically scan a particular disk drive when selecting the Anti-Virus icon, select *Program Item Properties* when the icon is highlighted in the Program Manager. Or, just highlight the Anti-Virus icon, then press Alt+Enter to also display the Properties dialog box. Make the desired drive the first parameter in the Command Line box. For example, to automatically scan drive C:, just type MWAV C: into the Command Line field.

➤ EXTRA!

Protect Your System with Continuous Virus Monitoring!

Whether you use the DOS (MSAV.EXE) or the Windows (MWAV.EXE) program for anti-virus protection, you must remember to initiate the program in order to receive its benefits. For continuous, "built-in" protection, take a moment to set up DOS's **VSAFE** program to run from your AUTOEXEC.BAT file. Depending on which options you turn on, different parts of your system will be protected from possibly virus-driven actions. (Refer back to Chapter 9 for discussion of all the possible options for this program.) Once you've run VSAFE, you can display the Warning Options screen by pressing Alt+V.

Windows users must additionally run the Windows MWAVTSR.EXE program. This program communicates with the VSAFE program to enable the display under Windows of any warning messages generated by VSAFE. To run MWAVTSR under Windows, you can add it to the **LOAD=** line in your WIN.INI file. Alternatively, if you are using Windows 3.1, you can include an icon for MWAVTSR.EXE in the Program Manager's Startup group.

In Figure 20.2, I've already clicked on two drives (C: and D:). The Status: portion of the screen updates itself as soon as the scan of the drives is completed. At this point, the Anti-Virus program has only read file information from whatever drives you've selected. To automatically detect *and* remove any discovered viruses, you would click on the *Detect and Clean* pushbutton. To simply alert you to any viruses discovered in your system, click on the *Detect* pushbutton. During this detection process, a status screen such as the one in Figure 20.3 is displayed and constantly updated.

FIGURE 20.3

During detection, the Anti-Virus program keeps you apprised of its progress. If any virus situations are discovered, the last virus found and the action you took are also identified here.

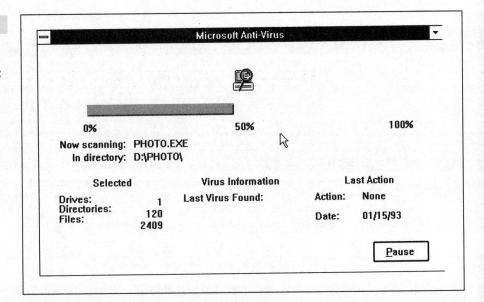

TIP

Windows 3.1 users can use drag-and-drop techniques to test a particular file for a hidden virus. Use this technique prior to copying unknown diskette files onto your system. To virus-test in this manner, drag the suspected file name(s) in the File Manager onto the Anti-Virus icon in the Microsoft Tools program group (seen in Figure 20.1), or onto an open Anti-Virus window (seen in Figure 20.2), or even onto the MWAV.EXE icon in the File Manager list for the \DOS directory.

A Virus Found box, such as the one shown in Figure 20.4, appears whenever an actual virus is discovered.

After the detection procedure is completed, you can pull down the Scan menu in the main Anti-Virus window (Figure 20.2) to learn more about

FIGURE 20.4

The Virus Found box appears whenever a virus is discovered during a Detection process. You can then decide whether to stop the detection sweep, clean up and remove the discovered virus, or simply continue searching for other possible viruses, keeping in mind that you must deal with this virus later.

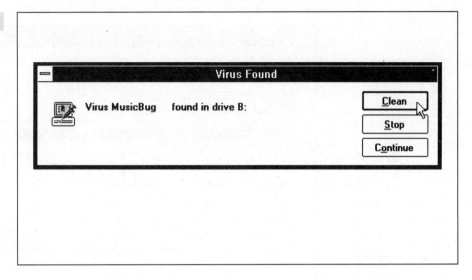

viruses that were discovered on your system. The Scan menu contains five choices:

- *Detect*
- *Clean*
- *Delete CHKLIST files*
- *Virus List*
- *Exit Anti-Virus*

The *Detect* choice offers the same processing as the *Detect* pushbutton, while the *Clean* choice provides the same processing as the *Detect and Clean* pushbutton. The *Exit* choice offers the obvious way to quit the Anti-Virus facility, removing it from the list of active Windows tasks.

The *Virus List* choice displays the dialog box seen in Figure 20.5. In it, you can scroll through the list box that shows known viruses and brief information about them. Each line item tells the type of virus (e.g., *Music Bug* is a boot-sector infector), its size, and the number of known variants of the virus. Additionally, as can be seen with the *MLTI* virus in Figure 20.5, any known aliases for a virus are also shown.

FIGURE 20.5

The Virus List box displays an alphabetical list of all known viruses, their types, sizes, and known variants. If the virus has any known aliases, these are also shown. You can scroll through the list, or type in a name to search directly for that virus entry.

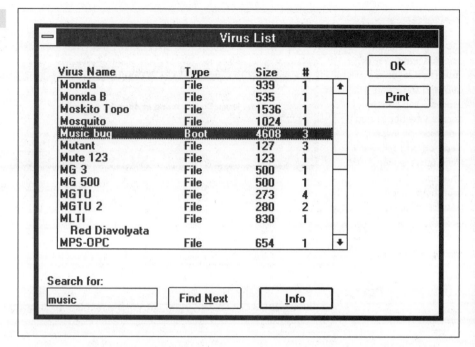

You can use the Virus List at any time. In this example sequence, I've used it to learn more about a Music Bug virus that was discovered on one of my client's computers. Figure 20.6 shows a typical Information screen for a discovered virus. As you can see, you can just click on the *Print* button to obtain a hardcopy printout of the information displayed.

Other settings and options available through this Windows version of the Anti-Virus program are similar to those seen in Chapter 9 for the DOS version of the program. For example, the Options pull-down menu offers two choices:

- *Set Options*
- *Save Settings on Exit*

Choose *Set Options* to display the Options box, shown in Figure 20.7, which contains a variety of customizing possibilities for the Anti-Virus program. You can use the online Help system to discover more about each of these options. Just press F1 or pull down the Help menu while the main

FIGURE 20.6

Clicking on the *Info* pushbutton in Figure 20.5 once the desired virus name is highlighted displays further details about an individual virus entry. Some viruses, like this one, are a lot scarier than others.

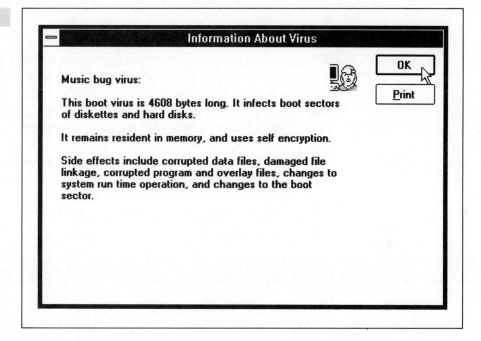

Information About Virus

OK

Print

Music bug virus:

This boot virus is 4608 bytes long. It infects boot sectors of diskettes and hard disks.

It remains resident in memory, and uses self encryption.

Side effects include corrupted data files, damaged file linkage, corrupted program and overlay files, changes to system run time operation, and changes to the boot sector.

FIGURE 20.7

Customizable options for the Anti-Virus program. Choose *Prompt While Detect* to receive an explanatory dialog box for each discovery of a possible virus intrusion. Choose *Create New Checksums* to reduce the repetition of virus alerts due to frequent software updates.

Options

OK

☒ Verify Integrity   ☒ Prompt While Detect

☒ Create New Checksums   ☐ Anti-Stealth

☐ Create Checksums on Floppies   ☒ Check All Files

☐ Disable Alarm Sound   ☐ Wipe Deleted Files

☐ Create Backup

Anti-Virus window is showing. The available help screens provide a good explanation of each option setting.

To toggle any one or more of these options on or off, just move the mouse pointer to it and click once. Alternatively, just move the highlight to an option and press the spacebar. To maximally protect your system, turn on the *Anti-Stealth* toggle. This will take some extra time, but will protect you against the latest virus types. These tricky bugs use what are called *stealth* techniques to change an .EXE file without making any observable adjustment in the disk size of the file. The anti-stealth toggle ensures that Microsoft Anti-Virus will use lower-level methods to check the current contents of the .EXE file against its former contents to determine if any of these more sophisticated viruses have infected your system.

► EXTRA!

Stay on the Trail of Brand New Viruses!

Microsoft Anti-Virus can definitely identify several hundred viruses. However, new viruses continue to be created all the time. To protect your system against these previously unidentifiable viruses, be sure to turn on the *Verify Integrity* option. (You will find this and all other toggle-type settings in the Options dialog box, which is displayed after selecting *Set Options* from the Options pull-down menu.)

The Verify Integrity feature causes the Anti-Virus program to generate a CHKLIST.MS file in each directory. This file contains size, date, attributes, and a checksum for each executable file in each directory. MWAV uses these statistics during detection scanning to alert you to any unexpected changes in executable files on your disk. If VSAFE is loaded, it will similarly alert you to a possible virus intrusion whenever you try to run a changed program.

If the space taken up by these files is too much for you to bear, you can erase all of them at once by selecting *Delete CHKLIST Files* from the Scan menu.

Just as with the DOS version of the Anti-Virus program, the final display after a detection procedure is a complete statistical summary. The summary includes information about the number of disks (hard and floppy) that were scanned, found to be infected, and subsequently cleaned. It also includes information about the number and type of files that were scanned, infected, and cleaned. The total time consumed by the detection and cleaning process is also displayed on this final summary screen.

Using the Windows Backup Facility

Chapter 11 covered in depth the DOS version of the Microsoft Backup software. It also explains the different types of backups, which include full, incremental, and differential backups. Refer to Chapter 11 for a fuller explanation of the fundamental characteristics of all DOS backups, whether done under Windows or not.

NOTE

When trying to use Backup, if you receive a message that your system's DMA buffer size is too small, you probably need to adjust the line in your CONFIG.SYS file that loads your EMM386.EXE driver. Use an editor to add a /D switch to the end of that line. Retain the EMM386.EXE line in your CONFIG.SYS file as it appeared; just append the /D switch to the line and rerun the Backup program. If the message still appears, reedit the line in CONFIG.SYS, using /D=64 instead of /D=32.

The Windows version of Backup offers exactly the same features as the DOS version, but does so using the standard Windows GUI (Graphical User Interface), just as the other programs discussed in this chapter. As you can see in Figure 20.8, you can prepare the same range of backup file copies as discussed in Chapter 11. The Windows version of the backup facility is MWBACKUP.EXE, while the DOS version seen in Chapter 11 is MSBACKUP.EXE.

The top portion of the main Backup window displays pushbuttons that enable you to select one of the Backup facility's primary functions. The bottom portion of the screen always displays commands, options, and status information that relate to your principal choice (i.e., Backup, Compare, Restore, or Configure).

FIGURE 20.8

Microsoft Backup for Windows offers a traditional GUI screen with pushbuttons for backup, comparison, restoration, and configuration; and pull-down menus, list boxes, and pushbuttons for options, actions, and file selection. Status information also appears for file selection.

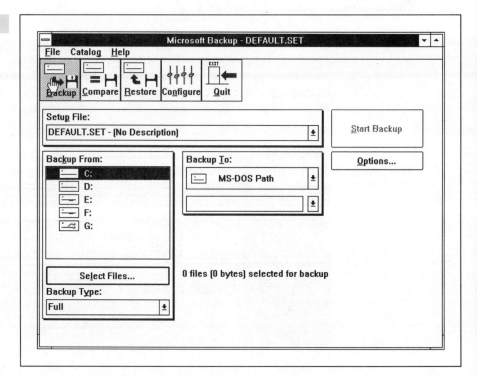

➤ EXTRA!

Set Up Your System for Automatic Backups!

Backup offers two ways in which to automate backup processing:

- via setup files
- via command-line options

A setup file stores a customized group of program settings and drive/file selections. Command-line options enable you to start the Backup program from a Program Manager icon, while directing it to use a predetermined setup file. Another command-line option might control whether or not the backups are performed in the background while other Windows processing is occurring.

To create a new setup file that can later control a backup procedure, first specify all the settings (e.g., source drives and files, destination drives or DOS paths, various customization options) in the way you'd like. Then pull down the File menu and choose *Save Setup As*. Type any name you like, using a standard .SET extension, and press Enter.

To automate a backup process under Windows, you can specify the *Command Line* property for a Program Manager icon to include a setup-file name. For example, to start Windows Backup using the WEEKLY.SET setup file, you would type:

```
MWBACKUP WEEKLY.SET
```

in the *Command Line* property field for the Backup icon in the Program Manager's Microsoft Tools group (seen in Figure 20.1).

You can customize your Microsoft Tools group further by creating separate icons for desired setup files. To do so, type a different setup-file name after MWBACKUP in the *Command Line* property field for each different icon. You can then double-click on the icon that represents the desired backup process. For example, one icon may run:

```
MWBACKUP MONTHLY.SET
```

which conceivably might run a *Full* disk backup, while another icon runs

```
MWBACKUP DAILY.SET
```

which conceivably might control a simple and fast *Incremental* backup.

On First Use, You Must Configure Backup for Your System

If you have never used the Windows Backup program, then the main window shown in Figure 20.8 will not immediately appear. Instead, an exclamation box will appear that informs you that Backup has not yet been configured. You will be asked whether or not you wish to spend the time necessary to configure it now. If you choose *Yes*, MWBACKUP will begin its automatic configuration sequence for your diskette drives. It can determine what type of drives your system has installed, but it needs your help to determine if the drive includes the ability to detect the opening and shutting of the drive doors. You'll then be directed to remove all diskettes from any drives in order for the "Disk-Change Test" to be performed.

TIP

To automatically configure your Windows Backup program for the diskette drives on your system, select the *Configure* button at the top of the main Backup screen, then choose *Auto Floppy Configure*. To save this automatic configuration for later backup sessions, pull down the File menu and choose *Exit*. Make sure that the *Save Configuration* choice has an x beside it before exiting the Windows Backup program.

This test determines whether or not your diskette drive can detect when a drive door has been closed. Such an ability helps to speed up backups because the program can then determine automatically when you've taken out and inserted different backup diskettes.

The disk change test is only one step in the overall configuration and compatibility testing for Microsoft Backup for Windows. The compatibility test itself consists of a small backup, with a comparison step afterwards to verify that the Backup program was correctly installed and configured for your hardware. This step is essential for guaranteeing the validity of your backup files on the drives that you test for compatibility. During backup, comparison, and restores, the Backup program needs exclusive access to your floppy drives.

Although Backup will guide you into performing the *Compatibility* test the first time you use the Windows version of the program, you can also run it any time you like. By choosing *Configure* from the main Backup window, your Backup screen will change to the one seen in Figure 20.9.

The Backup program will make the floppy drive unavailable to other applications until the procedure is complete. Naturally, you should avoid referencing the disk drive being used for a backup, a comparison, or a restore. During a *Compatibility Test*, you should simply follow the instructions on screen for inserting or removing diskettes. You'll be directed to insert one or more diskettes for the backup phase, then you'll be directed to sequentially insert the same diskette(s) during the comparison phase.

FIGURE 20.9

Configuring your system for the Backup program consists of two phases. First, you can identify what floppy drives your system contains and will use during backup operations. Second, you can perform a small backup-and-compare procedure to ensure accurate backups later.

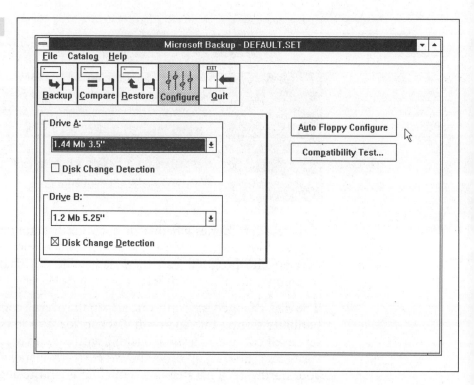

A complete progress window will appear during each phase as files are read, written, or compared. When and if the compatibility process is successful, you will be able to make reliable disk backups using the tested drive. The screen that was shown back in Figure 20.8 will then appear.

Selecting Files to Back Up

Note in Figure 20.8 that the *Start Backup* button on the right side of the screen is still grayed. This is because no files have yet been selected for backup, so there is no backup that can legitimately be started. To set up your Backup program for an actual backup, you should first select a setup file or highlight a disk drive in the Backup From: list box. Next, you should select the *Select Files...* button. This will display a screen similar to Figure 20.10.

FIGURE 20.10

Choosing *Select Files...* at the main Backup screen (Figure 20.8) displays a directory tree for the specified drive. Double-click on the files you want to back up. To select all the files in any directory, highlight the directory name and then press the spacebar.

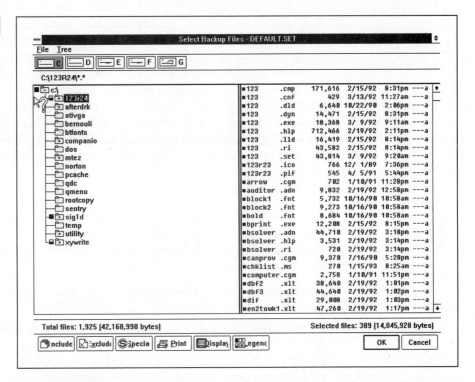

Select Backup Files - DEFAULT.SET				

File Tree

C D E F G

C:\123R24*.*

```
■☐ c:\                      ■123    .cmp    171,616   2/15/92   8:31pm ---a
  ■☐ 123r24                 ■123    .cnf        429   3/13/92  11:27am ---a
    ☐ afterdrk              ■123    .dld      6,640  10/22/90   2:06pm ---a
    ☐ ativga                ■123    .dyn     14,471   2/15/92   8:31pm ---a
    ☐ bernouli              ■123    .exe     18,368   3/ 9/92   9:11am ---a
    ☐ btfonts               ■123    .hlp    712,466   2/19/92   2:11pm ---a
    ☐ companio              ■123    .lld     16,419   2/15/92   8:14pm ---a
    ☐ dos                   ■123    .ri      43,582   2/15/92   8:14pm ---a
    ☐ mtez                  ■123    .set     43,814   3/ 9/92   9:20am ---a
    ☐ norton                ■123r23 .ico        766  12/ 1/89   7:36pm ---a
    ☐ pcache                ■123r23 .pif        545   4/ 5/91   5:44pm ---a
    ☐ qdc                   ■arrow  .cgm        702   1/10/91  11:28pm ---a
    ☐ qmenu                 ■auditor .adn     9,832   2/19/92  12:58pm ---a
    ☐ rootcopy              ■block1 .fnt      5,732  10/16/90  10:58am ---a
    ☐ sentry                ■block2 .fnt      9,273  10/16/90  10:58am ---a
  ■☐ sig1d                  ■bold   .fnt      8,684  10/16/90  10:58am ---a
    ☐ temp                  ■bprint .exe     12,208   2/15/92   8:15pm ---a
    ☐ utility               ■bsolver .adn    44,710   2/19/92   3:18pm ---a
  ■☐ xywrite                ■bsolver .hlp     3,531   2/19/92   3:14pm ---a
                            ■bsolver .ri        720   2/19/92   3:14pm ---a
                            ■canprov .cgm     9,370   7/16/90   5:28pm ---a
                            ■chklist .ms        270   1/15/93   8:25am ---a
                            ■computer.cgm     2,758   1/10/91  11:51pm ---a
                            ■dbf2   .xlt     38,640   2/19/92   1:01pm ---a
                            ■dbf3   .xlt     44,640   2/19/92   1:02pm ---a
                            ■dif    .xlt     29,008   2/19/92   1:03pm ---a
                            ■en2towk1.xlt    47,260   2/19/92   1:17pm ---a
```

Total files: 1,925 (42,168,998 bytes)   Selected files: 389 (14,045,928 bytes)

nclude xclude Special Print Display Legend   OK   Cancel

TIP

Setup files control what files are backed up, where they are written, and a number of other optional specifications. Computer administrators can standardize backup processing by defining these setup files and distributing them to all users. You should create a different setup file for different groups of files to be regularly backed up, or for backing up to different media than the current backup is set for.

A directory tree of the chosen disk drive appears on the left side of this screen window. To select the files you want to back up, press the Shift key and click on the individual file names in the files area of this screen, or just double-click your mouse on the file name you wish to include in the backup. A square bullet symbol appears beside each file name that has been selected for inclusion in the backup. To select all the files in any one directory for backup, just highlight the directory name on the left side and press the spacebar. You can select files for several different directories. The Backup program keeps track of how many files have been selected, and displays at the bottom of the screen that number as well as the total number of files on the current drive.

You may have noted in Figure 20.10 that a small icon appears beside each directory name that contains files selected for backup. The icon is a solid square if all files have been selected, and only a partially filled square if only some files have been selected for backup.

If you wish to discover how many files exist or have been selected in a particular directory, move the mouse pointer just to the left of a directory-name entry. You can see that I've done that in Figure 20.10. A large question mark (?) appears beside the mouse pointer. Click once and a Selection Information window appears, like the one in Figure 20.11, that provides detailed information about the selected directory and all its subdirectories. As you can see, the Selection Information window indicates how many total files exist in this subtree, and how many have already been selected for backup.

FIGURE 20.11

The Backup Directory Selection Information window indicates the total number of files in any directory and all its subdirectories. You can learn how many files in this subtree have already been selected for backup, as well as how much space these files take up.

Backup Directory Selection Information	
Directory: c:\123r24 and subdirectories	OK
Created On: 1/14/93 12:26pm	
Total Files: 205 (5,656,689 bytes)	Help
Selected Files: 86 (3,342,571 bytes)	
Backup Files: 86 (3,342,571 bytes)	

➤ EXTRA!

Use the Best Backup Type for Your Workload!

The *Backup Type* field in the main Backup window (Figure 20.8) offers three alternative choices: *Full, Incremental,* or *Differential* backups. Regardless of the choice, you must have first selected a group of files to back up. Backup then decides, according to the backup type, whether or not to spend the time writing a copy of each of your selected file choices.

In a *Full* backup, all your selections are copied to the backup media. Naturally, your selections may be all the files on a drive, or all the files with a particular extension, or just an eclectic group of chosen files. This can take the most amount of time, because so many files are written each time. However, it is easiest to later restore any one or more of the backed-up copies.

In an *Incremental* backup, the intent is to write copies of only those files that have changed since the last full or incremental backup. This allows you to maintain emergency backup copies of file versions as they change. You should use an incremental backup if you work with many different files. Each new incremental backup set will capture the latest version of all changed files. This is the method of choice if you need to have access to intermediate versions of your files.

Because fewer files are written during such a backup (unchanging files are not written), incremental backups are much faster than full backups and require less space (or fewer diskettes). However, since each incremental backup builds on the preceding full and incremental backup sets, you must retain the various sets. Later restorations will require the preceding full backup and each subsequent incremental backup set.

A *Differential* backup will copy to your backup media just the files that have changed since the last full backup. This is sort of a cross between a full and an incremental backup. You should use this method if you work with virtually the same set of files daily.

Differential backups are not as large as full backups, since only files that have changed since the last full backup are written. However, they are larger than incremental backups, since files that have changed since the last incremental backup are also written. Thus, this method is slower than an incremental backup, and requires more space or backup diskettes. Nevertheless, restoration will be faster because you will not have to use as many backup *sets* to reconstruct the latest version of your files.

Basically, if you can afford the space and time, use a full backup every time, and simply maintain separate sets of backup diskettes. If you don't mind the administrative overhead of maintaining multiple sets of incremental backups, save time by performing incremental backups. If you work with a limited number of different files daily, use the differential backup method as a balanced approach to save time and effort, both for initial backup and possible subsequent restoration.

Restoring Files

If it is ever necessary to restore files later, you will start by selecting the Restore icon at the top of the main Backup screen. If you have created multiple backup sets of files, you would first select the backup-set *catalog* you wish to use (see Figure 20.12). Next you would ensure that you've specified the source of the backed-up files (in the Restore From: list), as well as the destination of the files to be restored (in the Restore To: list).

As with the original backup process, you must specify the drives and files to be restored. You can also set a number of options that control the Restore process. In Figure 20.12, the backup set only contained files from drive C:, so the Restore Files: list box only contains that one drive possibility. Nevertheless, you can still choose the *Select Files...* button to potentially restore only some of the files from the backup set.

FIGURE 20.12

Restoring files is simple, and is essentially the reverse of the backup process. You first indicate the backup-set catalog that contains the information about which files were previously backed up, then you select the files to be restored from this backup set.

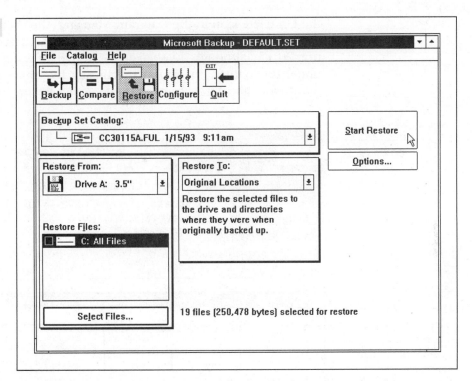

Using the Windows Undelete Facility

Chapter 19 explained the DOS version of the Undelete software. The Windows version of Undelete offers exactly the same features as the DOS version, but does so using the standard Windows GUI (Graphical User Interface). The Windows version of the Undelete facility is MWUNDEL.EXE, while the DOS version seen in Chapter 19 is UNDELETE.EXE.

Undelete for Windows is a particularly good example of an intuitively easy program to use. When you first run the program, by double-clicking on the Undelete icon in the Program Manager, the principal Microsoft Undelete screen appears. This is essentially the screen you see in Figure 20.13, although I've taken a couple of steps further along the undeletion path in this figure. Specifically, I've changed the current directory to C:\, and I've selected two file names for undeletion.

NOTE

If multiple versions of a similarly named (and currently existing) file have been deleted (as seen with QDOS.LOG in Figure 20.13), Undelete will prompt you for a new name to assign the undeleted file.

FIGURE 20.13

Undelete for Windows offers a traditional GUI screen, with pushbuttons for the major undeletion functions, pull-down menus for options and actions, and list boxes for identifying the specific files to recover.

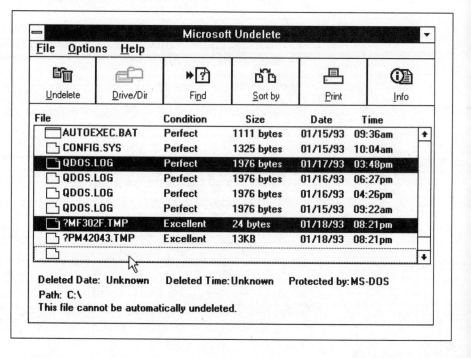

When the Undelete window first appears, the file portion of the screen contains a list of any deleted files found in the WINDOWS directory. To change to any other drive or directory, you can click on the *Drive/Dir* pushbutton. This displays a familiar browse-type window that enables you to choose any drive or directory on your system. After selecting a new drive and/or directory, you can press OK to redisplay Figure 20.13 with all file names found there that have been previously deleted.

Notice several things about Figure 20.13. First, *Undelete* indicates how good a chance you have of successfully recovering a file that was deleted. This information appears in the *Condition* column of the file list. If the condition is "Perfect," the file can be completely recovered with no loss whatsoever. If the condition is "Excellent," it means that all clusters previously in use by the file are currently available. You'll be able to completely recover this file as well if none of this space has been overwritten in the interim.

If the condition is listed as "Good," then the file is apparently fragmented on your disk. This means that some of the data in the file will probably be lost during the undeletion process. If the condition is "Poor," then you cannot recover the file with Undelete for Windows at all. However, if you really want to attempt recovery, it is possible that Undelete for MS-DOS may be able to recover some of the data in the file.

Finally, if the file is completely destroyed, as is the case with the last file indicated in Figure 20.13, you have no chance of recovery whatsoever. In this last entry, all that remains of the former file is the icon, Cheshire-like, that indicates something used to be there. The starting cluster of such a file has been overwritten on your disk, and the undeletion process cannot even start a recovery operation. In both the Poor and Destroyed conditions, you should refer to the Undelete for MS-DOS discussion of Chapter 19.

T I P

Press the *Sort By* button to arrange the file names that are eligible for undeletion. You can sort these names by name, extension, size, date and time of deletion or last modification, or current condition of the file. Condition refers to the likelihood of partial or complete file recovery. The Sort By dialog box also includes a checkbox that will arrange the files by directory. This is useful if you have previously used the *Sort By* button to find and display files from different directories, using one or more criteria.

To recover a file, you must first find it and mark it for recovery. If the file name does not appear in the files list in your Undelete window, you should scroll the window so that it appears. If you click on the *Print* push-button to send to the printer a complete copy of all the file names in the list, you can then make your decisions off-line about which files you wish to undelete. Use this technique if there are a great many files that are eligible for undeletion.

If the file name is not in the current drive and directory, press the *Drive/Dir* button and switch to the correct location where the file was located prior to its deletion. If you don't know where the file is located, use the *Find* button to scan the disk. This will display the Find Deleted Files dialog box seen in Figure 20.14.

You can type a specific file name into the File Specification: field, or you can use wild cards to find all files that meet your criteria. The matches will then appear in the file list in the main Undelete screen.

Similarly, you can find all files on the specified drive that contain any string of characters. Just type the desired character string into the Containing: field. You can refine your containment request by checking or not checking the *Ignore Case* and *Whole Word* boxes.

FIGURE 20.14

You can use wild cards to find deleted files on your disk. Use the Containing: field in this dialog box to find all files that contain particular text strings. Click on *Groups...* to find all files associated with a particular application. This option uses extensions to group files by executable file name.

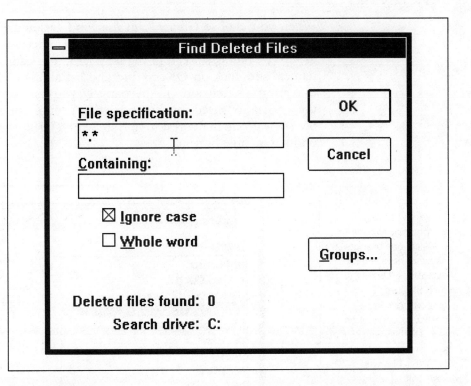

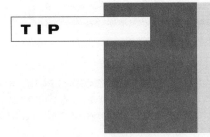

TIP

Sometimes, a deleted file was located within a directory that itself was deleted. In this case, you'll have to first find the deleted directory name and undelete it. Only then can you list and undelete one or more deleted file names from within that directory.

The *Groups...* button represents a most interesting selection facility. By choosing one of the existing group names, you can quickly select all files that, because of their extensions, are known to be associated with a particular application. Remember from Chapter 5 that you can use the DOS shell's File menu to associate file extensions with a specific .EXE file name. This Group option uses the same list of associations.

When you choose *Groups...* in the Find Deleted Files dialog box, Undelete displays a Search Groups dialog box. This box lists all known search groups by name, as seen in Figure 20.15. You can highlight one of these names, and click on OK, to find and list all associated file names using that group's extension(s). Alternatively, you can click on *Edit...* to change the association used for the undeletion group. You can even create your own new group in the resulting Edit Search Groups dialog box by clicking on its *New* pushbutton.

FIGURE 20.15

A search group enables you to rapidly undelete one or more files that have similar extensions. Usually, such files are associated with a particular application, like .TXT files with your word processor, or .WK1 files with your Lotus 1-2-3 spreadsheet application.

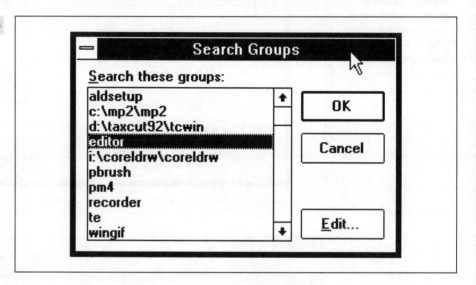

Nearly all of the choices in Undelete's pull-down menus are repetitions of the primary pushbuttons seen in Figure 20.13 just below the menu bar. However, the Options menu does contain the following important configuration choice:

• *Configure Delete Protection*

Selecting this choice leads to a series of configuration dialog boxes, beginning with the one shown in Figure 20.16. Usually this process must be done only once, at which time you indicate the range of files to be

FIGURE 20.16

Configure your system with the deletion sentry for the best chance of recovering deleted files. Deletion tracking is next best; it maintains a record of deleted file disk locations. The *Standard* method is not as useful, since it uses only the directory entry information.

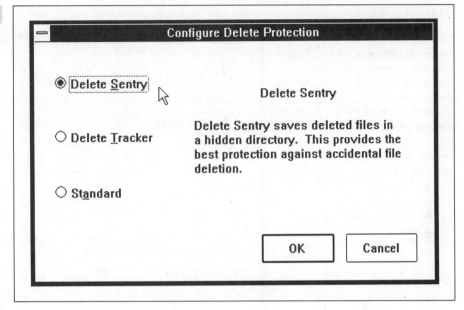

protected by one of the undeletion mechanisms. Chapter 19 explained the three different undeletion mechanisms in depth. I strongly suggest that you use *Delete Sentry* on your system; it is the best method for ensuring complete and easy recovery of the greatest possible number of undeleted files.

The deletion sentry method actually saves copies of your deleted files in a safe, read-only, hidden directory. As long as the file is maintained here, you have a 100% chance of recovering it when needed. After choosing *OK* for Delete Sentry in the box shown in Figure 20.16, a Configure Delete Sentry dialog box appears that allows you to customize the sentry operations. Figure 20.17 depicts all the controls you have over the sentry operations.

Although the easiest mechanism is to save all files, that is overkill. Most temporary files (.TMP) do not need to be protected. Neither should you save copies of Windows virtual-memory and swapping files. Add to the Exclude: list any known extensions of files that your applications create that are redundant, such as *.BAK files.

FIGURE 20.17

Deletion sentry offers maximum protection, but costs the most in disk space. Configure it effectively to minimize the burden on your system. You can specify a number of days after storage to purge the saved, hidden files, and you can specify which types of files to include or exclude.

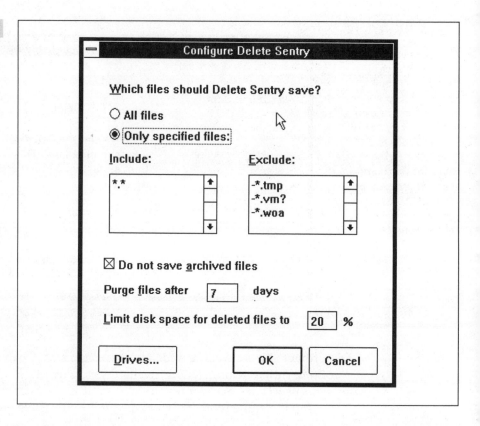

Depending on how active you are on your system, and how often your critical files change, you may be able to set the *Purge* time span to something smaller than the default 7 days. Files are cleared from the hidden directory after they have been protected there for the number of days indicated here.

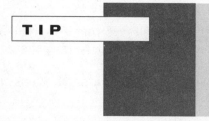

TIP

Recapture lots of disk space in a single go, if you are sure you no longer need the recovery protection, by purging all hidden, formerly deleted files. You can do this by pulling down the File menu and selecting *Purge Delete Sentry File* choice.

If your files are large, and you delete them or update them frequently, your available disk space may shrink rapidly. You can put a cap on the amount of disk space consumed by the hidden sentry file directory. Just type a percentage number into the field at the bottom of the Configure Delete Sentry dialog box. (The percentage you type is calculated from the amount of total disk space, not from the amount of unused disk space.) If this much space is used up before the number of days has gone by, Undelete will simply erase the oldest files first in order to make space for newly deleted files. In this way, your most recent deletions will always be protected.

After you dispense with the box seen in Figure 20.17, another dialog box appears that invites you to specify which drives are to be protected. You can click on as many drives as you like. A separate hidden Sentry directory will be created on each drive, and Delete Sentry will monitor file deletions on each specified drive. All of these configuration settings will be stored in an UNDELETE.INI file stored in the root directory of your boot drive.

The command to start up the UNDELETE.EXE file will then be placed in your AUTOEXEC.BAT file, specifying a **/LOAD** switch, which means that the startup configuration will be obtained from the stored settings in the UNDELETE.INI file. Optionally, you can specify in a follow-up dialog box that updates be stored in an AUTOEXEC.SAV file, which you must later look at and use to correctly update your AUTOEXEC.BAT file. In either case, your configuration will only take effect after AUTOEXEC.BAT is correctly updated (by you or by this configuration sequence) and you've rebooted your machine to reload the UNDELETE program with the new settings.

Monitoring the Efficiency of Disk Caching

The SMARTMON.EXE program is a Windows program that works in close concert with the SMARTDRV.EXE disk-caching program included both with DOS and with Windows. You can run the SMARTMON program by using the Run choice on the File menu in Windows, or you can set up an icon in your Microsoft Tools group, as I did for Figure 20.1. As you can see in Figure 20.18, the SmartDrive Monitor window provides information about your system's disk-cache setup and caching activities.

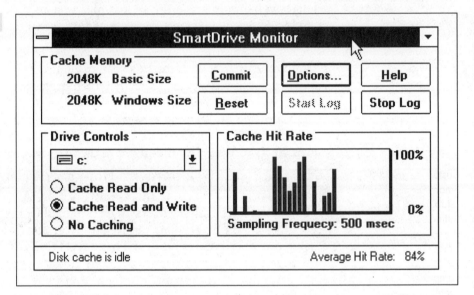

The Cache Hit Rate graphic shows a moving bar chart that depicts how often data that is requested by applications can be found in the cache. When data is found in the cache, it speeds up system throughput considerably, since the cache is found in memory, which is much faster than finding data on the disk. (There is more about the performance value of disk caching in Chapter 18.)

The overall average hit rate is shown numerically at the bottom right of this window. It appears as a total percentage of hits divided by data requests since the SMARTMON program was first started. The *histogram* (dynamic bar chart) is only updated with a new bar if there has been caching activity in the last 500 milliseconds, or whatever you set the sampling frequency to. To change the sampling frequency or otherwise influence the monitoring display, you can push the *Options...* button above the histogram, which will display the SmartDrive Monitor Options dialog box shown in Figure 20.19.

TIP

The SmartDrive Monitor window normally appears on top of any other Windows on your screen. If this placement is annoying or undesirable, you can ask Windows to treat it as it does other Windows. Just pull down the SmartDrive Monitor's control menu and click once on the *Always on Top* toggle switch.

FIGURE 20.19

Customize your Smart Monitor by establishing these settings, which are stored in the [smartmon] section of your WIN.INI file. Sampling Frequency controls how often the cache requests/hits are checked, and Histogram Display Intervals control how many vertical bars appear.

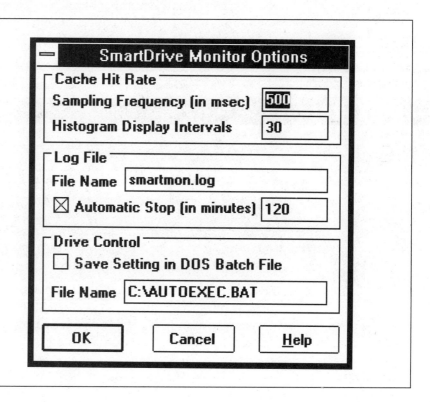

(SmartDrive Monitor Options)

Cache Hit Rate
Sampling Frequency (in msec) `500`
Histogram Display Intervals `30`

Log File
File Name `smartmon.log`
☒ Automatic Stop (in minutes) `120`

Drive Control
☐ Save Setting in DOS Batch File
File Name `C:\AUTOEXEC.BAT`

OK   **Cancel**   **Help**

The default *Sampling Frequency* in Figure 20.18 is 500 milliseconds, but you can change that in the Cache Hit Rate portion of the dialog box shown in Figure 20.19. The number can vary from 50 to 10,000 milliseconds, the smaller the number the greater the overhead in regard to your system performance. You can also vary the number of vertical histogram bars (in the *Histogram Display Intervals* field) that can appear in the Monitor screen, from a minimum of 3 to a maximum of 100, with the default value as 30.

If you wish to obtain numeric data about disk caching activities, you can also specify a Log File in the SmartDrive Monitor Options dialog box. This log will contain three entries. The first entry will be a simple timer tick count, from the start of the current Windows session. The second is the total number of cache accesses, and the third is the number of successful data discoveries (i.e., hits) in the cache. To limit the ongoing overhead, you can specify a number of minutes (from 1 to 960) for the logging to continue. If you've checked the Automatic Stop box here, the default is 120 minutes.

➤ EXTRA!

Reduce the SmartMon Screen to an Icon-Size Report!

Minimize the SmartMon program to see an icon that contains a percentage number and a small disk drive bitmap. The percentage is a numeric indicator that represents the average hit rate. The number is red (on color displays) or white (on monochrome displays) if the cache is active. The number appears in the current button-text color if the cache is idle.

The simple disk-drive bitmap on this icon flashes when the cache is active. However, this flashing is not a real-time indicator of disk or cache activity; it is just a cute indication that the activity is being monitored. Both the numeric indicator as well as the mini disk-drive indicator are updated at the same time, at an interval which depends on the sampling frequency. Therefore, this icon does not reflect the actual times of cache or disk access.

The final entry in Figure 20.19 is a checkbox to control the automatic loading of your SMARTDRV disk-caching program. If you have made changes to your drive cache settings, and you have completed the Drive Control section of Figure 20.19, then SMARTMON will update your batch file's activation line for the SMARTDRV program. If you wish your changes to hold only for the current session, then do not check the Save Setting box.

Returning to the main SmartDrive Monitor screen (refer to Figure 20.18), the Cache Memory section shows the amount of memory used under DOS (i.e., *Basic Size*) and currently under Windows (i.e., *Windows Size*). These sizes are specified on the SMARTDRV startup line when the disk-caching program begins. The two buttons in this section control how and when the contents of the cache are "flushed," or written back, to disk. Pressing *Commit* flushes all cache elements that have not yet been written automatically to disk. Pressing *Reset* flushes all cache elements to disk, and then discards the current contents of the cache. This has the effect of resetting the Average Hit Rate to zero.

Finally, you can move to the Drive Controls section of the main Monitor screen (again, refer to Figure 20.18) to see and possibly alter the current cache mode of your system's drives. All drives have a default cache mode, depending on their drive type. For example, a CD-ROM drive and a RAM drive cannot be cached, so you would see that the No Caching radio button would be selected for those drives on your system. If read-only or read-and-write caching is possible for a drive, you can set or reset the drive by clicking on the desired radio button in the Drive Controls area, after first highlighting the desired drive identifier.

NOTE   Floppy drives have a default caching mode of Read-Only. Hard drives default to Read-and-Write caching. CD-ROMs and RAM drives, as well as shared network drives, have no default caching at all.

Remember that you must check the *Save Setting in DOS Batch File* control in the Options dialog box if you wish the SMARTDRV startup line in

AUTOEXEC.BAT (or any other batch file that contains it) to be updated by SMARTMON. This will retain your SMARTMON settings adjustments for the next time SMARTDRV is started on your system.

Summary

In this chapter, you learned that DOS 6 goes well beyond the stand-alone operating system that it once was. It now includes:

- DOS and Windows versions of its Anti-Virus program, for detecting and optionally removing hundreds of possible viruses that may have intruded on your machine.

- DOS and Windows versions of its Backup facility, for making easy and fast backup copies of any group of specified files on one or more drives of your system.

- DOS and Windows versions of its Undelete program, for protecting your files from accidental erasure, as well as for easy recovery of deleted files.

- the Windows SMARTMON program, which provides monitoring and management capabilities for the SMARTDRV disk-caching software that is also included with DOS.

Appendices

Installing DOS 6

DOS 6 INCLUDES a SETUP.EXE program that makes it easy to successfully install DOS 6 onto your hard disk (or onto floppy disks if you don't want to put DOS 6 onto your hard disk, or if the system you're working with does not include a hard disk). DOS installation or upgrading is automatic when you turn on your computer with the DOS SETUP diskette in your A: drive. If you will be using the DOS program diskettes in your B: drive, you must first switch to the B: prompt and then type **SETUP** to start the process. If you have an earlier version of DOS, the DOS 6 SETUP program will update your earlier DOS system files, as well as automatically make protective backup copies of all DOS utility files.

This section will guide you through a typical installation sequence for DOS. The difference between installing DOS 6 on a new disk and upgrading an existing DOS system to version 6 is relatively minor. SETUP handles this distinction automatically for you. In this appendix, you'll concentrate on the flow of questions and answers that the DOS SETUP sequence presents.

TIP

Before initiating the SETUP procedure, you should take time to back up your existing hard disk files. Use whatever backup program you're comfortable with on your existing system.

Installing DOS 6 on Your Hard Disk

When you boot up your system with the first DOS program diskette in your A: drive, or when you type **SETUP** from a B: prompt with the diskette in your B: drive, SETUP.EXE runs automatically, displaying information and requesting entries from you as necessary. (Although the SETUP command recognizes a number of special-purpose switches, this appendix will concentrate on the standard SETUP sequence, which requires no switch settings at all. The switches are briefly described in Table A.1 at the end of this appendix.) In order to do as much as possible automatically, the first few moments of the SETUP operation are spent determining what hardware exists on your system. SETUP displays this message while it checks out the elements of your system:

```
Please wait.
Setup is determining your system configuration.
```

Once this information is known, SETUP displays a welcome screen that invites you to press Enter to go ahead and set up MS-DOS on your computer now. You can, alternatively, press F1 at this time to learn more about the Setup process before continuing, or you can press F3 to quit the Setup process without installing this new version of MS-DOS.

If you choose to continue with the installation here, Figure A.1 appears.

Notice that your primary key options are displayed at the bottom of the screen. At this point, they are the Enter key (for continuing the SETUP process from screen to screen), the F1 key (for obtaining online help text to explain any unclear step), and the F3 key (for canceling the installation process at any time). Initially, the F5 key is also active, and it appears on this status line as an option to remove screen colors for improving readability on your monitor. This makes all the remaining SETUP screens monochrome, which may be clearer, depending on your monitor. Later on, other key alternatives may be displayed on this bottom line as necessary.

SETUP will save your current DOS system and configuration information on one or two diskettes, which you must provide and should label UNINSTALL #1 and #2. When they are needed, SETUP will prompt you to insert them in your diskette drive.

```
Microsoft MS-DOS 6 Setup


        During Setup, you will need to provide and label one
        or two floppy disks. Each disk can be unformatted
        or newly formatted and must work in drive A. (If you
        use 360K disks, you may need two disks; otherwise,
        you need only one disk.)

        Label the disk(s) as follows:

            UNINSTALL #1
            UNINSTALL #2 (if needed)

        Setup saves some of your original DOS files on the
        UNINSTALL disk(s), and others on your hard disk in a
        directory named OLD_DOS.x. With these files, you can
        restore your original DOS if necessary.

          • When you finish labeling your UNINSTALL disk(s),
            press ENTER to continue Setup.


 ENTER=Continue   F1=Help   F3=Exit
```

At this point, DOS informs you that it will expect to use one (high-density) or two (low-density) floppy diskettes during the installation process. DOS will store system information on these UNINSTALL diskettes. The UNINSTALL diskette(s) will allow you to revert back to your former DOS version if you later choose to do so. In an emergency, you can even use the UNINSTALL diskettes to reboot your system if you experience hard-disk problems during or after DOS 6 installation.

In preparing or selecting diskettes to use as the UNINSTALL diskettes that are requested here, you must be sure to use unformatted or freshly formatted diskettes. If you simply use an old, previously formatted diskette, it may have developed some bad surface areas that will go unnoticed during the SETUP process. These bad disk areas may later prevent you from successfully being able to use the UNINSTALL diskettes to restore your former DOS system.

If you are installing DOS 6 onto a computer system that is part of a network, you must follow some additional steps prior to final installation. The next screen in the installation sequence asks whether or not you use a network. If you respond *Y*, you are directed to exit the SETUP procedure and to refer to the networking instructions in the DOS documentation. After following these instructions, you may reinitiate the SETUP program and continue from this point with your DOS 6 installation.

The next screen in the SETUP process is deceptively simple. As shown in Figure A.2, SETUP displays what it discovered about your system during the opening moments of its operation. Three aspects of operation appear in the window in the center of your screen.

If all of these entries are correct, you can accept them by simply pressing Enter. This accepts the default entry that is highlighted:

        The settings are correct.

In this example, SETUP automatically determined that my system was running MS-DOS. If the entry next to DOS Type: is not correct, or if you wish to change it, you can press the up arrow key to highlight the row containing DOS Type, then press Enter. A new screen would appear which lists all possible alternatives for your version of DOS. You can select one of them by highlighting the choice on the vertical list and then pressing Enter.

Similarly, if your DOS files themselves appear in another directory than C:\DOS, you can highlight the MS-DOS Path: entry in Figure A.2 and press Enter. You will be prompted to enter a corrected path. If your computer does not have a hard drive, SETUP assumes you are installing DOS 6 onto floppies, and the list of hardware and software components

FIGURE A.2

SETUP investigates your system's configuration and asks you to confirm that it's correct. If it isn't, you can display for each choice a list of alternative possibilities from which you can select. After making all modifications, highlight the bottom line and press Enter.

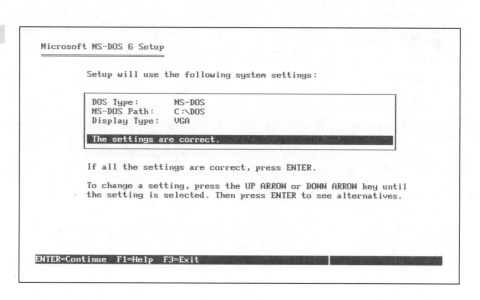

```
Microsoft MS-DOS 6 Setup

          Setup will use the following system settings:

        DOS Type:        MS-DOS
        MS-DOS Path:     C:\DOS
        Display Type:    VGA
        The settings are correct.

        If all the settings are correct, press ENTER.

        To change a setting, press the UP ARROW or DOWN ARROW key until
        the setting is selected. Then press ENTER to see alternatives.


ENTER=Continue  F1=Help  F3=Exit
```

would appear slightly different. For instance, the MS-DOS Path: choice would not be listed. Instead, an entry would appear that indicates which drive is being used for the new DOS diskettes that will be written:

```
Install to Drive: A:
```

The last choice concerns the type of monitor you will be using with DOS 6. If you highlight the Display Type: line in Figure A.2 and pressing Enter, SETUP will present a list of the possible types of monitors that MS-DOS can use with your hardware. You should highlight the monitor that most closely matches yours, then press Enter to select it, returning you to Figure A.2.

When you have made all necessary or desired adjustments to the entries first seen in Figure A.2, you should highlight the bottom line ("The settings are correct") and press Enter. Figure A.3 then appears.

If you are running Windows, as I am on my system, the default choices here are to load only Windows versions of the MS-DOS Backup, Undelete, and Anti-Virus programs. To install just those programs, press Enter. As suggested at the bottom of this screen, you can explore alternative options by pressing the up and down arrows to highlight one of the three choices, then press Enter.

FIGURE A.3

The SETUP program can install DOS and/or Windows versions of Backup, Undelete, and Anti-Virus. To help you decide which version(s) to install, this SETUP screen informs you as to how much disk space each choice would require, as well as how much free space remains on the drive.

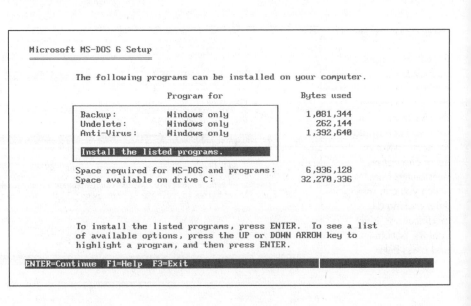

NOTE If you will want to run the Microsoft AntiVirus utility or the Undelete utility from your AUTOEXEC.BAT file, you must use the DOS versions of these utilities. This means that you must be sure to install the DOS versions during the SETUP procedure, even if you plan to use Windows as your primary operating environment.

For each of these three optional components of MS-DOS, a screen like Figure A.4 appears. In this case, I first highlighted the *Backup* feature in Figure A.3 and then pressed Enter.

On this screen, you can select one of four installation options before pressing Enter to return to Figure A.3. (However, you will be prevented from installing the Windows versions of these three components of DOS 6 if SETUP has not determined that your computer contains a version of Windows.) Depending on which choice you make on this screen, the Bytes Used column in Figure A.3 would instantly adjust to reflect the differing amount of space required.

FIGURE A.4

The SETUP program can install 1) the DOS command-prompt version, 2) the Windows graphical version, 3) both versions, or 4) no version of three important but optional MS-DOS utilities: Backup, Undelete, and Anti-Virus.

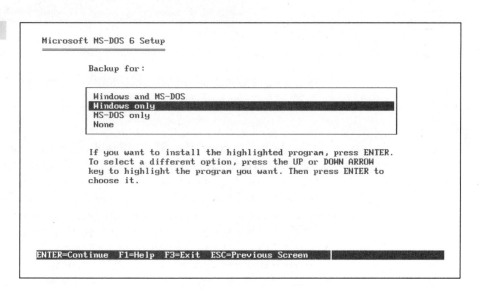

```
Microsoft MS-DOS 6 Setup


     Backup for :


     ┌──────────────────────────────────────────────────┐
     │ Windows and MS-DOS                               │
     │ Windows only                                     │
     │ MS-DOS only                                      │
     │ None                                             │
     └──────────────────────────────────────────────────┘

     If you want to install the highlighted program, press ENTER.
     To select a different option, press the UP or DOWN ARROW
     key to highlight the program you want. Then press ENTER to
     choose it.




 ENTER=Continue  F1=Help  F3=Exit  ESC=Previous Screen
```

If you have chosen to install one or more of the Windows components, the next screen that appears would display what SETUP believes to be your main Windows directory. You may either confirm this by pressing Enter, or type in the correct drive and directory location of your system's Windows directory. If your system does not contain Windows at all, you'll have to press Esc to return to Figure A.3 and change your selections.

After passing this screen, SETUP is ready to install the required files that constitute DOS 6. At this point, Figure A.5 appears and you only have two choices. Go ahead with the actual installation by pressing *Y*, or cancel the installation process by pressing F3.

FIGURE A.5

Beginning the final
stage of installation

```
Microsoft MS-DOS 6 Setup
════════════════════════════


          ┌──────────────────────────────────────────────┐
          │                                              │
          │  Setup is ready to upgrade your system to MS-DOS 6. │
          │  Do not interrupt Setup during the upgrade process. │
          │                                              │
          │   • To install MS-DOS 6 files now, press Y.  │
          │                                              │
          │   • To exit Setup without installing MS-DOS, press F3. │
          │                                              │
          └──────────────────────────────────────────────┘




 F3=Exit  Y=Install MS-DOS
```

If you choose to continue, SETUP will write all necessary files onto your hard disk. During this process, SETUP will successively prompt you to insert each of the DOS 6 program diskettes. If you are installing DOS 6 onto floppies, SETUP will prompt you at appropriate times to remove one disk or insert another. Follow the onscreen instructions carefully. To be safest, you should write-protect your original SETUP diskettes. While DOS 6 is being set up on your system (see Figure A.6), SETUP displays a progress indicator (e.g., "29% complete") at the bottom of the screen. Messages appear in the center of the screen that direct you as to

SETUP displays its progress during installation. It also directs you to insert or remove various diskettes during the process. As a bonus, it adds a little marketing pizzazz by displaying information about new DOS 6 features.

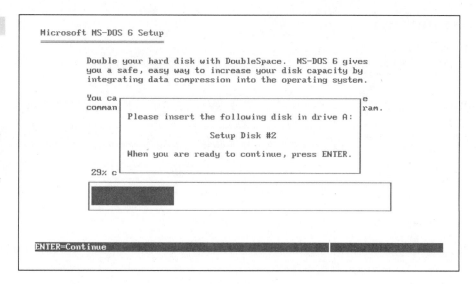

```
Microsoft MS-DOS 6 Setup

        Double your hard disk with DoubleSpace.  MS-DOS 6 gives
        you a safe, easy way to increase your disk capacity by
        integrating data compression into the operating system.

        You ca ┌────────────────────────────────────────────────┐ e
        comman │                                                  │ ram.
               │   Please insert the following disk in drive A:   │
               │                                                  │
               │              Setup Disk #2                       │
               │                                                  │
               │   When you are ready to continue, press ENTER.   │
        29% c  └────────────────────────────────────────────────┘

        ┌──────────────────────────────────────────────────────────┐
        │██████████████████████                                    │
        └──────────────────────────────────────────────────────────┘



ENTER=Continue
```

which diskette to insert. SETUP uses the top of the screen to display messages that reduce the boredom of the process while enticing you with information about new DOS 6 features.

If your system contains the appropriate and necessary hardware to run Windows in Enhanced mode, SETUP will store a special read-only file (WINA20.386) in the root directory of your boot disk. *Do not move this file*. Windows will expect to find it in the root directory in order to make effective use of the information stored within it.

When the final disk has been read, and the last disk files have been written, SETUP directs you to remove any floppy diskettes from your drives and press Enter one last time. Your system has now been installed, as seen in the final Figure A.7.

If you installed the program to your hard disk, press Enter now to have DOS 6 boot up automatically. If you installed DOS 6 onto floppies, you should place your first floppy (the one labeled *Startup*) into drive A: before rebooting your system.

FIGURE A.7

Copies of your previous CONFIG.SYS and AUTOEXEC.BAT files are saved on the UNINSTALL disk(s) in case you decide to revert to your former version of DOS. Pressing Enter now will restart MS-DOS using the updated DOS 6 system and the new CONFIG.SYS and AUTOEXEC.BAT files.

```
Microsoft MS-DOS 6 Setup



                    ┌──────────── MS-DOS Setup Complete ────────────┐
                    │ MS-DOS 6 is now installed on your computer.   │
                    │                                               │
                    │ Your original AUTOEXEC.BAT and CONFIG.SYS files, │
                    │ if any, were saved on the UNINSTALL disk(s) as │
                    │ AUTOEXEC.DAT and CONFIG.DAT.                  │
                    │                                               │
                    │  • To restart your computer with MS-DOS 6,   │
                    │    press ENTER.                              │
                    └───────────────────────────────────────────────┘



ENTER=Continue
```

TIP

Chapter 14 in this book explains how to create and modify an AUTOEXEC.BAT file. This file controls the sequence of programs and steps taken at power-up time. If you wish to run the MS-DOS shell at startup, you must be sure that the line DOSSHELL appears as the last line in your system's AUTOEXEC.BAT file to ensure that this happens.

Special Installation Considerations

As mentioned earlier in this appendix, the SETUP command recognizes a number of switches for extraordinary purposes. These are listed and briefly explained here in Table A.1.

TABLE A.1: Switches on the SETUP command

SWITCH	EXPLANATION
/N	Prepares shared copy of Windows on a network server
/I	Ignores hardware detection during Setup
/O:_FileSpec_	Specifies a SETUP.INF file that contains settings
/S:_FilePath_	Specifies a nonstandard path to the setup disk(s)
/B	Specifies monochrome display
/T	Searches for memory-resident TSRs
/C	Cancels search for memory-resident TSRs
/A	Administrative setup—places Windows on a network server. Setup expands and copies all files on every disk to a given directory, and marks them read-only.
/H:_FileSpec_	Batch-mode setup—sets up Windows with little or no user interaction. _FileSpec_ is the name of the system-settings file that contains user's configuration settings. If _FileSpec_ is not in the directory from which Windows is being set up, the path must be included.

It is possible to run SETUP more than once to reinstall DOS 6, or to reset the various aspects shown in this chapter. The first time that you install DOS 6 to a hard-disk system, all files stored in your original \DOS directory are written to a directory called OLD_DOS.1. These files will be needed, in conjunction with the information written to your UNINSTALL diskette(s), if later you want to revert to an earlier version of DOS. In order to do this, simply place the UNINSTALL diskette into drive A, close the drive door, and press Ctrl+Alt+Del to reboot. Follow the instructions on the screen once the Uninstall program begins.

Each succeeding time that you run the SETUP program, the current contents of your \DOS directory are written to the OLD_DOS.1 directory. If this directory already exists from an earlier installation sequence, a new directory is created called OLD_DOS.2, and the former OLD_DOS.1

files are first saved in this second-level backup. This will continue to directories OLD_DOS.3 and so on. In this way, you may also accumulate several UNINSTALL diskettes.

To revert to the most recent version of DOS, you'll need the most recent UNINSTALL diskette and the OLD_DOS.1 directory. The next most recent installation information resides in the OLD_DOS.2 directory, and the next most recent in OLD_DOS.3, and so on. When you are sure that you no longer will revert to an earlier version of DOS, you can discard the UNINSTALL diskette(s) and delete the OLD_DOS.x directory or directories.

APPENDIX

B

Partitioning Your Hard Disk

HARD disks are usually large enough to contain more than one type of operating system. For example, you can have DOS manage one part of a disk and UNIX manage another. Each of these sections is called a *partition*. You can have from one to four partitions on a disk.

Partitions make the hard disk, especially a very large one, a more economical investment by allowing you to have up to four completely different computer systems in one set of hardware. Unfortunately, since the resident systems do not share a common software environment, they cannot share data directly.

NOTE

DOS 6 can create partitions that are larger than 32Mb. However, you'll have to wait for a later version of DOS in order to exceed the maximum partition size of 2 gigabytes.

Two types of partitions can be set up for DOS: a primary DOS partition and an extended DOS partition. The primary DOS partition is the partition that contains DOS and is the first partition on the disk. Typically, this first partition on a disk is devoted completely to a DOS system. The extended DOS partition is a separate partition of your hard disk that cannot be used for booting, but can be divided into separate logical disk drives.

An extended partition helps you access data on a large physical drive more easily. For example, suppose that your system's backup media is limited to 60Mb (as are some tape drives) or 90Mb (as are some removable hard-disk cartridges). Your hard disk, however, may hold 120Mb, 240Mb, or even twice that once you incorporate the DBLSPACE compression facility included with DOS 6. If you use partitioning to create smaller, more manageable chunks of disk space, you can back up entire logical drives to your backup device with just one command.

When you create an extended DOS partition, it is assigned the next logical drive letter. For example, if you have a 100Mb hard-disk drive, you can create a 65Mb primary partition and a 35Mb extended partition. If DOS assigns drive C to the primary partition, the extended partition will be called drive D. You could also subdivide the extended partition into more logical drives (up to the letter Z), such as E or F and so on.

More and more computers have multiple hard drives on them. At the very least, you must use the FDISK command to first create a primary partition on the first hard drive. This will be drive C. As you'll see below, you can partition this first hard drive further, or you can leave it as a large single drive C as I have done on my system.

You can then partition the second drive into several smaller logical drives. The examples below will demonstrate how to use all of FDISK's features for any hard drive on your system.

You must create partitions before using a hard-disk drive. The easiest route is to simply use the FDISK program to make the entire disk into one primary partition, provided you will only use one operating system. To use multiple operating systems from the same disk, however, you need to leave room for additional partitions and then create those partitions with the other operating system. Each of these partitions will be a primary partition, but you must designate one as the active partition, the one that will gain control when your system boots up.

N O T E   FDISK assigns drive letters to the primary partitions of all physical drives before assigning letters to any logical drives.

Should you install a second hard-disk drive on your system and use FDISK to partition it, its primary partition will become drive D, and all drive identifiers of any logical drives in the first disk's extended partition will be bumped up by one letter. For example, if your first disk has a primary drive C and an extended partition for drive D, then adding a second hard disk will change the former drive D into drive E. The primary partition on the new hard drive will become your system's drive D.

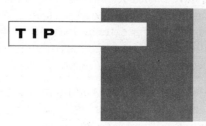

TIP

Eradicate a boot sector virus with an undocumented switch: Type FDISK /MBR to renew the boot sector, overwriting any possible virus that may have infiltrated your system's boot sector before installing virus protection.

You must always be careful not to lose any existing data on your hard disk during this required partitioning processing. If your disk is already being used and you wish to make a new partition, you should first back up all of your data and only then run FDISK from a system disk. Finally, you'll need to reformat your disk before restoring your files to it.

Setting Up Your Hard Disk

In this section, you will learn exactly how to use the FDISK command to partition your disk. This procedure is very important, and it will cause serious damage if done incorrectly. However, when you use FDISK properly, it can make your hard-disk system more efficient.

The FDISK command requires no arguments and can be easily invoked from the shell. After this command creates the appropriate partitions, you must then logically format each of the logical hard disks. Any existing data on them will be destroyed when you create partitions with FDISK.

WARNING   Any existing data on your disk will be destroyed when you create partitions with FDISK.

When you first invoke FDISK, the screen will clear and the FDISK Options screen shown in Figure B.1 will appear. As you can see, there are five choices in this initial FDISK screen. The fifth choice only appears if your system has more than one hard-disk drive. The number that appears in the *Current fixed disk drive* line (in the upper portion of the screen) will reflect which hard drive is currently the subject of your other partitioning commands.

You can work on only one hard-disk drive at a time, but you can switch from the drive you are working on to another drive. If your system has only one disk drive, then choice 5 will not appear and the current drive number will remain at as 1 during all subsequent FDISK operations. Throughout the remaining screens, you'll see drive 2 because I'll be partitioning my system's second hard-disk drive for demonstration purposes in this appendix.

FIGURE B.1

The FDISK Options menu provides four choices. A fifth choice appears if your system contains two or more fixed disks. You can divide up your disks into partitions, and into logical disks within these partitions.

```
                        MS-DOS Version 6
                      Fixed Disk Setup Program
                 (C)Copyright Microsoft Corp. 1983 - 1993

                          FDISK Options

Current fixed disk drive: 1

Choose one of the following:

1. Create DOS partition or Logical DOS Drive
2. Set active partition
3. Delete partition or Logical DOS Drive
4. Display partition information
5. Change current fixed disk drive


Enter choice: [1]




Press Esc to exit FDISK
```

Creating the Primary DOS Partition

You must select the first option on the FDISK Options menu to create a DOS partition, or to create a logical DOS drive (explained later in this chapter) in a secondary, or *extended*, partition. Since you are presently using DOS, and not another operating system like UNIX, you can only create DOS partitions. To put another operating system on the hard disk, you have to use that system's own version of FDISK, which would create its partitions next to DOS's.

After first using choice 5 on Figure B.1 to choose Fixed Disk 2, I chose option 1 on Figure B.1 to create a primary DOS partition on this second hard drive. This results in the screen shown in Figure B.2.

FIGURE B.2

The Create DOS Partition or Logical DOS Drive menu enables you to create at least one primary partition. You can also create an optional secondary (i.e., extended) partition, within which you can then create one or more logical disk drives of different sizes.

```
                Create DOS Partition or Logical DOS Drive

Current fixed disk drive: 2

Choose one of the following:

1. Create Primary DOS Partition
2. Create Extended DOS Partition
3. Create Logical DOS Drive(s) in the Extended DOS Partition



Enter choice: [1]




Press Esc to return to FDISK Options
```

TIP

If you plan to use your hard disk to later support another operating system, do not partition the whole disk. Leave some room so that you can later load another system on it.

Assuming you are starting from scratch, select choice 1 to create the primary DOS partition. You will then see the screen shown in Figure B.3. Answering Y at this screen tells DOS to use the whole disk. If your system has only a single hard drive, and you use the entire disk for a single partition, FDISK automatically makes it the active partition. This means that the system is immediately ready to reboot, using this single hard-disk partition. FDISK will prompt you with the following message:

```
System will now restart

Insert DOS system diskette in drive A:
Press any key when ready…
```

Since you just created the partition, there is nothing on the hard disk. Consequently, the system must be rebooted from a previously prepared system diskette, or from your first Setup diskette that is part of your DOS

FIGURE B.3

You can easily create a primary DOS partition that uses all available disk space, or you can answer N on this screen to then indicate a smaller size to make the primary partition.

```
                    Create Primary DOS Partition

Current fixed disk drive: 2

Do you wish to use the maximum available size for a Primary DOS Partition
(Y/N)....................................................? [Y]







Press Esc to return to FDISK Options
```

system diskettes. You can now format the entire hard disk as a system disk, just as you might do to a floppy disk.

If you are creating a primary DOS partition on a second hard drive, you will simply receive the following message:

```
Primary DOS Partition created,
drive letters changed or added
```

You can press Esc to return to the main FDISK Options screen. If you answer N in Figure B.3, another screen will appear (see Figure B.4). From this screen, you can create one or more smaller partitions from the total hard-disk space.

There are only two reasons why you would not accept the entire physical disk space for your primary DOS partition. First, you may want to reserve some space on the disk for another operating system. Second, you may want to create additional logical drives for use by DOS. As you can see in Figure B.4, you can define your primary DOS partition by entering into the square brackets either the desired number of megabytes, or the desired percentage of total disk space.

The sample disk I am partitioning in Figure B.4 has a total disk space of 100 megabytes. I entered the primary DOS partition size as 65Mb. The

FIGURE B.4

Specifying the size of the primary DOS partition. FDISK tells you how much space is available for partitioning. You tell FDISK how much space to use for the primary DOS partition.

```
                         Create Primary DOS Partition
         Current fixed disk drive: 2




         Total disk space is   100 Mbytes (1 Mbyte = 1048576 bytes)
         Maximum space available for partition is   100 Mbytes (100%)

         Enter partition size in Mbytes or percent of disk space (%) to
         create a Primary DOS Partition................................: [  65]

         No partitions defined


         Press Esc to return to FDISK Options
```

message near to the bottom of the screen:

```
No partitions defined
```

shows that I have not yet created any disk partitions. Pressing Enter now will create the primary DOS partition and produce the resulting status screen shown in Figure B.5.

This screen tells you that the partition you just created on drive C is a primary DOS partition (PRI DOS) which consists of 65Mb, or 65% of the entire physical disk. Pressing Esc at this point returns you to the FDISK Options menu.

NOTE

There can only be one primary DOS partition on any hard drive. When DOS boots up, the system files from the first hard drive's primary DOS partition are loaded into memory for your operations.

FIGURE B.5

Once a primary partition has been created, you can create a secondary (or extended) partition with some or all of the remaining space. Unless you plan to use the space for another operating system, you should always use the remaining space for the extended partition.

```
                        Create Extended DOS Partition
Current fixed disk drive: 2

Partition  Status    Type    Volume Label  Mbytes   System    Usage
  D: 1               PRI DOS                  65     UNKNOWN    65%




Total disk space is  100 Mbytes (1 Mbyte = 1048576 bytes)
Maximum space available for partition is   35 Mbytes ( 35%)

Enter partition size in Mbytes or percent of disk space (%) to
create an Extended DOS Partition............................: [  35]



Press Esc to return to FDISK Options
```

Setting the Active Partition

The active partition is the default partition on your system's first hard disk; it is used to boot the system. After creating your primary DOS partition on the first hard drive, FDISK warns you that you must specify at least one partition to be the controlling one when you power up your system:

```
WARNING!- No partitions are set active -
disk 1 is not startable unless a partition is set active
```

Choosing option 2 on the FDISK Options menu presents a screen that lists all specified partitions on the first hard drive. If you choose option 2 when dealing with a hard disk other than your system's first one, you'll receive a message telling you that only partitions on drive 1 can be made active.

Typically, at this Set Active Partition screen, you would type the number 1 so that the primary DOS partition will have control when your system comes up. However, if you partitioned your disk to include other operating systems, you can use the Set Active Partition choice to specify that another operating system gain control when your system next boots up. Entering a partition number and pressing Enter will result in a message that your selected partition has been made active.

Creating an Extended DOS Partition

In the example in this appendix, you have only used 65Mb out of a possible 100Mb. If this were the first hard drive, you could install a non-DOS operating system in the remaining space, or you could create an extended DOS partition and define logical DOS drives in that space. To create an extended DOS partition, which you can do on any hard drive you are partitioning, you select choice 1 on the FDISK Options menu (see Figure B.1 above) and then select choice 2 on the Create DOS Partition or Logical DOS Drive menu (see Figure B.2 above).

The screen shown in Figure B.5 then appears, telling you the current partitioning status. In Figure B.5, the maximum available space that remains for use in this partition is 35Mb (35% of the available physical disk). DOS initially displays the maximum available space in megabytes as the default entry in square brackets for this extended DOS partition size.

You only need to type a new value over the 35 to override the default. In Figure B.5, I pressed Enter to accept 35 as the partition's size, leaving no remaining space on this disk. Alternately, you can enter a smaller number. DOS will interpret your entry as megabytes if you simply enter a number, or as a percentage of the total physical disk space if you enter a number and a percent sign.

DOS then displays your current disk partition information, which includes sizing for both your primary and extended partitions (see Figure B.6). You can see that the 35 megabytes taken up by this extended

Disk status after creating an extended DOS partition.

```
                         Create Extended DOS Partition

      Current fixed disk drive: 2

      Partition  Status    Type    Volume Label   Mbytes   System   Usage
        D: 1                PRI DOS                  65     UNKNOWN   65%
           2                EXT DOS                  35     UNKNOWN   35%




      Extended DOS Partition created

      Press Esc to continue
```

DOS partition coincidentally represents 35% of the total hard-disk space. Pressing Esc at this screen will return you to the initial FDISK Options menu. You can then create logical drives in this extended partition.

Creating Logical Drives in an Extended Partition

To further define the drive structure of your disk, you should:

1. First select choice 1 on the FDISK Options menu:

   `Create DOS partition or Logical DOS Drive`

2. Then select choice 3 on the Create DOS Partition or Logical DOS Drive menu:

   `Create Logical DOS Drive(s) in the Extended DOS Partition`

DOS tells you that no logical drives have yet been defined in this extended partition (see Figure B.7). You are also told how much space is currently

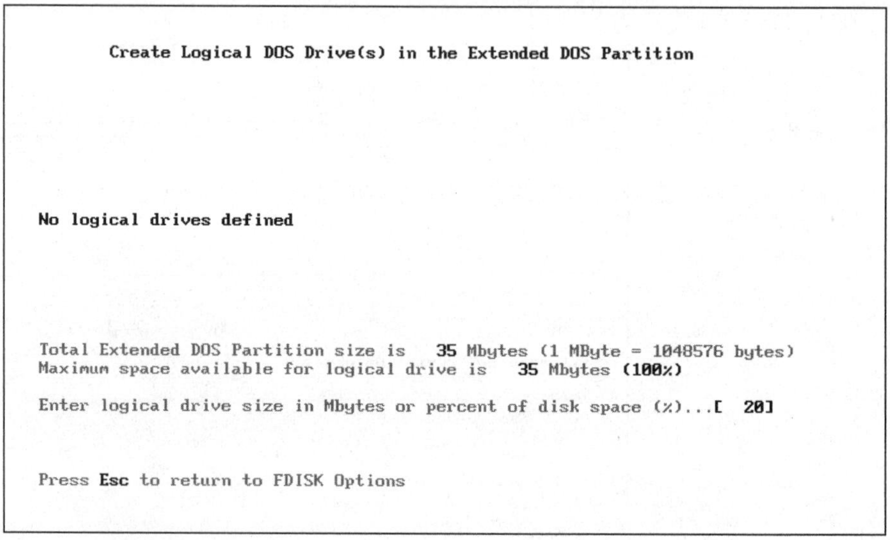

FIGURE B.7

You must first create an extended partition before you can create additional logical disk drives, beyond the one drive identifier representing the primary DOS partition. In this figure, you are about to create a 20Mb logical drive E in a 35Mb extended partition.

```
            Create Logical DOS Drive(s) in the Extended DOS Partition




No logical drives defined




Total Extended DOS Partition size is   35 Mbytes (1 MByte = 1048576 bytes)
Maximum space available for logical drive is   35 Mbytes (100%)

Enter logical drive size in Mbytes or percent of disk space (%)...[ 20]



Press Esc to return to FDISK Options
```

available for logical drives. This maximum amount is 35Mb in Figure B.7, all of which is available for defining logical drives. Your entry on this screen will define the size of the first logical drive. This will become drive E, since the primary DOS partition on this example hard drive has already been assigned to drive identifier D.

Let's say you enter 20, as shown in Figure B.7. This creates logical drive E, containing 57% of the available 35Mb in this extended partition. Since all available space in the extended partition has not been used, the resulting screen (see Figure B.8) lets you assign the remaining 15Mb (43%). Doing so will create drive F in the extended partition.

FIGURE B.8

After creating logical drive E with 20Mb, there remains 15Mb with which to create logical drive F in the extended partition.

```
              Create Logical DOS Drive(s) in the Extended DOS Partition

    Drv Volume Label  Mbytes  System   Usage
    E:                    20  UNKNOWN   57%













        Total Extended DOS Partition size is   35 Mbytes (1 MByte = 1048576 bytes)
        Maximum space available for logical drive is   15 Mbytes ( 43%)

        Enter logical drive size in Mbytes or percent of disk space (%)...[  15]

        Logical DOS Drive created, drive letters changed or added

        Press Esc to return to FDISK Options
```

You can simply press Enter to accept the default assignment of the remaining 15Mb to another logical DOS drive (F). The resulting screen (see Figure B.9) will then contain the completed logical drive information, telling you that all of your extended partition's space has been assigned.

Final status of your
logical DOS drives.
Note that the usage
column represents the
percentage of space
in the extended
partition (only 35Mb)
that is used by each of
the logical drives in
that partition.

```
                  Create Logical DOS Drive(s) in the Extended DOS Partition

     Drv Volume Label  Mbytes  System   Usage
     E:                   20    UNKNOWN   57%
     F:                   15    UNKNOWN   43%




            All available space in the Extended DOS Partition
            is assigned to logical drives.
            Press Esc to continue
```

Displaying Partition Information

Once you have set up your partitions, you can use choice 4 on the FDISK
Options menu to later display information about them. This option is useful because you don't have to execute any FDISK functions with it; you
can simply look at the information (see Figure B.10).

The information at the top of the screen is familiar by now. In the bottom
half of the screen, DOS also asks you if you want to see information about
the defined logical drives. Replying with Y results in a display of all known
information about these logical drives (see Figure B.11).

This information includes individual sizes for all logical drives on this particular hard drive, as well as percentage values for those logical disks.

FIGURE B.10

You can always display partition information if you get confused, or if you simply want to know the current status of your partitioning work.

```
                    Display Partition Information

Current fixed disk drive: 2

Partition  Status    Type    Volume Label   Mbytes    System    Usage
   D: 1              PRI DOS                   65      UNKNOWN    65%
      2              EXT DOS                   35      UNKNOWN    35%


Total disk space is   100 Mbytes (1 Mbyte = 1048576 bytes)


The Extended DOS Partition contains Logical DOS Drives.
Do you want to display the logical drive information (Y/N)......?[Y]




Press Esc to return to FDISK Options
```

FIGURE B.11

Displaying logical DOS drive information requires a second step, after displaying primary and extended partitioning information.

```
                  Display Logical DOS Drive Information

Drv Volume Label   Mbytes   System   Usage
E:                   20     UNKNOWN    57%
F:                   15     UNKNOWN    43%








       Total Extended DOS Partition size is    35 Mbytes (1 MByte = 1048576 bytes)




       Press Esc to continue
```

Deleting DOS Partitions

As always, you can revise what you set up in DOS—in this case, your partitions. To delete any of the partitions or logical drives you've set up on your hard disk, you should select choice 3 on the FDISK Options menu:

```
Delete partition or Logical DOS Drive
```

This displays Figure B.12, from which you can delete any of the information you've already set up.

You may wish to expand or contract other partitions, or you may no longer want to use a partition in the manner you originally planned. In any case, you can only make changes in a certain order. For example, you cannot delete the primary DOS partition without first deleting the extended DOS partition. If you tried to do so, SETUP would display a message informing you that you cannot delete a primary DOS partition when an extended DOS partition exists.

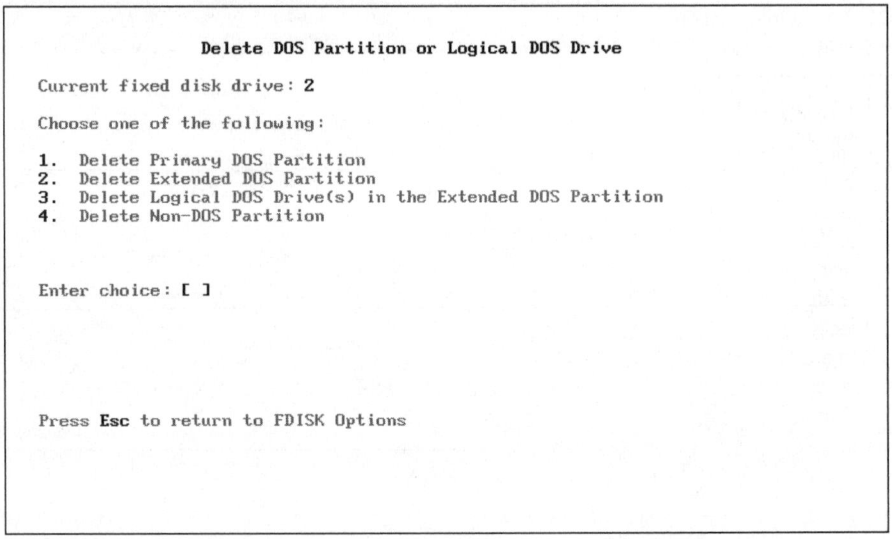

FIGURE B.12

Use the Delete DOS Partition or Logical DOS Drive menu to delete either the primary DOS, the extended DOS, or a non-DOS partition. Also, use this menu to delete entire logical disks within an extended DOS partition.

```
              Delete DOS Partition or Logical DOS Drive

Current fixed disk drive: 2

Choose one of the following:

1.   Delete Primary DOS Partition
2.   Delete Extended DOS Partition
3.   Delete Logical DOS Drive(s) in the Extended DOS Partition
4.   Delete Non-DOS Partition


Enter choice: [ ]




Press Esc to return to FDISK Options
```

You also cannot delete an extended DOS partition without first deleting the logical drives in that partition. Trying to delete the extended DOS partition before deleting the drives in it will simply display the current partition information with a message informing you that FDISK cannot delete extended DOS partition information while logical drives exist.

Choice 3 in the Delete DOS Partition or Logical DOS Drive menu is probably the first selection you will need to make. You must work backwards from the order in which you created things. When you select choice 3, a screen appears containing the logical drive information and the size of the extended DOS partition. You are also warned that any data contained in the logical disk drive to be deleted will be destroyed (see Figure B.13).

If you still want to delete the drive, enter its drive identifier. You will then be asked to enter the logical drive's volume label if it has one. You must enter the correct label, otherwise FDISK will not delete the logical drive. If it has no volume label, simply pressing Enter will suffice. In this example, the drives have never been assigned a volume label, so no entry is necessary for this field. Lastly, you will be asked to explicitly confirm this deletion request. Enter Y to do this. If you enter N, the deletion request is effectively canceled, and control returns to the FDISK Options menu.

FIGURE B.13

Deleting logical DOS drives can be hazardous to your data. You must explicitly type the drive identifier, correctly type any volume label on the drive, and then confirm the request itself.

```
                Delete Logical DOS Drive(s) in the Extended DOS Partition
    Drv Volume Label  Mbytes  System   Usage
    E:                   20   UNKNOWN   57%
    F:                   15   UNKNOWN   43%













    Total Extended DOS Partition size is   35 Mbytes (1 MByte = 1048576 bytes)

    WARNING! Data in a deleted Logical DOS Drive will be lost.
    What drive do you want to delete............................? [F]
    Enter Volume Label..............................? [         ]
    Are you sure (Y/N)..............................? [Y]

    Press Esc to return to FDISK Options
```

Figure B.13 displays the entire deletion sequence just described for this Appendix's example disk that contains a 20Mb drive E and a 15Mb drive F. Once FDISK deletes logical drive F, it updates the display at the top of the screen. If you have any remaining logical drives in your extended partition, FDISK asks you whether you want to delete another drive. You would then repeat the same procedure to delete other drives. When the last logical drive is deleted, as seen in Figure B.14, the display indicates which drives have been deleted and informs you that all the logical drives have been deleted from the extended DOS partition.

FIGURE B.14

FDISK shows the deletion status of logical drives. When they're gone, you have no recourse. Remember to back up any data on a drive before you delete partitioning information about that drive.

```
                  Delete Logical DOS Drive(s) in the Extended DOS Partition

    Drv Volume Label  Mbytes  System  Usage
    E:  Drive deleted
    F:  Drive deleted




                  




    All logical drives deleted in the Extended DOS Partition.

    Press Esc to continue
```

Pressing Esc twice at this point will bring you back to the main FDISK Options menu. Now that the logical drives are gone, you can delete the extended DOS partition itself by choosing option 3 on the FDISK Options menu and then option 2 on the Delete DOS Partition or Logical DOS Drive menu. As Figure B.15 shows, you are shown the partition information display, warned that data will be lost, and asked if you really want to delete the extended DOS partition.

Deleting the Extended
DOS partition is also
traumatic to your
data. It's a very rapid
way of saying
goodbye to everything
on every single disk
formerly contained
within that partition.

```
                    Delete Extended DOS Partition

Current fixed disk drive: 2

Partition  Status   Type    Volume Label  Mbytes  System    Usage
  D: 1               PRI DOS               65      UNKNOWN   65%
     2               EXT DOS               35      UNKNOWN   35%


Total disk space is  100 Mbytes (1 Mbyte = 1048576 bytes)

WARNING! Data in the deleted Extended DOS Partition will be lost.
Do you wish to continue (Y/N)................? [Y]




Press Esc to return to FDISK Options
```

If you reply Y, the screen will be updated to show only the primary DOS
partition and a message that the extended DOS partition has been
deleted. Press Esc to return once again to the FDISK Options menu. You
can now delete your primary DOS partition and then repartition your
hard disk as you see fit.

Yea, though I walk through the valley of the shadow of partitions, I shall
fear no data loss; For *Mastering DOS 6 Special Edition* is with me; Its chapters and appendices do comfort me; And do guide me into the land of
milk and honey and twenty megs of RAM.

At this point, of course, you would turn to the beginning of this appendix
to carefully guide yourself through the recreation of one or more partitions and logical disk drives. Give careful thought at this point to how you
or others will use the disk later. Deciding on one or more partitions, or
one or more logical disk drives, can make all your subsequent work with
DOS both easy and comfortable.

APPENDIX C

ASCII Codes and Numbering Systems

THIS appendix presents information on how ASCII codes are used in DOS. It also discusses the different numbering systems used by various aspects of DOS. With this information, you can both manage your DOS system more readily and manipulate file data for yourself.

ASCII Codes

A character is any letter, number, punctuation symbol, or graphics symbol. In other words, it is anything that can be displayed on a video screen or printed on a printer.

Each character in a *character set* has a number assigned to it, which is how the computer refers to the various characters in the set. The standard set of characters used by U.S. computers is shown in Figure C.1. In this set, code 65 refers to a capital *A*, and code 97 refers to a lowercase *a*. These codes are called ASCII codes; ASCII (pronounced *"ask-key"*) stands for American Standard Code for Information Interchange.

Codes 0 through 31 are used as *control codes*. Displaying one of these codes will cause something to happen instead of causing a symbol to be displayed. For example, displaying code 7 will result in the computer's bell or beeper being sounded. Displaying code 13 will result in a carriage return.

Codes 32 through 127 are ASCII character codes for numbers, letters, and standard punctuation marks and symbols. Codes 128 through 255, known as *extended ASCII* codes, vary from computer to computer. They

FIGURE C.1

ASCII numbers and their corresponding characters. The space at code 32 means that this code produces the space character. For code 255, the blank space means that this code produces a "null" character.

0-		2-		4-		6-		8-		A-		C-		E-	
0		32		64	@	96	`	128	Ç	160	á	192	└	224	α
1	☺	33	!	65	A	97	a	129	ü	161	í	193	┴	225	ß
2	☻	34	"	66	B	98	b	130	é	162	ó	194	┬	226	Γ
3	♥	35	#	67	C	99	c	131	â	163	ú	195	├	227	π
4	♦	36	$	68	D	100	d	132	ä	164	ñ	196	─	228	Σ
5	♣	37	%	69	E	101	e	133	à	165	Ñ	197	┼	229	σ
6	♠	38	&	70	F	102	f	134	å	166	ª	198	╞	230	µ
7	•	39	'	71	G	103	g	135	ç	167	º	199	╟	231	τ
8	◘	40	(	72	H	104	h	136	ê	168	¿	200	╚	232	Φ
9	○	41	)	73	I	105	i	137	ë	169	⌐	201	╔	233	Θ
10	◙	42	*	74	J	106	j	138	è	170	¬	202	╩	234	Ω
11	♂	43	+	75	K	107	k	139	ï	171	½	203	╦	235	δ
12	♀	44	,	76	L	108	l	140	î	172	¼	204	╠	236	∞
13	♪	45	_	77	M	109	m	141	ì	173	¡	205	=	237	ø
14	♫	46	.	78	N	110	n	142	Ä	174	«	206	╬	238	ε
15	☼	47	/	79	O	111	o	143	Å	175	»	207	╧	239	∩
16	►	48	0	80	P	112	p	144	É	176	░	208	╨	240	≡
17	◄	49	1	81	Q	113	q	145	æ	177	▒	209	╤	241	±
18	↕	50	2	82	R	114	r	146	Æ	178	▓	210	╥	242	≥
19	‼	51	3	83	S	115	s	147	ô	179	│	211	╙	243	≤
20	¶	52	4	84	T	116	t	148	ö	180	┤	212	╘	244	⌠
21	§	53	5	85	U	117	u	149	ò	181	╡	213	╒	245	⌡
22	▬	54	6	86	V	118	v	150	û	182	╢	214	╓	246	÷
23	↨	55	7	87	W	119	w	151	ù	183	╖	215	╫	247	≈
24	↑	56	8	88	X	120	x	152	ÿ	184	╕	216	╪	248	°
25	↓	57	9	89	Y	121	y	153	Ö	185	╣	217	┘	249	·
26	→	58	:	90	Z	122	z	154	Ü	186	║	218	┌	250	·
27	←	59	;	91	[	123	{	155	¢	187	╗	219	█	251	√
28	∟	60	<	92	\	124	¦	156	£	188	╝	220	▄	252	ⁿ
29	↔	61	=	93	]	125	}	157	¥	189	╜	221	▌	253	²
30	▲	62	>	94	^	126	~	158	₧	190	╛	222	▐	254	■
31	▼	63	?	95	_	127	⌂	159	ƒ	191	┐	223	▀	255	

usually comprise foreign characters, Greek and mathematical symbols, and graphics and "box-drawing" characters (small lines and curves that can be used to create geometric patterns).

You can view the characters in the extended ASCII set for your computer by using a technique available from the DOS command prompt and from within many DOS text editors. All you have to do is hold down the Alt key while you type in the ASCII number on your numeric keypad. (The NumLock key must be *on* for the key to register a number keypress instead of a cursor-movement keypress.) For example, on my computer, typing Alt+178 displays a shaded box character that I use for creating drop shadows in programs that display information in boxes.

TIP

See my ASCIICHR.BAT file (in an *EXTRA!* sidebar in Chapter 6) for an idea of how to display all the extended ASCII characters for your computer any time you want.

DOS has several available character sets, called code pages. The most common is the standard U.S. code page; the next most common is the Multilingual code page. These are discussed (with examples) in Appendix D.

Numbering Systems

Computers use a variety of numbering systems to operate. The most basic numbering system is the binary system, in which there are only two digits, 0 and 1. The digital circuitry used in computers operates by using small voltages that turn magnetic bits on or off. Therefore, 0 and 1 are used to represent the two states of off and on, respectively.

Counting in binary is not difficult, but it does require some adjustment from your standard decimal-numbering scheme. The progression of numbers and their matching decimal conversions are shown in Table C.1.

TABLE C.1: Binary-to-decimal conversion

BINARY	DECIMAL
0	0
1	1
10	2
11	3
100	4
101	5
110	6
111	7
1000	8
1001	9
1010	10

Chapter 9 contains a detailed explanation of the binary numbering system. The general rule for converting numbers from binary to decimal is to multiply the number in every binary number column by 2 raised to the column-number power. You count column numbers from the right, starting with 0. For the binary number 1101, for example, you would obtain

$$(1 \times 2^0)+(0 \times 2^1)+(1 \times 2^2)+(1 \times 2^3)$$

where any number to the 0 power (2^0 in this case) is defined as equal to 1. This is called *counting in base 2*. The above number, therefore, would be equal to 1+0+4+8, or 13 in our regular decimal notation.

The *decimal* system counts in base 10. Using the same method of converting binary numbers, you can see that breaking down the decimal number 2014 into its component parts works like this:

$$(4 \times 10^0)+(1 \times 10^1)+(0 \times 10^2)+(2 \times 10^3)$$
$$= 4+10+000+2000$$
$$= 2014$$

Another numbering system is called *octal,* or base 8. This system has only eight digits, 0–7. The octal number 701 is converted to base 10 (decimal) by the following computation:

$$(1 \times 8^0) + (0 \times 8^1) + (7 \times 8^2)$$
$$= 1 + 0 + 448$$
$$= 449$$

The last major numbering system in computers is called *hexadecimal,* which counts in base 16. This system has 16 digits in it: 0–9 and A–F, which form the counting sequence 0123456789ABCDEF. To count in this system, you use the same method you use for other numbering systems. The hexadecimal number BA7 translates to decimal as

$$(7 \times 16^0) + (A \times 16^1) + (B \times 16^2)$$

which is equal to

$$7 + (10 \times 16^1) + (11 \times 16^2)$$

which is also equal to

$$7 + 160 + 2816$$
$$= 2983$$

TIP

Hexadecimal notation is convenient for byte values because a hexadecimal digit is equivalent to 4 ($2^4 = 16$) binary digits (called a *nibble*) and there are 8 bits ($2^8 = 256$-character set) in a byte. A byte can therefore be represented by two hexadecimal digits.

APPENDIX

D

Setting Up DOS
for International Use

DOS HAS enjoyed worldwide popularity for years. Recognizing its international influence, DOS provides special features that allow you to customize your operating version to the needs of many languages. Although the specific commands and functions for national language support will be used primarily by only a small percentage of users, you may be one from that small group. This appendix is critical to understanding the intertwined requirements of country code pages and DOS setup.

Different countries use different symbols to represent their own systems. For example, currency symbols differ among countries—the $ in the USA, the £ in England, and the ¥ in Japan. Time formats also vary: the separator symbol between the hour and minutes is a colon in the U.S., but a period in Norway. Decimal numbers are also punctuated differently: in the U.S. they contain a period, but in Spain they contain a comma. You'll learn in this appendix how to set up your version of DOS to understand the default values for symbols used in different countries.

TIP

If you're a foreigner in the U.S., you can easily switch between the U.S. default key values and your own. In this way, you can avoid having to learning the U.S. keyboard layout in order to work on computers here. The same is true in reverse for Americans working abroad. This feature is explained in detail later in this appendix.

Different countries also employ different keyboard layouts. If you learned to type in the U.S. and then tried typing on a French typewriter or keyboard, you would type the letter *A* each time you meant to type a *Q*, and vice versa. This is because the key labeled *A* on an American keyboard is labeled *Q* on a French keyboard. You'll also learn in this appendix about the differences between keyboard layouts in different countries and how you can easily ask DOS to redefine all the keys properly. In addition, you'll learn how to rapidly switch between the various possible layouts.

Character Sets for Different Countries

The group of characters used in a country or on a computer composes the character set of that country or computer. Most countries share a common set of characters. However, some countries have enough different characters and symbols to justify creating a special character set just for them.

Along with the different character sets comes different placement of the characters on a computer keyboard. This is a result of making commonly used elements easy to use. For example, on a French keyboard certain keys are for accented letters.

A computer does not interpret letters as letters per se, but assigns an ASCII code to each letter. These codes range from 0 to 255, representing the 256 possible combinations of binary digits contained in an eight-bit byte.

Codes 0 through 31 are usually reserved for *control codes*, the codes that do not produce a visible character but perform some particular action. For example, printing the code #7 on most computers causes the computer to beep, and code #13 causes a carriage return. These codes control the functions of the hardware.

Codes 32 through 126 are standard characters and symbols (see Figure D.1). The capital alphabet starts at code 65, and the lowercase alphabet starts at code 97. Code 127 represents the deletion symbol. The control codes and the standard character codes together make up an entire set (from 0 to 127) called ASCII codes. The computer translates

Setting Up DOS for International Use

ASCII codes and their corresponding characters. The blank at code 32 indicates a space character, and the blank character at code 255 is actually the "null" character.

032	044 ,	056 8	068 D	080 P	092 \	104 h	116 t
033 !	045 -	057 9	069 E	081 Q	093]	105 i	117 u
034 "	046 .	058 :	070 F	082 R	094 ^	106 j	118 v
035 #	047 /	059 ;	071 G	083 S	095 _	107 k	119 w
036 $	048 0	060 <	072 H	084 T	096 `	108 l	120 x
037 %	049 1	061 =	073 I	085 U	097 a	109 m	121 y
038 &	050 2	062 >	074 J	086 V	098 b	110 n	122 z
039 '	051 3	063 ?	075 K	087 W	099 c	111 o	123 {
040 (	052 4	064 @	076 L	088 X	100 d	112 p	124	
041)	053 5	065 A	077 M	089 Y	101 e	113 q	125 }
042 *	054 6	066 B	078 N	090 Z	102 f	114 r	126 ~
043 +	055 7	067 C	079 O	091 [	103 g	115 s	127 ▮

128 Ç	144 É	160 á	176 ░	192 └	208 ╨	224 α	240 ≡
129 ü	145 æ	161 í	177 ▒	193 ┴	209 ╤	225 β	241 ±
130 é	146 Æ	162 ó	178 ▓	194 ┬	210 ╥	226 Γ	242 ≥
131 â	147 ô	163 ú	179 │	195 ├	211 ╙	227 π	243 ≤
132 ä	148 ö	164 ñ	180 ┤	196 ─	212 ╘	228 Σ	244 ⌠
133 à	149 ò	165 Ñ	181 ╡	197 ┼	213 ╒	229 σ	245 ⌡
134 å	150 û	166 ª	182 ╢	198 ╞	214 ╓	230 µ	246 ÷
135 ç	151 ù	167 º	183 ╖	199 ╟	215 ╫	231 τ	247 ≈
136 ê	152 ÿ	168 ¿	184 ╕	200 ╚	216 ╪	232 Φ	248 °
137 ë	153 Ö	169 ⌐	185 ╣	201 ╔	217 ┘	233 Θ	249 ·
138 è	154 Ü	170 ¬	186 ║	202 ╩	218 ┌	234 Ω	250 ·
139 ï	155 ¢	171 ½	187 ╗	203 ╦	219 █	235 δ	251 √
140 î	156 £	172 ¼	188 ╝	204 ╠	220 ▄	236 ∞	252 ⁿ
141 ì	157 ¥	173 ¡	189 ╜	205 ═	221 ▌	237 φ	253 ²
142 Ä	158 ₧	174 «	190 ╛	206 ╬	222 ▐	238 ε	254 ·
143 Å	159 ƒ	175 »	191 ┐	207 ╧	223 ▀	239 ∩	255

characters into these codes, and so does any other device using the characters. When a computer sends ASCII 65 to the printer, it expects an *A* to be printed out, so the printer must also translate from code 65 to *A*. You can see why it is important for these codes to be standardized; many pieces of equipment rely on the same code.

Codes 128 through 255 are computer/printer specific. IBM uses codes 128 through 255 for some graphics characters, while Epson, on some of its printers, uses them for italics.

The extended ASCII codes also represent certain specialized keys or key combinations, such as Alt+C or F1. These codes are defined by first sending an ASCII null character (code #0) to the device, and then another code. For example, sending code #0 then code #59 would have the same effect as pressing the F1 key.

The combinations of all these codes produce the complete visual and printed output you are used to seeing. Depending on where you live and work, however, you may have altogether different characters in your language and keys on your keyboard.

What Country Do You Call Home?

When DOS boots up, the system date and time are queried. Everybody agrees that any given date has a month, a day, and a year, but not everyone agrees on that order. In the U.S., dates are shown with the month first, the day next, and the year last. In Europe, the day is shown first, the month next, and the year last. In Japan, the year is first, the month next, and the day last. Hence, 11/04/07 can mean November 4, 1907; April 11, 1907; or April 7, 1911. It depends on who's writing the date *and* who's reading it. Again, that's why standards are so important.

The **DATE** function in DOS will display the system date according to the accepted custom in a specific country. Table D.1 shows the countries currently understood by DOS, along with their country and keyboard codes. You'll learn later in this appendix how to set up your version of DOS to understand which country or keyboard is in use.

TABLE D.1:　International country and keyboard codes for DOS

COUNTRY	COUNTRY CODE	KEYBOARD CODE
Arabic	785	*n/a*
Australia (English)	061	US
Belgium	032	BE
Canada (English)	061	US
Canada (French)	002	CF
Denmark	045	DK
English (International)	061	US

TABLE D.1: International country and keyboard codes for DOS (continued)

COUNTRY	COUNTRY CODE	KEYBOARD CODE
Finland	358	SU
France	033	FR
Germany	049	GR
Israel	972	*n/a*
Italy	039	IT
Japan	081	*n/a*
Korea	082	*n/a*
Latin America	003	LA
Netherlands	031	NL
Norway	047	NO
People's Republic of China	086	*n/a*
Portugal	351	PO
Spain	034	SP
Sweden	046	SV
Switzerland (French)	041	SF
Switzerland (German)	041	SG
Taiwan	088	*n/a*
United Kingdom	044	UK
United States	001	US

The order of the month, day, and year fields is only one of many things that differ among countries. Separator symbols between the month, day, and year values also vary from country to country. In fact, there are a host of special symbols that vary among countries: time separators (a colon or a period), list separators (a semicolon or a comma), decimal separators (a period or a comma), thousands separators (a comma or a period), and currency symbols (\$, £, ¥, and others). The U.S. shows time in 12-hour A.M./P.M. format, while most other countries use a 24-hour display. Most countries show two decimal places of accuracy in currency displays, while Italy shows none.

DOS maintains internal tables of these differing values according to which country has been set up as the system default. If you do nothing, the U.S. will be assumed to be the standard. However, if you wish to customize the system for some other country, you can simply use the proper country code from Table D.1 to add a line to your CONFIG.SYS file:

```
COUNTRY = Code
```

Figure D.2 shows the results of DOS date and time requests after adding **COUNTRY=41** to the system CONFIG.SYS file. This country represents Switzerland, and further assumes that the COUNTRY.SYS file is present in the root directory of your boot drive. Notice the changed format for both the date and time. The date now reflects the European standard of *dd.mm.yyyy*, while the time is shown in the common 24-hour format.

Getting the date and time was easy in this example. The real value of the **COUNTRY** code in CONFIG.SYS can only be realized fully by programmers using specialized assembly-language techniques. Thus, only a programmer can really obtain the specialized symbol and separator information necessary to customize an application program to the country it may run in. However, you can make a reasonable amount of adjustment yourself.

FIGURE D.2

Date and time formats for COUNTRY = Switzerland

```
C:\>DATE
Current date is Wed 16.06.1993
Enter new date (dd-mm-yy):

C:\>TIME
Current time is  18,34,34.58
Enter new time:

C:\>
```

Understanding Code Pages

DOS provides a complex ability to redefine its understanding of the keyboard you use. This is based on its feature called *code pages*. Code pages represent some complicated concepts, but with a little help and some extra knowledge, they can easily be understood. Let's start with the keyboard.

The Keyboard Translation Table

The keyboard is simply a segregated group of buttons, monitored by a microprocessor that sends a signal to DOS when any key is pressed. The signal that goes to DOS is called a *scan code*. A scan code is not a letter or an ASCII code, but it is a code that tells DOS which key has been pressed. It has nothing to do with what is printed on the physical key, but merely with the physical location of the key.

Whether DOS is busy or not, something will happen inside the computer when you press a key. This "something" is called an *interrupt*. One kind of interrupt occurs when a hardware device asks for the attention of the CPU. In the case of a keyboard, a small electrical signal—a scan code—is sent to DOS, indicating which key was pressed. The part of DOS that takes in the interrupt and processes it is called a *device driver* (or sometimes an *interrupt handler*).

When the keyboard device driver receives a signal, it processes the scan code to determine which key was pressed *and* to convert the scan code into an ASCII code. This translation is done through a table in memory that compares scan codes and ASCII codes. Figure D.3 diagrams this process.

Take a look at two different keyboards used in the United States and France, shown in Figure D.4. There are more than fifty other keyboard

Processing keyboard
interrupts

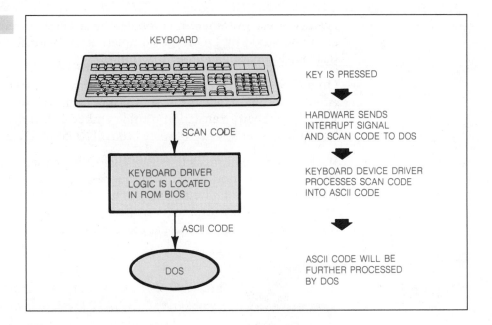

An extended, 101-key
keyboard commonly
used in the U.S., and
a French keyboard

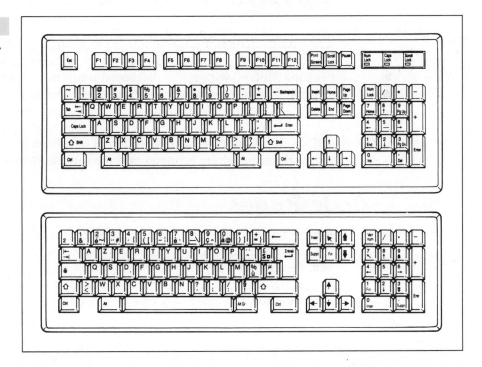

layouts in use on different computers in different countries. All of these are understood by DOS; the complete layouts for these alternatives are displayed in your DOS user's manual.

On a U.S. keyboard, if you press *A*, its scan code will be translated into ASCII code 65. However, if you hit the same key on a computer with a French keyboard translation routine embedded in the device driver, the same scan code will be converted to ASCII code 81, or the letter *Q*.

If a key combination such as Alt+Ctrl+2 is pressed with the U.S. translator installed, not much will happen, because the U.S. keyboard translator does not have an entry in its table for this scan code. However, if you press this key combination on a computer with the French keyboard translator in effect, you will get the @ symbol.

TIP Press Ctrl+Alt+F1 to return to the default keyboard layout. Press Ctrl+Alt+F2 to return to the alternate keyboard specified by a KEYB command.

The French translator understands this scan code and will match it up. The ASCII code generated will be 64, which is the same code generated by pressing Shift+2 with a U.S. keyboard translator. Both yield the same @ symbol. The two keyboard translation tables translate different keyboard scan codes to the same ASCII codes, allowing countries with different keyboards to use all the same characters, even though the keys are labeled differently. Countries that have different keyboard layouts but still use the same character set are grouped into the same code page.

Code Pages

After interpreting what key was pressed on the keyboard and converting the scan code into an ASCII code by means of a translation table, DOS next determines where the ASCII code should go. If it goes to a disk drive, it is simply routed there and stored on the disk. If, however, it is destined for a monitor or printer, it is first processed by a code page. A code page is yet another translation table that converts an ASCII code into a printable or displayable character.

There are five code pages available in DOS. The standard code page (numbered 437 in DOS) for the United States can be seen in Figure D.5.

FIGURE D.5

Standard code page 437, the default for U.S. computers.

0		32		64	@	96	`	128	Ç	160	á	192	∟	224	α
1	☺	33	!	65	A	97	a	129	ü	161	í	193	┴	225	ß
2	☻	34	"	66	B	98	b	130	é	162	ó	194	┬	226	Γ
3	♥	35	#	67	C	99	c	131	â	163	ú	195	├	227	π
4	♦	36	$	68	D	100	d	132	ä	164	ñ	196	─	228	Σ
5	♣	37	%	69	E	101	e	133	à	165	Ñ	197	┼	229	σ
6	♠	38	&	70	F	102	f	134	å	166	ª	198	╞	230	µ
7	•	39	'	71	G	103	g	135	ç	167	º	199	╟	231	τ
8	◘	40	(	72	H	104	h	136	ê	168	¿	200	╚	232	Φ
9	○	41	)	73	I	105	i	137	ë	169	⌐	201	╔	233	Θ
10	◙	42	*	74	J	106	j	138	è	170	¬	202	╩	234	Ω
11	♂	43	+	75	K	107	k	139	ï	171	½	203	╦	235	δ
12	♀	44	,	76	L	108	l	140	î	172	¼	204	╠	236	∞
13	♪	45	_	77	M	109	m	141	ì	173	¡	205	=	237	φ
14	♫	46	.	78	N	110	n	142	Ä	174	«	206	╬	238	ε
15	☼	47	/	79	O	111	o	143	Å	175	»	207	╧	239	∩
16	►	48	0	80	P	112	p	144	É	176	░	208	╨	240	≡
17	◄	49	1	81	Q	113	q	145	æ	177	▒	209	╤	241	±
18	↕	50	2	82	R	114	r	146	Æ	178	▓	210	╥	242	≥
19	‼	51	3	83	S	115	s	147	ô	179	│	211	╙	243	≤
20	¶	52	4	84	T	116	t	148	ö	180	┤	212	╘	244	⌠
21	§	53	5	85	U	117	u	149	ò	181	╡	213	╒	245	⌡
22	▬	54	6	86	V	118	v	150	û	182	╢	214	╓	246	÷
23	↨	55	7	87	W	119	w	151	ù	183	╖	215	╫	247	≈
24	↑	56	8	88	X	120	x	152	ÿ	184	╕	216	╪	248	°
25	↓	57	9	89	Y	121	y	153	Ö	185	╣	217	┘	249	·
26	→	58	:	90	Z	122	z	154	Ü	186	║	218	┌	250	·
27	←	59	;	91	[	123	{	155	¢	187	╗	219	█	251	√
28	∟	60	<	92	\	124	¦	156	£	188	╝	220	▄	252	ⁿ
29	↔	61	=	93	]	125	}	157	¥	189	╜	221	▌	253	²
30	▲	62	>	94	^	126	~	158	₧	190	╛	222	▐	254	■
31	▼	63	?	95	_	127	⌂	159	ƒ	191	┐	223	▀	255	

The other principal code page is the Multilingual code page, numbered 850. The first 128 characters are the same as those on code page 437; the remainder can be seen in Figure D.6.

The upper characters for the Multilingual code page (number 850), the second most commonly used code page.

128	Ç	160	á	192	L	224	Ó
129	ü	161	í	193	⊥	225	ß
130	é	162	ó	194	T	226	Ô
131	â	163	ú	195	⊦	227	Ò
132	ä	164	ñ	196	—	228	õ
133	à	165	Ñ	197	┼	229	Õ
134	å	166	ª	198	ã	230	µ
135	ç	167	º	199	Ã	231	þ
136	ê	168	¿	200	╚	232	þ
137	ë	169	®	201	╔	233	Ú
138	è	170	¬	202	╩	234	Û
139	ï	171	½	203	╦	235	Ù
140	î	172	¼	204	╠	236	ý
141	ì	173	¡	205	=	237	Ý
142	Ä	174	«	206	╬	238	¯
143	Å	175	»	207	¤	239	´
144	É	176	░	208	ð	240	-
145	æ	177	▒	209	Ð	241	±
146	Æ	178	▓	210	Ê	242	=
147	ô	179	│	211	Ë	243	¾
148	ö	180	┤	212	È	244	¶
149	ò	181	Á	213	ı	245	§
150	û	182	Â	214	Í	246	÷
151	ù	183	À	215	Î	247	¸
152	ÿ	184	©	216	Ï	248	°
153	Ö	185	╣	217	┘	249	¨
154	Ü	186	║	218	┌	250	·
155	ø	187	╗	219	█	251	¹
156	£	188	╝	220	▄	252	³
157	Ø	189	¢	221	¦	253	²
158	×	190	¥	222	Ì	254	■
159	ƒ	191	┐	223	▀	255	

You'll soon learn how to use and switch between these code pages, as well as the other three code pages also available in DOS (Portugese, Norwegian, and Canadian French). See your DOS user's manual for the precise layouts of these remaining code pages.

NOTE   Special code pages exist for the Hebrew language and for Asian languages. However, their use requires special supplemental software and/or hardware.

Code pages are simply character sets. As you saw in the last section, one character set (code page) can satisfy the needs of several different countries. Countries with significantly different character sets and keyboards are grouped into other code pages. The 25 different country codes (shown in Table D.1) correlate altogether with, at most, five different character sets, so only five different code pages are needed. For instance, even though in the U.S. you rarely use an accented e, it is included in one of the 256 entries in the U.S. character set.

After a scan code has been translated into an ASCII code, it is matched to the currently active code-page translation table. Now you're into the output side of DOS management. The device driver responsible for the output device now uses built-in logic to send a sequence of control instructions to the output device. These instructions describe precisely how to display the character represented by the ASCII code.

Devices and Their Drivers

All output consists of sequences of codes being sent to an output device like a monitor or printer. Unfortunately, not all monitors or printers act the same, have the same features, or can be controlled by the same device driver. In fact, sometimes the device driver consists of software instructions residing in your computer's main memory, while at other times these instructions reside in special memory built into the output device.

Each output device driver translates the requested output data into the specific commands needed to form the character for each device. As you might guess, you must have one of the special monitors or printers to access any special additional symbols not available on the standard U.S. code page.

Translation Tables and Device Drivers

DOS supports more than 50 different keyboard layouts and 11 languages. Microsoft has supplied all of the necessary keyboard translation tables in a file called KEYBOARD.SYS, which is loaded into the computer by using the **KEYB** command at the DOS prompt.

The output device drivers are loaded into memory from individual files contained on your startup or installation disks. The extension .CPI stands for Code-Page Information; you will usually find that the appropriate files have a base name that identifies the printer model and a .CPI extension.

DOS device drivers can have up to six different code pages to choose from. Any of these six character sets, or code pages, can be used in place of the default set used on your computer. Every computer uses a default set for your individual keyboard and monitor. Although the default set in the United States is code page 437, there are a number of unique international code pages that might very well constitute the default hardware character set on your computer. Each of these is referred to by a unique number, as shown in Table D.2.

TABLE D.2: Code-page identification numbers

LANGUAGE	CODE PAGE
United States	437
Multilingual	850
Slavic	852
Portuguese	860
Canadian French	863
Norwegian and Danish	865

Since code page 437 is the standard U.S. code page that can be used with any monitor, 437 is the default when DOS boots up. This is the only code page that can be used with devices other than the printers and monitors supported by special-purpose drivers included in your DOS version.

N O T E   Some computers manufactured solely for foreign use have the foreign character set built in, as well as a keyboard with the appropriate key labels in place. These computers will not respond at all when you try to switch keyboard layouts with either the KEYB command or the Ctrl+Alt+function-key combinations. No logic has been included in these keyboards to load in additional keyboard tables, since the necessary non-U.S. tables are already there.

Figure D.7 ties all of the preceding sections together. It shows the entire process of moving information from beginning to end—from the keyboard interrupt to the final display or printed output.

Let's quickly run through a last example of the process. Assume you've loaded the Canadian French keyboard-translation table into the computer (you'll learn how to do this in the next section). You've also loaded code page 863 and the 4201.CPI device driver, as you wish to print a character on an IBM Proprinter. The character you want to print is the ¾ symbol, which is not included in the normal ASCII character set of U.S. computers or printers. The ¾ symbol on the Canadian keyboard can be printed by using the key combination Alt+Shift+= (that is, Alt plus Shift plus the equals sign).

When this key combination is pressed, a scan code is sent to the keyboard device driver, which routes the scan code to the keyboard translation table. Here, the scan code is matched against the ASCII table, and an ASCII code (in this case, 173) is sent back to DOS. DOS sees that this character was destined for the printer and sends it on its way. The code is

FIGURE D.7

The overall code-page process. Read from top to bottom, this figure shows the sequence of commands necessary for preparing your system to use different code pages (the Configuration and Installation portions) and working with different code pages (the Operation portion of the figure).

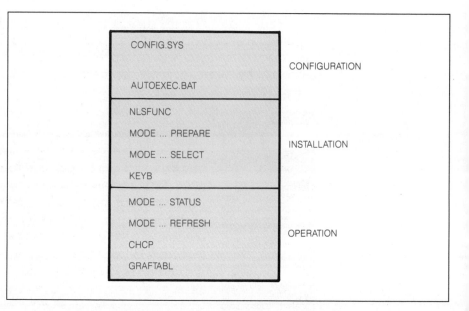

now processed by the Proprinter, which uses the installed code page. The Proprinter's driver now translates ASCII 173 to a set of hardware instructions that describe how to print a ¾ symbol.

Changing Your Code Pages

Now that you understand how code pages are used, you must learn the required sequence of DOS commands necessary to change them. You first need to learn how to tell DOS that you will be using the national language-support scheme (NLS), which is just another name for the code-page mechanism. You also need to learn how to prepare, select, and switch between the various code pages. The following sections will teach you the mechanics of the process. Figure D.8 provides an overview of the DOS command sequences necessary for a complete international setup.

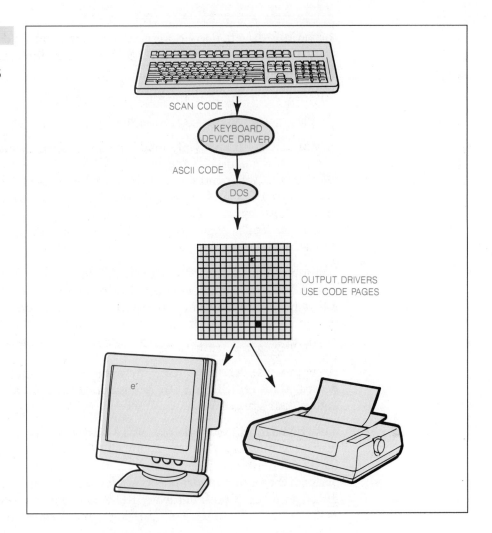

Command overview
for international DOS
operations

Step 1: Updating the CONFIG.SYS File for International Support

Before you can do anything with code pages, you must use one or more **DEVICE** configuration commands in your CONFIG.SYS file to load the various drivers needed for code-page switching. You need a different DEVICE line in your CONFIG.SYS for each different printer and display device.

Entering a command in the following format:

```
DEVICE=Drive:\DISPLAY.SYS CON:=(Type,CodePage,x)
```

in your CONFIG.SYS file loads the specialized display device drivers. *Drive* is the location of the DISPLAY.SYS file. *Type* is MONO, CGA, LCD or EGA, depending on the display being used. (An EGA type supports both EGA and VGA type monitors.) *CodePage* is the code-page number(s) supported directly by the hardware device, and x is how many additional code pages beyond the default are supported by your hardware.

You must also load the PRINTER.SYS file in your CONFIG.SYS file if you will be performing any output printing to the parallel ports. Use the following command syntax to load the specialized device driver information to support output to the LPTn port (n = 1, 2, or 3):

```
DEVICE=Drive:\PRINTER.SYS LPTn:=(Type,CodePage,x)
```

Except for the *Type* parameter, the parameters are the same as those just described for DISPLAY.SYS. *Type* is either 4201, 4208, or 5202, depending on your printer.

The IBM Proprinter models reserve a hardware memory area in their own read-only memory (ROM) specifically for code-page information. The IBM Quietwriter III Printer Model 5202 uses hardware font cartridges to perform the same support purpose. Hewlett-Packard's latest models offer the advantages of both hardware ROMs for built-in font creation as well as the opportunity to use both cartridges and plug-in boards for additional capabilities.

You can also have the country automatically set at the time your system boots up. The line to add to your CONFIG.SYS file is

```
COUNTRY=xxx
```

where *xxx* is the appropriate country code.

Step 2: Loading Code-Page Support Routines

You can type the **NLSFUNC** (short for national language-support functions) command from the DOS command prompt to allow for the use of extended country information provided with the code pages you have specified in the DISPLAY.SYS or PRINTER.SYS line(s) of your CONFIG.SYS file. Remember to run NLSFUNC from your original DOS command prompt only and not from a prompt obtained from within the DOS shell or from within Windows. This command will load all of the required country-specific information. It must be run *before* you attempt to select any code page other than the default (i.e., 437). As part of the format for the NLSFUNC command, you must tell DOS where it can find the COUNTRY.SYS file. This file contains information that defines the different country standards, such as the date and time format, the rules of capitalization, and special symbol usage for each of the available country codes (refer back to Table D.1). U.S. standards will be assumed if you neglect to specify the location of the COUNTRY.SYS file.

Assuming you accepted the default directory when you installed DOS, COUNTRY.SYS will be in the DOS directory, and the NLSFUNC command can be invoked as simply as typing:

```
NLSFUNC \DOS\COUNTRY.SYS
```

This loads the code-page support routines into memory. No direct action or messages will be shown on the screen.

Step 3: Loading Specific Code Pages

After preparing DOS for national language-support operations, you can select specific code pages to use. The primary command for this purpose is **MODE**. This command has several versions. You will need to enter two of these commands in sequence to use different code pages:

```
MODE DeviceName CODEPAGE PREPARE=Options
MODE DeviceName CODEPAGE SELECT=Options
```

DeviceName is any valid DOS-output reserved name, such as CON or LPT2. The *Options* for the PREPARE parameter tell DOS to install the code-page information necessary for the output drivers to handle the special international characters. With the *Options* for the SELECT parameter you then select the code page to be activated on the specified device.

PREPARE=

With the **PREPARE** parameter, you can load one or several code pages for the specified device. This requires that you specify the default and one or more allowable code pages and the file containing the output driver. Code page 437 is the default code page; although it is already automatically loaded into the device, you still must specify it as one of the code pages that may be invoked later, since it is possible to switch back and forth between or among all of them. The default is also the only code page that can access a nonspecified device (that is, one that Microsoft has not specifically written drivers for).

Think of it this way. A small buffer is set up for each device, and into this buffer you can enter a numeric list of code-page designations, one of which is active at a time. For example, entering

```
MODE CON CODEPAGE PREPARE=((850,437) C:\DOS\EGA.CPI)
```

will load the code-page information file EGA.CPI, specify that code pages 850 and 437 be selected for possible activation, and attach these code-page values to the EGA display.

TIP

In all of these versions of the MODE command, CODEPAGE can be contracted to CP. In addition, PREPARE can be abbreviated to PREP, SELECT to SEL, REFRESH to REF, and STATUS to STA. You can reduce your typing burden by using these abbreviations, as well as reduce the likelihood of errors. The full spelling is shown in this appendix for the sake of clarity only.

Suppose that later you decide that you want to replace 850 with 863, and that also you want to make code page 865 available. You would enter

```
MODE CON CODEPAGE PREPARE=((863,,865) C:\DOS\EGA.CPI)
```

The two commas hold the place of the second code page, thereby leaving 437 (the U.S. code page) as the second code page. If you had specified ((,850,437) instead, then the first code page would have been saved and the second and third written over and reset to 850 and 437.

If you execute this command and the requested device is unavailable (for instance, not hooked up), you will get the message:

```
Codepage operation not supported on this device
```

Assuming you really do have a device that supports code-page operations, check to see that it is connected properly to your system, that it is powered up.

WARNING

If the device driver for your output device is resident in hardware, don't use a PREPARE command for that device, since it will overwrite the hardware page. See your DOS user's manual for more detail on hardware code pages.

SELECT=

The **SELECT** parameter for the MODE command can only be used after you have properly prepared your code pages with PREPARE; or, in other words, the SELECT parameter will only work if the requested code-page device driver has been loaded. SELECT activates the specified code page on the specified device. For example, entering

```
MODE CON CODEPAGE SELECT=850
```

will make code page 850 the active code page for CON (the console or the display device). Using this command after the PREPARE version of the command in the example seen earlier would make 850 active for an EGA display.

Other Parameters for the MODE Command

Use the **/STATUS** parameter when you want to see information on the currently active code page, as well as a list of selectable code pages for a specific active device. All you need to enter is:

```
MODE DeviceName CODEPAGE /STATUS
```

DOS will then display information about the current code page assigned to the monitor and keyboard.

The last parameter, **REFRESH**, is very useful if for some reason you need to turn your printer off after setting it up for a specific code page or pages. The output device drivers stay resident inside the device they drive, but the available code pages and their related information are available through DOS, which is resident in your computer. So, when a device driver is installed, a copy is made of the code-page information in the computer and loaded into the memory of the device. If the device is turned off, then its memory is lost, and hence its modified driver. However, the original copy is still in the computer's memory. Instead of having to load the code page again with PREPARE, REFRESH just makes another copy and sends it out to the device's memory.

For example, suppose you've entered the following sequence of commands:

```
MODE LPT1 CODEPAGE PREPARE=((850,437) \DOS\4201.CPI)
MODE LPT1 CODEPAGE SELECT=850
```

This means you have installed code-page information for an IBM Proprinter model and that you have two code pages to choose from, with 850 the currently active code page. Selecting a code page (with SELECT) causes the code-page driver to be copied to the hardware device (in this case, the printer connected to LPT1). Now, if you decide to turn the Proprinter off and then back on (perhaps to reset some switches), it would lose its local memory copy of the code-page information. To reload the code-page driver without spending the system's time to retrieve it from the disk, you would issue the command

```
MODE LPT1 CODEPAGE REFRESH
```

Step 4: Loading a Keyboard Translation Table

If you have properly prepared your system to use national-language support with the NLSFUNC command, and you have also correctly installed the desired code-page information with MODE's PREPARE parameter and have selected a specific code page to use with MODE's SELECT parameter, the next step involves the **KEYB** command. This command is used to load in a new keyboard translation table for a specific country. In fact, it loads in a complete replacement for the keyboard driver resident in your computer's hardware (ROM BIOS). You can now select from the different country codes you saw in Table D.1.

The Multilingual code page (850) can support the primary character symbols used by all countries. If you switch between documents from different countries, it would be a good idea to load code page 850 in addition to your native code page so that you can view these other documents.

The general format for the **KEYB** command is

```
KEYB KeyCode, CodePage, FileSpec /ID:zzz
```

where *KeyCode* is one of the two-letter country codes in Table D.1, *CodePage* is one of the five three-digit code-page numbers, *FileSpec* is the full path name to the keyboard definition file KEYBOARD.SYS, and the optional **/ID** switch is used to specify the keyboard layout when there is more than one available. Most countries use only one standard keyboard, which you identify with your *KeyCode* entry. However, for countries that use more than one keyboard layout, you add the /ID switch to the KEYB command; the *zzz* parameter specifies which layout to use. For example, France can use 120 or 189, Italy can use 141 or 142, and the United Kingdom can use 166 or 168.

You can create a KEYB command for the Netherlands, a country that uses just one keyboard layout, with the following command:

```
KEYB NL, 850, \DOS\KEYBOARD.SYS
```

There is no need for the /ID switch, since there is only one keyboard available for the Netherlands. This will load the Netherlands keyboard translation table, based on code page 850, which is contained in the

KEYBOARD.SYS file. Located in the DOS directory, KEYBOARD.SYS contains all of the keyboard translation tables available for DOS setup.

Once you complete this initialization, the keys on the keyboard will no longer necessarily result in the letter, number, or character shown on the key. The assumption is that you will be using one of the scores of different keyboard layouts, each with its own key labels. In fact, if you're taking advantage of the keyboard reconfiguration capability but you are still using your original keyboard, it's a good idea to get new key labels, to switch the key labels around, or simply to put new labels on the keys that have been changed.

There are often more accented characters than there are possible keys to assign. In this case, DOS understands special two-key sequences to represent the specially accented character. For instance, certain foreign letters require a circumflex over them. On the French keyboard, this symbol looks like the ^, or "hat," symbol located over the 6 on the top row of a U.S. keyboard. In order to create this particular language-dependent effect, you must press the lowercase key just to the right of the letter *p* on the French keyboard and *then* press the letter you want to put the circumflex over. In other words, you must employ a two-keystroke sequence to generate the two-part character symbol (the circumflex and the letter).

The special keys that initiate a two-part character sequence are referred to as *dead keys* in DOS. If you make a mistake in typing the sequence, DOS will usually beep at you, show the erroneous result, and require you to erase the error and reenter the proper dead-key sequence. In this way, DOS provides yet another time-saving capability with the KEYB command, which saves you from having to touch up your text results with added accents and other special marks after the fact.

You can have up to two keyboard translation tables in memory at one time, but one of these must always be the standard U.S. table. To switch between the U.S. and another translation table, use these key combinations:

- Ctrl+Alt+F1 for the standard U.S. translation table
- Ctrl+Alt+F2 for a non-U.S. translation table

Step 5: Finally—Switching to a Different Code Page

Now that your system is prepared for code pages and you've selected one to be active for specified devices, you can finally switch to a different code page. The **CHCP** command allows you to change the currently loaded code page. It is a very simple command to use. For example, the command

```
CHCP 850
```

replaces the currently active code page with code page 850. Any of the other five possible code-page numbers can be used if they have been properly prepared with the MODE command first.

The CHCP command does not have a parameter indicating which output device is being selected. That's because CHCP works on all prepared output devices, changing the active code page on all of them to the requested number.

> **TIP**
>
> If you only want to change the code page on a particular device, use the MODE command with SELECT. Only use the CHCP command to change all prepared code-page devices at once.

Assigning Foreign Characters on a U.S. Keyboard

Now you understand how to load various code pages into your system and how to access characters via their table value (000 to 256 decimal).

I'll now show you another important technique. Often, you will have one code page loaded and a specified keyboard that does not have keys assigned for all possible characters. You can assign to the unused keys any foreign or graphic characters and incorporate them into your work without changing your code page each time.

To do this, you only need to run the **PROMPT** command (discussed in Chapter 9) one or more times to redefine the keys to your needs. For instance, suppose that you are writing a French manuscript about the British economy, and your analysis requires some mathematical equations with Greek symbols. You may want to use Alt+F8 to represent the French letter *e* with an accent grave (è), Alt+F9 to represent the Greek Sigma (Σ), and Alt+F10 to represent the British pound sign (£). By using the function-key redefinition codes in Table D.3, you can make all three key assignments with the following PROMPT command:

```
PROMPT $e[0;111;"'le"p$e[0;112;"&S"p$e[0;113;"£"p
```

TABLE D.3: Function-key redefinition codes

FUNCTION KEY AND CODE	WITH SHIFT	WITH CTRL	WITH ALT
F1: 59	Shift+F1: 84	Ctrl+F1: 94	Alt+F1: 104
F2: 60	Shift+F2: 85	Ctrl+F2: 95	Alt+F2: 105
F3: 61	Shift+F3: 86	Ctrl+F3: 96	Alt+F3: 106
F4: 62	Shift+F4: 87	Ctrl+F4: 97	Alt+F4: 107
F5: 63	Shift+F5: 88	Ctrl+F5: 98	Alt+F5: 108
F6: 64	Shift+F6: 89	Ctrl+F6: 99	Alt+F6: 109
F7: 65	Shift+F7: 90	Ctrl+F7: 100	Alt+F7: 110
F8: 66	Shift+F8: 91	Ctrl+F8: 101	Alt+F8: 111
F9: 67	Shift+F9: 92	Ctrl+F9: 102	Alt+F9: 112
F10: 68	Shift+F10: 93	Ctrl+F10: 103	Alt+F10: 113
F11: 133	Shift+F11: 135	Ctrl+F11: 137	Alt+F11: 139
F12: 134	Shift+F12: 136	Ctrl+F12: 138	Alt+F12: 140

As you learned Chapter 9, the $e[0; tells DOS that an extended key redefinition follows. The 111, 112, and 113 codes stand for the Alt versions of function keys F8, F9, and F10. Following each of the three-digit codes are quotation marks, which enclose the character to be assigned. You create each of these characters by holding the Alt key down on your keyboard and typing the decimal equivalent of the key's ASCII code on the numeric keypad.

In other words, the è is created by holding down the Alt key, pressing 138 on the numeric keypad, and then releasing the Alt key. Continue typing the PROMPT statement. When you reach the character inside the second pair of quotation marks, use the combination Alt+228 for the Σ symbol. Lastly, press Alt+156 to obtain the £ sign inside the third pair of quotation marks. Make sure you type the entire PROMPT command carefully, noting especially the semicolons and the lowercase *p*, which are critical separators in this single PROMPT statement.

Preparing a DOS System Disk for International Use

If you expect to work regularly with code-page switching, you should prepare your hard disk or a system diskette in such a way that international operations are automatically supported. With the following methods and commands, the delimiter format and keyboard information for each country can be installed permanently on a disk.

You can prepare the CONFIG.SYS and AUTOEXEC.BAT files with appropriate statements that will automate your international setup. You've already studied what's needed for your CONFIG.SYS file (earlier in this appendix). The changes needed for the AUTOEXEC.BAT file are outlined below.

Commands can be added to the AUTOEXEC.BAT file in the same way as they are for the CONFIG.SYS file. Including the **KEYB** command in the AUTOEXEC.BAT file lets the keyboard translation table and country codes be loaded automatically. For example, adding the following line to your AUTOEXEC.BAT file:

```
KEYB FR 033
```

will automatically load the keyboard and country information for France.

You can also include versions of the **NLSFUNC, MODE,** and **CHCP** commands to work in conjunction with the CONFIG.SYS statements. As an example, the following lines included in your AUTOEXEC.BAT file would initialize national-language support operations, prepare code pages 863, 437, and 850, load the keyboard information file for France, and then select 850 as the active code page for both output devices:

```
NLSFUNC
MODE CON: CP PREPARE=((863,437,850) \DOS\EGA.CPI)
MODE CON: CP PREPARE=((863,437,850) \DOS\4201.CPI)
KEYB FR 033
CHCP 850
```

APPENDIX

E

Glossary

THIS glossary defines all of the important Windows and DOS-related terms used in this book, as well as many more that are relevant to the latest developments in personal computing. Although many of these terms are defined in the text when they are first introduced, this glossary offers concise definitions that will refresh your memory when you read a chapter later in the book, or when you simply can't remember the meaning of a particular term.

386 Expanded Memory Manager *See* EMM386.EXE.

386 Enhanced mode The most advanced of Windows' operating modes. In this mode, Windows accesses the protected mode of the CPU chip for extended memory management and multitasking of both Windows and non-Windows applications.

8514 Refers to the 1987 high-resolution video standard introduced by IBM. It provides for the 8514 graphics coprocessor, and offers both 640x480 VGA resolution with 256 colors and interlaced 1024x768 resolution with either 16 or 256 colors.

accelerator key *See* shortcut key.

action bar A line at the top of a menu screen that contains the primary actions you can take.

activate To switch to a particular task.

active partition The section of a hard disk containing the operating system to be used when the hardware powers up.

active printer The hardware printer currently selected and connected to an output port.

Active Task List The area of the DOS shell screen that displays a list of suspended applications and facilitates switching and termination. *See also* Task List.

adapter segment *See* reserved memory.

alert message A dialog box that displays a critical situation message, such as a deletion confirmation or error situation. Also called alert box.

allocation The assignment of memory locations during the creation of graphical objects.

allocation unit *See* cluster.

ANSI character set The 256 characters defined by 8-bit codes by the American National Standards Institute. *See also* ASCII.

ANSI driver A device driver, contained in the ANSI.SYS file, that loads additional support for advanced console features.

API *See* Application Programming Interface.

applets A diminutive or affectionate term that is used to describe the collection of small, special-purpose utility programs included with Windows.

application *See* application program.

application program A program that performs a specific task or group of tasks for the user, such as checkbook management, word-processing, or inventory management programs.

Application Programming Interface (API) (Windows) The set of all operating-system service calls.

application shortcut key A key combination that performs a more complex preassigned series of keystrokes.

archive To store one or more files on backup media.

archive attribute A bit in a file specification used to indicate whether the file in question needs to be backed up. The bit is set to *ON* when the file is created or modified.

arrange *See* tile.

arrow keys The four directional keys that control cursor movement.

ASCII American Standard Code for Information Interchange; the coding scheme whereby every character the computer can access is assigned an integer code between 0 and 255.

assembly language A symbolic form of computer language used to program computers at a fundamental level.

associate (Windows) To connect all data file names having a particular extension to a specified application program.

asynchronous communications *See* serial communications.

attribute A characteristic (or *property*) of a disk file. *See* archive attribute, read/write attribute, hidden attribute, system attribute.

audible prompt (Windows) A program option that controls whether or not an audio sound accompanies a message box.

auto-answer mode A modem setup characteristic in which the modem will automatically answer an incoming phone call.

AUTOEXEC.BAT A batch file executed automatically whenever the computer is booted up.

backfill To disable some conventional memory and replace it with memory from an EMS board.

background (Windows) All the screen area behind the active window. Also, refers to all processing that occurs other than for the foreground task in Windows.

background application (task) (Windows) Any program that has been started but is currently not the foreground task.

backup cycle The time period that includes the creation of a full backup and all subsequent partial backups that use the same setup file.

backup media The group of diskettes, tape, or disk cartridges that contain your backed-up data.

backup catalog The file that contains an index of all files and directories that were backed up, as well as miscellaneous information about the backup itself.

bank switching A method of providing expanded memory by switching blocks (called *banks*) of memory into and out of the addressable range under one megabyte.

base name The portion of a file name to the left of the period or dot separator; it can be up to eight characters long.

batch program (or batch file) An ASCII file containing a sequence of DOS commands that will execute the commands when you invoke it.

baud rate The speed of data transmission, usually in bits per second.

BBS Bulletin Board System. An information system which offers file access and conference services. It is accessible from your computer via a modem using communications software.

binary A numbering system that uses powers of the number 2 to generate all other numbers.

binary file Any file that is not comprised solely of ASCII characters.

binary transfer A method for sending data files between computers. It transmits all data bits without processing any of the data as possible control characters.

bit One eighth of a byte. A bit is a binary digit, either 0 or 1.

bitmap A graphic file containing bitmapped information.

bit mapping Using storage bits to represent the color, location, and intensity of portions of graphic images.

bitmapped font Any character font which is fixed in size, device-specific, and stored as a group of bit values (i.e., a *bitmap*).

bits per second (BPS) The actual speed of data transmission over a communications port.

booting up *See* bootstrapping.

boot menu A menu of configuration choices that appears at power-up time, controlled by special subcommands available only within the CONFIG.SYS file.

boot record The section on a disk that contains the minimum information DOS needs to start the system.

bootstrapping When the computer initially is turned on or is rebooted from the keyboard with Ctrl+Alt+Del, it loads enough of its operating system into memory to get started; it "pulls itself up by its bootstraps." *See also* warm booting, cold booting.

border A side of a window or of the screen image.

branch A subportion of a directory tree.

branching The transfer of control or execution to another statement in a batch file. *See also* decision making.

break key The Ctrl-key combination that interrupts an executing program or command; you activate it by pressing the Break key while holding down the Ctrl key.

browse To explore the contents of files, or to list the files and subdirectories contained within a directory.

buffer An area in memory set aside to speed up the transfer of data, allowing blocks of data to be transferred at one time.

built-in font A font that is contained within the read-only memory of a printer. Sometimes called a hardware or resident font.

bulletin board *See* BBS.

bus The circuit wires or lines used for transferring data between various components of a command system.

byte The main unit of memory in a computer. A byte is an eight-bit binary-digit number. One character usually takes up one byte.

cache *See* disk cache, memory cache.

cartridge font A font that is included within a cartridge that slides into a printer slot. It has the advantages of a hardware font, but is not usually included with the original printer.

cascade An arrangement in Windows that displays each window overlapping the preceding window, but with the title bar always visible for each window.

cascading menu Any menu that appears after making a selection on another menu. Also known as a submenu.

case sensitivity Distinguishing between capital letters and lowercase letters.

CBT Computer-Based Training. Any instructional materials that use computer technology for presentation and interaction.

CD-I Compact Disk Interactive. A set of standards for merging data of various sorts (text, graphics, audio, video) on a single compact disk.

CD-ROM Compact Disk Read-Only Memory. A storage device that records data for retrieval by means of a laser rather than magnetically.

CD-ROM XA Compact Disk Read-Only-Memory Extended Architecture. An extension to the standard CD ROM format that specifies how to merge (*interleave*) audio with other data.

chaining Passing the control of execution from one batch file to another. This represents an unconditional transfer of control.

character set A complete group of 256 characters that can be used by programs or system devices. It consists of letters, numbers, control codes, and special graphics or international symbols. *See also* code page.

checkbox A square box that appears in dialog boxes. When selected, an X appears to indicate that the indicated option has been turned on or set.

clear To remove the X from a checkbox (a toggle option). To do this, move the mouse pointer over an existing X and click once. Alternatively, press Tab to select the option, then press the spacebar.

click To press and immediately release a mouse button.

client The computer (often a laptop) that redirects drive identifiers using the INTERLNK.EXE device driver to thereby gain access to the files on physical drives located on a separate (i.e., server) computer. The two computers must be connected by a compatible cable between like parallel or serial ports.

Clipboard The name given to the memory area assigned to temporary storage duties for information transfer between applications.

close (Windows) To terminate an application and remove its window from the screen.

cluster A group of contiguous sectors on a disk. Also known as an allocation unit, this is the smallest unit of disk storage that DOS can manipulate.

code page A character set that redefines the country and keyboard information for non-U.S. keyboards and systems.

cold booting Booting up DOS by turning the computer's power on. *See* bootstrapping.

collapse To remove from view, in the DOS Shell directory tree display, all subdirectory names below the currently highlighted one. When subdirectory structure is hidden in this way, a plus (+) sign appears in the icon just to the left of a directory name to indicate that there are more dirctories contained within.

COM port Shorthand phraseology for a communications, or serial, port. Windows and DOS support four serial ports, named COM1, COM2, COM3, and COM4.

COMMAND.COM The command processor that interprets your internal and external command requests.

command button A visual button that contains a selectable choice. Dialog boxes usually display several such buttons.

command line The line on which a command is entered. This line contains the command and all of its associated parameters and switches. It may run to more than one screen line, but it is still one command line.

command processor The program that translates commands and acts on them.

command prompt A visual indicator that DOS is waiting for input from you.

communications setting A value that represents one aspect of serial device configuration (i.e., for modems or serial printers).

composite video A video signal that contains all necessary color and timing information in a single input line.

compressed volume file (CVF) A hidden file that contains all the file and directory information from a disk drive that has been compressed with the DBLSPACE utility.

compressed print Printing that allows more than 80 characters on a line of output (usually 132 characters, but on newer printers up to 255 characters per line). To accomplish this, Windows uses a narrower-than-usual print font.

compression ratio A multiplicative factor that estimates how much file space can be squeezed onto a physical disk drive, using the compression technology of the DBLSPACE facility.

concatenation The placing of two text files together in a series.

conditional statement A statement in a batch file that controls the next step to be executed in the batch file, based on the value of a logical test.

CONFIG.SYS An ASCII text file containing system configuration commands.

configuration An initial set of system values, such as the number of buffers DOS will use, the number of simultaneously open files it will allow, and the specific devices that will be supported.

confirmation box A rectangular window that prompts you to confirm any request that may result in the loss of data. It helps to protect you from making irrevocable errors—for example, when deleting files.

console The combination of your system's monitor and keyboard.

context switching Making an inactive program into the active or foreground program.

contiguity The physical adjacency on a disk of the disk sectors used by a file.

control codes ASCII codes (from 0 to 31) that do not display a character but perform a function, such as beeping or deleting a character.

control focus *See* input focus.

conventional memory Physical memory located below the 640K addressing limit of DOS.

Copy To store a selected portion of the screen (i.e., text or graphics) in the Clipboard.

copy protection Special mechanisms contained in diskettes to inhibit the copying of them by conventional commands.

CPU Central Processing Unit. The main chip that executes all individual computer instructions.

critical message (Windows) A dialog box, which contains a red stop sign symbol, that appears when a severe error has occurred. The message announces the error and offers some advice on how to proceed.

crosshair pointer A screen positioning graphic, which consists of two crossing lines, that enables precise positioning during drawing applications.

Ctrl-Z The end-of-file marker, usually seen as ^Z in ASCII files.

current directory The directory in which file operations initiated from a command prompt or a Run line will be carried out unless another directory is specified.

cursor The blinking line or highlighting box that indicates where the next keystroke will be displayed or what the next control code entered will affect. *See also* selection cursor.

Cut To remove the selected portion of text or graphics from an application window, and store a copy of it in the Clipboard.

cutting and pasting Selecting a portion of one screen window and making a copy of it in another portion of the same window, or in a completely different document or application's window.

cylinder Two tracks that are in the same place on different sides of a double-sided disk. It may be extended to include multiple platters. For example, Side 0 Track 30, Side 1 Track 30, Side 2 Track 30, and Side 3 Track 30 form a cylinder.

CVF *See* Compressed Volume File.

DASD *See* Direct Access Storage Device.

data area Tracks on a disk that contain user information, as opposed to system information.

database A collection of data organized into various categories, such as can be found in an address or phone book.

database-management system A software program designed to allow the creation of specially organized files, as well as data entry, manipulation, removal, and reporting for those files.

data bits The bits that represent data when the computer is communicating.

data disk A disk that has been formatted without the /S or the /B switch. The disk can contain only data; no room has been reserved for system files.

data file A named storage area, used by applications to store a group of related information, such as a spreadsheet. Also called a *document*.

data stream The transmission of data between two components or computers.

dead key A reserved key combination on international keyboards, which outputs nothing by itself but forces the output device to produce an accent mark above or below the next keystroke's usual character.

debugging The process of discovering what is wrong with a program, where the problem is located, and what the solution is.

decimal A numbering system based on ten digits.

decision making A point in a batch file at which execution can continue on at least two different paths, depending on the results of a program test. It is also known as logical testing or branching.

defaults (or default settings) The assumed values, unless changed, of a variable or system parameter.

default button The command button in a dialog box that is selected when the dialog box first appears. To save time, this button may be selected by simply pressing the Enter key; it represents the most common and likely choice.

default printer (Windows) The active printer used by Windows applications when the Print command is selected.

deferred execution In a program or batch file, execution that is delayed until a value for some parameter is finally entered or computed.

deferred writes *See* staged writes.

defragmentation Rearranging the location of files stored on a disk into contiguous clusters in order to make the data in those files more quickly retrievable.

delimiter In data files, a special character, such as a comma or space, used to separate values or data entries.

delivery system The computer system used to play back a multimedia presentation.

demand loading Reading into memory a disk file when, and only when, the module is actually needed by the currently executing program.

desktop (Windows) The screen area which contains windows, icons, and dialog boxes.

desktop pattern (Windows) *See* wallpaper.

destination The targeted location for data, files, or other information generated or moved by a DOS command.

destination directory The intended directory location for files that are to be copied or moved.

destination document An OLE document that contains an iconic link to a data object in a source document.

device Any internal or external piece of peripheral hardware.

device contention (Windows) In 386 Enhanced Mode, when two or more devices attempt to use the same device.

device context (Windows) A special data structure used by application programs to connect the Windows API with a hardware-specific device driver.

device driver A special program that must be loaded at booting to use a device. Also known as an interrupt handler.

Device-Independent Bitmap (DIB) A monitor-independent format for graphic images.

device name Logical name that DOS uses to refer to a device.

dialog box A rectangular window that displays information and usually prompts you to make choices or to enter data.

DIB *See* Device-Independent Bitmap.

differential backup A type of backup that copies all files that have either been created or modified since the most recent full backup. The archive bit is not turned on. See *full backup* and *incremental backup*.

digital A representation based on a collection of individual digits, such as 0's and 1's in the binary number system.

dimmed Describes a menu option, or command button, that cannot be selected. It is either disabled or currently unavailable. Also referred to as *grayed*.

Direct-Access Storage Device (DASD) A disk drive.

Direct Memory Access (DMA) Very fast transfer of data between computer memory and a peripheral device (e.g., a disk drive) using a dedicated high-speed I/O channel.

direction keys The four arrow keys on a keyboard that control directional movement of the screen cursor.

directory A named group of files on disk. As part of DOS's file-management structure, this group may include other directories (i.e., subdirectories).

directory icon A mini icon that represents a disk directory.

directory path A combined sequence of directory names that locate a particular file on a disk. Also called a *full path* or a *pathname*.

directory tree A graphic depiction of the directories and subdirectories that represent the organization of files on a disk.

Directory Tree area In the DOS shell, the window that graphically depicts the subdirectories contained within the current (i.e., highlighted) directory.

disk cache A portion of memory reserved for the contents of disk sectors. It facilitates faster repeated access of the same sectors, as well as often enabling faster access of subsequently referenced sectors. It can be implemented with the SMARTDRV.EXE device-driver program.

disk drive A hardware device that accesses the data stored on a disk.

disk-drive icon A graphic icon that depicts a particular type of drive in the drives area of the DOS shell screen or the Windows File Manager. DOS uses different icons for floppy, hard, RAM, network, and CD ROM drives.

diskette A flexible, oxide-coated disk used to store data. It is also called a floppy diskette.

disk optimizer A program (such as DEFRAG.EXE in DOS 6) that rearranges the location of files stored on a disk in order to make the data in those files quickly retrievable. *See also* defragmentation.

disk-resident command *See* external command.

display adapter An add-in hardware board that sends video output signals to your monitor corresponding to the current contents of video memory.

display box A window that shows the current status of various selectable options.

dithering Generating a new (non-solid) color or gray scale by combining the dot patterns of available screen colors.

DLL *See* Dynamic Link Library.

DMA *See* Direct Memory Access.

document *See* data file.

document file Any document that is associated with an application program. Same as data file.

document file icon An icon that looks like a dog-eared piece of paper (one corner folded over) and appears beside a document filename in a files list.

DOS Disk Operating System. The main disk- and file-management software that facilitates computer/user interaction.

DOS environment A part of memory set aside to hold variables used by DOS and application programs, such as COMSPEC, PATH, and LASTDRIVE.

DOS memory Sometimes used to refer to the first 64K of conventional memory that is used by the typical DOS application.

DOS prompt *See* command prompt.

dot-matrix printer A printer that represents characters by means of tiny dots.

dot pitch The size in millimeters of each pixel on a video monitor. The smaller the dot pitch, the higher the allowable screen resolution and the clearer the colors.

double-click Pressing a mouse's button twice in rapid succession.

double-click speed The time frame within which two mouse button presses are registered as a double-click, as opposed to two successive single clicks.

double-density diskette A diskette on which magnetic storage material is arranged twice as densely as was true on the first available DOS diskettes, allowing the storage of twice the former amount of data.

downloadable font A printer font that can be copied from a disk file, or from system RAM, into a printer's memory. Also called a *soft font*.

draft quality An output technique that uses fewer pixels, dots, or display/printing features in order to improve output performance.

drag To move a screen item from one location to another by means of the mouse. Specifically, to first highlight an item with the mouse by pressing a mouse button, then moving the mouse to the new screen location without releasing the button.

DRAM Dynamic Random-Access Memory. Memory that will lose its contents when its power is interrupted.

drive icon An icon that represents an information-storage device (e.g., disk drives, RAM drives, and CD-ROM drives).

drive identifier A single letter assigned to represent a drive, such as drive A or drive B. It usually requires a colon after it, such as A:.

driver *See* device driver.

DRIVER.SYS A CONFIG.SYS device driver used to facilitate assigning logical-drive identifiers to extra physical-disk drives.

drop-down list box A dialog-box field that will display the choices available if you click on the arrow next to the field.

drop-down menu The menu that appears just below a menu name when you select that name on a window's menu bar. Same as pull-down menu.

Dynamic Link Library (DLL) A collection of executable procedures, grouped into one code file on disk, that can be shared at run time by multiple Windows applications. The procedures need not be separately linked into each application's .EXE file.

ECC *See* Error Correction Code.

echoing Displaying on your video monitor the keystrokes you type in.

EDIT DOS's primary full-screen text editor.

EISA Extended Industry Standard Architecture. An advanced 32-bit computer bus design that enables adapter memory addresses to be modified with simple configuration change requests, rather than by resetting switches on the adapter boards themselves.

EMM Expanded Memory Manager. A device driver that manages access to expanded memory, using either the physical characteristics of a particular memory board or the facilities of the 80386/80486 chip to emulate expanded memory.

EMM386.EXE A device driver for 80386 and 80486 computers that manages the allocation of upper memory blocks, as well as the emulation of expanded memory from available extended memory.

EMS memory Memory that conforms to the LIM (Lotus-Intel-Microsoft) Expanded Memory Specification (EMS) for addressing memory beyond the 1Mb maximum addressable DOS limit. LIM 4.0 is the current standard version, although LIM 3.2 (its predecessor) is still adhered to by many application programs and hardware boards.

emulation mode A machine state in which one device (usually a printer or terminal) mimics the electronic behavior of another device.

end-of-file marker A Ctrl-Z code that marks the logical end of a file. Usually seen as ^Z in ASCII files.

environment The settings DOS uses when it interfaces with you and with your commands.

environmental variable A symbolic name, such as PROMPT or PATH, that contains important system-wide textual data. Text values are assigned to these names with the SET command in DOS.

error correction code (ECC) A coding mechanism used by MSBACK-UP and MWBACKUP to write extra identifying data onto a backup diskette. The ECC can be used to help recover backup data if damage occurs to one or more of the diskettes in a backup set.

error level A code, set by programs as they conclude processing, that tells DOS whether an error occurred, and if so, the severity of that error.

executable file Any "runnable" application program with a file extension of .COM, .EXE, or .BAT. The term is sometimes extended to include files that don't run by themselves but do contain program code, such as .OVL and .PIF files.

expand To display subportions (hidden branches) of the Directory Tree.

expanded memory (EMS) Extra physical memory, generally found on separate, add-in boards, which is designed to conform to the industry standard LIM-EMS (Lotus-Intel-Microsoft Expanded Memory Specification). This memory is not directly addressable, and must be mapped into pages of conventional memory.

expanded memory emulation The simulation of expanded memory with extended memory, typically performed by a device driver.

expanded memory manager *See* EMM, EMM386.EXE.

expansion cards Add-on circuit boards through which hardware can increase the power of the system, such as adding extra memory or a modem.

expansion slots Connectors inside the computer in which expansion cards are placed so that they tie in directly to the system.

extended ASCII codes ASCII codes between 128 and 255, which usually differ from computer to computer.

extended DOS partition A hard-disk DOS partition, beyond the first hard disk drive C:, which can be divided into further logical disk drives (D:, E:, and so on).

extended memory Additional physical memory that offers general-purpose support beyond the DOS 1Mb addressing limit for 80286, 80386, and 80486 computers. It also enables Windows to support multiple, simultaneously initiated programs. This memory is directly accessible in protected mode, using 24-bit (on 80286 computers) or 32-bit (on 80386/80486 computers) linear addresses.

extended memory manager Any device driver (e.g., HIMEM.SYS) that manages and facilitates the use of extended physical memory.

Extended Memory Specification *See* XMS.

extended selection Multiple items selected for a subsequent action, such as moving more than one file at a time.

extension The one to three characters after the period following the base name in a file specification.

external buffer A device, connected between a computer and another device, that acts as a temporary holding area for data transmitted from the computer.

external command A DOS command whose procedures are stored in named disk files. When you run such a command, its associated instructions are read from the disk, then executed from memory. DOS includes the following external commands:

APPEND	DBLSPACE
ATTRIB	DEBUG
CHKDSK	DEFRAG
CHOICE	DELOLDOS
COMMAND	DELTREE

DISKCOMP	MSBACKUP
DISKCOPY	MSD
DOSHELP	MWAV
DOSKEY	MWAVTSR
DOSSHELL	MWBACKUP
EDIT	MWUNDEL
EMM386	NLSFUNC
EXPAND	POWER
FASTOPEN	PRINT
FC	QBASIC
FDISK	REPLACE
FIND	RESTORE
FORMAT	SETUP
GRAPHICS	SETVER
HELP	SHARE
INTERLNK	SIZER
INTERSVR	SMARTDRV
KEYB	SMARTMON
LABEL	SORT
LOADFIX	SUBST
MEM	SYS
MEMMAKER	TREE
MICRO	UNDELETE
MODE	UNFORMAT
MORE	VSAFE
MOVE	XCOPY
MSAV	

field A small box within a dialog box that allows text input from you for clarifying how to process a specified action. You may type parameters, switches, or actual commands, depending on the prompted request from the dialog box.

file A collection of bytes, representing a program or data, organized into records and stored as a named group on a disk.

file attribute One of several file status values that denote whether or not the file is read-only, system, hidden, or archived.

file allocation table (FAT) A table that records which clusters on a disk are being used, are empty, or are bad.

file extension *See* extension.

file filter A character pattern that is used to refine and restrict the selection of file names that will be acted upon by a program.

file fragmentation The storage of a file's clusters in noncontiguous disk locations.

File Manager The main Windows application program for managing files and disk structures.

file name The name of a file on the disk. File name usually refers to the base name only, but it can include the extension as well.

file version A term that refers to which developmental copy of a software program is being used or referenced.

filter A program that accepts data as input, processes it in some manner, and then outputs the data in a different form. *See also* file filter.

fixed disk IBM's name for a hard disk.

fixed-width font Any font whose characters are all the same horizontal width.

flicker A monitor image problem caused by insufficient video rewrite speed to create a steady image. Caused by either a slow refresh rate (i.e., the screen seems to blink) or by noticeable interlacing of the horizontal line output (i.e., one or more extraneous lines seem to move down the screen).

floppy diskette *See* diskette.

flow control The method used to control the starting and stopping of data transmission during serial communications. Sometimes called *handshaking*.

flow of control The order of execution of batch-file commands; how the control flows from one command to another, even when the next command to be executed is not located sequentially in the file.

font A graphic style applied consistently to all letters, numbers, and symbols in a character set.

font cartridge An electronic casing that plugs into a printer slot and which contains a set of hardware fonts in read-only memory.

font family A group of individual fonts, all of which display the same overall stylistic characteristics (e.g., all sans serif characters).

font set A group of fonts that have been selected for use with a particular application (i.e., a CAD program) or operating environment (i.e., Windows).

font size *See* point size.

footer Repeating text located at the bottom of document pages.

foreground application (or task) (Windows) The program running in the active (or foreground) window, as opposed to the less visible background tasks.

format The layout and appearance of an output document.

formatting The placement of timing marks on a disk to arrange the tracks and sectors for subsequent reading and writing.

fragmentation A condition in which many different files have been stored in noncontiguous sectors on a disk.

frame One complete video image.

full backup A type of backup that copies all files. The archive bit is turned off to indicate that the files have been backed up. See *differential backup* and *incremental backup*.

full path *See* directory path.

full-screen application (Windows) A non-Windows application that appears as it does under DOS alone. It uses the entire screen for its display, rather than appearing within a window.

function keys Special-purpose keys on a keyboard, which can be assigned unique tasks by DOS or by application programs. Also referred to as the F keys.

Generic printer A standard printer definition which uses no special characters or features.

GIF *See* Graphics Interchange Format.

gigabyte 1024 megabytes.

global characters *See* wild cards.

global memory RAM memory that Windows uses for information that may be accessed by all applications.

Graphics Interchange Format (GIF) CompuServe's compressed, device-independent, color image format. It supports color and gray-scale images and is used as a popular exchange mechanism by many electronic Bulletin Board users.

graphics coprocessor An additional processing chip, usually found on high-end video adapters, that takes over time-consuming graphics operations from the main CPU.

graphics mode The mode in which all screen pixels on a monitor are addressable and can be used to generate detailed images. Contrasts with text mode, which limits itself to a fixed number of rows and columns of textual characters.

graphics resolution The degree of detail (expressed as number of dots) used to display or print any image. Higher resolutions require special-purpose video or printer equipment, and invariably require more time to construct.

group In the DOS shell or Windows Program Manager, a named collection of application programs.

GUI Graphical User Interface.

handshake A communications signal used between two computers to regulate the coordinated sending and receiving of data. XON/XOFF is the most common of such software methods. Also called flow control.

hard disk A rigid platter that stores data faster and at a higher density than a floppy diskette. It is sealed in an airtight compartment to avoid contaminants that could damage or destroy the disk.

hardware The physical components of a computer system.

hardware interrupt A signal from a device to the computer, indicating that an event has taken place.

head A disk-drive mechanism that reads data from and writes data to the disk.

head crash Occurs when the head hits the disk platter on a hard disk, physically damaging the disk and the data on it.

header Repeating text located at the top of document pages.

header information The control information that is sent to a PostScript printer to prepare it for an application's printed output.

help Helpful textual information, obtained by selecting a choice from the Help menu or by pressing F1. Help text obtained by pressing the F1 key is context-dependent, relating directly to whatever item is currently highlighted.

help file A file of textual information containing helpful explanations of commands, modes, and other on-screen tutorial information. *See also* help.

hexadecimal A numbering system in base 16. A single eight-bit byte can be fully represented as two hexadecimal digits.

hidden attribute A bit in a file specification used to indicate whether the file in question is to be hidden from view and from all commands that search the DOS directory table.

hidden files Files whose names do not appear in a directory listing. This term usually refers to DOS's internal system files, disk-labeling file, deletion-tracking file, and partition-table image file. It can also refer to certain files used in copy-protection schemes.

high-bit characters All characters whose ASCII value exceeds 127 (i.e., the eighth, or *high*, bit is set on).

high-capacity diskette A 1.2Mb 5¼", 1.44Mb 3½", or 2.88Mb 3½" floppy diskette.

high DOS *See* reserved memory.

highlighting Displaying a portion of the screen in reverse video or in a combination of contrasting colors to indicate the item or screen area that has been selected for subsequent action.

high memory area (HMA) Refers to the first 64K of extended memory. Can be used by DOS to load internal tables and buffers, thereby freeing up additional conventional memory.

HMA *See* high memory area.

HIMEM.SYS The extended memory (XMS) memory manager used by both DOS and Windows.

horizontal frequency A measure of the time required to draw one horizontal line of pixels across the screen.

horizontal landscape When output to a printer is not done in the usual format, but rather with the wider part of the paper laid out horizontally, as in a landscape picture.

hotkey A key combination used to signal that a memory-resident program should begin operation.

housekeeping Making sure the directory stays intact and well organized, and that unnecessary files are deleted.

hub The center hole of a diskette. Also, the server in certain network or LAN situations.

IF A conditional statement in programming, such as in QBasic or in batch files.

inactive printer Any printer that is installed but not currently connected to a port.

inactive window Any on-screen window that is open but is not currently ready for input.

Industry Standard Architecture *See* ISA.

ink-jet printer A printer that forms characters by spraying ink in a dot pattern. *See also* dot-matrix printer.

increment box A text box or field that accepts numbers as input. Arrows usually appear beside the box to facilitate incrementation or decrementation by simply clicking on the appropriate arrow.

incremental backup A type of backup that copies all files that have either been created or modified since the most recent full or incremental backup. The archive bit is turned on to indicate that the files have been backed up. *See* full backup and differential backup.

input focus The portion of a graphic menu screen that the selection cursor is in. You can switch the input focus from one screen area to the next by pressing the Tab key or by using the mouse.

interface The boundary between two things, such as the computer and a peripheral. Also used to refer to the device used to pass communications between two parts of the computer system, and to the act of communicating with them.

interlacing A scheme whereby only half of the lines on a video screen are refreshed at a time.

interleaving The sequencing of sectors on the tracks of a hard disk. A 1:1 interleave means each successively numbered sector is physically located just after its predecessor. A 2:1 interleave means that each successively numbered sector is located one sector beyond the next physical sector.

internal command One of the following memory-resident commands that are part of the DOS COMMAND.COM file:

BREAK	LOADHIGH
CALL	MD
CD	MKDIR
CHCP	PATH
CHDIR	PAUSE
CLS	PROMPT
COPY	REM
CTTY	REN
DATE	RENAME
DEL	RMDIR
DIR	SET
ECHO	SHIFT
ERASE	TIME
EXIT	TYPE
FOR	VER
GOTO	VERIFY
IF	VOL
LH	

Interrupt A signal sent to the computer from a hardware device, indicating a request for service or support from the system.

I/O Address Memory location used for communicating information between a software program and a hardware device.

IRQ Interrupt Request Line. The hardware line which carries the interrupting signals (for sending or receiving data) from devices.

ISA Industry Standard Architecture. Refers to the most common hardware bus design used by the IBM AT and compatibles. It transfers 16 bits of data at a time, and requires you to flip DIP switches on plug-in boards to set or change adapter memory addresses.

ISO International Standards Organization, responsible for defining many computer-industry standards, such as the High Sierra (or ISO-9660) format for CD-ROM disks.

keyboard buffer A small area of memory that stores keystrokes until they can be processed by the active program.

keyboard translation table An internal table, contained in the keyboard driver, that converts hardware signals from the keyboard into the correct ASCII codes.

key combination When two or more keys are pressed simultaneously, as in Ctrl+ScrollLock or Ctrl+Alt+Del.

key redefinition Assigning a nonstandard value to a key.

key repeat rate The speed at which a character will redisplay if you keep the key depressed.

kilobyte 1024 bytes.

landscape mode A printer mode in which characters are printed horizontally along the length of the page. *See* portrait mode.

large page frame A misnomer that refers to the existence of bankable memory pages in conventional memory. This facilitates access to extra physical expanded-memory pages beyond the 64K limit provided by the standard page frame, which must always be located in reserved memory (between 640K and 1Mb).

laser printer A printer that produces images (pictures or text) by shining a laser on a photostatic drum, which picks up toner and then transfers the image to paper.

LCD Liquid Crystal Display. A method of producing an image using electrically sensitive crystals suspended in a liquid medium.

Least Recently Used (LRU) The algorithm used by Windows in 386 Enhanced Mode to decide which pages of physical memory are copied out to a swap file to make room for new pages associated with the currently running application.

LIM EMS The Lotus-Intel-Microsoft specification for accessing and managing expanded memory.

LIM 3.2 Version 3.2 of the LIM EMS specifications, which provides for a maximum expanded memory window of 64K (four contiguous 16K pages).

LIM 4.0 Version 4.0 of the LIM EMS specifications, which provides for a maximum expanded memory window of 1Mb (sixty-four 16K pages).

line feed A command to move the cursor on a screen to the next line, or to move the print head on a printer down the paper to the next line.

Line Wrap A display enhancement feature of the Windows Terminal accessory application that splits long lines into two or more lines on the screen.

list box A child window within a dialog box that displays a list of available choices.

literal Something that is accepted exactly as it was submitted.

local printer A printer that is connected to a port on your computer system, as contrasted to a network printer, which may be connected to a port on another computer in the network.

lockup The state in which the computer will not accept any input and may have stopped processing. It must be warm or cold booted to resume operating.

log file A separate file, created with the BACKUP command, that keeps track of the names of all files written to the backup diskette(s).

logging on Signing on to a remote system, such as a mainframe or telecommunications service.

logical Relating to something that is defined by decision, not necessarily by physical properties.

logical drives Disk drives, created in an extended DOS partition, that do not physically exist, but DOS thinks they do.

logical testing *See* decision making.

look-ahead buffers 512-byte memory buffers used by DOS or a caching program to read successively positioned disk sectors before those sectors are actually referenced by a program or command, thereby improving performance.

low DOS *See* conventional memory.

LPT port A parallel communications port. Windows supports up to three such ports, which are named LPT1, LPT2, and LPT3.

LRU *See* Least Recently Used.

luminosity The degree of brightness of a color, ranging from a minimum luminosity (i.e., black) to a maximum luminosity (i.e., white).

machine language The most fundamental way to program a computer, using instructions made up entirely of strings of 0's and 1's.

macro A set of memory-resident commands or actions that can be named and executed as a group, similar to the disk-resident mechanism known as batch files. The DOSKEY utility provides this service under DOS.

mark To select a portion of the screen in a DOS application running under Windows by using the Edit/Mark choice from the control menu. You select a screen area by moving the direction keys while keeping the Shift key depressed.

master catalog The one catalog that includes the names of all backup set catalogs used during a single backup cycle. There is always one master catalog (with .CAT extension) per setup file; the master catalog takes the same base name as the setup file in effect during the backup cycle.

maximize To increase a window to its largest size.

Maximize button The up-arrow symbol located at the right of the title bar in Windows. Clicking on this button expands the window to its largest possible screen size.

Media Control Interface (MCI) A specification for controlling multi-media devices and files. Windows includes drivers for MIDI devices and outputting sound (.WAV) files.

media file A disk file that contains multimedia instructions for creating sound, animation, or video output.

medium-resolution mode The mode on a Color Graphics Adapter in which only 320 x 200 pixels of resolution are allowed.

megabyte 1024 kilobytes.

memory The circuitry in a computer that stores information. *See also* RAM and ROM.

memory cache Data stored in a very fast type of memory (usually Static-Column RAM chips) that provides faster access to standard memory (usually Dynamic-RAM) locations.

memory-resident Located in physical memory, as opposed to being stored in a disk file. *See also* TSR.

menu A set of command choices displayed in tabular format.

menu bar The horizontal line, located just below the title bar, which contains the names of an application program's individual menus.

menu command A selectable word or phrase that appears on an application-program menu.

message passing The non-preemptive, cooperative, method of multitasking used in Windows.

meta symbols Special single-character codes used by the PROMPT command to represent complex actions or sequences to be included in the DOS prompt.

microfloppy diskette The $3^1/2"$ diskette format.

MIDI Musical Instrument Digital Interface. The specifications for communicating between computers and musical instruments.

MIDI file A file that contains the necessary instructions for outputting sounds on a MIDI device.

MIDI sequencer An application (such as the Windows Media Player accessory program) that plays music stored as MIDI files.

minimize To decrease the size of a window to a representative icon.

Minimize button The down-arrow symbol located at the right of the title bar in Windows. Clicking on this button removes the window from the screen, replacing it with a representative icon at the bottom of the screen.

MIPS Millions of Instructions Per Second. A comparative measure of a computer's speed.

modem A device that transmits digital data in tones over a phone line.

monitor The device used to display images; a display screen.

monochrome Using two colors only—the background and foreground.

monospaced font *See* fixed-width font.

mouse A device that moves the screen cursor in imitation of the movement of the device itself.

mouse pointer The screen symbol representing the symbolic location of the mouse. When in graphic mode, the mouse pointer is generally an arrow. When in text mode, it appears as a solid movable rectangle.

move pointer The graphic symbol that appears when you are moving a window on the screen. It consists of a cross hair with arrows pointing in all four directions.

MPC *See* Multimedia PC.

multimedia Any applications that employ sound, graphics, or video in combination with text information.

Multimedia PC (MPC) A personal computer that contains the necessary hardware and software to run CD-ROM–based multimedia applications.

Multiple Document Interface (MDI) A set of specifications that define how an application is to manage multiple child windows within the visual client area of a single Windows application.

multiprocessing *See* multitasking.

multitasking The execution of two or more computing applications simultaneously.

Musical Instrument Digital Interface *See* MIDI.

National Television Systems Committee (NTSC) The industry organization that produced the standards for color television displays in the United States. The U.S. standard consists of 525 horizontal lines per frame, displayed at a rate of 30 frames per second, using interlaced scan techniques.

national-language support operations The feature that supports video monitors and printers, for use with international language symbols and characters.

network Several computers, connected together, combined with specially designed software that facilitates sharing of common data files and peripheral devices.

network device Any shared device (e.g., large disk drive, laser printer, plotter, CD-ROM), located on a network and whose contents are available to any users logged-on to the network computers.

nibble Four bits, or half a byte.

noninterlaced mode A video display pattern in which an entire screen is drawn in one pass, drawing all horizontal screen lines in order from top to bottom.

non solid color A simulated color that is constructed of a pattern of colored pixels.

non-Windows application Any application that was not designed to use the windowing features or internal facilities of Windows. Typically, this refers to older DOS applications that may or may not have a Windows version available.

null-modem cable A serial cable with pins 2 and 3 reversed to enable two computers to communicate directly.

Object Linking and Embedding *See* OLE.

octal A numbering system in base 8.

OEM Original Equipment Manufacturer.

OLE (Windows) Object Linking and Embedding. A windows mechanism for transferring and sharing data among applications.

online help *See* help.

open 1) To run a highlighted program or 2) To run an executable program that has been previously associated with the extension of a file name that has been highlighted.

operating system *See* DOS or OS/2.

option Any selection alternative presented within a dialog box.

option button *See* radio button.

OS/2 IBM's Operating System/2. An advanced 32-bit multitasking, multithreading operating system.

overlay area A portion of memory reserved for storage and execution of overlay-file instructions.

overlay files Files containing additional command and control information for sophisticated and complex programs. An overlay file is usually too large to fit into memory along with the main .EXE or .COM file.

overlay manager Instruction code, usually built into a programming language, that controls the creation and subsequent loading (during execution) of independent and mutually exclusive code segments. This capability allows older DOS programs, which are constrained by a 640K address maximum, to include and execute more instructions than could fit at one time into the limited address space of conventional memory.

overwriting Typing or saving new data over what is already there.

page frame The reserved memory area (limited to 64K in upper reserved blocks) used for access to expanded memory pages.

paging A feature of 80386 (and successor) processors that organizes all possible memory into 4K blocks. Each block is assigned a table-resident base address (which effectively maps the virtual address location into available memory addresses) and an access status (e.g., paged to disk).

palette The set of colors offered by Windows for its desktop, or by an application program (like Paintbrush) for its own display.

parallel communications Data transmission in which several bits can be transferred or processed at one time. Also called parallel interface.

parallel port Any one of three computer connections (named LPT1, LPT2, or LPT3) used for parallel communications.

parameter An extra item of information, specified with a command, that determines how the command executes.

parameter passing Using variable parameters (%0 to %9) to pass startup information to a program.

parity bit The bit, added to the end of a sequence of data bits, and used to improve error checking, that makes the total of the data bits and the parity bit odd or even.

partition The section of a hard disk that contains an operating system.

password A sequence of characters that allows entry into a restricted system or program.

paste To copy the contents of the Clipboard into the insertion point of the current application.

path The list of disks and directories that DOS will search through to find a command file ending in .COM, .BAT, or .EXE.

pathname *See* directory path.

pels A synonym for pixels. Originally, *pel* was an abbreviated form of *picture element*.

peripheral Any physical device connected to the computer.

permanent swap file (Windows) A fixed, hidden swap file. It is created for the purpose of affording Windows an opportunity of writing directly to the known disk location, thereby enhancing performance as compared to writing to the disk file with conventional DOS file calls.

Pica A fixed-width font that outputs ten characters to the inch.

PIF (Program Information File) A file of specifications that define how a DOS application is to run from within Windows.

PIF Editor The Windows application, found in the Main group of the Windows' Program Manager, that enables you to create and modify the specifications (in a PIF file) for running DOS applications.

piping Redirecting the input or output of one program or command to another program or command by means of the ¦ symbol.

pixel The smallest unit of display on a video monitor—in short, a dot—which can be illuminated to create text or graphics images.

pixel depth The number of video-memory bits required to specify a pixel's color. Four bits are required for 16 ($2^4 = 16$) colors, eight bits are required for 256 ($2^8 = 256$) colors, and so on.

platter The rigid disk used in a hard-disk drive.

plotter A device that draws data on paper with a mechanical arm.

plotter font A font generated by scalable lines, or dots which make up lines. Also called a *vector font*.

point To use a mouse (or equivalent device) to move the screen pointer.

pointer The on-screen graphic representation of your mouse's location and status. Generally, the pointer is an arrow, although it changes appearance according to the task that an application (or Windows) is performing.

point size The number of points (one point equals $\frac{1}{72}$") used as the vertical height of the characters in a selected font.

pop-up program A memory-resident program that can be activated (i.e., popped up) while another application is running, by pressing a predefined hotkey.

port A computer connection for transferring data to and from external devices.

portrait mode A printer mode in which characters are printed horizontally along the width of the page. *See also* landscape mode.

primary DOS partition The first, logically named disk portion of a hard disk. Contains the boot record and other DOS information files.

primary mouse button The button (by default, the left one) on your mouse with which you make selections and control clicking.

printer driver The software program that manages the control interface between your computer and a particular printer.

printer fonts All fonts that are currently available (i.e., downloaded soft fonts or existing hard fonts) in your printer.

Print Manager The Windows application program that manages spooled output to your printer for all Windows applications.

print queue The list of file names that are to be printed by a particular printer.

priority (Windows) Refers to the relative proportion of time (from all possible processor time) that is to be allocated to an application.

process *See* task.

processor time (Windows) The overall CPU time available to divide up among applications. *See* priority and timeslice.

program file An .EXE, .COM, .BAT, or .PIF file that can run an application program.

program group A window containing a list of selectable programs.

Program Information File *See* PIF.

program item icon A graphic symbol that represents a "runnable" and selectable application program.

Program Manager The primary Windows shell program that manages program execution and application switching.

program startup command (PSC) Any DOS command (except GOTO) that is included in the Commands field of DOS's Add or Change Program dialog boxes. It may also include an option string enclosed in brackets.

proof quality The highest, most detailed, output resolution available for a particular printer.

proportional font Any font whose characters are defined to have variable widths for printing and display.

protected mode The principal operating mode of an Intel 80286, 80386, or 80486 chip that supports multitasking, process protection, and advanced memory management.

protocol A collection of conventions that govern the transfer of data between one computer and another.

public-domain Something not copyrighted or patented. Public-domain software can be used and copied without infringing on anyone's rights.

pull-down menu *See* menu.

pushbutton A symbolic button-shaped indicator seen in windows that can be selected by a mouse. Selecting it specifies the next operation to be performed.

QBasic A complete programming environment (including editor, programming language interpreter, tester, and debugger) for writing business or scientific application programs. It is included as a part of DOS.

queue A series of files waiting in line to be processed. *See also* print queue.

quick format A disk format that simply erases an existing File Allocation Table and root directory, but does not check for bad clusters. It saves time, but is not as safe.

radio button A small circle that appears beside each of several mutually exclusive options. (Borrowed from car radios: only one station can be selected at a time.) Also known as an option button.

RAM Random-Access Memory. The part of the computer's memory to which you have access; it stores programs and data while the computer is on.

RAM disk An area of RAM that acts as if it were a disk drive. All data in this area of memory is lost when the computer is turned off or warm booted. It is also known as a virtual disk.

RAMDRIVE.SYS Microsoft's device driver that emulates a physical disk drive in memory locations (i.e., a RAM disk).

range A contiguous series of values (minimum to maximum, first to last, and so on).

raster font A single-size character font created from a fixed pattern of dots.

read-after-write verification An extra level of validity checking, it is invoked with the VERIFY command or the /V switch. It rereads data after writing it to disk, comparing the written data to the original information.

read-only attribute A file with this attribute set *on* cannot be updated or deleted, but can still be read.

read/write attribute The bit in a file specification that indicates whether a file can accept changes or deletions, or can only be accessed for reading.

redirection Causing output from one program or device to be routed to another program or device.

reduce *See* minimize.

refresh rate *See* vertical frequency.

REM statement A line of text in a QBasic program, a CONFIG.SYS file, or a batch file, which contains only remarks or comments for program explanation or clarification.

reserved names Specific words, in a programming language or operating system, which should not be used in any other application context.

reserved memory System memory (between 640K and 1Mb) normally used only for video buffers. DOS can use it (with appropriate system configuration) for device drivers, memory-resident programs (TSRs), and ordinary application programs.

resident command *See* internal command.

resolution The density of dots per inch of a printer or video monitor.

resource allocation Making system facilities available to individual users or programs.

restore To return a window to its previous size.

RGB A video signal that consists of three separate signals to denote the red, green, and blue portions of the image.

ROM Read-Only Memory. The section of memory that you can only read from. This contains a small portion of the basic computer operating system, as well as certain hardware-support routines.

root directory The first directory on any disk.

RS232 communications *See* serial communications.

SAA *See* Systems Application Architecture.

sans serif font Any font whose characters are made of constant width lines, without fancy "feet" or "curls."

saturation A characteristic of a screen color expressing the purity of the color. It signifies how much of the actual color is used in the mix of pixels used, and how much gray is blended in.

scalable font *See* vector font. Also called a *scalable typeface*.

scaled point size An enlarged or contracted character size that is derived from an original, yet different, size.

scaling Enlarging or reducing a graphic image.

scan code The hardware code representing a key pressed on a keyboard. Converted by a keyboard driver into an ASCII code for use by DOS and application programs.

screen font A font designed for appearance around the precise resolution of a particular video mode.

screen capture To store a copy of the current screen image or active window image in the Clipboard or in a disk file.

screen font A character font designed for most effective and attractive screen display.

screen saver A variable pattern of colors or patterns that appears on your screen after a certain amount of time in which no keystrokes or mouse movements have been detected. There are also versions known as screen blankers.

scroll The act of rolling additional lines of text (or portions of a graphic image) onto the screen, while rolling data from the other side of the screen out of view.

scroll arrow An arrow at either end of a scroll bar that enables you to move the workspace contents by one line or one screen each time you click on the arrow.

scroll bars A vertical or horizontal bar that appears at the right or bottom of a window that is not large enough to display all necessary data. At either end of the scroll bar is an arrow that indicates the scrolling direction. Clicking on the arrow moves the slider box and the window contents in the indicated direction.

scroll box A small, movable rectangle (also called a *slider box*) that moves within a scroll bar to indicate your relative position within the data that appears inside the window's workspace.

scroll buffer The memory area that stores keystrokes, or other input, that is transmitted faster than it can be processed.

SCSI *See* Small Computer Systems Interface.

secondary command processor A second copy of COMMAND.COM, invoked either to run a batch file or to provide a new context for subsequent DOS commands.

sector A division of a disk track; usually 512 bytes.

select To specify, by highlighting, a screen item for a subsequent action (e.g., move, copy) to be performed.

selection cursor The extended highlighting that indicates that an item or a screen area has been selected.

serial communications Data transmission in which data is transferred and processed one bit at a time. It is also known as RS232 or asynchronous communications.

serial port A connection between your computer and one of up to four separate serial data devices. The port is labeled COM1, COM2, COM3, or COM4 for software access.

serif font A font whose individual strokes show finishing strokes or curls.

server On a network, a computer and shared device (typically a printer or disk drive) that processes requests from multiple nodes (computers) on the network. Also, a computer (often a desktop) that provides access to files on this computer's physical drives via the INTERSVR program to a connected (i.e., client) computer. The two computers must be connected by a compatible cable between like parallel or serial ports.

shadow RAM Any portion of RAM into which has been written a copy of instruction code from read-only memory (ROM). Typically, this is done in order to be able to later execute the frequently needed instructions from the RAM locations, which is normally faster than from the ROM locations.

shareware Copyrighted software that may be tried first, and paid for (and registered) later. *See also* public domain.

shell An application program that enables you to select and execute other application programs.

shortcut key A single key combination that replaces a sequence of steps or operations to effect some program action. Compare to hotkey.

shrink To reduce the screen representation of an active program to an icon at the lower portion of the screen.

slider box *See* scroll box.

Small Computer Systems Interface Known as SCSI, and pronounced "scuzzy," this 50-pin parallel interface is a fast data transfer standard (approximately 4 megabytes per second) for daisy-chain connection of up to seven peripherals to a single controller board. Many of the newest hard disks and CD-ROM drives use this interface.

small page frame A misnomer that refers to a standard page frame (64K) located in upper reserved memory, with no additional expanded memory access available through any conventional memory (below 640K).

SMARTDRIVE.SYS A disk-caching device driver that improves disk access and overall Windows performance.

snapshot program A program used in debugging to store the status of system or application-program variables.

soft font *See* downloadable font.

software The programs and instruction sets that operate the computer.

software interrupt A signal from a software program that calls up a routine that is resident in the computer's basic programming. It is also a software signal to the computer that the software program has finished or has a problem.

solid color A screen color that consists of pixels of the same color.

sound board An enhanced audio facility that enables you to support multimedia output of high-quality recorded music and voice.

sound driver A device controller that enables Windows and application programs to generate sounds on appropriate hardware.

sound file A disk file that contains audio data that represents playable sounds. Sound files have a .WAV extension.

source The location containing the original data, files, or other information to be used in a DOS command.

source directory The directory that contains the files to be moved or copied.

source document The document containing the data to be moved or copied elsewhere. In Windows, the document containing the object that is linked or embedded elsewhere.

special characters A group of unique graphic, mathematical, or international character symbols that cannot be generated from single keyboard presses. In DOS, you can usually generate such characters by holding down Alt (or Ctrl+Alt) and typing the character's ASCII code on the numeric keypad. You can also easily use such characters with the Character Map accessory program in Windows 3.1.

spooling Simultaneous Peripheral Operations On-Line. Using a high-speed disk to store input to or output from low-speed peripheral devices while the CPU does other tasks.

spreadsheet program An electronic version of an accountant's spreadsheet: when one value changes, all other values based on that value are updated instantly.

staged writes A caching technique which holds data in the cache until the CPU is free to manage the writes to disk, or until a fixed length of time passes by.

standard mode The Windows operating mode that provides task-switching ability, supports access to protected-mode operations, and access to as much as 16Mb of extended memory. It does not allow for multitasking of non-Windows applications (but does allow context switching).

standard settings The default values for actions or operations.

start bit The bit sent at the beginning of a data stream to indicate that data bits follow.

status bar Any line of miscellaneous information placed by an application in a line at the bottom of a window.

stop bit The bit sent after the data bits, indicating that no more data bits follow.

string A series of characters.

stroke font *See* vector font.

subcommands Several special commands used only within batch files.

subdirectory A directory contained within another directory or subdirectory. Technically, all directories other than the root directory are subdirectories, though those at the first level are usually referred to as directories.

Super VGA Any video resolution that exceeds the standard 640×480 VGA resolution. Most commonly, this term refers to 800×600 resolution at 16 colors.

S-video Separated video. A format that uses separate signals to denote the color and brightness of the image.

swap file In 386 Enhanced mode, a disk file used to store information about running applications that have been temporarily suspended from execution. *See* application swap file.

switch A parameter included in DOS commands, usually preceded by the slash (/) symbol, which clarifies or modifies the action of the command.

synchronization The coordination of sending and receiving devices, so that both send and receive data at the same rate.

synthesizer A musical device that generates sounds from a series of digital instructions, as opposed to using prerecorded sounds.

system attribute A bit in a file specification used to indicate whether the file in question contains special system information.

system disk A disk containing the necessary DOS system files for system booting.

system font (Windows) The type size and style used as the Windows default for desktop elements.

SYSTEM.INI The Windows initialization file that specifies characteristics of the hardware and internal operating environment.

system time The time of day stored in your computer's CMOS memory. It can be reset with the TIME command in DOS or with your individual computer's CMOS setup program.

Systems Application Architecture (SAA) A graphic interface developed by IBM that defines most of the elements of the Windows and OS/2 desktops.

Tagged Image File (TIF) The TIF Format (sometimes known as TIFF) is a graphics format used by most scanner and page layout applications. It includes compression techniques, and the ability to store multiple images in a single file. It provides color, gray-scale, and black-and-white capabilities.

target *See* destination.

task An active Windows or DOS application program, and the set of system resources that it uses.

Task List (Windows) The Windows control program that displays a list of running applications and facilitates switching, termination, and window/icon arrangement. *See also* Active Task List.

task switching Switching the foreground focus from one active program to another. *See also* context switching.

template The 127-character memory buffer in which DOS stores a copy of the most recent command-prompt entry.

temporary swap file (Windows) In 386 Enhanced mode, a file that is hidden but only created during Windows activities. No disk space is consumed when Windows is not running.

Terminate-and-Stay-Resident program (TSR) A program that is read into memory the first time it is used and then continues to reside in memory.

terminal emulation A group of communications settings that enable your computer to appear to a remote system as simply a connected terminal of a particular type.

text box A small box (or field) within a dialog box that allows text input from you for clarifying how to process a specified action. You may type parameters, switches, or actual commands, depending on the prompted request from the dialog box.

text file Any file that consists only of characters in the 256-character ASCII set.

text mode The mode in which standard characters can be displayed on a monitor.

TIF *See* Tagged Image File.

tile (Windows) To adjust the position and size of all open windows so that they appear adjacent (i.e., nonoverlapping) to each other.

timeout The amount of time that an application will wait for an event to occur before designating an error condition.

timeslice (Windows) The smallest unit of time that is allocated by Windows to each running DOS Windows application. This same unit of time is allocated to the Windows kernel, and is itself divided up among all running Windows applications.

title bar The thin rectangular portion at the top of a window that contains the name of the window.

toggle A switch or command that reverses a value from off to on, or from on to off.

track A circular stream of data on the disk. It is similar to a track on a phonograph record, except it does not spiral.

tracking speed The speed at which the on-screen mouse pointer keeps up with your movement of the actual mouse.

TrueType fonts (Windows) Fonts under Windows 3.1 and higher that can be sized to any height to appear the same on the printed page as they appear on your screen. Depending on your printer, a TrueType font may be generated as a bitmap or as a soft font.

TSR *See* Terminate-and-Stay-Resident program.

UART Universal Asynchronous Receiver/Transmitter. A fast buffering device that speeds up data reception in serial ports.

UMB Upper Memory Block. A reserved 384K area of system memory in the range 640 kilobytes to 1 megabyte. *See also* Reserved Memory.

utility A supplemental routine or program designed to carry out a specific operation, usually to modify the system environment or perform housekeeping tasks.

vaporware Software that has been announced but is not yet (and might never be) available for purchase.

variable parameter A named element, following a command, that acts as a placeholder; when you issue the command, you replace the variable parameter with the actual value you want to use.

vector font A character font that consists of a series of line definitions, representing the linear strokes necessary to create the desired character or symbol. Also called a stroke font.

verbose listing A listing of all files and subdirectories contained on the disk and path specified in the command. It is activated by the CHKDSK command with the /V switch.

vertical frequency A measure of the time required to draw, from top to bottom, all the horizontal lines of pixels on a screen.

vertical portrait The conventional 8-by-11-inch output for printed information, with the long side of the paper positioned vertically.

virtual disk *See* RAM disk.

virtual hard drive memory factor The amount of hard-disk space available for Windows to address as additional memory locations. *See* swap file.

virtual machine (VM) (Windows) In 386 Enhanced mode, the simulated software environment for each separately running application that creates the illusion to each application that it is running independently on its own computer.

Virtual memory (Windows) In 386 Enhanced mode, the apparent (but not actual) memory available to running applications. It is comprised of actual free memory plus a disk file (see *swap file*) used to simulate extra physical memory. See Chapter 4 for more details.

Virtual Memory Manager *See* VMM.

virus A small block of coded instructions that obtains control of your computer's CPU and directs it to perform unusual and often destructive actions.

visibility (Windows) Refers to which programs can access a memory object.

VM *See* virtual machine.

VMM Virtual Memory Manager. The management code built into Windows' 386 Enhanced Mode for managing the virtualization of memory addresses, using a page table to map logical application pages to actual physical memory pages.

volume label A one to eleven character name for identifying a disk. You can assign whatever label you want to a disk during a FORMAT operation or after formatting with the LABEL command.

wallpaper (Windows) The graphic pattern that appears on the screen desktop as a visual backdrop behind windows, icons, and dialog boxes.

warm booting Resetting the computer using the Ctrl+Alt+Del key combination. *See* bootstrapping.

warning box (Windows) A message box that warns you of an input error (such as an incorrect password) or a potentially dangerous consequence of a requested operation.

wide directory listing An alternate output format that displays file names in more than one column.

wild card A character or characters used to represent other characters. In DOS, * and ? are the only wild-card symbols.

window A rectangular portion of the screen that forms the fundamental graphic area within which Windows and analogous environments display information about applications.

Windows shell The graphic interface, which uses menus, windows, and icons, and facilitates both file and program management.

WIN.INI The Windows initialization file that contains specifications for desktop customization.

word processor An application program that allows the entry, correction, and reformatting of documents before they are printed.

word wrap An editing or word-processing feature that moves text and the cursor from the end of one line to the beginning of the next line. This feature activates when the end of a typed word would place it beyond the specified right margin.

work area *See* workspace.

workspace The central portion of a window, which is used for the primary information-display area.

wrapping around In menus, pressing the down arrow key at the end of a list will move the selection cursor to the top of the list, as if the two ends of the list were attached to each other.

write caching An algorithmic technique that analyzes disk-write requests, in order to reduce the amount of disk activity. This technique embodies a variety of techniques, implemented by different manufacturers, for avoiding multiple writes of unchanged data, and for ordering the actual writes to minimize disk head movement when writing changed data to disk.

write-protecting Giving a disk read-only status by covering the write-protect notch on a 5¼" diskette, or by sliding the write-protect switch on a 3½" diskette to a see-through position.

WYSIWYG What You See Is What You Get. An acronym that stands for the ability to print data that appears on paper exactly as it appears on your screen.

XMM *See* EMM.

XMS Extended Memory Specification: the set of accessing conventions that governs the use of extended memory.

INDEX

Note to the Reader: Boldfaced numbers indicate pages where the term is defined or is the primary topic of a discussion. Italic numbers indicate pages where the topic is mentioned in a figure caption.

D

S

X

Z

About the Author

Judd Robbins is a microcomputer applications expert specializing in training and consulting. He has trained personnel at such major corporations as IBM, AT&T, and Dupont. His other books include *Supercharging Windows*, *Windows Magic Tricks*, and *DOS Magic Tricks*, all from SYBEX. His previous editions of *Mastering DOS* have sold over 250,000 copies.

ORDER FORM

If you have found Mastering DOS 6 to be useful to you, you'll be glad to learn that **all one-hundred-plus batch files and DOSKEY macros** discussed, listed, and presented throughout this book are available on the MASTERING DOS 6 COMPANION DISKETTE. The QBasic CLARITY program discussed in Chapter 16 is also included on this diskette.

A second diskette, the QBASIC COMPANION DISKETTE, contains a wide range of additional QBasic examples and demonstration programs. Order it at the same time to learn even more about QBasic and save money as well.

Avoid the drudgery of typing any of these macros and batch files yourself. Save time and energy and begin to use these tools immediately by ordering the fully tested and complete working versions on these diskettes. Use the order form below to order today. Send a US dollar money order, or a check for US dollars *drawn on a United States bank only* to:

Judd Robbins

P.O.Box 9656

Berkeley, CA 94709

Mastering DOS 6 Companion Diskette   @ **US$24.95 =** _____
QBasic Companion Diskette   @ **US$24.95 =** _____
BOTH Companion Diskettes   @ **US$39.95 =** _____

Check Disk Format Preferred: _____3.5"_____5.25"
If not checked, 5.25" format will be sent.

Please add appropriate sales tax   _____

Please add Shipping/Handling charge:
Within United States $3.75
Outside USA $8.75
TOTAL ORDER   _____

Send Diskette(s) to:

Name: _____

Company: _____

Address1: _____

Address2: _____

City, State, Zip: _____

These materials are made available directly by the author. SYBEX is not responsible for their content.

SYBEX

FREE BROCHURE!

Complete this form today, and we'll send you a full-color brochure of Sybex bestsellers.

Please supply the name of the Sybex book purchased.

_____

How would you rate it?

_____ Excellent   _____ Very Good   _____ Average   _____ Poor

Why did you select this particular book?

_____ Recommended to me by a friend

_____ Recommended to me by store personnel

_____ Saw an advertisement in _____

_____ Author's reputation

_____ Saw in Sybex catalog

_____ Required textbook

_____ Sybex reputation

_____ Read book review in _____

_____ In-store display

_____ Other _____

Where did you buy it?

_____ Bookstore

_____ Computer Store or Software Store

_____ Catalog (name: _____)

_____ Direct from Sybex

_____ Other: _____

Did you buy this book with your personal funds?

_____ Yes   _____ No

About how many computer books do you buy each year?

_____ 1-3   _____ 3-5   _____ 5-7   _____ 7-9   _____ 10+

About how many Sybex books do you own?

_____ 1-3   _____ 3-5   _____ 5-7   _____ 7-9   _____ 10+

Please indicate your level of experience with the software covered in this book:

_____ Beginner   _____ Intermediate   _____ Advanced

Which types of software packages do you use regularly?

_____ Accounting	_____ Databases	_____ Networks
_____ Amiga	_____ Desktop Publishing	_____ Operating Systems
_____ Apple/Mac	_____ File Utilities	_____ Spreadsheets
_____ CAD	_____ Money Management	_____ Word Processing
_____ Communications	_____ Languages	_____ Other _____

(please specify)

Which of the following best describes your job title?

_____ Administrative/Secretarial   _____ President/CEO

_____ Director   _____ Manager/Supervisor

_____ Engineer/Technician   _____ Other _____
                                                        (please specify)

Comments on the weaknesses/strengths of this book: _____

_____

_____

_____

_____

Name _____

Street _____

City/State/Zip _____

Phone _____

PLEASE FOLD, SEAL, AND MAIL TO SYBEX

SYBEX, INC.
Department M
2021 CHALLENGER DR.
ALAMEDA, CALIFORNIA USA
94501

SYBEX

Using the DOS Shell

General-Purpose Keystrokes

up or down arrow Moves the cursor highlight up or down one item at a time

Tab (or Shift+Tab) Moves forward (or backward) from one screen area to the next

Enter Selects a command or operation, or rereads a drive

Ctrl+spacebar Selects or deselects the file at the current cursor location

Del Removes selected file(s) or program entry

plus Displays one directory level below the selected directory

minus or hyphen Hides any subdirectories below the selected directory

* (asterisk) Displays all subdirectories below the selected directory

Ctrl+asterisk Displays all directories in the selected drive's hierarchy

Esc Cancels a command or operation

F1 Displays context-sensitive help

F2 Copies program list entries with File Copy command

F3 (or Alt+F4) Exits the shell

F5 Refreshes a directory tree and file list. (Rereads from the disk.)

F7 Moves a selected file

F8 Copies selected file(s)

F9 Displays contents of a file. When contents are displayed, F9 acts as a toggle between ASCII and Hex display

F10 (or Alt) Selects the menu bar

Ctrl+drive letter Reads a drive and displays its directory tree

Ctrl+End Moves to last entry in a list

Ctrl+Home Moves to first entry in a list

Ctrl+/ Selects all files in a list

Ctrl+ Deselects all selected files

End Moves to end of a line or a list

Home Moves to beginning of a line or a list

PageDown Scrolls down one screenful

PageUp Scrolls up one screenful

Shift+F8 Turns Add mode on or off for non-consecutive file selections

Shift+spacebar When Add mode is on (Shift+F8), selects all files between the cursor and the last selected file

Shift+Ctrl+Enter Starts a program, or opens a selected file

Shift+F9 "Shells out" to a command prompt within the shell. To return to the shell, type EXIT from the command prompt

Shift+up or down arrow Extends current selection by adding preceding or following file-list entry

Shift+PageUp Extends current selection by adding files in previous window

Shift+PageDown Extends current selection by adding files in next window

spacebar When in Add mode (Shift+F8), adds highlighted file to the current selection

any letter Moves to next list item beginning with whatever letter you wish to type

Managing Multiple Active Tasks

Shift+Enter Adds a program from program group to active task list; actually starts the program behind the scenes while remaining at the DOS shell

Ctrl+Esc Switches from a program to the shell

Alt+Esc Switches from one active task to the next

Shift+Alt+Esc Switches from one active task to the previous

Alt+Tab Switches back and forth between two applications